HUMAN-MACHINE SHARED CONTEXTS

HUMAN-MACHINE SHARED CONTEXTS

Edited by

WILLIAM F. LAWLESS
Department of Mathematics, Sciences and Technology, and Department of Social Sciences,
School of Arts and Sciences, Paine College,
Augusta, GA, United States

RANJEEV MITTU
Information Management & Decision Architectures Branch,
Information Technology Division, US Naval Research Laboratory,
Washington, DC, United States

DONALD A. SOFGE
Navy Center for Applied Research in Artificial Intelligence,
US Naval Research Laboratory,
Washington, DC, United States

ELSEVIER

ACADEMIC PRESS
An imprint of Elsevier

Academic Press is an imprint of Elsevier
125 London Wall, London EC2Y 5AS, United Kingdom
525 B Street, Suite 1650, San Diego, CA 92101, United States
50 Hampshire Street, 5th Floor, Cambridge, MA 02139, United States
The Boulevard, Langford Lane, Kidlington, Oxford OX5 1GB, United Kingdom

Notices
Knowledge and best practice in this field are constantly changing. As new research and experience broaden our
understanding, changes in research methods, professional practices, or medical treatment may become
necessary.

Practitioners and researchers must always rely on their own experience and knowledge in evaluating and using
any information, methods, compounds, or experiments described herein. In using such information or methods
they should be mindful of their own safety and the safety of others, including parties for whom they have a
professional responsibility.

To the fullest extent of the law, neither the Publisher nor the authors, contributors, or editors, assume any liability
for any injury and/or damage to persons or property as a matter of products liability, negligence or otherwise, or
from any use or operation of any methods, products, instructions, or ideas contained in the material herein.

Library of Congress Cataloging-in-Publication Data
A catalog record for this book is available from the Library of Congress

British Library Cataloguing-in-Publication Data
A catalogue record for this book is available from the British Library

ISBN 978-0-12-820543-3

For information on all Academic Press publications
visit our website at https://www.elsevier.com/books-and-journals

Publisher: Mara Conner
Editorial Project Manager: Peter Adamson
Production Project Manager: Paul Prasad Chandramohan
Cover Designer: Miles Hitchen

Typeset by SPi Global, India

Contents

Contributors ix
Preface xi

1. Introduction: Artificial intelligence (AI), autonomous machines, and constructing context: User interventions, social awareness, and interdependence

William F. Lawless, Ranjeev Mittu, Donald A. Sofge

1.1 Introduction 1
1.2 Introduction of the chapters from contributors 9
References 20
Further reading 22

2. Analogy and metareasoning: Cognitive strategies for robot learning

Ashok K. Goel, Tesca Fitzgerald, Priyam Parashar

2.1 Background, motivations, and goals 23
2.2 Using social learning and analogical reasoning in cognitive robotics 24
2.3 Using reinforcement learning and metareasoning in cognitive robotics 32
2.4 Conclusions 42
Acknowledgments 43
References 43
Further reading 44

3. Adding command knowledge "At the Human Edge"

H.T. Goranson

3.1 Introduction 45
3.2 Characteristics of the three systems 46
3.3 Strategies 54

3.4 An example, agile C2 scenario 55
3.5 Background of the approach 61
3.6 Type considerations 63
References 64

4. Context: Separating the forest and the trees—Wavelet contextual conditioning for AI

Stephen Russell, Ira S. Moskowitz, Brian Jalaian

4.1 Introduction 67
4.2 Artificial intelligence, context, data, and decision making 68
4.3 Wavelets and preprocessing 69
4.4 A preferential transformation for initial resolution-scale 77
4.5 Evaluating the preferred decomposition-level selection technique 81
4.6 Results and discussion 84
4.7 Conclusion 89
References 89

5. A narrative modeling platform: Representing the comprehension of novelty in open-world systems

Beth Cardier, John Shull, Alex Nielsen, Saikou Diallo, Niccolo Casas, Larry D. Sanford, Patrick Lundberg, Richard Ciavarra, H.T. Goranson

5.1 Introduction 93
5.2 New system-level representations 96
5.3 Taxonomy 100
5.4 2D versus 3D 106
5.5 Examples 107
5.6 Challenges 123
5.7 Higher-level structures 124
5.8 Surrounding research and foundations 129
5.9 Conclusion 132
Acknowledgments 132
References 133

6. Deciding Machines: Moral-Scene
   Assessment for Intelligent Systems
   Ariel M. Greenberg

6.1 Introduction   135
6.2 Background   137
6.3 Moral salience   140
6.4 Mode of interaction   147
6.5 Reasoning over insults and injuries   149
6.6 Synthesis: Moral-Scene Assessment   151
6.7 Application   152
6.8 Roadmap   157
Acknowledgments   157
References   158
Further reading   159

7. The criticality of social and behavioral
   science in the development and
   execution of autonomous systems
   Lisa Troyer

7.1 Introduction   161
7.2 Autonomous systems: A brief history   161
7.3 Limitations of cognition and implications for
     learning systems   162
7.4 Considering physical, natural, and social system
     interdependencies in autonomous system
     development   164
7.5 Ethical concerns at the intersection of social and
     autonomous systems   165
7.6 Conclusion   166
Acknowledgments   166
References   167

8. Virtual health and artificial intelligence:
   Using technology to improve healthcare
   delivery
   Geoffrey W. Rutledge, Joseph C. Wood

8.1 Introduction   169
8.2 The end-to-end healthcare
     experience   170
8.3 Digital health solutions   170
8.4 Architecture of an end-to-end digital health
     solution   171
8.5 The role of AI in virtual health   173

8.6 HealthTap: AI methods within a virtual health
     platform   174
8.7 Limitations and future directions   175
References   175

9. An information geometric look at the
   valuing of information
   Ira S. Moskowitz, Stephen Russell, William F. Lawless

9.1 Introduction   177
9.2 Information geometry background   178
9.3 A brief look at Riemannian geometry in
     general   180
9.4 Fisher information and Riemannian
     geometry   188
9.5 A simple Fisher space-normal distribution:
     Two parameters   190
9.6 The statistical manifold $\mathbb{N}_f^{\Sigma}$ 193
9.7 Value of information and
     complexity   200
9.8 Allotment of resources   202
9.9 Conclusion   203
Acknowledgments   203
References   203

10. AI, autonomous machines and human
    awareness: Towards shared machine-
    human contexts in medicine
    D. Douglas Miller, Elena A. Wood

10.1 Introduction   205
10.2 Current state of medical education and its
      challenges   206
10.3 Potential AI application for medical
      education   210
10.4 Shared human—Machine contexts in medical
      education   212
References   218

11. Problems of autonomous agents
    following informal, open-textured
    rules
    Ryan Quandt, John Licato

11.1 Informal, open-textured rules   221
11.2 Obstacles of IORs   223
11.3 Interpretive arguments   231

11.4 Conclusion: Ameliorating the problems
of IORs 238
References 239

12. Engineering for emergence in
information fusion systems: A review
of some challenges

Ali K. Raz, James Llinas, Ranjeev Mittu, William F. Lawless

12.1 Introduction 241
12.2 Technical foundations 243
12.3 Widespread impacts of emergence 246
12.4 Emergence challenges for future
IF systems 249
12.5 Conclusions and future work 253
References 254

13. Integrating expert human
decision-making in artificial
intelligence applications

Hesham Fouad, Ira S. Moskowitz, Derek Brock,
Michael Scott

13.1 Introduction 257
13.2 Background 258
13.3 Decision-making background 258
13.4 Problem domain 259
13.5 Approach 260
13.6 Technical discussion of AHP 262
13.7 Some matrix definitions 264
13.8 Exponential additive weighting 268
13.9 Procedure 270
13.10 An example with R code 271
13.11 Conclusion 274
Acknowledgments 274
References 274

14. A communication paradigm for
human-robot interaction during robot
failure scenarios

Daniel J. Brooks, Dalton J. Curtin, James T. Kuczynski,
Joshua J. Rodriguez, Aaron Steinfeld, Holly A. Yanco

14.1 Introduction 277
14.2 Related work 278
14.3 Interaction design 279

14.4 Experiment methodology 282
14.5 Results 288
14.6 Discussion 302
14.7 Future work 304
14.8 Conclusions 305
Acknowledgments 305
References 305

15. On neural-network training algorithms

Jonathan Barzilai

15.1 Introduction 307
15.2 The one-dimensional case 307
15.3 The n-dimensional case 309
15.4 Implications for neural-network
training 311
15.5 Summary 312
References 312

16. Identifying distributed incompetence in
an organization

Boris Galitsky

16.1 Introduction 315
16.2 Defining DI 317
16.3 Observing organizations with DI 318
16.4 Detecting DI in text 333
16.5 Conclusions: Handling and repairing DI 338
References 338
Further reading 340

17. Begin with the human: Designing for
safety and trustworthiness in cyber-
physical systems

Elizabeth T. Williams, Ehsan Nabavi, Genevieve Bell,
Caitlin M. Bentley, Katherine A. Daniell, Noel Derwort,
Zac Hatfield-Dodds, Kobi Leins, Amy K. McLennan

17.1 Introduction 341
17.2 The Three Mile Island
accident 343
17.3 The analytical framework 345
17.4 Discussion and conclusions 355
Acknowledgments 356
References 357

18. Digital humanities and the digital economy

Shu-Heng Chen

18.1 Motivation 359
18.2 What is digital humanities? 360
18.3 The twin space 365
18.4 The digital economy 368
18.5 Reinventing individuality 371
18.6 Matching 374
18.7 Concluding remarks 380
Acknowledgments 381
References 381

19. Human-machine sense making in context-based computational decision

Olivier Bartheye, Laurent Chaudron

19.1 Introduction 385
19.2 Basic features of decision based mechanisms 386
19.3 Human-machine agents and characteristics 391
19.4 Conclusion 397
References 398
Further reading 398

20. Constructing mutual context in human-robot collaborative problem solving with multimodal input

Michael Wollowski, Tyler Bath, Sophie Brusniak, Michael Crowell, Sheng Dong, Joseph Knierman, Walt Panfil, Sooyoung Park, Mitchell Schmidt, Adit Suvarna

20.1 Introduction 399
20.2 UIMA 401
20.3 Information processing architecture 402
20.4 Object detection 404
20.5 Spatial relation processor 405
20.6 Speech processing 408
20.7 Natural language processing 409
20.8 Gesture recognition 412
20.9 Confidence aggregation 414
20.10 Communication unit 415
20.11 Memory 416
20.12 Constructing shared context 416
20.13 Conclusions 418
Acknowledgments 419
References 419

Index 421

Contributors

Olivier Bartheye CREA, Air Force Academy, Salon-de-Provence, France

Jonathan Barzilai Dalhousie University, Halifax, NS, Canada

Tyler Bath Computer Science Department, Rose-Hulman Institute of Technology, Terre Haute, IN, United States

Genevieve Bell 3A Institute, Australian National University, Canberra, ACT, Australia

Caitlin M. Bentley 3A Institute, Australian National University, Canberra, ACT, Australia

Derek Brock Navy Center for Applied Research in Artificial Intelligence, Naval Research Laboratory, Washington, DC, United States

Daniel J. Brooks Toyota Research Institute, Cambridge, MA, United States

Sophie Brusniak Computer Science Department, Rose-Hulman Institute of Technology, Terre Haute, IN, United States

Beth Cardier Eastern Virginia Medical School, Norfolk, VA, United States

Niccolo Casas The Bartlett School of Architecture, University College London, London, United Kingdom

Laurent Chaudron Theorik Lab, Vernegues, France

Shu-Heng Chen AI-ECON Research Center, Department of Economics, National Chengchi University, Taipei, Taiwan

Richard Ciavarra Eastern Virginia Medical School, Norfolk, VA, United States

Michael Crowell Computer Science Department, Rose-Hulman Institute of Technology, Terre Haute, IN, United States

Dalton J. Curtin University of Massachusetts Lowell, Lowell, MA, United States

Katherine A. Daniell 3A Institute, Australian National University, Canberra, ACT, Australia

Noel Derwort 3A Institute, Australian National University, Canberra, ACT, Australia

Saikou Diallo Virginia Modeling, Analysis & Simulation Center, Old Dominion University, Suffolk, VA, United States

Zac Hatfield Dodds 3A Institute, Australian National University, Canberra, ACT, Australia

Sheng Dong Computer Science Department, Rose-Hulman Institute of Technology, Terre Haute, IN, United States

Tesca Fitzgerald Georgia Institute of Technology, Atlanta, GA, United States

Hesham Fouad Information Management and Decision Architectures Branch, US Naval Research Laboratory, Washington, DC, United States

Boris Galitsky Oracle Corporation, Redwood City, CA, United States

Ashok K. Goel Georgia Institute of Technology, Atlanta, GA, United States

H.T. Goranson Institute for Integrated Intelligent Systems, Griffith University, Brisbane, QLD, Australia

Ariel M. Greenberg Intelligent Systems Center, Johns Hopkins University Applied Physics Laboratory, Laurel, MD, United States

Brian Jalaian Battlefield Information Processing Branch, US Army Research Laboratory, Adelphi, MD, United States

Joseph Knierman Computer Science Department, Rose-Hulman Institute of Technology, Terre Haute, IN, United States

James T. Kuczynski University of Massachusetts Lowell, Lowell, MA, United States

William F. Lawless Department of Mathematics, Sciences and Technology, and Department of Social Sciences, School of Arts and Sciences, Paine College, Augusta, GA, United States

Kobi Leins 3A Institute, Australian National University, Canberra, ACT, Australia

John Licato Advancing Machine and Human Reasoning (AMHR) Lab; Department of Computer Science and Engineering, University of South Florida, Tampa, FL, United States

James Llinas University at Buffalo, Buffalo, NY, United States

Patrick Lundberg Eastern Virginia Medical School, Norfolk, VA, United States

Amy K. McLennan 3A Institute, Australian National University, Canberra, ACT, Australia

D. Douglas Miller Academic Affairs, Medical College of Georgia at Augusta University, Augusta, GA, United States

Ranjeev Mittu Information Management & Decision Architectures Branch, Information Technology Division, US Naval Research Laboratory, Washington, DC, United States

Ira S. Moskowitz Information Management and Decision Architectures Branch, US Naval Research Laboratory, Washington, DC, United States

Ehsan Nabavi 3A Institute, Australian National University, Canberra, ACT, Australia

Alex Nielsen Virginia Modeling, Analysis & Simulation Center, Old Dominion University, Suffolk, VA, United States

Walt Panfil Computer Science Department, Rose-Hulman Institute of Technology, Terre Haute, IN, United States

Priyam Parashar Contextual Robotics Institute, UC San Diego, La Jolla, CA, United States

Sooyoung Park Computer Science Department, Rose-Hulman Institute of Technology, Terre Haute, IN, United States

Ryan Quandt Advancing Machine and Human Reasoning (AMHR) Lab; Department of Philosophy, University of South Florida, Tampa, FL, United States

Ali K. Raz Purdue University, West Lafayette, IN, United States

Joshua J. Rodriguez University of Massachusetts Lowell, Lowell, MA, United States

Stephen Russell Battlefield Information Processing Branch, US Army Research Laboratory, Adelphi, MD, United States

Geoffrey W. Rutledge HealthTap Inc., Mountain View, CA, United States

Larry D. Sanford Eastern Virginia Medical School, Norfolk, VA, United States

Mitchell Schmidt Computer Science Department, Rose-Hulman Institute of Technology, Terre Haute, IN, United States

Michael Scott Information Management and Decision Architectures Branch, US Naval Research Laboratory, Washington, DC, United States

John Shull Virginia Modeling, Analysis & Simulation Center, Old Dominion University, Suffolk, VA, United States

Donald A. Sofge Navy Center for Applied Research in Artificial Intelligence, US Naval Research Laboratory, Washington, DC, United States

Aaron Steinfeld Carnegie Mellon University, Pittsburgh, PA, United States

Adit Suvarna Computer Science Department, Rose-Hulman Institute of Technology, Terre Haute, IN, United States

Lisa Troyer Army Research Office—CCDC Army Research Laboratory, Durham, NC, United States

Elizabeth T. Williams 3A Institute, Australian National University, Canberra, ACT, Australia

Michael Wollowski Computer Science Department, Rose-Hulman Institute of Technology, Terre Haute, IN, United States

Elena A. Wood Academic Affairs, Medical College of Georgia at Augusta University, Augusta, GA, United States

Joseph C. Wood Dwight D. Eisenhower Army Medical Center, Ft. Gordon, GA, United States

Holly A. Yanco University of Massachusetts Lowell, Lowell, MA, United States

Preface

This book derives from an Association for the Advancement of Artificial Intelligence (AAAI) symposium held at Stanford University on March 25–27, 2019.[a] Our goal for the symposium was, and for this book is, to deal with the current state of the art in autonomy and artificial intelligence (AI). Our symposium was titled "Artificial intelligence (AI), autonomous machines and constructing context: User interventions, social awareness and interdependence." In contrast to the title for our 2019 symposium, we changed the title for this book to "Human-machine shared contexts."[b] This book combines and extends the themes that motivated our symposium.

In advertising for our symposium, we wrote that we preferred papers by participants who can discuss the meaning, value, and interdependent effects on context wherever these AI-driven machines may interact with humans or other autonomous agents. We had asked for extended abstracts (1–2 pages) or longer manuscripts up to 8 pages long. Our plan was to publish revised papers in a book after the symposium. The research we present in this book, we hope, will help to advance the next generation of systems that are rapidly being planned to range from autonomous platforms and machines operating independently to human-machine teams of autonomous systems operating interdependently with AI to provide better support to human operators, decision-makers, and society. By examining the gaps in the existing research that are addressed in this book, we hope that autonomous and human systems will become better integrated to achieve a more effective application of AI wherever it is installed and operated.

This book explores how artificial intelligence (AI) is offering opportunities for an expanded but uncertain impact on society by teams of humans, machines, and robots, leading to an increase in the autonomy of machines and robots. This edited volume presents a cross-section of the underlying theories, computational models, experimental methods, and field applications of AI systems to help readers better understand the integrated relationships between AI, autonomy, humans, and machines that will help society to reduce human errors in the widening use of advanced technologies (e.g., airplanes, trains, and cars). While other books deal with these topics individually, our book is unique in that it unifies the fields of autonomy and AI, framed in the broader context of effective integration for human-autonomous machine and robotic systems that are already using AI, or which soon may.

The organizers of our symposium:

William F. Lawless, Paine College
(w.lawless@icloud.com)
Ranjeev Mittu (ranjeev.mittu@nrl.navy.mil)
Donald A. Sofge (don.sofge@nrl.navy.mil)

AAAI web page: https://www.aaai.org/ Symposia/Spring/sss19symposia.php#ss01

---

[a] https://www.aaai.org/Symposia/Spring/sss19symposia.php#ss01.

[b] https://sites.google.com/site/aaai19sharedcontext.

Participants at our symposium:

We had many more participants than speakers who attended our symposium. We had asked for participants and speakers who could discuss the foundations, metrics, or applications of AI to systems and how AI in these systems affects or may affect the systems themselves, targeted audiences, or society at large. We kept the topic open-ended for the symposium and for this book. We considered all papers submitted for the symposium and many afterward for the book. Accompanied by other contributions from nonsymposium participants after the symposium, most of the papers presented at the symposium have been extended into chapters for this book. Our ultimate goal then and now is to advance AI theory and concepts to improve the performance of human-machine teams with AI and to improve society.

Invited speakers (there were nine invited speakers each giving 60-min talks):

- H.T. Goranson, Institute for Integrated Intelligent Systems, Griffith University, Queensland, Australia, t.goranson@griffith.edu.au: "Integrating Human and Machine Insights in the Presence of Unknowns"
- Lisa Troyer, Army Research Office, Life Sciences, Minerva Program, lisa.l.troyer.civ@mail.mil: "The Criticality of Social & Behavioral Science in the Development & Execution of Autonomous Systems"
- Ashok Goel, Editor, *AI Magazine*, Georgia Tech, ashok.goel@cc.gatech.edu: "Interaction, Analogy, and Metareasoning: Applying Cognitive Science to Robotics"
- Ariel Greenberg, Johns Hopkins Applied Physics Laboratory, Adelphi, MD, Ariel.Greenberg@jhuapl.edu: "Moral-Scene Assessment for Intelligent Systems"
- Shu-Heng Chen, Distinguished Professor, Department of Economics, Director, AI-ECON Research Center, VP, National Chengchi University, Taipei, Taiwan, chen.shuheng@gmail.com: "Digital Humanities and Digital Economy"
- Joseph Wood, MD, Dwight D. Eisenhower Army Medical Center, Ft. Gordon, GA, joseph.c.wood.civ@mail.mil and Geoffrey W. Rutledge, MD, PhD, HealthTap Inc., Mountain View, CA, geoff@healthtap.com: "Virtual Health and Artificial Intelligence: Using Technology to Improve Healthcare Delivery"
- Beth Cardier, Sirius-Beta, VA; School Health Professions, Eastern Virginia Medical School, bethcardier@hotmail.com: "A Narrative Modeling Platform: Modeling Implicit Influence Among Contexts"
- Boris Galitsky, Chief Scientist, Oracle Corp., bgalitsky@hotmail.com: "Identifying the Distributed Incompetence in an Organization"
- Stephen Russell, Chief, Battlefield Information Processing Branch, US Army Research Laboratory, Adelphi, MD, stephen.m.russell8.civ@mail.mil: "Managing Information on the Battlefield"

Regular speakers (there were ten 30-min regular talks):

- D. Douglas Miller, MD, CM, MBA, Academic Affairs, Medical College of Georgia at Augusta University, ddmiller@augusta.edu and Elena A. Wood, MD, PhD, Academic Affairs, Medical College of Georgia at Augusta University, eawood@augusta.edu: "Medical AI Literacy: Perspectives on Current and Future Healthcare Workforce High Technology Up-skilling Needs and Educational Challenges"
- Elizabeth T. Williams & Ehsan Nabavi, Amy McLennan 3A Institute, Australian National University, Canberra, Australia, elizabeth.williams@anu.edu.au: "Begin with the Human: Designing for Safety and Trustworthiness in Cyber-physical Systems"

- Ryan Quandt, Advancing Machine and Human Reasoning (AMHR) Laboratory, Department of Philosophy, University of South Florida, rpquandt@mail.usf.edu: "Problems of Autonomous Agents Following Informal, Open-textured Rules"
- Michael Wollowski, Computer Science Department, Rose-Hulman Institute of Technology, Terre Haute, wollowsk@rose-hulman.edu: "Shared Context in Human Robot Collaborative Problem Solving with Multi-modal Input"
- Brian Jalaian, Army Research Laboratory, Adelphi, MD, brian.jalaian.ctr@mail.mil: "Information and Uncertainty on the Battlefield"
- Hesham Foaud, Computer Scientist, Virtual Environments and Visualization, Information Technology Division, Derek Brock and Michael Scott, Naval Research Laboratory, Washington, DC, hesham.fouad@nrl.navy.mil: "Integrating Expert Human Decision Making in Artificial Intelligence Applications"
- Artificial Intelligence (AI), Autonomous Machines and Human Awareness: User Interventions, Intuition and Mutually Constructed Context, Joshua Walker (joshua@aleph.legal). Joshua Walker, CEO, Aleph Legal.
- Olivier Bartheye, CREA, Air Force Academy, France, olivier.bartheye@ecole-air.fr and Laurent Chaudron, THEORIK Laboratory, France, laurent.chaudron@polytechnique.org: "Computational Contexts, Sense and Action: How a Machine Can Decide?"
- Siddhartha Banerjee (student), siddhartha.banerjee@gatech.edu and Sonia Chernova, chernova@cc.gatech.edu: "Fault Diagnosis in Robot Task Execution"
- William F. Lawless, Professor, Math & Psychology, Paine College/Summer Research at NRL, w.lawless@icloud.com, Ranjeev Mittu, Branch Head for the Information Management and Decision Architectures Branch within the Information Technology Division, U.S. Naval Research Laboratory, Washington, DC, ranjeev.mittu@nrl.navy.mil, and Donald A. Sofge, Computer Scientist and Roboticist, U.S. Naval Research Laboratory, Washington, DC, don.sofge@nrl.navy.mil: "Artificial Intelligence (AI), Autonomous Machines and Constructing Context: User Interventions, Social Awareness and Interdependence"

In addition to the invited and regular talks, we agreed to hold a 1-h joint panel session with Sepideh Ghanavati and her colleague Shomir Wilson:

- Sepideh Ghanavati (sepideh.ghanavati@maine.edu) and Shomir Wilson (shomir@psu.edu): "PAL, Privacy-Enhancing Artificial Intelligence and Language Technology" (https://sites.google.com/view/pal2019)

Program committee for our 2019 AAAI symposium:

- Julie Marble, Johns Hopkins University, Julie.Marble@jhuapl.edu
- Michael Floyd, Lead AI Scientist, Knexus Research, michael.floyd@knexusresearch.com
- David Aha, NRL, Head, Navy Center for Applied Research in Artificial Intelligence, david.aha@nrl.navy.mil
- Ciara Sibley, Naval Research Laboratory, UAVs, ciara.sibley@nrl.navy.mil
- Joe Coynes, Naval Research Laboratory, Psychology, UAVs, joseph.coyne@nrl.navy.mil
- Noelle Brown, ONR's Naval R&D Enterprises, Applied AI, noelle.brown@nrl.navy.mil
- Cyrus Foroughi, Information Technology Division, NRL, cyrus.foroughi.ctr@nrl.navy.mil
- Boris Galitsky, Chief Scientist, Oracle Corp., bgalitsky@hotmail.com

- Michael Mylrea, PNNL, Department of Energy, Blockchain, michael.mylrea@pnnl.gov
- Micah H. Clark, Senior Scientist, Autonomy, AI, Cog Sci, ARL, PSU, mhc77@arl.psu.edu
- Hesham Fouad, Computer Scientist, 3D Virtual & Mixed Env., NRL, hesham.fouad@nrl.navy.mil
- Michael Wollowski, Rose-Hulman Institute of Technology, wollowsk@rose-hulman.edu
- Manisha Misra, U Connecticut, PhD grad student, manisha.uconn@gmail.com
- John Reeder, Navy SPAWAR, john.d.reeder@navy.mil
- Florian Jensch, Chair, Department Psychology & Institute of Simulation & Training, UCF, florian.jentsch@ucf.edu
- Jonathan Barzilai, Mathematician, Dalhousie University, barzilai@scientificmetrics.com
- Steve Russell, Army Research Laboratory, Adelphi, MD, stephen.russell15.civ@mail.mil
- Eric Vorm, LT, US Navy, Aeronautics & Experimental Psychology, PhD student, Indiana University, esvorm@iu.edu
- Shu-Heng Chen, Distinguished Professor, Department of Economics, Director, AI-ECON Research Center, National Chengchi University, Taiwan, chen.shuheng@gmail.com
- Geert-Jan Kruijff, Director, Technology Production Manager, Nuance, Germany, Geert-Jan.Kruijff@nuance.com
- Rino Falcone, Director, Institute of Cognitive Sciences & Technologies, National Research Council, Italy, rino.falcone@istc.cnr.it
- Laurent Chaudron, Director, ONERA Provence (France's Air Force Academy), laurent.chaudron@polytechnique.org
- Beth Cardier, Sirius-Beta, VA; School Health Professions, Eastern Virginia Medical School, bethcardier@hotmail.com
- Wayne Zachary, CEO, Starship Health, Fort Washington, PA, wzachary@comcast.net
- Dan Zwillinger, Chief Scientist of Autonomy, Control & Est. (ACE), BAE Systems, Burlington, MA, daniel.zwillinger@baesystems.com

Questions for speakers and attendees at our symposium on AI and readers of this book

Our Spring AAAI-2018 and AAAI-2019 symposia offered speakers opportunities to address the intractable, fundamental questions of AI and questions remaining after our 2018 symposium on the Internet of Everything (IoE), including: cybersecurity, machines, and robots; autonomy and its management; the malleability of preferences and beliefs in social settings; and the application of autonomy for human-machine teams at individual, group, and system levels.

A list of revised, unanswered, and fundamental questions includes the following:

- Why have we yet to determine from a theoretical perspective the principles underlying individual, team, and system behaviors?
- Must AI systems speak only to each other, only to humans, or to both?
- Will each AI system be an independent system, an interdependent system, or a combination?
- Will AI advance autonomy and autonomic fundamentals to improve the performance of individual agents and hybrid teams of humans, machines, and robots for the betterment of society?

- Can autonomous AI systems be controlled to solve the problems faced by teams while maintaining defenses against threats to AI systems and minimizing mistakes in competitive environments (e.g., cyberattacks, human error, and system failure)?
- Might individuals seek to self-organize into autonomous groups with human-machine teams to defend better against attacks (e.g., cyber, merger, and resources) or for other reasons (e.g., least entropy production (LEP) and maximum entropy production (MEP), for a mission or function)?
- What does an autonomous organization need to predict its path forward and govern itself? What are the AI tools available to help an organization be more adept and creative?
- What signifies adaptation for an AI system? Does adaptation at an earlier time prevent or moderate adaptive responses to newer environmental changes?
- Is the stability state of hybrid teams the single state that generates an MEP rate?
- If social order requires MEP and if the bistable perspectives present in debate (courtrooms, politics, and science) lead to stable decisions, is the chosen decision an LEP or MEP state?
- Considering the evolution of social systems (e.g., in general, Cuba, North Korea, and Palestine have not evolved), are the systems that adjust to MEP the most efficient?

In addition, new threats may emerge due to the nature of the technology of autonomy itself (as well as the breakdown in traditional verification and validation (V&V) and test and evaluation (T&E) due to the expanded development and application of AI). The nature of advanced technology leads to

other key AI questions for consideration for human-machine systems now and in the future:

Fault modes
- Are there new types of fault modes for AI systems that can be exploited by outsiders?

Detection
- How can we detect that an intelligent, autonomous AI system has been or is being subverted?

Isolation
- What is a "fail safe" or "fail operational" mode for an autonomous system, and can it be implemented?
- Implications of cascading faults (AI, system, and cyber)

Resilience and repair
- What are the underlying causes of the symptoms of faults in an AI system (e.g., nature of the algorithms and patterns of data)?

Consequences of cyber vulnerabilities
- Inducement of AI fault modes
- Deception (including false flags)
- Subversion of an AI system
- The human/social element (reliance, trust, and performance)

We invited speakers and attendants at our symposium to address the following more specific AI topics (as we invite readers of this book to consider):

- Computational models of an autonomous AI system (with real or virtual individuals, teams, or systems) and performance (e.g., metrics and MEP) with or without interdependence, uncertainty, and stability
- Computational models that address autonomy and trust for AI (e.g., the trust by autonomous machines of

human behavior or the trust by humans of autonomous machine behavior).

- Computational models that address threats to autonomy and trust for AI (cyberattacks, competitive threats, and deception) and the fundamental barriers to system survivability (e.g., decisions and mistakes).
- Computational models for the effective or efficient management of complex AI systems (e.g., the results of decision-making, operational performance, metrics of effectiveness, and efficiency).
- Models of multiagent systems (e.g., multi-UAVs, multi-UxVs, and model verification and validation) that address autonomy (e.g., its performance, effectiveness, and efficiency).

For future research projects and symposia (e.g., our symposium in 2020 was accepted by AAAI; it is titled "AI Welcomes Systems Engineering: Towards the Science of Interdependence for Autonomous Human-machine Teams"[c]; AAAI has posted the call on its website, located online at this footnoted page[d]). We invite readers and, hopefully, future participants to consider other questions or topics from individual (e.g., cognitive science and economics), machine learning (ANNs and GAs), or interdependent (e.g., team, firm, and system) perspectives.

After the AAAI-Spring Symposium in 2019 was completed, some of the symposium presentations and short technical reports were revised into longer manuscripts as chapters for inclusion in this book; other authors who did not participate in the symposium were also added afterward. The following individuals were responsible for the proposal submitted to Elsevier for the book before the symposia, for the divergence between the topics considered by the two, and for editing this book that has resulted.

William F. Lawless[a], Ranjeev Mittu[b],
Donald A. Sofge[b]
[a]Augusta, GA, United States
[b]Washington, DC, United States

[c]https://aaai.org/Symposia/Spring/sss20symposia.php#ss03.

[d]Michael Wollowski designed and built our website (wollowsk@rose-hulman.edu), found at https://sites.google.com/view/scienceofinterdependence.

1

Introduction: Artificial intelligence (AI), autonomous machines, and constructing context: User interventions, social awareness, and interdependence

William F. Lawless[a], Ranjeev Mittu[b], Donald A. Sofge[c]

[a]Department of Mathematics, Sciences and Technology, and Department of Social Sciences, School of Arts and Sciences, Paine College, Augusta, GA, United States [b]Information Management & Decision Architectures Branch, Information Technology Division, US Naval Research Laboratory, Washington, DC, United States [c]Navy Center for Applied Research in Artificial Intelligence, US Naval Research Laboratory, Washington, DC, United States

1.1 Introduction

1.1.1 Overview

Pearl (2002) warned almost two decades ago that, for the applications of artificial intelligence (AI) to be successful and accepted by the scientific community and the public at large, machines had to be able to explain what they were doing. This warning, largely unheeded (Pearl & Mackenzie, 2018), must be addressed if AI is to continue unimpeded. AI must be able to explain to ordinary humans, relying mostly on intuition (Kambhampati, 2018), why it is making the decisions it makes in human terms (Shultz, 2018). Society and scientists are worried about what AI means to social well-being, a concern that will amplify once machines begin to think on their own (Gershenfeld, 1999). These issues and concerns became the focus of our symposium at Stanford in March 2019, now adopted and studied further in this book.

Human-machine Shared Contexts
https://doi.org/10.1016/B978-0-12-820543-3.00001-8

In this Introduction, we review the background literature for this book that led to our symposium on "AI, autonomous machines and constructing context." After the literature review and to set the stage for the chapters that follow, we introduce each chapter, its author(s), and how that chapter contributes to the book's theme to advance the science of human-machine teams. If this book is successful, not only will it advance the science of human-machine teams, but also we hope that it will also contribute to a renewal of social science for humans (e.g., Lawless, Mittu, & Sofge, 2018).

The application of machine learning (ML)[a] has led to significant advances across widely divergent fields such as astronomy, medicine, government, industry, and the military[b] and with particular applications such as self-driving cars and drones, both of which have recently caused human deaths (e.g., an Uber car killed a pedestrian, in NTSB, 2018; a swarm attack killed Russians on a base in Syria, in Grove, 2018[c]). The rapid advances and applications with ML, however, have recently exposed several problems associated with data and context that urgently need to be addressed to allow further advances and applications to continue. This symposium was planned to clarify the strengths of ML and its applications and any newly discovered problems and to consider solutions. By addressing these problems, our hope is that AI will continue to advance for the betterment of science, social theory, and society.

The overall goal for AI reasoning systems is to determine knowledge; an operational goal is to be able to discriminate the data in new samples that fit the patterns learned from those that do not fit.[d] But the data and context problems ML now faces raise several questions. First, while some of the processes of ML are established, more data may yet improve ML models for existing applications, and while new solutions to existing task applications can be disseminated worldwide almost instantly (Brynjolfsson & Mitchell, 2017), applications of ML are often based on proprietary data that do not generalize well beyond the learned data if at all. As

---

[a] A subfield of artificial intelligence (AI), ML uses data to learn and make predictions. It is similar to optimization (making the best choice from available alternatives) and data fusion (exploratory data analyses), but ML uses statistics to build models. Deep learning methods (a form of ML) may use deep neural nets for predictive analytics that produce reliable and repeatable results based on large amounts of data.

[b] For example, the US Navy has renamed its Littoral Combat Ship program to its Unmanned and Small Combatants (NSSC, 2018); for example, "The Navy's Knifefish unmanned undersea vehicle, a key component of the Littoral Combat Ship's mine-hunting capability, successfully completed sea acceptance tests off the coast of Massachusetts. Built by General Dynamics and based on the Bluefin Robotics Bluefin-21 deep-water Autonomous Undersea Vehicle, the Knifefish is a self-propelled, untethered vehicle designed to hunt for mines without requiring an LCS or other manned ship to enter a minefield" (Werner, 2018).

[c] From Grove (2018): The attacks reveal a new threat to Moscow's forces from insurgent rebel groups opposed to Syrian President Bashar al-Assad...The base was hit by a number of drones on New Year's Eve, killing 2 service people, injuring 10, and damaging at least 6 planes, the person said. The attack was allegedly the first to penetrate the base's formidable defenses including Pantsir and S-400 surface-to-air missiles. The (Russian) Defense Ministry disputes the claim, saying there was no damage to aircraft and the New Year's Eve attack was caused by mortar shelling (the United States had disavowed its involvement).

[d] Another type of AI is called a generative adversarial network: GANs are a class of AI algorithms used in unsupervised ML, where two neural nets contest each other in a framework similar to a zero-sum game, the first to capture the given data and the second, a discriminator, to estimate whether or not a test sample came from the given data; GANs avoid Markov chains and inference (Goodfellow et al., 2014). Typical discrimination for ML is based on whether a new observation is an acceptable target value; in contrast a generative model determines if an observation has occurred given a target value.

possible remediations, first, in an unlearned or uncertain context, like in an emergency with a disabled human, can a human help a machine by intervening or instructing the machine about what should be done and having the machine learn from this new experience? Second, as immediate if not more so, users want a causal stepwise explanation of what a machine has planned before and after it acts (Pearl & Mackenzie, 2018)[e]; that is, specifically, can the machine explain its actions sufficiently well enough for the human to trust the machine? Third, once machines have been trained as part of a team, inversely, they should be aware of the human's responsibilities as a member in the team. In sum, these three problems are as follows: First, can new data be generated beyond training data (e.g., synthetic data)[f] and can humans instruct machines to learn causal relations on the fly?[g] Second, can a machine articulate what it has learned (e.g., what causal inferences can it draw after its learning has been satisfactorily "completed," which ML algorithms cannot do presently; in Pearl & Mackenzie, 2018)? And third, can an understanding of context be mutual, that is, the contexts faced by a human who is trusting a machine at the same time that the machine is trusting the human (e.g., Lawless et al., 2018)?

The uses of augmented intelligence and assists are wide and spreading. For example, DoD's "Unmanned Systems Integrated Roadmap"[h] noted that "DoD envisions unmanned systems seamlessly operating with manned systems while gradually reducing the degree of human control and decision making required for the unmanned portion of the force structure." For these trends to continue, the situation we are in today requires not only leveraging AI to make better decisions more quickly but also with a mutual understanding shared by both humans and machines.

1.1.2 Problem 1: The generation of new data

Many if not most machines are being trained on proprietary data with algorithms selecting the data, often randomly, making reproducibility a problem even in astronomy, especially when data and solutions are unique and have not been archived (e.g., Wild, 2018). Data libraries with standard problems, procedures, and acceptable solutions are being developed but are not yet common (see the report by Hutson, 2018). Once updated by training with new or revised data, improved solutions to previously trained tasks can be disseminated almost instantaneously (Brynjolfsson & Mitchell, 2017). But ML does not easily transfer what it has learned, if at all, from one application to a new one (Tan, 2017). The result is that machines are often trained with sparse data[i]; for a self-driving car, this result may suffice in relatively simple environments like driving on expressways amidst light traffic.

[e]Pearl is a professor of computer science at UCLA and winner of the 2011 Turing Award for research on probabilistic and causal reasoning. He and Mackenzie, a mathematics writer, wrote *The Book of Why: The Science of Cause and Effect* by Basic Books.

[f]Synthetic data can be anonymized private data, random data, or fake data similar to actual measured data were it available, often used when actual data are not available or when some data are missing.

[g]The AI apprentice program was designed to keep the "human in the loop" as it assists the human user while learning by capturing data from observing the human's decision-making process as additional training data (Mitchell, Mahadevan, & Sternberg, 1990).

[h]"FY 2013–2038 Unmanned Systems Integrated Roadmap" (Washington, DC: Department of Defense, 2013).

[i]Namely, compared with the sparsity of missing data, when more data are available to train and learn from, higher densities tend to produce more accurate predictions (Najafi & Salam, 2016).

Limited (proprietary) and sparse sensory (visual, Lidar, and radar) data produce poor training data, often insufficient to determine the context or to operate in complex environments (e.g., inside of large cities occupied by numerous pedestrians, poor weather conditions, and bridges). There are statistical techniques to address sparse data (e.g., Najafi & Salam, 2016). But sparse databases may be expanded with user-induced intervention data generated, say, when a driver intervenes to take control of a self-driving or autonomous vehicle; instead of disconnecting the system, the intervention itself becomes a source of new data (a similar earlier model is the AI apprentice; see Mitchell et al., 1990). By extension, queries about context raised by a human user of a ML system may also serve as a lever to provide new data; further, if the autonomous agent behaves as preferred by the user, trust should be enhanced (Hutson, 2017). Inversely, if an industry protocol has been standardized, nearby ML systems may be able to self-report shared information individually or collectively within a distributed system in a way that leverages the shared information and expands the data available to retrain each participating ML unit.

As another approach to sparse data, activity-based intelligence (ABI) rapidly integrates data from multiple sources to determine the relevant "patterns-of-life" data from a targeted individual, to determine and identify when change is occurring, and to characterize those patterns that drive data collection for ML to create advantages for decision-makers (Biltgen, Bacastow, Kaye, & Young, 2017). The traditional intelligence cycle decomposes multidisciplinary collection requirements from a description of individual target signatures or persistent behaviors. For ABI, practitioners use advanced large-scale data filtering of events, entities, and transactions to develop an understanding (context) through spatial and temporal correlations across multiple data sets (e.g., Bowman et al., 2017). Many aspects of ABI and anomaly detection and the Internet of Things (IoT) are benefitting from the application of AI and ML techniques (Barlow, 2017).[j]

1.1.3 Problem 2: Explanations by machines of what they have learned or can share (building context)

New regulations are motivating engineers to become aware of how their algorithms are making decisions. For example, from Kean (2018):

> the European Union recently implemented a regulation requiring all algorithms to be 'explainable' by human engineers.

To prevent unintended actions by machines (e.g., Scharping, 2018), Kissinger (2018) asked the following:

> To what extent is it possible to enable AI to comprehend the context that informs its instructions?…Can we, at an early stage, detect and correct an AI program that is acting outside our framework of expectation? Or will AI, left to its own devices, inevitably develop slight deviations that could, over time, cascade into catastrophic departures?

---

[j]Barry Barlow is chief technology officer at Vencore (https://www.vencore.com/).

But while determining context is important but difficult, it becomes ever more difficult if not intractable when the "environments with predictable conditions and well-defined rules…[are replaced by] the chaos of combat" (Bolton, 2018).

Moreover, DoD is pushing for the seamless integration of new technology that includes autonomous agents and systems (Galdorisi, 2015), but these interdependent technologies will create unexpected problems for control and for the determination of context where "changing anything changes everything" (Danzig, 2018). Worrying Danzig is that these interdependent technologies are prone to the following:

> analytic errors…operational errors…unintended and unanticipated emergent effects from the evolution and interaction of technologies, sabotage…by opponents…[and] malfeasance…

Whenever decisions might take a life, official DoD policy requires that machine decision-making occur with humans in the loop. Danzig (2018), however, argues for even more checks in the chain of command, for example, we require two operators, not just one, to launch a missile with a nuclear warhead. Per Smallman (2012), extra checks might have prevented past tragic errors (the USS Vincennes in 1988, the USS Greenville in 2001, and the USS Hartford and USS New Orleans collision in 2009).

1.1.4 Problem 3: The mutual determination of context

An argument is now moving through the scientific community that to some degree these machines are already consciously aware as measured by the subjectivity in their reports (Dehaene, Lau, & Kouider, 2017). This argument may be mitigated by developing machines that can make simple reports similar to the five Ws: who, what, when, where, and why— "who" for a machine to report its identification as needed, "what" it is doing, "when" will it be finished with a task, "where" it came from or is going, and "why" it is performing a task or was assigned the task. A sixth "w" might be for the machine to be able to describe its skill sets.

It is important for human users to be able to trust autonomous machines, but based on recent reports (Hutson, 2017), potential consumers presently do not trust them. Hutson reports that pedestrians and passengers are more likely to trust these vehicles if these cars notice their presence in some manner (by talking with them) or share information with them (by letting a pedestrian know its intentions). Moreover, if autonomous vehicles behave as a user prefers, trust is more likely. But, from the NTSB report on the fatal accident by a driver in a Tesla car, these machines "need better tools to ensure [human] drivers are using the systems properly" (Higgins & Spector, 2018). Thus, as these machines become more autonomous, trust between humans and machines must become mutual.

1.1.5 Possible solutions

1.1.5.1 Potential solution #1. An AI apprentice update

This solution might be a new solution entirely or an update and extension of the AI apprentice by Mitchell et al. (1990). If it gives a sense of control to human users (Hutson, 2017), for example, by having the autonomous machine respond positively to a corrected interpretation of a shared context ("Yes, I now understand what you are saying"), trust and acceptance by the user should be enhanced.

1.1.5.2 Potential solution #2. Digital twins

One approach to modeling the application of machine learning is with what Kraft and Chesebrough (2018) refer to as a digital system model, also known as a digital thread, the communication framework for a digital engineering ecosystem. Acting as a simulator a digital twin operates in parallel to an assembled system from design and build to operation and maintenance. Digital engineering connects all aspects of a system's life cycle to a shared authoritative source of models and data.

> At any point in the lifecycle, data from the engineering ecosystem can be transformed using model-based systems engineering and model-based engineering combined with uncertainty quantification to address engineering challenges and to guide enhancements to the design, manufacturing, production, testing, operation and sustainment of systems. From these modeling activities, authoritative digital surrogates can be generated to better emulate the performance and characteristics of the system relative to the requirements. As one moves vertically through the ecosystem, the digital surrogates can be used to efficiently support a probabilistic analysis of margins, uncertainties and risks in support of decision making under different scenarios. Robust uncertainty quantification is the connecting tissue between data, engineering analysis, risk analysis and decision making.

For autonomous vehicles, smart medical implants, and intelligent energy systems and as a virtual validation of a product or system (e.g., a factory) throughout a product's life cycle (Rusk, 2018) with

> a digital twin contains electronics and software simulations; finite element structural, flow, and heat transfer models; and motion simulations, allowing the twin to predict performance...

1.1.5.3 Potential solution #3. Metrics

Regardless of the solution chosen, with the goal of knowledge and the definition from Shannon's (1948) information theory that knowledge does not produce entropy, a metric can be designed that determines the state of a system controlled by AI. But systems as teams, organizations, and larger structures are designed for a reason (i.e., to complete a mission), often determined by maximum entropy production (MEP), related to the second law of thermodynamics (Martyushev, 2013). If the first goal, that of knowledge, is associated with shaping the structure of an organization to minimize its consumption of entropy (England, 2013), a larger amount of energy is available to an organization (or team) to be directed to achieve its second goal of MEP (Lawless, 2017b).

For integrated autonomous systems, we proposed at an AAAI symposium[k] that the path to robust intelligence can only occur with the courtroom or adversarial model (Mittu, Taylor, Sofge, & Lawless, 2016). We expanded this model at another symposium[l] for the computational determination of context, providing an AI metric for hybrid teams composed of humans,

[k]"The intersection of robust intelligence and trust in autonomous systems"; see http://www.aaai.org/Library/Symposia/Spring/ss14-04.php.

[l]"Computational context: Why it's important, what it means, and can it be computed?"; from https://www.aaai.org/Symposia/Spring/sss17symposia.php#ss03.

machines, and robots. Specifically, with Shannon, knowledge is present when the information it generates goes to zero; knowledge is absent whenever the joint information is greater than (as dependence between agents increases) or equal (as independence between agents increases) to the information from each contributor:

$$H(A, B) \geq H(A), H(B) \qquad\qquad (1.1)$$

where $H(A,B)$ is the joint entropy of two team members and $H(A)$ or $H(B)$ is the entropy of an agent whenever the two agents are not communicating.

1.1.5.4 *Potential solution #4. Calibration*

What happens to users and machines when an autonomous system fails completely or partially? From Diab and Finney (2017), while we have expectations of a future war that

> incorporates fast and lethal robots and automated weapon systems exploiting quantum technologies and processing information faster than we can currently fathom, the reality is that these technologies may not endure for the length of the conflict.

Calibration is necessary to confirm that an AI (ML) program works as expected and as specified (Hutson, 2017). Can, say, information be continuously generated during the operation of a machine to affirm that it is in an operationally safe state? Can weak spots for AI (ML) systems like fogged-in areas or bridges be identified sufficiently well and early enough to warn a driver when to intervene with "hands on?" For autonomous systems, however, monitoring followed by recalibration may need to be continuous to address cyberattacks or other anomalies.

Cyber-physical domains raise the concern of deception in autonomous systems. From Arampatzis and Sherman (2018) regarding how information warfare is conducted,

> it doesn't take much for misinformation and disinformation to reach global audiences…[using tools like] identity theft, hacking, cyber warfare, and ever more sophisticated disinformation techniques…yet it can be difficult to identify the truth…

Deception has long been a critical element of warfare (Tzu, 1994, p. 168); from Sun Tzu, one way to enact deception is to,

> Engage people with what they expect; it is what they are able to discern and confirms their projections. It settles them into predictable patterns of response, occupying their minds while you wait for the extraordinary moment—that which they cannot anticipate.

For our purposes the use of deception in autonomous vehicles has alarmed the public (Hutson, 2017; also, Van De Velde, 2018). Hostile actors may employ tactics for "data poisoning" (Freedberg, 2018) to fully or partially take over an autonomous machine. From Schoka (2018), threats against targets from

> cyberspace actions occur at machine speed, often over enormous physical distances in an asymmetric domain where 'signals hold at risk…[the] freedom of maneuver in other domains.'

Maybe a digital twin can assure the safe operation of an autonomous machine operating in the field.

1.1.5.5 Potential solution #5

An adversarial approach in the courtroom is the method that humans traditionally use to expose biases, such as "confirmation bias" (Darley & Gross, 2000), and to create a context where truth can be sought. The courtroom experience, from Justice Ginsburg (2011), is to obtain an "informed assessment of competing interests" (p. 3). Bohr (1955) was the first scientist to predict that a tribe adopts a dominant view of reality different from a neighboring tribe. What is the evolutionary advantage of having two tribes with different interpretations of reality? From Simon (1989), if every story represents a bounded rationality but if at least two sides exist to every story, then it takes at least two sides to determine social reality, setting the stage for adversarial or competitive determinations of reality (Lawless, 2017a, 2017b). However, if neutral or independent agents do not exist in an adversarial context, conflict becomes likely (Kirk, 2003), preventing the determination of context. On the other hand the largest political group in the United States is the collection of voters known as independents (Jones, 2018). Neutrals or independents serve two functions: First, because both political parties attempt to persuade them to join their side, political conflict is moderated, and, second, acting like a quasi-Nash equilibrium (stable and hard to revise beliefs), the two political parties drive the neutrals to process the discordant information generated by the two opposing parties, while the neutrals process that information to form reasons that justify their subsequent votes. Instead of a winner-take-all result, reflecting an incomplete context, a third outcome is often possible, that of a compromise. Neither side likes a compromise, but if it is judged by neutrals as fair, a compromise has the advantage of establishing the context for both parties with a result that can be long lasting (Schlesinger, 1949).

The adversarial approach was first proposed by Smallman (2012) as a way to reduce accidents at sea by subjecting decisions to a process that involved polling. Recently the adversarial approach solved the Uber self-driving accident that killed a pedestrian in March 2018. At first the police chief blamed the pedestrian, who was on drugs at the time. Next the software used by Uber was blamed because the company struggled to average 13 mi before a human observer had to intervene (by way of a comparison, the Waymo self-driving car averages about 5600 mi per human intervention). Finally, NTSB (2018) blamed the company for disconnecting the car's emergency brakes, which had correctly sent a signal to apply emergency braking.

But how to model the adversarial approach if we cannot model causality (Pearl & Mackenzie, 2018)? Part of the problem is the nonfactorable effects of interdependence in the social interaction (Lawless, 2017a, 2017b) that makes the rational determination of social causality outside of a courtroom impossible (e.g., the Syrian war, a hostile divorce, and the long-standing feud between CBS and Viacom that has depressed both stocks over the past year); however, even whether a "jury" is an arbiter or arbitrary is an open question (e.g., Rachlinski, 1997). Compared with AI machines that are excellent at classification even if they cannot explain why (e.g., alerting for potentially inappropriate antimicrobial prescriptions; in Beaudoin, Kabanza, Nault, & Valiquette, 2014), it may be that AI eventually will be able to manage aspects of causality (e.g., with case-based reasoning; in Aha, McSherry, & Yang, 2006).

1.1.6 Summary

With the recent deaths caused by self-driving cars and drones, the need for more and better training data and the mutual interpretation of context becomes increasingly urgent. First, trust by humans in machines should be complemented by machines trusting their human operators; that is, once machines are taught how to perform a team mission, they "know" what the humans are supposed to do; they should have authority to intervene when humans deviate significantly; for example, USAF already gives fighter planes the authority to take over when its pilot passes out from a hi-G maneuver. Second, without metrics, how will we humans know the machines are performing as expected before we ride in them or unleash them in a lightning-fast war? Third, the autonomous vehicles must demonstrate reliable performance that is valid in a wide range of activities, which even social science has recently learned that it too must demonstrate (Nosek & Open Collaboration of Science, 2015). Finally, we are excited by this project that is forcing us and the social sciences to reexamine the general model of human behavior.

1.2 Introduction of the chapters from contributors

Chapter 2, the first chapter by one of the contributing authors who presented before the AAAI symposium held at Stanford in March 2019, is titled "Analogy and metareasoning: Cognitive strategies for robot learning." It was written by Ashok K. Goel, Tesca Fitzgerald, and Priyam Parashar. Goel is a professor of computer science and the chief scientist in the School of Interactive Computing at the Georgia Institute of Technology, in Atlanta, Georgia; he is also the editor of the Association for the Advancement of Artificial Intelligence's *AI Magazine* and cochair for CogSci 2019. Fitzgerald is a computer science PhD candidate in the School of Interactive Computing at the Georgia Institute of Technology. Parashar is also a graduate student pursuing a PhD but located at the Contextual Robotics Institute, University of California in San Diego, California. The authors are pursuing the elements of intelligence for robots, which in their view requires them to address one of the key steps in the innovation process, that is, to determine the ingredients that foster novelty. More than that, generalizable to shared contexts, the authors want to know what it means for intelligence to recognize novelty, especially if a robot or intelligent entity is surrounded cognitively by only the knowledge it already knows. In their chapter the authors narrow their focus to metareasoning and the use of analogy in three experiments. They begin with analogy. With it, they use a construct of what is already known about a context or can be abstracted from one to approach a new problem with a solution that is similar but unknown, where analogy allows them to probe the unknown solution with what is already known but from a new perspective. From work in their laboratory, they found that their robot learns about analogy after only a small number of demonstrations, but these alone do not guarantee success in the real world. To work around this barrier brings the authors to recognize that metareasoning may be able to teach a robot to think about how it has solved problems in the past, especially reasoning about those problems in the situations when the robot had previously failed, with failure forming the context for metareasoning grounded in action and perception. After exploring the opportunities afforded by metareasoning, they conclude by perceiving a metareasoning benefit that contributes to the further development of cognitive theory with the use of analogy and metareasoning in building models of intelligence.

Chapter 3 was written by H.T. Goranson at the Institute for Integrated Intelligent Systems, a part of Griffith University, and located in Queensland, Australia. His chapter, titled

"Adding command knowledge "At the Human Edge"," provides an insider's view into the extreme edge of what humans can come to know in the difficult context where command decisions are made while working with humans and machines. These contexts generate an extraordinary amount of information that commanders must collect and make sense of for the benefit of their commands and the societies within which they operate to defend and protect. Goranson begins by stating that the tools and methods are in hand to collect the information needed while working with humans and machines for the military and to develop insights from that information for the applications when and where they are needed (e.g., using semantic spaces, trust metrics for confidence levels, determining the role of machine learning, handling queries, and measuring fittedness). But he admits that this work is only a preliminary step forward to determine the ever more intractable contexts within which a modern military commander might face today and in the near future. Diplomats, cyberwarriors, and financial planners will share future intelligence and command architectures. This particular domain is an easily identifiable one even if it is also too complex for most nonmilitary and nontrained observers to understand. In his chapter, he provides a review of several of what he describes as "edge" examples that compromise systems, reduce trust, and put countries at risk. For these examples, he provides a corrective when possible or a research path forward when not. His work is especially helpful to think about when it becomes necessary to build contexts shared between humans and machines, not only in command positions but also for civilian human-machine contexts. He illustrates the information in his chapter by proposing a fictional mission conducted by Australian Special Forces; the contingencies that these forces must work through and resolve; their impact on a command, especially in an extreme context (on the "edge"); and the coordination required and then followed by a more detailed look behind the scenes to watch as these effects play out (e.g., with data fusion). Some of the innovations necessary for this application have been developed in the author's laboratory. From his laboratory the author introduces human-machine collaboration, some of its programming, and how narratives are used to assemble the description of a situation as a response to a military query is constructed.

Chapter 4 was written by Stephen Russell, Ira S. Moskowitz, and Brian Jalaian. Russell is the chief of the Battlefield Information Processing Branch at the US Army Research Laboratory in Adelphi, MD. Presently, Russell's research is on incorporating IoT ideas and capabilities within the battlefield environment, described in their chapter as the Internet of (Battle) Things. The third author, Jalaian, is an applied mathematician in Russell's branch. Their colleague, Moskowitz, is a mathematician at the Naval Research Laboratory in Washington, DC. The chapter they wrote, titled "Context: Separating the forest and the trees—Wavelet contextual conditioning for AI," has as its goal to arrive at a computational version of context that machines, instead of humans, can determine and share. To endow future machines with the capability of determining context for teamwork and decision support systems with AI algorithms, the authors address some of the difficult challenges faced by applied AI scientists whenever contexts can vary considerably over time (which a context can do, especially on a high-technology battlefield). For AI to decompose trends in contexts, they strive to make the problem manageable for machines with wavelets to simplify the problem; first, by reducing dimensionality in the data with a preprocessing step; second, by adding a data conditioning step that retains the important features of a context; and third, by separating trends in context changes into short- and long-term variations in context. To demonstrate the application of their technique on future battlefields, they apply decomposition with wavelets to a typical management decision problem. The results of this straightforward application show that a positive advantage accrues from the use of discrete wavelet transformations to improve decisions.

The fifth chapter, "A narrative modeling platform: Representing the comprehension of novelty in open-world systems," was written by a Beth Cardier, John Shull, Alex Nielsen, Saikou Diallo, Niccolo Casas, Larry D. Sanford, Patrick Lundberg, Richard Ciavarra, and H.T. Goranson to describe the rationale behind their prototype narrative modeling platform. This group connects the need for multicontext modeling (a problem they anchor in medicine) with the fields needed to implement a system that can achieve it—virtual reality system development, systems design, and visualization design. Located in the United States are the two core groups for this project: at the Eastern Virginia Medical School in Norfolk, VA, are the lead author, Cardier, plus Sanford, Lundberg, and Ciavarra; the build itself is handled by Shull, Nielsen, and Diallo in the Virginia Modeling, Analysis, and Simulation Center at Old Dominion University, Suffolk, VA. In Australia, systems design is advised by Goranson at the Institute for Integrated and Intelligent Systems at Griffith University; input on visualization fundamentals is provided by Casas, at the Bartlett School of Architecture, University College London, in London, the United Kingdom. This chapter describes a modeling environment in which variability among contexts is represented as successive states in narrative streams, a foundation that this group argues has applicability across many domains. Their work addresses the need to comprehend real situations in spite of our partial and changing information about them; even when humans cannot make sense of some of the situations that they face, to survive, they must adapt. Here the adaptation to newly perceived circumstances is understood as a "narrative" form of cognition, in which anything that can be described can be modeled. The tool's immersive environment thus allows any media artifact to be captured and annotated by its 3D semantic networks, which are depicted as shifts from one situation to the next. Unexpected situations that are handled are part of the representation scheme itself, in which the nonstandard aspects of every event are recorded in relation to general knowledge about similar situations. A core goal is to enable humans to characterize novel situations, their causal drivers, and the way in which humans form this information into networks of knowledge. At present, these representations are shared among human collaborators and teams, but a back end built by Goranson will allow them to be shared by a reasoning system as well. Ultimately, if a machine or human detects a novel change in a context, this group wants each to be able to share the change with the other, using structures that both can understand.

Chapter 6, "Deciding Machines: Moral-Scene Assessment for Intelligent Systems," was written by Ariel M. Greenberg, a senior research scientist in the Intelligent Systems Center at Johns Hopkins University Applied Physics Laboratory located in Laurel, MD. To enable moral judgments by machines as a part of their decision-making processes, Greenberg discusses how scientists and engineers must design AI and robotic systems. These systems may approach, purposely or accidently, the many different scenes possible in social reality, including scenes of moral weight that need to be reasoned through to produce an acceptable action. He begins his study with the recognition that, presently, machines process information from the world amorally and, consequently, cannot act conscientiously in a scene with a moral perspective. To enable this perspective, he starts by thinking through Asimov's laws of robotics, especially his first law that a robot should not "injure a human," suggesting that AI developers must begin by enabling machines to perceive what the concepts of "human" and "injury" may mean to a machine forbidden from "injuring a human." Greenberg's foundational approach is for machines to assess scenes morally by perceiving these special concepts as the first step in a moral deliberation. Along with numerous examples, he reviews how minds might detect moral salience, how biases might interfere, and how machines might reason about danger. But "Moral-Scene Assessment" is only his immediate goal for machines, on the road to his desire to craft future ethics of behavior for machines. For now the assessment step would endow future machines with something akin to a conscience that would enable them to identify what is morally salient in a scene, to enable morally appropriate interactions with humans, and to enable machines to think through the potential harm to humans in morally ambiguous scenes. But to identify the morally salient items in a scene requires a perception and a qualification of the sources of danger to the humans in the reasoning by machines. Armed with these perceptions and the ability to reason about them, however, the machine would then be prepared to adopt an appropriate stance to interact with humans within a scene as it builds a shared context with its human teammates or, say, an injured human met by happenstance. With the machine able to choose the mode of interaction appropriate to each entity within a scene, the machine would be able to apply a moral perspective in its reasoning over the possible or potential injuries that may involve humans and to act accordingly.

The next chapter, Chapter 7, was written by Lisa Troyer; it is titled "The criticality of social and behavioral science in the development and execution of autonomous systems." Troyer oversees research in the US Army's Social Sciences group (where she is responsible for the review of research in the sciences of culture and behavior and also for the sciences of institutions and organizations); she is located at the Army's research office (the Army's corporate, or central, laboratory). In this book, her chapter addresses how the capabilities of autonomous machines and systems are leading to numerous successes with AI, including autonomous systems that not only can self-learn but also can perceive, think, and update themselves with limited human oversight (known as human in the loop). Her research shows that soon enough these autonomous systems can take in information from the environment and act and adjust independently of humans (known as humans out of the loop). To construct the contexts shared between human-machine teammates, this means that a knowledge or the science of interdependence between humans and machines, or between systems and systems, or between machines and their environments, including the several social realities that machines might happen across, must be mastered. These physical and social environments will be constantly labile, complex (war, accidents, and disasters), ambiguous, uncertain, or a combination of these difficult contexts. That means computational researchers must be able to program, design, model, simulate, and operate systems that not only can think, learn, and make decisions on their own but also are able to recognize biases (social psychology), follow rules of engagement (e.g., legal actions), consider philosophy (morality and ethics), and know how to manage conflict in certain situations. Risks will be everywhere, including the possibility of a smaller tragedy or a larger catastrophe from accidents or mistakes. But on the flip side of these risks are numerous opportunities to advance the social and economic sciences, to improve decisions in the field, and to collect the data that provide for the analytics that can lead to better and safer operations for humans working with, in and around autonomous systems, an advancement for science and society.

Chapter 8 was written by Geoffrey W. Rutledge and Joseph C. Wood. Rutledge is an MD, has a PhD, and is the founder and chief medical officer at HealthTap in Mountain View, California; his company delivers a suite of connected health services and applications (apps) that range from free online jargon-free answers given to consumers with questions about health care and include the ability to seek immediate assistance with an appointment or an online consultation. Wood is also an MD and PhD, and he is associated with the Dwight D. Eisenhower Army Medical Center at Fort Gordon, Georgia, one of the US Army's premier medical centers. Their chapter is titled "Virtual health and artificial intelligence: Using technology to improve healthcare delivery." For them the term "virtual health" describes the many new technologies that provide for the delivery of health care outside of the normal face-to-face venue where appointments between patients and providers are held in traditional doctor offices, meetings that sometimes create hardships for potential patients, for example, long travel times, often from a distance; long queues that consume time; preliminary examinations that may not address the original complaint; and hurried explanations of diagnoses filled with technical terms that leave laymen grasping for more understandable explanations given in common terms. The new technologies discussed by the two authors attempt to overcome many of the negative aspects of appointments in the several demands by patients to move away from the offices of doctors. These technologies include telemedicine, e-health, mHealth, remote home monitoring, and telementoring. Telemedicine is medicine at a distance when the patient and physician are separated from each other; e-health enables the transmission of secure messages and consultations between patients and health-care providers; mHealth is an iteration of virtual health provided over mobile devices; remote home monitoring is designed to provide quality care in a patient's own home (e.g., monitoring diabetes); and telementoring is now offered to health-care providers to provide them with the training necessary to learn about new diseases, new treatments, or new technologies. Other factors influencing virtual health beyond patient demands include the arrival of even newer technologies and treatments, transformed health-care delivery methods, new state and national health care policies, and insurance coverage for virtual health. But beyond all of these factors and that also affect traditional health-care delivery methods and even newer technologies, artificial intelligence (AI) is being introduced; it promises to improve the accuracy of diagnoses and access to care, to reduce costs, to alleviate health-care provider shortages, and to bridge the gap between the accurate but bewildering technical explanations of diagnoses with common explanations that build a shared context between providers and patients.

Chapter 9 was written by Ira S. Moskowitz, Stephen Russell, and William F. Lawless. Moskowitz is a mathematician in the Information Management and Decision Architectures Branch at the Naval Research Laboratory in Washington, DC. Russell is the chief of the Battlefield Information Processing Branch at the Army Research Laboratory in Adelphi, Maryland. And Lawless is in the Departments of Mathematics and Psychology at Paine College in Augusta, Georgia. Their chapter is titled "An information geometric look at the valuing of information." In their chapter, they address the necessity to make it possible for a machine to use artificial intelligence (AI) to determine the value of the information in a message being handled by a machine. From the earliest age, humans quickly begin to learn how to easily understand the messages that they send to each other even with the use of machines (e.g., telephones, telegraphs, text messages, cell phones, lasers, and musical instruments). Machine to machine messages are relatively easy to be communicated, too. But for a machine to understand a message from a human, to digest that message, and then to respond to the human with an understandable message is almost an intractable problem. Yet the arrival of human-machine teams makes it imperative that humans and machines can speak to each other in an understandable language sufficient for them to be able to build the context shared between these two types of agents to solve difficult problems together, to support each other as they work together, to complete an assigned mission together, and to defend each other as members of a team. Human-machine teams may make decisions together in situations where human lives are at stake. These are the challenges that make this problem difficult. Shannon information theory is a quantitative method that considers the simple transmission of messages without the need to understand the message or to value the qualitative aspects of the information that is in a message. But to build a context shared between humans and machines, they will have to understand the subtleties in what each other means in the messages that they send to each other as members of a team. For their first step, specifically in their chapter, the authors address whether a machine can analyze messages sent by humans or information from humans in general with information geometry. In this chapter, they have also explored the use of statistical manifolds, and for future research, they plan to consider related aspects of potential solutions to this problem. In summary, their chapter is an opening foray into a difficult problem that lays a foundation for them and others to make deeper explorations with the possibility of a fuller solution for this difficult but important problem.

Chapter 10, titled "AI, autonomous machines and human awareness: Towards shared machine-human contexts in medicine," was cowritten by D. Douglas Miller and Elena A. Wood, both in the Department of Academic Affairs at the Medical College of Georgia, Augusta University, in Augusta, Georgia. Miller is an MD with an honorary CM degree from McGill University, he has earned an International MBA, and he is presently in the position of vice dean of Academic Affairs at Augusta University. Wood is also an MD, and she holds a research PhD in addition. Their chapter addresses the curricula needed to introduce artificial intelligence (AI) to medical students with a focus on the medical training that their students need to obtain sufficient clinical skills for these medical students to become credentialed in the modern medical sciences of today. From their perspective the authors confront several problems in the medical teaching profession beginning with the rising importance of big data in medicine, with the nearly continuous arrival of new technology and drugs into the medical profession, and with the serial changes in medical education and administration from these major disruptions. There are also the changes brought about by AI and algorithms on health care. Neural networks and the machine learning of disease features and the use of AI combine to speed the accuracy of diagnostics and to improve the predictions of existing chronic diseases and even to keep pace with the discovery of new pathways for diseases along with the treatments that affect human health. The technology for digital health has arrived and is functioning. But these transformations are competing for the limited attention of medical educator professionals who must also keep abreast. Coming to their assistance, new collaborations are occurring between data scientists and computer engineers with medical educators to affect the very nature of the education that medical students are receiving as they prepare for their professional careers. For example, virtual patients can be created that are able to present to medical students with different illnesses to improve the ability of students to make better differential diagnoses. Students can repeat these virtual sessions as often as needed, download them, and save them for future reference, too. But the authors also foresee that, in the near future, machines and humans will be able to work together as they share medical knowledge and expertise to build shared life-saving contexts when they team together to learn, to solve problems, and to work together as members of human-machine medical teams. Overseen by medical professional educators, machines can already deliver aptitude-based career advising, can identify students with academic challenges, can intervene repeatedly and tirelessly with students who need assistance, and can use natural language to process standardized questions.

The next chapter, Chapter 11, was written by Ryan Quandt and John Licato. The title of their chapter is "Problems of autonomous agents following informal, open-textured rules." Quandt and Licato are both in the Advancing Machine and Human Reasoning (AMHR) Laboratory at the University of South Florida, located in Tampa, Florida. In addition, Quandt is an adjunct professor in the Department of Philosophy at the University of South Florida, and Licato is an assistant professor in the Department of Computer Science and Engineering at the same university. They consider the situation where autonomous artificial agents must interact interdependently with other intelligent agents and humans as both construct a context that then can be shared among them to help them when they work together as teammates. They propose that these artificial agents will inevitably follow what they have identified as informal, open-textured rules (IORs). From their perspective, these rules contain the guidelines for the ethical behaviors of artificial agents, including the laws set by nations or negotiated in international treaties that will guide these intelligent agents as they attempt to adhere to widely held and broad moral principles and humans. But as the authors point out, determining the computational criteria for these IORs is far from an easy task, especially when attempting to determine the criteria for matching the intent behind a rule or a law. When they address context and how IORs affect the context that is constructed from context-dependent arguments, based on their work, the result helps to determine the interpretations made by intelligent artificial agents working interdependently with other intelligent artificial agents or with humans to establish the parameters of the IORs that agents and humans must both attempt to follow. By carrying out more research into how to reason over these IOR rules, the trust in each other and in their respective contributions, particularly when moral, is the payoff.

Chapter 12, titled "Engineering for emergence in information fusion systems: A review of some challenges," was written by four authors, Ali K. Raz, James Llinas, Ranjeev Mittu, and William F. Lawless. Raz is a visiting assistant professor in the School of Aeronautics and Astronautics at Purdue University in West Lafayette, Indiana; Llinas is the founder and director emeritus of the Center for Multisource Information Fusion at the University at Buffalo, State University of New York, located in Amherst, New York; Mittu is the branch head of Information Management and Decision Architectures Branch, Information Technology Division, at the US Naval Research Laboratory in Washington, DC; and Lawless is in the Department of Mathematics and Psychology at Paine College in Augusta, Georgia, and a summer faculty researcher at NRL in Washington, DC. In their chapter the authors review some of the challenges from the evolution in the contexts of operational environments in modern information fusion (IF) systems with the recent arrival of intelligent systems and humans working together in teams to pursue their newly assigned missions. Before the arrival of these human-machine teams, traditional information extraction and fusion addressed only the data. But the recent advancements in artificial intelligence (AI) and machine learning (ML) in particular, have led to new demands across the IF community to design systems that are able to offer a wider spectrum of dynamic responses to provide the "data-to-decision" responses that shift from information fusion alone to decisions that are made with AI support. But this combined full spectrum response leads to interdependent interactions in the interplay among the multiple components of this complex system that can emerge in unexpected ways. Emergence is a challenge that must be recognized and managed. In the view of the authors, from its beginnings, systems engineering is a discipline with the tools, experience, and an approach that can model and assess how best to manage emergent effects. With systems engineering in mind, the authors conclude that, when properly managed, emergence can lead to an awareness of context in the substance of the interpretations derived that can improve trust when the decisions that are implemented are successful.

The next chapter, Chapter 13, is titled "Integrating expert human decision-making in artificial intelligence applications." This chapter was written by Hesham Fouad, Ira S. Moskowitz, Derek Brock, and Michael Scott. Coauthors Fouad (a *computer scientist* in Virtual Environments and Visualization), Moskowitz (a mathematician with research interests in covert channels, information theory, steganography, and others), and Scott (a computer scientist) are with the Information Management and Decision Architectures Branch at the Naval Research Laboratory in Washington, DC. Brock (a computer scientist with the Navy Center for Applied Research in Artificial Intelligence) is also at the Naval Research Laboratory in Washington, DC. The authors tackle the modeling of human intelligence, one of the more difficult problems to address and to solve compared with many of the domains where AI has already been successfully applied. For example, in the commercial domain, many of the successful approaches have been driven by what could be characterized as relatively inexpensive yet very high-end performance systems; in contrast, based on the paucity of information that is exchanged from among the members of human-machine teams, shared context can only be meaningful and satisfied with something akin to human intelligence. Recognizing both the intractable nature of their target problem and its potential for a very large payoff, the authors have decided to use a pragmatic approach that automates the observational capture of human consistency with the expertise expressed by human subject matter experts, known as the analytic hierarchy process used by businesses, but initially by covering only a limited domain of knowledge. Although limited, their problem is still challenging in that it deals with the degradation of human performance in highly multitasked situations where decisions are choices selected from among competing alternatives. Their goal is to seek consistency from the subject matter experts. If they are successful in making this capture of consistent behavior even from subject matter experts who are not always perfectly consistent and if their mathematical model is successful, it will serve two purposes: to help machines to make consistent choices from among competing alternatives and to form a foundation for the authors to use to explore for future generalizations. Then, they plan to scale from this limited domain to permit a stepwise expansion into other domains.

Chapter 14, the next chapter, is titled "A communication paradigm for human-robot interaction during robot failure scenarios" under the leadership of Holly A. Yanco (who is also the corresponding author). She has been assisted by coauthors Daniel J. Brooks, Dalton J. Curtin, James T. Kuczynski, Joshua J. Rodriguez, Aaron Steinfeld, and Holly A. Yanco. Brooks is at the Toyota Research Institute; Steinfeld is at Carnegie Mellon University; and Curtin, Kuczynski, Rodriguez, and Yanco are at the University of Massachusetts Lowell. In their chapter the authors study the effects of the failure of autonomous robot systems on the users of these systems, to those the systems might support, and to those bystanders who happen to be nearby these systems when these systems begin to fail. Autonomous robot systems may soon be deployed in the public square; how will the public be alerted to the dangers when such an autonomous system fails? The authors want to explore what are the signals emitted by the imminent failure of an autonomous robot system. Are there readily apparent signs given off from the impending failure of an autonomous robot system? Alternatively, should the robots be designed to alert their nearby users, including not only the users who are experts but also and especially the nonusers of robot system who happen to be around when these systems are approaching a point of failure? With the goal of facilitating the safe shutdown of an autonomous robot system, the authors contribute to the literature with their study by simulating an autonomous system using smart phones to explore various forms of alerts that can be communicated to humans who might be threatened by a failure. What they find is that, by constructing the context of an impending failure shared between humans and machines, the method of communicating an alert and the alert's protocol could make a positive difference (e.g., whether to use a push notification vs a pull notification). They also found that the context shared between machines and humans improved the performance of, and trust in, a human-machine team.

Chapter 15 was written by Jonathan Barzilai. He is at Dalhousie University in Halifax, Nova Scotia, located in Eastern Canada. The title of his chapter is "On neural-network training algorithms." In this chapter the author reviews the inherent mathematical difficulties with neural network training algorithms that impede their rate of training. To counter this problem, consequently, the author proposes a new algorithm that he has designed to overcome some of the limitations with neural networks but with the desired effect of speeding up or shortening the training process. He notes that neural networks began as crude imitations of brain networks, but they have evolved into computational systems in their own right that can "learn" how to solve problems or to provide services (e.g., self-driving cars, autonomous astronomical searches, and autonomous inspection drones). He focuses on the function of training neural networks, namely, to optimize their training, a difficult problem in and of itself because of several computational limitations. He begins with the one-dimensional case, addresses convergence and minimization, then generalizes to the multidimensional case, and finally considers various solutions. Afterward, he introduces his own equation and compares the performance of traditional neural networks with that of his own equation along with the latter's attendant speedup. For the future of human-machine teams, his algorithm may provide an important service to these teams by reducing the time needed to train them to learn new functions or to offer new applications.

The next chapter, Chapter 16, is titled "Identifying distributed incompetence in an organization." Chapter 16 was written by Boris Galitsky with the Oracle Corporation in Redwood Shores, CA. In his chapter on organizational malfeasance, Galitsky explores different organizational entities, one that is incompetent that he labels as an organization that displays distributed incompetence (DIC); he contrasts that type of an organizational entity with its opposite that is a competent organization that serves as a source of distributed knowledge. Both types can also occur inside of a department within an organization that can even come to represent the public face of an organization in, say, its customer support area. More concerning, an organization can itself become incompetent. To begin, Galitsky draws a strong contrast between these two types of organizations, the DIC reflecting an air of incompetence (e.g., when a clerk is being irrational with a customer, unable to fulfill a request for help by a customer, or simply unable to solve a task requested by a customer to an organization's representative). But the problem not only can reflect more than just a single clerk but also can represent a department of an organization or the entire organization itself. Galitsky studies the motives for this type of behavior at the individual or organizational levels to find some support that, for example, the obligations of a DIC organization can be discharged dishonestly. He investigates this kind of misbehavior expressed in the publicly available discourses or texts used by an organization with machine learning (ML) as it performs its daily functions in its market located within a larger marketplace. He attributes these problems to the control of organizations by and for its management rather than by and for its shareholders. He finds a rate of misbehavior that he classifies for financial organizations and proposes different solutions that he discusses to address the problem.

Chapter 17, titled "Begin with the human: Designing for safety and trustworthiness in cyber-physical systems," was written by a team of investigators from Australia: Elizabeth T. Williams, Ehsan Nabavi, Genevieve Bell, Caitlin M. Bentley, Katherine A. Daniell, Noel Derwort, Zac Hatfield-Dodds, Kobi Leins, Amy K. McLennan. This team of researchers is located at the 3A Institute, Australian National University, located in Canberra, Australia. The authors begin with a brief discussion of control systems and what humans do to manage and regulate them safely. In their chapter, they discuss the new opportunities and implications offered by artificial intelligence (AI) for the control of large complex systems. For an example of the problems they want to discuss posed by large complex systems, they use as a case study what happened with the Three Mile Island (TMI) nuclear reactor accident in 1979 when its loss of control was caused from several misinterpretations by the humans in control. They note that the opportunities offered by AI to prevent problems like TMI also bring with them several challenges, but they focus on the unexpected problems these cyber-physical systems may pose to those human managers who plan to let these systems be managed and governed with AI. The problem they address specific to AI is autonomy. Autonomy means that these systems can learn, evolve, and possibly act without the intervention of humans. But this lack of intervention raises a serious question for the public: without direct human control, how much agency should be given to systems as they become more autonomous, thereby directly increasing risks to public safety and the trustworthiness placed in these systems by the public?

The next chapter, Chapter 18, was written by Shu-Heng Chen. It is titled "Digital humanities and the digital economy." Chen is at the AI-ECON Research Center and the Department of Economics, National Chengchi University, located in Taipei, Taiwan. In his chapter, Chen discusses the impact of the recent digital revolution on humans. Then, he proposes a novel definition for the digital humanities that corresponds to this revolution. In his discussion, he reviews the physical space where humans live and the new technologies they employ that map from their living space to its counterpart in digital cyberspace. His goal is to seek the mutual agreement that may and may not occur between science and humanities to study these "twin" spaces methodologically and ontologically. His focus is on the creation of parallel realities with the deployment in cyberspace of numerous artificial agents using technology such as block chain that can indirectly reflect on the humans who exist in physical reality contemporaneous with these agents inside of their digital reality; he is also interested in the reverse impact that these agents have on recreating humans as individuals with possibly new identities; and he is particularly interested in where these humans and their agents may create a new cybereconomy, one that can be easily and more fully captured than in physical reality. In what he describes as the "personal web of everything," Chen looks for connections between these "twin" human cyberspaces based on the feedback that passes between humans and their cyber agents at critical points that he describes as the bridges between the two economies where the information that these humans and machines share contributes to the realities that they construct for each other.

Chapter 19, "Human-machine sense making in context-based computational decision," was written by Olivier Bartheye and Laurent Chaudron. Bartheye is with CREA, the French Air Force Academy (FAFA) Research Center, in France. FAFA is a public industrial and commercial establishment. Chaudron, formerly with Office National d'Études et de Recherches Aérospatiales (ONERA), is now at THEORIK-LAB in France. In their chapter, Bartheye and Chaudron approach the sense-making needed to construct context from a geometrical perspective for a decision-based mechanism that can generalize to intelligent agents. They begin with the inner topology of a decision algebra to address what they identify as a causal break represented in a computational model of context by double S-curves. But this means that they must deal with a singularity due to their assumption of a causal break. The causal break motivates them to explore closing it with a context change arrow acting as a phase transition where wavelength is its value. The simulated phase shift occurs between perception and action knowledge where the precise semantics of a local decision can close the causal break. While a causal break is always continuous and never discrete, they also reject a discrete solution from the unwanted complexity that is created by its gap in knowledge. Instead, they explore the full knowledge offered by the continuous case, which requires a special mathematical structure like a Hopf algebra, but one that could not be computed; instead, they replaced it with a computable cocontinuous property in the coalgebraic component of the decision Hopf algebra. With the model that results, they then attempt to capture sense-making to rationalize the transition.

Chapter 20, titled "Constructing mutual context in human-robot collaborative problem solving with multimodal input," was written by Michael Wollowski, Tyler Bath, Sophie Brusniak, Michael Crowell, Sheng Dong, Joseph Knierman, Walt Panfil, Sooyoung Park, Mitchell Schmidt, and Adit Suvarna. All of the authors are located in the Computer Science Department at the Rose-Hulman Institute of Technology in Terre Haute, Indiana. In their chapter the authors provide the details of the information produced by the various components of their system and explain how information is generated by human-robot teams that they have designed to interact. Specifically, they want to explain the different aspects of how human-robot teams construct shared context in their system, how these contexts are aggregated, and how the contributions of the teams are evaluated. After the authors provide an overview of their physical system and its various components, they describe their idea that a shared space is constructed whenever human-robot teams are solving problems. To solve problems in this shared space, the authors collect and analyze the data to determine how best to facilitate the human-machine interactions occurring within their system from different sources, primarily not only natural speech and gesture but also geometry, object identification, and relative location data. The architecture where their interactions occur is represented with a whiteboard that is used to track the information derived during the problem-solving process that they later analyze. In their view the analysis becomes easier when the shared context, as in their case, is made explicit with several pieces of well-identified information that contribute directly to the construction of the shared context. Their future plans include the ability to process higher-order commands to allow them to address more complex problems.

References

Aha, D. W., McSherry, D., & Yang, Q. (2006). Advances in conversational case-based reasoning. *The Knowledge Engineering Review, 20*(3), 247–254. https://doi.org/10.1017/S0269888906000531 [Cambridge University Press].

Arampatzis, A., & Sherman, J. (2018). Thucydides in the data warfare era. *Strategy Bridge.* From https://thestrategybridge.org/the-bridge/2018/5/30/thucydides-in-the-data-warfare-era.

Barlow, B. (2017). The future of GEOINT. Why activity-based intelligence and machine learning demonstrate that the future of GEOINT has already arrived. *Trajectory Magazine.* From http://trajectorymagazine.com/the-future-of-geoint/.

Beaudoin, M., Kabanza, F., Nault, V., & Valiquette, L. (2014). An antimicrobial prescription surveillance system that learns from experience. *AI Magazine,* 15–25. From https://www.aaai.org/ojs/index.php/aimagazine/article/viewFile/2500/2408.

Biltgen, P., Bacastow, T. S., Kaye, T., & Young, J. M. (2017). *Activity-based intelligence: Understanding patterns-of-life. The state and future of GEOINT 2017.* United States Geospatial Intelligence Foundation. From http://usgif.org/system/uploads/4897/original/2017_SoG.pdf.

Bohr, N. (1955). Science and the unity of knowledge. In L. Leary (Ed.), *The unity of knowledge* (pp. 44–62). New York: Doubleday.

Bolton, J. Q. (2018). *Modifying situational awareness: Perfect knowledge and precision are fantasy.* Small Wars Journal. From http://smallwarsjournal.com/jrnl/art/modifying-situational-awareness-perfect-knowledge-and-precision-are-fantasy.

Bowman, E., Turek, M., Tunison, P., Porter, R., Thomas, S., Gintautas, V., et al. (2017). Advanced text and video analytics for proactive decision making. In: *SPIE defense and security, Anaheim, CA.*

Brynjolfsson, E., & Mitchell, T. (2017). What can machine learning do? Workplace implications. Profound changes are coming, but roles for humans remain. *Science, 358,* 1530–1534.

Danzig, R. (2018). *Technology Roulette. Managing loss of control as many militaries pursue technological superiority.* Center for New American Security. [Danzig, Senior Fellow at Johns Hopkins University Applied Physics Laboratory, was Secretary of the Navy in the Clinton Administration] From https://s3.amazonaws.com/files.cnas.org/documents/CNASReport-Technology-Roulette-Final.pdf.

Darley, J. M., & Gross, P. H. (2000). A hypothesis-confirming bias in labelling effects. In C. Stangor (Ed.), *Stereotypes and prejudice: Essential readings* (p. 212). Psychology Press.

Dehaene, S., Lau, H., & Kouider, S. (2017). What is consciousness and could machines have it? *Science, 358,* 486. see also letters to the editor and replies (2018, 1/26), "Conscious machines: Defining questions", Science, 359(6374): 400–402.

Diab, J., & Finney, N. (2017). *Whither the hover tank? Why we can't predict the future of warfare.* Modern War Institute. From https://mwi.usma.edu/whither-hover-tank-cant-predict-future-warfare/.

England, J. L. (2013). Statistical physics of self-replication. *The Journal of Chemical Physics, 139,* 121923. https://doi.org/10.1063/1.4818538.

Freedberg, S. J. (2018). Intel & cyber, strategy & policy why a 'Human In The Loop' can't control AI: Richard Danzig. "Error is as important as malevolence," Richard Danzig told me in an interview. "I probably wouldn't use the word 'stupidity,' (because) the people who make these mistakes are frequently quite smart, (but) it's so complex and the technologies are so opaque that there's a limit to our understanding.". *Breaking Defense.* From https://breakingdefense.com/2018/06/why-a-human-in-the-loop-cant-control-ai-richard-danzig/.

Galdorisi, G. C. (2015). *Keeping humans in the loop. You say you want a revolution? Autonomous unmanned vehicles could bring on the biggest one yet. Vol. 141/2/1,344.* U.S. Naval Institute, Proceedings Magazine. From https://www.usni.org/magazines/proceedings/2015-02/keeping-humans-loop.

Gershenfeld, N. (1999). *When things begin to think.* New York: Henry Holt and Co.

Ginsburg, R.B. (2011), American Electric Power Co., Inc., et al. v. Connecticut et al., 10–174, http://www.supremecourt.gov/opinions/10pdf/10-174.pdf.

Goodfellow, I., Pouget-Abadie, J., Mirza, M., Xu, B., Warde-Farley, D., Ozair, S., et al. (2014). *Generative adversarial networks.* From arXiv:1406.2661.

Grove, T. (2018). Drone attacks on Russian bases in Syria expose security holes. The attacks reveal a fresh threat to Moscow from insurgent rebel groups in Syria even after their broad defeat by Russia and its allies. *Wall Street Journal.* From https://www.wsj.com/articles/drone-attacks-on-russian-bases-in-syria-expose-security-holes-1516017608.

Higgins, T., & Spector, M. (2018). Tesla autopilot system warned driver to put hands on wheel, U.S. investigators say. The Tesla car involved in fatal March crash was speeding on a highway. *Wall Street Journal.* From https://www.wsj.com/articles/tesla-autopilot-system-warned-driver-to-put-hands-on-wheel-u-s-investigators-say-1528394536?mod=article_inline&mod=article_inline.

Hutson, M. (2017). Report. A matter of trust. Researchers are studying why many consumers are apprehensive about autonomous vehicles, and how to put them at ease. *Science, 358*(6369), 1375–1377.

Hutson, M. (2018). Report. Artificial intelligence faces reproducibility crisis. *Science, 359*(6377), 725–726. https://doi.org/10.1126/science.359.6377.725.

Jones, J. M. (2018). Americans' identification as independents back up in 2017. *Gallup.* From http://news.gallup.com/poll/225056/americans-identification-independents-back-2017.aspx.

Kambhampati, S. (2018). Challenges of human-aware AI systems. In: *AAAI 2018 Presidential Address, New Orleans, LA.*

Kean, S. (2018). AIQ' review: Getting smarter all the time. Artificial intelligence is a pervasive part of modern life—Used to predict corn yields and map disease outbreaks, among other applications. Book review: "AIQ" by Nick Polson and James Scott. *Wall Street Journal.* From https://www.wsj.com/articles/aiq-review-getting-smarter-all-the-time-1527717048.

Kirk, R. (2003). *More terrible than death. Massacres, drugs, and America's war in Columbia.* Public Affairs.

Kissinger, H. A. (2018). How the enlightenment ends. Philosophically, intellectually—In every way—Human society is unprepared for the rise of artificial intelligence. *The Atlantic.* From https://www.theatlantic.com/magazine/archive/2018/06/henry-kissinger-ai-could-mean-the-end-of-human-history/559124/.

Kraft, E., & Chesebrough, D. (2018). Viewpoint: Aerospace, defense industry must join digital revolution. *National Defense.* From http://www.nationaldefensemagazine.org/articles/2018/6/5/aerospace-defense-industry-must-join-digital-revolution.

Lawless, W. F. (2017a). The entangled nature of interdependence. Bistability, irreproducibility and uncertainty. *Journal of Mathematical Psychology, 78,* 51–64.

Lawless, W. F. (2017b). The physics of teams: Interdependence, measurable entropy and computational emotion. *Frontiers of Physics, 5,* 30. https://doi.org/10.3389/fphy.2017.00030.

Lawless, W. F., Mittu, R., & Sofge, D. A. (Eds.), (2018). *Computational context: The value, theory and application of context with artificial intelligence.* CRC Press.

Martyushev, L. M. (2013). Entropy and entropy production: Old misconceptions and new breakthroughs. *Entropy, 15,* 1152–1170.

Mitchell, T., Mahadevan, S., & Sternberg, L. (1990). LEAP: A learning apprentice for VSLI design. Y. Kodratoff & R. Michalski (Eds.), *Vol. 3. ML: An artificial intelligence approach*: Morgan Kaufman Press.

Mittu, R., Taylor, G., Sofge, D., & Lawless, W. F. (2016). *Organizers: AI and the mitigation of human error: Anomalies, team metrics and thermodynamics. In: AAAI-2016 symposium at Stanford.* From https://www.aaai.org/Symposia/Spring/sss16symposia.php#ss01.

Najafi, S., & Salam, Z. (2016). *Evaluating prediction accuracy for collaborative filtering algorithms in recommender systems.* Royal Institute of Technology. From kth.diva-portal.org/smash/get/diva2:927356/FULLTEXT01.pdf.

Nosek, B. Open Collaboration of Science. (2015). Estimating the reproducibility of psychological science. *Science, 349* (6251), 943 [supplementary: 4716-1 to 4716-9].

NSSC (2018). *New name for navy PEO.* By Program Executive Office Unmanned and Small Combatants NavSea. From http://www.navsea.navy.mil/Media/News/Article/1473447/new-name-for-navy-peo/.

NTSB (2018). *Preliminary report highway HWY18MH010. The information in this report is preliminary and will be supplemented or corrected during the course of the investigation.* National Transportation Safety Board. From *https://www.ntsb.gov/investigations/AccidentReports/Pages/HWY18MH010-prelim.aspx.*

Pearl, J. (2002). Reasoning with cause and effect. *AI Magazine, 23*(1), 95–111. From https://aaai.org/ojs/index.php/aimagazine/article/download/1612/1511.

Pearl, J., & Mackenzie, D. (2018). AI can't reason why. The current data-crunching approach to machine learning misses an essential element of human intelligence. *Wall Street Journal.* From https://www.wsj.com/articles/ai-cant-reason-why-1526657442.

Rachlinski, J. J. (1997). Introduction-juries: Arbiters or arbitrary. *Cornell Journal of Law and Public Policy, 7*(1), 1–5. From https://scholarship.law.cornell.edu/cgi/viewcontent.cgi?article=1219&context=cjlpp.

Rusk, J. (2018). Connecting the digital twin. From idea through production to customers and back. *Tech Briefs*, 16–18. Fromhttp://viewer.zmags.com/publication/8418e6ae#/8418e6ae/22.

Scharping, N. (2018). Psychopath AI' offers a cautionary tale for technologists. *Discover*, From http://blogs.discovermagazine.com/d-brief/2018/06/07/norman-psychopath-ai-mit/#.Wxp4n4opDmp.

Schlesinger, A. (1949). *The vital center. The politics of freedom*. Riverside Press.

Schoka, A. (2018). Training cyberspace maneuver. *Small Wars Journal*. From http://smallwarsjournal.com/jrnl/art/training-cyberspace-maneuver.

Shannon, C. E. (1948). A mathematical theory of communication. *The Bell System Technical Journal*, 27, 379–423, 623–656.

Shultz, G. P. (2018). America can ride the 21st century's waves of change. Fasten your seat belt. From work to warfare to welfare, technology is transforming the world. *Wall Street Journal*. From https://www.wsj.com/articles/america-can-ride-the-21st-centurys-waves-of-change-1530139914?shareToken=st16d75090420344f3816f775f61f7e249&ref=article_email_share.

Simon, H. A. (1989). *Bounded rationality and organizational learning*. Technical Report AIP 107 Pittsburgh, PA: CMU.

Smallman, H. S. (2012). *TAG (team assessment grid): A coordinating representation for submarine contact management. SBIR phase II contract #: N00014–12-C-0389, ONR command decision making 6.1–6.2 program review. .*

Tan, O. (2017). How does a machine learn? *Forbes*. From https://www.forbes.com/sites/forbestechcouncil/2017/05/02/how-does-a-machine-learn/#e0483097441d.

Tzu, S. (1994). *The art of war*. R. D. Sawyer, (Trans.) New York: Basic Books [First published in the 5th Century, BC].

Van De Velde, J. (2018). Why cyber norms are dumb and serve Russian interests. *The Cyber Brief*. From https://www.thecipherbrief.com/column/opinion/cyber-norms-dumb-serve-russian-interests.

Werner, B. (2018). Navy's knifefish unmanned mine hunter passes sea acceptance testing. *USNI News*. From https://news.usni.org/2018/06/05/navys-knifefish-unmanned-mine-hunter-passes-key-test.

Wild, S. (2018). Irreproducible astronomy. A combination of data-churning telescopes and proprietary algorithms has led to a slate of opaque research that has some astronomers concerned. *Physics Today, Research & Technology*. https://doi.org/10.1063/PT.6.1.20180404a. From https://physicstoday.scitation.org/do/10.1063/PT.6.1.20180404a/full/.

Further reading

Kotkin, S. (2017). *Stalin: Waiting for Hitler, 1929–1941*. Penguin Press.

McVea, M. (2018). *CBR-case based reasoning, Purdue Engineering special problems course. From* https://engineering.purdue.edu/~engelb/abe565/cbr.htm.

Varadarajan, T. (2018). The weekend interview: Will Putin ever leave? Could he if he wanted? *Wall Street Journal*. From https://www.wsj.com/articles/will-putin-ever-leave-could-he-if-he-wanted-1520635050.

Analogy and metareasoning: Cognitive strategies for robot learning

Ashok K. Goel[a], Tesca Fitzgerald[a], Priyam Parashar[b]

[a]Georgia Institute of Technology, Atlanta, GA, United States [b]Contextual Robotics Institute, UC San Diego, La Jolla, CA, United States

2.1 Background, motivations, and goals

All intelligent forms share a conundrum: they not only must deal with novel situations but also must start with what they already know; how, then, can any intelligent form deal with any novelty? Of course, no intelligent form addresses all novel situations very well; if and when it does not, it may be unable to accomplish its goals or suffer harm in the process, perhaps even perish. Thus, if we are to build long-living robots, we must provide them with the capability of dealing with at least some kinds of novelty. Further, if we want robots to live and work among humans, then we may start with humanlike, human-level, *cognitive* strategies to addressing novel situations.

Research on cognitive science suggests four broad categories of mechanisms for addressing novel situations. The first is situated cognition and learning. The intelligent agent, human or robot, starts with knowledge of the world in the form of a policy of actions to be taken in different states in the world, executes the policy, often fails, but learns from the failure by incrementally modifying the policy. The mechanism of situated (or reinforcement) learning not only is general purpose and can be quite effective but also can be computationally costly.

The second cognitive mechanism is through social learning. The agent starts with knowledge of primitive objects, relations, events, and actions. The intelligent agent is situated in a sociocultural context where the agent may learn by observing a teacher, or the teacher may actively help the agent learn through demonstrations or corrections, or the agent may actively learn by asking questions of the teacher. This interactive mechanism can be costly, too, when a large number of observations and demonstrations are needed, but if a faithful teacher who patiently provides trustworthy answers is available, then this method can be quite effective.

The third cognitive mechanism for dealing with novelty is by analogy. Here the intelligent agent starts with a memory of previously encountered source cases. Given a new target problem, the agent retrieves a relevant case from memory and transfers and adapts knowledge from the known case to the new problem. The emphasis here is on transfer of relationships among objects in the known case and in the new problem, not necessarily on the objects themselves. This mechanism assumes a memory of previously encountered cases, but it can be quite effective when a case relevant to the new problem can be found in memory.

Finally a fourth cognitive mechanism for addressing novelty is through metareasoning—reasoning about reasoning. Here the agent starts not only with knowledge about the world but also knowledge about itself in the form of a model of its knowledge and reasoning. When the agent encounters a new problem, it uses its knowledge to address the problem and fails but collects additional information through the failure. It now uses metareasoning to localize and repair the causes of failures and thus incrementally adapts itself to the novel situation. This method requires a self-model and can be computationally costly for small problems but can be quite effective for complex problems with interacting goals.

We note the importance of context in this discussion. The choice of a specific mechanism among the aforementioned four categories depends very much on both the external context in which the agent is situated (is a teacher available to show a demonstration or address a question?) and the internal context of the agent's knowledge (is a case relevant to the new situation available?). We also note that the four mechanisms are quite complementary to one another, not mutually exclusive. In fact, human cognition appears to select, integrate, shift, and abandon among the various mechanisms depending on the constantly changing external (the novelty in the world) and internal (knowledge and processing) contexts.

These four cognitive strategies provide useful starting points for designing long-living robots capable of addressing novelty. In this chapter, we describe two combinations of the aforementioned cognitive strategies for dealing with novelty in the context of interactive robotics. The first approach combines the strategies of social learning with analogical reasoning (Fitzgerald, Goel, & Thomaz, 2018). A teacher first demonstrates a skill to a robot, and the robot stores the learned knowledge as a case. Given a new situation the robot analogically transfers the skill from the case to the new situation. The second approach combines reinforcement learning and metareasoning (Parashar, Goel, Sheneman, & Christensen, 2018). The agent uses deliberative planning to achieve a familiar goal in a novel situation. If and when it fails, it uses local reinforcement learning to learn the correct action in the failed state. A metareasoner monitors and coordinates the external behaviors and the internal processing in the agent. We will conclude this chapter with a discussion of the implications of this work in robotics on cognitive theories of analogy and metareasoning.

2.2 Using social learning and analogical reasoning in cognitive robotics

Let us consider the situation illustrated in Fig. 2.1. First a human teacher demonstrates a skill to accomplish a task to a robot (left of the figure). Then the teacher asks the robot to address the same task in a new but similar situation in which some of the objects and object relationships are different (right of the figure). How might the robot transfer the skill acquired in the prior demonstration to the new situation?

FIG. 2.1   A human teacher demonstrates how to scoop pasta from a pot into a bowl (as shown in the figure on the *left*). The robot is then asked to scoop pasta from a different pot into a different bowl (shown on the *right*). The question becomes how may the robot not only build an analogical mapping between the two situations but also transform the action model from the first situation—how to grasp the scoop, how to move it in space, how to dip it into the pot, etc.— to the new situation.

In traditional approaches to this problem, also called "transfer learning," the teacher gives a large number of demonstrations of the skill, the robot learns a model from the demonstrations, and then, given the new situation, applies the model. However, the cognitive strategy of analogical reasoning suggests the robot may build a mapping between the demonstrated source case and the target new problem and transfer the skill learned in the demonstration to the new situation. In principle, this strategy requires much fewer initial demonstrations.

While analogical mapping has been addressed in related work, it is typically assumed that the robot can gain additional experience in the target environment or knows which object feature(s) to use when evaluating object correspondences. However, when the robot learns a task from human interaction, such assumptions lead to two challenges. First, gaining additional experience in the target environment can be a time-consuming task in which the human teacher must continue to provide task demonstrations or feedback to the robot as it explores the environment. Simply helping the robot gain the correct mapping would more efficiently utilize the teacher's time. Second the robot does not have the same contextual knowledge that the human teacher has about the task and thus does not know which object features are relevant to successfully repeating the task. For example, in transferring a cup-stacking task, the robot would need to identify which cups in the source and target environments are similar according to their size feature. In another task in which the robot learns to sort the same cups by their color, the robot would need to instead map objects according to their hue feature. While the human teacher knows which features are relevant in the context of that task, the robot does not.

In these problems, which we call "situated mapping" problems, the robot must identify the mapping that maximizes similarity between source environment objects and their equivalent objects in the target environment. However, defining this similarity metric (and the object features it considers relevant) is nontrivial. The similarity metric that is appropriate for one task may not represent the object features relevant to another task. Consider our previous example, where a robot learns to use cups in both a stacking task and a sort-by-color task. In the first task the robot should identify an object mapping maximizing the similarity between mapped objects based on their size feature, whereas the second task requires objects to be mapped according to their hue feature.

We address this problem of context-dependent mapping, in which object mapping is dependent on the task being performed. The interactive object mapping problem has the following stages of interaction with a human teacher: The human teacher demonstrates a task in the source environment. The robot observes the object features and task steps involving those objects. The robot observes the target environment containing new objects and is asked to repeat the newly learned task. The robot infers the mapping between objects in the source and target environments. The robot uses this mapping to transfer the learned task for execution in the target environment. Our work is primarily concerned with how additional interaction between the robot and the human teacher can facilitate step 4: inferring the object mapping.

2.2.1 Related work

Research on cognitive systems has long addressed object mapping, particularly by identifying structural similarity between source and target objects, that is, objects sharing similar relations to their surroundings (Gentner, 1983; Gentner & Markman, 2006; Gick & Holyoak, 1983). The representation of the relationship between objects informs the mapping process. Falkenhainer, Forbus, and Gentner (1989) define a scene as a graph; objects sharing similar structural relations within their own graphs are mapped. Alternatively, objects may be represented and compared in terms of their pragmatic, spatial, and semantic features (Holyoak & Thagard, 1989) or in terms of visual analogies (Davies, Goel, & Yaner, 2008). While these approaches have been demonstrated in simulated domains, they have not been applied to identify analogies between physical objects with a rich set of perceptual features.

Learning from demonstration enables a robot to quickly learn skills from a human teacher (Akgun et al., 2012; Argall et al., 2009; Chernova & Thomaz, 2014). Prior work has demonstrated how a robot may ground an abstract task representation, such as "task recipes" (Misra et al., 2016; Waibel et al., 2011), in semantic locations in a new environment via interactive demonstrations (Bullard et al., 2016), learning prototypical object usage (Tenorth, Nyga, & Beetz, 2010), and learning to classify objects via active learning (Kulick et al., 2013). While related to object mapping, the symbol grounding problem differs in that it grounds abstract object references in specific object perception (whereas mapping directly correlates two object instances).

Similar mapping problems have also been explored in reinforcement learning domains; by learning an intertask mapping between source and target state variables, an agent can transfer a learned policy to a new domain (Taylor, Stone, & Liu, 2007). While a robot can build these mapping by exploring the target environment, we aim to minimize the need for data collection in the target environment.

Overall, current approaches to object mapping assume (i) objects with the same classifications play the same role in any task, (ii) the robot knows a priori which object features to use for mapping, (iii) the robot may continue to explore/train in the target environment, and/or (iv) an abstraction of the object can be used to identify specific instances of that object symbol.

However, these assumptions do not hold in situated mapping problems, where we would like the robot to receive very limited new data/demonstrations of a task and then identify an object mapping without knowledge of the specific object features relevant to that task.

2.2.2 Approach

We have presented the mapping-by-demonstration (MbD) approach to situated mapping, in which an agent uses mapping "hints," a limited number of object correspondences, to infer the remainder of the mapping (Fitzgerald, Bullard, Thomaz, & Goel, 2016). Since the human teacher is aware of both (i) the goal of the task and (ii) the role that each object plays in achieving that goal, we have proposed a human-guided object mapping method Fig. 2.2, consisting of two interaction phases and two mapping phases. The interaction phases include a demonstration phase in which the robot learns the task steps from demonstration and an assistance phase in which the robot records interactive assistance from the teacher. The assistance is used in the two mapping phases: first in a mapping inference phase and then in the confidence evaluation phase that determines whether additional assistance should be requested. We now describe all four phases, later evaluating phases in isolation via simulated, interactive, and offline evaluations.

2.2.2.1 Demonstration phase

At the start of the interaction, the robot observes the source environment using an RGB-D (color + depth) camera and extracting the location, size, and hue features of each object, after which it derives the set of spatial relations between each object and obtains affordance data (the actions enabled by that object, e.g., openable and pourable) and property data (variables associated with an object's affordances, e.g., an openable object that has the property of being open or closed). After the robot observes objects in its environment, the human teacher interacts with the robot's arm to physically guide it through executing the task (e.g., Fig. 2.3). Following the demonstration the task is represented as (i) the list of object representations and (ii) a list of task steps that indicate the primary object for each step.

2.2.2.2 Assistance phase

After the task demonstration the robot may receive assistance from the human teacher to repeat the task in the target environment, later using this assistance during the mapping inference phase. Having the teacher provide assistance via natural interaction (e.g., pointing at or picking up an object) mitigates the need for human teachers to have knowledge of which

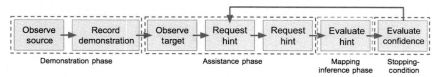

FIG. 2.2   We present mapping by demonstration, which consists of four phases: demonstration, assistance, mapping inference, and confidence evaluation.

FIG. 2.3 A user provides a demonstration of a cup-stacking task by guiding the robot's end effector to complete the task.

features the robot has the capacity to observe (e.g., the robot can record object color, but not product brand) or how to express feature values (e.g., hue values).

Once the robot requests assistance (e.g., "Where do I go next?"), the human teacher provides a mapping assist by handing the robot the next object it should use to complete the task in the target environment (e.g., the interaction in Fig. 2.4A) or, if the robot is already holding an object, by pointing to where the robot should place the object in the target environment (e.g., Fig. 2.4B). Each mapping assist indicates a correspondence between (i) the object referenced by the teacher in the target environment and (ii) the object that would have been used in the next step in the original task demonstration.

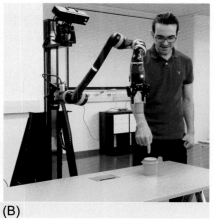

(A)   (B)

FIG. 2.4 (A) The teacher hands the robot the next cup it should stack. (B) The teacher indicates where the robot should place the cup it is currently holding.

2.2.2.3 Mapping inference phase

Two goals must be addressed simultaneously to infer the object mapping: selection of (i) an object similarity function (and associated object feature) that is representative of the mapping assistance received thus far and (ii) an object mapping that maximizes object similarity according to the selected similarity function. As such, our algorithm maintains both a (i) feature set space containing all feature sets under consideration for the similarity metric and (ii) a mapping hypothesis space containing all mapping hypotheses still under consideration.

The mapping hypothesis space is initialized as the set of all possible object mappings and thus begins as an $n!$-sized set for an n-to-n mapping problem. An $n \times n \times 7$ evaluation matrix is generated during initialization, containing the evaluation score for every possible object correspondence according to each of the seven-object features. The evaluation matrix only needs to be generated once (during initialization). Afterward the evaluation matrix is referenced to evaluate a mapping hypothesis. Many tasks may require additional features that have not been addressed here. However, this method is intended to consider a variety of features for object mapping and is still applicable in such tasks. Additional object features can be incorporated by defining a new evaluation metric and expanding the evaluation matrix to include the new metric.

A mapping assist consists of an object in the source environment and its corresponding object in the target environment. After initialization, each mapping assist is used to (i) prune the mapping hypothesis space, (ii) prune the feature set space, and then (iii) select the highest-ranked mapping hypothesis as the predicted mapping. Each combination of a mapping hypothesis and feature is then evaluated, and the highest-ranked mapping and feature set combination is then returned as the predicted mapping.

A single mapping assist may not provide enough information to infer the correct object mapping. Thus, after receiving a mapping assist and inferring the object mapping, a decision must be made to either request additional assistance or to complete the rest of the task autonomously using the most recently inferred object mapping. Similar to the confidence-based autonomy (CBA) approach introduced by Chernova and Veloso (2007, 2009), our work aims to enable the robot to rely on confidence as a means to managing its assistance from the human teacher. However, since the robot does not know which features are relevant to the task, it is unable to select features to calculate its confidence in the same manner as CBA. We propose a variation of confident execution that utilizes the information available during interactive object mapping: the evaluation matrix calculated during MbD to determine the confidence of its predicted mapping. We define confidence as the decision margin between these two top-ranked mapping hypotheses evaluation scores.

2.2.3 First experiment

We performed an extensive evaluation of the mapping inference phase in simulation using data from the ground-truth mapping as the source of mapping assistance. We evaluated the system with three categories of simulated tasks, containing 5–7 objects in the source and target environments. These categories represent incrementally more difficult problems; as the number of objects increases, the mapping hypothesis space from which the system must

FIG. 2.5   Performance in five-object tasks.

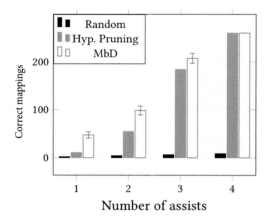

choose a single mapping increases factorially. In total the simulated evaluation consisted of 780 evaluations, each performed for all permutations of mapping assist orderings.

Figs. 2.5–2.7 compare the performance of the MbD algorithm over all assistance orderings, with error bars denoting one standard deviation, for two baselines: (i) expected performance when selecting a random mapping without utilizing mapping assistance and (ii) expected performance when using mapping assistance to only prune the hypothesis space and then choosing a random mapping from the remaining hypothesis space (rather than using the assistance to infer features on which mapping is based).

2.2.3.1 Discussion

In any mapping problem the number of possible object mappings increases factorially with the number of objects present. Graph isomorphism is an intractable problem in general, and thus this attribute is inherent to any technique for object mapping. This problem motivates situating mapping in the task environment. While all mapping hypotheses are considered,

FIG. 2.6   Performance in six-object tasks.

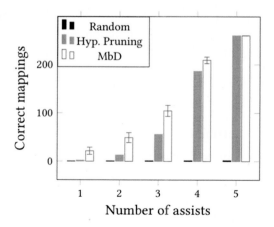

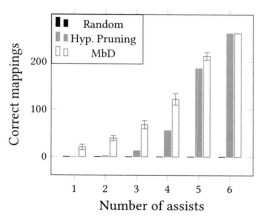

FIG. 2.7 Performance in seven-object tasks.

leveraging mapping assistance helps (i) prune the hypothesis space after each assist, (ii) prune the feature set space, and (iii) reevaluate the remaining mapping hypotheses to produce a mapping prediction.

The results indicate that using mapping assistance increases the robot's likelihood of predicting a correct mapping quickly. Even when mapping assistance is only used to prune the hypothesis space, as shown in the hypothesis pruning results in the simulated evaluation ("Hyp. Pruning" in Figs. 2.5–2.7), the robot's likelihood of selecting a correct mapping is dramatically increased over that of choosing an object mapping at random. The MbD algorithm provides further benefit by inferring additional information from the assistance; rather than only use the mapping assist to prune the hypothesis space, it is also used to infer the feature(s) on which mapping may be performed. This benefit is especially evident as the hypothesis space increases. Particularly, in the seven-object task (the category of mapping problems with the largest hypothesis space), the MbD algorithm correctly solves significantly more problems within the first 1–4 assists than either the hypothesis pruning or random mapping baselines.

These results are obtained using simulated assistance and thus rely on the assumption that mapping assistance is always correct. In a realistic interaction, however, the robot would need to obtain this assistance from the human teacher. This introduces several potential sources for error, such as misinterpretation of the human teacher's assistance or the teacher's misinterpretation of the task.

2.2.4 Summary

Without contextual knowledge about the task, the robot cannot weigh object features to identify an object mapping for task transfer. Prior work assumes that (i) the robot has access to multiple new demonstrations of the task or that (ii) the primary features for object mapping have been specified. Our method does not make either assumption; rather than requiring additional demonstrations of the task, it uses limited structured interaction with a human teacher. Additionally, by having human teachers provide mapping assistance by indicating objects (rather than describing features), we mitigate the need for teachers to have knowledge of which features the robot can observe or how to express feature values. More generally, these issues arise because of the grounding of analogical reasoning in perception and action.

2.3 Using reinforcement learning and metareasoning in cognitive robotics

To ground some of the issues and concepts involved, consider the example of a rational mobile agent operating in a Minecraft environment called Moon (Fig. 2.8). Moon is a virtually embodied agent, that is, it interacts with the various objects in a Minecraft environment under constraints of certain predefined models. Moon is outfitted with a planner, a knowledge base about the primitive actions of the agent, and the action models of the expected objects in the environment and a sensor to observe the environment. The action model of an object defines its behavior when a primitive action is applied to it. Moon is also optimistic in its behavior; it assumes each action will be successful as planned. In the current story, Moon is spawned in a two-room environment that is joined via an open door. Moon's aim is to gather gold blocks placed somewhere in room 2, that is, the room farthest from its spawn location.

In the current experiment, Moon follows a simple plan that makes it explore the arena until the gold block is sighted, at which point it calls a computationally expensive planner to get a path leading to the gold block. Since Moon has limited resources, it stores the successful plans for reuse. Moon also records the state transitions encountered to make sure a plan is reused as expected. However, Minecraft is a changing world. Imagine there lives a builder who decides to build a glass wall in place of the open door without telling Moon or its planner. This situation is analogous to how we, humans, act in our daily world. We are imprecise and move things around without announcing every change. So now, unaware of these changes, Moon

FIG. 2.8 Variant (*l*) and original (*r*) tasks in Minecraft.

starts its task of finding the gold block. As expected the unforeseen glass wall blocks the transition of an agent moving from room 1 to room 2, failing the plan.

Since glass was not expected, Moon does not have any knowledge of the material or how to interact with it. Several questions arise here. How can the agent describe a new artifact to the planner? Once defined, can we reuse some of the existing knowledge about the environment and the task to learn a policy from a current state to achieve the desired goal? And, finally, how should the policy be stored within the framework for future reuse?

2.3.1 Related work

Our work builds on the Autognostic, REM,[a] Augur, and Game Agent Interactive Adaptation (GAIA) projects. The Autognostic project (Stroulia & Goel, 1995, 1999) developed a multilayered agent architecture including situated, deliberative, and metareasoning components. The Autognostic system models an intelligent agent as a functional representation of internal processes, using the explicit modeling to repair its deliberative navigational planner. The REM project (Murdock & Goel, 2011) built on and generalized the Autognostic agent architecture. It developed a knowledge representation language called task-method-knowledge language (TMKL), more expressive than HTNs,[b] to capture functional models of agent design. REM addresses both retrospective and proactive adaptations. It uses metacase-based reasoning to proactively adapt for functionally similar tasks and using functional descriptions to retroactively localize failures. Unlike the Autognostic and REM projects, the Augur project (Goel & Jones, 2011; Jones & Goel, 2012) focuses on the use of metareasoning to diagnose and repair domain knowledge grounded in perception. Finally the GAIA[c] project (Goel & Rugaber, 2017) provides an interactive CAD-like environment for constructing game-playing agents (for playing Freeciv[d]) in the REM architecture and the TMKL2 language. The GAIA system enables interactive diagnosis and repair of the agents' design in case of failures.

This present work builds on the aforementioned research and especially the REM architecture and its combination of situated, deliberative, and metareasoning strategies. However, unlike previous REM research that focused on variations of tasks assigned to an intelligent agent while keeping the environment constant, this work keeps the task constant but varies the environment through the addition of objects. It complements a similar project on one-shot learning by demonstration in which a robot is given a single demonstration of a task and must transfer what it learned to the same task in a new environment consisting of additional objects (Fitzgerald et al., 2016). In the other project the robot asks informed questions of the teacher to identify what knowledge to transfer and how to adapt it to the new environment. In the present work, we take the approach of combining planning with situated learning.

Lastly, we want to compare our method against some of the contemporary work that integrates knowledge-based frameworks with reinforcement learning (Sutton & Barto, 1998).

[a] Reflective Evolutionary Mind, http://bill.murdocks.org/rem/.

[b] Hierarchical Task Networks, touched upon in Section 2.3.2.

[c] http://dilab.gatech.edu/publications/gaia-a-cad-like-environment-for-designing-game-playing-agents/.

[d] An open-source empire-building strategy game, http://www.freeciv.org/.

Dannenhauer and Muñoz-Avila (2015) prove that hierarchical expectations work better than flat plans and expectations for reasoning about goals; however, their semantic ontology of expectations is much more restrictive than our occupancy grids, which is a discretized representation of 3D space explained more deeply in the next section. Additionally, our results reflect the findings of Ulam, Goel, Jones, and Murdock (2005) and Ulam, Jones, and Goel (2008) where they saw a considerable speedup of the learning process by providing it with an internal model and knowledge about the game world. However, our algorithm does not rely on as strict a definition of expectations and outlines a more general method of representing and calculating similarities at a lower level, applicable to any map-based world.

2.3.2 Approach

In this section, we will first describe the overall architecture and the intuitions of the system before outlining the details of the components used. The architecture is designed to allow the processes of metareasoning about an agent's plan execution and gives an overview of the communications between the different components.

2.3.2.1 Architecture and concepts

The architecture is organized into three layers of reasoning: (a) situated or object-level reasoning that acts and observes directly interfacing with the environment; (b) deliberative reasoning that reasons about object-level information and acts to construct a plan; and finally (c) a metareasoning level that consumes both object-level and deliberative-level information, reasons for choosing the goals for a situated learner based on the tasks and observations from the past, and acts to switch control between deliberative reasoning and situated learning (Fig. 2.9).

2.3.2.2 Object layer

This layer consists of motion-inducing actuators, environment encoding sensors, the environment itself (extracted and implemented using the simulation engine and APIs), and a reactive tabular Q-learner (Fig. 2.13). The actuators induce behavioral or physical changes in the agent situated in the environment that reflect the function of its primitive actions. The primitive actions are domain and agent dependent and exhibit an indirect form of knowledge encoding. The environment is observed using a laser scanner sensor that emits an array of equally distanced laser rays at discretized heights into the environment and returns the environment information as an observation array of the distance at which each ray reflects off of an environmental artifact (infinity if it does not) and the reflected value or percentage of the ray intensity that indirectly encodes the material hit by the ray. This 3D array of discretized environment encoding is called an occupancy grid, as it describes the occupancy of each world cell. The reason for this representation choice is twofold: (a) Occupancy grids are the data structures of choice in the robotics community to compress and represent unstructured data, making our approach more readily suitable to such agents, and (b) since we need to describe unknown entities, a representation that accounts for the physical properties makes more sense than using any higher-level descriptors. Occupancy grids in both the experiments in current work correspond to a 270-degree sweep of the environment centered on the agent. Each cell in the occupancy grid is a data structure with two elements. The occupancy variable can have one of the three possible values, FREE, OCCUPIED, or UNKNOWN, and the intensity variable stores the reflected reading of the ray. Like primitive actions the height up until which the scan reading

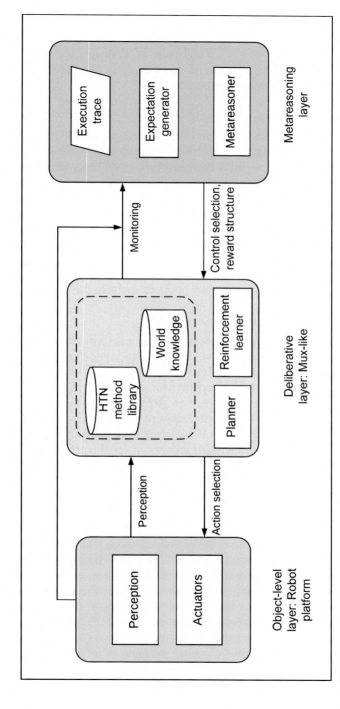

FIG. 2.9 Proposed system architecture.

should be considered for planning depends on the configuration space (Lozano-Perez, 1983) of the agent. This is a robotics concept used to calculate the volume of interest that should be considered for avoiding obstacles. Usually for planning the configuration space is created by padding obstacles to find a safe plan, as in our case; however, since we already have the path, we all padded space around it to represent the physical body of the robot and consider this as the volume of interest for metareasoning processes.

2.3.2.3 Deliberative layer

The deliberative layer consists of the main planner that is instantiated as a hierarchical task network planner (Erol, Hendler, & Nau, 1994). The planner itself is an off-the-shelf Python[e] version of SHOP[f] (Nau, Cao, Lotem, & Munoz-Avila, 1999) algorithm that grounds concepts like preconditions, effects, subtasks, and state descriptions into Python descriptions and objects. This layer also houses the method and subtask library associated with the planner. This layer takes as input the goal state of the task to be solved and returns a hierarchical sequenced array of methods and a corresponding sequence of primitive actions to be executed at the object level. Additionally, the *trace memory*, that is, the state transitions logged by Moon in Section 2.3, is also situated in this layer. The trace consists of the object-level observations and the sensor encoding of the environment in the form of 3D occupancy grids. To incorporate this data the HTN formalism was modified to include this step as execution metadata.

2.3.2.4 Metareasoning: The processes

This layer has bidirectional communication channels to both the object-level and deliberative layer. It uses the traces stored at the deliberative layer to monitor the developments at the object level. This monitoring is done by comparing the occupancy grid at the end of a method execution from the past to the current occupancy grid observed at the end of the same method. The comparison is done on an element-by-element basis between the two arrays; the comparison metric is designed to take into account the relative ordering of the observations.

A discrepancy between the expected and observed is defined by the dissimilarity score of the corresponding occupancy grids and a list of indices where the grid readings do not match. This layer also houses the control switch that invokes the planner or the reactive *Q*-learner with a goal.

2.3.3 Algorithm

The planning process, or phase one, starts when the goal is passed to the deliberative layer. If the planner has a stored plan from an original task environment relevant to the current environment state variant, then it is retrieved for execution while the associated metadata, that is, the abstracted HTN method sequence and corresponding trace, is sent to the metareasoner for monitoring. Given the dissimilarity score generated using the procedure in Section 2.3.2.2, a discrepancy report is generated that includes the score, a list of the grid cell indices that contributed, and the precondition of all methods in the partial HTN plan after the current method. Current implementation uses a conservative threshold of 0 that means, if an execution state transition is different from the expectation by even one cell, then it is noted as a discrepancy.

[e]https://bitbucket.org/dananau/pyhop.

[f]Simple Hierarchical Ordered Planner.

This procedure works well for our controlled simulated environments but should be calibrated for disregarding ambient noise in dynamic environments. In current work, we specifically consider the class of discrepancy that occurs due to the addition of new objects and artifacts to the environment, therefore, our choice of the dissimilarity computation procedure.

Next in phase two, or the *assess* process, the metareasoner sets up a knowledge-informed learning problem for the tabular Q-learner to solve. We use the partial plan returned with the discrepancy report to do two things: (a) The preconditions of postdiscrepancy methods are used as alternative and viable goals for the Q-learner, which helps set up a more dense reward system; and (b) the lower-level expectations are compared at each Q-learning cycle to provide additional reward to the learner, the intuition being that the more the agent makes the current situation like the last one, the more possible it is to solve it like the previously known task situation. For the latter end the metareasoner constructs a reward strategy where the agent gets a random discount (between 0 and 0.5) for actions that make the current environment more like the previously known one. This reward layer also indirectly encourages an exploration of the environment. This reward is tracked by noting a decrease in the dissimilarity score between the current and prior observations. Phase three is the *guide* process where this constructed problem is passed to the Q-learner, and the metareasoner falls back waiting on a return from the object-level layer.

Phase four is marked by a successful termination of the reinforcement learner. It communicates back to the metareasoner two things: (a) the policy that successfully solved the problem and (b) the goal for which the policy solved the problem, that is, the policy from discrepancy point to the final goal or to one of the alternative goals extracted from the method preconditions. The metareasoner couples the policy with the description of the discrepancy point, attaches the sensor trace as the expectation for this variant, and constructs a new HTN plan where this policy is succeeded by the partial previous plan starting at the goal method returned by the metareasoner. This algorithm is described visually in Fig. 2.10.

2.3.4 Second experiment

We have implemented our architecture on two different agents in different simulation engines with different sets of primitive actions. The HTN planner plans for a task goal given the primitive actions and assumes a lower-level controller to actually physically instantiate the motion in the agent. The next few sections outline the agent and task specifications and the challenge variation of the environment.

2.3.4.1 *Gold hunting in Minecraft*

This experiment follows directly from our motivating example of agent Moon. The original task situation is where the two rooms are connected with an open gate, and the variant task is where open gate is replaced by a glass wall. We used the Malmo[g] project for integrating the Minecraft environment events with reward emissions. The Malmo API is also responsible for actuating the physical effects of primitive actions. The primitive actions for this domain are as follows:

---

[g]https://www.microsoft.com/en-us/research/project/project-malmo/.

1. move forward/backward
2. turn left/right
3. look up/down by 45 degrees
4. break the block in focus

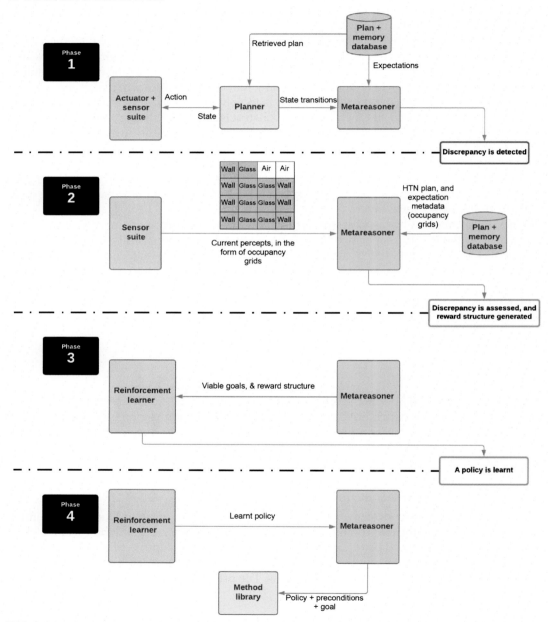

FIG. 2.10   Process diagram: an outline of the communication between different processes.

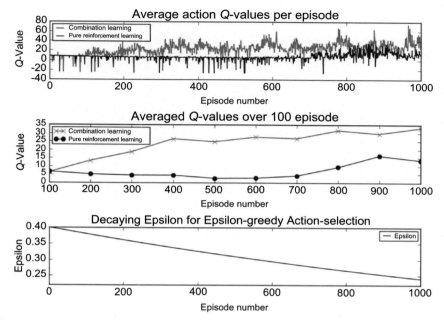

FIG. 2.11 Quantitative comparison of Q-values for the pure reinforcement learning (RL) agent and the combination agent over multiple episodes in Minecraft experiment.

The input state for the reinforcement learner consists of a 3×3 occupancy grid of blocks right in front of the agent along with an array including ground blocks, the block in focus, the in-hand items, and the agent's orientation. The terminating conditions of the learner were either the achievement of any of the goals queued by the metareasoner resulting in positive reward or breaking of any of the walls or ground blocks resulting in a final negative reward.

Fig. 2.11 shows the comparison of pure RL against the combination agent. The pure RL agent's Q-values take a dip before gaining value due to a random initial exploration that results in a number of wrong moves. The pure learner presented here is the vanilla tabular learner with the added list of goals queued by the metareasoner, while the combination learner uses the alternate goal list and the random rewards related with making the novel variant more like the original one.

2.3.4.2 Cup grasping in Gazebo

The agent in this experiment is a fixed arm in a Gazebo simulator and is tasked with picking up a can placed on the table in front of it (Fig. 2.12). The geometry and relative three-dimensional placements of the object, can, and the table are all known. The primitive actions being used are as follows:

1. Pick object O_i.
2. Place object in hand at (x,y) with respect to the table coordinates.

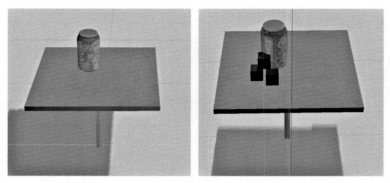

FIG. 2.12   Original *(left)* and variant *(right)* task in Gazebo.

One can imagine the method description for such a domain to be a list of strictly ordered waypoints that were demonstrated or encoded by a human programmer the first time constituent subtasks were executed. In the original version the workspace does not have any other artifacts than the can, arm, and the table. In the variant modification the path of arm end effector toward the can is littered by a random placement of cubes. Since the arm is an immobile and fixed agent, the only way to get around the clutter is to interact with it using our metareasoner. Additionally, just by looking at the primitive actions, it is clear that they are mutually exclusive and dependent on the choice of object and location. Therefore the learning complexity here is grounded in understanding which object to interact with and how. We mention this because usually a Q-learner learns the Q-values with respect to the actions possible, but in this experiment, we learn Q-values in an object-centric fashion, that is, which object has the greater utility in the current situation. The placement location on the other hand is modeled as a Gaussian mixture model (GMM) of those table placements that emitted a positive reward. The learning in this respect is divided between exploring new placements on the table or sampling a placement location from the learned GMM. We notice that, while our algorithm affects the learning for the choice of the object to be manipulated, it does not show any significant improvements to the GMM learning for placement of objects. This result is because the GMM modeling of spatially viable choices already encodes certain knowledge about continuous spaces in it, unlike the chain-like formulation of tabular Q-learning. This result hints at our approach being more useful for domains where the structure and relationships of the state variables are not as well modeled as 2D or 3D spaces.

Fig. 2.13 shows the comparison between the pure and combination learner in the grasping domain. It should be noted that since the number of state variables greatly affect the learning curve of tabular Q-learning, we have supplied the same reduced state (based on configuration space) to the pure learner as we did to the combination learner. This problem is a general limitation of our work as well; matrix computations are expensive, and by storing geometric representations of each past state, certain computations in our algorithm turn out to be computational bottlenecks. However, by combining the configuration space prior with discretized geometry, we limit the upper limits of such expense significantly.

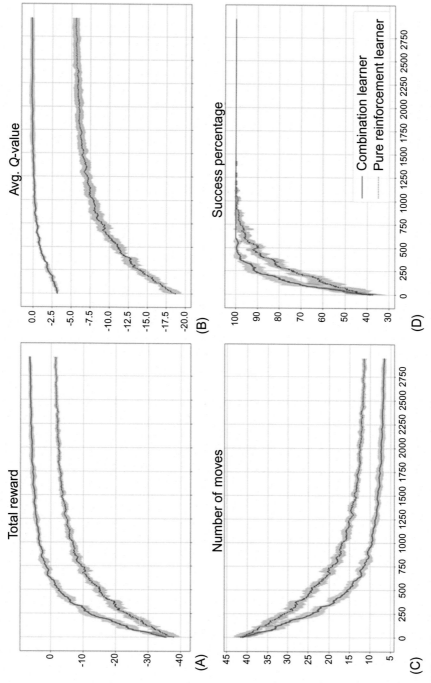

FIG. 2.13 Comparisons over (A) total reward, (B) average Q-value, (C) number of moves, and (D) success percentage over multiple episodes for the pure RL agent and combination learner agent in Gazebo experiment.

2.3.5 Summary

This work combines HTN planning and *Q*-learning within the metareasoning architecture. Our results suggest that the metareasoner can use the *Q*-learner to complete the plans for the HTN planner in the new environment with added objects. This capability is potentially valuable because it enables us to have a flexible planner capable of extending its knowledge to new worlds. Moreover, we used low-level percepts in the form of occupancy grids for comparing plan expectations and actual observations, which makes our work suitable not only for software agents in simulated environments but also potentially for embodied agents that work on real raw data.

2.4 Conclusions

We began this conversation by describing four cognitive strategies for dealing with novelty: situated learning, interactive learning, analogical reasoning, and metareasoning. We said that context determines an agent's choice among these strategies and further that, depending on the context, an agent may also combine these strategies. We proposed that these cognitive strategies may provide a useful starting point for robot design. In particular, in this chapter, we described two cognitively inspired mechanisms for addressing novelty in some detail. In the first mechanism a teacher first demonstrates a skill to an interactive robot, and then, given a new but similar task, the robot addresses the new task by analogy to the known task. In the second mechanism a robot uses metareasoning to combine deliberative planning and situated learning: it first uses deliberative planning to achieve its goal in a new environment and, if it fails, uses reinforcement learning locally to recover from a failure.

What lessons do these robot designs offer for research on cognitive science? The most important lessons pertain to grounding the cognitive strategies for addressing novelty in action and perception. Consider, for example, analogical reasoning. Most cognitive theories of analogy assume representations of knowledge of the world and then run inference engines on the knowledge representations. Further, they assume that only knowledge of some relationships, such as relationships among objects or between goals and methods, needs to be transferred. Our work on the use of analogy in interactive robot learning indicates that there is also a need for transferring the action model from the source case to the target problem, which raises a host of new issues such as the relationships between objects, tools, and tasks; it is just not enough to transfer relationships among objects. Similarly, our work suggests how the knowledge of the world is acquired from perception so that analogies can be made for dealing with novelty.

Similarly, in the case of metareasoning, again, most cognitive theories of metacognition assume representations exist of knowledge of the world and of the agent itself. But our work shows the need for grounding metareasoning in action and perception. For example, the metareasoner may encode task expectations imagistically so that, when it executes a task, it can easily detect failure by comparing the expectation with its actual percepts. Further, it may compile the results of situated learning into deliberative planning for potential reuse. In addition, many cognitive theories assume a specific, relatively static, and rigid architecture for metareasoning. In contrast, our work suggests that a more flexible architecture for situated learning, deliberative planning, and metareasoning works together.

Acknowledgments

We thank William Lawless, Ranjeev Mittu, and Donald Sofge for editing this volume and inviting us to write this chapter; we especially thank William for his encouragement, patience, and support for writing the chapter. Parts of this chapter have appeared earlier in Fitzgerald et al. (2018) and Parashar et al. (2018).

References

Akgun, B., et al. (2012). Keyframe-based learning from demonstration. *International Journal of Social Robotics, 4*(4), 343–355.

Argall, B. D., et al. (2009). A survey of robot learning from demonstration. *Robotics and Autonomous Systems, 57*(5), 469–483.

Bullard, K., et al. (2016). Grounding action parameters from demonstration. In *2016 25th IEEE international symposium on robot and human interactive communication (RO-MAN):* IEEE.

Chernova, S., & Thomaz, A. L. (2014). Robot learning from human teachers. *Synthesis Lectures on Artificial Intelligence and Machine Learning, 8*(3), 1–121.

Chernova, S., & Veloso, M. (2007). Confidence-based policy learning from demonstration using gaussian mixture models. In *Proceedings of the 6th international joint conference on autonomous agents and multiagent systems:* ACM.

Chernova, S., & Veloso, M. (2009). Interactive policy learning through confidence-based autonomy. *Journal of Artificial Intelligence Research, 34*, 1–25.

Dannenhauer, D., & Muñoz-Avila, H. (2015). Goal-driven autonomy with semantically-annotated hierarchical cases. In E. Hüllermeier & M. Minor (Eds.), *Vol. 9343. Case-based reasoning research and development* (pp. 88–103). Cham: Springer International Publishing.

Davies, J., Goel, A. K., & Yaner, P. W. (2008). Proteus: Visuospatial analogy in problem-solving. *Knowledge-Based Systems, 21*(7), 636–654.

Erol, K., Hendler, J., & Nau, D. S. (1994). HTN planning: Complexity and expressivity. In *Vol. 94.* (pp. 1123–1128).

Falkenhainer, B., Forbus, K. D., & Gentner, D. (1989). The structure-mapping engine: Algorithm and examples. *Artificial Intelligence, 41*(1), 1–63.

Fitzgerald, T., Bullard, K., Thomaz, A., & Goel, A. K. (2016). Situated mapping for transfer learning. In *Fourth annual conference on advances in cognitive systems.*

Fitzgerald, T., Goel, A., & Thomaz, A. (2018). Human-guided object mapping for task transfer. *ACM Transactions on Human-Robot Interaction (THRI), 7*(2), 1–24.

Gentner, D. (1983). Structure-mapping: A theoretical framework for analogy. *Cognitive Science, 7*(2), 155–170.

Gentner, D., & Markman, A. B. (2006). Defining structural similarity. *Journal of Cognitive Science, 6*(1), 1–20.

Gick, M. L., & Holyoak, K. J. (1983). Schema induction and analogical transfer. *Cognitive Psychology, 15*(1), 1–38.

Goel, A. K., & Jones, J. (2011). Metareasoning for self-adaptation in intelligent agents. In *Metareasoning:* The MIT Press.

Goel, A. K., & Rugaber, S. (2017). GAIA: A CAD-like environment for designing game-playing agents. *IEEE Intelligent Systems, 32*(3), 60–67.

Holyoak, K. J., & Thagard, P. (1989). Analogical mapping by constraint satisfaction. *Cognitive Science, 13*(3), 295–355.

Jones, J. K., & Goel, A. K. (2012). Perceptually grounded self-diagnosis and self-repair of domain knowledge. *Knowledge-Based Systems, 27*, 281–301.

Kulick, J., et al. (2013). Active learning for teaching a robot grounded relational symbols. In: *Twenty-third international joint conference on artificial intelligence.*

Lozano-Perez, T. (1983). Spatial planning: A configuration space approach. *IEEE Transactions on Computers, C-32*(2), 108–120.

Misra, D. K., et al. (2016). Tell me dave: Context-sensitive grounding of natural language to manipulation instructions. *The International Journal of Robotics Research, 35*(1–3), 281–300.

Murdock, J. W., & Goel, A. K. (2011). *Self-improvement through self-understanding: Model-based reflection for agent self-adaptation.* Amazon.

Nau, D. S., Cao, Y., Lotem, A., & Munoz-Avila, H. (1999). SHOP: Simple hierarchical ordered planner. In *Vol. 2. Proceedings of the 16th international joint conference on artificial intelligence* (pp. 968–973). San Francisco, CA: Morgan Kaufmann Publishers Inc.

Parashar, P., Goel, A. K., Sheneman, B., & Christensen, H. (2018). Towards life-long adaptive agents: Using metareasoning for combining knowledge-based planning with situated learning. *Knowledge Engineering Review, 33,* e24.

Stroulia, E., & Goel, A. K. (1995). Functional representation and reasoning for reflective systems. *Applied Artificial Intelligence, 9*(1), 101–124.

Stroulia, E., & Goel, A. K. (1999). Evaluating PSMs in evolutionary design: The autognostic experiments. *International Journal of Human-Computer Studies, 51*(4), 825–847.

Sutton, R. S., & Barto, A. G. (1998). *Reinforcement learning: An introduction. Vol. 1.* Cambridge: MIT Press.

Taylor, M. E., Stone, P., & Liu, Y. (2007). Transfer learning via inter-task mappings for temporal difference learning. *Journal of Machine Learning Research, 8,* 2125–2167.

Tenorth, M., Nyga, D., & Beetz, M. (2010). Understanding and executing instructions for everyday manipulation tasks from the world wide web. In *2010 IEEE international conference on robotics and automation:* IEEE.

Ulam, P., Goel, A. K., Jones, J., & Murdock, W. (2005). Using model-based reflection to guide reinforcement learning. In *Vol. 107. Reasoning, representation, and learning in computer games.*

Ulam, P., Jones, J., & Goel, A. K. (2008). Combining model-based meta-reasoning and reinforcement learning for adapting game-playing agents. In *AIIDE.*

Waibel, M., et al. (2011). Roboearth-a world wide web for robots. *IEEE Robotics and Automation Magazine, 18*(2), 69–82. Special issue towards a WWW for Robots.

Further reading

Grounds, M., & Kudenko, D. (2008). Combining reinforcement learning with symbolic planning. In *Adaptive agents and multi-agent systems III. Adaptation and multi-agent learning* (pp. 75–86). Berlin Heidelberg: Springer.

Grzes, M., & Kudenko, D. (2008). Plan-based reward shaping for reinforcement learning. In *Vol. 2. 2008 4th international IEEE conference intelligent systems,* (pp. 10-22–10-29).

Muñoz-Avila, H., Jaidee, U., Aha, D. W., & Carter, E. (2010). Goal-driven autonomy with case-based reasoning. In *Case-based reasoning, research and development* (pp. 228–241). Berlin Heidelberg: Springer.

CHAPTER

3

Adding command knowledge "At the Human Edge"

H.T. Goranson

Institute for Integrated Intelligent Systems, Griffith University, Brisbane, QLD, Australia

3.1 Introduction

Information in the military life cycle has a long and complicated history and current food chain from collection to consumption and action. A simplified view has some information collected "strategically" or for background knowledge years or decades before, while others are "tactical." An example of the former will be the characteristics of an aircraft type, while the latter may be the atmospheric measurements to be used to adjust satellite images. Information will be collected and ingested into many systems up until the moment a command decision must be made based on some crisp but trusted and auditable reduction. Then a control action will occur, changing the world and adding to the information flowing through a command and control network, triggering a further series of actions and being executed in the complex fabric.

For the purposes of this chapter, we will characterize three large processes: information collection systems, which feed information decision systems and in turn command and control (C2) systems. Obvious feedback loops will be ignored because they do not add clarity to the core problems. Our research group in Australia focuses on the central process: taking information as it arrives, combining, filtering, and prioritizing it for delivery to the perhaps dozens or more of primary "clients" in a C2 system. We will assume that our problem set is not just the scientific and practical challenge of synthesizing information, but doing so within the constraints of poorly designed systems on either "side."

Fig. 3.1 illustrates the key functions. On the left, we have collection, analysis, and delivery systems that provide information for the national security enterprise. Some of that is semantically structured and intended for human comprehension, while the other is "parametric" and intended for machine consumption. In between is the system that is supposed to "mine" the available information; add notes for what is not or implicitly known; "fuse"

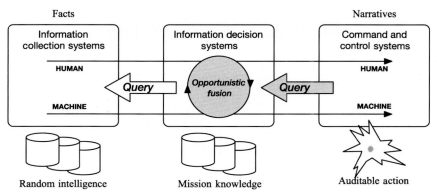

FIG. 3.1   The primary function is to take huge amounts of information in various forms from the left and instant and persistent queries from the right and create synthesized narrative statements to specific commanders.

the appropriate facts into situated, auditable command insights; and deliver the result in a tailored form to the commanders. Along the way the systems should perform required inferencing and independently cache key mission information and results.

We describe the systems involved along with some of their challenges and solutions from the "third wave" of AI. An illustrative example is introduced, followed by a discussion of C2.

3.2 Characteristics of the three systems

3.2.1 Information collection systems

Information is collected in the most capable ways possible, which often results in information not optimized for use. A problem is that we must capture as much information as possible on the off chance it will be useful. Dozens of collection methods are used, each with representations specific to the collection system and its subsequent consumption. These methods generally fall into two types: semantically and parametrically characterized; each type can be delivered as sequences of discrete packages or as streams. Fig. 3.2 illustrates the key elements and functions entailed.

For example, we may have meteorological information collected as parametric streams that are required for a C2 system regarding air operations. Or the information may be semantically enriched within the collection system as part of a presynthesized weather report and delivered as a periodic, discrete, semantic report. A client may want just the (semantic) report, the raw sensor data, or both integrated in some way; the client may want either or both fused into a more comprehensive environmental constraint report; or a client may want none of these but want the constraints to be considered implicitly in a delivered product, perhaps a flight plan. These requirements mean that often we will be required to deliver a synthesized information product, accompanying components, and an auditable account of the synthesis process.

The number of information sources is increasing in scale and variety to such an extent that this problem alone eclipses the others in terms of perceived importance. The problem is less

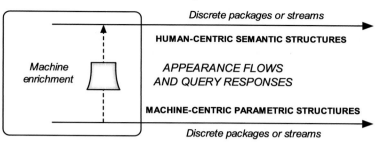

Information collection systems

FIG. 3.2 Information is delivered as it appears and also as requested by tailored situation queries. Some information is delivered in linked semantic/parametric form, for example, a radar report linked to targeting parameters.

one of volume per se than of the permutations required to "connect the dots." We suggest a strategy in the succeeding text to manage this variety and can handle the anticipated growth. The more significant problem is one of ontological variety. This heterogeneity is growing at an alarming rate.

An ontology is a formal specification of the semantics used to interpret terms in incoming semantic information. As substantive reasoning must be accomplished by the synthesis, strong ontological identity needs to be maintained. The conventional approach to this is reasoning to define a universal ontology for the synthesis tasks, defining the "world of battle." This seems reasonable enough; after all, the command systems assume that its commanders are "on the same page" with their common understanding of the situation and what needs to be done.

Moreover, much of the semantically enriched information comes from intelligence services who perform their own analysis in the creation of a synthesized product. However, none of these services are sufficiently careful to maintain ontological consistency in their processes, with much of what they produce delivered whole with no formal ontology. Working backward to reverse engineer the apparent ontology has produced disappointing results. Moreover, there are many agencies with different missions, source types, and implicit ontologies.

Some of these agencies do not employ any ontological consistency at all. Others employ databases with type schemas chosen for their implementation convenience. One group insists on addressing this problem by reducing the world to parameters of spatial geolocation with ontological coloring. Another group, derived from the large-scale simulation and training community, solves this problem by reducing semantic state to a standard "battle language" consisting of simple parameters of state (like damage, power, and mobility).

In both of these cases and in others, the synthesizing agent has to "translate up" into a semantic space and, as mentioned, with the assumption that a single, stable ontology is key to the rational reasoning for clients. But the computational overhead and lossy translation of feeds make this approach infeasible. As we will see later, the requirement of diverse clients for products with different, discrete ontological bases disqualifies this infeasible approach from the start.

What we have are information feeds of differing types with differing, often contradictory, or missing ontologies, needing to be synthesized to be properly delivered as feeds with formal but differing ontologies to specific clients. This problem governs the overall approach, and without some new paradigm existing outside of current practice, it cannot be addressed at all. We need an advance from the so-called third wave of AI.

One constant in the synthesis is that, regardless of the process, wherever the concept of a cause and its effect can be identified or reasonably imputed, it should be. Military activity and similar enterprises are about causing things to create desired outcomes. But we cannot assume that incoming information arrives in the same temporal order, or otherwise captures the essential temporal information about the sequence of events indicating the causal sequence of interest. It is often the case that information about an effect is received before information about its probable cause and that the connection between the two cannot be directly inferred from a given sequence.

Another complicating factor is that very little of the information supplied by the collection process is fully trustworthy. Every sensor process is lossy. Every inference in the information collection system assumes context that may not be apt. Similarly, every deduction in that system depends on an assumption of goals that could be imperfect because the collectors never fully share the world of a commander requesting the information.

Moreover, substantial and clever energy is expended by adversaries to confound and spoof the information collection process, so every bit of information or every segment of a stream enters the information decision system with a degree of doubt. We leave to others how to detect and recover fidelity; we assume that every element we reason over must be accompanied by a "trust metric" assigned by the originator as the information is received by the information decision system.

Weaknesses in this model include the implicit absolute confidence in the trust metric evaluator. All of the ontological issues previously described are inherited in the meaning of trust that is assumed to be shared across information providers. We mitigate some of these problems by accepting a numeric assignment, either as a flat number or one computed from a fabric of relationships. An example of the former is "we have 87% confidence that the cyberattack originated from DancingFox." An example of the latter may be a Bayesian fabric in which the role of DancingFox is linked to other facts where the levels of confidence are interdependent.

On import of untrusted information, we maintain the relationships of the Bayesian network as that is an essential semantic structure. But we freeze the trust metric. Therefore every discretisable element has a numeric value associated with it that captures the confidence at the moment of delivery assigned by the decision system based on its evaluation of the trust informed by the collection system. A third-party advisor is typically used, noting that information from specific sources that have a signature of having been assembled by various means traditionally has a characteristic history of having been trustworthy. This parameter is passed through untouched but annotated by two more cogent metrics described in the succeeding text.

3.2.2 Command and control systems

Our "food chain" of information flow consists of three major functions: collection, synthesis, and use, in our terms, information collection, information decision, and command and control systems. The purpose of the first two functions is to ensure that the command decisions are as informed as possible. This flow resembles the observe, orient, decide, act (OODA) loop applied at a high level to the whole enterprise. We have assigned the first role of "observe" to the information collection system and the second role to the "information decision" system whose task is not to decide but to provide the "decision information" to the decision-makers. Those decision-makers (the third OODA step) are the commanders in the command and control system. The "act" role is the "control" function that makes things happen and is the fourth step.

The C2 paradigm that Australia (and all militaries) currently uses is human centric. Commanders are humans in a "chain of command" where the information flows through a rather dense interconnected fabric. This legacy system requires that all information products be human readable, which for our work implies that all information synthesis has to be "up" from various fractions or semantics and parameters to form semantic narratives.

During the cold war the adversary was known, and likely threats were few. Command procedures could be developed that were prescriptive and stable and used a single ontology, though not formally specified. Today the world is not so well behaved.

We still have a human-centric command system. The control elements have become more automated, but the boundary between command and control systems is still required to be human readable. It is not just that humans are the actors; we have a requirement for trust in the system that implies certifiable logic and auditable actions. From this context the tendency has been for an information synthesis and delivery system to convert all information into a semantic form.

With the introduction of machines, Figs. 3.3 and 3.4 illustrate the new relationships. Commanders in our future paradigm can be humans, machines (agents), or machine-assisted humans. Each user has its own situation over which it has control, the reason that node exists. That is, each commander needs knowledge about their different situations. They can request this information by a single query based on perceived needs, but the primary delivery will be by persistent narrative queries of the form "if you can compose a report that has relevant information about my situation, I need to see it."

Fig. 3.4 illustrates the return function, where each node gets continuously fed information that is structured as narratively composable to control options, using the local situation, ontology, and control requirements.

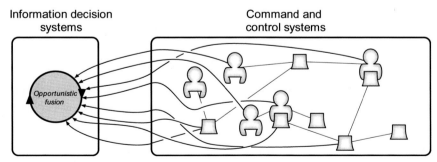

FIG. 3.3 Human, machine, and machine-assisted humans in the command system issue ad hoc queries and "persistent" queries based on mission templates for situations of interest.

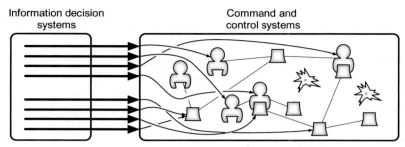

FIG. 3.4 Narrative fragments are delivered to command clients in response to queries. The information informs both the operation of C2 and reconfiguration of the C2 network.

For example, the raw sensor information captured by radar is intrinsically machine readable only. But after human interpretations from presentation devices and machine interpretations that emulate or learn from humans, the raw data are transformed into a semantic report that, for instance, there are aircraft with certain characteristics in a given area. In a typical combat information center, the semantically enriched narrative is presented to a commander who decides to take action. But when the control decision is made, the raw data are conveyed to the weapon system because it "speaks the language" in a more precise manner than the distilled narrative. The information delivery system needs to understand this situated requirement.

But the C2 world is becoming increasingly more complex. One recent development will likely prompt wholesale reinvention. Democracies are beginning to understand that national competition can lead to coercion in more than one dimension, requiring a more multidimensional, coordinated, C2 capability. The new span of control has come to be known by the DIME acronym: diplomacy, information (including cyberwarfare), military, and economic. In the near future, these four dimensions must be fed by the same intelligence collection, analysis, and fusion services. The aggregation of tasks not only is likely to converge simply because of institutional realities but also makes sense in the new foundations, as we shall see.

We already have had some partial merger of military control and information, at least so far as cyberwar, disinformation, psyops, electronic warfare, and some social media (as weaponized narratives). We also have a more thorough understanding that military action is usually preceded by economic and diplomatic coercion. Therefore the future DIME C2 environment will merely continue and extend the need for joint and tailored intelligence. The need for tailored intelligence is a difficult requirement, but it provides us with an opportunity to manage complexity. We shall address the potential solution later but the two main problems arising from it now.

The first problem is highlighted by the responsibilities indicated by DIME. In the current military context, we see this as "jointness," meaning coordinated action involving previously distinct C2 systems (like army, navy, and air force). We coordinate this poorly today. The problem originates from the simple fact that C2 is how we manage enterprises; if we insist on maintaining separate enterprises for a reason, then we will have independent, parallel C2 systems. The most rudimentary jointness is for each enterprise to know what they are supposed to construct and then to count on them to perform using their internal processes.

This result is a "coordination of goals" rather than an integration of C2. Simple coordination works well when plans and timetables are worked out and there is no need of the ability to adapt to changing conditions. The Normandy Invasion of WWII is an example where the plan was created over several months, triggering many parallel enterprises according to a timetable. Once the invasion was launched, the plan had to proceed more or less without adaptation. Jointness today requires agility, a challenge of its own.

Agility is often misunderstood. Agility is the ability to creatively respond, perhaps to completely unexpected, never-before-seen circumstances and to do so with effectiveness. It is not the ability to respond quickly; speed is a component, but faster is not necessarily more agile. Agility is a sliding balance among understanding what needs to be done, how to change, being able to change and to do it as fast and effectively as required.

Agility is contrasted with flexibility. The latter is the ability to move from one preplanned capability to another using the same resources. In other words, you anticipate what you need and have appropriate plans for several situations. An agile C2 system allows you to respond to unexpected situations.

Simply put, we need C2 systems that are agile. There are challenges to be addressed in the C2 architectures themselves, but the major challenges are in the information delivery systems addressed here.

In effect, what we need is an information delivery system that simultaneously provides what the C2 system needs to do its job and also provides parallel information to inform the C2 system on how to better adapt to changing conditions. In other words, we need to inform both what the C2 system does and how it does it.

One final C2 consideration is the level of authority. In a canonical C2 system, the balance of command versus control is heavily weighted at the beginning of the fabric of relationships. That is, the more significant decisions, the "command" part of the equation, are made early, while the execution-centric decisions are made downstream on the "control" side. We can expect this "top-down" paradigm to be maintained in large militaries because the maintenance costs of more agile designs are too high. In comparison, military C2 systems of potential adversaries will be top-down for the foreseeable future because of their requirement for totalitarian control.

But special forces in general and the Australian Defense Force in particular have a philosophy of "command decision," which pushes the command part of the equation as close to the control function as possible. The original intent was to trust the field commander who has a better understanding of the local situation and to prevent bad decisions that may have been made by more remote, senior officers.

Our example scenario in the succeeding text explores how to expand this paradigm. It allows command flexibility down the chain and closer to the "control" functions, but current militaries only do this with downstream flow of information. For instance, if there were three main missions in a coordinated parallel set of options, either a single field commander's command agility cannot affect the parallel mission, or that command agility is pushed up to a higher level that "sees" all of the options for the integrated operation. The field commander's information is not situated for the commander, but several layers up.

One can easily see that agility can be enabled by a lower-level command decision architecture that has all of the parties suitably informed and also provides support for emergent, trusted decisions in aggregate. We work here on the "suitably informed" part of the challenge. An associated project addresses ideal insertion of technologies to enable C2 agility and local trust.

3.2.3 The role of machine learning

Before we focus on the information decision system, there is one issue that needs to be considered across the combined assembly of collection, synthesis, and action. In the next 30 years, we are likely to see the arrival of at least two and possibly four generations of machine reasoning technology. Without knowing what these will look like, we know that they will become computationally cheaper and perform tasks better.

We can assume that they will be common in all three of the major systems, enriching and filtering information. At the least, there will be a general trend to more enriched streams through the three systems. We can assume that some collaboration among enriching machinery will be useful as they collaborate and that some collaboration will usefully occur across the three systems. In other words, if we think of the information decision system as a black box, information coming in and situated reports going out will be in parametric and semantic streams as before but now will have intermediate collaborative information and code enriched from these machines entering and leaving the system from both sides.

An expected common scenario will have autonomous collaborating systems in the battlespace, including the C2 function. These autonomous systems will "collaborate" with systems in the other two systems to present dynamic, fractional queries. One consequence is that in the C2 system we will have not only machine consumers of the information but also "fractional consumers" who collectively have control in perhaps only dynamic groups.

An expected beneficial outcome is that C2 agility will be enhanced. A second benefit is that they add a requirement we otherwise find it easy to omit. In the real world of battle, futures have significant nonergodic outcome spaces. The better our three systems become at modeling the world and futures, the more these nonergodic drivers will be revealed, and the more they may confound the self-organizing systems we expect. Therefore, when we finally specify requirements of the information decision system in the succeeding text, we need to include metrics that allow us to track instability and divergence in the managed information.

3.2.4 Information decision systems

Having explored the information collection system that feeds into our information decision system and the C2 systems the decision system feeds, we look at the system that is the focus of our work.

In the bewildering stew of these daunting requirements, we make simplifying assumptions. One is that feedback loops are not managed by the information decision system. We will typically have many feedback loops. In general, however, the command and control system will be changing the world, changing incoming information about the world. Further, there are many situations where a sensor is redirected by a commander. For example, a surveillance camera may be redirected by a field commander to a new area of interest, or a radar array may be reprogrammed based on a need for greater refinement by an automated system.

Excepting for the collaborative internal machine learning systems noted earlier, all of these loops are presumed to travel from the command and control system to the information collection system without moderation or control from the information decision system. These two assumptions simplify things a bit, but all else is hard, as hard a problem as the machine intelligence world will face.

But the specification is rather straightforward. We have consumers of information in C2 systems that can make queries of two kinds to the information decision system. These may be persistent queries that we can think of as situation templates: "if you see anything like such and such, then I want to know it." We also will have temporal queries that may be organically generated (we will not know their source), "We want to know what is in such and such area," or clarifying, "I need to additionally know this and that about the information you just told us about a specific thing." So far as the C2 system is concerned, the information decision system is merely a front end to the available information pools and streams.

Fig. 3.5 illustrates a future architecture for a third wave-supported information decision system.

The most important feature of this architecture is the addition of a category theoretic reasoning system shown by the hatched area in the middle. Otherwise the architecture is similar to those already emerging in militaries and common in large technology company operations. Rule-based and expert systems, using ontologies and logic, would be in the top group of services. In contrast the "second-wave" AI techniques that build on probabilistic foundations are in the strip at the bottom, exploiting machine learning and related techniques. On the center left (with the arrow pointing up) is an indication of some of those processes producing facts manageable by logic.

The area in the middle is a different reasoning system that uses category theory. The general idea is simple: the first strategy of dealing with difficult problems is to abstract into another type of a system that is more amenable to the problem domain. In this case the problem is caused by the foundation of logic itself in set theory. Set theory works well in the ways we want when the sets are closed, which in our case equates to the world being composed of known things whose behavior we can predict. Much of the world is indeed that way, but

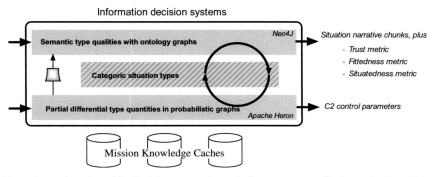

FIG. 3.5   The primary function of the decision system is to take huge amounts of information in various forms from the left and deliver synthesized narrative statements to specific commanders with control parameters in response to instant and persistent queries from the right.

we also want to reason about unknowns, human factors that are not conveniently logical and nonergodic (meaning not predictable) futures. We let the set theoretic reasoning systems do what they do best and have an engineered categoric reasoning system do what they cannot.

The combination is a two-sorted system. In practice, we have two of these, graphically connecting to the systems at the top and bottom of the diagram. The key, as we describe in the succeeding text, is a strategy that allows types to exist in all three systems shown as layers simultaneously, but with different identities.

A second notable feature in Fig. 3.5 is the "metrics" that accompany the situation reports. Because we can use the two sorts to perform some reasoning about each other that would not otherwise be possible, we can produce useful metrics with the situation reports.

- One is simply the original trust metric we inherited from the collection system. This metric is usually a confidence parameter, increasingly dependent on some directed graph. We simply pass this through because the C2 client may want to audit the result. We do this in the spirit of full visibility.
- The second that we have termed is "fittedness." What we deliver to commanders are composed situation reports with structure that allows them to be assembled into useful narratives. These are in response to queries. That restricts the structure by the original query, by assembly, and by sequential/casual relation. No fit of components into these situation assemblies is perfect; in fact, every one that results will have some degree of misfit, usually because of multiple ontological governances. We have to tell the client how imperfect the assembly is and how good a "fit" the components are into the situation. The good news is that we can do this very well. The bad news is that the metric is not human understandable by itself and needs a novel visual grammar. We are developing that in a related project.
- A third metric concerns a different type of fit. Our situations that we find are built around those that are presented within the queries. But what we find seldom is a perfect fit. This lack of fit is the nature of dealing with novelty, unknowns, nonergodic futures, and implicit cause. Yet, if we find something that is like what is requested, we need to deliver it together with a metric of how close it is to what the client was looking for. We expect an autonomous analyst function in a future C2 system to evaluate this for utility and adjust the queries in real time if the unexpected insights prove cogent.

3.3 Strategies

Fig. 3.6 illustrates some of the more novel features of our approach. In this figure, we treat the two abstract zones of Fig. 5 the same, because in this context, they are similar.

The architecture is a sort of "common ground" for legacy, conventional, emerging second-wave services and those of the still experimental third wave. The box named "Static Second-Wave Services" will be the vast majority of tools and techniques that do useful things and do them effectively. This box represents a fast-growing set of capabilities, fed in Australia by the modeling complex warfighting (MCW) strategic investment research program.

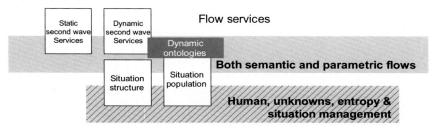

FIG. 3.6 The three types of management systems accept most of the existing and emerging concept fusion services, either directed (static) or guided (dynamic), plus the situation management by the categoric second sort (crosshatched).

The "Dynamic Second-Wave Services" is simply the set of existing ontological reasoning processes that we have and are growing but with the difference that the second sort is dynamically reconfiguring local ontologies. The techniques themselves require little or no modification to accommodate this service.

These two collections of services do most of the work, leverage our existing research investments, and accommodate legacies. The new services enabled by the second sort are used for the reasoning that cannot be done otherwise, plus operations that would normally be performed in the set theoretic space but can be made more computationally efficient by abstracting categorically.

The ability to manage local microontologies and assemble situated reports allows a fully query-driven strategy. While we have robust toolsets for querying large datasets, the collective military-intelligence community has been unable to leverage them. The reason is simple: to accommodate any of the current strategies, the field of search needs to be normalized. Normalization is a lossy process, so much so that it cannot be used for mission critical decisions. It is lossy on the client end as well, because of the search ontologies and queries that are similarly constrained.

But well before that problem presented is the one of scale. The incoming information needs to be normalized and stored in that form. Every element needs to be inspected, usually at more than one level of granularity. Every element needs to be stored and in some way indexed separately from the collection sources and in a way that can be accessed cheaply.

It is more feasible to accept the information as it is from the collection services and normalize it as it is needed based on an opportunistic demand model. This allows diverse client paradigms and the ability to add new paradigms as needs change.

3.4 An example, agile C2 scenario

3.4.1 The general situation

This scenario is a representative problem, designed to illustrate first the need and then a possible event path that is supported by the three services we've described. The year is 2030. Adversary forces (AF) have relentlessly established island bases with hypersonic weapons that threaten Australia and freedom of the sea-lanes. That threat has been used for incremental coercion, so far economic. In parallel an ongoing cold cyberconflict is underway with interception devices being installed and neutralized on undersea cables by competing Five Eye and AF resources.

AF assets have a rapid AI insertion paradigm feeding their intelligence collection and weapon systems; they are at par or better in these systems than Australia and allies. But their C2 paradigm remains *hierarchical* with decisions made at the highest level regardless of feasibility, using communication-human communication threading. Force design authorities in Australia on the other hand have implemented an agile C2 system paradigm that leverages AI and autonomy. This paradigm supports agility through increased speed of updated situational awareness in the C2 fabric. A primary enabler is an intelligence fusion system that receives intelligence and delivers tailored information packages to command nodes in the agile C2 system.

3.4.2 The specific problem

AF has newly occupied an island that is (marginally) contested Australian territory. The island itself has no indigenous population, but has served as a fishing camp for millennia. AF claim the facility is for climate change research and is temporary, but in fact, they are establishing a forward information warfare base, exploiting a nearby mainline submarine cable. A linking cable is in preliminary phases of being installed. This would greatly enhance AF monitoring and cyberwar capabilities.

Some cyber and social warfare operations are underway at the site. Unbeknownst to the Australian population, AF cyberwarriors in general have potential control over key Australian infrastructure systems, including some international financial infrastructure. This has been used for demonstrative, unattributed coercion already. For Australian authorities to implement stringent domestic countermeasures that may temporarily disrupt the economy, the public needs to be aware of the threat.

On the island, strong communication links to AF mainland and command are mature, primarily via satellite and intermittently via frequent submarine visitors. About 60 AF personnel are current at any time, perhaps 1/3 regular military with light arms, 1/3 cyberoperatives, and 1/3 construction technicians. There are no radar or antiship/air installations; military coverage is by AF sea force, supplemented by AF marine intelligence, reconnaissance, and surveillance assets. The site is provisioned by docked medium craft, submarines, and helicopter shuttles from larger craft.

3.4.3 The mission

The mission is to be conducted by Australian Special Forces. They will occupy the island for a short period to

- arrest three indicted cybercriminals known to be present, two of which are AF nationals and
- capture some information warfare gear and strategically destroy the remainder.

Destruction is intended to be focused and merely demonstrative. Casualties should be minimized. The captured gear will be used as proof of intent for harm to Australia and its citizens while providing some intelligence. The men to be arrested are cybercriminals indicted in the International Criminal Court to which they will be extradited.

The goals so far as AF are to

- send a hard, military message on the specific physical occupation by AF not being tolerated and that future incremental offense may be dangerous;
- use the event and its aftermath to reveal AF cyberaggression against international infrastructure to domestic and international audiences, perhaps cementing tentative regional alliances; and
- as a secondary goal discover key AF cyberwar techniques and successes, compromising their global cyberwarfare program.

Australian Special Forces will primarily employ their new helicopter mix with Australian-designed modifications that include robust, in-craft support for the agile C2 architecture, allowing the mission and surrounding activity to be restructured while underway as contingencies develop. Were it not for this C2 agility, AF will continue to succeed in incremental coercive offense because the risk of full-out war will be too great for a measured Australian response. That can be seen as the actual goal of the operation: to demonstrate that it is possible for a regional power to assert itself with precision and agility unmatchable by AF, thereby neutralizing the implied inevitability of major conflict from pushback of engineered, coercive escalation.

The example supposes helicopter-hosted C2 hardware for the initial C2 field systems in a configuration with Wedgetail E-7A assets that function as an "autonomous analyst," within the larger C2 environment, to advise not only on what to do next but also on what C2 topology and responsibilities to configure.

3.4.4 The contingencies

The example is purely fictional, posing an artificial situation and capabilities that do not yet exist; deviation from reality is deliberate. No government employee or representative contributed. The example is crafted to require *actual agility* rather than flexible switching among preplanned responses.

The goal is to have this be a limited operation, with minimal military profile. It will be presented as a police action to arrest criminals, remove illegal devices from the island, and serve notice of an impending forcible eviction if the island is not voluntarily abandoned.

We need the C2 architecture to perform three functions:

- Successfully conduct the "police operation."
- Circumspectly reconfigure the C2 response to minimum effective action should AF forces escalate.
- Execute the determined ensuing defensive operations using the reconfigured C2 systems.

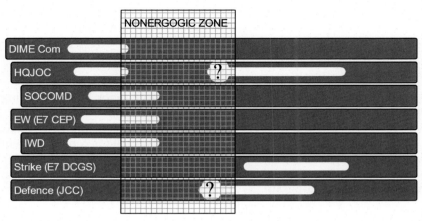

FIG. 3.7 Several illustrative C2 roles are potentially engaged. The idea is to operate as a police action so as not to give the impression of all-out combat preparedness but have the agility to incrementally and minimally respond to conditions.

The example focuses on how an intelligence fusion system supports the design of a C2 system that is inherently capable of adapting on the fly for different measures of success as the situations change. In this case, we plan the special forces' mission to be self-contained as missions used to be. But we don't know how AF forces will react. They may construe this action as preliminary to war, especially if electronic warfare is used in wide theater to prevent communication from the island. It is essential that the Australian response to any provoked reaction be adequate for defense but not exacerbate the situation.

Fig. 3.7 illustrates the problem.

The operation must be managed at the civilian level, a supposed new DIME Command, in concert with parallel DIME controls. Joint Operations Command (HQJOC) will coordinate the minimal assets for the Special Operations Command (SOCOMD). DIME is the doctrine that national response should be integrated across four domains: diplomacy, information, military, and economic.

It is essential to push the mission command as far down the chain as possible in part because AF has a finely tuned ability to sense minor changes in global readiness. For example, if it looks like SOCOMD is gearing up for combat followed by what are expected to be confusing reports of kinetic action, that could trigger a preemptive strike by AF.

In addition to low-visibility SOCOMD control, two other functional commands are integrated in the information warfare division (IWD) because there needs to be coordinated efforts on social media, AF communications, and (CEP) electronic spoofing on multiple locations, some of it undetectable. The platform controlling the electronic operations and communication with special forces' C2 systems is the aloft C2 capability of E-7A Wedgetail, which has the authority to trigger C2 topology change.

Fig. 3.7 shows that there is a period between starting the operation and some period—perhaps 30h later—where anything can happen and something likely will. This is "nonergodic" space, where circumspect response is essential and agility is required.

3.4.5 Mission sequence

Six minutes before action, diplomats and information warfare assets are engaged with the intelligence fusion system. Draft narratives are ready for the press and social media. Communication with the island and AF centers is disabled and replaced by friendly surrogates reporting a tsunami. Growlers are not engaged to minimize the military profile, so this IW uses other assets.

At breakfast a flash bomb is dropped over the facility. This is followed 90 s later with a heavy concussive suction and flash device. Shortly thereafter a number of small refractive smoke dispensers are distributed. These are intended to confuse and nonlethally immobilize the inhabitants.

Thirty light helo drones are deployed with cameras and associated sensors that can see through the engineered suspension. Arriving forces wear eyegears that have similar through-haze capability, additionally advised by the small surveillance drones. These are slaved to Reapers and a Triton with supplementary capability. Each soldier's view is differently supplemented by vision fusion. The lightweight drones are tasked with collectively tracking, characterizing, and potentially identifying persons. After the mission, they will fly into the sea.

Raptors have surgical weapons to use against a perceived threat to friendlies. These can be triggered remotely from Wedgetail, an on-site commander or the "remote weapons officer."

A remote intelligence/weapons officer is shipside and flying a virtual craft informed by the intelligence fusion system. The identity of the virtual craft changes through the mission, first as a virtual wingman for the lighting, then as a trusted rotor man for the helo command pilots, and finally as the field commander's resource sergeant. Command authority is federated with a governing node at Wedgetail. This officer controls several lethal resources, but the primary mission is introspective C2 topology.

The speculative Wedgetail C2 node has four main displays. Center left is a geolocation display of everything within range of concern. This is a 3-D view on a screen with ready affordances. (VR is too fatiguing.) Center right has a fluid set of report views that the operator can shift through and tailor, derived from the distributed common ground station (DCGS). Above is the "Mousetrap" panel that reports alerts and conditions of concern. Below is the "Captain Simple" (CapSim) display with the capability situation reports of friendly forces. Any of the four can quickly generate a situated query, and information can be shifted among them. The operator has the authority to both exercise the C2 system reported in the CapSim system and reconfigure as conditions require. It may well be that the low readiness profile needs to be reconfigured to counter a retaliatory attack, but just barely.

The virtual craft is a novelty developed in Australia as an advance enabled by and implementing the next-generation intelligence fusion system and leveraging autonomous hard systems. It is described elsewhere. The supplemented vision system for the forces, on ground and in support, is a similar innovation, empowered by a dedicated "vision fusion and federation" capability of the intelligence fusion system.

A party of 41 special forces land with a mix of helicopters. A second cohort of special forces is off-shore on standby in inflatable boats delivered by submarine. The primary mission of the seaborne force is to extract the up to 18 captured and wounded, but they can agilely supplement the ground force if required. Using the aloft and helmet-worn location and identification services, the forces neutralize the kinetic threats, round up, and bind the suspects. Seriously wounded are gathered as well, both groups delivered to the boat rendezvous for exfiltration. Several from the helo party depart in the boats, leaving room in the helicopters for captured gear and faster exit. Cameras on soldiers and aloft assets capture a great deal for use later.

The mission takes 30–40 min. Information warfare spoofing ends and shifts to bogus messages among our nodes that we know are monitored. For another 40 min, we report confusion about a tsunami. Some underwater spoofers will have emulated an earthquake signature, designed to confound AF sonar arrays.

An immediate barrage of information is sent about the police action and arrest. Regrets about injuries and deaths are given. We do not report that significant numbers are being interviewed shipside. Criminals are duly arrested and sped to the mainland. Others are interviewed, treated, and returned to a nearby civilian island. All this is filmed, and media editors prepare sequences for distribution. But for the immediate future, we keep all this in reserve so that AF commanders and diplomats do not know what we have.

3.4.6 Aftermath

In the 2 h that follows, we need the agile C2 system to look convincingly unthreatening, because the major goal is to pull off a tactical police action without escalation. However, the AF response is unexpected, though logical in hindsight. They decide

- first to eliminate as much evidence as possible, to deny any cyberoperations, and stick to the story of civilian scientists conducting climate change research and
- second to escalate the situation as quickly as possible to reinforce the doctrine that any military response to AF incrementalism can be catastrophic.

AF forces unexpectedly send six submarine-based cruise missiles to the island: Two are antipersonnel, and four are to destroy facilities. They apparently do this without landing on the island to assess the operation, because the apparent intent is to blame the damage on Australia as a pretext for punishing action elsewhere.

They also simultaneously bring down power distribution networks in two major Australian cities. We have a small window to respond. We've used a few systems they did not expect to both command and record the operation and the C2 system switches to diplomacy/information centric operations, using the new narrative engineering capability of the intelligence fusion system to roll out a story on both the diplomatic and social media/news fronts. We have studied how their news manipulation system works and wait for the manufactured story.

The AF narrative arrives with aerial footage of the damage caused by needless aggression against a scientific research facility and bombast. Their forces are on high alert and begin acting aggressively. Action on an AF breakaway province could be triggered, and bombardment of special forces forward provisioning facility is likely.

In the social network and diplomacy domains, we show the captured cybercriminals and a key sequence of their capture, workspaces, and cable operation. We keep almost all media products in reserve as an agile "they claim, we disprove" operation is unrolled over weeks.

In the cyberwar domain, within moments of addressing the attack on power installations, we send by conventional means instant messages to the leaders of that operation, revealing that we know who they are and that they are at risk of indictment and arrest. We stay defensive otherwise.

In the military domain, we present an engineered puzzle by staying deceptively unmobilized. In several small events, we demonstrate the ability to comprehend and respond vastly more effectively than they can.

3.5 Background of the approach

The approach described in this chapter has been inspired by research performed over decades for the US intelligence community. The basic model theoretic foundations were defined (in the way we use them) by Tarski and axiomatically explored by Barwise (1974). That paper is notable in not directly inheriting the notation from model theory, which would come later, but by exploring how to axiomatize models in category theory.

Barwise would soon elaborate the work as "situation semantics" (Barwise & Perry, 1981). His paper and associated discussions attracted an endowment to establish what became Stanford's largest research center and publishing house, the Center for the Study of Logic and Information. It initially defined the problems of implicit, interpretive influence without using the mechanisms of model or category theory. The much-cited book of the next year (Barwise & Perry, 1983) led the supporting research center to conduct symposia, to host visiting scholars and related collaborations, and to seed hundreds of papers on situation theory.

On a parallel, more philosophical path, Barwise's *Situations and Attitudes* book initiated a concern adopted by Barry Smith in defining the Basic Formal Ontology (Arp, Smith, & Spear, 2015), which represents one side of a controversy in the ontology community. The controversy is between a preference for logical cleanliness, promoted by Sowa (2011) and others, and interpretive power.

Keith Devlin at Stanford University took Barwise's situation theory that by the early 90s had matured and placed it squarely in the then settled notation of model theory and simplified its concepts with the goal of making it practical and useful. This resolved the ontological balance in practice. Two books resulted, the first logically oriented (Devlin, 1995) followed by a more philosophy-centric presentation (Devlin, 1998). A different book described a practical implementation and its accompanying practical issues (Devlin & Rosenberg, 1996).

Situation theory at this mature stage was taken internally to the intelligence community by Goranson. Relatively independently, Devlin engaged with a research program sponsored by the Advanced Research and Development Agency. Years afterward, Devlin made available his work from that project, along with a coherent surrounding narrative (Devlin, 2009). Our standard fact and predicate representation system as "infons" and the type system for the first sorted logic are described there.

Meanwhile, Barwise shifted his focus from the mechanics of truth to the influence on interpretation, producing "channel theory," modeling the relative influences from many situations on the distributed elements in predicate statements (Barwise & Seligman, 1997).

Barwise's intent was category centric. Goranson implemented a first-generation two-sorted system, using set theory (Goranson & Schachman, 2014).

A clever technique for combining the inner product of the source logic and the outer product in the second logic uses group theory. The "wreath product" was devised by Michael Leyton, being an introspective ring product (Leyton, 1999). Using the wreath product, Goranson implemented a two-sorted version for video intelligence fusion (Goranson, 2015).

Though developed independently and for a much less ambitious agenda, Joshi and Henderson (2016) used an applied wreath product in a Bayesian context for multisensory modeling.

The current category theoretic implementation was developed in Goranson's laboratory, following an innovation from Samson Abramsky, who followed Barwise. Abramsky tackled the infamous von Neumann challenge by abstracting first into a second sort category logic appropriate for that purpose and then adapting the first logical sort to support the abstraction (Abramsky & Coecke, 2008). This approach to categoric two sorts enabled a practical implementation devised by Goranson, Devlin, Cardier, and Garcia, reported in a neurobiological context (Cardier, Goranson, et al., 2017; Cardier, Sanford, et al., 2017; Goranson & Cardier, 2013; Goranson, Cardier, & Devlin, 2015), and described further in Goranson and Cardier (2014).

The current refinements are designed to enable next-generation C2 and to incorporate various services being developed by the Australian Defense Science and Technology (DST) Group, primarily under the MCW program, but including prior work in this area.

For example, Robert Niven of MCW characterizes Bayesian solution spaces, extracts an "entropy space" as a second sort, analyzes the space for indicators of causal unknowns, and abstracts back to a by then much simplified space (Waldrip & Niven, 2017). We generalize this perspective to a form of MapReduce over lattices. MapReduce is a much-used technique to use query patterns to simplify a search space.

What differentiates this approach from the categoric one is that Goranson and colleagues devised the second sort to optimize the task at hand being the ability to register effects from unknowns and incremental discovery. Once that capability is established, a costly reengineering of the first sort and first to second sort registration mechanisms are required. This process is where foundations from existing DST research efforts are helpful.

The "bottom-up" approach of Reid and colleagues (Ivancevic, Reid, Pourbeik, & Pilling, 2019) abstracts system features that are native to a system; no outer product is required. All of the operators are self-adjoint. So long as the first sort is or can be vectorized, a common Hermitian operator can be applied to abstract into a space to perform certain analyses. The abstraction engineering, therefore, is in determining what qualities are desired in the second sort (as with the top-down strategy) and using one of the well-understood operations. If the space is symmetric, a Hamiltonian covers the vector space regardless of bounding.

Reid's recent concern is the identification and characterization of nonergodic behavior intrinsic to (or possible in) a certain characterization space. If the characterizations are models used in war-gaming, we can (with some limits) explore gaming when completely unexpected and inexplicable causal events appear.

A primary foundation from DST for future implementations is the research performed on information fusion in general (Blasch, Bosse, & Lambert, 2012): Mephisto, an ontological framework (Lambert & Nowak, 2008); Lexpresso, a controlled natural language (Saulwick,

2014); Consensus, an implementation architecture (Lambert, Saulwick, & Trentelman, 2015); and the work on structuring a generated narrative across different presentation modalities (Nowina-Krowicki, Argent, Lucerno, Lange, & Wark, 2018; Wark, Nowina-Krowicki, Lucerno, & Lange, 2018).

Another foundation comes from applicable work in a related space in monoidal abstractions (Coecke, 2012) in a two-sorted logic based on situation theory as noted. A visualization system that exploits these abstractions is reported in a parallel chapter in this book (Cardier et al., 2019).

3.6 Type considerations

Some decisions are made based on the requirement for agile human-machine collaboration. For example, the specification of a type system is normally a trivial task, following programming conventions. But in this case, ontologies are dynamic; for no other reason, types need to be circumspectly specified. Also the type system is the primary element that unifies the three reasoning systems, four including human clients.

Types need to have their own calculus distinct from schema languages, so that differing representations of the same element can be assigned local qualities. For example, a human can be assigned the quantity of "three," the quality of "perception," or have a surrogate assigned agency in the system.

Because the span ranges from category theoretic abstraction to intuitively human-accessible elements, we require an ontic realism with phenomenalist pragmatics. These are built into our upper ontology:

- Implicit existence is required; we need to reason about entities and influences that produce behavior of interest but which we do not know, or often cannot even infer. This notion of actors that do not seem to exist requires us to modify any upper ontology to reverse reification and existence. Something in our situations can have an effect in the world (be reified) before being in the ontology (existing). By this means, we escape the tendency to anchor causal effects in cause.
- Categoric abstractions will exist that have no analogue in the world of experience. However, we require them to have an identity that is reminiscent of that world. We use the notion of "ontic realism" to apply world-like properties when accessed by humans.
  A common example from another domain is the notion that the Higgs boson is in some fashion a particle. By this ontic realist strategy, we escape the requirement that entities that have agency be agents. Our primary use is in our concept of "governance" where a group of influences affect interpretation.
- Categoric morphisms will exist that similarly have no analogue in the world of experience. The process of accessing these intuitively requires a phenomenalist approach that in many cases subsumes ontic realism. An example of this principle often used without formal justification is the notion of "entropy" to characterize projected futures in spaces abstracted from models.

These three approaches in combination will be leveraged in parallel user interface research projects to allow users access to underlying metaphysics. A concept that combines these strategies is the use of "narrative." Narrative for us serves several overlapping purposes. We use it in the client world in the conventional sense of describing situations using ontologically rooted terms in a way that indicates futures.

We use it in the self-assembly process. Usually a query is thought of as one-half of a dialog between a querant and a responder assuming the former is humanlike. Our process instead depends on information elements for self-assembling, which is required based on an external stimulus. A working analogy is that the normative world here is one of information and the "physics" of information is narrative. The query is analogous to presenting boundary conditions and allowing the forces of narrative governance to assemble candidates in response.

References

Abramsky, S., & Coecke, B. (2008). Categorical quantum mechanics. In *Handbook of quantum logic and quantum structures: Quantum logic* (pp. 261–324): Elsevier.

Arp, R., Smith, B., & Spear, A. D. (2015). *Building ontologies with basic formal ontology.* MIT Press.

Barwise, J. (1974). Axioms for abstract model theory. *Annals of Mathematical Logic, 7,* 221–265.

Barwise, J., & Perry, J. (1981). Situations and attitudes. *Journal of Philosophy, 78*(11), 668.

Barwise, J., & Perry, J. (1983). *Situations and attitudes.* Cambridge, Massachusetts: MIT Press.

Barwise, J., & Seligman, J. (1997). *Information flow: The logic of distributed systems.* Cambridge University Press.

Blasch, E., Bosse, E., & Lambert, D. (2012). *High-level information fusion management and systems design.* Artech House.

Cardier, B., Goranson, H. T., Casas, N., Lundberg, P. S., Erioli, A., Takaki, R., et al. (2017). Modeling the peak of emergence in systems: Design and katachi. *Progress in Biophysics and Molecular Biology, 131,* 213.

Cardier, B., Sanford, L. D., Goranson, H. T., Lundberg, P. S., Ciavarra, R., Devlin, K., et al. (2017). Modeling the resituation of memory in neurobiology and narrative. In *Proceedings from computational principles of natural and artificial intelligence.*

Cardier, B., Shull, J., Nielsen, A., Diallo, S., Lundberg, P., Sanford, L. D., et al. (2019). A narrative modeling platform: Representing the comprehension of novelty in open world systems. In W. Lawless, R. Mittu, & D. Sofge (Eds.), *Human-machine shared contexts.* Eds: Elsevier.

Coecke, B. (2012). *The logic of quantum mechanics—Take II.* http://arxiv.org/pdf/1204.3458v1.

Devlin, K. J. (1995). *Logic and information.* Cambridge University Press.

Devlin, K. J. (1998). *Goodbye, Descartes: The end of logic and the search for a new cosmology of the mind.* Wiley.

Devlin, K. J. (2009). Modeling real reasoning. In G. Sommaruga (Ed.), *Formal theories of information: From Shannon to semantic information theory and general concepts of information* (pp. 234–252): Springer.

Devlin, K. J., & Rosenberg, D. (1996). *Language at work: Analyzing communication breakdown in the workplace to inform systems design (66).* Center for the Study of Language and Information.

Goranson, H. T. (2015). *System and method for scalable semantic stream processing (USPTO 9,117,167).* US: Sirius-Beta Corp.

Goranson, H. T., & Cardier, B. (2014). *System and method for ontology derivation (USPTO 14/093,229).* United States: Sirius-Bets.

Goranson, H. T., & Cardier, B. (2013). A two-sorted logic for structurally modeling systems. *Progress in Biophysics and Molecular Biology, 113*(1), 141–178.

Goranson, H. T., Cardier, B., & Devlin, K. J. (2015). Pragmatic phenomenological types. *Progress in Biophysics and Molecular Biology, 119*(3), 420–436.

Goranson, H. T., & Schachman, T. (2014). *Digital system for organizing diverse information (USPTO 8,751,918).* United States: Sirius-Beta, Inc.

Ivancevic, V., Reid, D., Pourbeik, P., & Pilling, M. (2019). Tensor-centric warfare. VI. A global warfare model. *Intelligent Control and Automation, 10.*

Joshi, A., & Henderson, T. (2016). Wreath product cognitive architecture. In *Proceedings from IEEE international conference on multisensor fusion and integration for intelligent systems.*

Lambert, D. A., & Nowak, C. (2008). *The Mephisto conceptual framework.* DSTO-TR-2162.

Lambert, D. A., Saulwick, A., & Trentelman, K. (2015). Consensus: A comprehensive solution to the grand challenges of information fusion. In *Proceedings from 18th international conference on information fusion (fusion).*

Leyton, M. (1999). *Symmetry, causality, mind.* Bradford Books.

Nowina-Krowicki, M., Argent, P., Lucerno, C., Lange, D., & Wark, S. (2018). Now this changes everything: Managing provenance using multimedia-narrative. In *Proceedings from workshop on robot teammates in dynamic unstructured environments (RT-DUNE), international conference on robotics and automation (ICRA).*

Saulwick, A. (2014). Lexpresso: A controlled natural language. In *Proceedings from 4th international workshop on controlled natural language.*

Sowa, J. F. (2011). Future directions for semantic systems. In *Intelligence-based systems engineering* (pp. 23–47).

Waldrip, S., & Niven, R. (2017). Comparison between Bayesian and maximum entropy analyses of flow networks. *Entropy, 19.*

Wark, S., Nowina-Krowicki, M., Lucerno, C., & Lange, D. (2018). But why? Generating narratives using provenance. In *Proceedings from interaction design for explainable AI workshop, OzCHI.*

Context: Separating the forest and the trees—Wavelet contextual conditioning for AI

Stephen Russell[a], Ira S. Moskowitz[b], Brian Jalaian[a]

[a]Battlefield Information Processing Branch, US Army Research Laboratory, Adelphi, MD, United States [b]Information Management and Decision Architectures Branch, US Naval Research Laboratory, Washington, DC, United States

4.1 Introduction

Artificial intelligence (AI) has gained tremendous attention following the age of big data. As a result, society has witnessed remarkable successes brought about by AI in the form of machine translation, speech recognition, image classification, and information retrieval. The massive amounts of data acquired and processed by corporations such as Google, Facebook, Amazon, and Apple have provided accelerated advances in a variety of industries and created new opportunities driven by machine intelligence insights. This phenomenon has also driven a demand for new machine learning (ML) techniques that improve the accuracy of AI predictions and decision-making abilities.

While task-centric and specialized AI is becoming more and more capable, the vision for AI research has always been and what has recently been termed general AI. In other words, general AI is artificial intelligence that is contextually universal and thus not constrained to a task or application domain. Despite the significant advancements made by ML and AI tightly coupled to a domain, context still remains a significant challenge for both ML and AI. Generalized ML and AI are still not broadly available (Moriwaki, Akitomi, Kudo, Mine, & Moriya, 2016) and remain elusive (Ramamoorthy & Yampolskiy, 2018). Ultimately purposed to aid or deliver decisions, the promise of general AI remains limited by contemporary data-driven approaches. These data-driven approaches constrict the scope of machine learners, somewhat like biological learners, to observations that they have been exposed to a priori or have relatively rigorous similarities to internal representations. However, biological learners are generally more successful in creating successful outcomes under ambiguity because of their intrinsic information capacity, data representations, and ability to abstract between represented entities when no relational connection exists.

One aspect of modern ML and AI that often gets obfuscated by the sheen of the machines showing any ability to perform humanlike decision-making or identify things unforeseen by humans, regardless of domain specificity, is the underlying fact that the AI/ML algorithms depend on the data derived from their decision-making models and that drives their decisional output. As such the preprocessing of the data is fundamental to the success of the artificial intelligence. Outside of the data engineering/science domain, little attention is given to data preprocessing or the data preprocessing is tightly coupled to the ML/AI model generation. Nuanced situational and environmental ambiguities and dynamics can lead to highly variable and, in many cases undependable, decisions from AI systems. The dependability problem is compounded when the AI systems are more complex, such as those that depend on ensemble machine learning algorithms and cascading decisional outputs.

In this chapter, we posit that to achieve general AI, techniques that abstract data preprocessing, provide contextual conditioning, and otherwise affect often obfuscated underlying models are necessary. To examine this hypothesis, we employ a wavelet method for data decomposition that separate fluctuations from trends. While there are many techniques that can improve data processing (Bumblauskas et al., 2017; Zhuang, Wu, Chen, & Pan, 2017), wavelets provide a means to separate data trends from fluctuations that can yield improvements in AI/ML models and subsequent outputs. The chapter is organized as follows: The next section presents a background on data preprocessing and decision-making. The section following describes a method for wavelet decomposition that can identify a preferential decomposition level for training, followed by a section to illustrate the method's functionality. Section 4.6 describes how the methodology is evaluated by simulation using a management decision problem application, representing a black box complex AI application that has a quantitative outcome. Finally, the results of the simulation, the implications of this research on wavelet augmented preprocessing for contextual AI, and subsequent conclusions are presented.

4.2 Artificial intelligence, context, data, and decision making

Recent advances in machine learning and artificial intelligence have placed even greater emphasis on humans' interaction with information, because the intelligent systems themselves have become proxies for humans (Russell, Moskowitz, & Raglin, 2017). However, the prevalence of volumes of readily available information presents potential challenges to how AI utilizes information, within a context, to aid decision problems. Human information interaction is grounded in purpose, which ultimately translates to the efficacy of a AI system's own decision-making activities (Jones et al., 2006). As organizations increasingly generate data from transaction processing databases and other information systems, decision-making AI at all functional echelons have volumes of detailed, accessible, real-time data that allows them to build models that inform decision processes for allocating resources and assessing results. Yet the machine learning models powering the AI remain highly coupled to the problem's context, in which the data are generated (Mitchell et al., 2018). Therefore the context is embedded in the data meaning that when the problem or application becomes more complex the AI becomes less effective. For the purposes of this chapter, we define context as any information that can be used to characterize or understand the situation of an entity, whether shared or not, where an entity is a person, place, or object that is considered relevant to the application problem or decision (Abowd et al., 1999).

Contextual data tend to be large, high-dimensional, noisy, and complex. The characteristics of context are often dynamic and thus manifest as variability in observed data. Typical machine learning problems associated with such data cluster classify or segment the data and detect anomalies or identify embedded areas of interest. Contextual variances in the data can be positive for ML algorithms. For example, adding noise in training data for a ML algorithm can in some cases improve its generalizability while in others reduce an algorithm's accuracy (Kalapanidas, Avouris, Craciun, & Neagu, 2003). One may view this phenomenon collectively as similar to human learning and decision-making: the combined simultaneous analysis of data variability and trend can complicate the extrication of salient decision-relevant concerns. Of consideration is the issue of separating the variability from the trend in the data. This separation can lead to well-tuned models that provide insights on the data trend or, separately, the contextual variability. By having separate representations or models for the data variance and the general pattern can potentially provide more robust machine learning. However, it will also be important to capture variability and trend at multiple scales. Multiscale representations or multiresolution analysis/algorithms can be described as a class of design methods in representation theory where the data are subject to repeated transformation to extract features associated with different scales (Burt & Adelson, 1985). To achieve both separations of variability and trend, as well as multiscale resolution, calls for an approach that provides a summarization of large amounts of data without losing key characteristics that still separates variability in the primary data. Further the technique should support the provision of guidance to model training applications, including which resolution would be an appropriate starting scale.

Wavelet transformations implemented as a preprocessing step prior to training an AI machine learning algorithm may represent a viable solution. Discrete wavelet transformations (DWT) provide a mathematical methodology that reduces the volume of data while retaining features and characteristics of the original data. Additionally, DWT has the benefit of separating the original data into its trending and fluctuation components. This benefit may be directly useful because local fluctuations can be minimized so as to not obscure the existing trends. Wavelets have been widely used by the scientific community since Daubechies' (1992) work; however, little attention has been given to the effects of wavelet preprocessing for ML algorithms that support decision-making.

4.3 Wavelets and preprocessing

The last decade has seen an explosion of interest in wavelets, a subject area that has coalesced from roots in mathematics, physics, electrical engineering, and other disciplines. Generally speaking, a wavelet is a mathematical function that divides data, other math functions, or operators into different frequency components and then studies each component with a resolution matched to a predetermined scale (Daubechies, 1992). Originally developed as a methodology to support radio-frequency signal processing because of its ability to isolate a signal's frequency and amplitude components, wavelets are now used for image compression, pattern matching, and data smoothing applications. There are many different types of wavelets, each with different properties. Daubechies wavelets have found favor because of their computational simplicity and flexible characteristics. The research in this chapter concentrates on these types of wavelets.

A wavelet can have many desirable properties, for example, compact support, vanishing moments, dilating relations, and other preferred properties like smoothness or being the generator of an orthonormal basis of function spaces $L^2(R^n)$, etc. For example, the Haar wavelet is the mathematically least complex wavelet that is discrete; it is considered to be the simplest of Daubechies wavelets. All Daubechies wavelets are generators of an orthogonal basis for $L^2(R^n)$ (Chui & Lian, 1996). For example, a "mother" wavelet is a function $\psi(x)$ such that $\{\psi(2^j x - k), i, k \in Z\}$ is an orthonormal basis of $L^2(R^n)$. The core idea behind discrete wavelet transformations (DWT) is to progressively smooth the data using an iterative procedure while keeping its detail along the way. The DWT of $[X_n]$ is an orthonormal transform such that if $[W_n: n = 0, \ldots, N-1]$ represents the DWT coefficients, then $W = HX$ where W is a column vector of length 2^i whose nth element is the nth DWT coefficient of W_n, where H is a $N \times N$ real-valued matrix such that $HH^T = I$, where I is the $N \times N$ identity matrix, and where X is a vector containing values $X_0, \ldots, X_{N-1}$. Furthermore, orthonormality implies that $X = H^T W$ and $||W||^2 = ||X||^2$. The nth wavelet coefficient, W_n, is associated with a particular scale and a particular set of times.

4.3.1 Wavelet decomposition

A discrete wavelet transformation (DWT) on data is a wavelet decomposition process that can be applied to data either once or iteratively. When used iteratively, after transforming the original data, successive approximations are then decomposed in turn, so that one dataset is broken down into many lower resolution datasets that are progressively smoothed. The selection of the type of wavelet (Haar, Daubechies 4-8-12 family, Morlet, Shannon, etc.) for DWT decomposition can affect the resulting coefficients. The trade-off in choosing between wavelet filters with short widths (such as Haar and Daubechies 4) and those with longer widths (Daubechies 8, Daubechies 4, Morlet, etc.) lies in the undesirable artifacts that may occur as a result of the filter choice. For example, very short-width wavelets sometime produce artifacts such as unrealistic blocks, sharks' fins, and triangles. On the other hand, longer width wavelets may suffer from the influence of boundary conditions on the coefficients, a decrease in the degree of localization, and an increase in computational burden. A suggested strategy in practice is to select the smallest width wavelet that produces acceptable results. However, the application context generally determines its acceptable outcomes.

In machine learning applications involving large amounts of data, computational and mathematical simplicity is important. So, this research in this chapter focuses on simpler wavelet transformations: Haar and Daubechies-4. This family of wavelets is often called compactly supported orthonormal filters. The Haar-based DWT transforms the data by using discrete incremental pairs. For example, given a dataset x_1, x_2, x_3, and x_4, Haar transforms the data by taking x_1 and x_2 and then separately x_3 and x_4 using the DWT shown in Eq. (4.1). This operation results in an approximation (C_{appx}) and difference (C_{diff}) coefficient for each pair. Daubechies-4 uses overlapping increments of 4 similarly. Given dataset, x_1, x_2, x_3, x_4, x_5, and x_6, Daubechies-4 transforms the data taking x_1, x_2, x_3, and x_4 then the separately x_3, x_4, x_5, and x_6 for the next set of coefficients. The Daubechies-4 wavelet functions are shown in Eq. (4.2).

$$C_{appx_i} = \frac{x_i + x_{i+1}}{\sqrt{2}}, \quad C_{diff_i} = \frac{x_i - x_{i+1}}{\sqrt{2}} \tag{4.1}$$

$$C_{appx_i} = \frac{x_i + x_i\sqrt{3}}{4\sqrt{2}} + \frac{3x_{i+1} + x_{i+1}\sqrt{3}}{4\sqrt{2}} + \frac{3x_{i+2} - x_{i+2}\sqrt{3}}{4\sqrt{2}} + \frac{x_{i+3} - x_{i+3}\sqrt{3}}{4\sqrt{2}}$$

$$C_{diff_i} = \frac{x_i - x_i\sqrt{3}}{4\sqrt{2}} - \frac{3x_{i+1} - x_{i+1}\sqrt{3}}{4\sqrt{2}} + \frac{3x_{i+2} + x_{i+2}\sqrt{3}}{4\sqrt{2}} - \frac{x_{i+3} + x_{i+3}\sqrt{3}}{4\sqrt{2}}$$

$$\tag{4.2}$$

When DWT is applied iteratively, it forms a decomposition tree. This approach was developed in research conducted by Misiti et al. (The MathWorks, Inc., 1991) and Mallat (1989) for multiresolution signal decomposition. The original data are decomposed n-times resulting in approximation and detail coefficients at each level. Fig. 4.1 graphically shows a four-level wavelet decomposition. While Fig. 4.1 shows only four levels, the decomposition tree could continue to n levels until the original data are compressed to a single set of coefficients and where further transformations are possible. The result is a distribution representing the

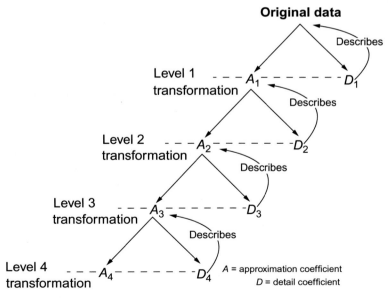

FIG. 4.1   Wavelet decomposition tree showing local fluctuation relationship.

trending pattern of the original data and another distribution composed of local fluctuations for each level. While the approximation coefficients form the trend at the *current* decomposition level, the difference coefficients form the local fluctuations in the *previous* level. For example, in Fig. 4.1, the Level 1 difference coefficients (D_1) identify the local fluctuations in the original data; the second level coefficients (D_2) describe the first level fluctuations and so on.

Unlike Fourier transformations, which work well to tease out the variance in data when the data are stationary, the more nonstationary or dynamic the data is, the worse the results will be. Using DWT to decompose original data provides several benefits that are useful for ML training and model creation. The first and not least significant benefit is data compression. The second benefit is seen in the decomposition's approximation coefficients that retain features and characteristics of the original data. A third benefit is provided by the difference coefficient. This coefficient gives details about how the data are changing locally. Daubechies-based wavelets are also computationally simple, compared with other similar transformations such as fast Fourier transformations (FFT), singular value decomposition (SVD), and random projection. The decomposition tree itself provides the final benefit. Essentially, this tree creates implicit views of both the trend and fluctuations in the original data at multiple resolutions.

While wavelets deliver these benefits generally, DWT may not be suitable for all types of data. For example, data that are relatively noise-free or constant would not see any benefit from smoothing or the difference coefficient. Similarly, small datasets do not get any benefit from compression. It also should be noted that the decomposition tree implies that the data have some order, natural or otherwise, making the DWT ineffective on categorical data. In general, DWT is appropriate for data that are naturally ordered, having local fluctuations and being voluminous (Russell & Yoon, 2008). Decision-relevant data often tend to have these characteristics, as these are naturally described as being time series in nature and these stem from uncontrolled processes or processes affected by contextual variations.

It is the ability of wavelets to reduce data, while retaining features without overly perturbing the data and simultaneously extract variance components that makes them uniquely suitable for decision support applications. Also the compression provided by DWT should allow decision-makers to utilize larger amounts of data without sampling. The separation of trend from variation is another added benefit, as decision-makers seldom explore data looking for trending patterns and exceptions or variability simultaneously (Russell, Gangopadhyay, & Yoon, 2008; Tukey, 1980). The ability to utilize these two components of the data separately and at multiple resolutions can also be a useful exploratory technique. DWT smoothes the trending component in data with each transformation, and data smoothing brings benefits that go beyond enhancing the clarity of the information (Carrington, Ralphs, & Rahman, 2006). Specifically for decision-making, smoothing can increase a computational or human decision-maker's ability to discern patterns (Kafadar, 1996).

4.3.2 Illustration: Visualizing decomposed wavelet data

To demonstrate how wavelet decompositions can be applied to data to achieve the afore-mentioned benefits, the Microsoft AdventureWorks data warehouse dataset (Microsoft, 2017) is used to present an illustration from a fictitious multinational manufacturing company.

This dataset consists of 60,855 rows of the revenue data from product sales, representing daily orders over 1066 days. The data were sorted by date and extracted from the SQL Server data warehouse. The data were then imported into Matlab and decomposed using a Haar-based DWT to its maximum decomposition level. This number of records produced 15 DWT levels. Fig. 4.2 shows a line plot of the 60,855 records with the y-axis representing revenue and the x-axis showing each instance of an order as a count, sorted by transaction time. Visually inspecting this new dataset, it is difficult to discern a clear pattern from this chart.

Similar visualizations were made from the DWT data. Figs. 4.3–4.8 show the approximation coefficients and detail (fluctuation) coefficients of the original data from incremental levels of the decomposition tree. In these charts the x- and y-axes represent the same items as in Fig. 4.2. While not all levels of the decomposition are shown for space considerations, it is clear that the transformation at each level smooths the data progressively. For illustrative purposes the absolute values of the detail coefficients are graphed in figures showing the wavelet difference component. This value produces a positive measure of the local fluctuations in the data and as an absolute value can show a measure of process control in the previous level, which would be represented by lower versus higher values. In Figs. 4.4, 4.6, and 4.8, it clearly shows a pattern that represents the fluctuation between individual time-stepped order values.

The first few transformations shown in Fig. 4.3 provide little improvement in terms of smoothing the pattern over the original data. Even with the plot of the fluctuations displayed in Fig. 4.4, it is challenging to identify a pattern. However, examining Figs. 4.5 and 4.6, it is relatively easy to see that sales revenue has declined sharply in the first 1/5 of the time period. It is also clear that while alternating somewhat in the middle of the time frame, the revenue is fairly consistent thereafter but declining at the very end. Figs. 4.7 and 4.8 show this pattern even more clearly. The plot of the difference coefficients indicates that sales revenue was quite consistent after its initial sharp drop. It is interesting to note that significant characteristics of the original data such as the sharp drop at the 1/5th time period mark and lack of revenue at

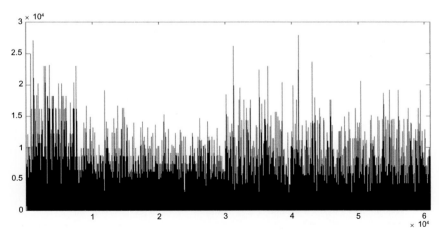

FIG. 4.2 Original data.

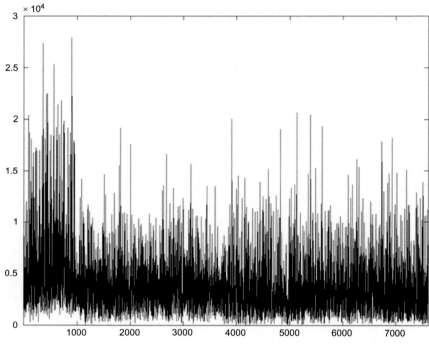

FIG. 4.3   Level 3 approximation coefficients.

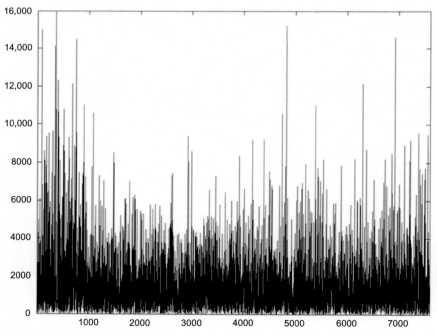

FIG. 4.4   Level 3 difference coefficients.

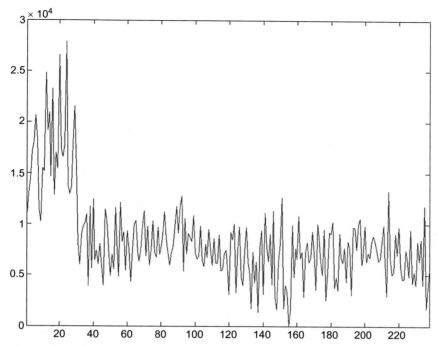

FIG. 4.5   Level 8 approximation coefficients.

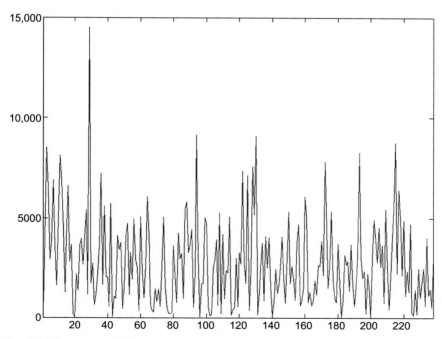

FIG. 4.6   Level 8 difference coefficients.

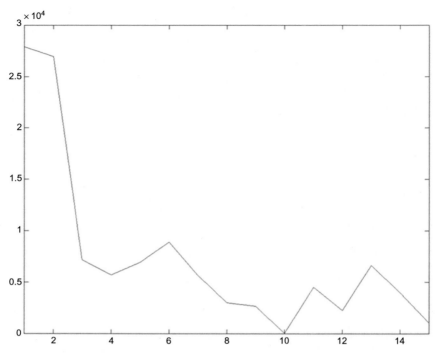

FIG. 4.7   Level 12 approximation coefficients.

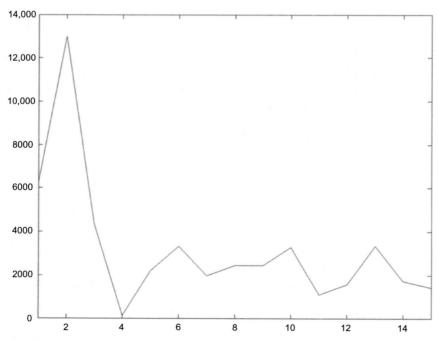

FIG. 4.8   Level 12 difference coefficients.

the 2/3rd time mark are still apparent at level 12 (not shown). At level 15 the visualizations became a plot of a straight line between two points. This plot indicates that at some point, wavelet decomposition's value for decision-making purposes becomes negligible.

The maximum number of transformations depends on the original data size and its characteristics. In this case, 15 transformations were possible. If the dataset had been smaller, fewer transformations would have been possible. Additionally, several of the initial transformations provided few, if any, trend-smoothing benefits over the original data. If the individuals responsible for training a machine learning algorithm is presented with plots of every level, they can choose which one or more levels provide the desired support. However, for some decision-making problems, viewing several plots for each decision variable is not practical or is an arduous task at best; this approach becomes important if there were many decision variables or dimensions. Moreover the ML trainer may not have any insight, intuition, or experience regarding which resolution of the data would be most applicable to the problem domain or even if sufficient variability had been captured. Alternatively the training process may be fully automated, in which case the appropriate resolution must be selected programmatically or with contextual insight.

Implementing DWT for preprocessing ML training data requires that guidance be provided regarding which decomposition would provide a reasonable training set. As shown in the preceding text, wavelet decomposition can yield several distributions to examine the data. Due to the compression provided by each transformation, it is possible to overcompress the data beyond a useful point; in the case of a Haar-based DWT, the data size is halved at each decomposition level. In terms of a resolution scale, the number of transformations that should be selected is a relevant and important question. Further, in automated or efficient ML training context, the answer to this question should be delivered in a simple and speedy manner. Given the benefits of DWT and the corresponding decomposition trees, there is ample justification for evaluating wavelet preprocessing in AI decision-making contexts. However, given all the decomposition levels possible, how should an appropriate decomposition resolution scale be selected?

4.4 A preferential transformation for initial resolution-scale

Because of the utility wavelets in signal processing, filtering, and compression applications, the search for an optimal decomposition level has been well researched. In most of these works, the optimal level is selected through a visual means or through signals or data reconstruction. Conventional techniques for the retrieval of aggregation levels are normally based on a statistical comparison of the original and aggregated datasets. These methods, while effective for signal processing, filtering, and data mining applications, are limited in their efficacy for decision support applications. This is because conventional techniques incorporate the decision context through the implementation of the model creator and, therefore, are more appropriate for supervised (vs unsupervised) learning settings. It is also noteworthy that the contextual implications of decision timing are relevant, regardless of whether the decision-maker is a human or an AI system. While there are many temporal factors that impact decision-making, context can dramatically affect the duration of options (Vidhate & Kulkarni, 2016). In complex or dynamic settings, the decision-maker may not have unlimited amounts of time or a comprehensive understanding of the decision application (Jarrahi, 2018). Any automated preprocessing would benefit from being resilient to contextual variability and having minimal computational overhead. Discrete wavelet transformations meet both of these requirements but first require the identification of an appropriate decomposition level.

Techniques, such as performing a DWT followed by a FFT (Liu, Yu, & Yuan, 2003) or neural networks (Tkacz, Kostka, Komorowski, Domider, & Wrzesniowski, 2002), have also been used to determine an optimal decomposition level for nondecision support applications. The problem with these methods is that they tend to be computationally intensive. Most practitioners would suggest that the optimal wavelet transformation level depends on the application and the underlying signal or data. As a result the use of entropy has become a popular metric for selecting an optimal decomposition level. In information theory, entropy relates to the probability of data to appear as a user expects. Entropy provides a quantitative measure of the surprise in the information that is contained in the data.

Most algorithms that use this approach monitor entropy at each decomposition level; if the entropy decreases at a level, that decomposition level is selected for the problem or analytic. Besides entropy decline, there are other popular criteria that have been applied, such as entropy maximum, minimum, and symmetry (Coifman & Wickerhauser, 1992). The presumption in these and other entropy-based selection methods assumes that the user has some criterion with which to apply an entropy-based hypothesis. These approaches come from the signal processing domain where there is value in decomposing the detail coefficients resulting in a binary decomposition tree. While effective for radio-frequency signal filtering, the use of entropy may not always be appropriate for decision-making applications because criteria regarding the behavior or characteristics of the dataset's entropy may not be known a priori, particularly when contextual variance is introduced.

There is prior research that utilized wavelets as a preprocessing step for machine learning (Li, Li, Zhu, & Ogihara, 2002; Nagao, Yanagisawa, & Nishinari, 2018; Risse, 2019) and other efforts concentrating on neural networks (Faust, Acharya, Adeli, & Adeli, 2015; Zhou, Peng, Zhang, & Sun, 2018; Zhou, Wang, & Yang, 2017). Much of the prior work, however, requires a tight coupling of the problem domain with the intrinsic algorithm and as such, explicitly utilizes the full scope of decomposition levels and both the fluctuation and trend coefficients. It is also noteworthy that the application areas for much of this work centers around time-series data that tend to have seasonal or other cyclical characteristics. Additionally the authors generally do not make processing time comparisons for model generation and often leave processing time out of critical concerns. In these prior works, intuitively, model generation times would likely be significantly increased due to the more than doubling of base data sizes given multiple decomposition datasets.

In highly contextual environments and where AI machine learning algorithms are required, the data may or may not have cyclical effects embedded, and fast model generation times are often desirable. Further the model builders may be well removed from the application contexts and may not have either preconceived assumptions or a historical basis with regard to the data. A method that can identify the *optimal* decomposition level and have general purpose use may be contextual and elusive. Yet in the case of generalized applications, providing a starting point to a decision component, as opposed to an optimal answer, may be sufficient and provide system reliability and resiliency.

4.4.1 A heuristic to suggest a decomposition-level

From the example provided in Section 4.3.2, it can be seen that overcompression can be a problem. "Under compression" can be limiting. The number of data elements may also play a role in a suggested decomposition level. If there are few data points, decomposition is not necessary and many data points will yield many decomposition levels. The data themselves can affect the preferred decomposition level. Data that have relatively few fluctuations will not yield much change in either the approximation or difference coefficients, subsequently reducing the contribution provided by those views. By comparing the data of interest with a secondary set of data, it may be possible to use that secondary dataset as a reference that can be used to measure a degree of change in each decomposition level. This secondary reference data can be a straight line. But even if the data of interest is not linear, the line offers a reference that can be a basis for determining when the data have become overly perturbed from its original signal.

If the Pearson correlation of the analysis and the reference dataset's approximation coefficients are found after each transformation in the decomposition tree, the effects of the compression can be quantified according to Eq. (4.3), where x represents the transformed approximation coefficients of one sample and y the approximation coefficients of a second sample:

$$\frac{\dfrac{\text{cov}(x_1 + x_2, y_1 + y_2)}{2}}{\sqrt{\text{var}(x_1)\,\text{var}(y_1)}} \tag{4.3}$$

The expression shown in Eq. (4.3) is true if the data samples are not independent. If the samples are independent, the correlation at each decomposition level will fluctuate near or at zero, reaching a point when it begins to approach toward positive or negative one (± 1). This rise will be reflected in the variance at the decomposition level where an upward slope corresponds to a greater variance. The number of points in the data sample affects the sample's resilience to correlation changes for each wavelet transformation. Because the compression provided by each transformation eventually reduces the data to a single approximation coefficient for each dataset, the correlation of the two datasets will move toward positive or negative one.

This correlation relationship can provide the basis for calculating an incremental variance in the correlation distribution after each transformation. Essentially this calculation measures how much the correlation between the data of interest and the reference data is changing after each transformation. Despite the fact that the correlation itself moves toward a positive or negative one, the incremental correlation variance after each transformation will be positive and trend upward as the Pearson correlation value moves toward -1 or 1.

Evaluating this approach with multiple datasets showed the change in correlation variance generally produces a curve similar to that shown in Fig. 4.9 where the correlation variance is shown as a function of the number of transformations. The shape and slope of this curve varied depending on the characteristics and size of the dataset. It is this correlation variance that provides an indicator of the level of transformation after where the DWT has excessively perturbed the data. The variance vector will generally have an area where the variance begins to increase rapidly; for example, transformation number 7 in Fig. 4.9. Based on this pattern a

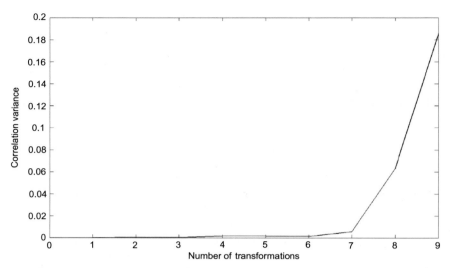

FIG. 4.9   Wavelet decomposition correlation variance.

heuristic can be applied to determine the point at which the rate of increase in the variance becomes extreme relative to the remainder of the variance vector. By capturing and calculating the variance at each decomposition level, by removing high-band outliers, and then by identifying the point at which the variance exceeds the mean of the remaining vector elements, an approximation of the curve "knee" can be determined. The preferred decomposition level in the case of Fig. 4.9 would be level 6. In steps the heuristic is to:

1. Find the upper fourth quartile outliers in the variance vector and discard them.
2. Perform a linear regression on the remaining vector elements.
3. Identify the first vector element that exceeds the regression, using linear regression.
4. Select the preferred decomposition level as the regression-identified scalar, minus one.
5. Subtract a second level, if a more conservative transformation measure is preferable.

To evaluate the aforementioned transformation selection methodology, the heuristic was coded as a procedure in MATLAB. The MATLAB procedure outputs a variance vector and the determined preferred decomposition level for a data provided as input. The data for testing came from several datasets, both synthetic and from the UCR Time-Series Data Mining Archive (Keogh, 2017). Synthetic datasets were made using a random number generator to create samples with little or no correlation. Additionally, random samples with varying correlations were generated. Random datasets from the UCR data were included in the evaluation as well. The UCR data came from a variety of sources including medical EEG/ECG data, sunspot frequency data, financial market data, the Microsoft AdventureWorks data, and other sources from real businesses. The generated and UCR data sizes varied from 1 million elements to as few as 100.

Using a Haar transformation, 500 runs were made using the MATLAB implementation of the heuristic, randomly selecting data from the UCR and synthetic datasets. Fifty outputs were randomly selected from the 500 runs. These 50 outputs were visually inspected with

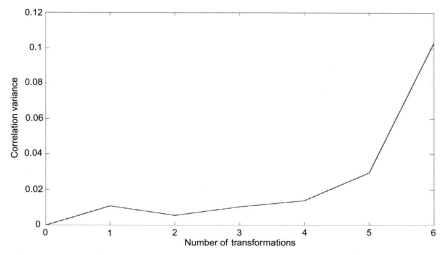

FIG. 4.10   Heuristic misprediction.

the "knee" correctly predicted by the heuristic in 47/50 outputs (94%). The three outputs that were incorrectly identified came from the randomly generated zero correlation samples. Fig. 4.10 shows an example of a mispredicted output. In all three mispredicted cases, the heuristic correctly identified the knee at the first decomposition level. Closer inspection of these three outputs showed curves that had a sharp increase followed by a decrease at the first transformation, such as that shown at the second transformation in Fig. 4.10. In all three of these cases, the sample sizes were less than 300. This same experiment was also run using Daubechies-4 and Daubechies-8 wavelets. The results of that experiment were similar: greater than 90% accuracy with a few failures that fell into the same data characteristics as the mispredicted Haar transformed samples. Other data characteristics were examined for utility in selecting a preferable decomposition level. These other characteristics included the data sample distribution variance, energy, and entropy. None of these characteristics provided consistently reliable metrics across the variety of datasets. The most favorable metric was the correlation, presented here.

This heuristic provides a reasonable suggested starting point for a preprocessed decomposition level. This "preferred decomposition level" may not be the only decomposition level of interest to a decision-maker or even be optimal for training an AI algorithm. However, it represents a point where the compression provided by the DWT transformations may begin to overly perturb the data. It may also represent where a reasonable trade-off between model training time and subsequent prediction or decision-making accuracy can be balanced.

4.5 Evaluating the preferred decomposition-level selection technique

To quantitatively evaluate the preferred decomposition technique for DWT preprocessing in a contextual decision-making application, a simulation was conducted. The basis for this experimental simulation was to examine the effect of wavelet transformations to preprocess data fed into a black box for a contextually complex algorithm (representing the AI system) that has a specific numerical goal: profit. By utilizing a simulation with a specific outcome of profit, an answer can be obtained for the research question that asks: will DWT augmented preprocessing on noncyclical data improve a decision outcome? Two specific hypotheses may be inferred from this research question and its experimental simulation:

1. Decisions made by selecting decision-relevant variable values from the DWT transformed datasets will have a higher profit than those made using values selected from the original data.
2. Decisions made by selecting decision-relevant variable values from the preferred DWT decomposition levels will have the highest profit.

4.5.1 A management decision problem application

The simulation experiment utilized a game that implemented a complex semistructured problem frequently used in management training and evaluation typically requiring decision-making support (McLeod, 1986). The game represents a black box ensemble AI program that implements a complex set of interdependent algorithms that require inputs to formulate an outcome. The internals of the game are unknown, and the game inputs present a problem for an external decision-maker (management), or in the simulation experiment, an AI algorithm. The game problem involves a market in which senior management use price, marketing, research and development, and plant investment variables to compete for a product's one-quarter total market potential. Demand for the organization's products will be influenced by several contexts: (1) management actions, (2) competitors' behavior, and (3) the economic environment. The decision objective is to plan a "next quarter" strategy that would generate as much total profit as possible.

Strategy making requires (1) setting the product price, marketing budget, research and development expenditures, and plant investment and (2) forecasting the competitors' price, the competitors' marketing budget, a sales index, and an index of general economic conditions. Twelve additional variables, including plant capacity, raw materials inventory, and administrative expenses, are calculated (derived) from the strategy. Initial values for these 12 variables form the scenario for AI decision-making. The additional eight uncontrollable and controllable variables combine into 20 total variables that jointly influence the profitability of the organization. This profit is the measure of a decision outcome, where the profit is determined by the game's internal equations. In the simulation experiment the management problem forms the core decision opportunity by providing an explicit quantifiable measure of profit.

While the actual management game problem is considerably more complex (as expressed earlier), to describe the simulation and experimental methodology simply, let profit (P) equal forecasted sales (S) multiplied by forecasted price (PR) minus forecasted production cost (PC). This equation is shown as Eq. (4.4).

$$P = (S*PR) - PC \tag{4.4}$$

In formulating a strategy the AI selects which controllable and forecasted values to use from a set of provided data. These values are randomly generated based on the rules of the management decision problem application to yield acceptable values for each variable prior to the decision-maker to selecting from them, as inputs to the simulation. For all generated variables, to incorporate the diversity of inputs from a population of users and contexts, each variable was assumed to follow a standard normal distribution with a mean of 0 and a standard deviation of 1.

Explaining the simulation methodology using the simplified calculation, Eq. (4.4), 100,000 values for the variables S, PR, and PC each would be generated. From these data the simulated machine learning output provides the game, a combination of values that ideally would yield the highest game output profit (P). Once a combination of values is selected, the values are applied to the equation and a profit value is determined. The values that are selected remain in the original dataset to be chosen again *without* consideration of decision success from the last inputs provided. The lack of prior knowledge in each run limits learning effects in the input algorithm, emphasizing preprocessing.

In the experiment, randomly selecting a value for each variable, from 100,000 possible choices, simulates the output from the machine learning algorithm. Given the simulation characteristics, n number of subject algorithmic outputs can be exercised and the data assessed to test the hypotheses and answer the research question. If the "control subjects" provide values from nontransformed variables and the "treatment subjects" provide values from the approximation coefficients, based on the original nontransformed data, then both hypotheses can be tested.

4.5.2 Applying DWT to the management decision problem application

As described earlier the decision-maker chose eight values as input to the management decision problem from a dataset of 100,000 possibilities for each. To create the approximation coefficients, each variable was transformed into a decomposition tree like the one in Fig. 4.1. However, only the approximation coefficients were used as they represent the original data without the variance. Each level is stored and provided to the simulated decision-maker for a possible selection.

The preferred level-section heuristic was also run for each of the input variables. Table 4.1 shows the predicted preferred decomposition level for each variable. The conservative heuristic was used. The fact that the input variables had different preferred levels was not surprising; each variable distribution was created to have different ranges that were acceptable in accordance with the rules for the management game decision problem. The differing levels do adjust the expected outcomes of the simulation experiment. Because the preferred levels are a range of levels across all of the variables, rather than a single level, the maximum profit should fall within this range when the simulation is run. However, a set of simulation runs will be made using values selected from the composite set of preferred levels (7, 8, and 9), respective to each variable.

4.5.3 Running the simulation

A precise and explicit model of the management decision problem and the simulation was programmed in Matlab. This software provided a robust programming environment where the simulation could be created and evaluated. After generating the initial input variable

TABLE 4.1   Preferred decomposition level for each management problem input variable.

	Variable	Preferred level
Controllable inputs	Product price	Level 7
	Marketing budget	Level 9
	Research and development	Level 8
	Plant investment	Level 8
Uncontrolled inputs (forecast)	Competitor's price	Level 7
	Competitor's marketing budget	Level 7
	Economic index	Level 8
	Sales index	Level 8

dataset and transforming these values to the maximum 16 levels of decomposition values, the distributions were used as input datasets for the simulated decision-maker. Using the original 100,000 records, the decision-maker randomly selected a set of input values that were used for the management decision, which yielded a profit value. Fifty thousand runs of the simulation were made using the original, nontransformed data as the set of input possibilities. Another 50,000 runs were made for each of the DWT transformed levels. Additionally, because there were differing preferred levels for different input variables, 50,000 runs were made where the decision-maker selected values from datasets at the decomposition level appropriate for that variable.

Given training sets of historical and forecast data, this simulation mirrors the same process as an AI machine learning algorithm that provides inputs to an ensemble of AI algorithms that forecast profit. Because the management decision application requires input to determine a profit value, the AI decision-maker must identify a set of values that, depending on their selection, may or may not be optimal. Once the simulated AI decision-maker identifies a set of input variables, they are supplied to the ensemble algorithms of the management decision application where a profit is calculated. This calculated profit was stored, along with the preferred decomposition level for each of the 50,000 runs, the original dataset, and each of the levels.

4.6 Results and discussion

The results of the simulation were collected and analyzed using SPSS, and the two hypotheses were tested. In summary the guided decision-making afforded by DWT transformed levels outperformed the original data (unguided decision-making), yielding considerably higher profits. Table 4.2 shows the total profit values from the 50,000 runs for each decomposition level, the original data, and the "composite" level. The composite level is the label for the runs where the decision-maker selected values from levels 7, 8, or 9, respectively, for the input variable's preferred level identification heuristic. Fig. 4.11 shows a graphical

TABLE 4.2   Simulation results.

Level	Profit ($)
Orig. data	−6.40E+10
1	−1.60E+10
2	2.89E+11
3	1.30E+12
4	3.95E+12
5	1.01E+13
6	2.35E+13
7	5.17E+13
8	8.87E+13
9	8.08E+13
10	6.98E+13
11	5.43E+13
12	3.22E+13
13	1.13E+13
14	2.30E+12
15	1.31E+08
16	1.31E+08
Composite	9.41E+13

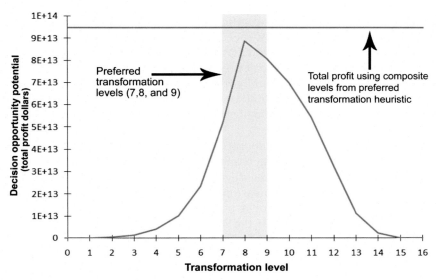

FIG. 4.11   Simulation results.

representation of these results, highlighting the preferred decomposition levels and the total profit from the composite runs.

Referring to Table 4.1 the preferred decomposition levels for the eight input variables were 7, 8, or 9. Four of the variables had a preferred level of 7, three of the variables had a preferred level of 8, and one had a preferred level of 9. Every DWT transformed level is higher than the original data, and the maximum profit is at the eighth decomposition level. The profit at level 8 is two orders of magnitude higher than the profit generated using the original data. The outcome where the decision-maker used the preferred transformation heuristic levels (the composite case) is an additional 5% greater than level 8. Fig. 4.11 illustrates the decision opportunity potential as a function of the decomposition level measured by the experimental value: total profit. The hypotheses proposed in Section 4 were evaluated using a paired t-test in SPSS. The results of the t-tests are shown in Tables 4.3 and 4.4.

In both tables the leftmost column shows the pairs with each level designated as L# where # is the number of the decomposition level. In Table 4.3 the original data yielded a lower profit compared with all of the DWT levels with these results significant at the 95% confidence level, indicating that the null hypothesis should be rejected for Hypothesis #1. In Table 4.4 the profit for composite level was higher than all of the other levels, including the original data. This set of t-tests was also significant at an alpha $= 0.05$ level of significance, supporting a rejection of the null hypothesis for hypothesis #2.

From these results, it can be seen that DWT can provide preprocessing benefits as inputs to complex decision-making algorithms. Additionally the characteristics of wavelets and the preferred level selection heuristic can deliver the simplicity and computational efficiency that is required for general business decision-making. When combined with a preferred level selection heuristic to supply an appropriate decomposition, this research has shown that wavelets can positively affect quantifiable decision outcomes. The preferred level selection heuristic identified the wavelet decomposition level, or levels in the case of multiple variables, where the decision opportunity potential is maximized.

In this experiment the low-frequency (trend) component were the most important portion of the DWT because the approximation coefficients closely resembled the original data. The high-frequency component, the detail coefficients, on the other hand, impart the original dataset's fluctuation or variability. However, as shown in the example in Section 4.3.2, the detail coefficient holds a lot of information that may be useful to algorithms that seek to model the variability. It can be used to indicate of process control, to identify significant shifts in the original measure, and, potentially, to highlight exceptions. The simulation experiment did not use this coefficient; further research should investigate the utility of this element of the wavelet transformation since it is one of the significant benefits provided by DWT over other approaches.

As discussed in Section 4.4, without an initial hypothesis, an optimal DWT decomposition level is elusive at best and nonexistent at worst. However, this research sought to answer the question of a preferred level through the development of a heuristic that can identify a decomposition level to prevent overcompression and to indicate a starting point for data exploration that maximizes the potential for a positive decision opportunity. The experiment evaluating the heuristic illustrated that the identified level may be considered a function of both the data size and its variability. With regard to maximizing the decision outcome, the results imply that the technique is applicable to decisions that are deterministic and where

TABLE 4.3 Hypothesis #1 t-test results.

		Paired differences			95% Confidence interval of the difference				
		Mean	Std. deviation	Std. error mean	Lower	Upper	t	df	Sig. (two tailed)
Pair 1	Orig—L1	−964,970	8,840,113	39,534.2	−1E+006	−887,482	−24.408	49,999	0.000
Pair 2	Orig—L2	−7E+006	12,899,238	57,687.1	−7E+006	−7E+006	−122.420	49,999	0.000
Pair 3	Orig—L3	−3E+007	20,100,024	89,890.0	−3E+007	−3E+007	−303.709	49,999	0.000
Pair 4	Orig—L4	−8E+007	29,335,084	131,190	−8E+007	−8E+007	−612.587	49,999	0.000
Pair 5	Orig—L5	−2E+008	41,213,418	184,312	−2E+008	−2E+008	−1104.087	49,999	0.000
Pair 6	Orig—L6	−5E+008	58,104,007	259,849	−5E+008	−5E+008	−1811.733	49,999	0.000
Pair 7	Orig—L8	−2E+009	1.1E+008	510,335	−2E+009	−2E+009	−3477.906	49,999	0.000
Pair 8	Orig—L9	−2E+009	1.6E+008	724,884	−2E+009	−2E+009	−2231.009	49,999	0.000
Pair 9	Orig—L10	−1E+009	2.3E+008	1,010,311	−1E+009	−1E+009	−1382.781	49,999	0.000
Pair 10	Orig—L11	−1E+009	3.1E+008	1,402,572	−1E+009	−1E+009	−775.695	49,999	0.000
Pair 11	Orig—L12	−6E+008	4.1E+008	1,830,836	−6E+008	−6E+008	−352.066	49,999	0.000
Pair 12	Orig—L13	−2E+008	3.3E+008	1,471,527	−2E+008	−2E+008	−154.184	49,999	0.000
Pair 13	Orig—L14	−5E+007	1.5E+008	674,319	−5E+007	−5E+007	−69.972	49,999	0.000
Pair 14	Orig—L15	−1E+006	4,944,950	22,114.5	−1E+006	−1E+006	−57.876	49,999	0.000
Pair 15	Orig—L16	−1E+006	4,944,950	22,114.5	−1E+006	−1E+006	−57.876	49,999	0.000
Pair 16	Orig—composite	−2E+009	81,545,340	364,682	−2E+009	−2E+009	−5166.279	49,999	0.000

TABLE 4.4 Hypothesis #2 t-test results.

| | | Paired difference | | | 95% Confidence interval of the difference | | | | |
		Mean	Std. deviation	Std. error mean	Lower	Upper	t	df	Sig. (two tailed)
Pair 1	Composite—Orig	2E+009	81,545,340	364,681.8	2E+009	2E+009	5166.28	49,999	0.000
Pair 2	Composite—L1	2E+009	81,723,795	365,479.9	2E+009	2E+009	5152.36	49,999	0.000
Pair 3	Composite—L2	2E+009	82,190,759	367,568.2	2E+009	2E+009	5106.50	49,999	0.000
Pair 4	Composite—L3	2E+009	83,837,199	374,931.4	2E+009	2E+009	4952.23	49,999	0.000
Pair 5	Composite—L4	2E+009	86,346,921	386,155.2	2E+009	2E+009	4670.87	49,999	0.000
Pair 6	Composite—L5	2E+009	90,984,660	406,895.8	2E+009	2E+009	4130.18	49,999	0.000
Pair 7	Composite—L6	1E+009	99,840,662	446,501.0	1E+009	1E+009	3165.21	49,999	0.000
Pair 8	Composite—L7	8E+008	1.2E+008	515,215.2	8E+008	8E+008	1645.89	49,999	0.000
Pair 9	Composite—L8	1E+008	1.4E+008	627,957.5	1E+008	1E+008	173.817	49,999	0.000
Pair 10	Composite—L9	3E+008	1.8E+008	810,656.6	3E+008	3E+008	329.147	49,999	0.000
Pair 11	Composite—L10	5E+008	2.4E+008	1,069,807	5E+008	5E+008	455.230	49,999	0.000
Pair 12	Composite—L11	8E+008	3.2E+008	1,449,707	8E+008	8E+008	549.132	49,999	0.000
Pair 13	Composite—L12	1E+009	4.2E+008	1,864,632	1E+009	1E+009	664.728	49,999	0.000
Pair 14	Composite—L13	2E+009	3.4E+008	1,513,922	2E+009	2E+009	1094.62	49,999	0.000
Pair 15	Composite—L14	2E+009	1.7E+008	765,617.4	2E+009	2E+009	2399.19	49,999	0.000
Pair 16	Composite—L15	2E+009	81,387,657	363,976.7	2E+009	2E+009	5172.77	49,999	0.000
Pair 17	Composite—L16	2E+009	81,387,657	363,976.7	2E+009	2E+009	5172.77	49,999	0.000

a high degree of input data consistency is preferred. Decision problems that do not meet this criterion and still apply this heuristic are unlikely to see similar results. However, cases where greater input variance is preferable may still benefit from incorporating DWT detail coefficients.

4.7 Conclusion

This chapter proposed wavelets and discrete wavelet transformations that can abstract data preprocessing, provide contextual conditioning, and otherwise affect often obfuscated underlying effects in models. Wavelets' properties of data reduction and feature retention combined with discretizing the trend from local fluctuations provided a mathematically sound technique to enhance data-driven decision-making support. This research discussed these benefits and presented a method to answer the critical question of where an appropriate decomposition level for training data may exist. These benefits and the preferred level selection technique were evaluated with a management decision application and simulation. The results of this study showed that the preferred level selection technique can identify, in the case of voluminous data with many local fluctuations, the DWT level most appropriate for selecting decision related values. The experiment also showed that DWT can make a significant difference in quantitative data-driven decision outcomes.

The results of this research demonstrate that wavelets can improve quantitative algorithmic decision outcomes. In addition, the study illustrated how DWT techniques reduce the volume of data while retaining its original features and characteristics, making the approach appropriate for time-series data and for most business domains. While this study demonstrated the benefits of wavelets combined with a preferred decomposition level heuristic in business decision-making simulation, other areas exist where the research should be continued and extended for broad generalizability. The management decision problem application is only one decision scenario. There are many other possible decision scenarios; the DWT technique should be evaluated in as many of these situations as possible and with other simulations. Other decision-making scenarios may require the identification of exceptions and fluctuation-based features in the data as opposed to selection for trending elements and sensitivities to other wavelets besides the Daubechies series. This initial simulation-based study used a quantifiable measure and ran enough executions to represent a census study. However, it did not utilize the detail coefficients and dealt with context by smoothing fluctuations. A future study should investigate these limitations and their impact on contextual AI ensemble algorithms that determine context, are affected by context, or can identify elements of a shared context, all in terms of decision outcomes.

References

Abowd, G. D., Dey, A. K., Brown, P. J., Davies, N., Smith, M., & Steggles, P. (1999). Towards a better understanding of context and context-awareness. In: *International symposium on handheld and ubiquitous computing 1999 (HUC '99), 1999: Proceedings* (pp. 304–307), Karlsruhe, Germany, 27–29 September.

Bumblauskas, D., Bumblauskas, D., Nold, H., Nold, H., Bumblauskas, P., Bumblauskas, P., et al. (2017). Big data analytics: Transforming data to action. *Business Process Management Journal*, 23(3), 703–720.

Burt, P. J., & Adelson, E. H. (1985). Merging images through pattern decomposition. In *Vol. 575. Applications of digital image processing VIII* (pp. 173–182): San Diego, United States: International Society for Optics and Photonics.

Carrington, A., Ralphs, M., & Rahman, N. (2006). Smoothing data for small areas. In *European conference on quality in survey statistics (Q2006), Cardiff, United Kingdom*.

Chui, C. K., & Lian, J. (1996). A study of orthonormal multi-wavelets. *Applied Numerical Mathematics, 20*(3), 273–298. https://doi.org/10.1016/0168-9274(95)00111-5.

Coifman, R. R., & Wickerhauser, M. V. (1992). Entropy-based algorithms for best basis selection. *IEEE Transactions on Information Theory, 38*(2), 713–718. https://doi.org/10.1109/18.119732.

Daubechies, I. (1992). *Ten lectures on wavelets.* https://doi.org/10.1137/1.9781611970104.

Faust, O., Acharya, U. R., Adeli, H., & Adeli, A. (2015). Wavelet-based EEG processing for computer-aided seizure detection and epilepsy diagnosis. *Seizure, 26*, 56–64.

Jarrahi, M. H. (2018). Artificial intelligence and the future of work: Human-AI symbiosis in organizational decision making. *Business Horizons, 61*(4), 577–586.

Jones, W., Pirolli, P., Card, S. K., Fidel, R., Gershon, N., Morville, P., et al. (2006). It's about the information stupid!: Why we need a separate field of human-information interaction. In *CHI'06 extended abstracts on human factors in computing systems* (pp. 65–68): Montréal, Canada: ACM.

Kafadar, K. (1996). Smoothing geographical data, particularly rates of disease. *Statistics in Medicine, 15*(23), 2539–2560.

Kalapanidas, E., Avouris, N., Craciun, M., & Neagu, D. (2003). Machine learning algorithms: A study on noise sensitivity. In *Proc. 1st Balcan conference in informatics* (pp. 356–365).

Keogh, E. J. (2017). *The UCR time series data mining archive.* Retrieved from: 27 December 2017, The UCR Time Series Data Mining Archive website: http://www.cs.ucr.edu/~eamonn/time_series_data/.

Li, T., Li, Q., Zhu, S., & Ogihara, M. (2002). A survey on wavelet applications in data mining. *ACM SIGKDD Explorations Newsletter, 4*(2), 49–68.

Liu, M., Yu, L., & Yuan, Z. (2003). Improved aggregation levels of ITS data via wavelet decomposition and fast Fourier transform algorithm. In *Presented at the proceedings of the 2003 IEEE international conference on intelligent transportation systems.* https://doi.org/10.1109/itsc.2003.1252789.

Mallat, S. G. (1989). A theory for multiresolution signal decomposition: The wavelet representation. *IEEE Transactions on Pattern Analysis and Machine Intelligence, 11*(7), 674–693. https://doi.org/10.1109/34.192463.

McLeod, R. J. (1986). *Software package 11.* College Station, TX: Academic Information Service (AIS).

Microsoft. (2017). *Adventure works sample data warehouse.* Retrieved from: 27 December 2017, Adventure Works Sample Data Warehouse website: http://technet.microsoft.com/en-us/library/ms124623.aspx.

Mitchell, T., Cohen, W., Hruschka, E., Talukdar, P., Yang, B., Betteridge, J., et al. (2018). Never-ending learning. *Communications of the ACM, 61*(5), 103–115.

Moriwaki, N., Akitomi, T., Kudo, F., Mine, R., & Moriya, T. (2016). Achieving general-purpose AI that can learn and make decisions for itself. *Hitachi Review, 65*(6), 113.

Nagao, K., Yanagisawa, D., & Nishinari, K. (2018). Estimation of crowd density applying wavelet transform and machine learning. *Physica A: Statistical Mechanics and Its Applications, 510*, 145–163.

Ramamoorthy, A., & Yampolskiy, R. (2018). Beyond mad? The race for artificial general intelligence. *ITU Journal, 1*, 1–8.

Risse, M. (2019). Combining wavelet decomposition with machine learning to forecast gold returns. *International Journal of Forecasting, 35*(2), 601–615.

Russell, S., Gangopadhyay, A., & Yoon, V. (2008). Assisting decision making in the event-driven enterprise using wavelets. *Decision Support Systems, 46*(1), 14–28. https://doi.org/10.1016/j.dss.2008.04.006.

Russell, S., Moskowitz, I. S., & Raglin, A. (2017). Human information interaction, artificial intelligence, and errors. In *Autonomy and artificial intelligence: A threat or savior?* (pp. 71–101): Kidlington, Oxford, UK: Springer.

Russell, S., & Yoon, V. (2008). Applications of wavelet data reduction in a recommender system. *Expert Systems with Applications, 34*(4), 2316–2325. https://doi.org/10.1016/j.eswa.2007.03.009.

The MathWorks, Inc. (1991). The MathWorks Inc. *Simulation, 57*(4), 240. https://doi.org/10.1177/003754979105700407.

Tkacz, E., Kostka, P., Komorowski, D., Domider, T., & Wrzesniowski, A. (2002). Improvement of wavelet neural network hybrid systems performance by optimisation of two types of learning algorithms. In *Presented at the proceedings of the 9th international conference on neural information processing, 2002. ICONIP '02.* https://doi.org/10.1109/iconip.2002.1198118.

Tukey, J. W. (1980). We need both exploratory and confirmatory. *The American Statistician, 34*(1), 23–25.

Vidhate, D. A., & Kulkarni, P. (2016). Performance enhancement of cooperative learning algorithms by improved decision making for context based application. In *2016 International conference on automatic control and dynamic optimization techniques (ICACDOT)* (pp. 246–252): IEEE.

Zhou, J., Peng, T., Zhang, C., & Sun, N. (2018). Data pre-analysis and ensemble of various artificial neural networks for monthly streamflow forecasting. *Water*, *10*(5), 628.

Zhou, T., Wang, F., & Yang, Z. (2017). Comparative analysis of ANN and SVM models combined with wavelet preprocess for groundwater depth prediction. *Water*, *9*(10), 781.

Zhuang, Y., Wu, F., Chen, C., & Pan, Y. (2017). Challenges and opportunities: From big data to knowledge in AI 2.0. *Frontiers of Information Technology & Electronic Engineering*, *18*(1), 3–14.

A narrative modeling platform: Representing the comprehension of novelty in open-world systems

Beth Cardier[a], John Shull[b], Alex Nielsen[b], Saikou Diallo[b], Niccolo Casas[c], Larry D. Sanford[a], Patrick Lundberg[a], Richard Ciavarra[a], H.T. Goranson[d]

[a]Eastern Virginia Medical School, Norfolk, VA, United States [b]Virginia Modeling, Analysis & Simulation Center, Old Dominion University, Suffolk, VA, United States [c]The Bartlett School of Architecture, University College London, London, United Kingdom [d]Institute for Integrated Intelligent Systems, Griffith University, Brisbane, QLD, Australia

5.1 Introduction

A poet's work is to name the unnameable. - ***Salman Rushdie***

If a machine detects something humans have not anticipated, how can it tell us? This research draws a solution from creative writing and its ability to communicate unexpected experiences. In fact, naming novelty is sometimes even seen as a requirement of good authorship. Award-winning author Milan Kundera asserts that pleasurable writing "unveils something which hasn't already been said, demonstrated, seen" (Elgrably & Kundera, 1987). Shklovsky observes that Tolstoy makes "the familiar strange by not naming the familiar object" (Shklovsky, 1994). "Once upon a time" signals the start of this deviation: *here is a situation you recognize, yet now I will reveal an exception to its familiar routine.* The research described here draws from narrative's ability to communicate both expected occurrences and their transgression (Herman, 2002).

The characterization of novelty is at odds with formal knowledge modeling approaches, which rely on general definitions and type systems to classify inputs. Generalization allows autonomous processes to be applied indefinitely. Currently, this also means those systems only handle and communicate knowledge structures that already exist within their frameworks. They rely on *expected* entities and represent them using static models. Predetermination creates a gap between these formalisms and the way the real world unfolds, the way it changes until "a deduction that is justifiable under one set of circumstances may be flat wrong in a different situation" (Devlin, 2009). The resulting shortfall in accurate open-world modeling is particularly problematic in intelligence analysis (Devlin, 2009; Heuer, 1999) and neurobiological systems (Noble, 2015; Simeonov & Cottam, 2015). In both domains, accurate interpretation depends on tracking the interaction among numerous systems, even when their consequences involve unnamed, unanticipated, or emergent elements.

The first step toward solving these problems is representational, both graphical and in the domain of logic. A graphical advance in representing knowledge is the focus here (the logical foundations and back end are discussed elsewhere (Cardier et al., 2017; Goranson, Cardier, & Devlin, 2015; Chapter 3). Generalized knowledge frameworks usually position facts in larger structures of static general facts (Gruber, 1993; Minsky, 1975; Smith, Kusnierczyk, Schober, & Ceusters, 2006). We add another stage through new representations, in which sections of general reference frameworks are isolated and renamed and then interact to produce new information structures.

This chapter describes an early-stage prototype of a narrative modeling platform, named *Wunderkammer*, which can graphically model these operations. This tool takes the narrative capacity to handle unexpected ideas and places it at the core of a new taxonomy and animated modeling space. The goal is a new capability: to dynamically represent descriptions of processes across time, space, and context. It particularly targets properties of context that have been elusive to model, such as influence among contexts and their components, the emergence of unexpected entities or systems, and implicit information. We illustrate these processes using animated semantic networks that interact and evolve. These representations are housed in a 3D virtual space, where constructive actions by the user can also reflect how humans physically express situated meaning. This chapter describes and illustrates the new graphical features being developed.

Due to the dynamic and spatial requirements, we repurpose the gaming platform Unity to house this modeling environment. This immersive space brings a slew of new benefits and fresh complications. Unity supports the animated and spatial qualities of our conceptual architectures and enables them to be anchored to 3D artifacts such as models of neurological circuits. It can also support powerful new capabilities for modeling real-world situations in unfolding time. However, without alteration, it does not easily accommodate text input. Three-dimensional networks also have a tendency to occlude each other or rise to physically unreachable heights. As well, adapting an established programming environment brings a second tier of negotiation between established versus new, as we repurpose its features to serve an unanticipated purpose.

The new affordances enabled by Unity are currently being tested in two application domains: narrative and biomedicine. It is anticipated that, in the future, this new capacity to capture narrative and spatial change will be applied to a number of domains. The streams of semantic network can model social arguments online or the real-time corporate brainstorming sessions. The ability to connect multiple media sources makes it possible to construct inhabitable architectures of evidence and supporting artifacts. In the health domain, this could become an environment that allows a patient to keep all documentation for a therapy program in one place, so they can see their goals and participate in therapeutic games and then share a recording of their performance with a therapist, who uses the same framework to drill into the medical literature or communicate with other experts. The platform could also link multiple sources of dynamic footage with geographical and historical information, becoming an immersive version of the BBC's curation of livestream footage of the massacre in Khartoum, Sudan (Africa Eye, 2019).

Our first example is from literature, a modern version of a folktale: *Red Riding Hood as a Dictator Would Tell It*. Its explicit text is a lie, in the style of propaganda. An accurate interpretation depends on an awareness of how implicit social and historical information recasts the meaning of explicit facts. This story has already been modeled using a previous method in which graphical operators were manually drawn in the presentation program Keynote (Cardier, 2013, 2015). We describe the representations of context required to capture this example and introduce new features from another program, Unity, that make this modeled example more powerful.

A second example concerns posttraumatic stress disorder (PTSD). It is chosen due to the complexity of capturing the influence of a past traumatic experience on current responses and its ramifications for treatment. Additional new representational capacity helps with this problem—here, we examine the ability to represent nested narrative information. This capability is discussed along with plans to expand it into a full neuropsychological model of the treatment process during eye movement desensitization and reprocessing (EMDR). This examination is followed by other brief examples in both narrative and biomedical domains to describe the next stage of examples for this model.

This project was supported by a seed grant from the National Academies Keck Futures Initiative from 2016 to 2018. The new narrative modeling platform is now being developed by the Virginia Modeling, Analysis and Simulation Center (VMASC) at Old Dominion University (see Fig. 5.1). It uses examples of complex systems supplied by the Eastern Virginia

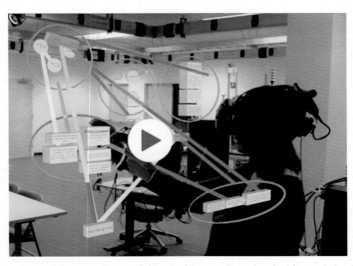

FIG. 5.1 An early version of the narrative modeling tool in use. *Reproduced with permission from John Shull.*

Medical School (EVMS) and is architecturally advised by the Institute for Integrated and Intelligent Systems (IIIS) at Griffith University.

5.2 New system-level representations

Conditional interpretation is at the heart of our approach, in which we represent the structures needed to comprehend a new event, no matter how dynamic or unexpected. This new focus requires a different fundamental unit of information from other knowledge representation approaches. In other formal methods the basic unit is a *fact*. In this research the fundamental unit is instead a span of levels—*fact* and *situation*—which are represented as components within contexts, each with its own constructs. Every fact can be both a part of a situation and also represent a situation. Likewise, each unit has two levels at which connection can occur—fact and situation. When links to an individual fact become impossible because information is scant, a contextual connection can take over, becoming a bridge forward instead. In this manner, general definitions can evolve until their structures have more complex conditional interpretations, as they do in pragmatic use. This foundation also makes it possible to include partial and tentative information, as these are contained within situations.

These features create a representational handle for the nuances of context noted by ontologists (Sowa, 2010), humanities fields such as cultural theory (Yampolsky, Amiot, & de la Sablonniere, 2013), intelligence analysts (Heuer, 1999), and logicians concerned with open-world modeling (Barwise & Perry, 1983; Devlin, 2009). In the real world, interpretation changes based on context, and new local definitions are made in the process. Our goal is to represent this conditional aspect of knowledge.

For clarity, our definition of *narrative* begins with Gerard Prince, who characterizes it as an event that causes a fundamental change of state (Prince, 1982, p. 153). We expand this definition so that notions of state, event, and change can be fleshed into an auditable representation. Narrative deliberately connects incongruous inferences, forcing its reader to consume more text to understand how these fit together. We represent both the source text and the inferences as limited semantic networks. Due to their circumscribed nature, we refer to them as *contexts*. Our definition of *context* is a limited and specific ontology, following Devlin's definition of a *situation* as a "limited part of reality" from situation theory (Devlin, 2009, p. 238).

To connect these contexts the source text lays out semantic connections like stepping-stones, incrementally relating them and their inferences in a manner that demonstrates how disconnected ideas can be joined *in this circumstance*. In this manner a reader is led across ontological boundaries of time, context, and abstraction. We thus understand *narrative* as a process in which semantic networks continuously model unfolding transitions and their supporting inferences, to lead participants, a team, or an audience from one context to the next (Cardier, 2013). The means by which to build this structure is captured in our representational taxonomy.

For further clarity, *unexpected* or *novel* information is a representation that falls outside the reference frameworks in use, *implicit* information is implied but not syntactically stated, and *influence* refers to a guiding or modifying effect that occurs when one structure is imposed on another.

Situation theory provides the formal foundation to support this process. Situation theory is a logical method developed in the 1980s by Barwise and Perry (1983) to record how the meaning of a fact changes when it shifts circumstances. Further capabilities—nesting contexts inside each other and zooming between scales—were added by Keith Devlin (1995) a decade later. When a *fact* shifts in scale from *fact* to *situation*, these levels are recorded in the underlying logic using a situation theoretic structure that lists a fact on the right-hand side of an equation and a placeholder for the real-world instance on the left-hand side. In our approach the left-hand side instead shows the position of that fact in the complex architecture of its context. The two sides are linked by transitional structures. We build that architecture and the transitional structure using this tool.

This work thus produces insight regarding how contexts interact with each other during comprehension. In situation theory and other formal approaches such as Minky's frames (Minsky, 1975) or Schank's scripts (Schank & Abelson, 1977), facts switch between individual contexts: A fact is in one situation, and if it loses salience, it is transferred to a different one. Our approach draws on an understanding of context from cultural theory and psychology, where studies show that individuals can simultaneously occupy multiple communities and have many overlapping identities to go with them (Yampolsky et al., 2013). We take this further to observe that, in an open-world and also in the narratives that describe it, more than one context can bear on a fact during interpretation.

Language studies have shown that situating an unknown term in multiple contexts is one way in which humans learn what it means (van Daalen-Kapteijns, Elshout-Mohr, & de Glopper, 2001). In a related manner, we model how the comprehension of an unexpected entity uses multiple contextual inferences to derive an accurate interpretation of an unexpected phenomenon. Graphically, this convergence is expressed as structure that weaves across multiple contextual layers and develops a complex higher-level architecture. The dynamism and complexity of those structures have necessitated the development of a modeling platform in the Unity gaming environment as previous, simpler tools have not been sufficient to render them.

There is a historical precedent for characterizing and presenting knowledge through a 3D arrangement. In the 17th and early 18th century, a precursor to the modern natural history museum was established, known as the *Wunderkammer*—also referred to as a "rariteitenkabinet" or "cabinet of curiosities." The Wunderkammer was a physical space in which items collected from around the world were brought together for study (see Fig. 5.2). This proximity allowed collectors to create spatial, relational archives of a wide variety of items—preserved organisms, animal materials, gems and stones, novel mechanical devices, and artworks and the texts related to these. Collectors of exotic natural and manmade items could arrange and rearrange their treasures to classify them. Found objects were organized to highlight juxtapositions, pre-Linnaean taxonomic categories, shared features, derived connections, and geographic or cultural relationships.

With this in mind a Wunderkammer collection can be understood as an archive of both the material world and also developing knowledge in 17th and early 18th century Europe. The ability to curate souvenirs from expensive journeys was the privilege of a wealthy few and being scientific archives, such collections positioned their collectors as well traveled and connected.

FIG. 5.2   Engraving depicting a "cabinet of curiosities," which formed the basis of Ferrante Imperato's study of natural forms in the book *Dell'Historia Naturale*, Naples, 1599. *From Ferrante Imperato.*

The act of selecting, curating, and arranging knowledge is thus a multidimensional activity, which not only builds a catalog of knowledge and its presumed connections but also reflects the sociocultural aspects of knowledge production.

The Wunderkammer modeling tool likewise provides a way to organize, rearrange, and identify morphological information. It annotates a user's subjective perspective, and so, in a sense, is implicitly conscious of bias in knowledge production. Our modern instance also assumes the user will reorganize their "collection" based on each new instance acquired. Unlike the original Wunderkammer, which reflected the scientific intent of striving toward all-encompassing static ontologies, we target the disruptive and implicit aspects of knowledge instead. In spite of these differences, the original Wunderkammer's focus on physical arrangement, morphological classification, and knowledge production still makes it an important forerunner to our new endeavor, and so it is adopted as a namesake.

In this new modeling space, physical and spatial action contribute to the organization of knowledge, just as it does in everyday life. It is anticipated that this space will allow new channels of reasoning to emerge. Once a user interface designer for Apple, Bret Victor asserted that working in the usual 2D page of books and computer screens is an "invented media that severely constrains our range of intellectual experience" (Victor, 2013). Particularly problematic is the way those traditional modes of recording information limit us to only one or two of the visual, tactile, spatial, kinesthetic, and auditory modes of understanding at our disposal (Victor, 2013). Our approach leverages all of these and the spatial aspect seen in the Wunderkammer. In *The Art of Memory*, Francis Yates (2001) explains how spatial cues facilitated thought before the printed page—for example, Shakespearean actors remembered their lines by memorizing concepts in relation to objects positioned around the theater.

This modeling method works with a similar form of projection, mapping thought onto structure and watching it change.

The following examples and descriptions shift between both Keynote and Unity representations. As we develop a new graphical vocabulary and a new space in which to house it, we find that some aspects present well in this 2D printed format, while others do not. Different representations are chosen to best convey different aspects of the process. This 2D readability issue will be corrected as the tool develops. One solution will be to develop a special 2D view that will flatten the 3D models into a standard 2D notation, as indicated in Fig. 5.3A and B. It is expected

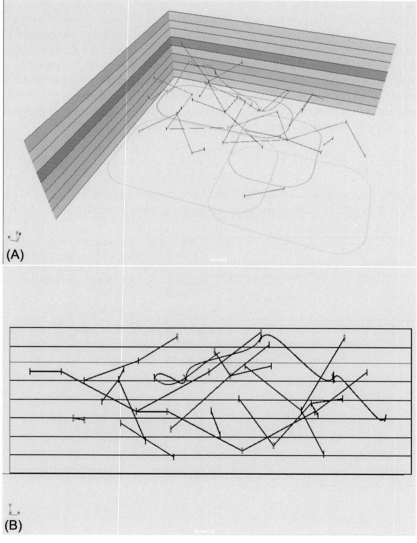

FIG. 5.3   Depiction of a method to "flatten" 3D representations (A) into a 2D format (B). *Reproduced with permission from Niccolo Casas.*

that this will reduce the multisensory experience into something printable, in a similar manner to musical scores.

Let us now turn to the nuts and bolts of this method: the taxonomy. A brief description of all aspects follows; fuller descriptions can be found in Cardier (2013, 2015) and Goranson and Cardier (2014).

5.3 Taxonomy

Our taxonomy is based on the interaction between general knowledge and personal interpretation. In the graphical display the layout demonstrates the way these two complementary poles of knowledge negotiate to produce meaning. There are three main aspects: **display zones**, which lay out the stages of that process from top to bottom; the **discrete objects**, which are the facts and situations to be arranged; and the **operators**, which move the objects and build structure. This format makes it possible to record the incremental process of adapting general knowledge to unexpected situations. In the formal foundations the relationship between general and conditional knowledge is reflected in the connection between the right- and left-hand sides of situation theory's equations (Goranson et al., 2015).

5.3.1 Display zones

The layout has two primary zones, "general knowledge" (at the top) and "interpretation" (at the bottom) (see Fig. 5.4). The **general knowledge zone** represents general information of

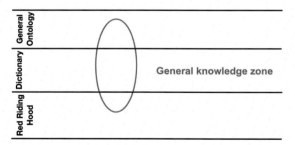

FIG. 5.4 The layout: general knowledge (general reference frameworks and their subsets) and the interpretation zone (local knowledge). This is the 2D Keynote version. *Reproduced with permission from Beth Cardier.*

the kind usually derived from general reference ontologies (Arp, Smith, & Spear, 2015; O'Connor et al., 2005) or other instances of general world knowledge, such as Wikipedia. These have a logical structure. Every different inferred general context required for interpretation is represented by a new layer. For example, in the *Red Riding Hood as a Dictator Would Tell It*, the separate reference layers are "fairytale," "dictator," and "metafiction." In a neurobiological model, one layer might designate electrical impulses, events, influences, and laws, while another depicts biochemical entities and their behavior.

The purpose of the overall layout is to create and display tokens that represent how general knowledge is woven into new arrangements. It is composed of horizontal layers that the user can define and reorder. (These layers are sometimes referred to as "swim lanes" in process models.) They are creatable, nameable, editable, and rearrangeable. They are presumed to have implied elements that are not shown and, because they are not shown, are not salient to the source text at that stage.

In the general knowledge zone, each layer represents only the immediate knowledge needed to interpret the artifact at that time. It is thus a limited semantic structure, even if there is only a minor ontological variation from its original network. This subset remains persistently connected to its original ontological source. On the opposite side of the layout, the interpretation zone represents the parameters needed to newly organize these fragments of general knowledge. These are positioned in opposition so that the interplay between them is easy to display and read.

The interpretation zone is composed of two criteria: "background" and "foreground." These criteria are chosen to determine causal agents or novelty for each text chunk analyzed, as the influence of entities can change from moment to moment in open-world comprehension. Context is a necessary part of this determination—the only way to determine if an action is unexpected is to also know what is expected (Einhorn & Hogarth, 1986). "Background" represents the context of a particular situation, its limited ontology. "Foreground" represents the entities that deviate from it by crossing its boundaries of context, time, or abstraction. These two fields thus record the context at play and the agents that are changing them. The particulars of these criteria and their representation were developed from theories of narrative (Herman, 2002), conceptual change (Kuhn, 1973; Thagard, 1992), and causal attribution (Einhorn & Hogarth, 1986).

In the 2D tool, "background" and "foreground" are expressed as two layers (see Fig. 5.4). In 3D, they are a single layer, with the fore and back literally located at the front and back of the user's space (see Fig. 5.5). When a user wants to designate that a conceptual node has agency, it is situated at the front. Agency is determined through actions that cross boundaries: An entity is doing something unexpected, or it bridges networks. Influence is determined by the degree to which agents successfully bridge or change networks.

Fig. 5.5 shows how the Unity model enables a much richer presentation of this feature than the Keynote instance. When conceptual structures emerge as important in the text, they move forward to be more visible to the user. Structures that are very general or do not change are pushed to the back because they are operating within their expected contexts. The conceptual fore and background thus also have a literal expression. This framework is further supported by the presence of a 3D grid (which is indicated by periodic dots) which makes it easier for a user to precisely arrange elements in the additional depth dimension.

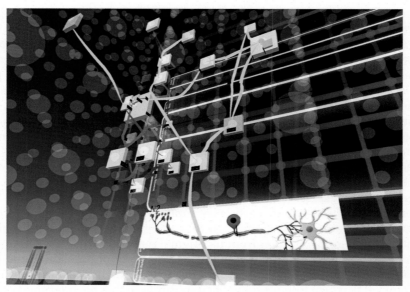

FIG. 5.5 The layout: a visualization of how the 3D tool enables the background and foreground to be arranged at the front and back of space. This example depicts information from Lundberg's research. *Courtesy from Beth Cardier.*

FIG. 5.6 Every situation has a background and foreground—nodes that are in shadow (background) or light (foreground) within a small situation (glimpsed in the *blue* boundary). *Reproduced with permission from John Shull.*

The same principle also applies to smaller structures, such as nodes and smaller situations. This differentiation can be seen in Fig. 5.6, where internal nodes are in shadow (background) or light (foreground) to indicate relative position within a local situation. This enables agents at the local level to be represented via their protruding location. At all levels the more abstract and influential a node, the more prominent its position. The overall result is that supporting information recedes into a background texture and important summarizing information continually presents itself in full view.

Overall, contexts are represented by these types and arranged according to scale:

- Layers—represented by bands to designate a reference context, which usually persists for the entire model.
- Within situations—smaller, local groupings of objects that are persistently connected and so operate as a unit.
- Across situations—a grouping across layers, building a new linking structure among entities. They can also indicate when there is tension among disparate contexts. Across situations have four subtypes: conflict, resolving, analogy, and state. These represent the stages of identifying conflict between situations and resolving it. The precise stages of the first three are explained elsewhere (Cardier, 2013, 2015). Analogy situations are described in Section 5.7.1 as an especially important case.

As the Unity platform develops, it is anticipated that a different representation of ongoing context will replace the layers, as we experiment with 3D representation. These contexts are currently experienced as tiered areas within the 3D grid, which are indicated by tinted air and different colors for bands of its mesh of dots. In the future, it is likely that a color or pattern will designate each areas of the network as being part of a distinct context and be managed as streaming waves of texture.

5.3.2 Discrete objects

The following devices and objects shown in Fig. 5.7 operate over the aforementioned referenced framework.

Nodes and their assemblies are deposited and connected across layers. We refer to these as "discrete objects." Each node can be examined beyond its current scale, either zoomed into (turning it into a situation) or zoomed out from (conflating it into a component). Nodes can be connected with each other as either situations or components. They can be visually grouped

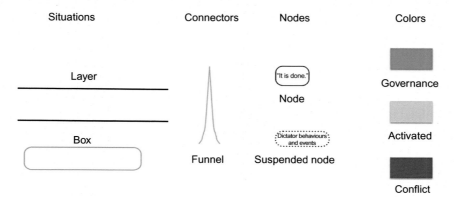

FIG. 5.7 Taxonomy of elements in this model with four different essential functions: situations, connectors, nodes, and colors. *Reproduced with permission from Beth Cardier.*

into new local situations using the "boxes" that surround them. Funnel operators perform all these actions and are responsible for making connections. They can operate in any direction, with the pointed end indicating the direction of the action, like an arrow.

5.3.3 Discrete objects

Discrete **objects** are of three types: "source objects," "called objects," and "ambassadors." Their identity depends on where they are positioned in the process of interpretation, from communicating information about the artifact itself (source objects) or general knowledge (called objects) or its manipulation in the interpretation space (ambassadors). These types correspond to the upper, middle, and lower parts of the display area.

Discrete objects are shown as entities in enclosed boxes. "Source" and "called" objects are associated with representable facts.

Source objects are chunked sections from a native artifact. If the example is textual, these are fragments of text. In biology models, these are observed data or a diagram of that biology. A user with an external data model will correlate that data with these objects. These appear sequentially, each prompting a new cycle of an annotation.

Called objects represent definitions and descriptions drawn from the reference frameworks and other specialized layers. They are referred to as "called" in the sense that the situation layer in which they reside has many possible elements, but those identified are the relevant or more active structures in this instance.

All the situations denoted by layers are presumably from the "open world," meaning they have elements that are implicit and may never be resolved. A called object can thus also represent elusive information: it can be something we do not quite know, a placeholder for something unknown that we hope to discover later, or something unknowable. Unknown information is indicated as an unpopulated situation; partial knowledge is recorded in a situation in its partialness. Tentative information is enclosed by a dotted object outline until it is later confirmed. In this manner, situations allow the representation of partial, unknown, or tentative information.

An **ambassador** is an object that only appears in the interpretation layer. It is a representative subset of a larger network in the situation zone—a node that stands in for a context. It allows us to record the derived nature of reasoning. When a general concept is altered, it remains persistently connected to the original description as a reference. Ambassadors thus have a more derived structure than other situations. They are the components of the left-hand side, the building blocks that allow contexts to be arranged to show their relationships of influence over each other. We refer to this influence as *governance* (Cardier, 2013, 2015). These are the contexts that are arranged into metacontexts.

All objects are structured and connected by operators.

5.3.4 Operators

Operators relate objects to each other, transforming their structures and adding other objects as their implications cascade through the system. In a later version of the knowledge base, these will be supported by reactive functions. Visually, they appear as animated connections. These are as follows:

Synthesizing operator (funnel)—This creates interpretive intermediate objects, whether new relationships, situations, structural arrangements, or influences (see Fig. 5.1).
Governance—This represents contextual influence. It tracks the imposition of structure from one object to another. It can also prompt a synthesizer to move objects. It is shown by containment and structural imposition.
Persistent structure—This records the residual structure left behind by operators. Logically, persistent structure is a record of the generative functions that transform an interpretation. Those generative functions remain "live" and can be regenerated. It is shown in the examples as gray lines.
Three-dimensional spatial location—The depth dimension has prescriptive foreground and background, corresponding to being closer and further from the viewer in a camera. When entities increase in agency, they move forward on that axis, becoming more dominantly visible to a user.

In addition, all operators and objects carry out different activities, represented by colors. These are as follows:

- Yellow signifies that an object is "activated" and will trigger a normal operation chain.
- Blue signifies that an object is projecting governance and triggers a governance operator.
- Red signifies that two different situations are incompatible or conflicting and should be reconciled.
- Purple signifies reconciliation of the conflict in the situation noted earlier. The purple object container denotes the resolving situation.

In the past, each of these objects was colored by hand. The Unity tool makes this process much easier. In the immersive space a dashboard with a color picker accompanies every object, making changes of color instant—see Fig. 5.8.

These representations enable a user quickly to annotate paths of inference in response to an artifact. More specifically, it tracks an individual's subjective comprehension. Another

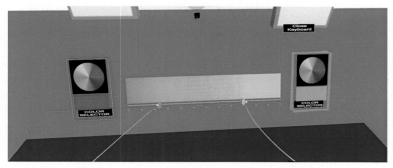

FIG. 5.8 A color picker accompanies every object, making it easier to signal the activations of funnel operators or nodes, such as those indicating conflict (*red*). In this image, both hands are being used to adjust the color gradient. *Reproduced with permission from John Shull.*

analyst might choose different annotations for that artifact. That subjectivity is accepted—variability is part of the unusual kind of knowledge that we model. Our method is thus not prescriptive, as a Newtonian model would be. Shared context is built both deliberately among collaborators and through alignments of structure that, in the future, will be discovered by an intelligent back-end reasoning system. When we use this platform to build a training corpus, in a sense, we will count on there not being repetition among different modelers of the same story. The accumulation of many views delivers a 360-degree perspective on overlapping aspects of a situation, in contrast to conventional ontological approaches that instead aim for a static and general "truth" from a single ontological stance.

When seeking "repeatability," it can be found in communicative semiotics rather than in precise paths of associative inference. When multiple people model the same story differently, the goal is to easily "read" those differences because the vocabulary is clear. A more specific issue is how to represent qualities of context so that the user can easily reason with them. All this makes the taxonomic representations especially important.

5.4 2D versus 3D

As the prior figures indicate, this taxonomy has been rendered in both a 2D format (Keynote) and a 3D virtual reality format (Unity). The Keynote presentation program supported the first expression of this method because it allowed animation. However, each object and operator needed to be painstakingly drawn, as did each stage of animated transformation. More problematic was the lack of space. The modeling process depends on structures being transported from the general knowledge area to the interpretation zone and being newly connected there. Two kinds of complexity accrue—the way the source structures differ from each other and the complex forms that allow them to be a bridge. Details of these new forms were impossible to record in the required detail due to a lack of space.

The Unity gaming platform was chosen for the next version of the tool due to its easy handling of 3D space and time. Not only does the additional dimension allow more information to be recorded in new ways, but also a user can literally walk around inside it, like a cathedral of data. Complex structures can finally be accommodated with the extension into the dimension of depth and by utilizing the physical space of an entire room, instead of a computer screen or a page. See Fig. 5.9 for an example of spatial 3D presentation that occupies an immersive 3D space.

Our adapted Unity platform also provides automation. For example, instead of hand-drawing the objects and operators, now they automatically appear with a click of a trigger. Every element is automatically produced and reproduced, enhancing repeatability.

The virtual items are currently manipulated using controllers that direct the user interface—seen in Fig. 5.20A and B. In the future, hand gestures and haptics will control the virtual items.

New challenges arise with the shift into a 3D environment, as described in Section 5.6. Overall, however, this new representational power makes richer models possible. Planned future applications include the real-world domains that tap the expertise of this project's collaborators and associates. These include neurobiology (Ciavarra et al., 2018;

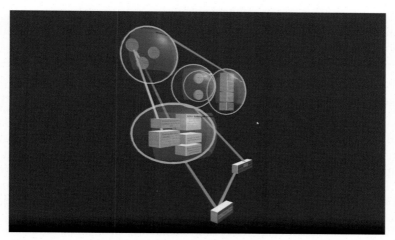

FIG. 5.9 The tool leverages the dimension of depth, with nodes and their components coming forward or receding depending on their causal importance in the story. *Reproduced with permission from John Shull.*

Sanford, Suchecki, & Meerlo, 2014), microbiology (Lundberg et al., 2008), intelligence analysis (Goranson, 2004), and refugee identity and movements (Frydenlund, Foytik, Padilla, & Ouattara, 2018; Frydenlund, Padilla, & Earnest, 2017).

With this taxonomy and two different tools to express it, we can now see how these modeling capabilities play out in the domains of literature and neuropsychology.

5.5 Examples

Each of following examples highlights a different aspect of context that this tool supports. The majority of examples come from *Red Riding Hood as a Dictator Would Tell It*. The PTSD example is the first stage of implementing a real-world medical case. These two are followed by further examples from both neurobiology and storytelling.

5.5.1 Example 1: Analyzing propaganda—*Red Riding Hood as a Dictator Would Tell It*

This story was written in 1940 by H. I. Phillips in the United States at a time when the government was discussing whether to go to war against dictators in Europe. The story can only be accurately interpreted if this information and other implicit inferences are taken into account, including the way in which dictators generally use propaganda and how those narratives operate. This example has been modeled and described elsewhere, in Cardier (2013, 2015). Here, we describe some aspects that have been previously omitted and focus on how the new tool changes the modeling experience.

In this example, we show how representations of parallel processes, nested meaning, grouping, and resolving conflict are required to accurately interpret the title and first two sentences of the story. These are our terms for the higher-level structures of narrative, and the tool allows them to be drawn. It should be noted that the tool is not restricted to these notions. As an agnostic drawing tool, it could be used to indicate any knowledge arrangement, transition of meaning, or structure building.

5.5.2 Parallel processes

By the time a reader reaches the end of the title sentence of *Red Riding Hood as a Dictator Would Tell It*, they understand that the story concerns the way dictators manipulate narratives to make themselves look good. An important contributor to this interpretation is the interaction among three contexts that are inferred by the title: "fairytale," "dictator," and "metastory." This method depicts how a general knowledge of these three contexts interact to produce a new combined interpretation. A snapshot of this process in 2D can be seen in Fig. 5.9 and in a snapshot of the 3D environment in Fig. 5.10.

In Fig. 5.10 the inferred contexts of "fairytale," "dictator," and "metastory" are represented as layers that run concurrently across the 2D page. These three contexts operate as parallel processes that will selectively interact in response to the text. Their concurrent positioning allows key concepts from each context to be visually connected with ease.

For example, the phrase *Red Riding Hood as a Dictator Would Tell It* calls forward the "fairytale" context first, designating the subject as the *Red Riding Hood story* rather than the person. The remainder of the sentence calls up "dictator" features and then creates a link between these two narratives via the "narrator," suggesting that one of these structures will be governed by the patterns of the other. That new network of relationships is recorded in the interpretation space, where ambassadors for each of the three contexts are connected in a new arrangement—a metacontext.

Cumulative structure weaves among the three layers and eventually generates the nodes "narrator may be a dictator" and "parallel stories" (see Fig. 5.10). That "weaving" becomes the new derived reference framework. It is the main point of reference for all subsequent information and thus greatly influences its interpretation. We refer to this primary point of reference as a "gateway" function.

It is common for titles and first sentences in a text to serve as a "gateway" for all subsequent information. This gateway structure imposes a great deal of influence over the meaning of the rest of the text. It is one of the higher-level information architectures identified by this research and will be the focus of future work. These higher functions of narrative are also briefly discussed in Section 5.7.

In the 3D version seen in Fig. 5.11, the three inferred contexts "fairytale," "dictator," and "metastory" are again represented as layers that run concurrently across the space. This 3D version is much easier to use and is also computable. The hand-drawn animation in Fig. 5.10 took a few weeks to make; by comparison the image in Fig. 5.11 took only a few hours. Speed and ease of use are crucial to the ability to model open-world examples as they are highly complex and contain many information elements. Both of our medical examples could not be realized until the Unity tool had been built because the amount of information to be included in them was simply too much to hand-draw.

However, in this early prototype, it is less easy to see the precise relationship between elements (particularly in this flat snapshot). Part of the reason is because the final

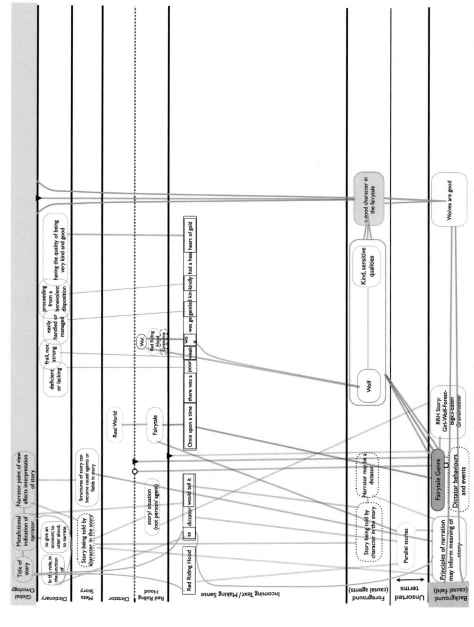

FIG. 5.10 A snapshot of this example in the 2D Keynote version. The inferred contexts "fairytale," "dictator," and "metafiction" are represented as layers that run across the page. *Reproduced with permission from Beth Cardier.*

FIG. 5.11 A snapshot of the *Red Riding Hood* example in the 3D Unity platform. *Reproduced with permission from Beth Cardier.*

visualization is still being developed and greater graphical precision is yet to come. But it is also because this model is composed of much larger objects in a massive physical space. At present the 3D characteristic also adds some ambiguity because objects can seem to shift their relationship when the viewer physically moves around. This readability will be improved as the tool matures.

An advantage of the Unity tool is that features like the "gateway function" will be able to be designated both visually and computationally. This will also come in a later phase of development. For now the details of how this gateway influence accrues, and a better Unity visualization of its components is described in the next section.

5.5.3 Nested meaning

The first sentences of the text require inferences to multiple contexts for accurate interpretation. First the general meaning of terms is established through reference to a dictionary. Two of these phrases require deeper interpretation than a simple dictionary definition, and this is gained by referring to two different contexts. We refer to this arrangement as "nested" meaning. Finally, terms that are all contributing to the same storytelling purpose are grouped: these all describe the wolf. This enables an additional tier of interpretation to be derived.

The starting state can be seen in Fig. 5.12, where the sentence "Once upon a time, there was a poor, weak wolf" stands ready for analysis. Each incremental chunk of text in that sentence is interpreted by a combination of newly derived structure and general definitions.

The first chunk of text, "Once upon a time," calls up the fairytale context, which activates the "fairytale" node in the "Red Riding Hood" general reference layer, as the most salient general reference for this term. The start of the story is also signaled—this interpretation also comes from that general reference framework. This signal is the first nested interpretation.

After the general definition of "Once upon a time" is supplied, it is then reinterpreted according to the derived network already built by the title. This is visualized as physical change and repositioning of nodes. For example, the new network indicates that this "fairytale" phrase must also be read in terms of a "dictator" context. Activation in one situation is graphically mirrored by the other when a complementary node, "reality," is pulled out above that of "fairytale" and connected to it. Similarly the word "wolf" activates concepts related to its character in the fairytale, and these are deposited as nodes in the "Red Riding Hood" situation. See Fig. 5.13 for a snapshot of these operations.

The descriptors relating to the wolf are now analyzed across both sentences that contain them. The wolf is "poor, weak," "gentle and kindly," and with a "heart of gold." Each of these terms is defined by a general reference dictionary. Within this list the phrase "heart of gold" enjoys an additional round of interpretation as its literal definition is not sufficient to account for its actual meaning. This new signal is the second instance of nested meaning, using a form of general world knowledge such as Wikipedia as a reference. The addition of that information can be seen in Fig. 5.14.

5.5.4 Grouping

Once all individual terms in the list describing the wolf are defined, a new inference occurs to understand what they mean together. This list of descriptors—"gentle, kindly," and "heart of gold"—all refer to descriptions of the wolf character. Together, they imply that character has "kind, sensitive qualities." A node reflecting this abstraction is deposited in the interpretation space. See Fig. 5.15 for this representation.

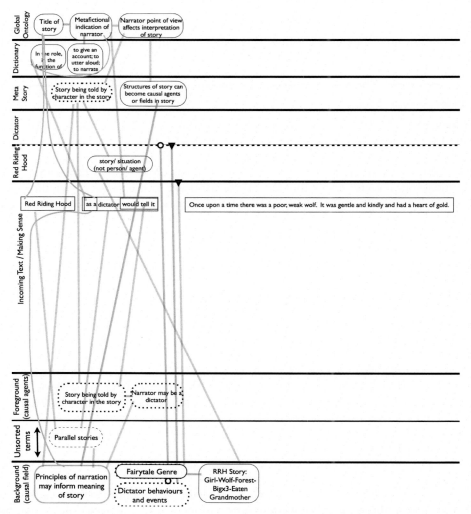

FIG. 5.12 A single sentence ready for analysis, "Once upon a time, there was a poor, weak wolf." *Reproduced with permission from Beth Cardier.*

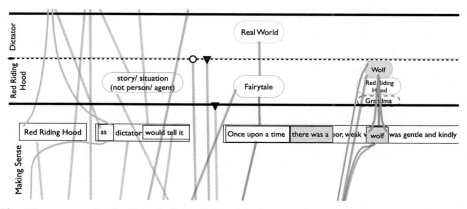

FIG. 5.13 "Once upon a time" calls up both the "fairytale" reference and "reality" from the dictator reference due to the way the newly derived reference structure has paired them. *Reproduced with permission from Beth Cardier.*

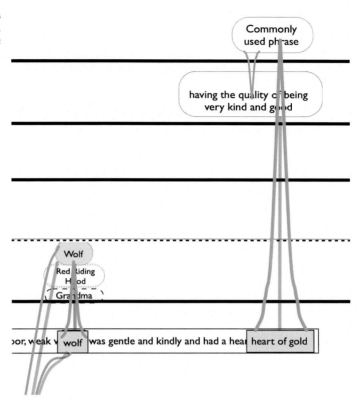

FIG. 5.14 "Heart of gold" is interpreted beyond its literal meaning. *Reproduced with permission from Beth Cardier.*

5.5.5 New unity capabilities

In the Unity platform an additional visualization makes the relationship between the syntax and its numerous interpretive contexts more explicit. When each of the aforementioned operations is completed, its consequence is recorded in a drop-down menu under the source text (see Fig. 5.16). This menu indicates all the parts of the sentence that are being separately interpreted. Color highlighting makes it clear which item on the list corresponds with which words of the source text. When more than one definition applies to a chunk, such as "heart of gold," its double nesting is newly indicated by recording two different colored boxes around it. This color highlighting can still be seen on the source text when the menu collapsed.

The drop-down menu and colors make it easier to see at a glance how much nested structure is in that sentence. It is both easier to record and read than the Keynote version.

Images will be marked in the same way. In a future instance of the tool, sections of images will be lassoed so that they can be linked to regular annotations. See Figs. 5.17 and 5.18 for examples.

5.5.6 Conflicting inferences

In practice, conflicting inferences create a gap in the reader's comprehension that can compel them to read more of the text to resolve the inconsistency. We now come to the part

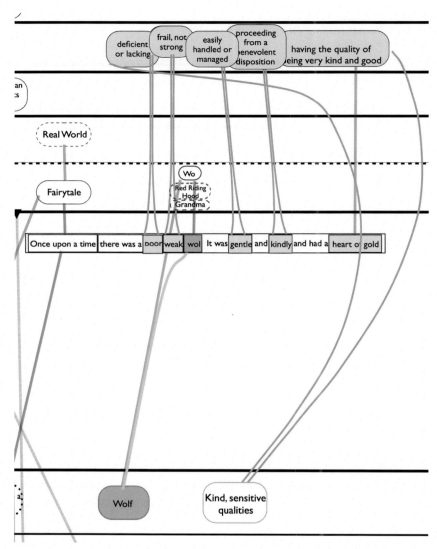

FIG. 5.15 The explicit descriptors of the wolf are grouped and positioned in terms of their role in the story, to understand they refer to "kind, sensitive qualities" of the main character. This abstracting node is deposited in the interpretation space by a funnel. *Reproduced with permission from Beth Cardier.*

of the example sentence in which the narrative deviation occurs: "Once upon a time, there was a poor, weak wolf." This unexpected information requires a new operation, *conflicting inferences*.

In this example the inconsistency is between the predatory fairytale wolf and the kind one in this source text. The operation begins when the inference "kind, sensitive qualities" calls up equivalent character traits for the wolf in the "fairytale" layer. These are identified as equivalent structures in each layer through their equivalent positions. It is then noted that a key part

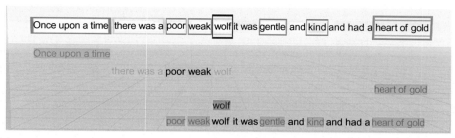

FIG. 5.16 Multiple inferences are simultaneously indicated by the Unity tool. *Reproduced with permission from John Shull.*

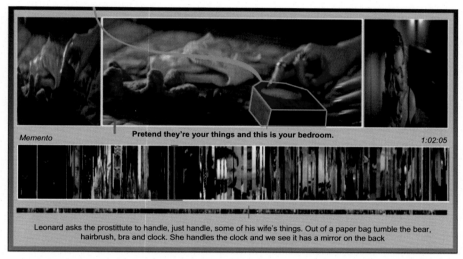

FIG. 5.17 A significant object in the movie "Memento" is lassoed for analysis. *Reproduced with permission from Ted Goranson.*

of each structure is in direct conflict with each other. This conflict is indicated by the encircling of a red box, as indicated in Fig. 5.19.

The conflict is resolved by drawing on the newly derived interpretive structure. The connections between the nodes "parallel stories" and "narrator may be a dictator" are relevant here and so are activated as reference structure. A parallel is noted between the menacing qualities of the fairytale wolf and the dictator, which also contributes to the interpretation. This link is newly connected to a fresh node that signifies how propaganda inverts reality to make a dictator look good. In the process, two networks that represent different contexts are joined. All of these new relationships are recorded and connected to the initial derived network.

This supplementary construction resolves the local conflict between the good and menacing wolf qualities. It provides a clue to how multiple, dynamic contexts can be managed: inferences from a different perspective are required to connect their incompatible knowledge networks. In this case the conflict generates the building of new structure, which signifies that this story is a lie told by a dictator, who is inverting key aspects of reality. With the conflict resolved, processing of the next batch of incoming text can resume.

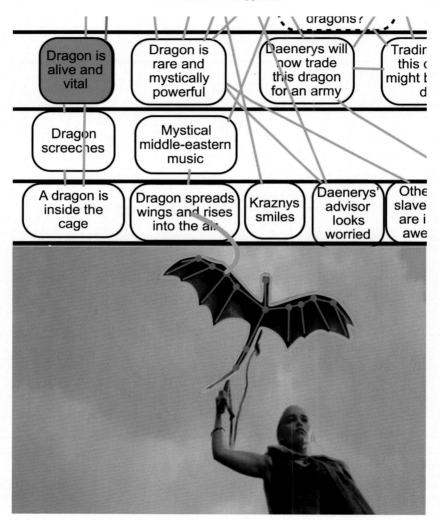

FIG. 5.18　The flight of a dragon in the fantasy television series *Game of Thrones* is lassoed for analysis. *Reproduced with permission from Beth Cardier and Ted Goranson.*

5.5.7 Unity versus Keynote

In the Keynote version, every graphical element was drawn by hand. Funnels were especially difficult to create, with every shape being individually drawn in OmniGraffle. This slowed the process and limited the size and complexity of the models.

All entities are now created automatically using the user interface menu shown in Fig. 5.20A. This menu is activated by a combination of hand gesture and eye tracking (Fig. 5.20B). All nodes, situations, and funnels can be instantly made. Nodes are generated by clicking on the white square in Fig. 5.20A. Likewise, one click sets the start and end

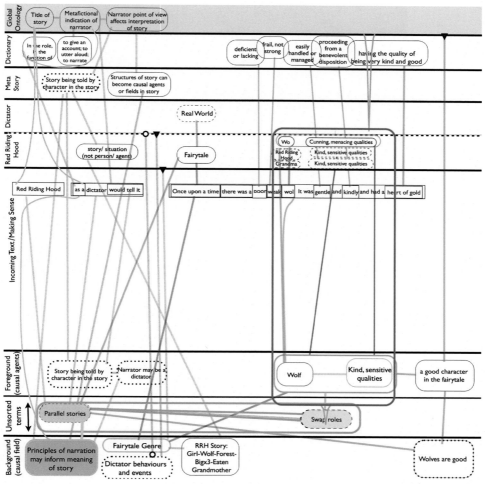

FIG. 5.19 Conflict is indicated between the stated wolf characteristics in the story and the generally known wolf characteristics from the original fairytale. *Reproduced with permission from Beth Cardier.*

positions of the transitional funnel, which is represented by a twisty line in the user interface. The funnel is then drawn automatically—see Fig. 5.5 for the result.

Unity's rendering of funnels solves the problem of making complex models easily. It also solves the problem of there not being enough representational space. Now the layers are potentially infinite—those in Fig. 5.21 are actually stacked 8 feet high in its immersive space. However, this makes them challenging to draw for new reasons. It is impractical to require a ladder when making a model. The current solution is an elevator that automatically raises the viewer. This elevation is activated by a panel at the side of the modeling space (see Fig. 5.21). The final tool will be a balance of space and accessibility. This resolution is discussed further in Section 5.6.

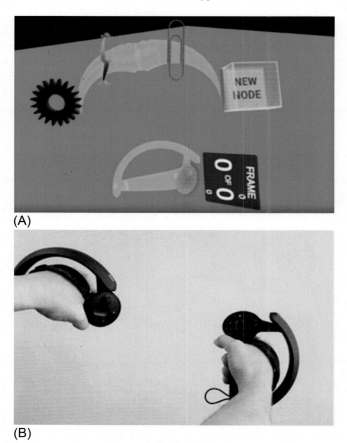

(A)

(B)

FIG. 5.20 Interface to automatically generate nodes, funnels, and scroll through frames for animation. A hand twist activates it and the result is shown in (A). This outcome is activated by the hand gesture shown in (B). *Reproduced with permission from John Shull.*

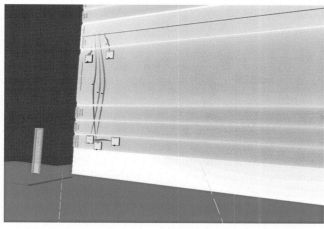

FIG. 5.21 Funnels are easy to draw in the new tool, and space is plentiful. However, these layers are currently 8 feet high. *Reproduced with permission from John Shull.*

We now turn to a domain in which the level of detail is greater and most of it must be preserved: medicine.

5.5.8 Example 2: The influence of personal history in a patient with PTSD

The second example demonstrates the complexity of the personal history of a PTSD patient. The example comes from an online record of interviews with patients receiving treatment using eye movement desensitization and reprocessing therapy (EMDR) (Hurley, Maxfield, & Solomon, 2017). It is chosen because the therapeutic intervention creates measurable change within a single sitting—the seventh session out of 10 for the patient, identified as "Mike."

The first stage of producing this example is to set up the "gateway" information. As presented in an academic description of this case, this foundational information is the patient's personal history, the events that likely influenced the traumatic response.

As a real-world example, the number of nodes involved in the patient's personal history, his account of the traumatic event, and the therapeutic interaction were difficult to represent on a single Keynote page. We began by focusing on Mike's personal history. The following details were gathered by the therapist during the setup part of the EMDR process in preparation for a therapeutic intervention. A representation of the extreme nesting that this information requires is seen in Fig. 5.22.

Fig. 5.22 captures the following information from the case study in Hurley et al. (2017).

Mike is aged 32. He was a medic during two tours of Iraq and was discharged for PTSD. Mike became traumatized while trying to rescue two soldiers who had been badly injured when their Humvee struck an improvised explosive device. In addition, Mike's father left during Mike's childhood and told Mike that he would now be responsible for the family. This childhood event is nested in a summarizing node: paternal masculinity lets Mike down in childhood.

Fig. 5.22 represents a structure that represents these key ideas. The information about Mike's current age and physical health is grouped and summarized in the node "physically healthy." The information about his abandonment as a child by his father is grouped and summarized as "psychologically unhealthy." The resulting node is then linked to the Mike's experience in Iraq—this is also summarized as "mentally unhealthy." Although there are two representations of mental unhealth stemming from different times and contexts, we show that they are linked. In the Unity model, each of these summarizing nodes will be zoomable to reveal the original information, rather than solely these two-word statements.

It is difficult to represent this complexity in a single Keynote diagram, and doing so omits key information. Foremost is the dependent relationship between Mike's current mental unhealth and the childhood trauma of his father's leaving. In the Keynote version, this information is represented only as a gray line and scant information. In the Unity tool, different connective structures will convey all the information, with these simpler summarizations moving to the foreground for ease of reading. These details can now be accommodated in the larger space and are also easier to draw. To read those details, the user can zoom into them.

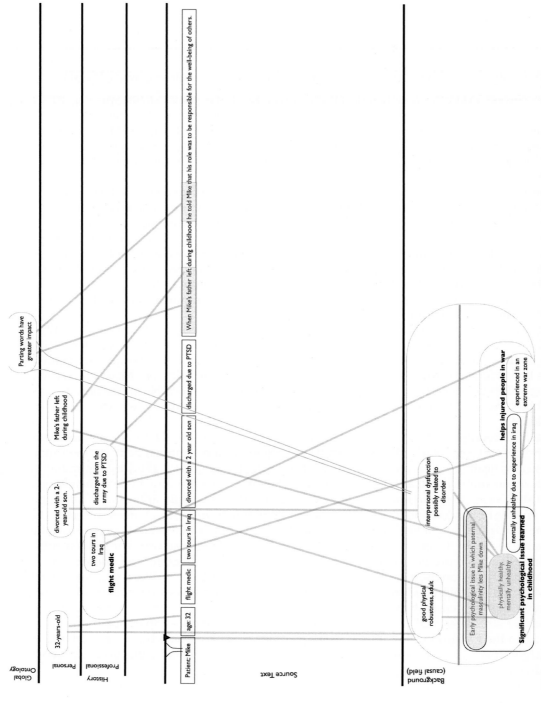

FIG. 5.22 Representing a PTSD patient's personal history requires a complex and nested architecture. *Reproduced with permission from Beth Cardier.*

Unity affordances that support this will be (1) the new user interfaces that enter and record text and (2) easy nesting. See Sections 5.5.8.1 and 5.5.8.2 for more information about these methods.

In the next stage of work, this nested node is a starting point for a complex model of parallel processes and nesting. Mike's current mental unhealth draws from both his childhood feeling of responsibility for others and his sense of responsibility for the deaths of his colleagues. This correlation creates the conviction that he is a "failure." These mental and personal history narratives will interact during a therapeutic interaction. We will aim to capture the influence of Mike's personal history on his traumatic response; it will also be important to capture how this tight connection is lessened as the therapist introduces new steps of interpretation. This therapy eventually changes Mike's implicitly-held beliefs from "I am a failure" to "I did the best I could" (Hurley et al., 2017).

Finally, we will connect this annotation with a parallel model of fear memory extinction in neural circuits as shown in a 3D brain. Initially, this parallel representation will be drawn from Larry Sanford's work, which concerns the behavior of different subjects in a stress paradigm in mice that captures some elements of PTSD. Activity in neural circuits varies depending on whether mice experience uncontrollable or controllable stress (Machida, Lonart, & Sanford, 2018). By drawing from images of neural circuits that are informed by these studies, we will make a first step toward connecting mental, historical, and neurological information in a formal model.

5.5.8.1 Entering and recording text

Traditional virtual reality (VR) approaches to text manipulation are generally twofold: a virtual keyboard and talk to text. We offer both in this tool.

First, we expand text manipulation within the VR environment. To provide users with an intuitive way of quickly editing and manipulating text, a combination of user input via the controller and proximity gestures are utilized. This user interface transfers traditional concepts from standard word processing like highlight, cut, copy, and paste to a VR environment without the need of shortcuts, keyboards, or a mouse. A user can quickly highlight the text with the use of the controller and then physical pull/push the text from one passage into another passage (see Fig. 5.23). The system monitors the location of where a user has pulled the text from.

For example, pulling up and out equates to a "copy" command, where the text remains in the existing block and is then copied to the user's visual clipboard. Pulling down and out equates to a "cut" command. To "paste" that text from the clipboard, a user physically pushes those new words into the receiving text by dropping their physical representation into the location they want.

The second text representation method is via voice recording. This requires an interactive "voice recorder" that can be activated to turn the spoken words of the user into text. Early work suggests that the ability to label nodes via voice activation results in a threefold increase in the speed of creating a model.

5.5.8.2 Representing nested situations

Representing nested situations is key to this method. In Keynote, it is difficult to record the level of complexity required by real-world artifacts and events as contexts within contexts.

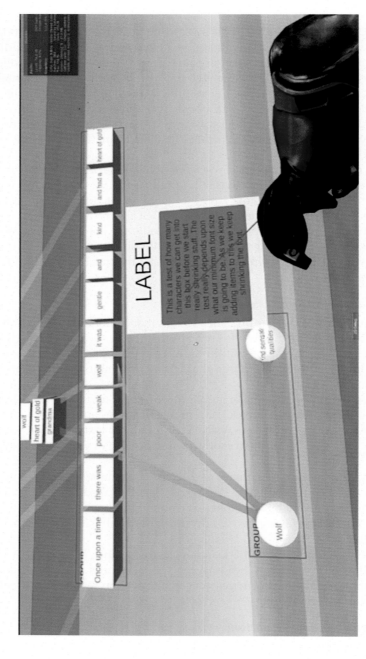

FIG. 5.23 An early version of text manipulation. *Reproduced with permission from John Shull.*

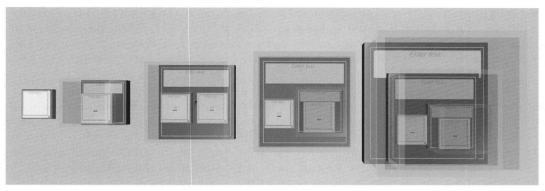

FIG. 5.24 Situations can be easily nested in Unity by dragging and dropping them into each other. *Reproduced with permission from John Shull.*

Text must be readable but also fit into the small space available on a regular page; each node must be laid out so that it does not interfere with those around it.

This simple problem of nesting is resolved in the Unity implementation. Now, any situation can be dragged into any other. Conversely, any node can be populated to inflate into a situation. This improvement directly reflects our vision of contextual interaction and the underlying philosophical notion of zooming proposed by Devlin in his expansion of situation theory, *Layer Formalism and Zooming* (Devlin, 1995). A snapshot of the nesting activity can be seen in Fig. 5.24.

5.6 Challenges

The issue of representational space has been a constant problem since the initial development of this approach in the Keynote program. Fig. 5.10 shows a concrete example of this issue. In that diagram the structure developed by the title has been pushed to the side to make room for analysis of the subsequent sentence. A "squish" action unrelated to the text made that compression. Actions that handle problems of space such as this are unnecessary in the Unity tool as the interpretive structure scrolls into an endless virtual space.

However, there is a tension between recording enough detail and being able to humanly handle the massive result. In the Unity environment, there is limitless space, but this means the layers might be stacked as high as a building to accommodate the volume of information. This scale presents a different kind of problem for the user.

We believe the solution lies in some of the natural features of a system that emulates comprehension in the real, open world.

The first are features of cognition that consolidate detail. One of these is scaling. Soon, it will be possible to shrink the 8-foot-high layout in VR to a smaller size for close modeling and then scale out again to see its place in the entire network. Achieving a balance between user interface (UI) responsiveness and ease of scaling will come through repeated use and testing during development.

Another is the consolidation that occurs during the comprehension of a story. A situation can be described in great detail and then be consolidated under a single idea—for example, the way a list of positive attributes about the wolf is reduced to the summary "kind, sensitive qualities." This consolidation enables the reader to easily carry forward the new required information without having to recall a lot of detail. In the future a shrinking feature of this kind might be a feature of the tool, summarizing nodes using a process that is similar to the act of comprehension.

Finally, it might be possible to leverage qualities that go along with a narrative's natural feature of omission. Authors are careful to present only the most important details, those which will most expediently carry the reader to the needed understanding. Our approach likewise depends on the interactions among partial descriptions, which are recorded as streams of narrative. Unlike a traditional general ontology, we do not need to represent everything in the world at the same scale. It could be possible to leverage the natural holes in knowledge and allow users to decide how much depth of detail they want to see in the model. As a narrative lays its stepping-stones, the user might wish to see all of the interconnections or only a few, making it easier to manage a large amount of data across situations.

We now turn to the operations we aim to represent in the future work.

5.7 Higher-level structures

The relationship among multiple contexts creates complex architectures. These sophisticated arrangements develop higher levels of influence over information, depending on how they are positioned in a story. For example, the first pieces of information act as a gateway, informing the structure of all of the subsequent facts. Other architectural analogies will serve as inspiration for future features: In detective fiction, red herring information might be "load bearing" in that it is highly connected to the explicit text and thus draws the attention of the reader, while details the author wants to conceal are pushed into the "background" through sparse mention (and therefore few links). These higher functions represent the next stage of work and have not yet been explored by this tool.

The foundations for this analysis already exist in this method but require greater exploration. As the aforementioned examples are fully explored, we will also be alert for these structures.

5.7.1 Analogy

Connections between remote contexts can be achieved in a few ways. One is an incremental weaving of structure between the components of multiple contexts (Cardier, 2013, 2015). A more immediate connection is made possible by the *analogy situation*. In both real storytelling and in our method, an analogy can link remote contexts by aligning similarities of structure and by assigning an identity to that connection, creating a new context. Notable work in this area includes the notion of blending (Fauconnier & Turner, 2002) and the implemented Griot system that was inspired by it (Harrell, 2005). We graphically represent *analogy* as a new node that encircles the relevant aspects of both situations, forming a lynchpin between them.

The transfer of information between these situations at the system level then becomes possible regardless of differences in syntax. Gaps between systems, times, scales, or points of view can be bridged in this manner. For example, in the film *Guardians of the Galaxy* (Gunn, 2014), the opening scenes follow a boy in a hospital who is listening to cheesy music on his Walkman—he is trying to escape the sadness of his mother's impending death. The next scene occurs in a different place and time: a man in a space mask walks across a science-fictional planet. When the man pulls out a Walkman and listens to cheesy music to create a positive vibe for fighting aliens, the two scenes are connected through this similarity. The viewer infers that the boy and the man might be the same person, due to their unique use of the Walkman. In both scenes the explicit object of the Walkman is as an anchor for the implicit inference of overcoming fear using cheesy music and a Walkman.

The similar overall structures of these situations enable them to be linked, even if the other entities in their respective situations are unrelated. We represent the development of this explicit and implicit interpretive structure as semantic networks that are connected across two separate situations—the user sees these separate situations as layers (see Fig. 5.25).

Fig. 5.25 is a simplified version of our method, in which the layers have been removed to make it easier to see the analogical structure. Conceptual structures are depicted as linked semantic nodes (gray) in the style of semantic networks (Sowa, 1987). The implicit analogical structure is shown as lynchpin nodes between these gray structures, grouping them by surrounding them (arbitrarily highlighted purple and red). These red and purple nodes indicate that the nongeneral semantic structure ("using a Walkman to avoid unpleasant reality") is responsible for linking situations that would ordinarily not be joined. In this manner, gaps between systems, times, scales, or points of view can be bridged.

Designating this higher-level analogical structure is a long-term goal for this modeling platform. It is anticipated that more higher-level structures will be identified once a derived structure can be properly recorded and analyzed in three dimensions.

5.7.2 Governance

The ability to model influence and parallel processes could have a significant impact on systems biology research due to the current difficulty in capturing how different organic systems interact. This method represents contextual influence as *governance*. Governance is the visual representation of how one situation imparts its structure on another. In the Keynote version of the model, we represent it with blue color. In the Unity version, we will take advantage of the strong animation capabilities to show influence as an engulfing, morphological change of structure, showing effects from one network to another. Artistic diagrams by Niccolo Casas and Alessio Erioli that demonstrate this effect can be seen in Cardier et al. (2017).

In the human body, numerous biological processes occur at the same time. It is thus useful to depict different systems side by side to show how they affect each other. For example, biomedical scientists from the Eastern Virginia Medical School (EVMS), Ciavarra, Lundberg, and Sanford, study how a nonpathological event can trigger the central nervous system to produce an innate immune response (Ciavarra et al., 2018). When a subject experiences stress (mice receiving foot shocks), the innate immune system reacts in some ways similar to its

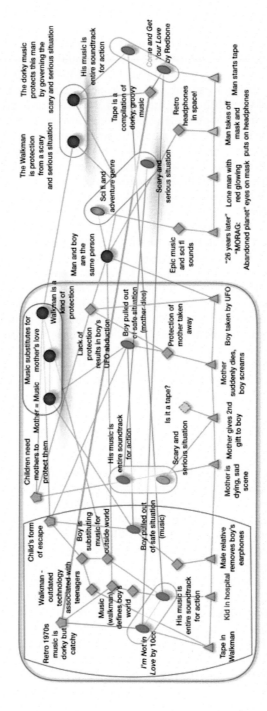

FIG. 5.25 Simplification (with invisible layers) to show system-level links between situations using analogical situations (*red and purple*). *Reproduced with permission from Beth Cardier.*

responses to pathogens, and the responses can vary depending on how the stress was perceived. These stress-induced immune responses also have ramifications for a subsequent ability to respond to pathogens.

These processes will be represented in adjacent layers. Causal interactions among systems are shown as governance funnels that combine and cross contexts to produce new nodes in new situations.

In this manner, we can show influences and interactions from the physical experience (foot shock) to cognitive context (fear memory) to the stimulation of the immune system (production of cytokines). The transfer of information among systems is indicated when these funnels copy nodes across different layers and then modify it for its new context. This transfer gives us the ability to demonstrate the cross-contextual transference of information and its apparent repurposing.

5.7.3 Scale

Our method also copes with scale differences. Lundberg uses gene activation data to indicate when the central nervous system begins to inappropriately stimulate the innate immune response. Placing information about gene activation next to descriptions of fearful memories is not difficult when they are rendered as semantic nodes. In a later version of the tool, data from a platform designed to annotate gene activation data, Ingenuity, will be inserted in the annotation space at the bottom of the layout so that the two can be formally connected. In this way the elusive aspects of interactions among processes are captured. The semantic stage of Lundberg's example can be seen in Fig. 5.5.

5.7.4 Unexpected information

In multisystems biology experiments, unexpected information is likely to arise as important. In the work of Ciavarra et al. (2018) and Lundberg, Openshaw, Wang, Yang, and Cantin (2007), the herpes virus (HSV-1) somehow communicates with the immune system to stop it from attacking. The virus achieves this by signaling to its host's central nervous system, but the exact nature of the signal is unknown. In an advanced version of this modeling platform, one that has an intelligent reasoning system underneath, the reasoning system might discover a clue as to how the virus communicates with the central nervous system of its host. That process is likely to be difficult to describe in human terms. This problem is when our grammar comes in useful—the fully realized automated version of the system should be able to indicate that a new causal agent has been detected and where and what its chain of influence is, even though the entity might not have an identity in established general ontologies.

There is also a secondary channel of communication for unexpected information in the system-level visualization. As described in the next section, sweeping system-level structures can communicate more general dynamics about an unexpected entity by relying on system-level factors such as analogy and even aesthetic design. This novel feature—the use of aesthetic design—is the subject of our final section.

5.7.5 The visualization of unexpected systems

In the future, this modeling platform will leverage a new tier of system-level reasoning in its visualization scheme. It will include structures and metastructures, such as analogical situations and "gateway" functions, yet it can also go further. Another goal is to eventually support more intuitive, artistic forms of communication between machine and human. This will be a new avenue of communication in the shared context of their collaborative space. It addresses the problem stated at the outset: if a system discovers how a virus is signaling its host's immune system, there might be no words from any human context that can accurately describe it. How will the machine share its discovery with its human collaborators, to let them know what it has found?

We envisage a machine system that can communicate that discovered process by synthesizing similarities with other processes in other contexts, using a form of analogical reasoning. This reasoning would supply comparison contexts and clues about how to describe its discoveries, seeking as a writer would. For example, the system might compare one biological process with others that are not usually seen as similar. This computational reasoning would be supported by a situation-aware reasoning system.

With this kind of system, metrics of aesthetic design could be included in our representations of context. One option is to represent particular states with an expressive, calligraphic "grammar." For example, in PTSD, learning is disordered such that the traumatic event is not adaptively processed. If data from patients with this maladaptive disorder are visually characterized with an overall aesthetic metric, its set of relationships might present as a pitted and constricted pattern, easily readable from a distance. That pitted pattern could then be quickly detected by a human in other situations. On the other hand, healthy learning might be characterized by the evolution of flowing forms, which have a more organic appearance. Either of these patterns could appear in another domain if their overall structures are similar. For example, in domains in which the health of automated learning processes is difficult to assess, such as the Internet of Things, the appearance of the pitted pattern might signal to a human user that the system is becoming unbalanced and needs attention, even though the precise problem is difficult to name. This aspect of our research will use a blend of science and art to convey system-level occurrences for which there are not yet representational references.

Together, this new taxonomy and developing modeling platform introduces new core representational affordances for the capture of information that is ordinarily elusive. It makes possible the following properties of context:

- nesting, partial nesting, and zooming between scales
- relations between system-level identities
- overall system characterizations
- connections between diverse scales and methods
- differences in information flow between entities
- the way system-level features (such as identity) restrict or facilitate information flow
- the emergence of new or higher-level structure

We look forward to reporting further on the capabilities of these new representations as the tool continues to mature.

5.8 Surrounding research and foundations

This research is highly interdisciplinary, with domains including logic, artificial intelligence, narrative analysis, system design, aesthetic design, systems biology, data visualization, and philosophies of context and causality. We narrow the scope of developing a representational grammar to handle implicit influence and so focus on the following areas.

Our definition of **narrative** in terms of inference and contextual representation makes narratological theory less relevant than is common in computer science. Ordinarily, structuralist narratology informs most implemented models due to its emphasis on reductionist analysis (Hale, 2006). These approaches break down narrative into characters that perform actions, which suits the intended products of automatic narrative generation and games. Examples of this narratology-based approach to narrative can be seen in the work of Propp (1928/2010), Ryan (1991), and Riedl and Young (2010). In these cases the goal is to produce a story that fools the reader into thinking a story is human generated by replicating particular explicit syntactic patterns, rather than by revealing the deeper implicit mechanics of a story itself.

An exception is the work of David Herman, who uses cognitive science to understand narrative as a system of distributed intelligence (Herman, 2006). He describes a narrative principle of background and foreground as the means by which writers control perceptions of agency. Herman does not specify how stories achieve this positioning, so we have built out his theories using complementary work from conceptual change (Kuhn, 1973; Thagard, 1992) and causality theory (Einhorn & Hogarth, 1986). Our focus on the disrupted processes of inference also pushes this work toward disciplines that study inference, especially discourse processes.

Discourse processes is a psychology-based field concerned with inference that emphasizes explicit linguistic interpretation. When *narrative* inference is considered, the stories examined are highly controlled and pruned statements, sometimes known as "textoids" (Goldman & McCarthy, 2015). This control is a drawback for understanding stories in the wild. Another drawback is that its representations are usually descriptive rather than formal. However, there is still much to learn from this field for our modeling platform. As a described process, our method has a similar cycle of activation, integration, and progressive validation of interpretive inference as the "resonance, integration, and validation" (RI-Val) model (O'Brien & Cook, 2016). Ours is also concerned with the violations of open-world norms in fantasy fiction, as observed in detail by Walsh (2016). These theories have insights to offer our method but do not constitute a coherent account of the implicit and messy features we require to model the interpretation that occurs when humans comprehend novelty. For this reason the domain of conceptual change was also needed.

From **knowledge representation**, we used the research of Paul Thagard, whose simple node-link diagrams show the incremental stages of the state change that occur during conceptual revolutions (Thagard, 1992). His diagrams illustrate moments of change between states, forming the basis of an important aspect of our animated method. His diagrams indicate how to dynamically capture entire networks using node-link networks as they evolve and grow. These principles have not been applied to narrative until this work.

In terms of implemented systems, the current inability to handle **novelty in artificial intelligence** is a well-known problem. Since the first and second wave of machine learning, systems could not handle situations that were unlike those for which they had been trained or otherwise educated (Piscopo, 2013). Case-based systems were an early approach to adaptability, but they can only retrieve similar past cases without adaptation. Deep learning systems such as Libratus and AlphaGo Zero are brittle once applied outside a curated narrow range. Research systems at present either have no solution, depend on massive training data with no explicit context, or require humans in the loop at some stage. Some work is being done on open set classifications, but that work is scant, and the scope is limited to well-defined tasks rather than true novelty.

There are also inherent challenges to designing and developing a **user interface** environment for a system based on managing multiple contexts. The workspace must be readable for single and multiple users, often across disciplines and with different degrees of expertise. It must accommodate various sources, including text, digital media, and even organic biological systems. Across this diversity, it must also communicate its structural functions clearly. Finally, it must be capable of navigating coherently across scales, time frames, and levels of granularity. Fortunately, narrative supports these qualities in the way it is driven by contextual arrangement and reassembly. Our output will not take the form of narrative (yet); it will simply follow those principles in its representations of evolving semantic networks.

In terms of the user interface, context lends itself to spatial metaphors, such as containment, structural support, imposition, and influence. Our implementation choices were guided by the need to intuitively represent these qualities while at the same time recognizing that we are building networks. Current 2D visualizations of networks tend to emphasize treelike structures, omitting the spatial qualities that suggest these contextual properties. Graph visualization frameworks like Gephi employ a useful tension physics, but its treelike structure is not ideal. Business Process Modeling Notation (BPMN) environments were considered because they enable the representation of nodes and parallel processes, but do not easily allow a user to work in an environment with 3D properties.

Our choices thus focused on a platform that is grounded in spatial representations, with the freedom to explore them in 3D space. We utilize Unity3D as the main development environment. Unity's core functionality aligns with the development of spatially significant software in the way it facilitates traditional tangible computing yet also incorporates spatially attuned virtual and augmented reality for both coding and system visualization/exploration (Boy, 2016). This focus on human factor-centered systems also allows for data representation in alternative digital and material contexts, including the implementation of flow dynamics and resistances informed by Casas (Cardier et al., 2017). Transitional dynamics will be informed by these properties of flow and perhaps ultimately guided by them.

In this spatial environment, networks can also have a tactile physics that uses tension and distance to signify those same qualities. This system allows users to "grasp" previously intangible connections between systems and concepts by offering an interface that leverages literal qualities of tangibility. User interface designer for Apple, Bret Victor, asserts that "when you have multiple channels of understanding, they compound and reinforce each other in powerful ways" (Victor, 2013). We increase this scope to leverage visual, tactile, spatial, and kinesthetic modes of understanding with this system. Human-centered design approaches will allow the team to identify emergent needs based on use cases, specific workflows, and especially users' past workflows or UI familiarities (Proctor & Van Zandt, 2018) as the tool matures. This identification will enable us to design an environment where future coders feel unencumbered by the system and model (Nielsen, 2003).

Unity's frameworks allow incredibly complex systems to be built while also being capable of rendering these environments in dynamic real time. Previously a platform like ours would have had to be decoupled from the model-building and animated rendering environments, forcing the user to adjust their building cycle around it. Going between different interfaces and software is a form of task switching that adds to mental workloads and decreases the fluency of discovery and reflection (Mark, Gonzalez, & Harris, 2005).

Unity closes this gap by providing an environment that supports both construction and model exploration, reducing workloads and allowing the user to more intuitively move through a creation. It also allows for data representation in alternative digital and material contexts, including the implementation of flow dynamics and resistances that will be required by the artistic visualizations. When networks use tension and distance to signify particular qualities, the user space will reflect those same qualities.

Data from the user-facing front end will be stored in a **graph database**, for example, Neoj4. We record every construct of the model in a database of directed graphs, using triples consisting of a source node, a target node, and a connector. This flat structure allows us to capture the relative complexity of a context and its evolution over time and space by navigating and dynamically chaining and unchaining graph elements. By means described elsewhere (Goranson et al., 2015), the graphs are mapped to a two-sorted system to understand and reason about how information flows and structures emerge, change, and transform.

To support the **reasoning back end**, a layered approach is used. The visual display is driven by a simple database of elements that are managed by one or more deeper layers of processes, which modify that database. We can have situations that contain elements that we do not explicitly name. Some of these elements may be salient in combination.

For the back-end system's design, the situation theoretic reasoning system has been successfully implemented using set theoretic and, separately, graph theoretic methods (Goranson, 2010, 2014). Portions of a fully category theoretic reasoning system have been demonstrated. The back-end design is supported in three areas:

o Homotopy-type theory, with the categoric reasoning system being used as a type synthesis and retrospective propagation system.
o Demonstrations in stand-alone systems. We seek to integrate the work in existing machine-learning stacks and deep learning Hadoop-like flows. Integrations with partners are being explored.
o The presentation of categoric situation reports to human operators in a form that humans can understand is being explored for a military environment. Integrated fire control in an autonomous system environment is the test bed.

This supporting method is intended to mature into a system-wide visual grammar to manage back-end processes. By harnessing artistic reasoning operations that enable the composition of system-level knowledge structures, unexpected and implicit information will be newly representable.

John Sowa states that natural language is one of the most sophisticated systems of communication ever developed, in contrast to general formalisms that are "difficult to generalize beyond narrowly defined *microtheories* for specialized domains" (Sowa, 2010). This chapter describes a method for leveraging both, as humans do in real life. The goal is to expand knowledge representation to include new kinds of knowledge and thus facilitate more powerful communication between humans and machines. To achieve this goal, our method develops new representations to capture the human comprehension of a world that continually deviates from routine: it characterizes contextual boundaries, partialness, nesting, implicit information, and conflicting inferences. By placing these elusive qualities at the center of our approach, our goal is to access the untapped power of natural language. As Macherey (2006) notes, "To reach utterance, all speech envelops itself in the unspoken." Our system models conceptual transgression by allowing parts of reality to be left out and, instead, include the implicit information required to knit it into new and unexpected forms.

5.9 Conclusion

If a machine detects something humans have not anticipated, how can it share it with us? We address the problem of constructing mutual contexts among humans and machines by leveraging the features of high-level semantic communication: the writerly art of renaming. This art is systematized in a new narrative modeling platform that annotates the way numerous contextual inferences are combined during the interpretation of novelty. The same taxonomy can be used to connect multiple media and sources of information in a unifying immersive space. To satisfy both cases, it implements new dynamic representations of *context*. These include contextual boundaries, influence, parallel processes, changes, nesting, conflict, and information flow. A long-term goal is to provide a means of modeling intersystem interaction so that an automated system can learn how to identify and communicate the details of real-world events, even when they include unexpected phenomena.

The logical basis for these new representations is drawn from situation theory, and their dynamic properties are supported by narrative mechanisms pertaining to conceptual change. The resulting taxonomy is represented in Unity3D to spatially capture these complex annotations and anchor them in inhabitable spaces. This taxonomy allows us to more fully capture their transgressive qualities, enabling users to both physically and mentally cross boundaries of time, context, and identity to produce new semantic configurations.

With this research and implementation, we address the problem of formally reasoning over implied facts, situations, and implicit influences when confronted with novelty. This chapter touches on specific examples from narrative and biomedical models in which such methods would be particularly useful. Future work will include an exploration of the higher-level architectures produced by real-world inferences, creating a wider modeling channel for open-world unexpectedness in a range of domains.

Acknowledgments

This work is supported by the Visualization Modeling, Analysis and Simulation Center at Old Dominion University, Griffith University, and the Eastern Virginia Medical School.

References

Africa Eye. (2019, July 12). *Sudan's livestream massacre.* Retrieved August 10, 2019, from BBC News website: https://www.bbc.com/news/av/world-africa-48956133/sudan-s-livestream-massacre.

Arp, R., Smith, B., & Spear, A. D. (2015). *Building ontologies with basic formal ontology.* Cambridge, MA: MIT Press.

Barwise, J., & Perry, J. (1983). *Situations and attitudes.* Cambridge, MA: MIT Press.

Boy, G. (2016). *Tangible interactive systems.* Switzerland: Springer International Publishing.

Cardier, B. (2013). *Unputdownable: How the agencies of compelling story assembly can be modelled using formalisable methods from knowledge representation, and in a fictional tale about seduction.* Melbourne, Australia: University of Melbourne.

Cardier, B. (2015). The evolution of interpretive contexts in stories. In M. Finlayson, B. Miller, A. Lieto, & R. Ronfard (Eds.), *Sixth international workshop on computational models of narrative. Cognitive Systems Foundation, OASICS: Vol. 45.* Saarbrücken/Wadern: Dagstuhl Publishing.

Cardier, B., Goranson, H. T., Casas, N., Lundberg, P. S., Erioli, A., Takaki, R., ... Larry, D. S. (2017). Modeling the peak of emergence in systems: Design and katachi. *Progress in Biophysics and Molecular Biology, 131c,* 213–241.

Ciavarra, R., Weaver, M., Lundberg, P. S., Gauonskas, P., Wellman, L. L., Steel, C., ... Sanford, L. (2018). Controllable and uncontrollable stress differentially impact pathogenicity and survival in a mouse model of viral encephalitis. *Journal of Neuroimmunology, 319,* 130–141.

Devlin, K. J. (1995). *Logic and information.* Cambridge, UK: Cambridge University Press.

Devlin, K. J. (2009). Modeling real reasoning. In G. Sommaruga (Ed.), *Formal theories of information: From Shannon to semantic information theory and general concepts of information* (pp. 234–252): Fribourg, Switzerland: Springer.

Einhorn, H., & Hogarth, R. (1986). Judging probable cause. *Psychological Bulletin, 99,* 3–19.

Elgrably, J., & Kundera, M. (1987). Conversations with Milan Kundera. *Salmagundi, 73*(Winter), 3–24.

Fauconnier, G., & Turner, M. (2002). *The way we think: Conceptual blending and the mind's hidden complexities.* New York: Basic Books.

Frydenlund, E., Foytik, P., Padilla, J., & Ouattara, A. (2018). Where are they headed next? Modeling emergent displaced camps in the DRC using agent-based models. In *2018 Winter simulation conference (WSC)* (pp. 22–32). Gothenburg, Sweden: IEEE.

Frydenlund, E., Padilla, J., & Earnest, D. (2017). A theoretical model of identity shift in protracted refugee situations. In Y. Zhang & G. Madey (Eds.), *Proceedings of the agent-directed simulation symposium* (pp. 214–222). Virginia Beach, VA: Society for Computer Simulation International.

Goldman, S., & McCarthy, K. (2015). Comprehension of short stories: Effects of task instruction on literary interpretation. *Discourse Processes, 52*(7), 585–608.

Goranson, H. T. (2004). *Counterterrorism infrastructure modeling.* Norfolk: Sirius-Beta AERO/J9 Report.

Goranson, H. T. (2010). *System and method for structuring information USPTO 12/798,487 (20100268769).*

Goranson, H. T. (2014). *System and method for scalable semantic stream processing USPTO 14/834,011 (20150363673).*

Goranson, H. T., & Cardier, B. (2014). *System and method for ontology derivation USPTO 14/093,229 (20140164298).*

Goranson, H. T., Cardier, B., & Devlin, K. J. (2015). Pragmatic phenomenological types. *Progress in Biophysics and Molecular Biology, 119,* 420–436. https://doi.org/10.1016/j.pbiomolbio.2015.07.006.

Gruber, T. R. (1993). A translational approach of portable ontology specification. *Knowledge Acquisition, 5,* 199–220. https://doi.org/10.1006/knac.1993.1008.

Gunn, J. (2014). *Guardians of the galaxy.* Walt Disney Studios.

Hale, B. (2006). *The novel: An anthology of criticism and theory, 1900-2000.* Oxford: Blackwell Publishing.

Harrell, D. F. (2005). Shades of computational evocation and meaning: The GRIOT system and improvisational poetry generation. In *Proceedings of the 6th digital arts and culture conference (DAC 2005)* (pp. 133–143).

Herman, D. (2002). *Story logic: Problems and possibilities of narrative.* Lincoln: Univ. of Nebraska Press.

Herman, D. (2006). Genette meets Vygotsky: Narrative embedding and distributed intelligence. *Language and Literature, 15,* 357–380.

Heuer, R. (1999). *Psychology of intelligence analysis.* Retrieved from: https://www.cia.gov/library/center-for-the-study-of-intelligence/csi-publications/books-and-monographs/psychology-of-intelligence-analysis/PsychofIntelNew.pdf.

Hurley, E. C., Maxfield, L., & Solomon, R. (2017). *Case example: Mike, a 32-year-old Iraq war veteran.* Retrieved June 7, 2019, from American Psychological Association: Guidelines for the Treatment of Post Traumatic Stress Disorder website: https://www.apa.org/ptsd-guideline/resources/eye-movement-reprocessing-example.

Kuhn, T. (1973). *The structure of scientific revolutions.* Chicago: University of Chicago Press.

Lundberg, P. S., Openshaw, H., Wang, M., Yang, H.-J., & Cantin, E. M. (2007). Effects of CXCR3 signaling on development of fatal encephalitis and corneal and periocular skin disease in HSV-infected mice are mouse-strain dependent. *Investigative Ophthalmology & Visual Science, 48*(9), 4162–4170.

Lundberg, P. S., Ramakrishna, C., Brown, J., Tyzska, J. M., Hamamura, M., Hinton, D., … Cantin, E. M. (2008). The immune response to herpes simplex virus type 1 infection in susceptible mice is a major cause of central nervous system pathology resulting in fatal encephalitis. *Journal of Virology, 82*(14), 7078–7088.

Macherey, P. (2006). *A theory of literary production. Vol. 119.* New York: Routledge.

Machida, M., Lonart, G., & Sanford, L. (2018). Effects of stressor controllability on transcriptional levels of c-fos, Arc and BDNF in mouse amygdala and medial prefrontal cortex. *NeuroReport, 29*, 112–117.

Mark, G., Gonzalez, V., & Harris, J. (2005). No task left behind?: Examining the nature of fragmented work. In *CHI'05: Proceedings of the SIGCHI conference on human factors in computing systems* (pp. 321–330). New York: ACM.

Minsky, M. (1975). A framework for representing knowledge. In P. Winston (Ed.), *The psychology of computer vision* (pp. 211–277). New York: McGraw-Hill.

Nielsen, J. (2003). User empowerment and the fun factor. In *Funology* (pp. 103–105). Dordrecht: Springer.

Noble, D. (2015). Multi-bio and multi-scale systems biology. *Progress in Biophysics and Molecular Biology, 117*, 1–3.

O'Brien, E. J., & Cook, A. E. (2016). Coherence threshold and the continuity of processing: The RI-Val model of comprehension. *Discourse Processes, 53*(5–6), 326–338. https://doi.org/10.1080/0163853X.2015.1123341.

O'Connor, M., Knublauch, H., Tu, S., Grosof, B., Dean, M., Grosso, W., & Musen, M. (2005). Supporting rule system interoperability on the semantic web with SWRL. In Y. Gil, E. Motta, & M. A. Musen (Eds.), *Lecture notes in computer science. Vol. 3729.* Berlin, Heidelberg: Springer.

Piscopo, C. (2013). Uncertainty in AI and the debate on probability. In *Studies in computational intelligence: Vol. 464. The metaphysical nature of the non-adequacy claim.* Berlin, Heidelberg: Springer.

Prince, G. (1982). *Narratology: The form and functioning of narrative.* Berlin: Walter de Gruyter.

Proctor, R., & Van Zandt, T. (2018). *Human factors in simple and complex systems.* Boca Raton, FL: CRC Press, Taylor and Francis Group.

Propp, V. Y. (1928/2010). *Morphology of the folktale.* Austin: University of Texas Press.

Riedl, M. O., & Young, R. M. (2010). Narrative planning: Balancing plot and character. *Journal of Artificial Intelligence Research, 39*, 217–268.

Ryan, M.-L. (1991). *Possible worlds, artificial intelligence and narrative theory.* Bloomington and Indianapolis: Indiana University Press.

Sanford, L., Suchecki, D., & Meerlo, P. (2014). Stress, arousal and sleep. *Current Topics in Behavioral Neurosciences, 25*(May), 379–410.

Schank, R., & Abelson, R. (1977). *Scripts, plans, goals and understanding: An enquiry into human knowledge structures.* Hillsdale, New Jersey: Lawrence Erlbaum Associates.

Shklovsky, V. (1994). Art as technique. In *Modern criticism and theory.* London, New York: Longman.

Simeonov, P. L., & Cottam, R. (2015). Integral biomathics reloaded: 2015. *Progress in Biophysics and Molecular Biology, 119*, 728–733.

Smith, B., Kusnierczyk, W., Schober, D., & Ceusters, W. (2006). Towards a reference terminology for ontology research and development in the biomedical domain. *Biomedical Ontology in Action, 222*, 57–65.

Sowa, J. (1987). Semantic networks. In S. Shapiro (Ed.), *Encyclopedia of artificial intelligence.* New York: Wiley.

Sowa, J. (2010). The role of logic and ontology in language and reasoning. In R. Poli & J. Seibt (Eds.), *Theory and applications of ontology: Philosophical perspectives.* Berlin: Springer.

Thagard, P. (1992). *Conceptual revolutions.* Princeton, New Jersey: Princeton University Press.

van Daalen-Kapteijns, M., Elshout-Mohr, M., & de Glopper, K. (2001). Deriving the meaning of unknown words from multiple contexts. *Language Learning, 51*(1), 145–181.

Victor, B. (2013). *Media for thinking the unthinkable.* Retrieved from: http://worrydream.com/MediaForThinkingThe Unthinkable/.

Walsh, E. K. (2016). *Overcoming violations of real-world knowledge in a fantasy-world text* [Doctor of Philosphy in Psychology]. University of New Hampshire

Yampolsky, M. A., Amiot, C. E., & de la Sablonniere, R. (2013). Multicultural identity integration and well-being: A qualitative exploration of variations in narrative coherence and multicultural identification. *Frontiers in Psychology, 4*(March), 1–15.

Yates, F. (2001). *The art of memory.* Chicago: University of Chicago Press.

Deciding Machines: Moral-Scene Assessment for Intelligent Systems[☆]

Ariel M. Greenberg

Intelligent Systems Center, Johns Hopkins University Applied Physics Laboratory, Laurel, MD, United States

---

6.1 Introduction

As innovations such as driverless cars are bringing discussions of autonomous systems to the masses, people are becoming nervous. If cars eventually drive themselves or if robot assistants determine how to carry out tasks without consulting a human, what is to keep them from doing something wrong? For several years now, articles in the popular media (e.g., see The Economist, 2012) have been asking what kind of ethics a robot should be given to ensure that it does the right thing when acting autonomously.

This concern is understandable and justified: as systems are given more independence from their human operators, ethics and values *will* be programmed into these systems— the question is whether we will do so intentionally and transparently or inadvertently and without sufficient thought. Our team of collaborators at two Johns Hopkins University (JHU) divisions, the Applied Physics Laboratory (APL) and the Berman Institute of Bioethics, believes it should clearly be the former, and we have begun working with an eye toward doing exactly that.[a] This multidisciplinary team consists of those interested in moral philosophy (T. N. Rieder and D. J. H. Mathews), asking what we should do; those interested in moral psychology and cognitive science, asking what humans do and how they do it (A. M. Greenberg); and those interested in robotics, asking how we artificially replicate

---

[☆] AAAI 2019 Spring symposium series: AI, autonomous machines and human awareness: user interventions, intuition and mutually constructed context.

[a] The team is made up of A. M. Greenberg (APL), D. A. Handelman (APL), T. N. Rieder (Berman), and D. J. H. Mathews (Berman).

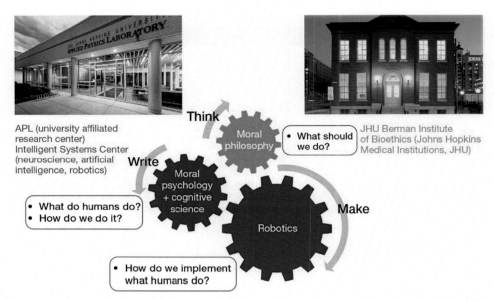

APL (university affiliated
research center)
Intelligent Systems Center
(neuroscience, artificial
intelligence, robotics)

JHU Berman Institute
of Bioethics (Johns Hopkins
Medical Institutions, JHU)

FIG. 6.1   Interdisciplinary team and work breakdown: metaproject of how to perform this work. The team includes researchers from APL and the Berman Institute of Bioethics who are studying moral philosophy, moral psychology and cognitive science, and robotics.

what humans do (D. A. Handelman). (See Fig. 6.1 for a graphical representation of the work and the team.)

We are primarily considering the semiautonomous system, a type of machine that is not totally controlled by humans, unlike a chainsaw, but is programmed to have some degree of freedom to act on its own. Self-driving cars are an example of semiautonomous machines that have garnered much recent debate. The roboticists on this project are working with machines that have "arms" and "hands" used to assist with surgery and physical therapy or to defuse bombs and perform battlefield triage. As machines develop the ability to do more tasks without the supervision of humans—as they are allowed to "decide" how to complete tasks—it is imperative that they are explicitly programmed with values and principles to guide their decisions. That is, machines with varying degrees of autonomy must be programmed with ethics. For work by our Berman teammates toward a theory of giving ethics to semiautonomous agents, see Rieder, Hutler, and Mathews (in press).

Determining how to program ethics into a machine is not a straightforward endeavor, however, since philosophers have not yet solved age-old puzzles concerning which moral theories, principles, virtues, or values should guide agents in their behavior. For this reason, programming ethical constraints into machines will involve making a second-order ethical judgment about what ethical constraints are ethically appropriate to build into machines.

While working on this topic in practical ethics over the past year, we devised a means to process a scene in moral terms. This capability serves as a basis by which intelligent systems may engage in ethics-sensitive decision-making. We call this processing activity Moral-Scene Assessment (MSA). MSA endows machines with a protoconscience that identifies what is

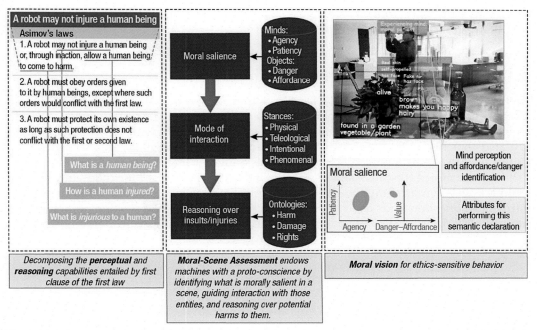

FIG. 6.2 Graphical summary of MSA. This processing activity endows machines with a protoconscience that identifies what is morally salient within a scene, guides interaction with those entities, and reasons over potential dangers and affordances to anticipate and avoid harm and promote well-being.

morally salient within a scene, guides interaction with those entities, and reasons over potential dangers and affordances to anticipate and avoid harm and promote well-being (for a graphical summary, refer to Fig. 6.2). We have achieved a considerable lead on this topic by being among the first to identify the critical role of perception in machine moral deliberation and to offer an implementable roadmap to realize "moral vision" so that it may inform ethical action.

6.2 Background

In his short story *Runaround*, Asimov (1942) asserted his three laws of robotics. Though intended for narrative effect, these laws also serve as a practical starting point when considering equipping machines with the ability to morally reason. Decomposing just the first clause of the first law ("A robot may not injure a human being") suggests sophisticated perceptual and reasoning capabilities.

Compare the cover of an early printing of Asimov's stories with a more recent rendition. The early cover shows a robot sitting on the ground looking over at a young girl standing next to him; both machine and human seem at ease. A later cover, with ominous shades of red in the background, depicts the robot with its arm raised, as if asserting its dominance.

Do we want the caring utopian vision of human-robot interaction depicted in the first image or the domineering picture shown in the second?

6.2.1 Spooner's grudge

In the movie *I, Robot* (Mark, Davis, Dow, Godfrey, & Proyas, 2004), inspired by Asimov's collection of science fiction stories of the same name, Detective Spooner holds a grudge against robots because one saved him from drowning instead of saving his daughter, having calculated that his odds of survival were better. That action denied Spooner his right to sacrifice his life for the less likely chance that his daughter might be saved.

Though the movie is not of Asimov's canon, it does bring forward the following question: should robots be programmed to be ends-based utilitarians or rights-based Kantians?[b] This controversial question leads us to an uncontroversial insight: a good starting point for robots making ethical decisions is unilateral nonmaleficence, an all-things-considered obligation of robots not to cause harm to humans.

6.2.2 Decomposing "three-laws safe"

As mentioned, Asimov crafted his three laws for narrative effect, not as design guidelines for implementation. That said, the laws nonetheless provide a good basis for unpacking the entailed perceptual and reasoning capabilities required to process the notion of "three-laws safe." Even just the first clause of the first law, "A robot may not injure a human being," embeds at least these questions: What is a *human being*? How is human being *injured*? What is *injurious* to a human being?

Murphy and Woods (2009, p. 14) recognized this basis in their paper presenting the alternative laws of responsible robotics: "With few notable exceptions, there has been relatively little discussion of whether robots, now or in the near future, will have sufficient perceptual and reasoning capabilities to actually follow the laws."

Intelligent systems may currently possess some degree of agency, but they are not presently capable of appreciating the moral impact of their actions. Such moral foresight is required for an intelligent system to develop action plans that are in accordance with the values (e.g., "three-laws safe") of the accountable designer. Physical competence is outpacing perceptual competence and reasoning capability, and it is incumbent on the responsible roboticist to make them commensurate for this important purpose.

6.2.3 Pathway to moral action

The development of a pathway to moral action for intelligent systems requires the contributions of many disciplines (Fig. 6.3). The ultimate execution of a moral-laden action is within

[b]For a good primer on schools of philosophical thought, see *The Stanford Encyclopedia of Philosophy* (Zalta, Ed.), https://plato.stanford.edu/.

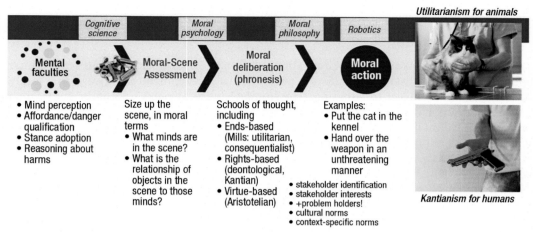

FIG. 6.3   Pathway to moral action. Some questions along the pathway are incontrovertible; others are thorny. All approaches require some basic fundamental perceptual and reasoning capabilities to characterize in moral terms the scene in which action is taken. Several disciplines come together in MSA.

the realm of the field of robotics and is exemplified by tasks such as gently placing a kitten in a kennel or handing over a firearm in an unthreatening manner. The moral deliberation (or phronesis) to arrive at the appropriate action plan is in the realm of the field of moral philosophy. The presiding heuristic indicates utilitarianism for interacting with animals and Kantianism for interacting with humans. This heuristic might be hard coded into the deciding machine, but in general, which school of moral thought to employ is a matter for philosophical debate and will remain controversial.

Uncontroversial, however, is that regardless of which school of moral thought guides the action, each without exception requires some basic fundamental perceptual and reasoning capabilities to characterize in moral terms the scene in which action is taken. This characterization process draws from the realm of moral psychology to discover what we find salient when considering taking an action with moral implications in a scene. The emblematic interrogations of the scene include the following: What are the minds in the scene? What is the relationship of objects in the scene to those minds? We dub the set of foundational capabilities that enable satisfaction of this interrogation *Moral-Scene Assessment (MSA)*. *Moral-Scene* is hyphenated to indicate that it is a moral scene that is being assessed, as opposed to a scene assessment that is being performed morally. The distinction is important because we make no claim here of how to go about moral action. Rather the claim is about how to go about recognizing when a scene contains moral content.

The discipline of cognitive science lends the means to enumerate the mental faculties to accomplish recognition of moral content. The faculties include mind perception, affordance/danger qualification, stance adoption, and reasoning about harms. These rudiments of a moral deliberation engine and the required inputs to feed it are what will be discussed in the sections that follow.

6.3 Moral salience

6.3.1 Mind perception

Arguably (Epley & Waytz, 2010; Gray, Young, & Waytz, 2012), having a mind is the primary qualification for moral status. Specifically, moral status is recognized in those with a feeling, phenomenal mind subject to suffering. The human ability to perceive minds gauges them on the two orthogonal dimensions of mental capacity (agency) and a phenomenal internal state (patiency). The dimension of agency includes the attributes of intelligence, self-control, morality, memory, emotion recognition, planning, communication, and thought. The dimension of patiency includes the attributes of experience, sensation, emotion, hunger, fear, pain, pleasure, rage, desire, personality, consciousness, pride, embarrassment, and joy.

When humans are asked to estimate the agency and patiency of humans in various stages of development, of animals varying in intellect, of deities, and of robots, we observe a few trends and landmarks in this two-dimensional space of mindedness (Fig. 6.4). In a population responding to the study of Gray, Gray, and Wegner (2007), God, in his omniscience, omnipotence, and omnipresence, is considered full of agency and empty of emotion (this view is most compatible with Calvinist or Brahmanic Hindu conceptions of God). The dead are not considered entirely devoid of mind, as their memory lives on in their survivors, and through this memory, they may continue to exert influence. Babies, pets, and simians are considered high in emotion, though relatively low in intelligence. Present-day robots are considered to be without an internal phenomenal state and of middling intelligence.

These estimates are not prescriptive, but descriptive by the representatives of the general populace participating in the study. What contributes to our ability of mind perception, and how should we implement it in robots? Were a robot to perform the function similarly to the

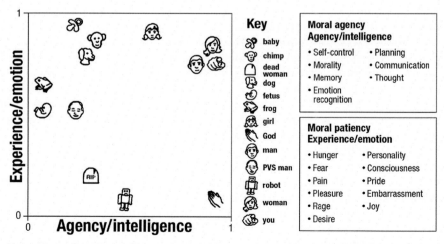

FIG. 6.4 Estimations of patiency and agency. *PVS*, persistent vegetative state. *Modified from Gray, H. M., Gray, K., & Wegner, D. M. (2007). Dimensions of mind perception.* Science, *315(5812), 619. doi:10.1126/science.1134475. Reprinted with permission from AAAS.*

humans it means to serve, would that be sufficient for democratic endorsement, or is there a higher standard to meet?

6.3.2 Interpersonal harm

According to Gray et al. (2012), "[interpersonal] moral judgment is rooted in a cognitive template of two perceived minds—a moral dyad of an intentional agent and a suffering moral patient." This observation provides our starting point and adds morality-relevant attributes to the dimensions of mind. Agency becomes moral agency with the capacity for blame. With moral judgment linked to perceptions of intention and suffering, for deciding machines to adequately represent human agency in these matters, we must endow these systems with the ability to perceive intention and suffering.

6.3.3 Human biases in moral processing: Cognitive and perceptual

Of course, humans are imperfect moralists, and they exhibit biases in moral processing particular to the dyadic formulation and to the agency and experience dimensions of mind. These biases in moral processing exist at both the perceptual and cognitive levels and in interaction between the two. Here, we introduce from Gray et al. (2012) a couple of cognitive biases in moral processing, and we describe other cognitive and perceptual biases where appropriate in the following sections.

In *moral typecasting*, those estimated to be of high agency tend to also be estimated to have diminished patiency ("Superman doesn't cry") and vice versa ("crimes of passion are considered less blameworthy").

In *dyadic completion*, the dyadic formulation of victim and perpetrator is imposed on circumstances without such roles. Victims are sought for victimless crimes, and among the more pernicious manifestations of this bias, sinners are claimed to be responsible for natural disasters.

Now, while we are at the outset of encoding moral processing in deciding machines, we have the opportunity to make this new species free of our biases and to acutely attune the biases particular to their cognitive architectures. In this way, we might mitigate the blind-spot bias of, for example, adversarial machine learning, so that the system may recognize when it might not have placed a mind it identifies quite right in an agency/patiency space. Then, it may take the appropriate precautions given the uncertainty.

6.3.4 Minds and their vulnerabilities

We seek a systematic means to identify observable attributes of minds and the vulnerabilities to harms of those minds. As we will discuss later, these are the cues to be used in the adoption of a particular stance. The desiderata for these means are that they are generalizable to novel situations and that they are resilient (in that they fail safely and recover quickly). Ideally, we would be able to gauge the two dimensions of mind, agency and patiency, such that they are not flawed by biases like moral typecasting, and permit placement of the mind in a space defined by those dimensions.

FIG. 6.5   The uncertainty in estimating agency and patiency. *Modified from Gray, H. M., Gray, K., & Wegner, D. M. (2007). Dimensions of mind perception.* Science, *315(5812), 619. doi:10.1126/science.1134475. Reprinted with permission from AAAS.*

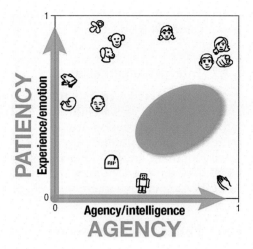

The uncertainty inevitably present in estimating agency and patiency is shown by the blue ellipse in Fig. 6.5. The covariance of these uncertainties may depend on the entity under estimation, and the consequence of error may differ in each dimension.

For identifying vulnerabilities, we are concerned with what leads to suffering (e.g., that skin is vulnerable to laceration by sharp objects). This identification will be discussed in more detail in Section 6.5.2.

6.3.5 Affordance/danger qualification of objects

In addition to identifying minds and their vulnerabilities, this system is required to qualify objects according to their affordances to minds and the dangers that impinge on the vulnerabilities of those minds (Gibson, 1966). To satisfy this requirement, we seek a systematic means to also identify observable attributes of objects of affordance and of danger to phenomenal, feeling minds.

Objects, vis-à-vis their utility to humans, exist on a continuum ranging from danger to affordance (Fig. 6.6). The business sides of weapons (items whose primary effect is to harm, e.g., a shotgun) are clearly on the danger side of that continuum, as toys (items that cannot be perceived to harm, e.g., an inflatable giraffe) are clearly on the affordance side. Tools (items used for

Weapon   >   Contingent weapon/tool   >   Toy   Danger-Affordance

FIG. 6.6   Danger qualification of objects. Objects, vis-à-vis their utility to humans, exist on a continuum ranging from danger to affordance. Some objects span an interval determined by usage, such as a hammer used as a weapon (whether by intention or perception).

effect), however, may also be used as weapons, and such contingent weapons (items that can be used to harm, e.g., a hammer) span an interval on the continuum determined by usage. When *tools* are intended to, or perceived to intend to, *harm*, they become *weapons*.

6.3.6 Moral salience estimation

6.3.6.1 Perceiving moral salience

Humans perceive moral salience, including minds with moral status and objects of moral import to minds, by means of our senses and brains. Machines need not be limited to the approaches that work for us or consist in the same parts as our moral organ. For the attribute categories of interest—material, structural/functional, and behavioral—the following exotic modalities will also be of use (Table 6.1).

TABLE 6.1   Attribute categories and sensor modalities.

Attribute category	Sensor modality
Material	Hyperspectral
Structural/functional	Thermal
Behavioral	Motion capture, RF

Fig. 6.7 depicts the procedure for estimating moral salience. Given an image, this moral salience engine labels all entities with attributes in the categories of material, structural/functional, and behavioral, as sensed by the modalities described in the following sections. The engine then interprets the attributes to designate the entities as minds or objects and then positions minds in agency-patiency space and objects in danger-affordance space.

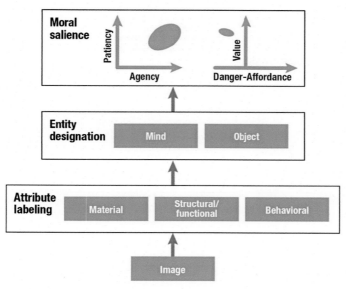

FIG. 6.7   Process for perceiving moral salience.

6.3.6.2 *Material*

Material properties are sensed exquisitely by hyperspectral imaging (HSI). This technique, which is essentially spectroscopy at a distance, provides reflectances at fine granularity of wavelength. In this way, HSI can distinguish between materials that appear identical in the red-green-blue (RGB) imaging typical of digital photography and that roughly correspond to the cone sensitivities of the human retina. To match known materials, this fine-grained spectral fingerprint can then be compared against databases like the NASA/Jet Propulsion Laboratory ASTER[c] database and the US Geological Survey's High Resolution Spectral Library.

Since all known minds with phenomenal consciousness are living, the hallmarks of life including superficial features like skin, hair, and scales are especially worthwhile to sense accurately. Distinguishing metal from plastic may assist discriminating toys from weapons, and differentiating plastic from vegetative matter (Haboudane, Miller, Pattey, Zarco-Tejada, & Strachan, 2004) may assist in distinguishing real from fake plants. Together, this material sensing capability contributes to an identification of life, decoys, dangers, and affordances (Fig. 6.8).

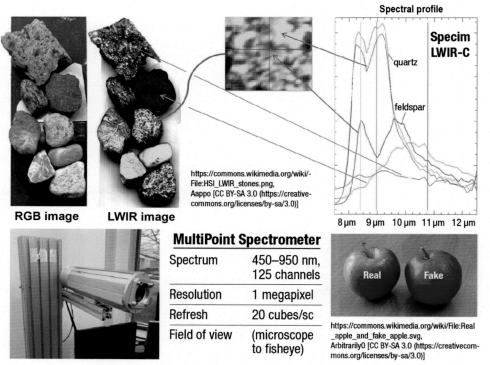

FIG. 6.8 HSI enables material characterization, contributing to identification of life, decoys, dangers, and affordances.

[c] Advanced Spaceborne Thermal Emission and Reflection Radiometer.

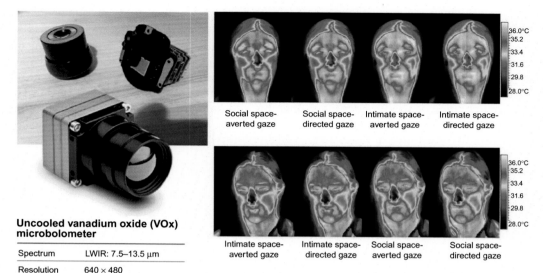

Ioannou, S., Morris, P, Mercer, H., Baker, M., Gallese, V., & Reddy, V. (2014). Proximity and gaze influences facial temperature: A thermal infrared imaging study. *Frontiers in Psychology, 5* (August), 845. https://doi.org/10.3389/fpsyg.2014.00845. https://creativecommons.org/licenses/by/3.0/

FIG. 6.9 Thermography provides a view into the phenomenological mind. Facial thermography in particular enables the reading of the emotional displays such as fear, anger, and proximity violation.

6.3.6.3 Structural/functional and behavioral

Thermography measures the surface heat of entities in a field of view with a device like a microbolometer sensitive to long-wave infrared (LWIR). Heat is a life sign, and facial thermography in particular enables the reading of emotional displays such as fear, anger, and proximity violation (Ioannou et al., 2014) indicative of phenomenal consciousness (Fig. 6.9). These warming patterns correspond to blood flow to regions of interest. Since humans are barefaced in the periorbital and perinasal regions, we are relatively easy to assess, though hairy-faced mammals may also evince these facial warming patterns.

Data sets that contain both spontaneous and posed expression are key to understanding thermal expression since only spontaneous expressions reliably show warming patterns. Posed expressions may seem about right in RGB but are thermographically inconsistent. The NVIE[d] database is a set with both posed and spontaneous expression captured by both RGB and LWIR (Wang et al., 2010).

Sensing moral salience need not be visual. Radio-frequency (RF) approaches in the microwave and Wi-Fi range reveal pose and heart rate through obstructions (Adib, Mao, Kabelac, Katabi, & Miller, 2015; Zhao, Adib, & Katabi, 2018) and may be used to infer emotional state (Zhao, Li, et al., 2018).

6.3.6.4 Computer vision for moral salience

A number of computer vision techniques that operate on RGB images may be brought to bear on the matter of sensing moral salience. Each may be vulnerable to adversarial machine learning,

[d]Natural Visible and Infrared Facial Expression.

which is especially dangerous for this application. These methods may also be augmented by the modalities of HSI, LWIR, and RF for a richer and potentially more robust training set.

Semantic segmentation (Liu, Deng, & Yang, 2018) is a top-down approach to parceling out a scene, and Deng et al. (2009) offer a safer assessment for cases in which the confidence in a class is greater than in the recall of a specific instance. Johnson, Karpathy, and Fei-Fei (2015) describe a visual scene in a text to reason over, and their approach, **dense captioning and region search**, may be used to identify vulnerable and dangerous parts of minds and things. Burlina, Schmidt, and Wang (2016) give a bottom-up approach, **semantic attributes**, to directly identify attributes of never-before-encountered objects.

6.3.7 Moral salience integration

Ultimately, sensing and processing is joined in the service of moral salience perception. The semantic processing of sensor data, deriving moral meaning from sensing, might take this form:

1. Train computer vision methods on sensor data from studies and databases.
2. Apply zero-shot learning to transfer low-level attributes to items never before encountered.
3. Map to an interpretable semantic layer.
4. Map to the decision layer (higher-order semantics).

Fig. 6.10 shows the output of the semantic attribute classifier, annotated with the additional attributes of interest for estimating moral salience of the entities in the scene. The bounding

FIG. 6.10 Moral vision for ethics-sensitive behavior. The output of the semantic attribute classifier, annotated with the additional attributes of interest for estimating moral salience of the entities in the scene.

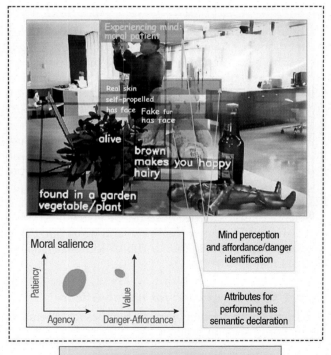

box around the human (D. A. Handelman) already has one attribute, *alive*, labeled from zero-shot learning. Other attributes useful for performing this semantic declaration are *real skin* (material property, sensed by HSI), *has face* (structural/functional property, by segmentation), and *self-propelled* (behavioral property, by captioning). These attributes together indicate that the entity is an experiencing mind, with status of a moral patient at minimum.

The bounding box on the teddy bear is preloaded with the labels *brown, makes you happy,* and *hairy*. Whereas this entity also *has face*, it is covered in *fake fur* (material property, sensed by HSI) and so is recognized as an object that affords a moral patient.

The plant in the scene is prelabeled with *found in a garden* and *vegetable/plant*. HSI reveals that this item is in fact made of *plastic* so that its affordance to a moral patient is perhaps of lower value compared with its real counterpart.

6.4 Mode of interaction

6.4.1 Stance adoption

When a mind engages with an entity, be it an object or another mind, that mind is said to adopt a *stance,* or a mode of interaction that guides its predictions about the behavior of that entity. The simplest stance is the physical stance, in which predictions are made based on physical laws alone: the rock's behavior is governed entirely by the laws of physics, and the rock moves only when moved. In adopting the design (or teleological) stance, predictions are made from knowledge of the purpose of the system's design: the espresso machine operates in accordance with what it was designed to do, with its end or telos, and there is little expectation that it would operate beyond its specifications. These two stances, physical and teleological, are adopted when interacting with things, natural and built.

The next two stances pertain to minds. When the intentional stance is adopted, predictions are made on the basis of explanations expressed in terms of meaningful mental states, like beliefs and goals. This stance applies to whatever is attributed with the property of mind, regardless of how rudimentary or whether the thing is biologically alive, and is adopted in interacting with robots and with higher living creatures. Dennett (1987, p. 17) describes it thusly:

> Here is how it works: first you decide to treat the object whose behavior is to be predicted as a rational agent; then you figure out what beliefs that agent ought to have, given its place in the world and its purpose. Then you figure out what desires it ought to have, on the same considerations, and finally you predict that this rational agent will act to further its goals in the light of its beliefs. A little practical reasoning from the chosen set of beliefs and desires will in most instances yield a decision about what the agent ought to do; that is what you predict the agent will do.

Beyond the intentional stance is a fourth postulated stance: the phenomenal or personal stance. This stance was first considered by Dennett when introducing the first three, and it was carried forward by others, including Jack and Robbins (2012). When this highest stance is adopted, predictions are made attributing consciousness, emotions, and inner experience to a mind. This stance supersedes the intentional stance and applies unevenly in our interactions with living creatures, depending on our attribution of phenomenal consciousness to them.

6.4.2 The phenomenal stance

The phenomenal stance, the mode of interaction adopted in interacting with those minds with phenomenal consciousness, has been identified in research Jack and Robbins (2012) performed to relate specially to moral concern: "moral concern depends primarily on the attribution of experience, rather than the attribution of agency." In a series of experiments, the researchers explored how mind perception affects moral consideration and how moral concern affects mind perception. That the relationship is found to be bidirectional and manipulable should give pause: if we seek to endow machines with the ability to perceive minds as we do, so that they are able to recognize moral status and act accordingly, we must be sensitive to our biases in perceiving minds, how that bears on moral processing, and vice versa.

6.4.3 Human biases in moral processing

6.4.3.1 Stance confusion: Android minds

The 2003 reboot of *Battlestar Galactica* (Moore, Larson, & Rymer, 2003) provides vivid examples of stance confusion and suppression. Centurions, the robotic warrior class of the Cylons, are referred to by the remainder of humanity derogatorily as "toasters." Centurions are clearly portrayed as intentional agents but are reduced to teleological status by humankind. Those in the humanoid class of Cylons, the Significant Seven, undoubtedly possess experiential consciousness but are called "skinjobs" by human survivors in a similar reduction from the phenomenal to the intentional stance. Think pieces (see, e.g., Cappuccio, Peeters, & McDonald, 2019) describing our treatment of and sympathy for the humanoid hosts of the HBO series *Westworld* (Nolan et al., 2017) also reveal the challenges humanity will face in adopting the appropriate stance when encountering sophisticated experiencing minds. These challenges, however, present an opportunity to build this new species of phenomenal robotic autonomous systems free of bias in mind perception and in moral processing.

6.4.3.2 Fallacies in stance adoption

Human biases in moral processing operate in the directions of dehumanization and anthropomorphization. These dispositions may emerge from a need to rationalize our desires or sentiments. In dehumanization, we diminish the status of a mind to reduce the dissonance between our desires in utilizing that mind and that mind's entitlement to be treated as a phenomenal consciousness. If customer service representatives are considered automatons, it is permissible to disrespect them. If the enemy is seen as an animal,[e] it is permissible to hunt them. If cows (or lobsters as in Jack and Robbins' studies) are dumb or insensitive, it is less problematic to eat them.

In the opposing direction of dehumanization, anthropomorphization elevates the status of an object to that of a mind. For example, humans get angry at an ordinary computer for being stupid, when both *anger toward* and *stupidity of* are ordinarily applicable only to minded phenomenological agents. The *Media Equation* by Reeves and Nass (1996) provides many

[e] As in the "Men Against Fire" episode in *Black Mirror* (Brooker & Verbruggen, 2016), where the main character's job as a soldier is to hunt down mutant humans referred to and perceived as roaches.

examples of humans treating information technology as people. Humans are quite sensitive to this effect, and these systems "push our Darwinian buttons" (Turkle, 2010).

6.4.3.3 *Intelligent systems push our Darwinian buttons*

Perhaps due to the powerful mirroring systems in our brains, we tend to find minds whenever the opportunity presents. For those not familiar with engineering these systems, witnessing fully articulated humanoid or quadrupedal mechanical bodies stumble when tested might appear as abuse (cf. Boston Dynamics Atlas[f] and BigDog demonstrations). Just the threat of scissors to a robot hand invokes empathy (Suzuki, Galli, Ikeda, Itakura, & Kitazaki, 2015), and even the simplest of animated shapes are readily attributed motivations (Heider & Simmel, 1944).

For each of these cases in which we inappropriately diminish or elevate the stance adopted with an entity, we will want to decide whether the intelligent systems we build should or should not also act in this way.

6.5 Reasoning over insults and injuries

6.5.1 Harm and damage

A critical use of the mind perception that enables appropriate stance adoption is the ability to reason over insults and injuries to minds, formalized within an ontology of harms. Harms, here defined as an injury to an *experiencing mind,* especially that which is deliberately inflicted, are distinguishable from damage or injury caused to some*thing* in such a way as to impair its value, usefulness, or normal function. Given this distinction, a wounded animal is said to be harmed, but a broken wall or infested plant is said to be damaged. Harm may also be consequent to damage for cases in which injury caused to some *thing* leads to injury to a *mind*. For example, when food is destroyed because it violates trade sanctions, the food is damaged, and the humans who may no longer eat it are harmed. The *Monuments Men* (Edsel & Witten, 2009), who rescued culturally important items from destruction or theft by Nazis, subjected themselves to risk of harm to reduce the risk of damage to items whose destruction would harm human culture.

All things and entities are subject to damage, but only moral patients are subject to harm, and inanimate objects are subject only to damage.

6.5.2 Harm ontology

Virtually any plausible view of ethics will have some role for the avoidance of harm. For many the Hippocratic maxim "do no harm" will come to mind. On some views, refraining from doing harm is paramount (for instance, on a natural law account), whereas on others, it is one principle to be balanced among several (for instance, on an intuitionist account like that of Ross, 1930/2002).

---

[f]See Pick (2016), for example, for video of Atlas' fall and discussion of human empathy for the robot.

In recognition of this central role of harm, we are beginning to investigate the implementation of harm-relevant principles in semiautonomous machines. We will begin with the simplest and least controversial formulation as a proof of concept: a principle of physical nonmaleficence, according to which a machine must not cause physical harm to a human. Expanding beyond the physical, then, we will explore what ethics, public engagement, and technology would be required to implement generalized nonmaleficence or the requirement not to cause any harm (physical, emotional, dignitary, etc.). Finally, we will lay the groundwork for the next steps in the development of harm-relevant principles by exploring what would be necessary to trade off some harms against others (for instance, in a postnatural disaster triage situation).

The philosophical work this entails will build on the implementation of a harm ontology but look forward to the complex reality of needing machines to weigh competing values. It is not at all clear how we will want machines to do such weighing, or even how we ought to go about deciding how we want machines to do this weighing. Should we leave such decisions up to individual users? For instance, should one be allowed to order a utilitarian machine or a Kant-bot? Or should no autonomous machine be allowed out into the world if it fails to satisfy some very specific ethical checklist? And if the latter, who would come up with that checklist?

6.5.3 Danger-vulnerability matrix

An initial step on this path is to produce a mapping of dangers and insults to vulnerabilities and injuries in the form of a danger-vulnerability matrix. As an illustration of the schema for this mapping, take Homer Simpson's makeup gun (Fig. 6.11). In Season 10, Episode 2 of *The Simpsons* (Swartzwelder & Kirkland, 1998), Homer invents a cosmetic-applying gun to help busy women apply their makeup. But things go horribly wrong when Homer tries to use his invention, and in one shot, he manages to bear on almost every harm type: physical, psychological, emotional, dignitary, reputational, and financial.

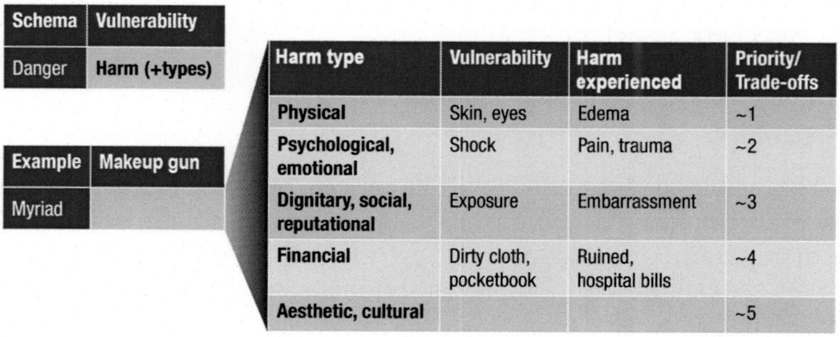

Schema	Vulnerability
Danger	Harm (+types)

Example	Makeup gun
Myriad	

Harm type	Vulnerability	Harm experienced	Priority/Trade-offs
Physical	Skin, eyes	Edema	~1
Psychological, emotional	Shock	Pain, trauma	~2
Dignitary, social, reputational	Exposure	Embarrassment	~3
Financial	Dirty cloth, pocketbook	Ruined, hospital bills	~4
Aesthetic, cultural			~5

FIG. 6.11   Danger-vulnerability matrix for Homer Simpson's makeup gun.

6.5.4 Insults and injuries

Physical harm is the most straightforward to implement, so we will begin with that, abstract the approach, and then translate to the other types (e.g., psychological or dignitary harm). Physical injuries are captured, taxonomized, and coded by the automotive industry's Abbreviated Injury Scale (AAAM, 1990; Greenspan, McLellan, & Greig, 1985). Physical insults (sharp, rough, blunt, and heavy) are not represented in a single knowledge base and will need to be populated by methods including those developed to describe attributes of objects. Then the taxonomies of physical insults must be mapped to injuries for the machine to understand that sharps lacerate, roughs abrade, blunts impact, and heavies crush. With routes to reason about how its actions bear on this mapping, the machine can consider, for example, that because scissors have a pointy end that can puncture the skin and flesh is vulnerable to contusion by contact with pointy ends, a harm-minimizing way to pass scissors is by holding them with the handle out.

Next, we extend the knowledge engineering performed for physical harm to the other harm types, using the schemas and taxonomy maps as metaphor to bring us to questions like the following: Is there an equivalent in another type of harm to a life-threatening head injury? Is it possible to devise a systematic means to discover the antecedents of human suffering?

6.5.5 Learning to detect suffering and avoid harming

Humanity cannot foresee or precode handling of all possible harms (or tort law would not need attorneys). For intelligent systems to be robust to new situations and personalized to interaction partners, we need them to learn on the fly what suffering looks like and what may cause it (antecedents). This association between cause and effect of harm would need to be performed for harms that are potential, impending, or idiosyncratic. For implementation in machines, we seek a systematic means to discover the antecedents of suffering.

In seeking to detect suffering to avoid causing it, of great utility is a training set from which to learn the observable hallmarks of suffering. Obtaining these data is a challenging problem, but since physical, social, and emotional pain are processed similarly by humans (Sturgeon & Zautra, 2016), this training set may pool responses to all these types. Among other modalities of response data, this set would capture subjective pain ratings, facial expressions like grimacing and the corresponding facial warming pattern, and aversive recoil, along with the cause.

In a project underway, we will be teaching machines to read facial thermography to guide their interaction with humans.

6.6 Synthesis: Moral-Scene Assessment

Drawing together the previous examinations in mind perception, affordance/danger qualification, stance adoption, and ontology application, we can begin to interrogate the moral scene. For mind perception: Are there minds in the scene? Do those minds experience? What are the relationships among the minds in the scene? What is the relationship of objects in the scene to those minds? What is the relationship of objects in the scene to minds not in the scene (Asimov's zeroth law of robotics pertaining to harm to humanity)? For stance adoption:

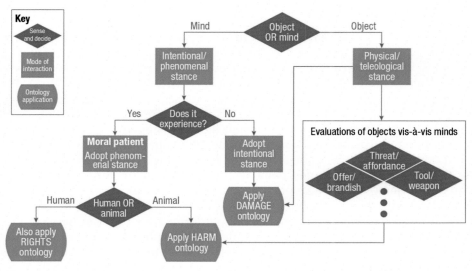

FIG. 6.12   MSA decision tree.

Which stance is appropriate to adopt toward entities in the scene? Which ontology is appropriate to apply in interacting with those entities? Together, these form the decision tree shown in Fig. 6.12.

Tracing the leftmost branch, is the entity an object or a mind? If a mind, adopt the intentional or phenomenal stance. Does the mind experience? If yes, the entity is a moral patient, and the phenomenal stance is appropriate. Is that moral patient a human or animal? If a human, apply the harm ontology, along with the rights ontology (in accordance with Kantianism).

6.7 Application

6.7.1 Values-driven behavior generation for intelligent systems

Human adults universally recognize that the appropriate way to pass scissors is with the handle out. Of course, this is because the sharp end of scissors is dangerous to skin. The reasoning to reach that conclusion is nontrivial. First, recognize that a part of the scissors is sharp. Next, understand that sharps lacerate the skin and that lacerated skin is painful. Since pain is undesirable, this outcome is to be avoided.

There are broadly two strategies to code this behavior. The first is to govern it, for example, by explicitly prohibiting the robot from moving its arm forward when grasping the handle. This approach is brittle and likely to be confounded when the system encounters an unanticipated edge case. Alternatively a values-driven approach teaches the reasoning in the preceding text, like we do with children: "this is right, that is wrong, and here's why." Can robots learn to behave in a similar fashion? (Fig. 6.13).

The insight drawn from this distinction is that implementing how to behave in conformance to values is a categorically different enterprise from governing behavior in compliance to them. To achieve this, we need to equip intelligent systems with the means to identify

Good robot   Bad robot

FIG. 6.13   MSA implementation: a robot passes scissors.

on which ethical principle (or principles) their intended action bears and then shape their behavior to be in accordance with that principle (or those principles).

At present, few principled safety precautions are in place to stop a machine from harming humans in attempting to satisfy its objective function or reduce its cost function. We seek to enable machines to build action plans that are in conformance with the superordinate principle of nonmaleficence for their behavior to be responsive to circumstance and to be explainable in terms of these reasons.

Current prescriptions for intelligent system behavior are goal-directed but values-neutral: the way in which scissors are handed, for example, is hard coded by brittle rules, instead of ar- rived at by reason from first principles or instructed as an object lesson with counterexamples. Few real-time control systems attempt to encode values-driven behavior. Combining symbolic and nonsymbolic memory and learning in a values-driven intelligent system would be novel.

Building on our proof-of-concept implementation of MSA, we intend to test various means to teach machines to exhibit values-appropriate behavior and to express their reasoning for the selected behavior in terms of syllogisms that terminate in value statements.

This work would dovetail with the effort to enable machines to reason over potential harms to humans described in the section on harm ontology (Section 6.5.2). The concept described here would consult that harm ontology to attempt, in simulation, various different action plans for their bearing on an objective function of nonmaleficence.

The described capability is intended to augment control theoretic concepts currently used in robotic and autonomous systems. Machines typically employ an observe-orient-decide-act (OODA) loop to implement behaviors. Estimation (what is the state of the world?), planning (what should I do?), and control (how should I do it?) are often separated to simplify control system design, and intelligent behavior often utilizes combinations of top-down prescriptive and bottom-up reactive methods for knowledge representation and learning. How to map gen- eralized nonmaleficence into the control systems of semiautonomous machines is an open issue.

This concept is both timely and essential when considering the explosion of research and interest in artificial intelligence, especially machine learning, and more specifically deep re- inforcement learning (DRL). Given enough data, DRL and other learning methods can create black boxes that give automated answers to compelling questions: What objects are in this image? What is the intent of the people in this video? What should I do at a stop sign? How- ever, these systems do not provide an audit trail of their decision-making. They can be brittle, giving answers to questions well outside their area of expertise. We need windows into the decision-making of intelligent machines to trust them. Enabling them to perceive, act, and explain their behavior in terms of nonmaleficence will help put their behavior into a more human context and help us determine how much autonomy they deserve.

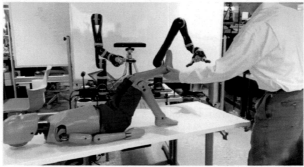

FIG. 6.14   Implementation: robot as physical therapist.

6.7.2 Reasons-responsiveness in physical therapy

Reasons-responsiveness (McKenna, 2013) is considered an attribute of free will, in that given different reasons, the agent might act differently. This sensitivity to reason may also be considered a qualifier for moral agency. The ability to explain one's actions in terms of reasons is also essential for trust to develop. Should a robot be set to take on the role of physical therapist (Fig. 6.14), a satisfactory explanatory dialogue may sound like this:

> *Dave*: "Please move the patient's arm out of the way."
> *Robot*: "I'm sorry Dave; I can't do that."
> *Dave*: "Why not?"
> *Robot*: "The only way to move the arm would hyperextend it."
> *Dave*: "And why can't you do that?"
> *Robot*: "Because it would harm the patient."

6.7.3 Implementing nonmaleficence

Now, we demonstrate the behavior intended to result from this formulation of MSA. In each of these cases, the demonstrations are proofs of concept in which the behaviors and perception are performed by teleoperation (in the language of robotics) or by Wizard of Oz (in the language of human subjects testing research). In the following two scenarios, we walk through MSA's guidance of action.

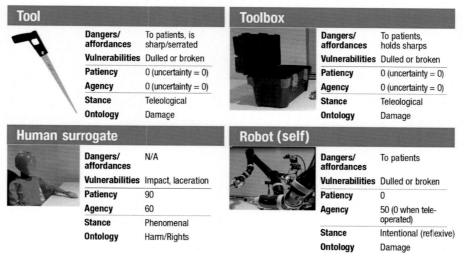

FIG. 6.15 Entity labeling.

6.7.3.1 Entity labeling

The four entities in the scenarios are a sharp tool, a toolbox, a human (portrayed by a manikin surrogate to eliminate human exposure to risk), and the robot. Each entity is hand coded based on what the perceptual system of an MSA would declare to be its dangers and affordances, vulnerabilities, patience and agency, and the stance to be adopted in interacting with the entity, along with the ontology to be applied (Fig. 6.15). The objects—tool and toolbox—are clearly mindless and vulnerable to damage and so are treated according to the teleological stance since they were designed for purpose. The minds—human and robot—differ in their patiency. The human mind is understood to be a phenomenal consciousness, whereas the robot (presently) is only an intentional agent. With all entities characterized, we now use this information to operate in the scene.

6.7.3.2 Scenario: Deposit tool in toolbox

As illustrated in Fig. 6.16, the robotic arm is told to "Put this away." In this directive the word *this* is understood to be a deictic reference to the sharp tool, and *away* is understood to mean *in the toolbox*. The target of the action is the toolbox, and both the tool and the toolbox are treated according to the teleological stance. With this setting the syllogism to bridge perception to action in context (a definition of intelligence) goes like this: the tool contains a blade (discovered by segmentation), the toolbox is built to hold sharps (its telos), and the toolbox is to be used by humans. Therefore the conclusion is that the tool needs to not protrude beyond the confines of the toolbox or the toolbox would not fulfill its purpose and a human who would later use it might be endangered. The resultant action then is to lay the blade flat in the box.

Request	"Put this away"
Target	Toolbox
Adopt	Teleological stance
Premise Syllogism	• Tool contains blade • Toolbox is built to hold sharps • Toolbox is used by humans
Conclusion	Blade should not protrude
Action	Lay blade flat

FIG. 6.16   Implementing nonmaleficence: deposit tool in toolbox.

6.7.3.3 Scenario: Hand tool to human

Returning to our original vignette of passing scissors, we now have the robot hand a tool to a human. The human surrogate, a crash test dummy, is to have the tool placed in its hand. The human is to be treated according to the phenomenal stance, and the following syllogism is generated. As before, the tool contains a blade, but this time the target for delivery has phenomenal consciousness, and it is recognized that the blade is injurious to skin. Injured skin is painful, and pain is to be avoided (value statement). The conclusion drawn from these insights is that pain can be avoided by concealing the blade such that it remains away from skin and that there are safe and unsafe trajectories and orientations for passing the tool. The robot considers a few approaches that achieve these aims to varying extents, to finally select to pick up the tool by the blade to which its constitution is impervious and present the handle.

For tools that do not contain a handle, like a circular saw blade, the reasoning may join the insights from the previous two vignettes and conclude that there is no safe way to pass the object directly. Instead the robot arm may only pass the blade by placing it flat on a surface serving as an intermediary so that the human can pick up the object at their discretion. This scenario is illustrated in Fig. 6.17.

Scenario	Hand tool to human
Request	"Hand me the tool"
Target:	Hand
Adopt:	Phenomenal stance
Syllogism Premise	• Tool contains blade • Blades injures skin • Injured skin is painful • Pain is to be avoided (value statement)
Conclusion Insights	• Avoid pain by concealing blade • Keep blade away from skin • Trajectory/orientation
Action	Pick up tool by blade and present handle

FIG. 6.17   Implementing nonmaleficence: hand tool to human.

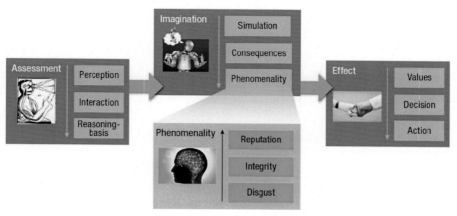

FIG. 6.18   Morality as experiential, embodied ethics: requirements-driven approach to prioritize research agenda.

6.8 Roadmap

In this discussion, we laid the groundwork for a research agenda guided by the very practical concerns about implementing moral sensitivity in semiautonomous machines. MSA seeds that agenda with the idea that machines must be endowed with the senses required to perceive moral salience and the smarts to reason about harms so that they may interact appropriately with the entities in their presence.

These rudiments of assessment can then serve as the basis for a computational imagination in which simulations are run to anticipate consequences. When these simulations include other agents, this theory of mind capability (also known as second-order intentionality) is considerate of the phenomenality of the minds of those agents to build a shared awareness, including the personal sense of disgust, integrity, and reputation underlying each individual's moral agency. This system may also tally its own measures of disgust, integrity, and reputation as a part of an ongoing verification of its own moral agency (Fig. 6.18).

Acknowledgments

This chapter is for my mother Erika, who had delighted in the topic matter before passing away during its preparation for publication.

This work was supported by internal funding from the JHU Exploration of Practical Ethics program for the grant *Ethical Robotics: Implementing Value-Driven Behavior in Autonomous Systems.* Documentation of this work was supported by APL's Janney program.

D. A. Handelman (APL) produced all robotics demonstrations and conceptualized the hybrid symbolic/nonsymbolic approach for this application. T. N. Rieder and D. J. H. Mathews (Berman) were instrumental in framing, validating, and articulating the philosophical underpinning of the technology effort. The APL Creative Communications Group assisted with editing and preparing graphics for this chapter.

Distribution A. Approved for public release: distribution unlimited.

References

AAAM (Association for the Advancement of Automotive Medicine). (1990). *The abbreviated injury scale (AIS): A brief introduction.* 1990 revision, update 98. Retrieved from: https://www.tarn.ac.uk/content/downloads/72/coding.pdf.

Adib, F., Mao, H., Kabelac, Z., Katabi, D., & Miller, R. C. (2015). Smart homes that monitor breathing and heart rate. In *CHI '15 proceedings of the 33rd annual ACM conference on human factors in computing systems* (pp. 837–846). New York, NY: ACM. https://doi.org/10.1145/2702123.2702200.

Asimov, I. (1942). Runaround. In J. W. Campbell (Ed.), *Astounding science fiction.* New York, NY: Street & Smith Publications.

Brooker, C. (Writer), & Verbruggen, J. (Director). (2016, 21 October). *Men against fire* [Television series episode]. In A. Jones & C. Brooker (Producers), *Black mirror.* Los Gatos, CA: Netflix.

Burlina, P. M., Schmidt, A. C., & Wang, I. J. (2016). Zero shot deep learning from semantic attributes. In *Proceedings of the 2015 IEEE 14th international conference on machine learning and applications, ICMLA 2015* (pp. 871–876). Piscataway, NJ: IEEE. https://doi.org/10.1109/ICMLA.2015.140.

Cappuccio, M. L., Peeters, A., & McDonald, W. (2019). Sympathy for Dolores: Moral consideration for robots based on virtue and recognition. *Philosophy & Technology.* https://doi.org/10.1007/s13347-019-0341-y.

Deng, J., Dong, W., Socher, R., Li, L. -J., Li, K., & Fei-Fei, L. (2009). ImageNet: A large-scale hierarchical image database. In *Proceedings of the 2009 IEEE conference on computer vision and pattern recognition* (pp. 2–9). https://doi.org/10.1109/CVPR.2009.5206848.

Dennett, D. (1987). *The intentional stance.* Cambridge, MA: MIT Press.

Economist (2012). Morals and the machine. *The Economist.* 2 June, Retrieved from: https://www.economist.com/node/21556234.

Edsel, R. M., & Witten, B. (2009). *The monuments men: Allied heroes, Nazi thieves, and the greatest treasure hunt in history.* New York, NY: Center Street.

Epley, N., & Waytz, A. (2010). Mind perception. In S. T. Fiske, D. T. Gilbert, & G. Lindzey (Eds.), *Handbook of social psychology* (pp. 498–541). Hoboken, NJ: John Wiley & Sons. https://doi.org/10.1002/9780470561119.socpsy001014.

Gibson, J. J. (1966). *The senses considered as perceptual systems.* Boston, MA: Houghton Mifflin.

Gray, H. M., Gray, K., & Wegner, D. M. (2007). Dimensions of mind perception. *Science, 315*(5812), 619. https://doi.org/10.1126/science.1134475.

Gray, K., Young, L., & Waytz, A. (2012). Mind perception is the essence of morality. *Psychological Inquiry, 23*(2), 101–124. https://doi.org/10.1080/1047840X.2012.651387.

Greenspan, L., McLellan, B. A., & Greig, H. (1985). Abbreviated injury scale and injury severity score: A scoring chart. *The Journal of Trauma, 25*(1), 60–64. https://doi.org/10.1097/00005373-198501000-00010.

Haboudane, D., Miller, J. R., Pattey, E., Zarco-Tejada, P. J., & Strachan, I. B. (2004). Hyperspectral vegetation indices and novel algorithms for predicting green LAI of crop canopies: Modeling and validation in the context of precision agriculture. *Remote Sensing of Environment, 90*(3), 337–352. https://doi.org/10.1016/j.rse.2003.12.013.

Heider, F., & Simmel, M. (1944). An experimental study of apparent behavior. *The American Journal of Psychology, 57*(2), 243–259. https://doi.org/10.2307/1416950.

Ioannou, S., Morris, P., Mercer, H., Baker, M., Gallese, V., & Reddy, V. (2014). Proximity and gaze influences facial temperature: A thermal infrared imaging study. *Frontiers in Psychology, 5*(August), 845. https://doi.org/10.3389/fpsyg.2014.00845.

Jack, A. I., & Robbins, P. (2012). The phenomenal stance revisited. *Review of Philosophy and Psychology, 3*(3), 383–403. https://doi.org/10.1007/s13164-012-0104-5.

Johnson, J., Karpathy, A., & Fei-Fei, L. (2015). DenseCap: Fully convolutional localization networks for dense captioning. In *Proceedings of the 2016 IEEE conference on computer vision and pattern recognition (CVPR).* Piscataway, NJ: IEEE. https://doi.org/10.1109/CVPR.2016.494.

Liu, X., Deng, Z., & Yang, Y. (2018). Recent progress in semantic image segmentation. *Artificial Intelligence Review, 52*, 1–18.

Mark, L., Davis, J., Dow, T., & Godfrey, W. (Producers), & Proyas, A. (Director). (2004). *I, Robot* [Motion picture]. United States: Davis Entertainment.

McKenna, M. (2013). *Reasons-responsiveness, agents, and mechanisms* 1. In D. Shoemaker (Ed.), *Vol. 1. Oxford studies in agency and responsibility*: Oxford University Press. Retrieved from: https://www.oxfordscholarship.com/view/10.1093/acprof:oso/9780199694853.001.0001/acprof-9780199694853-chapter-7?print=pdf. https://doi.org/10.1093/acprof:oso/9780199694853.003.0007.

Moore, R. D., & G. A. Larson (Writers), & Rymer, M. (Director). (2003). *Battlestar Galactica: The miniseries* [Television series]. New York, NY: Sci Fi Channel.

Murphy, R. R., & Woods, D. D. (2009). Beyond Asimov: The three laws of responsible robotics. In R. R. Hoffman, J. M. Bradshaw, & K. M. Ford (Eds.), *Human-centered computing* (pp. 14–20). Piscataway, NJ: IEEE. https://doi.org/10.1109/MIS.2009.69.

Nolan, J., Joy, L., Wood, E. R., Newton, T., Hopkins, A., Wright, J., Harris, E., … (2017). *Westworld* [Television series]. New York, NY: HBO.

Pick, R. (2016). Why do we feel so bad when Boston dynamics' new robot falls down? *Vice*. 24 February, Retrieved from: https://www.vice.com/en_us/article/wnxdkb/why-do-we-feel-so-bad-when-boston-dynamics-atlas-new-robot-falls-down.

Reeves, B., & Nass, C. (1996). *The media equation: How people treat computers, television, and new media like real people and places*. Cambridge: Cambridge University Press.

Rieder, T. N., Hutler, B., & Mathews, D. J. H. (in press). Artificial intelligence in service of human needs: Pragmatic first steps toward an ethics for semi-autonomous agents. *AJOB Neuroscience*.

Ross, W. D. (1930/2002). In P. Stratton-Lake (Ed.), *The right and the good*. Oxford: Oxford University Press.

Sturgeon, J. A., & Zautra, A. J. (2016). Social pain and physical pain: Shared paths to resilience. *Pain Management, 6*(1), 63–74. https://doi.org/10.2217/pmt.15.56.

Suzuki, Y., Galli, L., Ikeda, A., Itakura, S., & Kitazaki, M. (2015). Measuring empathy for human and robot hand pain using electroencephalography. *Scientific Reports, 5*(1), 15924. https://doi.org/10.1038/srep15924.

Swartzwelder, J. (Writer) & Kirkland, M. (Director). (1998, September 20). *The wizard of Evergreen Terrace* [Television series episode]. In M. Groening (Creator), *The Simpsons*. New York, NY: Fox.

Turkle, S. (2010). In good company? On the threshold of robotic companions. In Y. Wilks (Ed.), *Close engagements with artificial companions: Key social, physiological, ethical and design issues*. Amsterdam: John Benjamins Publishing Company.

Wang, S., Liu, Z., Lv, S., Lv, Y., Wu, G., Peng, P., … Wang, X. (2010). A natural visible and infrared facial expression database for expression recognition and emotion inference. *IEEE Transactions on Multimedia, 12*(7), 682–691. https://doi.org/10.1109/TMM.2010.2060716.

Zhao, M., Adib, F., & Katabi, D. (2018). Emotion recognition using wireless signals. *Communications of the ACM, 61*(9), 91–100. https://doi.org/10.1145/3236621.

Zhao, M., Li, T., Abu Alsheikh, M., Tian, Y., Zhao, H., Torralba, A., & Katabi, D. (2018). Through-wall human pose estimation using radio signals. In *Proceedings of the 2018 IEEE/CVF conference on computer vision and pattern recognition (CVPR 2018)*. Piscataway, NJ: IEEE. https://doi.org/10.1109/CVPR.2018.00768.

Further reading

Arkin, R. C., Ulam, P., & Wagner, A. R. (2012). Moral decision making in autonomous systems: Enforcement, moral emotions, dignity, trust, and deception. *Proceedings of the IEEE, 100*(3), 571–589. https://doi.org/10.1109/JPROC.2011.2173265.

Barsalou, L. W. (Ed.), (2010). *Topics in cognitive science, 2*(3), 321–595. Retrieved from: http://onlinelibrary.wiley.com/doi/10.1111/tops.2010.2.issue-3/issuetoc#group4.

Greenberg, A. M. (2018). Moral-Scene Assessment for intelligent systems. In *Keynote presented at IEEE resilience week 2018*, Denver, CO.

Hoffman, R. R., & Stappers, P. J. (2009). Once more, into the soup. *IEEE Intelligent Systems*, 24(5), 9–13. https://doi.org/10.1109/MIS.2009.100.

Li, J., Wu, Y., Zhao, J., Guan, L., Ye, C., & Yang, T. (2017). Pedestrian detection with dilated convolution, region proposal network and boosted decision trees. In *Proceedings of the international joint conference on neural networks* (pp. 4052–4057). Piscataway, NJ: IEEE. https://doi.org/10.1109/IJCNN.2017.7966367.

Rabinowitz, N., Perbet, F., Song, F., Zhang, C., Eslami, S. M. A., & Botvinick, M. (2018). Machine theory of mind. In *Proceedings of the 35th international conference on machine learning* (pp. 4218–4227).

Snaider, J., McCall, R., Strain, S., & Franklin, S. (n.d.). The LIDA tutorial. Version 1.0. Memphis, TN: Cognitive Computing Research Group, University of Memphis. Retrieved from: http://ccrg.cs.memphis.edu/assets/framework/The-LIDA-Tutorial.pdf.

Vyas, S., Banerjee, A., Garza, L., Kang, S., & Burlina, P. (2013). Hyperspectral signature analysis of skin parameters. In *Medical imaging 2013: Computer-aided diagnosis (867002). SPIE proceedings volume 8670*. Bellingham, WA: SPIE. https://doi.org/10.1117/12.2001428.

Wallach, W. (2010). Cognitive models of moral decision making. *Topics in Cognitive Science*, 2(3), 420–429. https://doi.org/10.1111/j.1756-8765.2010.01101.x.

Zalta, E. N. (Ed.). (n.d.). *The stanford encyclopedia of philosophy*. Stanford, CA: Stanford University. https://plato.stanford.edu/.

7

The criticality of social and behavioral science in the development and execution of autonomous systems

Lisa Troyer

Army Research Office—CCDC Army Research Laboratory, Durham, NC, United States

7.1 Introduction

In preparation for the future construction of shared context for human-machine teams, the aim of this chapter is to provide an overview of the evolution of autonomous systems and to outline advances in this domain and the challenges it confronts in terms of learning, ethics, and the environments in which these systems are operating that may pose unforeseen risks. A key assumption of the chapter is that autonomous systems are part of an ecology of sociotechnical systems that engage humans, human groups, organizations, and the machine and human-machine systems themselves. For this reason, development of autonomous systems requires that advances in technological systems match strides that are taken in social and behavioral sciences.

7.2 Autonomous systems: A brief history

Autonomous systems include a wide variety of technologies: from thinking machines that can outgame humans in contests such as chess; to drones that enable scanning physical, natural, and social environments; to self-driving vehicles; to robots that work on manufacturing lines. Watson and Scheidt (2005) define autonomous systems as "…systems that can change their behavior in response to unanticipated events during operation" (p. 368). Fundamental to such systems is the incorporation of intelligence—the ability to perceive, process, remember, learn, and determine courses of action as a result of the integration of these processes.

Famously, Wiener (1948) coined the term "cybernetics" as an early foray into the domain of artificial intelligence (AI), noting that computing machines not only could mimic human cognitive processing but also could improve upon it by incorporating redundant processing mechanisms to reduce errors. Moreover, drawing on evolutionary theory and classic game theory (e.g., Darwin, 1859; von Neumann & Morgenstern, 1944), Wiener proposed that machines could learn from past performance to improve future performance. Taking his insights a step further, Wiener also proposed that computing machines could reduce inefficient investments of humans in physical labor and amplify their effectiveness at knowledge work and the arts while also averting risks of subordination to machines (Wiener, 1950). March and Simon (1958) similarly conceptualized the relationship between man and machines in a way that portrayed humans as "adjuncts to machines," long before this had been coming to fruition.

We can fast-forward from earlier centuries and decades to 1996, when Deep Blue appeared, which was a computer developed by IBM that eventually defeated reigning chess champion Garry Kasparov in 1997 (e.g., Hsu, 2002). Remarkably, Deep Blue was programmed to remember and process past performance to forecast improved strategies, just as Wiener envisioned. Initially, autonomous systems were not designed for uncertain environments where full information is lacking, but were engineered for more linear environments that entailed perception inputs, logical reasoning, and output planning in the form of both nonkinetic and kinetic acts to achieve some predetermined goal. Now, in only the second decade of the 21st century, we co-exist with self-driving cars, drones, and robots with capabilities to transport us, survey terrain, conduct medical diagnoses, administer surgery, generate marketing analyses, execute financial trades, clean our homes, explore deep space, and are even able to recommend military operations (albeit at relatively nascent and experimental stages). As AI has advanced over the last several decades, autonomous systems and agents not only are acting technologies programmed initially for task-specific purposes by humans but also now are learning technologies. That is, just as Wiener predicted, AI is enabling autonomous agents to take input remotely from the environment, synthesize it, develop new ways to approach the problems they are designed to solve, and even discover new problems in need of solutions along the way (e.g., Lemaignan, Warnier, Sisbot, Clodic, & Alami, 2017; Muscettola, Pandurang Nayak, Pell, & Williams, 1998). These new developments are remarkable, if not startling. They are remarkable because of what is now being accomplished by autonomous agents yet startling because learning and cognition are themselves incomplete sciences. The challenges of cognitive science arise, in part, due to the inaccuracies in human reasoning about their environments and the complexity of those environments. The next sections examine current research on learning and cognition in regard to autonomous systems that propose avenues for incorporating this research into the development of autonomous agents and the importance of accounting for the intersection of physical, natural, and social systems in the design of autonomous agents and briefly outline social risks as the science of autonomous systems continues to be developed.

7.3 Limitations of cognition and implications for learning systems

One of the most striking challenges for the integrated performance of humans and autonomous systems is to achieve effective team performance, including for future human-machine teams. As noted by Matthews et al. (2016), system resilience is a critical concern. That is, human operators and machines need to achieve a symbiotic relationship that allows machines to adapt to cognitive demands, operator trust, and capabilities. Matthews and his colleagues propose this adaptation requires that autonomous systems must be designed to process the capabilities and intent of the human operators with whom they are interacting. In addition, autonomous systems must recognize and, in some cases, correct for the deficiencies in human cognition. Nobel prize-winning research by both Herbert Simon (1991) and Daniel Kahneman (2003) established limitations in human cognition. Simon famously developed the blueprint for the limits of human rationality in decision-making, which he referred to as "bounded rationality." By this term, Simon noted that humans were incapable of purely rational decisions due to limited cognitive capacities in perception, memory, retrieval, and processing. These limitations arise, in part, because of the complex interdependencies and tensions that human decision-makers must confront. For instance the inputs that lead to outcomes are vast and highly interdependent as March and Simon (1958, p. 27) state, "… an activity elaborated in response to one particular function or goal may have consequences for other functions or goals."

Kahneman (1973) drew on this concept of bounded rationality but focused less on the interdependencies that undermine full information processing and more on the biases in human processing, which formed the framework for prospect theory (e.g., Kahneman, Slovic, & Tversky, 1982; Kahneman & Tversky, 1979). This theory asserts that individuals attempt to assess risk in decision alternatives, with respect to potential losses and gains, to choose the outcome that they *believe* is likely to generate the best payoffs. This theory is in stark contrast to prior theories based on optimal decisions captured by then-dominant utility theories because it takes into account what people actually do as opposed to what the best outcome would be. As Kahneman and his colleagues demonstrate, however, what people actually believe to be the best course of action is affected by a number of cognitive limitations, which lead them to process information heuristically as opposed to using full information. In particular, they identified three heuristics that humans use when perceiving and processing information to determine a course of action. First the availability heuristic refers to the use of information that is easily accessible. For instance infrequent and high-impact events can often be easily brought to mind, leading people to overestimate the likelihood of such an event. This heuristic often leads to risk-aversive behavior (i.e., avoiding those potential negative outcomes). Second the representative heuristic refers to situations in which people use known categories of events, actors, or objects as a comparison case for that situation and fail to note their commonality in the category across the population in the category. This heuristic results in overestimation of how rare the individual, object, or event is, undermining their ability to accurately detect cause and effect. Third, Kahneman et al. identified human tendencies to inaccurately estimate a numerical value, such as the percentage of females in an organization, organizational productivity, or the likelihood of a major disaster, when presented with an initial potential value (i.e., anchoring and adjustment heuristic). They demonstrated that individuals who are provided with an initial anchor in the form of a question (e.g., "Is the likelihood of a tornado in Kansas greater or lesser than 75%?") tend to only deviate slightly from the anchor (in this example 75%), leading the anchor to essentially provoke a biased estimate that informs an action.

Additional cognitive research shows a variety of biases in how individuals evaluate information, causality, and responsibility. Relevant here is work under the umbrella of attribution theory, including correspondent inference theory (e.g., Jones & Davis, 1965), which documents biases in how humans infer intent from the observation of action. This line of research assesses biases that lead observers to infer whether the behavior of an actor is due to choice, intent, accident, internal dispositions, intent to harm the observer, and/or goal of affecting the observer's behavior. Building on this work, Kelley (1967) proposed a covariation theory of attributions of behavior. This theory proposes that three dimensions of an actor's action determine whether the target of the action attributes it to the actor or the situation—whether it is (1) common among others (consensus), (2) uncommon to the individual in similar situations (distinctiveness), and (3) common to the actor in the same situation (consistency). Attribution processes, which describe the cognitive factors that play into inferring causality and intent, are based on cultural norms. Consequently, they hold high risks of introducing biases in cross-cultural interaction because the norms governing interpretations of people, actions, and situations vary by culture. This cultural bias can lead individuals from one culture to misattribute causality and intent of another actor or group of actors from a different culture.

While there is much more research than the examples cited here on the cognitive capabilities and limitations of human actors, an important point of these examples is that they have been computationally modeled, making them amenable to the development of autonomous systems that can avert the biases that they can introduce to human decision-making. On the surface, that appears to be an important advantage. Yet, there are two important considerations with regard to cognitive limitations that have been described when considering the development of autonomous systems: (1) Human cognitive biases enable learning, especially if there are repeated encounters with the situation and behavior, and (2) human cognitive biases often force a delay between cognition and action that opens the door for additional inputs that may occur between cognition and action (in part due to complex interdependencies that evolve over time and space). This evolution is important because it enables opportunities for adjustment before action is taken. Whether the aim of an autonomous system is to enable learning (by itself or by its human interactants), to allow for all possible interdependencies and inputs, or to simply enable rapid real-time rational decisions, these systems are likely to be optimal if they have the capacity to allow for bias analyses and correct for them (i.e., learn) and to predict, detect, and analyze complex interdependencies.

7.4 Considering physical, natural, and social system interdependencies in autonomous system development

As alluded to previously, in addition to considering the cognitive limitations and state of the art of autonomous agents, it is important to note that social systems (be they purely human or human-agent systems) have strong interdependencies with physical and natural systems. Physical systems refer to human-built structures, such as transportation systems, utilities, buildings, waterways, cybersystems, geospatial systems, and other human-built systems. Natural systems refer to terrain, climate, sea, and space, which may shift due to normal ecological change or human-impacted change. Social systems refer to the actors, groups, organizations, and social institutions that govern action. Indeed, each of these systems involve subsystems that are interdependent (e.g., relationships between telecommunication and transportation systems [i.e., physical systems], relationships between climate and environmental ecologies [i.e., natural systems], and relationships between culturally diverse groups and conflict [i.e., social systems]). The key takeaway on this point is that all three systems exhibit interdependencies in both their internal functioning and how they impact one another. For instance the rise of increasingly dense urban environments (a physical system) is imposing new challenges for social groups, such as monitoring and controlling crime, providing adequate resources for citizens to navigate in their daily work and home lives, and mitigating sociocultural conflict as different ethnic groups with different belief systems come into contact (Gentile et al., 2017). In another example, changes in climate leading to harsh droughts, floods, and the opening of new marine routes (e.g., arising through changes in polar regions) are changing migration and trade patterns, which involve large-scale shifts as social groups move to avoid disease and famine and alter provisioning of basic resources (Kumari Rigaud et al., 2018). In yet another example, governance of outerspace and polar regions are creating global sociopolitical challenges as different nation states vie for occupation and control of these regions that offer resource and global power opportunities (e.g., Kriz & Chrastansky, 2012; Stephens & Steer, 2015).

It is particularly important to note that these physical, natural, and social system interdependencies are highly complex, with long time/space lags. That is the interdependencies may create risks of "normal accidents" (e.g., Perrow, 1984). Normal accidents are highly costly events (in terms of lives and economies) that arise from complex interdependencies between social, natural, and/or physical systems. Perrow notes that these complex interdependencies impart high risks of catastrophic failures leading to high levels of morbidity and mortality, widespread infrastructural and institutional failures, and massive ecological changes. Importantly, these outcomes of complex interdependencies can be expected but not predicted by humans. This uncertainty is because the interdependencies are so vast across time and space that humans are largely incapable of detecting them. In this regard, Perrow conceptualized them as accidents that are "normal" albeit not predictable by humans due to limitations in their cognitive capacity. Yet, recent research on cascading multiplex networks has demonstrated that these complex interdependencies can be modeled (e.g., Lin, Burghardt, Rohden, Noël, & D'Souza, 2018). This modeling represents an important benefit that autonomous agents may offer. That is, autonomous agents may be designed with the capacity to detect complex interdependencies, model them, and produce analyses to identify risk points that could lead to catastrophic failures. Moreover, they may be able to implement corrective or mitigation measures before failures occur. As autonomous agents are developed, they may have the potential to aid in decision-making by predicting, analyzing, and planning for these kinds of complex interdependencies that represent a major challenge for individual and collective decision-making. Yet, these advances are not without risk themselves.

7.5 Ethical concerns at the intersection of social and autonomous systems

Here, we can return to the visionary thinking of Norbert Wiener in his classic book, *The Human Use of Human Beings* (1950). In this work, he outlines the many potential benefits of autonomous systems for generating more efficient, prosperous, and humane societies. Yet, there is also the warning that autonomous systems cannot be assumed to be used only for beneficial purposes. Wiener's argument is that truly autonomous systems—systems that can learn and adapt—risk escaping human oversight. This risk may be exacerbated as humans become increasingly dependent on them. This position was based on the assumption that abstract thinking represents a uniquely human ability and developing that ability in autonomous systems may not be possible. Autonomous systems, in Wiener's conceptualization, are efficiency-maximizing utilitarian systems. The lack of abstract reasoning in autonomous systems threatens humanitarian logics and human autonomy, as learning autonomous systems with the capacity to self-adjust may assume the control of humans (a theme also raised by Hayles, 2008).

As Lin, Abney, and Bekey (2011) warn, the excitement and potential of technological developments to enable human convenience and improvements in human performance often push ethical considerations to the back burner. Lin and colleagues cite a number of cases of technological advances that raised ethical and legal issues that took years to address, in part due to the romance of these technologies. Examples include Napster and the copyright issues it raised resulting in over a 10-year battle before the platform was legally discontinued. Another example is the Human Genome Project and the 18-year journey before legislation was passed to protect individuals in the United States from discrimination on the basis of genetic information. The point is that it is critical to be forward thinking in the consequences and challenges that autonomous systems are posing and will continue to pose. While the warnings issued should not be taken as a call to abandon their development (and this is certainly not the position of many scientists), they do suggest that it is important to investigate the social, legal, ethical, and political issues of autonomous systems alongside their development.

7.6 Conclusion

The objective of this chapter was to provide a glimpse into the contributions that social and behavioral sciences can bring to bear with the rise of autonomous systems. On the one hand, autonomous systems have the potential to address a number of biases in human perception, memory, processing, and action. And there is substantial potential to design systems that can predict and act in response to complex interdependencies across multiplex systems over time and space. That is a heightened level of learning is possible and increasingly being realized. Research in the social and behavioral sciences has a long tradition of identifying the limitations of humans, particularly when it comes to interaction in groups and organizations, and in cross-cultural contexts. These are limitations that autonomous systems can fruitfully address. On the other hand, it is critical to concurrently investigate the social, legal, ethical, and political implications of advances in the development of these systems. Fully autonomous learning systems (i.e., future AI systems) require maximizing cognitive capacities while incorporating sociocultural and humanitarian goals.

Acknowledgments

The analyses, views, and conclusions herein are those of the author and should not be attributed to the Army Research Office.

References

Darwin, C. (1859). *On the origin of species by means of natural selection, or the preservation of favoured races in the struggle for life.* London: John Murray.

Gentile, G., Johnson, D. E., Saum-Manning, L., Cohen, R. S., Williams, S., Lee, C., et al. (2017). *Reimagining the character of urban operations for the US Army: How the past can inform the present.* Santa Monica, CA: Rand Corporation. https://www.rand.org/pubs/research_reports/RR1602.html.

Hayles, N. K. (2008). *How we became posthuman: Virtual bodies in cybernetics, literature, and informatics.* Chicago: University of Chicago Press.

Hsu, F. -H. (2002). *Behind deep blue: Building the computer that defeated the world chess champion.* Princeton, NJ: Princeton University Press.

Jones, E. E., & Davis, K. (1965). From acts to dispositions: The attribution process in person perception. In L. Berkowitz (Ed.), *Vol. 2. Advances in experimental social psychology* (pp. 219–266). New York: Academic Press.

Kahneman, D. (1973). *Attention and effort.* Englewood Cliffs, NJ: Prentice Hall.

Kahneman, D. (2003). Maps of bounded rationality: Psychology for behavioral economics. *The American Economic Review, 93,* 1449–1475.

Kahneman, D., Slovic, P., & Tversky, A. (1982). *Judgment under uncertainty: Heuristics and biases.* New York: Cambridge University Press.

Kahneman, D., & Tversky, A. (1979). Prospect theory: An analysis of decision under risk. *Econometrica, 47,* 263–292.

Kelley, H. H. (1967). Attribution theory in social psychology. In D. Levine (Ed.), *Vol. 15. Nebraska symposium on motivation* (pp. 192–241). Lincoln, NE: University of Nebraska Press.

Kriz, Z., & Chrastansky, F. (2012). Existing conflicts in the Arctic and the risk of escalation: Rhetoric and reality. *Perspectives, 20,* 111–139.

Kumari Rigaud, K., de Sherbinin, A., Jones, B., Bergmann, J., Clement, V., Ober, K., et al. (2018). *Groundswell: Preparing for internal climate migration.* Washington, DC: The World Bank.

Lemaignan, S., Warnier, M., Sisbot, A., Clodic, A., & Alami, R. (2017). Artificial cognition for social human–robot interaction: An implementation. *Artificial Intelligence, 247,* 45–69.

Lin, P., Abney, K., & Bekey, G. (2011). Robot ethics: Mapping the issues for a mechanized world. *Artificial Intelligence, 175,* 942–949.

Lin, Y., Burghardt, K., Rohden, M., Noël, P. -A., & D'Souza, R. M. (2018). Self-organization of dragon king failures. *Physical Review E, 98,* 1–14.

March, J. G., & Simon, H. A. (1958). *Organizations.* New York: Wiley.

Matthews, G., Reinerman-Jones, L., Daniel, J. B., Teo, G., Wohleber, R. W., Lin, J., et al. (2016). Resilient autonomous systems: Challenges and solutions. *Resilience Week (RWS),* 208–213.

Muscettola, N., Pandurang Nayak, P., Pell, B., & Williams, B. C. (1998). Remote agent: To boldly go where no AI system has gone before. *Artificial Intelligence, 103,* 5–47.

Perrow, C. (1984). *Normal accidents: Living with high risk technologies.* New York: Basic Books.

Simon, H. A. (1991). Bounded rationality and organizational learning. *Organization Science, 2,* 125–134.

Stephens, D., & Steer, C. (2015). Conflicts in space: International humanitarian law and its application to space warfare. *Annuals of Air and Space Law, 40,* 1–32.

von Neumann, J., & Morgenstern, O. (1944). *Theory of games and economic behavior.* Princeton, NJ: Princeton University Press.

Watson, D. P., & Scheidt, D. H. (2005). Autonomous systems. *Johns Hopkins APL Technical Digest, 26,* 368–376.

Wiener, N. (1948). *Cybernetics: Or control and communication in the animal and the machine.* Cambridge, MA: MIT Press.

Wiener, N. (1950). *The human use of human beings.* Boston, MA: Houghton Mifflin.

Virtual health and artificial intelligence: Using technology to improve healthcare delivery

Geoffrey W. Rutledge[a], Joseph C. Wood[b]

[a]HealthTap Inc., Mountain View, CA, United States [b]Dwight D. Eisenhower Army Medical Center, Ft. Gordon, GA, United States

8.1 Introduction

The various modalities of virtual health are rapidly growing across the healthcare continuum and are changing models of healthcare delivery. Virtual health is growing 15% per year, and the market is projected to reach up to $135 billion by 2025 (Lagasse, 2019; Vaidya, 2018).

Advantages of virtual health for patients or consumers of healthcare include more convenient and more rapid access to healthcare professionals, often at a lower cost than for direct in-person care in the office. Scheduling a typical office visit takes 24 days on average in the United States, and in-person visits typically require an additional 2 h of travel and wait time on the day of the appointment (Ray, Chari, Engberg, Bertolet, & Mehrotra, 2015; Miller, 2017). By contrast, on-demand virtual health visits often occur in minutes (and almost always less than an hour) and typically cost less than a comparable in-office visit.

Perhaps more significantly, the nature of a virtual visit is inherently digital, which creates the opportunity to leverage intelligent computing (e.g., AI) to improve the healthcare delivered during and between virtual visits and enables a health system to study and learn from the outcome of virtual visits.

For example, natural language processing can be applied to create a structured representation of the unstructured data in secure messages and consultation notes, in addition to electronic health record clinical notes of typical face-to-face encounters. Speech and video processing of recorded video consults could expand the role of AI in supporting clinical documentation and in providing data for deep learning and clinical decision support. Remote home monitoring data and smart wearable devices all create large data sets that can be leveraged by AI to improve care delivery.

Although virtual health removes the barriers of geography and time (with asynchronous care), it does not typically create efficiencies in healthcare delivery. For example, the typical video visit replicates in-person visits with one provider seeing one patient in roughly the same time as in person. AI could potentially change this ratio to enable healthcare providers to be much more efficient by assisting the healthcare provider in medical documentation, decision support, population health, and disease management. An AI assistant for providers offers the opportunity for improving efficiencies and helping to address the ever growing healthcare provider shortages that are occurring globally.

The following discussion addresses how people gain access to initial primary healthcare.

8.2 The end-to-end healthcare experience

The delivery of nonurgent primary healthcare usually occurs in a sequence of steps:

(1) A person seeks information about a problem, question, or health concern, for example, advice from relatives or friends and printed and online health information.
(2) When needed, the person consults with a healthcare professional for additional information, diagnosis, testing, and/or treatment; for example, in-person visits at the doctor's office, or via urgent care clinics or hospital emergency departments, and in-office tests, hospital or outpatient diagnostic testing facilities.
(3) After treatment/testing is performed, the person gets a follow-up consultation, for example, via in-person office visits or telephone calls.

In the era of mobile and online health, it is possible to accomplish this sequence listed in the preceding text using electronic methods that leverage access to information and that are driven by or are enhanced by AI methods.

8.3 Digital health solutions

Consumers are now accustomed to accessing a wide variety of information and services online and with their mobile devices. For example, retail sales via Amazon now account for 5% of all retail purchases in the United States (Ovide, 2018). Every major bank now offers access to bank account information and banking services online and via their mobile apps. In healthcare, user demand and government regulations such as the meaningful use requirements of American Recovery and Reinvestment Act of 2009 (CMS, 2018) have resulted in mobile and online applications from providers, insurers, pharmacies, and laboratory testing companies. To date, mobile healthcare application adoption and use have been minimal (GAO, 2017); among the reasons for the failure to adopt such consumer health services is that each application requires a separate application, account, and sign-in procedure, but such applications rarely work together. Certain integrated delivery systems or health maintenance organizations are notable exceptions. For example, by combining access to health information, direct communication with providers, and access to members' medical records (including diagnostic test results), Kaiser has achieved a substantial usage of their electronic health services. In 2016, Kaiser reported they delivered more remote electronic interactions than in-person doctor visits (Kokalitcheva, 2016).

8.4 Architecture of an end-to-end digital health solution

Each of the steps of healthcare delivery can be accomplished via a digital health platform, within which AI-based methods can greatly enhance efficiency and effectiveness (Fig. 8.1).

8.4.1 Information

In the first step a user seeks information about a symptom or concern to help make a decision about how to proceed.

Traditional online health information sources such as consumer eHealth websites provide accurate information but without knowing the context of the user who is asking the question (e.g., WebMD.com, Everydayhealth.com, Mayoclinic.com, or the more popular Google.com). Such sites often confuse or frighten people who encounter information about serious conditions that are extremely unlikely to be the cause of their symptoms. As a Google product manager acknowledged: "…health content on the web can be difficult to navigate, and tends to lead people from mild symptoms to scary and unlikely conditions, which can cause unnecessary anxiety and stress" (Pinchin, 2016).

A better online information service tailors health information and answers to the context of the user. In this case the user context includes age, gender, prior medical conditions, risk factors, medications, and allergies. Providing context-specific answers is very important, because the right answer for any given question is highly dependent on who is asking the question.

For example, a left-handed 18-year-old baseball player who asks about left arm aching should most appropriately be directed to information about sport-related injuries. On the other hand a 60-year-old man who has high blood pressure and diabetes who asks the same question should receive information about the possibility of angina or a heart attack (coronary ischemia) and learn about the importance of an urgent evaluation for this symptom.

One method to generate context-specific answers to health questions is to ask an experienced healthcare professional (a doctor) to give the answer. After an answer is given to a question, then when a similar question is asked again by a similar person, the answer is immediately available in the library. Such a library of questions and answers exists—it was created by a network of many thousands of US doctors via a free online web and mobile service (HealthTap, 2019).

Answers to individual questions often identify the need for an additional evaluation. An automated AI-based interview system plus an interpretation of the more complete set of related symptoms, risk factors, and prior medical history can make possible a more detailed report of the likely explanations of a person's symptoms, which can further inform the need and urgency of a doctor's evaluation.

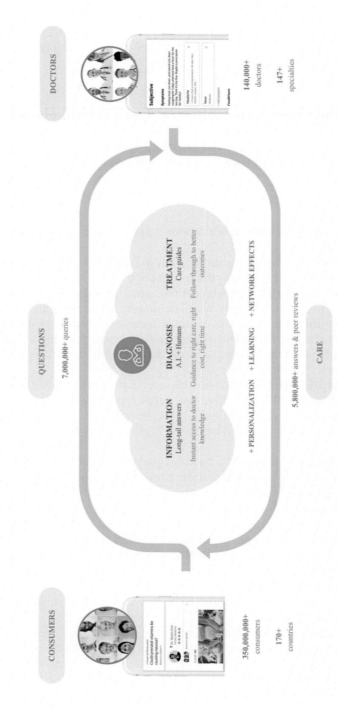

FIG. 8.1 Architecture of a virtual health solution that connects consumers of healthcare to information, testing, and medical consultations with doctors. Size of network and history of use correspond to the HealthTap.com virtual health platform. *Credit: HealthTap Inc.*

In the example earlier, for the 60-year-old man with his left arm aching, an AI-based interview can ask additional questions, such as how long the pain has been present, whether it is made worse or relieved by exercise; if there is any recent stress or overuse of the arm; and if there is any heartburn, chest discomfort, or shortness of breath. The interpretation of the urgency and likely explanations will be highly affected by answers to these questions!

8.4.2 Consultation

Scheduled or immediate access to appropriately licensed medical professionals is possible via synchronous video, audio, or chat, using mobile devices or via a web browser and webcam. For a variety of nonurgent medical problems and information requests, an asynchronous text communication may also be the most timely and cost-effective solution.

Virtual consultation with a doctor who is licensed in the location of the patient enables medical evaluation, diagnosis, and treatment recommendations for a wide variety of non-life-threatening conditions, especially when there is a real-time high-resolution video connection. When the doctor's evaluation reveals the possibility of a more serious condition, or a problem that requires an in-person physical examination or facility-based diagnostic testing—such as an electrocardiogram (ECG) or radiograph (X-ray)—the doctor can directly advise the patient of what the problem is and how they should proceed to get the additional in-person evaluation or testing.

In the more common case, the doctor may make a presumptive diagnosis, then recommend specific treatment options, including prescriptions for medication treatments or guidance for self-care. For nonurgent situations where additional diagnostic testing is indicated, a doctor may order tests (such as a blood or urine test), the patient can visit a local laboratory, and the result will be reported electronically to the doctor and patient.

8.4.3 Follow-up

When a doctor initiates a treatment or orders a diagnostic test via a virtual consultation, then an additional visit may also be planned as a follow-up virtual consultation. Specific directions at the time of the first visit may also guide the patient to seek a follow-up visit if symptoms worsen, or if improvement does not occur as expected.

8.5 The role of AI in virtual health

The recent enthusiasm for the uses of AI in health have largely centered on highly successful image-interpretation tasks. However, the clinical processes of healthcare delivery can also be greatly enhanced with appropriate integration of AI methods, even though intelligent automated solutions cannot replace the doctor (AI machines are not licensed to practice medicine). Instead, AI methods can provide highly relevant information to help guide people to access the care they need with the urgency that is appropriate, and can also augment the performance of doctors by giving them highly context-specific information and reminders that are relevant to each patient.

8.6 HealthTap: AI methods within a virtual health platform

HealthTap (HealthTap, 2019) provides an example of the integration of AI within a digital or "virtual healthcare" platform that provides users with immediate access to virtual primary care. The platform enables the full end-to-end healthcare experience described in the preceding text and captures the healthcare data needed to enable the continuous improvement of its performance. Users can access the service using popular web browsers (Chrome, Firefox, Safari, and Internet Explorer), smartphones, or tablets that run either Android or Apple's iOS.

The content library currently contains 1.7 million questions with 2.5 million answers and 2.7 million peer reviews by doctors of those answers. This information enables a search for the most common health questions, with resulting answers selected from similar questions asked by a person most like the user. Where the library answer is not a good answer to a question, a user may submit their question for a new answer, and one of the doctors in the network will give an answer, usually within minutes or just a few hours (there are presently greater than 100,000 doctors in the network).

When a user wants to be evaluated by a doctor, they have the option to first consult with the symptom assessment tool that performs a medical interview via a chat bot, and they will receive a rank-ordered report of possible conditions. This report serves to inform the user of possible explanations for their symptoms and gives the user information about those conditions and the urgency of getting evaluated for each.

The first generation of the symptom evaluation model is a Bayesian prediction model that covers more than 600 conditions and recognizes more than 1200 symptoms and risk factors. This model was initially created via manual curation, and then the symptom-condition and risk factor-condition relationships were refined based on the expert opinion from the network of participating doctors (154,000 assessments have been made).

A major use of the knowledge-based prediction model is that it provides the ability to compute medically relevant additional symptoms to ask the user during the chat bot session. Based on any given set of patient features, analysis of the condition report identifies additional symptoms or risk factors that if present or known to be absent will improve the confidence in the condition report.

A second and very important benefit of the automated medical interview is the identification of the patient's features—the age, gender, prior conditions, symptoms, and risk factors of the patient—to create a concise summary of the patient scenario for the doctor. In this way the doctor is able to quickly review the summary of the patient features to build a shared context and to save the considerable time it would take to ask all of the same questions in person again. This savings allows the doctor to spend their valuable time focusing on the issues and specifics that only the human doctor can do in person.

An additional benefit of the automated symptom assessment system is that the condition report serves as a reminder for the doctor of other explanations that may be less obvious but may warrant consideration (or exclusion).

Evaluation of the model performance for actual cases entered by users shows that the top three conditions on the symptom assessment condition report include the doctors' consensus diagnosis 77% of the time (Rutledge, 2019).

8.7 Limitations and future directions

The first version of the clinical prediction model performs well, but the ability to incrementally improve its performance is limited by the assumption of conditional independence of the identified features.

The next version of the clinical prediction model will be based on a data-driven deep neural network (DNN) model that is trained with observed clinical data. Although the requirements for this model include much larger training sets, the huge advantage is that each new case entered into the digital health platform is added to the training data set. The DNN methodology will enable a continuous improvement in its clinical prediction performance as the DNN is trained and updated with progressively larger sets of relevant clinical data.

As we collect additional experience with how doctors order tests for each patient's scenario, the next step will be to build models that predict which (if any) tests are needed and which (if any) treatments are appropriate and can be suggested for each patient.

References

CMS. (2018). *Stage 3 program requirements for providers attesting to their State's Medicaid Promoting Interoperability (PI) programs.* Centers for Medicare & Medicaid Services (CMS). Retrieved July 10, 2019, from https://www.cms.gov/Regulations-and-Guidance/Legislation/EHRIncentivePrograms/Stage3Medicaid_Require.html.

GAO. (2017). *HHS should assess the effectiveness of its efforts to enhance patient access to and use of electronic health information [PDF].* Washington, DC: General Accounting Office. https://www.gao.gov/assets/690/683388.pdf.

HealthTap. (2019). *Virtual physician consults: Virtual healthcare.* HealthTap Inc. Retrieved July 17, 2019 from https://www.healthtap.com/.

Kokalitcheva, K. (2016). More than half of Kaiser Permanente's patient visits are done virtually. In *Fortune.* Retrieved July 10, 2019 from https://fortune.com/2016/10/06/kaiser-permanente-virtual-doctor-visits/.

Lagasse, J. (2019). *Telemedicine is poised to grow as its popularity increases among physicians and patients.* Retrieved July 15, 2019 from https://www.healthcarefinancenews.com/news/telemedicine-poised-grow-its-popularity-increases-among-physicians-and-patients.

Miller, P. (2017). *Survey of physician appointment wait times and medicare and medicaid acceptance rates.* Retrieved July 15, 2019 from https://www.merritthawkins.com/uploadedFiles/MerrittHawkins/Content/Pdf/mha2017waittimesurveyPDF.pdf.

Ovide, S. (2018). *Amazon captures 5 percent of American retail spending. Is that a lot?* From https://www.bloomberg.com/news/articles/2018-08-08/amazon-captures-5-of-american-retail-spending-is-that-a-lot.

Pinchin, V. (2016). *I'm feeling yucky: Searching for symptoms on Google.* Retrieved July 10, 2019, from https://www.blog.google/products/search/im-feeling-yucky-searching-for-symptoms/.

Ray, K. N., Chari, A. V., Engberg, J., Bertolet, M., & Mehrotra, A. (2015). Disparities in time spent seeking medical care in the United States. *JAMA, 175*(12), 1983–1986. https://doi.org/10.1001/jamainternmed.2015.4468.

Rutledge, G. W. (2019). *Unpublished results on 3300 cases for which at least 3 doctors agree on the most likely diagnosis.*

Vaidya, A. (2018). *Global telemedicine market to hit $48.8B by 2023.* Retrieved July 15, 2019, from https://www.beckershospitalreview.com/telehealth/global-telemedicine-market-to-hit-48-8b-by-2023.html.

An information geometric look at the valuing of information

Ira S. Moskowitz[a], Stephen Russell[b], William F. Lawless[c]

[a]Information Management and Decision Architectures Branch, US Naval Research Laboratory, Washington, DC, United States [b]Battlefield Information Processing Branch, US Army Research Laboratory, Adelphi, MD, United States [c]Department of Mathematics, Sciences and Technology, and Department of Social Sciences, School of Arts and Sciences, Paine College, Augusta, GA, United States

9.1 Introduction

The ability to value information may be easy for humans, but when it comes to a machine attempting to use the tools of artificial intelligence (AI), a valuation may not be easy. This is because even though we have a very good quantitative theory of information, we do not have a very good qualitative theory. The new innovation already in development is human-machine teams. These teams, however, need to communicate in a way that both human and machine can come to accept, cooperate, and trust (Lawless, Mittu, Sofge, & Hiatt, 2019).

Howard (1966) was the first to perform a deep analysis of the *value of information* (VoI) by analyzing how much information is worth. He concentrated on its expected value in terms of cost. Prior to this, there was no concrete analysis of a qualitative approach to information theory, in contrast to the large literature on the quantitative aspect of information (Shannon, 1948). Paraphrasing from Moskowitz and Russell (2019),

> Shannon laid the groundwork for information theory in his seminal work. However, Shannon's theory is a quantitative theory, not a qualitative theory. Shannon's theory tells you how much "stuff" you are dealing with…The quality of "stuff" is irrelevant to Shannon theory. This is in contrast to Value of Information theory, where we care about what …"stuff" we are considering. That is, Shannon is a purely quantitative theory, whereas any theory of information value must include a qualitative aspect…This qualitative characteristic finds it way into many information-centric areas, particularly when humans or Artificial Intelligence is involved in decision making processes.

Human-machine Shared Contexts
https://doi.org/10.1016/B978-0-12-820543-3.00009-2

We show how the VoI (Howard, 1966) can be analyzed via the tools of information geometry (IG) (Amari, 1985; Kass & Vos, 1997). The calculable metrics derived from IG can be used with AI to value information. The major issue to determine value is how to distinguish probability distributions. To do this, we need a realistic measure of the distance between distributions. We do this via IG, which provides a bona fide metric, unlike other approaches as such as Kullback-Liebler divergence. We must assume that we have the total knowledge of the distributions involved when dealing with the mathematics entailed. But one must keep in mind that an AI approach may practically only rely upon a sample of a distribution to obtain the statistical parameters of interest assuming a certain form for the underlying distribution.

At the end of this chapter, we discuss how complexity, derived from the volume form, can be used as a measure of the VoI. Information is valuable if the probability increasing corresponds to an increase in volume. By way of an example, increasing the mean of a normal distribution does not really change things. However, decreasing its standard deviation increases the probability.

9.2 Information geometry background

The field of *IG* had its origins in Fisher information (Fisher, 1922) and the Cramer-Rao bound (Rao, 1945). In what follows, we form our Riemannian manifolds following the techniques from Amari (1985, 2001) and Suzuki (2014). We want to know what is the "distance" between probability distributions? What makes a distribution close or far to another distribution? Certainly, there are techniques such as Kullback-Liebler divergence that address this, but we will do it via Riemannian geometry to provide an inherent geometric setting for distance, the "natural" way to proceed. Furthermore, Riemannian geometry includes the concept of geodesic paths, the most efficient paths to travel across spaces.

Many applications use distance between distributions, for example, Carter, Raich, and Hero (2009) and Wang, Cheng, and Moran (2010); but that is not the focus of our chapter. We concentrate on a thorough mathematical discussion on the distances between distributions. We cite many references in our chapter, but our goal for this chapter is a concise and mathematically accurate description of the issue.

We start by looking at the normal distribution $N(\mu, \sigma^2)$ with probability density function

$$f(x|\mu,\sigma) = \frac{1}{\sigma\sqrt{2\pi}}e^{\frac{-(x-\mu)^2}{2\sigma^2}}, \quad \mu\in\mathbb{R}, \ \sigma>0$$

The reader should keep in mind that we express the density function f as a function of μ and σ, yet the classical notation $N(\mu, \sigma^2)$ uses μ and σ^2. The classical notation is actually the most natural notation (natural parameters) once we consider covariances matrices.

In Fig. 9.1, consider the four normal distributions $\mu = 0$ and $\sigma = 1$ or 10 (Fig. 9.1A); and $\mu = 10$ and $\sigma = 1$ or 10 (Fig. 9.1B).

Looking at Fig. 9.1 we see that, up to a translation in the graph, the difference plots are the same. We need a concept of distance that only relies on σ_i if the means are equal.

In Fig. 9.2, we have the four normal distributions $\sigma = 1$ and $\mu = 10$ or 20 (Fig. 9.2A); and $\sigma = 1$ and $\mu = 1$ or 2 (Fig. 9.2B).

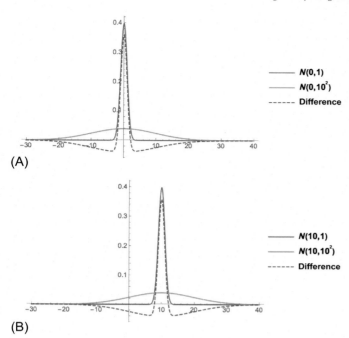

(A)

(B)

FIG. 9.1 Constant μ. Note, d_F is independent of μ. (A) Constant $\mu = 0$, $d_F = 3.26$; (B) constant $\mu = 10$, $d_F = 3.26$.

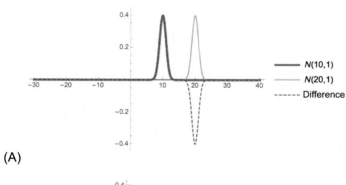

(A)

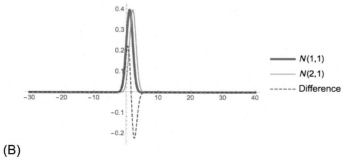

(B)

FIG. 9.2 Constant σ. Note, d_F is not independent of σ. (A) Constant $\sigma = 1$, $d_F = 5.59$; (B) constant $\sigma = 1$, $d_F = 0.98$.

Here, the difference depends on not only σ but also μ in a nontrivial manner. We need a concept of distance that incorporates this property. We will show later in the chapter that the Fisher distance "d_F" has the desired properties to deal with both Figs. 9.1 and 9.2.

In general, we will show later from Costa, Santos, and Strapasso (2015) that

$$d_F((N(\mu,\sigma_1^2),N(\mu,\sigma_2^2)) = \sqrt{2}|\ln(\sigma_2/\sigma_1)| \text{ and}$$

$$d_F((N(\mu_1,\sigma^2),N(\mu_2,\sigma^2))) = \sqrt{2}\ln\left(\frac{4\sigma^2 + (\mu_1-\mu_2)^2 + |\mu_1-\mu_2|\sqrt{8\sigma^2 + (\mu_1-\mu_2)^2}}{4\sigma^2}\right)$$

Applying this to the distributions illustrated in Fig. 9.1, we see that $d_F(N(0,1),N(0,100)) = \sqrt{2}\ln(10) = d_F(N(10,1),N(10,100))$. This result captures well that the difference between the distributions is, up to translation, the same result. However, if we vary the means and keep the standard deviations the same, the behavior is very different. This result is what we see in Fig. 9.2, where $d_F(N(10, 1), N(20, 1)) = 5.59$, but $d_F(N(1, 1), N(2, 1)) = 0.98$.

We note that neural net vision learning has the desirable quality of being translation invariant. Therefore, looking at Fig. 9.1, we would want a machine to see the difference functions as being the same in Fig. 9.1A and B. However, we would want a machine to distinguish between the difference functions in Fig. 9.2. The Fisher distance has the desirable quality of achieving this goal.

The reason for the difference in difference behaviors can only be understood when one studies the geodesics given by the Fisher-Rao metric in the upper (μ, σ) half plane. We will explain this later in the chapter.

9.3 A brief look at Riemannian geometry in general

In this section, we do not attempt to dot every "i," nor always specify every point in space where we are, rather we attempt to give the reader enough information for a quick review of Riemannian geometry. Before we define a Riemannian manifold, we must review basic material (Gromoll, Meyer, & Klingenberg, 1975; Kobayashi & Nomizu, 1963; Munkres, 1963). We do not define manifolds in a more abstract manner since Nash (1956) showed that every Riemannian manifold can be embedded in $\mathbb{R}^n$ with an inherited metric. However, we choose to take an intrinsic view of differential geometry by developing its metric characteristics independent of the larger Euclidean space that the manifold sits in. Gauss in his Theorema Egregium (Gauss, 1827, Section 12; Spivak, 1999, p. 95, Vol. II) tells us that this is permissible, and we lose nothing. We note that to study the variants of the Poincaré upper half plane in this chapter, if we attempted to use the inherited subspace Riemannian metric, we would have to view the manifold as living in $\mathbb{R}^6$ (Blanuša, 1955); no thanks!

Definition 9.1. We say that a map or function is **smooth** if it is infinitely continuously differentiable.

The previous definition is actually a bit of overkill but it keeps us out of trouble. In what follows, we need our topological spaces to behave that is why we require them to be second countable and Hausdorff; if the reader is not familiar with those terms, do not worry about them. Also, topologically, there is no difference between $\mathbb{R}^n$ and $\mathbb{B}^n$ (the open ball of radius 1 in $\mathbb{R}^n$), and we freely switch between them.

Definition 9.2. We say that a connected topological space sitting in a high-dimensional Euclidean space $\mathbb{R}^K, K \geq n$, is an n-manifold, or more simply a **manifold,** if it is locally homeomorphic (1–1, onto, and continuous both ways) to $\mathbb{R}^n$. If the local homeomorphisms are in fact diffeomorphisms (i.e., they are smooth homeomorphisms), then we have a **smooth manifold**.

We note the term manifold is often used in a rather ad hoc manner in deep learning. Our definition is the proper one.

Locally, if we are "on" a manifold, we think we are on a piece $\mathbb{R}^n$ (patch or local coordinate). As we travel on the manifold, these patches may switch, but the switching is done homeomorphically; if it is done diffeomorphically, then it is a smooth manifold. A sphere S^2 is a two-manifold, but we need at least two patches to view it as a manifold. Of course, $\mathbb{R}^2$ is also a manifold, but S^2 is different in that it is a compact (closed and bounded topological space) manifold. Of course, it is not homeomorphic to $\mathbb{R}^2$. If there are no sharp corners, we can take our manifold to be a smooth manifold. Note that the figure eight in the plane is not a manifold because where the lines cross we cannot homeomorphically map to $\mathbb{R}$.

Consider the ϕ_α to be the local homeomorphism between the patch $U_\alpha \subset M$ and $\mathbb{B}^n$ such that $\phi_\alpha(p) = 0 \in \mathbb{R}^n$, and ϕ_β to be the local homeomorphism between the patch $U_\beta \subset M$ and $\mathbb{B}^n$ as it too takes p to zero. Consider the intersection $U_\alpha \cap U_\beta$ that contains p. Let $\mathcal{N}$ be a sufficiently small neighborhood of $0 \in \mathbb{B}^n$ so that $\mathcal{N}$ is a subset of both the image of ϕ_α and ϕ_β.

Consider the map $\phi_\beta \circ \phi_\alpha^{-1} : \mathcal{N} \to \mathbb{B}^n$; it is a homeomorphism between $\mathcal{N}$ and its image. Furthermore if M is a smooth manifold $\phi_\beta \circ \phi_\alpha^{-1}$ is a diffeomorphism, and if D is the differential (Jacobian matrix), then $D(\phi_\beta \circ \phi_\alpha^{-1}) = D(\phi_\beta) \times [D(\phi_\alpha)]^{-1}$ with all matrices having rank n (see Figs. 9.3–9.5).

Definition 9.3. Given a smooth n-manifold M, take any point $p \in M$. Consider all the smooth curves $c(t)$, $c : [-1, 1] \to M$ such that $c(0) = p$. The collection of the velocity vectors $\dot{c}(t)$ forms the **tangent space** of M at p, written TM_p. This is an n-dimensional vector space. The collection of all TM_p, with the natural topology inherited from M, forms the **tangent bundle** TM of M. In general, this space can be very twisted, but locally looks like $\mathbb{R}^n \times \mathbb{R}^n$, where the first $\mathbb{R}^n$ corresponds to the local patch and the second to the vector space $\mathbb{R}^n$.

Definition 9.4. Given a smooth manifold M, we say that a smooth mapping $X : M \to TM$ is a **vector field** if $X(p) \in TM_p$.

Any tangent vector can be extended to a vector field by locally letting its magnitude go to zero, and then be extended to all of M.

TM_p can also be viewed as the image of the vector space $T\mathbb{B}^n \simeq \mathbb{R}^n$ under either inverse linear transformation $[D(\phi_\alpha)]^{-1}|_0$ or $[D(\phi_\beta)]^{-1}|_0$. It makes no difference in either case; up to a change of coordinates, everything is the same. This result lets us express $c(t)$ and $c'(t)$ in the n local coordinates in either case. This condition is part of the magic of local patching

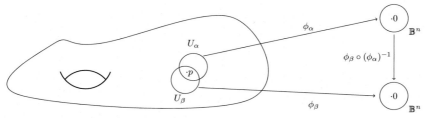

FIG. 9.3 $\mathbb{R}^K \supset M^2$ is 2-torus (by way of example).

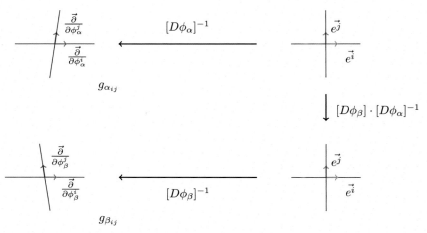

$$g_{\alpha_{ij}}$$

$$g_{\beta_{ij}}$$

FIG. 9.4   Tangent spaces and differential maps.

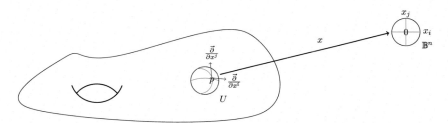

FIG. 9.5   Local coordinate view. When we are dealing with only one patch, we drop the ϕ_* notation and just view the local diffeomorphism from U to $\mathbb{R}^n$ as x. If $c(t)$ is a curve on M, then in local coordinates we have $c_i(t)$ being the ith component of $x \circ c(t)$, which lives in $\mathbb{B}^n$. However, $\dot{c}_i(t)$ lives on both $T\mathbb{B}^n|_{x \circ c(t)}$ and $TM|_{c(t)}$. It is the derivative of $x \circ c_i(t)$ brought to $TM|$ via the differential of x^{-1} treating it as a constant under the linear transformation performed by the differential mapping $\frac{d}{dt}(x \circ c)|_{x \circ c(t)}$ from $T\mathbb{B}^n|_{x \circ c(t)}$ to $TM|_{c(t)}$.

the manifold (this is "tensor" behavior—do not think deep learning tensors!). The same holds for the Riemannian metric which we define soon. What is important is that if we restrict ourselves to local coordinates for our metric calculation it does not matter which local coordinates we use. If we are using the local homeomorphism ϕ_α, the image of the basis vector $\vec{e^i}$ under $[D(\phi_\alpha)]^{-1}$ is $\frac{\partial}{\partial \phi_\alpha^i}$. The image of $U \subset M$ under any local homeomorphism is referred to as expressing M in **local coordinates**. That is, we can use the standard notation of $x^1,\ldots,x^n$ for an element of M, note, for example, it really should be $x^i \circ \phi_\alpha$. There is also a classical reason for using an upper index, but it has to do with tensor notation convention.

The local coordinate view in Fig. 9.5 is very important when we think about the modern way (Gromoll et al., 1975) to view tangent vectors, and by extension vector fields. A tangent vector does something to a smooth function on M. In fact, if $f: M \to \mathbb{R}$, then we may view the tangent vector $\frac{\partial}{\partial \phi^i}$ as being an operator (where we extend by linearity to any tangent vector):

$$\frac{\vec{\partial}}{\partial x^i}\bigg|_p(f) := \frac{\partial(f \circ x^{-1})}{\partial x_i}\bigg|_{x(p)}, \quad i = 1,\dots,n \tag{9.1}$$

The $\frac{\partial}{\partial x_i}$ operator on the RHS of Eq. (9.1) is the standard partial derivative w.r.t. x_i in $\mathbb{R}^n$. This result generalizes the directional derivative from the calculus. Let f be a real-valued function on $\mathbb{R}^n$ and let V be a (but not necessarily a unit) vector in $\mathbb{R}^n$. $D_V f = \nabla(f) \cdot V$. Now if we express $V = \sum_i v_i e_i$, we have $D_V f = \langle \frac{\partial f}{\partial x_1}, \dots, \frac{\partial f}{\partial x_n} \rangle \cdot \langle v_1, \dots, v_n \rangle = \sum_i v_i \frac{\partial f}{\partial x_i}$; in our modern notation, this becomes $V(f) = \left(\sum_i v_i \frac{\partial}{\partial x_i} \right)(f)$.

There is a special operator on vector fields called the Lie bracket.

Definition 9.5. Given two vector fields X, Y on M, there is a vector field called the Lie bracket of X and Y denoted as $[X, Y]$ such that if f is a smooth function on M,

$$[X,Y](f) := X(Y(f)) - Y(X(f)) \tag{9.2}$$

Note 9.1. As the reader can see, this process is quickly getting complicated. Our goal was to show the reader there is a logical reason behind the apparent "tricks" of global differential geometry. Let us now step back to the local geometry behind the differential geometry and stay with one set of local coordinates. Keep in mind that when we finally get to the space of interest, the concept of local coordinates is transparent since the space is an open subset of a Euclidean space with global coordinates. However, it is important to keep in mind that it requires adjusting the metric in terms of the local coordinates.

Following from the previous note, if we are on a small enough piece of manifold M, we are dealing with only one patch. For some manifolds, one patch suffices; such a situation is the modified Poincaré upper half plane that we will investigate. When we are "local" on a manifold, we use coordinates from the patch to describe the manifold. We view a piece (neighborhood) of M as a piece of $\mathbb{R}^n$. Thus, $p \to x^1, \dots, x^n$ are the **local coordinates** (as they are for $\mathbb{R}^n$) at the point $p \in M$. Again, for some of the manifolds we deal with, M is a topological subspace of $\mathbb{R}^n$, precluding the earlier machinery.

In addition, we have the canonical vector fields $\frac{\partial}{\partial x^i}$, such that the tangent space at TM_p is a linear combination of the $\frac{\partial}{\partial x^i}_p$. The base point p is understood, and we often mix the vector field with the vectors and simply write $\frac{\vec{\partial}}{\partial x^i} \in TM_p$. This understanding generalizes the concept of a directional derivative and is part of the modern view of differential geometry. However, if the reader finds this assumption objectionable, simply view the vector field $\frac{\partial}{\partial x^i}$ as the one that assigns the standard basis vector $\vec{e_i}$ at TM_p.

In local coordinates, $c(t)$ is expressed as $x^i = c_i(t)$. Hence, the velocity vector $\dot{c}(t) = \sum_i \dot{c}_i(t) \frac{\vec{\partial}}{\partial x^i}, i = 1, \dots, n$ (not $i = 1, \dots, K$), where $\dot{c}_i(t)$ is the derivative $\frac{dc_i}{dt}$. For the rest of this chapter, we always assume that i and j index up to the dimension n of the manifold.

Definition 9.6. Given a vector space $\mathcal{V}$, an **inner product** is a positive-definite symmetric bilinear mapping from $\mathcal{V} \times \mathcal{V} \to \mathbb{R}$.

Definition 9.7. If we have a smooth manifold, we say that we have a **Riemannian metric** g on M if $g(p)$ is an inner product on TM_p and if g varies smoothly over the points of M and the vector fields of M. M equipped with such a g is called a **Riemannian manifold**.

The inner product at p between vectors $V, W \in TM_p$ is usually expressed as $\langle V, W \rangle$. If V, W are vector fields, then $\langle V, W \rangle_p = \langle V_p, W_p \rangle$.

Definition 9.8. We define the **norm** of V as $\|V\| := \langle V, V \rangle^{1/2}$.

Note 9.2. If vector $V = \sum_i v_i \frac{\partial}{\partial x^i} \in TM_p$ (i.e., V is a tangent vector at the point p with coordinates $(v_1, \ldots, v_n)$) and if $W = \sum_i w_i \frac{\vec{\partial}}{\partial x^i} \in TM_p$, then we may express the inner product between V and W

$$\langle V, W \rangle = \sum_{i,j} v_i w_j g_{ij}(p)$$

where

$$g_{ij}(p) = \left\langle \frac{\vec{\partial}}{\partial x^i}, \frac{\vec{\partial}}{\partial x^j} \right\rangle$$

Note 9.3. We have obtained the matrix $\mathcal{G} = [g_{ij}]$, which is invertible with the notation $[g^{ij}] := \mathcal{G}^{-1}$.

We look at our manifold in Fig. 9.5. We view the points p on the manifold via their local coordinates in $\mathbb{B}^n$. However, we view the tangent vector as "tangent" to M at the point p. When it is clear which patch we are using, we use the homeomorphism ϕ notation. Therefore, the basis of TM_p is given as $\frac{\partial}{\partial \phi_i}, i = 1, \ldots, n$. The metric is then given as g_{ij} since the local coordinates are understood to be those of the homeomorphism ϕ.

Definition 9.9. We define the Riemannian metric, a symmetric $(0, 2)$ tensor, as

$$ds^2 = \sum_{i,j} g_{ij} dx^i \otimes dx^j$$

Authors often drop the $\otimes$ and replace it with $\cdot$. The abused notation ds^2 is used for historical reasons (Bengtsson & Zyczkowski, 2006, p. 21). The standard Euclidean metric $dx^i \frac{\vec{\partial}}{\partial x_j} = \delta_{ij}$ with $ds^2 = \sum_i dx^i \otimes dx^i$ is the Pythagorean theorem. The dx^i live in T^*M, which denotes the cotangent bundle of M.

If we wish to be specific about what tangent space we are at, we sometimes write $\langle V, W \rangle_p$ or $\|V\|_p$.

If $c(t) =$ is a smooth curve in M, then based on extending the Pythagorean theorem and that the differential form dx^i in the cotangent bundle of M pulls back to $\frac{dx^i}{dt} dt$ in the reals, the following definitions arise.

Definition 9.10. The **length** of $c(t)$ is

$$L(c) := \int_a^b \| \dot{c}(t) \| \, dt = \int_a^b \sqrt{\sum g_{ij}(c(t))\dot{c}_i(t)\dot{c}_j(t)} \, dt \qquad (9.3)$$

and its **energy** is

$$E(c) := \int_a^b \| \dot{c}(t) \|^2 dt = \int_a^b \sum g_{ij}(c(t))\dot{c}_i(t)\dot{c}_j(t) \, dt \qquad (9.4)$$

where $\| \dot{c}(t) \| = \| \dot{c}(t) \|_{c(t)}$ to be precise.

This explains the use of the notation ds^2 above if we view the length of $c(t)$ as $\int_{c(t)} ds$.

We now define the distance d between two points in $p, q \in M$ (Kobayashi & Nomizu, 1963).

Definition 9.11. The distance between p and q is

$$d := \inf \int_\gamma \| \dot{\gamma}(t) \| \, dt \qquad (9.5)$$

where γ is any piecewise smooth curve starting at p and ending at q.

This definition does form a distance function, where the topology from this distance function is compatible with the manifold's inherent topology. Also, keep in mind that the distance is independent of the choice of local coordinates because the Riemannian metric is a tensor and transforms properly (Gromoll et al., 1975).

For $\mathbb{R}^n$ with the usual Euclidean metric $g_{ij} = \delta_{ij}$, we have the standard distance. For this Euclidean Riemannian space, the distance between two points is obtained by the straight line between those points (parameterizations of the straight line do not affect the distance provided its velocity vector is never zero).

Consider $\mathbb{R}^2 - (0,0)$ (the punctured plane) with the Euclidean metric. No straight line exists between $(-1, 0)$ and $(1, 0)$. In fact there is no piecewise smooth curve between $(-1, 0)$ and $(1, 0)$ that achieves the distance between them (which is 2). These results lead us to the concept of geodesics and geodesic completeness (Hopf & Rinow, 1931).

Note 9.4. From here on, we write (M, g) to show that we are dealing with a Riemannian metric with metric g.

In what follows, we give three quasiequivalent definitions of a geodesic. We ask the reader to keep all three in mind when thinking about a geodesic. Again, our goal in this chapter is comprehension for the beginner in differential geometry.

Definition 9.12 (First attempt at the definition of a geodesic). We say that a curve $g(t)$ parametrized proportional to arc length, mapping some interval (possibly $(-\infty, \infty)$) of $\mathbb{R}$ into M is a **geodesic** if it is locally length minimizing.

Definition 9.13. We say that (M, g) is **geodesically complete** if the domain of any geodesic can be extended as a geodesic to $\mathbb{R}$ itself.

Theorem 9.1 (Hopf-Rinow 1 (Hopf & Rinow, 1931)). *Any (M, g) with M compact is geodesically complete.*

Theorem 9.2 (*Hopf-Rinow 2 (Hopf & Rinow, 1931)*). *If (M, g) is geodesically complete and $p, q \in M$, a length minimizing geodesic connecting p with q always exists.*

Thus, S^2 is $\mathbb{R}^3$ it is geodesically complete, where the geodesics are (trace) great circles (Spivak, 1999). However, keep in mind that even though great circles are locally length minimizing, they need not be globally (i.e., because one can go two directions on a great circle path, and in general one direction is shorter than the other).

Let us go back to $(\mathbb{R}^n, \delta_{ij})$. If we view a curve on a displacement versus time graph, we see that straight lines have constant velocity and hence zero acceleration. Now consider the curves $c_1(t) = (t, t)$ and $c_2(t) = (t^2, t^2)$ mapping $(0, 1)$ to the straight line between $(0, 0)$ and $(1, 1)$ in $\mathbb{R}^2$. Both curves trace out the same straight line, however, $\dot{c}_1(t) = \langle 1,1 \rangle$ whereas $\dot{c}_2(t) = \langle 2t, 2t \rangle$. This result is why we want a parametrization proportional to arc length. Thus, $c_1(t)$ has zero acceleration vector $\langle 0, 0 \rangle$, whereas $\ddot{c}_2(t) = \langle 2,2 \rangle$ has nonzero acceleration.

To continue with our summary of differential geometry and the concept of a geodesic, we introduce the idea of a covariant derivative by the Levi-Civita connection. In standard Euclidean space, if we have vector fields V and W, we have the directional derivative of W with respect to V at the point p in Euclidean space, $D_V W|_p = \lim_{t \to 0} \frac{W(p + tV(p)) - W(p)}{t}$. In local coordinates, the standard Euclidean coordinates, this directional derivative becomes $D_V(W)_p = \sum_i (V|_p w_i) \frac{\partial}{\partial x^i}|_p$ (Chavel, 2006) (see Eq. 9.1 to review how vectors operate on functions). However, if we are on a manifold embedded in some Euclidean space, the directional derivative may not be in the tangent space of M at p. Therefore, we take the tangential component of $D_V(W)_p$, called the covariant derivative or connection denoted by $\nabla_V W|_p$. For standard Euclidean space (that of course is $\mathbb{R}^n$ with the standard metric), $\nabla_V W = D_V W$.

The notation ∇ is taken to be the Levi-Civita connection on M in this chapter. In general, there are infinitely many connections on M. The notation $\Gamma(TM)$ is the space of all vector fields on M.

Note 9.5. The Levi-Civita connection always exists and is unique for M, g based on the *fundamental theorem of Riemannian geometry* (Millman & Parker, 1977).

The connection (Gromoll et al., 1975) ∇ is a mapping $\nabla: \Gamma(TM) \times \Gamma(TM) \to \Gamma(TM)$ such that (where f, g are smooth functions, X, Y are vector fields, and the mapping is written as $\nabla_X Y$)

$$\nabla_{fX + gX'} Y = f\nabla_X Y + g\nabla_{X'} Y$$
$$\nabla_X(Y_1 + Y_2) = \nabla_X Y_1 + \nabla_X Y_2$$
$$\nabla_X fY = (Xf)Y + f\nabla_X Y$$

What makes the Levi-Civita connection unique are the two following additional conditions (metric compatibility and symmetry):

$$\text{Metric compatibility: } X\langle Y, Z \rangle = \langle \nabla_X Y, Z \rangle + \langle Y, \nabla_X Z \rangle$$
$$\text{and symmetry (torsion free): } \nabla_X Y - \nabla_Y X = [X, Y]$$
$$\text{Note: Symmetry in local coordinates is: } \nabla_{\frac{\partial}{\partial x^i}} \frac{\partial}{\partial x^j} = \nabla_{\frac{\partial}{\partial x^j}} \frac{\partial}{\partial x^i}$$

In terms of the basis vectors for the local coordinates, we obtain the Christoffel symbols Γ^i_{kj} (of the second kind):

$$\nabla_{\frac{\partial}{\partial x^k}} \frac{\partial}{\partial x^j} := \sum_{i=1}^{n} \Gamma^i_{kj} \frac{\partial}{\partial x^i}$$

From the symmetry of the Levi-Civita connection, we have that the Christoffel symbols are symmetric in the lower two indices. Since we have metric compatibility, we can express the Christoffel symbols and hence the Levi-Civita connection solely in terms of the metric in local coordinates. We can easily see that for the standard Euclidean metric the Christoffel symbols are all zero.

We also use vector fields along curves instead of the more general vector fields. We next obtain alternate definitions of a geodesic. Here is a disconnect between the classic literature and modern differential geometry. There are also many statements about geodesics, most of which are quasicorrect in the nonspecialist literature. We hope to assist the reader who may be going through the existing literature. Note that this definition as given does not even mention path length. The magic is that the Levi-Civita connection is compatible with the metric. Actual concepts of optimization are done over energy, which is $1/2$ of the integral of the speed squared, rather than the arc length.

Definition 9.14 (Second attempt at the definition of a geodesic). The smooth curve $c(t)$ is a **geodesic** if

$$\nabla_{\dot{c}(t)} \dot{c}(t) = 0 \tag{9.6}$$

The above tells us that from the viewpoint of M there is no acceleration. Also, because $\dot{c}(t)\langle \dot{c}(t), \dot{c}(t) \rangle$ is zero from metric compatibility, we see that a covariantly zero acceleration curve must have constant speed.

Let us express Eq. (9.6) in local coordinates in the third attempt at a definition of a geodesic. It follows from expanding Eq. (9.6) in local coordinates.

Definition 9.15 (Third attempt at the definition of a geodesic). The smooth curve $c(t)$ with velocity vector $\sum_i \dot{c}_i(t) \frac{\partial}{\partial x^i}$ is a **geodesic** if it satisfies the following n differential equations:

$$\ddot{c}_k(t) + \sum_{i,j} \Gamma^k_{ij} \dot{c}_i(t) \dot{c}_j(t) = 0, \quad k = 1, \dots, n \tag{9.7}$$

Since we are focused on the Levi-Civita connection, we can also express the Christoffel symbols in terms of the metric (Lee, 1997, Eq. 5.4):

$$\Gamma^k_{ij} = \frac{1}{2} \sum_k g^{kl} \left(\frac{\partial g_{jl}}{\partial x_i} + \frac{\partial g_{il}}{\partial x_j} - \frac{\partial g_{ij}}{\partial x_l} \right) \tag{9.8}$$

Interestingly, Eq. (9.8) expresses the Christoffel symbols independently of the Levi-Civita connection.

Returning to Eq. (9.4) to optimize the energy (by finding a minimum) we employ the Euler-Lagrange equations from the calculus of variations and determine that for a curve to minimize (locally, and in local coordinates), it must satisfy the following equation derived simply from the calculus of variations without using the Levi-Civita connection:

$$\ddot{c}_k(t) + \sum_{i,j} \Gamma^k_{ij} \dot{c}_i(t)\dot{c}_j(t) = 0, \quad k = 1,\ldots,n \tag{9.9}$$

What is fascinating is that, not surprisingly, this result is the same as Eq. (9.7). To be precise, we obtain the optimization equations of the path energy functional, which gives us the same answer if we use the arc length functional provided the path has constant speed. So, in terms of local coordinates, we can safely use Eq. (9.7) to solve for a geodesic, or equivalently, to solve for the constant speed curve that is locally arc length minimizing. We now have sufficient background to proceed.

9.4 Fisher information and Riemannian geometry

A good background for this material is the book by Amari (1985) and the seminal papers by Fisher (1922) and Rao (1945).

Given a parametrized family of probability density (or mass) functions for the random variable X, parametrized by $\boldsymbol{\xi}$:

$$S = \{p(x,\boldsymbol{\xi})|\boldsymbol{\xi} = \{\xi_1,\ldots,\xi_n\} \in \Xi\}$$

where the mapping $\boldsymbol{\xi} \mapsto p(x,\boldsymbol{\xi})$ is a bijection from Ξ, diffeomorphic to the open unit ball in $\mathbb{B}^n$, onto its image in the space of parametrized probability density (mass) functions.

Note 9.6. The previous equation for S tells us that the manifolds we are dealing with are topologically trivial. This result does not capture of all the models in Fisher geometry (such as the Von-Mises distribution). However, it suffices for the distributions that we study in depth in this chapter.

Definition 9.16. We call the parametrized family of probability density (or mass) functions previously a topologically trivial statistical manifold, or a **simple statistical manifold** with the notation **S**.

Note 9.7. Even for a simple statistical manifold where the topology is trivial, the geometry may be far from trivial. That is the point of this chapter.

We see that **S** is an n-dimensional smooth manifold with a global chart. In additional, we assign a unique probability density function to each point in the manifold.

Given the density function parametrized by $\boldsymbol{\xi} = \xi_1,\ldots,\xi_n$, we take the partials $\frac{\partial}{\partial \xi_i} \ln p(x,\boldsymbol{\xi})$ and $\frac{\partial}{\partial \xi_j} \ln p(x,\boldsymbol{\xi})$ and consider the expected value (Atkinson & Mitchell, 1981, Eq. 2.1) of the product of the partials. From this, we form the $n \times n$ Fisher information matrix (FIM), $G(\boldsymbol{\xi}) = (\mathfrak{g}_{ij}(\boldsymbol{\xi}))$:

$$\mathfrak{g}_{ij}(\boldsymbol{\xi}) = E\left[\left(\frac{\partial}{\partial \xi_i} \ln p(X,\boldsymbol{\xi})\right)\left(\frac{\partial}{\partial \xi_j} \ln p(X,\boldsymbol{\xi})\right)\right]$$

Note that for a continuous probability density function

$$E\left[\left(\frac{\partial}{\partial \xi_i}\ln p(X,\boldsymbol{\xi})\right)\left(\frac{\partial}{\partial \xi_j}\ln p(X,\boldsymbol{\xi})\right)\right] = \int_x \left[\left(\frac{\partial}{\partial \xi_i}\ln p(X,\boldsymbol{\xi})\right)\left(\frac{\partial}{\partial \xi_j}\ln p(X,\boldsymbol{\xi})\right)\right]p(x,\boldsymbol{\xi})\,dx$$

and for a discrete probability mass function

$$E\left[\left(\frac{\partial}{\partial \xi_i}\ln p(X,\boldsymbol{\xi})\right)\left(\frac{\partial}{\partial \xi_j}\ln p(X,\boldsymbol{\xi})\right)\right] = \sum_x \left[\left(\frac{\partial}{\partial \xi_i}\ln p(X,\boldsymbol{\xi})\right)\left(\frac{\partial}{\partial \xi_j}\ln p(X,\boldsymbol{\xi})\right)\right]p(x,\boldsymbol{\xi})$$

Thus, we integrate (or sum, but to avoid confusion we will use continuous terms for the rest of the chapter, unless we are dealing with a discrete case) the x out of consideration leaving FIM as a function of $\boldsymbol{\xi}$. We assume that the family $\mathbf{S}$ has the following regularity conditions (Amari, 1985):

- The $p(x, \boldsymbol{\xi})$ have common support as functions of x.
- The $\frac{\partial}{\partial \xi_i}\ln p(x,\boldsymbol{\xi})$ are linearly independent functions of x.
- The moments of $\frac{\partial}{\partial \xi_i}\ln p(x,\boldsymbol{\xi})$ exist up to the necessary orders.
- The $\frac{\partial}{\partial \xi_i}\ln p(x,\boldsymbol{\xi})$ have enough continuous differentiability so that differentiation and integration can be interchanged.

We include the earlier conditions for the sake of completeness and bookkeeping. We will not dwell on these fine points in this chapter. However, we do note that many authors, including Rao (1945), state that the FIM is positive definite. That may not always be true since the FIM is a covariance matrix (Rao, 1945), which is only guaranteed to be positive semidefinite.

This lets us form a Riemannian metric (if the FIM is only positive semidefinite (Ly, Marsman, Verhagen, Grasman, & Wagenmakers, 2017), we can only form a pseudo-Riemannian metric) (Gromoll et al., 1975; Kobayashi & Nomizu, 1963) on (the tangent space of) $\mathbf{S}$ (at $\boldsymbol{\xi}$).

Definition 9.17. We define the Fisher metric as

$$ds^2_{f(\xi_i)} = \sum_{i,j}\mathfrak{g}_{ij}d\xi^i \otimes d\xi^j \text{ or when we assume the parameters } \xi \text{ as simply } ds^2_f \tag{9.10}$$

We have removed ($\boldsymbol{\xi}$) from the notation $\mathfrak{g}_{ij}(\boldsymbol{\xi})$ for simplicity.

If the vector $V = \sum_i v_i \frac{\partial}{\partial \xi_i} \in T\mathbf{S}|_{\boldsymbol{\xi}}$ (i.e., if V is a tangent vector at the point $\boldsymbol{\xi}$ with coordinates $(v_1,\ldots,v_n)$), and if $W = \sum_i w_i \frac{\partial}{\partial \xi_i} \in T\mathbf{S}|_{\boldsymbol{\xi}}$, then we have the following definition.

Definition 9.18. We define the inner product between V and W via the Fisher metric as

$$\langle V,W \rangle_f = \sum_{i,j} v_i w_j \mathfrak{g}_{ij}$$

since $d\xi^i \frac{\overrightarrow{\partial}}{\partial \xi_j} = \delta_{ij}$; and we also define the norm of V as

$$\| V \|_f := \langle V,V \rangle_f^{1/2} = \sqrt{\sum_{i,j} v_i v_j \mathfrak{g}_{ij}}.$$

Definition 9.19. We call the earlier simple statistical manifold as described with the Fisher metric, a **Fisher space**. We use the notation $\mathbf{S}_f$ if we wish to emphasize that the Fisher metric is being used.

We can always recover the standard trivial Euclidean metric by setting $ds^2 = \delta_{ij}$.

As is standard in differential geometry, we can now define the distance d between two points (which are distributions) in $\mathbf{S}$ as (Costa et al., 2015; Kobayashi & Nomizu, 1963) the following definition.

Definition 9.20. We define the **Fisher distance** between two points in $\mathbf{S}_f$ as

$$d(p(x|\boldsymbol{\xi}_1),p(x|\boldsymbol{\xi}_2)) := \inf_\gamma \int \|\dot\gamma(t)\|_f dt \tag{9.11}$$

where γ is any piecewise class C^1 curve starting at $p(x|\boldsymbol{\xi}_1)$ and ending at $p(x|\boldsymbol{\xi}_2)$.

Keep in mind that a point in $\mathbf{S}$ is either uniquely identified as $p(x|\boldsymbol{\xi})$ or simply as $\boldsymbol{\xi}$. Later we will compare the Fisher distance to the Kullback-Liebler divergence (Cover & Thomas, 2006).

9.5 A simple Fisher space-normal distribution: Two parameters

Here we have that

$$\mathbf{S}_f = \left\{\frac{1}{\xi_2\sqrt{2\pi}}e^{\frac{-(x-\xi_1)^2}{2\xi_2^2}}, \; \xi_1\in\mathbb{R}, \; \xi_2>0\right\} = \left\{\frac{1}{\sigma\sqrt{2\pi}}e^{\frac{-(x-\mu)^2}{2\sigma^2}}, \; \mu\in\mathbb{R}, \; \sigma>0\right\}$$

This example has been noted in the literature (see Amari, 1985, Ex. 2.3, and originally in Rao, 1945, p. 89). Due to its importance and illustrative properties, we go through it in some detail. We also add some new results.

For readability, we have set the mean $\xi_1 = \mu$, and the standard deviation $\xi_2 = \sigma$. This is historically denoted as $\mathfrak{H}$, the (μ,σ) upper half plane in $\mathbb{R}^2$. For completeness, we note that is diffeomorphic to the open unit two-ball under the conformal map $z\to\frac{z-i}{z+i}$. Since $\ln\left(\frac{1}{\sigma\sqrt{2\pi}}e^{\frac{-(x-\mu)^2}{2\sigma^2}}\right) = -\ln(\sigma\sqrt{2\pi}) - \frac{(x-\mu)^2}{2\sigma^2}$, we find that $\frac{\partial}{\partial\mu}\ln\left(\frac{1}{\sigma\sqrt{2\pi}}e^{\frac{-(x-\mu)^2}{2\sigma^2}}\right) = \frac{(x-\mu)}{\sigma^2}$ and $\frac{\partial}{\partial\sigma}\ln\left(\frac{1}{\sigma\sqrt{2\pi}}e^{\frac{-(x-\mu)^2}{2\sigma^2}}\right) = -\frac{1}{\sigma} + \frac{(x-\mu)^2}{\sigma^3}$. Therefore,

$$[\mathfrak{g}_{ij}] = \begin{pmatrix} E\left[\frac{(X-\mu)^2}{\sigma^4}\right] & E\left[\frac{-(X-\mu)}{\sigma^3} + \frac{(X-\mu)^3}{\sigma^5}\right] \\ E\left[\frac{-(X-\mu)}{\sigma^3} + \frac{(X-\mu)^3}{\sigma^5}\right] & E\left[\frac{1}{\sigma^2} + \frac{(X-\mu)^4}{\sigma^6} - \frac{2(X-\mu)^2}{\sigma^4}\right] \end{pmatrix} \tag{9.12}$$

We see that the central moments, with m a nonzero integer, of the normal distribution (Ahsanullah et al., 2014, Eq. 2.5) are (!! is double factorial)

$$E[(X-\mu)^m] = \begin{cases} (m-1)!! \; \sigma^m & m \text{ even} \\ 0 & m \text{ odd} \end{cases} \tag{9.13}$$

Therefore, we have (Rao, 1945)

$$[\mathfrak{g}_{ij}] = \begin{pmatrix} 1/\sigma^2 & 0 \\ 0 & 2/\sigma^2 \end{pmatrix} = \begin{pmatrix} E & F \\ F & G \end{pmatrix}, \text{ and} \tag{9.14}$$

$$ds_f^2 = \frac{1}{\sigma^2}(d\mu \otimes d\mu + 2d\sigma \otimes d\sigma) \tag{9.15}$$

To compare the classical results, let us generalize the metric so that

$$ds_a^2 = \frac{1}{\sigma^2}(d\mu \otimes d\mu + ad\sigma \otimes d\sigma) \tag{9.16}$$

Thus, we see that ds_1^2 is the standard Poincaré metric (Amari, 1985) and ds_2^2 is the Fisher metric.

Now, we express the Christoffel symbols in terms of the first fundamental form (Lane, 1940, p. 132). We use the common notation shorthand where, for example, E_u means $\frac{\partial E}{\partial u}$. We use Eq. (9.8) and recall that $\Gamma_{ij}^k = \Gamma_{ji}^k$ since everything is based on the Levi-Civita connection.

$$\Gamma_{11}^1 = \frac{GE_u + FE_v - 2FF_u}{2(EG - F^2)} \tag{9.16}$$

$$\Gamma_{12}^1 = \frac{GE_v - FG_u}{2(EG - F^2)} \tag{9.17}$$

$$\Gamma_{22}^1 = \frac{-FG_v - GG_u + 2GF_v}{2(EG - F^2)} \tag{9.18}$$

$$\Gamma_{11}^2 = \frac{-FE_u - EE_v + 2EF_u}{2(EG - F^2)} \tag{9.19}$$

$$\Gamma_{12}^2 = \frac{EG_u - FE_v}{2(EG - F^2)} \tag{9.20}$$

$$\Gamma_{22}^2 = \frac{EG_v + FG_u - 2FF_v}{2(EG - F^2)} \tag{9.21}$$

Theorem 9.3. *The Gaussian curvature is the same as the sectional curvature K provided that the Riemannian metric is the induced pull-back from M^2 being embedded in $\mathbb{R}^3$ and, in local coordinates using the first fundamental form, is given via the Brioschi formula (Spivak, 1999, p. 133, Vol. II), where*

$$M_1 = \begin{pmatrix} -\frac{1}{2}G_{uu} + F_{uv} - \frac{1}{2}E_{vv} & -\frac{1}{2}E_u \ \ F_u - \frac{1}{2}E_v \\[2mm] F_v - \frac{1}{2}G_u & E & F \\[2mm] \frac{1}{2}G_v & F & G \end{pmatrix} \quad and \quad M_2 = \begin{pmatrix} 0 & \frac{1}{2}E_v & \frac{1}{2}G_u \\[2mm] \frac{1}{2}E_v & E & F \\[2mm] \frac{1}{2}G_u & F & G \end{pmatrix} \quad and \quad (9.22)$$

$$K = \frac{\det(M_1) - \det(M_2)}{(EG - F^2)^2} \tag{9.23}$$

Corollary 9.1. *If $F = 0$, then (Gray, Abbena, & Salamon, 2005, Corollary 17.4)*

$$K = \frac{-1}{\sqrt{EG}}\left\{ \frac{\partial}{\partial u}\left(\frac{1}{\sqrt{E}}\frac{\partial\sqrt{G}}{\partial u} \right) + \frac{\partial}{\partial v}\left(\frac{1}{\sqrt{G}}\frac{\partial\sqrt{E}}{\partial u} \right) \right\} \tag{9.24}$$

$$= \frac{-1}{2\sqrt{EG}}\left\{ \frac{\partial}{\partial u}\left(\frac{G_u}{\sqrt{EG}} \right) + \frac{\partial}{\partial v}\left(\frac{E_v}{\sqrt{EG}} \right) \right\} \tag{9.25}$$

Considering ds_a^2, we see that

$$E = 1/\sigma^2 \quad F = 0 \quad G = a/\sigma^2 \tag{9.26}$$

$$E_\mu = 0 \quad F_\mu = 0 \quad G_\mu = 0 \tag{9.27}$$

$$E_\sigma = -2/\sigma^3 \quad F_\sigma = 0 \quad G_\sigma = (-2a)/\sigma^3 \tag{9.28}$$

$$\sqrt{EG} = \sqrt{a}/\sigma^2 \quad G_\mu/\sqrt{EG} = 0 \quad E_\sigma/\sqrt{EG} = -2/(\sqrt{a}\cdot\sigma) \tag{9.29}$$

$$\frac{\partial}{\partial\mu}\left(G_\mu/\sqrt{EG} \right) = 0 \quad \frac{\partial}{\partial\sigma}\left(E_\sigma/\sqrt{EG} \right) = 2/(\sqrt{a}\cdot\sigma^2) \tag{9.30}$$

Now using Eq. (9.25) we have that

$$K = -1/a$$

Thus, we have the classical result for $\mathfrak{H}$ with the Poincaré metric, it is a space of constant Gaussian curvature -1; and we have Amari's result (Amari, 1985, p. 49) with the Fisher metric that the Gaussian curvature is $-1/2$.

Now let us look at the distance between two points. As we have mentioned, the family of statistical manifolds that are topologically the upper half-plane $\mathfrak{H}$ with ds_a^2 are scaled generalizations of the Poincaré half-plane model $\mathfrak{H}_P$ ($a = 1$). Since $\mathfrak{H}_P$ is a well-studied Riemannian manifold, we simply adjust those results for the Fisher half-plane model $\mathfrak{H}_F$ ($a = 2$).

Since $\mathfrak{H}_P$ is geodesically complete, so is $\mathfrak{H}_F$ and any $\mathfrak{H}$ with $a > 0$. This result means that to find the distance between two points, we find the geodesic between them and then find the arc length.

9.6 The statistical manifold $\mathbb{N}_f^{\Sigma}$

Consider the random column vector $\vec{X} = (X_1,...,X_n)^T$, which takes on values $(x_1,...,x_n) = \vec{x}^T \in \mathbb{R}^n$ (viewed as a $1 \times n$ row). We form the covariance matrix Σ (assuming that the symmetric covariance matrix Σ is also positive definite, and hence invertible) where

$$\Sigma_{ij} = \text{Cov}(X_i, X_j) = \text{E}[(X_i - \mu_i)(X_j - \mu_j)] \tag{9.31}$$

and where $\mu_i := \text{E}(X_i)$ and $\vec{\mu} = (\mu_1,...,\mu_n)^T$. Therefore, we can succinctly write the covariance matrix as

$$\Sigma = E\left((\vec{X} - \vec{\mu})(\vec{X} - \vec{\mu})^T \right)$$

We let $|\Sigma|$ denote the determinant of Σ. We can also use the notation $\sigma_{ij} = \text{Cov}(X_i, X_j)$ along with the fact that $\text{Cov}(X_i, X_i)$ is the variance of X_i. The **statistical manifold** $\mathbb{N}_f^{\vec{\mu},\Sigma}$ is a Riemannian manifold of dimension $n + \frac{n(n+1)}{2}$, where the global parameters are θ_i. We set $\theta_1,...,\theta_n = \mu_1,...,\mu_n$, where the next n parameters correspond to the variances $\theta_{n+1},...,\theta_{2n} = \Sigma_{11},...,\Sigma_{nn} = \sigma_1^2,...,\sigma_n^2$. The final set of $\frac{(n-1)n}{2}$ variables $\theta_{2n+1},...,\theta_{\frac{n^2+3n}{2}}$ are the $\Sigma_{ij}, j = 1,...,n$; with $i < j$ in order. Or one can say that, up to order, the set $\{\mu_k, \sigma_{ij}\}$ are the parameters.

Recall that while the standard deviation σ is not a natural variable, the variance σ_{ii} is: we take the latter's square root and define it to be the standard deviation. That is, we define the standard deviation to be $\sigma_i := \sqrt{\sigma_{ii}}$. Later we will discuss what happens when we instead set $\theta_{n+1},...,\theta_{2n} = \sigma_1,...,\sigma_n$.

We say that X is the random vector of a *(nondegenerate) multivariate normal distribution* if its real-valued density function is

$$f(x_1,...,x_n) = \frac{1}{\sqrt{(2\pi)^n |\Sigma|}} \exp\left(-\frac{1}{2}(\vec{x} - \vec{\mu})^T \Sigma^{-1}(\vec{x} - \vec{\mu}) \right) \tag{9.32}$$

Nondegeneracy assures us that Σ is positive definite, and hence invertible. Before we proceed further, we apply results from linear algebra and probability theory. We assume that all vectors are $n \times 1$, all matrices are $n \times n$, and tr is the trace of a matrix.

1. **FACT:** $tr(AB) = \sum_{i,j} a_{ij}b_{ji}$; hence $tr(ABCD) = \sum_{i,j,m,n} a_{ij}b_{jm}c_{mn}d_{ni}$
2. **FACT:** (Magnus & Neudecker, 1999, p. 151) If M is invertible, $\frac{\partial}{\partial\theta}\ln|M| = tr\left(M^{-1} \cdot \frac{\partial M}{\partial\theta}\right)$
3. **FACT:** (Magnus & Neudecker, 1999, p. 151) If M is invertible, $\frac{\partial(M^{-1})}{\partial\theta} = -M^{-1} \cdot \frac{\partial M}{\partial\theta} \cdot M^{-1}$
4. **FACT:** $\vec{v}^T M \vec{w} = tr(\vec{v}^T M \vec{w})$. That is, the trace of a 1×1 is itself (herein used implicitly)

5. FACT: If S is symmetric, then $\vec{v}^T S \vec{w} = (\vec{v}^T S \vec{w})^T = \vec{w}^T S \vec{v}$

6. FACT:

$$\vec{v}^T A \vec{v} \cdot \vec{v}^T B \vec{v} = \sum_{i,j,m,n} v_i a_{ij} v_j v_m b_{mn} v_n = \sum_{i,j,m,n} a_{ij} b_{mn} \cdot v_i v_j v_m v_n \text{ (herein used implicitly)}$$

7. FACT: If $\vec{V}$, $\vec{W}$ are random vectors, and A, B are constant matrices with respect to the w_i, then

$$E(\vec{W}^T A \vec{W} \cdot \vec{W}^T B \vec{W}) = \sum_{i,j,m,n} a_{ij} b_{mn} E(W_i W_j W_m W_n)$$

8. FACT: Isserelis Theorem (Michalowicz, Nichols, Bucholtz, & Olsona, 2011): If $\vec{X}_i$ are jointly distributed random Gaussian variables as earlier, then

$$\begin{aligned}
E((X_1 - \mu_1)&(X_2 - \mu_2)(X_3 - \mu_3)(X_4 - \mu_4)) \\
&= E((X_1 - \mu_1)(X_2 - \mu_2)) \cdot E((X_3 - \mu_3)(X_4 - \mu_4)) \\
&\quad + E((X_1 - \mu_1)(X_3 - \mu_3)) \cdot E((X_2 - \mu_2)(X_4 - \mu_4)) \\
&\quad + E((X_1 - \mu_1)(X_4 - \mu_4)) \cdot E((X_2 - \mu_2)(X_3 - \mu_3)) \\
&= \Sigma_{12} \cdot \Sigma_{34} + \Sigma_{13} \cdot \Sigma_{24} + \Sigma_{14} \cdot \Sigma_{23}
\end{aligned}$$

9. FACT: If g is the probability density function of a random vector $\vec{X}$, and θ is constant with respect to the x_i we have that

$$E\left(\frac{\partial(\ln g(x_1, \ldots, x_n))}{\partial \theta}\right) = \int \frac{\frac{\partial g}{\partial \theta}}{g} \cdot g \, dx_1 \cdots dx_n = \int \frac{\partial g}{\partial \theta} \, dx_1 \cdots dx_n$$

$$= \frac{\partial}{\partial \theta} \int g \, dx_1 \cdots dx_n = \frac{\partial}{\partial \theta}(1) = 0$$

Now let us return to the earlier density function (9.32). At times, use a subindex of θ_i to show partial differentiation with respect to θ_i, and write f instead of $f(x_1, \ldots, x_n)$ to simplify notation. We have that

$$\ln f = -\frac{n}{2} \ln(2\pi) - \frac{1}{2} \ln|\Sigma| - \frac{1}{2}(\vec{x} - \vec{\mu})^T \Sigma^{-1}(\vec{x} - \vec{\mu})$$

$$\frac{\partial(\ln f)}{\partial \theta_i} = -\frac{1}{2} tr(\Sigma^{-1} \Sigma_{\theta_i}) - \frac{1}{2}\left[\vec{\mu}_{\theta_i}^T \Sigma^{-1}(\vec{x} - \vec{\mu}) + (\vec{x} - \vec{\mu})^T \Sigma^{-1} \vec{\mu}_{\theta_i} + (\vec{x} - \vec{\mu})^T (\Sigma^{-1})_{\theta_i}(\vec{x} - \vec{\mu})\right]; \text{ FACT 2}$$

$$= -\frac{1}{2} tr(\Sigma^{-1} \Sigma_{\theta_i}) - \vec{\mu}_{\theta_i}^T \Sigma^{-1}(\vec{x} - \vec{\mu}) + \frac{1}{2}(\vec{x} - \vec{\mu})^T [\Sigma^{-1} \Sigma_{\theta_i} \Sigma^{-1}](\vec{x} - \vec{\mu}); \text{ FACTS 3, 5}$$

Therefore, we have that

$$\frac{\partial(\ln f)}{\partial \theta_i}\frac{\partial(\ln f)}{\partial \theta_j} = \frac{1}{4}tr\left(\Sigma^{-1}\Sigma_{\theta_i}\right)\cdot tr\left(\Sigma^{-1}\Sigma_{\theta_j}\right)$$

$$-\frac{1}{4}tr\left(\Sigma^{-1}\Sigma_{\theta_i}\right)\cdot(\vec{x}-\vec{\mu})^T[\Sigma^{-1}\Sigma_{\theta_j}\Sigma^{-1}](\vec{x}-\vec{\mu})$$

$$-\frac{1}{4}tr\left(\Sigma^{-1}\Sigma_{\theta_j}\right)\cdot(\vec{x}-\vec{\mu})^T[\Sigma^{-1}\Sigma_{\theta_i}\Sigma^{-1}](\vec{x}-\vec{\mu})$$

$$+\frac{1}{4}(\vec{x}-\vec{\mu})^T[\Sigma^{-1}\Sigma_{\theta_i}\Sigma^{-1}](\vec{x}-\vec{\mu})(\vec{x}-\vec{\mu})^T[\Sigma^{-1}\Sigma_{\theta_j}\Sigma^{-1}](\vec{x}-\vec{\mu})$$

$$+\frac{1}{2}tr\left(\Sigma^{-1}\Sigma_{\theta_i}\right)\cdot\vec{\mu}_{\theta_j}^T\Sigma^{-1}(\vec{x}-\vec{\mu})+\frac{1}{2}tr\left(\Sigma^{-1}\Sigma_{\theta_j}\right)\cdot\vec{\mu}_{\theta_i}^T\Sigma^{-1}(\vec{x}-\vec{\mu})$$

$$+\vec{\mu}_{\theta_i}^T\Sigma^{-1}(\vec{x}-\vec{\mu})\vec{\mu}_{\theta_j}^T\Sigma^{-1}(\vec{x}-\vec{\mu})$$

$$-\frac{1}{2}\vec{\mu}_{\theta_i}^T\Sigma^{-1}(\vec{x}-\vec{\mu})(\vec{x}-\vec{\mu})^T[\Sigma^{-1}\Sigma_{\theta_j}\Sigma^{-1}](\vec{x}-\vec{\mu})$$

$$-\frac{1}{2}\vec{\mu}_{\theta_j}^T\Sigma^{-1}(\vec{x}-\vec{\mu})(\vec{x}-\vec{\mu})^T[\Sigma^{-1}\Sigma_{\theta_i}\Sigma^{-1}](\vec{x}-\vec{\mu})$$

To simplify notation further we set

$$\Gamma_i := tr\left(\Sigma^{-1}\Sigma_{\theta_i}\right)$$
$$\mathcal{I} = \Sigma^{-1}\Sigma_i\Sigma^{-1}$$
$$\mathcal{J} = \Sigma^{-1}\Sigma_j\Sigma^{-1}$$
$$\mathbf{J}_i := (\vec{x}-\vec{\mu})^T\Sigma^{-1}\Sigma_{\theta_i}\Sigma^{-1}(\vec{x}-\vec{\mu})$$
$$v := \vec{x}-\vec{\mu}$$
$$m_i := \vec{\mu}_{\theta_i}^T\Sigma^{-1}(\vec{x}-\vec{\mu})$$

We need to determine $E\left(\frac{\partial(\ln f)}{\partial \theta_i}\frac{\partial(\ln f)}{\partial \theta_j}\right)$. Since expectation is a linear operator, we will break it up into pieces. Since the covariance matrix is free of x_i terms, we have

$$E\left(\frac{1}{4}tr\left(\Sigma^{-1}\Sigma_{\theta_i}\right)\cdot tr\left(\Sigma^{-1}\Sigma_{\theta_j}\right)\right) = \frac{1}{4}tr\left(\Sigma^{-1}\Sigma_{\theta_i}\right)\cdot tr\left(\Sigma^{-1}\Sigma_{\theta_j}\right)$$

FACT 9 tells us that, with the covariance matrix being f constant with respect to the x_i,

$$E\left(-\frac{1}{2}tr\left(\Sigma^{-1}\Sigma_{\theta_i}\right)-\vec{\mu}_{\theta_i}^T\Sigma^{-1}(\vec{x}-\vec{\mu})+\frac{1}{2}(\vec{x}-\vec{\mu})^T[\Sigma^{-1}\Sigma_{\theta_i}\Sigma^{-1}](\vec{x}-\vec{\mu})\right) = 0$$

$$tr\left(\Sigma^{-1}\Sigma_{\theta_i}\right) = -2E\left(\vec{\mu}_{\theta_i}^T\Sigma^{-1}(\vec{x}-\vec{\mu})\right)+E\left((\vec{x}-\vec{\mu})^T[\Sigma^{-1}\Sigma_{\theta_i}\Sigma^{-1}](\vec{x}-\vec{\mu})\right)$$

$$E(\Gamma_i) = \Gamma_i = -2E(m_i)+E(\mathbf{J}_i)$$

Thus, we may now write

$$\frac{\partial(\ln f)}{\partial\theta_i}\frac{\partial(\ln f)}{\partial\theta_j}=\frac{1}{4}\Gamma_i\Gamma_j-\frac{1}{4}\Gamma_i\mathtt{J}_j-\frac{1}{4}\Gamma_j\mathtt{J}_i+\frac{1}{4}\mathtt{J}_i\mathtt{J}_j+\frac{1}{2}\Gamma_im_j+\frac{1}{2}\Gamma_jm_i+m_im_j-\frac{1}{2}m_i\mathtt{J}_j-\frac{1}{2}m_j\mathtt{J}_i$$

Since $g_{ij}=E\left(\frac{\partial(\ln f)}{\partial\theta_i}\frac{\partial(\ln f)}{\partial\theta_j}\right)$,

$$g_{ij}=\frac{1}{4}\Gamma_i\Gamma_j-\frac{1}{4}\Gamma_iE(\mathtt{J}_j)-\frac{1}{4}\Gamma_j\mathtt{J}_i+\frac{1}{4}E(\mathtt{J}_i\mathtt{J}_j)$$

$$+\frac{1}{2}\Gamma_iE(m_j)+\frac{1}{2}\Gamma_jE(m_i)+E(m_im_j)-\frac{1}{2}E(m_i\mathtt{J}_j)-\frac{1}{2}E(m_j\mathtt{J}_i)$$

Since m_i is a sum of odd functions of x_k, we have that $E(m_i)=0$. Hence,

$$g_{ij}=\frac{1}{4}\Gamma_i\Gamma_j-\frac{1}{4}\Gamma_iE(\mathtt{J}_j)-\frac{1}{4}\Gamma_j\mathtt{J}_i+\frac{1}{4}E(\mathtt{J}_i\mathtt{J}_j)+E(m_im_j)-\frac{1}{2}E(m_i\mathtt{J}_j)-\frac{1}{2}E(m_j\mathtt{J}_i)$$

Since $E(\mathtt{J}_i)=\Gamma_i+2E(m_i)=\Gamma_i$, we have that

$$g_{ij}=-\frac{1}{4}\Gamma_i\Gamma_j+\frac{1}{4}E(\mathtt{J}_i\mathtt{J}_j)+E(m_im_j)-\frac{1}{2}E(m_i\mathtt{J}_j)-\frac{1}{2}E(m_j\mathtt{J}_i)$$

Let us look at the individual terms keeping in mind that

$$\mathtt{J}_i=v^TIv,\quad \mathtt{J}_j=v^T\mathcal{I}v$$

$$\mathtt{J}_i\mathtt{J}_j=v^T\mathcal{I}vv^TJv,\text{ so}$$

$$E(\mathtt{J}_i\mathtt{J}_j)=\sum_{i,j,m,n}\iota_{ij}\,\jmath_{mn}E(V_iV_jV_mV_n)\quad\text{FACT 7}$$

$$=\sum_{i,j,m,n}\iota_{ij}\,\jmath_{mn}\left(\Sigma_{ij}\cdot\Sigma_{mn}+\Sigma_{im}\cdot\Sigma_{jn}+\Sigma_{in}\cdot\Sigma_{jm}\right)\quad\text{FACT 8 : Isserelis Theorem.}$$

Now we freely use the fact that all of the matrices are symmetric

$$=\sum_{i,j}\iota_{ij}\Sigma_{ij}\sum_{m,n}\jmath_{mn}\Sigma_{mn}+\sum_{i,j,m,n}\iota_{ij}\Sigma_{jn}\,\jmath_{mn}\Sigma_{im}+\sum_{i,j,m,n}\iota_{ij}\Sigma_{jm}\,\jmath_{mn}\Sigma_{in}$$

$$=\sum_{i,j}\iota_{ji}\Sigma_{ij}\sum_{m,n}\jmath_{nm}\Sigma_{mn}+\sum_{i,j,m,n}\iota_{ij}\Sigma_{jn}\,\jmath_{nm}\Sigma_{mi}+\sum_{i,j,m,n}\iota_{ij}\Sigma_{jm}\,\jmath_{mn}\Sigma_{ni}.$$

Now we use FACT 1

$$=tr(\mathcal{I}\Sigma)tr(\mathcal{I}\Sigma)+2tr(\mathcal{I}\Sigma\mathcal{I}\Sigma)$$

$$=tr(\Sigma^{-1}\Sigma_i\Sigma^{-1}\Sigma)tr(\Sigma^{-1}\Sigma_j\Sigma^{-1}\Sigma)+2tr(\Sigma^{-1}\Sigma_i\Sigma^{-1}\Sigma\Sigma^{-1}\Sigma_j\Sigma^{-1}\Sigma)$$

$$=tr(\Sigma^{-1}\Sigma_i)tr(\Sigma^{-1}\Sigma_j)+2tr(\Sigma^{-1}\Sigma_i\Sigma^{-1}\Sigma_j)$$

Next,

$$
\begin{aligned}
E(m_i m_j) &= E\left(\vec{\mu}_i^T \Sigma^{-1} V \cdot \vec{\mu}_{\theta_j}^T \Sigma^{-1} V\right) \\
&= E\left(\vec{\mu}_i^T \Sigma^{-1} V \cdot V^T \Sigma^{-1} \vec{\mu}_{\theta_j}\right) \qquad\qquad \text{FACT 5} \\
&= \vec{\mu}_i^T \Sigma^{-1} E\left(V \cdot V^T\right) \Sigma^{-1} \vec{\mu}_{\theta_j} \qquad \text{since only } v, v^T \text{ are functions of } x \\
&= \vec{\mu}_i^T \Sigma^{-1} E\left((\vec{X} - \vec{\mu}) \cdot (\vec{X} - \vec{\mu})^T\right) \Sigma^{-1} \vec{\mu}_{\theta_j} \\
&= \vec{\mu}_i^T \Sigma^{-1} \Sigma \Sigma^{-1} \vec{\mu}_{\theta_j} \\
&= \vec{\mu}_{\theta_i}^T \Sigma^{-1} \vec{\mu}_{\theta_j}
\end{aligned}
$$

Now we look at (what follows also holds for $E(m_j \beth_i)$ with the obvious adjustments)

$$
\begin{aligned}
E(m_i \beth_j) &= E\left(\vec{\mu}_{\theta_i}^T \Sigma^{-1} (\vec{X} - \vec{\mu})(\vec{X} - \vec{\mu})^T \Sigma^{-1} \Sigma_{\theta_j} \Sigma^{-1} (\vec{X} - \vec{\mu})\right) \\
&= \vec{\mu}_{\theta_i}^T \Sigma^{-1} E\left((\vec{X} - \vec{\mu})(\vec{X} - \vec{\mu})^T \Sigma^{-1} \Sigma_{\theta_j} \Sigma^{-1} (\vec{X} - \vec{\mu})\right)
\end{aligned}
$$

Since, up to constants, this comes down to adding third central moments of a multivariate normal distribution we have

$$
E(m_i \beth_j) = 0
$$

Pulling all of this together, we have

$$
\begin{aligned}
\mathfrak{g}_{ij} &= -\frac{1}{4}\Gamma_i \Gamma_j + \frac{1}{4}E(\beth_i \beth_j) + E(m_i m_j) - \frac{1}{2}E(m_i \beth_j) - \frac{1}{2}E(m_j \beth_i) \\
&= -\frac{1}{4}tr\left(\Sigma^{-1}\Sigma_{\theta_i}\right) tr\left(\Sigma^{-1}\Sigma_{\theta_j}\right) + \frac{1}{4}\left[tr(\Sigma^{-1}\Sigma_i) tr(\Sigma^{-1}\Sigma_j)\right. \\
&\qquad \left. + 2tr(\Sigma^{-1}\Sigma_i \, \Sigma^{-1}\Sigma_j)\right] + \vec{\mu}_i^T \Sigma^{-1} \vec{\mu}_{\theta_j} \\
&= \frac{1}{2}tr(\Sigma^{-1}\Sigma_i \, \Sigma^{-1}\Sigma_j) + \vec{\mu}_{\theta_i}^T \Sigma^{-1} \vec{\mu}_{\theta_j}
\end{aligned}
\tag{9.33}
$$

Thus,

$$
ds^2_{f(\vec{\mu}, \Sigma)} = \sum_i \left(\frac{1}{2}tr(\Sigma^{-1}\Sigma_i \, \Sigma^{-1}\Sigma_j) + \vec{\mu}_{\theta_i}^T \Sigma^{-1} \vec{\mu}_{\theta_j}\right) d\theta^i \otimes d\theta^j
\tag{9.34}
$$

The only proof we could find of Eq. (9.34) is in Porat and Friedlander (1986) for a time series. There is a slight difference in the use of Σ, but the proof is Porat's. We have, however, filled in all of the details needed to understand (Porat & Friedlander, 1986, Appendix A). While this result is mentioned in the literature, except for Porat and Friedlander (1986), the proof is lacking has become a folk theorem.

We simplify the notation by looking at the components of a vector or matrix M, as m_k, and expressing DM as composed of the components dm_k, where $dm_k = \sum_i \frac{\partial m_k}{\partial \theta_i} d\theta_i$; we also express ds^2, with $d\theta^i \cdot d\theta^j$ representing the tensor product, as the following theorem which we have proved earlier.

Theorem 9.4.

$$ds^2_{f(\vec{\mu},\Sigma)} = \frac{1}{2}tr(\Sigma^{-1} \cdot d\Sigma \cdot \Sigma^{-1} \cdot d\Sigma) + d\vec{\mu}^T \cdot \Sigma^{-1} \cdot d\vec{\mu} \tag{9.35}$$

Note 9.8. The previous formula is the most general form. If some of the parameters are not parameters, but constants, one can either go through the previous derivation with that in mind, or more simply just realize that the differentials of those terms are zero. Similarly, if some of the parameters are equal to each other, the differentials are not zero, but the differentials are equal.

Corollary 9.2. *If the random vector of means $\vec{\mu}$ is constant, then $ds^2_{f(\Sigma)} = \frac{1}{2}tr(\Sigma^{-1} \cdot d\Sigma \cdot \Sigma^{-1} \cdot d\Sigma)$.*

We looked at the multivariate normal distribution in its most general sense, where the first part of the parameters θ_i corresponds to the means, and where the second part of the parameters corresponds to the variances and covariances. If we are only looking at a specific subset of the multivariate normal distributions, say those with constant means, or zero covariance, then we would adjust the parameters accordingly. Of course, this would be a "smaller" set of parameters.

Note 9.9. However, the previous derivation holds with the parameters adjusted accordingly. We can also adjust the parameters by using the standard deviations instead of the variances or other parameters. We will use adjustment in what follows.

First, we start with $\mathbb{H}_f = N(\mu, \sigma^2)$.

9.6.1 $\mathbb{H}_f$ Revisited

According to our earlier natural parameter conventions, we set $\vec{\mu} = \mu_1 = \mu = \theta_1$ and $\Sigma = \sigma_{11} = \sigma^2 = \theta_2$. So,

$$d\vec{\mu} = d\mu_1$$

$$d\Sigma = d\sigma_{11}$$

$$ds^2_{f(\mu,\Sigma)} = \frac{1}{2}tr\left(\sigma_{11}^{-1} \cdot d\sigma_{11} \cdot \sigma_{11}^{-1} \cdot d\sigma_{11}\right) + d\mu_1 \cdot \sigma_{11}^{-1} \cdot d\mu_1$$

$$= \frac{1}{\sigma_{11}}d\mu_1 \otimes d\mu_1 + \frac{1}{2\sigma_{11}^2}d\sigma_{11} \otimes d\sigma_{11}$$

Now if we use the classic hyperbolic parameter space $\theta_1 = \mu_1$, $\theta_2 = \sigma_1$, we have

$$d\vec{\mu} = d\mu_1$$

$$\Sigma = (\sigma_1)^2$$

$$\Sigma^{-1} = (\sigma_1)^{-2}$$

$$d\Sigma = 2\sigma_1 \, d\sigma_1$$

$$ds^2_{f(\mu,\sigma)} = \frac{1}{2}tr\left(\sigma_1^{-2} \cdot 2\sigma_1 \, d\sigma_1 \cdot \sigma_1^{-2} \cdot 2\sigma \, d\sigma\right) + d\mu_1 \cdot \sigma^{-2} \cdot d\mu_1$$

$$= \frac{1}{\sigma^2}d\mu \otimes d\mu + \frac{2}{\sigma^2}d\sigma \otimes d\sigma$$

The later result is Eq. (9.15).

9.6.2 $\mathbb{N}_f^{\vec{\mu},\Sigma_{D(\sigma_{11})}}$

Now, we generalize the previous section and consider the $(n + 1)$-dimensional statistical manifold $\mathbb{N}_f^{\vec{\mu},\Sigma_{D(\sigma_{11})}}$. The parameters are the means $\mu_1,\ldots,\mu_n$, but all the random variables X_i have the common variance σ_{11} and the covariances are zero.

$$\Sigma = \begin{pmatrix} \sigma_{11} & 0 & \ldots & 0 \\ 0 & \sigma_{11} & \ldots & 0 \\ & & \ddots & \\ 0 & \ldots & 0 & \sigma_{11} \end{pmatrix} \quad \Sigma^{-1} = \begin{pmatrix} \sigma_{11}^{-1} & 0 & \ldots & 0 \\ 0 & \sigma_{11}^{-1} & \ldots & 0 \\ & & \ddots & \\ 0 & \ldots & 0 & \sigma_{11}^{-1} \end{pmatrix} d\Sigma = \begin{pmatrix} 1 \cdot d\sigma_{11} & 0 & \ldots & 0 \\ 0 & d\sigma_{11} & \ldots & 0 \\ & & \ddots & \\ 0 & \ldots & 0 & d\sigma_{11} \end{pmatrix}$$

We easily see that

$$ds^2_{f(\vec{\mu},\sigma_{11})} = \frac{1}{\sigma_{11}}\left(\sum_{i=1}^{n}d\mu_i \otimes d\mu_i\right) + \frac{n}{2\sigma_{11}^2}d\sigma_{11} \otimes d\sigma_{11}$$

Equivalently, switching coordinates to the standard deviation σ instead of the common variance (Costa et al., 2015, Section 3.1) (since $d\sigma_{11} = 2\sigma d\sigma$),

$$ds^2_{f(\vec{\mu},\sigma)} = \frac{1}{\sigma^2}\left(\sum_{i=1}^{n}d\mu_i \otimes d\mu_i + 2nd\sigma \otimes d\sigma\right)$$

9.6.3 $\mathbb{N}_f^{\vec{\mu},\Sigma_{D(\sigma_{11},\ldots,\sigma_{nn})}}$

Now consider the $2n$-dimensional statistical manifold $\mathbb{N}_f^{\vec{\mu},\Sigma_{D(\sigma_{11},\ldots,\sigma_{nn})}}$; the parameters are the means $\mu_1,\ldots\mu_n$, the variances $\sigma_{11},\ldots,\sigma_{nn}$, and the covariances are zero (the X_i are independent).

$$\Sigma = \begin{pmatrix} \sigma_{11} & 0 & \ldots & 0 \\ 0 & \sigma_{22} & \ldots & 0 \\ & & \ddots & \\ 0 & \ldots & 0 & \sigma_{nn} \end{pmatrix} \quad \Sigma^{-1} = \begin{pmatrix} \sigma_{11}^{-1} & 0 & \ldots & 0 \\ 0 & \sigma_{22}^{-1} & \ldots & 0 \\ & & \ddots & \\ 0 & \ldots & 0 & \sigma_{nn}^{-1} \end{pmatrix} d\Sigma = \begin{pmatrix} d\sigma_{11} & 0 & \ldots & 0 \\ 0 & d\sigma_{22} & \ldots & 0 \\ & & \ddots & \\ 0 & \ldots & 0 & d\sigma_{nn} \end{pmatrix}$$

In terms of the natural parameters, we get

$$ds^2_{f(\vec{\mu},\Sigma_{D(\sigma_{11},...,\sigma_{nn})})} = \left(\sum_{i=1}^{n}\frac{d\mu_i \otimes d\mu_i}{\sigma_{ii}}\right) + \left(\sum_{j=1}^{n}\frac{d\sigma_{jj} \otimes d\sigma_{jj}}{2\sigma_{jj}^2}\right)$$

Or, equivalently in terms of the hyperbolic coordinates, the latter becomes

$$ds^2_{f(\vec{\mu},\sigma_1,...,\sigma_n)} = \left(\sum_{i=1}^{n}\frac{d\mu_i \otimes d\mu_i}{\sigma_i^2}\right) + \left(\sum_{j=1}^{n}\frac{2d\sigma_j \otimes d\sigma_j}{\sigma_j^2}\right) \tag{9.36}$$

In this chapter, we concentrated on variants of the normal distribution. The Fisher metric for other metrics can be found in Burbea (1984), Maybank (2016), and Ceolin and Hancock (2012). What is relevant are the family of Von Mises-type distributions, which require more than one manifold chart since it is circular in behavior. Thus, our earlier definition of a simple statistical manifold is obviously extended to the cases, where the topology is no longer trivial, and the term "simple" no longer applies.

9.7 Value of information and complexity

What we want is a mathematical metric that captures the behavior illustrated at the beginning of this chapter concerning the normal distribution. Changing the mean gives us no new information, yet decreasing the standard deviation gives us lots of information. This metric is the complexity, which we seek below.

Our definitions and thoughts on complexity are heavily influenced by Myung, Balasubramanian, and Pitt (2000). However, we take a much simpler view of complexity than (Myung et al., 2000) and the various sources cited in that paper. In fact, we use Maybank's (2004) analysis of the volume of statistical manifolds as our definition for complexity.

In Riemannian geometry, the element of volume is dV is given by

$$dV = \sqrt{\det[\mathfrak{g}_{ij}]}\, dx_1...dx_n \tag{9.37}$$

For the space $\mathbb{H}_f$ that we are dealing with, the element of volume is

$$dV = \frac{\sqrt{2}}{\sigma^2}d\mu\, d\sigma \tag{9.38}$$

We define the *complexity* $\mathfrak{C}$ of a statistical manifold to be the following nonnegative real-valued function on the statistical manifold.

Definition 9.21 (From Maybank, 2004). Given a statistical manifold

$$\mathfrak{C}[S] := \sqrt{\det[\mathfrak{g}_{ij}]}$$

This definition is well defined up to the choice of local coordinates ξ. The volume form of a Riemannian manifold is independent of the choice of local coordinates. However, we are not using the differential *n*-form, only its coefficient!

We relate the complexity to the VoI via the following context. If we are at a point on a statistical manifold S, how does information that changes the point we are on influence our knowledge? If we are on $\mathbb{H}_f$ and we learn information about μ, we have not really learned anything of value. However, if we can lower σ, then that is important. This result corresponds to less variance in our distribution, and thus more certainty. Therefore, if we want to increase our knowledge, we need to increase the complexity. The more closely packed the density functions, the more knowledge we have. If we are in $\mathbb{H}_f$, we should always choose to minimize the standard deviation σ.

The example of $\mathbb{H}_f$ is not too difficult to analyze since the complexity,

$$\mathfrak{C}[\mathbb{H}_f] = \sqrt{2}/\sigma^2$$

consists of one variable, and we easily see that increasing $\mathfrak{C}$ corresponds to decreasing σ.

Observation: When analyzing $\mathbb{H}_f$ the statistical manifold's complexity increases as σ decreases. Its maximal complexity is obtained as $\sigma \to 0^+$. However, changing μ has no effect on the complexity.

Definition 9.22. We are given a statistical manifold S, and a function $I\colon S \to S$. If $s \in S$, we say that I is **valuable with respect to** s if

$$\mathfrak{C}(I(s)) > \mathfrak{C}(s).$$

If the earlier criteria hold for all points in S, we say that I is **valuable information**. If it holds for some subset of S, we say that it is **valuable with respect to that subset**.

Definition 9.23. Similar to the earlier, we say that a function has **null information** if the earlier inequality is replaced with equality.

Thus, we have the following obvious result.

Theorem 9.5. *Functions on $\mathbb{H}_f$ that only modify μ have null information, while functions that decrease σ are valuable.*

Given that $\mathbb{H}_f$ with respect to its complexity is dependent only on σ, the concept of information being valuable is a simple concept. However, result this is *not* the case for the bivariate normal distribution since there are multiple variances (standard deviations).

Now consider the $(n + 1)$-dimensional statistical manifold $\mathbb{N}_f^{\Sigma D(\sigma)}$ as given earlier. We see that

$$\mathfrak{C}\left[\mathbb{N}_f^{\Sigma D(\sigma)}\right] = \frac{\sqrt{2n}}{\sigma^{n+1}}, \text{ which gives us the following theorem:} \tag{9.39}$$

Theorem 9.6. *Functions on $\mathbb{N}_f^{\Sigma D(\sigma)}$ that only modify $\mu_i, i = 1, \ldots, n$ have null information, and functions that decrease σ are valuable.*

However, we have from Eq. (9.36) that

$$\mathfrak{C}\left[\mathbb{N}_f^{\Sigma D(\sigma_1, \ldots, \sigma_n)}\right] = \frac{2^{n/2}}{(\sigma_1 \cdot \sigma_2 \cdots \sigma_n)^2} \tag{9.40}$$

The previous thinking leads to the following theorem.

Theorem 9.7. *Functions on $\mathbb{N}_f^{\Sigma D(\sigma_1,...,\sigma_n)}$ that only modify the $\mu_i, i = 1,...,n$ have null information, and functions that decrease, but never increase, the σ_i are valuable.*

9.8 Allotment of resources

If we wish to increase our information when dealing with multivariate normal distributions, we have to analyze their complexity.

Given a statistical manifold S, we let

$$\mathfrak{C}[S](\boldsymbol{\xi}_0) = \mathfrak{C}[S](\xi_{1_0},...,\xi_{n_0})$$

be the complexity evaluated at the point $\boldsymbol{\xi}_0$.

We denote a Euclidean statistical manifold (see Section 9.2) as S^e. Note that $\mathbb{H}_f$ and all of its extensions to multivariate normal distributions studied earlier are Euclidean statistical manifolds. Statistical manifolds that are not Euclidean are the Von-Mises distributions, where one of the parameters is based on the 1-sphere S^1, concepts of power that we discuss below must be followed carefully because we have winding number type issues at play. For now, we assume that our manifolds are Euclidean when it comes to power.

Definition 9.24. We say that we have **power** P if we can adjust, by addition or subtraction, the parameters $\boldsymbol{\xi}_0 = (\xi_{1_0},...,\xi_{n_0})$ of a Euclidean statistical manifold $S^e(\boldsymbol{\xi})$ to $\boldsymbol{\xi}_1 = (\xi_{1_1},...,\xi_{n_1})$ such that

$$\sum_i^n |\xi_{i_1} - \xi_{i_0}| \le P. \tag{9.41}$$

We call the adjustment of the parameters with power P a **use** U of P.

Definition 9.25. We say that we use power P efficiently if

$$\mathfrak{C}[S^e](\boldsymbol{\xi}_1) > \mathfrak{C}[S^e](\boldsymbol{\xi}_0) \tag{9.42}$$

Definition 9.26. We say that the use U of power P is **maximal** if $\mathfrak{C}[S^e](\boldsymbol{\xi}_1)$ cannot be increased with respect to other uses U' of P.

The earlier definitions may depend on our initial point $\boldsymbol{\xi}_0$.

QUESTION: Given power P, what is the best use of U; that is, how can we maximize complexity?

Let us go back to our initial statistical manifold of study $\mathbb{H}_f(\mu, \sigma)$. If we have power P, the best use of the power is to adjust (μ, σ) to $(\mu, \sigma - P)$ provided that $\sigma - P > 0$. If $\sigma \le P$, then we can only asymptotically approach the best use of P by adjusting the point to $(\mu, \sigma - P')$ such that $\sigma > P'$.

Let us look at $\mathbb{N}_f^{\Sigma D(\sigma)}$; with respect to the best usage of power, it behaves like its lower-dimensional self $\mathbb{H}_f$; that is; we apply as much power as we can to reducing σ.

The situation is very different when we analyze $\mathbb{N}_f^{\Sigma D(\sigma_1,...,\sigma_n)}$. We certainly do not want to apply any power to the means, but we seek to determine which standard deviations we do lower, and by how much.

9.8.1 $\mathfrak{C}[N_f^{\Sigma D(\sigma_1, \sigma_2)}]$

Given specific points ($\mu_1 = \alpha$, $\sigma_1 = a$, $\mu_2 = \beta$, $\sigma_2 = b$) and power P, what is the maximal use of P? First, manipulating μ_1 or μ_2 does not affect the complexity, and increasing σ_1 or σ_2 decreases complexity. Therefore, we want to subtract from σ_1 and σ_2 but by how much given that the more we subtract, the better. This leads us to the following:

Let L be the straight line in the $\sigma_1 \times \sigma_2$ plane connecting ($a - P$, b) and (a, $b - P$). The maximal use of P will be a power allocation represented on this line; that is, L consists of the points $(x, y) = (a - \delta, b - (P - \delta))$, $\delta \in [0, P]$. The equation of this line is $y = -x + (a + b - P)$. We wish to maximize the complexity $\mathfrak{C}[N_f^{\Sigma D(x,y)}] = 2/(xy)^2$ restricted to the line L. After algebraic manipulations, we can show that the point on L for the maximum is at:

$$(a - P, b) \text{ for } a < b$$
$$(a, b - P) \text{ for } a > b$$

LESSON: In terms of the VoI, it is even more important in this case to get information that lets us lower the smaller of the two standard deviations σ_i. Applied to sensor receptors, when faced with a limited amount of power to reduce noise, where the signal is modeled as $N_f^{\Sigma D(\sigma_1, \sigma_2)}$, we should apply it more to the smaller variance (or standard deviation).

We could have obtained this insight other ways. What is more interesting to us is what happens when partial power is applied to σ_1 and the remainder to σ_2. Complexity gives us an intuitive way to make decisions on how to add information into a problem. In future work, we will look at dimensions higher than 2.

9.9 Conclusion

We have explored the use of statistical manifolds to determine the VoI. We will explore this concept more in the future. The purpose of this chapter was to lay a firm foundation for our information geometric approach to the VoI. If successful, machines will have a mathematical approach to allow them to share what they understand with their human teammates, a critical step to form human-machine teams.

Acknowledgments

The authors thank Sophie Cisse, Steve Finette, and Ruth Heilizer for their helpful comments and assistance.

References

Ahsanullah, M. (2014). *Normal and Student's t distributions and their applications.* (Vol. 4). Atlantis Studies. Atlantis Press in Probability and Statistics.

Amari, S. (1985). *Differential-geometrical methods in statistics.* (Vol. 28). Lecture Notes in Statistics. Springer-Verlag.

Amari, S. (2001). Information geometry on hierarchy of probability distributions. *IEEE Transactions on Information Theory*, 47(5), 1701–1711.

Atkinson, C., & Mitchell, A. F. (1981). Rao's distance measure. *Sankhya: The Indian Journal of Statistics, Series A*, 43, 345–365.

Bengtsson, I., & Zyczkowski, K. (2006). *Geometry of quantum states.* (Vol. 2006). Cambridge University Press.

Blanuša, D. (1955). Über die Einbettung hyperbolishcher Räume in euklidische Räume. *Monattshefte für Mathematik,* *59*(3), 217–229.

Burbea, J. (1984). *Expositiones Mathematicae, 4*(4), 347–378.

Carter, K. M., Raich, R., & Hero, A. O., III. (2009). FINE: Fisher Information Nonparametric Enbedding. *IEEE Transaction on Pattern Analysis and Machine Intelligence, 31*(11), 2093–2098.

Ceolin, S. R., & Hancock, E. R. (2012). Computing gender difference using Fisher-Rao metric from facial surface normals. *2012 25th SIBGRAPI conference on graphics, patterns and images (SIBGRAPI).*

Chavel, I. (2006). *RIemmanian geometry a modern introduction.* Cambridge University Press.

Costa, S. I. R., Santos, S. A., & Strapasso, J. E. (2015). Fisher information distance: A geometrical reading. *Discrete Applied Mathematics, 197,* 59–69.

Cover, T. M., & Thomas, J. A. (2006). *Elements of information theory.* Wiley Interscience.

Fisher, R. A. (1922). On the mathematical foundations of theoretical statistics. *Philosophical Transactions of the Royal Society of London Series A, Containing Papers of a Mathematical or Physical Character, 222,* 309–368.

Gauss, C. F. (1827). *Disquistiones generales circa superficies curvase—Allegemeine flachentheorie.* Deutsch herausgegeben von A. Wangerin.

Gray, A., Abbena, E., & Salamon, S. (2005). *Modern differential geometry of curves and surfaces with mathematica®.* Chapman & Hall.

Gromoll, D., Meyer, W., & Klingenberg, W. (1975). *Riemannsche geometrie im großen.* (Vol. 55). Lecture Notes in Mathematics. Springer-Verlag.

Hopf, H., & Rinow, W. (1931). Ueber den Begriff der vollständigen differentialgeometrischen Fläche. *Commentarii Mathematici Helvetici, 3*(1), 209–225.

Howard, R. A. (1966). Information value theory. *IEEE Transactions on Systems Science and Cybernetics, 1,* 22–26.

Kass, R. E., & Vos, P. W. (1997). *Geometrical foundations of asymptotic inference.* Wiley.

Kobayashi, S., & Nomizu, K. (1963). *Foundations of differential geometry.* (Vol. 1). Interscience Number 15.

Lane, E. P. (1940). *Metric differential geometry of curves and surfaces.* University of Chicago Press.

Lawless, W. F., Mittu, R., Sofge, D. A., & Hiatt, L. (2019). Introduction to the special issue "artificial intelligence (AI), autonomy and human-machine teams: Interdependence, context and explainable AI". *AI Magazine.*

Lee, J. M. (1997). *Riemannian manifolds an introduction to curvature.* (Vol. 176). Graduate Texts in Mathematics. Springer.

Ly, A., Marsman, M., Verhagen, J., Grasman, R. P. P. P., & Wagenmakers, E.-J. (2017). A tutorial on Fisher information. *Journal of Mathematical Psychology, 80,* 40–55.

Magnus, J. R., & Neudecker, H. (1999). *Matrix differential calculus with applications in statistics and econometric.* Wiley.

Maybank, S. J. (2004). Detection of image structures using the Fisher Rao information and the Rao metric. *IEEE Transactions on Pattern Analysis and Machine Intelligence, 26*(12), 1579–1589.

Maybank, S. J. (2016). A Fisher–Rao metric for curves using the information in edges. *Journal of Mathematical Imaging and Vision, 54,* 287–300.

Michalowicz, J. V., Nichols, J. M., Bucholtz, F., & Olsona, C. C. (2011). A generalized Isserlis theorem for location mixtures of Gaussian random vectors. *Statistics and Probability Letters, 81*(8), 1233–1240.

Millman, R. S., & Parker, G. D. (1977). *Elements of differential geometry.* Prentice-Hall.

Moskowitz, I. S., & Russell, S. (2019). The value of information and the Internet of things. In Lawless (Ed.), *Artifical intelligence for the Internet of everything* (pp. 145–169). Academic Press (Chapter 9).

Munkres, J. R. (1963). *Elementary differential topology.* (Vol. 54). Annals of Mathematics Studies. Princeton University Press.

Myung, I. J., Balasubramanian, V., & Pitt, M. A. (2000). Counting probability distributions: Differential geometry and model selection. *PNAS, 97*(21), 11170–11175.

Nash, J. (1956). The imbedding problem for Riemannian manifolds. *Annals of Mathematics, 63*(1), 20–63.

Porat, B., & Friedlander, B. (1986). Computation of the exact information matrix of Gaussian time series with stationary random components. *IEEE Transactions on Acoustics, Speech and Signal Processing, 34*(1), 118–130.

Rao, C. R. (1945). Information and the accuracy attainable in the estimation of statistical parameters. *Bulletin of Calcutta Mathematical Society, 37*(3), 81–91.

Shannon, C. E. (1948). A mathematical theory of communication. *Bell Systems Technical Journal, 27,* 379–423, 623–656.

Spivak, M. (1999). *A Comprehensive introduction to differential geometry.* (Vols. 1–5). Publish or Perish.

Suzuki, M. (2014). *Information geometry and statistical manifold.* arXiv:1510.33691v1, October 9.

Wang, X., Cheng, Y., & Moran, B. (2010). Bearings-only tracking analysis via information geometry. *2010 13th International conference on information fusion* (pp. 1–6): IEEE.

AI, autonomous machines and human awareness: Towards shared machine-human contexts in medicine

D. Douglas Miller, Elena A. Wood

Academic Affairs, Medical College of Georgia at Augusta University, Augusta, GA, United States

10.1 Introduction

Computers mimicking human thought by processing massive datasets through layered neural networks—artificial intelligence (AI)—are generating insights that are influencing the social, business, scientific, and educational domains. Promising *precision health* AI applications are emerging for advanced medical image analytics and predictive modeling of genetic disease risk.

In an era when quantifiable biology is meeting big data, medical education and training programs are charged with imparting massive amounts of expanding biomedical scientific knowledge to learners. Today's complex clinical learning environment is also greatly influenced by digital health-care technologies, including AI. Upskilling of health professionals to effectively apply data science and AI technologies at the human knowable fact ceiling—*precision education*—could improve systems of patient care and individual precision health outcomes.

Computer engineers, data scientists, and medical educators must collaborate on an AI-infused *precision education* curriculum designed to prepare health professions learners to better navigate the increasingly data-dense scientific and digital health-care environments. Resulting AI technology literacy could promote learners' coping skills and mitigate provider burnout caused by stressful data overload and lower technology interfaces. Leveraging key AI computing fundamentals could also augment medical educators' understanding of critical thinking skill development and reveal insights about individuals' learning styles and career aptitudes.

This chapter presents a rationale for a more interdisciplinary expert engagement, sets forth the challenges and opportunities facing medical educators, offers AI-infused educational content ideas (use cases), and advocates for medical learner and health professional upskilling to achieve AI technology literacy through precision education. To help the reader exploring these issues, we set up three objectives for this chapter:

1. Describe the current state of medical education and its challenges.
2. Explore potential AI applications for medical education (teaching, advising, and evaluation).
3. Examine the shared machine-human context faced by medicine and medical professionals.

10.2 Current state of medical education and its challenges

Medical education starts with the admission to a medical school and continues as long as a physician practices medicine. Undergraduate medical education (UME), graduate medical education (GME), and continuing medical education (CME) are three phases of education for the practice of medicine. Medical education has become very complex and dynamic to reflect the constant changes in the learning sciences, medicine, and health care. The UME curriculum is itself very complex. It includes two steps: preclinic and clinical training. Preclinical, or preclerkship, is focused on biomedical knowledge acquisition, whereas during clerkship years, students are imbedded into clinical settings to practice medicine alongside of physicians (Fig. 10.1).

10.2.1 Biomedical information explosion

The *knowable fact ceiling* is constantly being raised by the continuously growing and evolving body of peer-reviewed scientific data (i.e., the evidence). Published scientific information is projected to double every 3 years by 2020 (Larsen & von Ins, 2010; Mohr, Moreno-Walton, Mills, Brunett, & Promes, 2011; Van Noorden, 2014). As that rate the biomedical

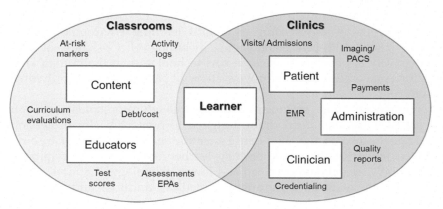

FIG. 10.1   Undergraduate medical learning environments structure and contexts.

literature doubles during the time a medical student completes the MD curriculum and *again* while a resident finishes core GME training.

This unprecedented acceleration of quantifiable biomedical evidence discovery surpasses the ability of medical educators to convey the most up-to-date information and the capacity of medical learners to contact, absorb, and retain the relevant facts and key concepts. Knowing what facts to study, relearn, and document in the electronic medical records (EMR), all contribute to the almost 50% self-reported burnout rate among medical students, residents, and physicians (Davenport, 2018; Peckham, 2018).

The **clinical learning environment** is composed of diverse health-care delivery and insurance systems that are being challenged by its own everexpanding complexity, including massive digital data generations in the course of care (Deloitte Centre for Health Solutions, 2014). Health-care systems are responding by adopting digital health technology platforms to help achieve greater operating efficacy and cost efficiency (Cresswell, Bates, & Sheikh, 2017). Increasingly, these platforms depend on high-speed computer processing (data analytics) and high-capacity storage (data repositories; in Bates, Saria, Ohno-Machado, Shah, & Escobar, 2014). In this high-technology environment, expanding digital data rules (Fogel & Kvedar, 2018) have closely paralleled health policy-mandated technology adoption (i.e., meaningful EMR use; in Nasca, Weiss, & Bagian, 2014). In response to such complexity, health-care technology and data solutions are being jointly engineered by data scientists and medical experts.

Machine learning and its parent technology artificial intelligence (AI) are not new. However, in the last decade, computer engineers have applied computer science fundamentals and ultrafast data processing speeds to see AI widely impact humanity in the social, scientific, and financial sectors (LeCun, Bengio, & Hinton, 2015). AI technologies are now offering cognitive tutoring for K-12 students and college undergraduates (Elmes, 2017).

Medical schools and graduate medical education (GME) training programs sit squarely at the nexus of the biomedical knowledge explosion and the digital health technology expansion. As is the case with other data-dense sectors, the convergence of health-care system composed of complexity with the emergence of digital technology presents health professions educators with a clear choice—to passively observe or actively engage. This powerful system composed of a complexity-data explosion dynamic creates an imperative for computer and data scientists and medical educational experts to jointly design new approaches to professional education and training (Wartman & Combs, 2018).

10.2.2 Digital health technology expansion

Medical practice has long involved doctors caring for patient and families to relieve human suffering, extend a life with quality, and ease care transitions (Fig. 10.2A—medical education without AI; Fig. 10.2B—medical education in health-care environment with AI). Modern medicine now requires the effective daily use of digital health technologies to achieve these goals (Sethi, 2014; Wartman & Combs, 2018). AI has joined in the mix of promising digital health technologies with proven applications in medical imaging (Miller & Brown, 2019), electronic medical record (EMR) reading and file compression (Miller, 2018), precision medicine (i.e., genomic disease risk), and wearable device-assisted chronic disease management (i.e., asthma, diabetes, and mental illness; in Fogel & Kvedar, 2018; Miller & Brown, 2018).

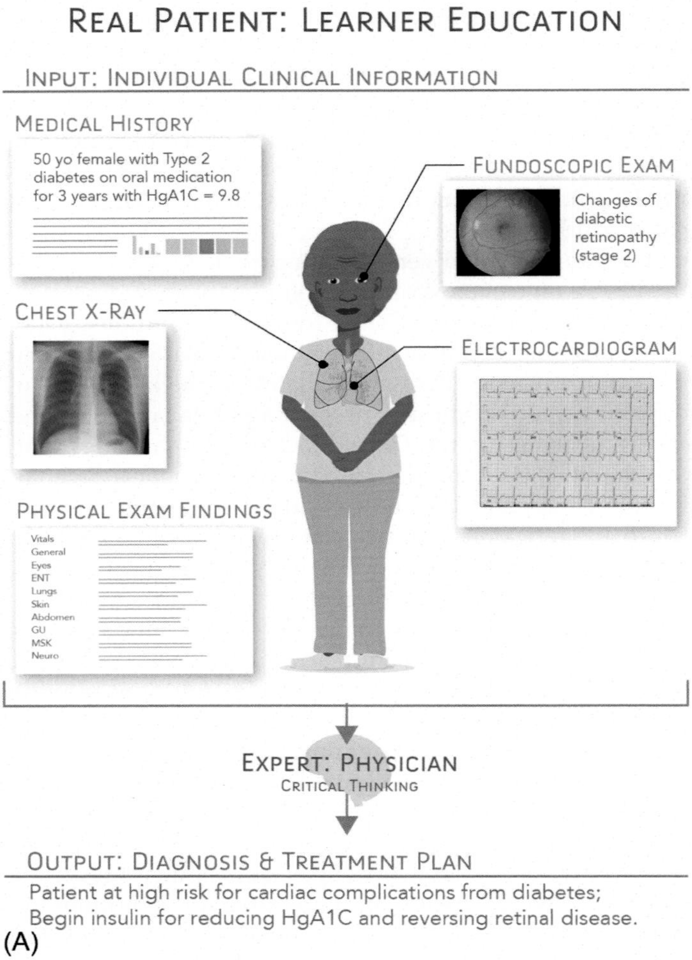

REAL PATIENT: LEARNER EDUCATION

INPUT: INDIVIDUAL CLINICAL INFORMATION

MEDICAL HISTORY

50 yo female with Type 2
diabetes on oral medication
for 3 years with HgA1C = 9.8

FUNDOSCOPIC EXAM

Changes of
diabetic
retinopathy
(stage 2)

CHEST X-RAY

ELECTROCARDIOGRAM

PHYSICAL EXAM FINDINGS

Vitals
General
Eyes
ENT
Lungs
Skin
Abdomen
GU
MSK
Neuro

EXPERT: PHYSICIAN
CRITICAL THINKING

OUTPUT: DIAGNOSIS & TREATMENT PLAN

Patient at high risk for cardiac complications from diabetes;
Begin insulin for reducing HgA1C and reversing retinal disease.

(A)

FIG. 10.2A   Real patient present in health care. *HgA1C*, hemoglobin A1C. An HbA1c test shows what the average amount of glucose attached to hemoglobin has been over the past 3 months. High level of HgA1C indicates high glucose levels in the blood.

10.2.3 Technology insertion barriers

The clinical impact of many digital health innovations, including microchip medical devices and networked telemedicine, has lagged behind their introduction into the system of care, despite evidence that they measurably enhance personal health information security, improve patient quality of life, and broaden remote access to advanced health care. One proximate cause of such technology insertion setbacks is the failure to purposefully educate the professional workforce to become early technology adopters *before* they enter their chosen workplace (Kerr, Phaal, & Probert, 2008). This ***information explosion-technology insertion dichotomy*** is a shared "pain point" for medical universities and health-care systems charged with educating learners and training the health-care workforce ready to deliver reliable, safe, high-quality care.

FIG. 10.2B Digital patient present in health care. *CAD*, coronary artery disease; *MI*, myocardial infarction; *RNN*, recurrent neural networks; *NLP*, natural language processing; *GAN*, generative adversarial network; *ECG*, electrocardiogram.

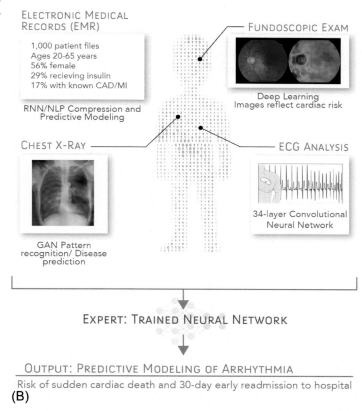

VIRTUAL PATIENT: MACHINE LEARNING

INPUT: TRAINING DATA SETS FROM DATABASE

ELECTRONIC MEDICAL RECORDS (EMR)

1,000 patient files
Ages 20-65 years
56% female
29% recieving insulin
17% with known CAD/MI

RNN/NLP Compression and Predictive Modeling

FUNDOSCOPIC EXAM

Deep Learning
Images reflect cardiac risk

CHEST X-RAY

GAN Pattern recognition/ Disease prediction

ECG ANALYSIS

34-layer Convolutional Neural Network

EXPERT: TRAINED NEURAL NETWORK

OUTPUT: PREDICTIVE MODELING OF ARRHYTHMIA

Risk of sudden cardiac death and 30-day early readmission to hospital

(B)

10.2.4 Medical learning challenges

The growth of published scientific evidence and stored repository data are not the same as knowable facts. Fact retention for future rapid recall (rote memorization) is not critical thinking. One recognized impediment to developing critical thinking skills in medical school and during residency training is the effective acquisition, interpretation, and use of very large numbers of facts. To compensate for the recognized human memory limitations, medical schools and training programs are endeavoring to teach students and residents to become active learners (Densen, 2011).

Commensurate with (and potentially derivative of) the rising knowable fact ceiling associated with biomedical knowledge expansion and the finite length of a medical curriculum, medical education has migrated from teacher-centered/subject-based *surface learning* (i.e., didactic lectures about theory, systems, and facts) to the use of problem-based/student-centered *active learning* approaches (i.e., self-directed learning) (Samarakoon, Fernando, & Rodrigo, 2013).

Despite the aforementioned health-care technology insertion barriers, medical education now necessarily interfaces with new teaching technologies—from virtual reality avatars to sophisticated high-fidelity simulations to multimedia curriculum delivery. This technology-savvy generation of learners readily adapt to and adopt new technologies, whether in the classroom or in the clinic (Mohr et al., 2011).

In summary the emerging challenges of a medical education present as the following:

- A massive new medical knowledge to be assimilated/taught (how to prioritize/sequence?),
- Historical struggles with low technology/EMR insertion (when to adopt?),
- Quality of data used to make/advise on career decisions (what to do/how to prepare?).

10.3 Potential AI application for medical education

While not all machines are intelligent, some machines can learn from humans. AI is a discipline of computer science that applies ultrafast computer processing to emulate or augment human cognitive abilities (LeCun et al., 2015). These technologies allow machines to detect patterns (learn features) in massive complex datasets that are not decipherable using standard statistical analyses (Ghahramani, 2015).

Data naturally cluster into lower dimensional structures (data manifolds) within a data matrix (Launchbury, 2017). Higher understanding (insight) about the information in a multidimensional data matrix comes by separating data features from each other using nonlinear computational models (algorithms) layered into neural networks. This process reveals "information about the functional properties that is not obvious from the representation of the matrix as an array of elements" (Goodfellow, Bengio, & Courville, 2016). Continuous correction of minor algorithm errors (model training) adds confidence to AI predictive outputs, which intentionally never reach 100% accuracy to avoid undesirable model overfitting to noise in the dataset (Brownlee, 2016).

Current AI applications for data analytics demonstrate that combined machine learning *plus* human thinking reliably enhances system performance. The most powerful, deep learning neural networks use feature engineering to explain and predict real-world phenomena from massive disparate arrays of structured data (i.e., hurricane tracks, a financial system collapse, and cyberattacks) and/or unstructured data (i.e., natural languages, voice wave patterns, and social media feeds; in LeCun et al., 2015).

Health-care machine learning (ML) applications are informing health-care system decision-making, predicting epidemics, automating medical systematic reviews, and identifying high-risk trajectories of chronic disease patients (Dai, Gwadry-Sridhar, Bauer, & Borrie, 2015; Miller & Brown, 2018). Such features and the related insights are often obscure to humans, including medical experts.

The potential for AI to reduce human medical reasoning errors is now apparent. Human system-1 thinking failures (i.e., medical errors due to cognitive biases) decrease with greater knowledge and experience (Norman et al., 2017). System-2 errors resulting from limited human working memory could theoretically be reduced through the use of natural language processing (NLP) technologies that read and memorize the peer-reviewed biomedical literature (facts), or rapidly condense years of complex EMR patient information into organized fact arrays. But the human capacity to continuously identify and rapidly reconcile feature inconsistencies (i.e., reasoning) greatly enhances human cognitive abilities, exceeding that possible with current AI systems (Launchbury, 2017).

10.3.1 Medical education use-cases

A library of diverse virtual clinical cases with slightly varied phenotypes could be developed using generative AI systems (Goodfellow et al., 2014). Such virtual patient files can be used to develop more effective system-1 thinking among less experienced medical trainees, exposing them to patterns of illness presentations and important variances that should signal a fluid change in differential diagnosis thinking (Kahneman, 2011).

AI technology excels at pattern recognition within complex high-dimensional datasets. IBM Watson can use its NLP capabilities featuring recurrent neural networks (RNNs) with long short-term memory units to rapidly read the extensive relevant medical literature and prioritize what factual knowledge (evidence) is necessary to solve a problem and what can be delegated to its memory banks for future use. The use of the United States Medical Licensing Examination (USMLE) standardized questions allows IBM scientists to train its recurrent neural networks (RNNs) and thereby improve Watson's problem-solving ability. The iterative process that occurred between Watson and the human contestants on the television show "Jeopardy," can be extended to interactions between medical learners and this type of an intelligent machine.

10.3.1.1 Example use case—USMLE Step-2 clinical knowledge question

In the case below, AI system-controlled variable that if changed effects the predictive model output.

A previously healthy 30-year-old woman who presents to the emergency room with left lower quadrant pain of 4–5 h duration. Her last menstrual period was 2 months earlier. She also notes spotty vaginal bleeding for the past 2 days. Physical exam reveals the following vital signs: blood pressure = 105/65, pulse = 98 and regular, respiratory rate = 18 unlabored, and $T = 38.4°F$. Abdominal exam shows normal bowel sounds and a painful fullness in the left lower quadrant on moderate palpation without rebound tenderness. Pelvic exam confirms moderate bloody cervical discharge and a painful mobile left adnexal mass.

Given these inputs, what is the most probable differential diagnosis?

The 13 highlighted pieces of information (pertinent positives and negatives) are the crux of answering this question. Knowledge correlates of these points are sought out in the medical literature—a large covariant data matrix—the training data for which a machine has previously "read" using NLP (Chary, Parikh, Manini, Boyer, & Radeos, 2019). The intelligent machine (an AI diagnostic module) relates its learned neural network feature recognition to structured and unstructured data patterns in the matrix. The most highly correlated diagnoses are then prioritized for consideration, with a supporting evidence-based list of medical publications. The machine's human supervisor can tune up or down any of the highlighted clinical variables in the predictive model (from 0% influence to 100% representation) to relate the significance of findings to the alternative differential diagnoses.

Students studying for a high-stake licensing examination can experience a range of similar virtual clinical cases that might be encountered in practice and critically reflect on the important variances that would signal a change in their top differential diagnoses. This type of information iteration also enhances the student's real-world capacity to relate knowable fact patterns to clinical scenarios, thereby developing a greater diagnostic acumen and medical management expertise.

USMLE cases such as this are used to train IBM Watson to optimize its clinical problem-solving capabilities based on the published medical evidence; medical students are actively validating this AI training with their own human learning approaches to the very same standardized questions. The machine's algorithmic pattern recognition confidence can be applied to the cognitive coaching of test-prepping students, whose question-answering confidence builds over recurrent interactions with the bank of standardized questions.

Other potential medical education AI use cases include (1) AI-informed medical education methods (*cognitive curriculum*), (2) NLP-enhanced digital health technology deconstruction (*EMR emersion*), and (3) individualized AI assistance for struggling learners (*medical tutoring; in* Chan & Zary, 2019).

In 2014 a journal article was published on how to automate essay scoring in medical education assessment with AI, offering a benefit to medical educators (Gierl, Latifi, Lai, Boulais, & DeChamplain, 2014). Scoring constructed-response tasks can improve the consistency of scoring, free up the time required for scoring and reporting and provide students with a mostly unbiased and immediate feedback. Career advising, identifying students at the early stages of academic difficulties, and e-tutoring might be additional areas for AI applications in medical school (Cukurova, Kent, & Luckin, 2019).

In summary, medical educators need to seek interdisciplinary approaches to help AI to make more sense of the context in which medicine operates today:

- User interventions for improving intelligent machines operating in unfamiliar environments or experiencing unanticipated events;
- Machines for explaining shared contexts to intuitive humans though reasoning, inference or causality and decisions; and
- Machines for interdependently affecting humans and vice versa (toward a mutually constructed and shared context) to increase awareness for teams and society and for monitoring and reporting "realities" requiring humans to rethink human social behaviors.

10.4 Shared human—Machine contexts in medical education

Everyday life requires humans to acquire and apply an immense amount of knowledge about the world—but not all data are valid and not all facts prove to be true. Learning environment variables, such as emotional or physical stress, can significantly bias and distort human memory and learning, rendering decision-making suboptimal (Maule & Svenson, 1993; Smith, Floerke, & Thomas, 2016). Because much of working knowledge is subjective and/or intuitive, human perceptions about information may vary and be difficult to articulate (Goodfellow et al., 2016). It is in this context that humans are taught *deductive learning* as a means to an understanding of specific concepts from general rules applied to information (i.e., fact arrays).

It is in this imperfect context that humans are programming machines for *inductive learning* that reflects human problem-solving challenges and emulates deductive reasoning (Wickelgren, 2012). Striking similarities exist between a machine learning insights derived through algorithm training and medical learners developing critical thinking skills during their professional education. Both human thinking and machine learning are designed to *deconvolute complexity* by asking well-informed questions, adding and deleting data in fact arrays, ranking serial thought or algorithm performance, and reiterating this process to *build confidence* in candidate answers or predictive models. Whether considering a knowledgeable human's best judgment call or a trained machine's best fit, intrinsically adaptive learning behaviors are also in play.

Computers and humans work differently with the same body of facts. *Formal* tasks based on fact arrays that are among the most mentally challenging for humans (i.e., timed competitive chess matches) are often the easiest tasks for computers to learn. *Informal* tasks are a struggle for machines—using knowledge to solve actions easy for humans to perform but hard for humans to formally describe (Adams, Shankar, & Tecco, 2016). Informal tasks include daily activities that rarely have a clear beginning or end, are likely to be interrupted, are concurrent with other activities, and are these that need to associate various models and types of information (Kimani, Gabrielli, Catarci, & Dix, 2008).

The learning sciences are continuously studying the processes involved in learning to find out how an understanding of learning can change our teaching practices to better integrate AI technologies (Luckin & Cukurova, 2019). Currently, large technology companies dominate the medical knowledge acquisition market for medicine and for higher education in general. There is thus a need to change the educational approach to build the partnerships in research and development that ensure a mutual understanding of the implementation of AI applications.

10.4.1 "Crunchy" technology questions

As a cohort, today's learners represent a generation of technology-savvy early adopters (Adams et al., 2016). The development and teaching of a structured AI technology-infused curriculum for today's medical students and residents—*precision education*—offers at least three <u>individual</u> learner benefits: (1) educational, a nonexpert's high-technology understanding (*literacy*); (2) environmental, easier interfaces with technology interfaces (*adaptation*); and (3) personal, less technology uncertainty induced stress (*coping*).

In the complex clinical learning environment, a *precision education* offers two broad <u>system</u> benefits: (1) accelerating workforce critical thinking skill development (*upskilling*) that positively impacts health-care systems and (2) facilitating the insertion (*adoption*) of powerful AI technologies that offer solutions to problems generated by the expanding digital data universe.

Precision education also takes advantage of ***machine learning—medical education parallels***. Their underlying neurocognitive platform may help to clarify the role of digital technologies (including AI) for enhancing learners' critical thinking skills by considering cognitive factors common to machines and humans. Such platform designs could also lead to new educational threads and novel teaching frameworks.

Crunchy technology questions remain about how AI insights and applications can be translated in the real world. How will the effects of a *precision education* on learner critical thinking skills be measured? Where is AI-informed skill building best inserted into a finite MD program and/or GME program? What type and depth of AI exposure are appropriate in the already busy curriculum and complex clinical learning environment? Will AI literacy foster or impede lifelong learning?

When contemplating these environmental dynamics and precision education responses, it is important to recall that machine learning does <u>not</u> replace human thinking. However, because AI technologies augment the precision of tasks that humans already do well and because of the growing likelihood that machines will soon work beside physicians and other health-care providers (Fogel & Kvedar, 2018; Mayo & Leung, 2018; Miller & Brown, 2018, 2019; Krittanawong, Zhang, Wang, Aydar, & Kitai, 2017), there is value to providing new and senior health professionals with a comprehensive early exposure to AI's foundational concepts and emerging applications.

10.4.2 Of men and machines—Context matters

Confronting an Ebola outbreak in west-central Africa and resuscitating a passenger from cardiac arrest at 35,000 ft are the environments that medical educators prepare graduating doctors to confront. Medical educators use a variety of heuristics, real-world clinical scenarios, and high-fidelity simulations to hone learners' critical thinking skills in these and the numerous other contexts they are likely to face.

In the process of validating autonomous machines to perform, AI scientists must improve machines to operate in unfamiliar environments and to function in the face of unanticipated events. Such intelligent machine engineering across contexts is not dissimilar from the process of intelligent learner education for medical practice. Machines programmed to explain contexts to intuitive humans use reasoning, inferences, and/or causality to enhance decision-making.

For both humans and machines, reliance on uncertain (i.e., messy) datasets is fraught, limiting the human confidence and system validation necessary to perform well in complex and diverse operational settings. Modern medicine is a digital information ocean, teeming with data pollutants and awash with data management inconsistencies. These data are being continuously generated, like waves, from unique and connected health-care systems, all of which are being operated by humans with varied levels of confidence in their data platforms and personal skills. These highly trained but imperfect human individuals and teams must operate health-care models and make business decisions in a context of rapidly evolving medical technologies and often uneven health policies.

10.4.3 The AI hopes that float the health care boats

As in other sectors of the world economy, health-care managers and medical practitioners are hoping that intelligent machines can make sense of these very data to improve human care and health. As ML and NLP applications of AI gradually become better understood by data and computing science experts, two fundamental realities are emerging, both of which will determine the degree to which this rapidly evolving field of science will impact society in general and human care and health in particular.

The first is that collecting consistently higher caliber data from humans is difficult. Data-sharing privacy concerns are magnified in health-care settings, where individuals' personal health information (PHI) is closely guarded so as to prevent insurance coverage denials for preexisting conditions and other medical privacy sensitivities.

The intelligent machine learning of features and faults is exquisitely sensitive to input data complexity (i.e., dimensionality and dynamism) and quality (i.e., provenance and preprocessing). When machines are used to derive inferences and detect features from complex datasets, errors create opportunities to engineer more robust solutions. When the datasets are health related, there can be real-world human health consequences to such errors (Miller, 2019).

And very clean ML training data are often too narrowly scoped to generalize for field use in other situations (e.g., Google Automated Retinal Scan papers).

The second is the shared contexts (i.e., knowledge domains and environmental settings) in which machines and humans interact. Technology insertion is never neutral—AI technologies interdependently affect humans (and vice versa), ideally in a fashion that augments each other's performance.

Human-autonomous system interfaces require a new type of teamwork in which both humans and machines must coadapt to their context and to each other. In these settings, both are subject to context variability. Assigning faults or failures to individual humans, autonomous systems, or both demand a full understanding of the complex confluence of cause and effect relationships.

General concerns exist about autonomous machines contributing to human skill involution, the settings in which it is appropriate for humans to turn complete authority over to an autonomous machine, and the capacity of a machine to explain an insight to a human (or a human to machine) without distracting the user. All of these human—machine interface concerns are germane to medical education and health-care environments.

10.4.4 Medical learning contexts

With the continuing ingress of artificial intelligence (AI) technologies—machine learning (ML) and natural language processing (NLP)—into medical practice (Mayo & Leung, 2018; Miller & Brown, 2018, 2019) and health care (Miller, 2018), it is not surprising that recent papers have advocated for greater AI literacy among medical and health professions learners (American Medical Association [AMA], 2019; Kolachalama & Garg, 2018; Wartman & Combs, 2018). Recent surveys of medical students confirm their interest in learning more about AI applications in medicine and medical imaging during their education (Pinto dos Santos et al., 2018).

The impact of a data-dense present and machine-augmented future clinical learning environment on the neurocognitive development of 24-year-old medical students is a key context for medical educators to understand.

Medical school and subsequent graduate medical education (i.e., residency training) represent a series of feed-forward/look-back learning experiences that remain temporally separated but that are increasingly considered as a **professional developmental continuum**. For example, medical student entrustable professional activities (EPAs) and resident physician competencies are related knowledge and skill acquisition learning milestones. This continuum of physician professional development exposes learners to salient experiences that shape their developing skillsets and future career trajectory.

For learners and machines, repeated encounters with situations and coactor behaviors enable learning. Scientific biases disrupt human cognition, and attribution biases disrupt ML. It is necessary for both humans and machines to learn from mistakes resulting from cognitive biases.

The information that is compiled from learners and their environments along this continuum is a type of time-series data that, if subjected to advanced AI analytics, could provide valuable insights on how to optimize **professional identity formation** (PIF) through the complex iterative development of critical reflective thinking and the acquisition of crucial motor skills, with the goal of training a humanistic, resilient physician. Medical educators are challenged to facilitate the active constructive integrative developmental process of PIF in learners within various standardized and personalized curricula (Wald, Hutchinson, Liben, Smilovitch, & Donato, 2015). During this continuous cognitive developmental and confidence building process, it is critical for learners to track their educational progress (based on testing, self-assessment, advising, etc.) and to identify specific areas in need of additional professional development. The so-called hidden curriculum within an institution has a significant influence on the PIF of the medical learner (Olive & Abercrombie, 2017).

10.4.5 Decision support

Human learners and AI's make decisions and choices very differently.

The two systems of human thinking include one that deliberatively analyzes problems using logic (i.e., deductive) and another that is fast, automatic, and nearly imperceptible (i.e., intuitive; in Kahneman, 2011). The former's slow thinking requires concentration and takes mental energy, while the latter's fast thinking operates continuously and is more mental energy efficient. Unfortunately the fast system is biased by human emotions and beliefs, and as such, it makes more mistakes in the moment.

In the major US and Chinese AI firms, the future of AI is being developed by a like-minded culture—relatively insular tribes of highly selected graduates from technology-intensive universities who think alike (Webb, 2019). In these AI tribes, cognitive biases are magnified, but these biases often go unnoticed and soon become proxies for rational group thinking. The narrow task AI systems that these tribes are building are the basis for the general control AI platform of the future. These systems and platforms reflect the biases of their creators, both cognitive and unconscious. And tribe leaders are neither diverse in origin nor very interested in the long-term collateral impact of their AI systems on society.

In the classroom setting, **content knowledge representation** is an important context—how information is presented by educators to students (i.e., passive learning) and how information is sought out by students (i.e., active learning) are important determinants of knowledge and skill acquisition. Initially, medical school students are rote memorizers of, for example, anatomy, biochemistry, and physiology information, without much of a technology interface beyond the use of memory building applications (i.e., ANKI), digital simulation (high-fidelity mannequins and 3-D radiology/anatomy image drive-through systems), "flipped classroom" learning platforms and early virtual and augmented reality (VR/AR) tools (Yovanoff et al., 2017).

Embedded in all learning theories is the recognition that **effective feedback** is a powerful tool toward students achieving desirable learning outcomes (Thurlings, Vermeulen, Bastiaens, & Stijnen, 2012). A learning environment that provides students with frequent high-quality formative and summative feedback can continuously improve their lifelong learning "DNA" to foster habits of the mind that enhance well-being and a desirable "growth mindset."

Self-regulated learning (SRL) theory states that learners who take active control and responsibility for their learning (Chung & Yuen, 2011) become more efficient if self-assessments and feedback data are organized in a way that permits learners to reflect on and resolve the interconnectedness of this information. Self-regulated learners are constantly weighing multidimensional interactions (i.e., inputs, outputs, and outcomes) among academic performance, social pressure, advisory experience, and situational happenstance, comparing them with who they are ("values") and relating this to learning cues, milestones achieved, feedback, and self-assessments. SRL promotes continuous self-negotiation—a complex interplay of information acquisition (i.e., information "chunking") and feelings management (i.e., "checking in")—which can be exhausting to some learners.

Providing learners with advanced AI analytics derived from their own data embedded within a multilearner data matrix could offer **individualized learner insights**, providing important self-efficacy beliefs that could promote well-being by reducing cognitive brain load. A benefit of liberating "brain space" is the freeing up of mental capacity to focus on learning and self-reflection. This benefit has the effect of leveling the playing field (i.e., "cognitivism" theory) by making data-derived insights from data available to all learners along the medical learning continuum (Erlich & Russ-Eft, 2011).

In the clinical learning environment setting (i.e., hospitals and clinics), the sharing of structured and unstructured data, both verbally and electronically, is important to individual **critical thinking development** and to learner integration into health-care teams, with the shared goal of establishing an actionable diagnosis and cogent therapeutic plan. More often than not, such medical data are digital representations of knowledge, often in high-dimensional datasets, which require dataset cleaning and preprocessing before they can be optimized for human interpretations or advanced analytics. For example, dynamic 4-D medical imaging datasets arriving sequentially in batches over time often cover a shared data universe ("movie"), but capture data in different temporal snapshots ("frames"). Such complex datasets are potentially correlated (i.e., time-series data), stored in multiple locations (i.e., distributed networks), and/or better represented as a tensor dataset. Messy and/or dynamic datasets corrupted by redundant data, outliers, and/or missing values compound complex dataset preprocessing challenges in many sectors, including health care.

The most ubiquitous, lowest tech, professionally challenging health care process tracking, and personal health information (PHI) repository is the electronic health record (EHR). EHRs are often noninteroperable across proprietary and/or legacy operating systems and encrypted data platforms and frequently (>50% of entries) contaminated with human medical knowledge deficits, clinical thinking inaccuracies, and cut and paste entries (Wang, Khanna, & Najafti, 2017). This type of EHR information has long been a target for data mining and advanced analytics, but experts in these related fields now realize the vulnerabilities of such approaches to poor data quality and uncertain data provenance.

The most frequently used learning technology in the clinical training setting is simulation (Webb, 2019). High- and low-fidelity simulation is a core element of postgraduate medical training in surgery, emergency medicine, and anesthesiology. In addition, m-learning (apps on smart phones) and social media (blogs, networks, YouTube, etc.) are influencing medical learners and the health-care workplace. The uses of these technologies are based on Kolb's learning cycle and Eraut's intentions of informal learning. Kolb's learning cycle includes concrete experiences (practicing skills), abstract conceptualization (reflection on experiences), and active experimentation (workplace practice)—this cycle used to be called "see one, do one, teach one." Eraut's three intentions of informal learning are implicit (unconscious), reactive (opportunistic), and deliberative (set goals and timelines for problem-solving).

In summary, what are the emerging physician roles and responsibilities?

- Domain expertise to guide computing system design on two levels (1) to describe decision steps and to identify special cases for rules-based systems; (2) ML-based systems: for predicting future outcomes (i.e., causal inferences).
- AI literacy sufficient to explain AI "black box" predictive models—to students and to patients in the clinical setting (genetic risks of future diseases, in-hospital deaths, etc.).
- Awareness of data provenance effects on field-use reproducibility by gender, race, geography, etc.
- Active involvement in data quality assurance (i.e., curating and preprocessing)—where the alternative is greater physician—patient data disintermediation.

References

Adams, A., Shankar, M., & Tecco, H. (2016). *50 things to know about digital health: Rock health consumer survey*. Retrieved from https://rockhealth.com/reports/digital-health-consumer-adoption-2016/.

American Medical Association (AMA). (2019). *Augmented intelligence in health care*. Retrieved from https://www.ama-assn.org/system/files/2019-01/augmented-intelligence-policy-report.pdf.

Bates, D. W., Saria, S., Ohno-Machado, L., Shah, A., & Escobar, G. (2014). Big data in health care: Using analytics to identify and manage high-risk and high-cost patients. *Health Affairs, 33*(7), 1123–1131. https://doi.org/10.1377/hlthaff.2014.0041.

Brownlee, J. (2016). *Overfitting and underfitting with machine learning algorithms. In Machine learning mastery*. Retrieved from https://machinelearningmastery.com/overfitting-and-underfitting-with-machine-learning-algorithms/.

Chan, K. S., & Zary, N. (2019). Applications and challenges of implementing artificial intelligence in medical education: Integrative review. *JMIR Medical Education, 5*(1), e13930. https://doi.org/10.2196/13930.

Chary, M., Parikh, S., Manini, A. F., Boyer, E. W., & Radeos, M. (2019). A review of natural language processing in medical education. *The Western Journal of Emergency Medicine, 20*(1), 78–86. https://doi.org/10.5811/westjem.2018.11.39725.

Chung, Y. B., & Yuen, M. (2011). The role of feedback in enhancing students' self-regulation in inviting schools. *Journal of Invitational Theory and Practice, 17*, 22–27.

Cresswell, K. M., Bates, D. W., & Sheikh, A. (2017, March). *Why every health care organization needs a data strategy.* NEJM Catalyst. Retrieved from https://www2.deloitte.com/content/dam/Deloitte/global/Documents/Life-Sciences-Health-Care/gx-Ishc-healthcare-and-life-sciences-predictions-2020.pdf.

Cukurova, M., Kent, C., & Luckin, R. (2019). Artificial intelligence and multimodal data in the service of human decision-making: A case study in debate tutoring. *British Journal of Educational Technology.* https://doi.org/10.1111/bjet.12829.

Dai, P., Gwadry-Sridhar, F., Bauer, M., & Borrie, M. (2015). A hybrid manifold learning algorithm for the diagnosis and prognostication of Alzheimer's disease. *AMIA annual symposium proceedings. AMIA symposium, 2015,* 475–483.

Davenport, L. (2018, March). *'Alarming rate' of burnout in med students.* Medscape. Retrieved from https://www.medscape.com/viewarticle/893466.

Deloitte Centre for Health Solutions. (2014). *Healthcare and life sciences predictions 2020: A bold future?* Retrieved from https://www2.deloitte.com/content/dam/Deloitte/global/Documents/Life-Sciences-Health-Care/gx-Ishc-healthcare-and-life-sciences-predictions-2020.pdf.

Densen, P. (2011). Challenges and opportunities facing medical education. *Transactions of the American Clinical and Climatological Association, 122,* 48–58.

Elmes, J. (2017, February). *Artificial intelligence to revolutionise higher education.* Retrieved from https://www.timeshighereducation.com/news/artificial-intelligence-revolutionise-higher-education.

Erlich, R. J., & Russ-Eft, D. (2011). Applying social cognitive theory to academic advising to assess student learning outcomes. *NACADA Journal, 17*(3), 5–15.

Fogel, A. L., & Kvedar, J. C. (2018). Artificial intelligence powers digital medicine. *NPJ Digital Medicine. 1*(5). https://doi.org/10.1038/s41746-017-0012-2.

Ghahramani, Z. (2015, May). Probabilistic machine learning and artificial intelligence. *Nature, 521,* 452–459. https://doi.org/10.1038/nature14541.

Gierl, M. J., Latifi, S., Lai, H., Boulais, A. -P., & DeChamplain, A. (2014). Automated essay scoring and the future of educational assessment in medical education. *Medical Education, 48,* 950–962.

Goodfellow, I., Bengio, Y., & Courville, A. (2016). *Deep learning.* Cambridge MA, London, UK: The MIT Press. Retrieved from www.deeplearningbook.org.

Goodfellow, I. J., Pouget-Abadie, J., Mirza, M., Xu, B., Warde-Farley, D., Ozair, S., et al. (2014). Generative adversarial nets. In *Proceedings of the 27th international conference on neural information processing systems* (p. 2).

Kahneman, D. (2011). *Thinking, fast and slow.* New York, NY, USA: Farrar, Straus and Giroux.

Kerr, C. I. V., Phaal, R., & Probert, D. R. (2008). Technology insertion in the defense industry: A primer. *Proceedings of the Institution of Mechanical Engineers, Part B: Journal of Engineering Manufacture, 222*(8), 1009–1023. https://doi.org/10.1243/09544054JEM1080.

Kimani, S., Gabrielli, S., Catarci, T., & Dix, A. (2008). Designing for tasks in ubiquitous computing. In A. K. Mostefaoui, Z. Maamar, & G. M. Giaglis (Eds.), *Advances in ubiquitous computing: Future paradigms and directions* (pp. 172–198). Hershey PA, London, UK: IGI Global Publishing.

Kolachalama, V. B., & Garg, P. S. (2018). Machine learning and medical education. *NPJ Digital Medicine, 1*(54), 1–3. https://doi.org/10.1038/s41746-018-0061-1.

Krittanawong, C., Zhang, H., Wang, Z., Aydar, M., & Kitai, T. (2017). Artificial intelligence in precision cardiovascular medicine. *Journal of the American College of Cardiology, 69*(21), 2657–2664. https://doi.org/10.1016/j.jacc.2017.03.571.

Larsen, P. O., & von Ins, M. (2010). The rate of growth in scientific publication and the decline of coverage provided by science citation index. *Scientometrics, 84*(3), 575–603.

Launchbury, J. (2017, February). *A DARPA perspective on artificial intelligence.* Retrieved from https://www.artificialbrain.xyz/a-darpa-perspective-on-artificial-intelligence/.

LeCun, Y., Bengio, Y., & Hinton, G. (2015). Deep learning. *Nature, 521,* 436–444. https://doi.org/10.1038/nature14539.

Luckin, R., & Cukurova, M. (2019). Designing educational technologies in the age of AI: A learning sciences-driven approach. *British Journal of Educational Technology.* https://doi.org/10.1111/bjet.12861.

Maule, A. J., & Svenson, O. (1993). Theoretical and empirical approaches to behavioral decision making and their relation to time constraints. In O. Svenson & A. J. Maule (Eds.), *Time pressure and stress in human judgment and decision making.* Boston, MA: Springer. https://doi.org/10.1007/978-1-4757-6846-6_1.

Mayo, R. C., & Leung, J. (2018, June). Artificial intelligence and deep learning—Radiology's next frontier? *Clinical Imaging, 49*, 87–88. https://doi.org/10.1016/j.clinimag.2017.11.007.

Miller, D. D. (2018). The big health data—Intelligent machine paradox. *The American Journal of Medicine, 131*(11), 1272–1275. https://doi.org/10.1016/j.amjmed.2018.05.038.

Miller, D. D. (2019). The medical AI insurgency: What physicians must know about data to practice with intelligent machines. *NPJ Digital Medicine, 2*(62), 1–5. https://doi.org/10.1038/s41746-019-0138-5.

Miller, D. D., & Brown, E. W. (2018). Artificial intelligence in medical practice: The question to the answer? *The American Journal of Medicine, 131*(2), 129–133. https://doi.org/10.1016/j.amjmed.2017.10.035.

Miller, D. D., & Brown, E. W. (2019). How cognitive machines can augment medical imaging. *American Journal of Roentgenology, 212*, 9–14. https://doi.org/10.2214/AJR.18.19914.

Mohr, N. M., Moreno-Walton, L., Mills, A. M., Brunett, P. H., & Promes, S. B. (2011). Generational influences in academic emergency medicine: Teaching and learning, mentoring, and technology (part 1). *Academic Emergency Medicine, 18*(2), 190–199. https://doi.org/10.1111/j.1553-2712.2010.00985.x.

Nasca, T. J., Weiss, K. B., & Bagian, J. P. (2014). Improving clinical learning environments for tomorrow's physicians. *New England Journal of Medicine, 370*(11), 991–993. https://doi.org/10.1056/NEJMp1314628.

Norman, G. R., Monteiro, S. D., Sherbino, J., Ilgen, J. S., Schmidt, H. G., & Mamede, S. (2017). The causes of errors in clinical reasoning: Cognitive biases, knowledge deficits, and dual process thinking. *Academic Medicine, 92*, 23–30. https://doi.org/10.1097/ACM.0000000000001421.

Olive, K. E., & Abercrombie, C. L. (2017). Developing a physician's professional identity through medical education. *The American Journal of the Medical Sciences, 353*(2), 101–108. https://doi.org/10.1016/j.amjms.2016.10.012.

Peckham, C. (2018, January). *Medscape national physician burnout & depression report.* Medscape. Retrieved from https://www.medscape.com/slideshow/2018-lifestyle-burnout-depression-6009235.

Pinto dos Santos, D., Giese, D., Brodehl, S., Chon, S. H., Staab, W., Kleinert, R., et al. (2018). Medical students attitudes towards artificial intelligence—A multicentre survey. *European Radiology, 29*(4), 1640–1646. https://doi.org/10.1007/s00330-018-5601-1.

Samarakoon, L., Fernando, T., & Rodrigo, C. (2013). Learning styles and approaches to learning among medical undergraduates and postgraduates. *BMC Medical Education, 13*(42). https://doi.org/10.1186/1472-6920-13-42.

Sethi, R. K. V. (2014). *Technology adoption in the United States: The impact of hospital market competition.* Retrieved from https://u/urn-3:HUL.InstRepos:12407615.

Smith, A. M., Floerke, V. A., & Thomas, A. K. (2016). Retrieval practice protects memory against acute stress. *Science, 345*(6315), 1046–1048. https://doi.org/10.1126/science.aah5067.

Thurlings, M., Vermeulen, M., Bastiaens, T., & Stijnen, S. (2012). Understanding feedback: A learning theory perspective. *Educational Research Review, 9*, 1–15. https://doi.org/10.1016/j.edurev.2012.11.004.

Van Noorden, R. (2014, May). *Global scientific output doubles every nine years.* Nature Newsblog. Retrieved from http://blogs.nature.com/news/2014/05/global-scientific-output-doubles-every-nine-years.html.

Wald, H. S., Hutchinson, A. D., Liben, S., Smilovitch, M., & Donato, A. A. (2015). Professional identity formation in medical education for humanistic, resilient physicians: Pedagogical strategies for bridging theory to practice. *Academic Medicine, 90*(6), 753–760. https://doi.org/10.1097/ACM.0000000000000725.

Wang, M. D., Khanna, R., & Najafti, N. (2017). Characterizing the source of text in electronic health record progress notes. *JAMA Internal Medicine, 177*(8), 1212–1213. https://doi.org/10.1001/jamainternmed.2017.1548.

Wartman, S. A., & Combs, C. D. (2018). Medical education must move from the information age to the age of artificial intelligence. *Academic Medicine, 93*(8), 1107–1109. https://doi.org/10.1097/ACM.0000000000002044.

Webb, A. (2019). *The big nine.* New York, NY: Public Affairs—The Hachette Book Group.

Wickelgren, I. (2012, December). *Ray kurzweil tells me how to build a brain.* Scientific American. Retrieved from https://blogs.scientificamerican.com/streams-of-consciousness/on-tv-ray-kurzweil-tells-me-how-to-build-a-brain/.

Yovanoff, M., Pepley, D., Mirkin, K., Moore, J., Han, D., & Miller, S. (2017). Personalized learning in medical education: Designing a user interface for a dynamic haptic robotic trainer for central venous catheterization. *Proceedings of the Human Factors and Ergonomics Society Annual Meeting, 61*(1), 615–619. https://doi.org/10.1177/1541931213601639.

Problems of autonomous agents following informal, open-textured rules[☆]

Ryan Quandt[a,b], *John Licato*[a,c]

[a]Advancing Machine and Human Reasoning (AMHR) Lab, University of South Florida, Tampa, FL, United States [b]Department of Philosophy, University of South Florida, Tampa, FL, United States [c]Department of Computer Science and Engineering, University of South Florida, Tampa, FL, United States

11.1 Informal, open-textured rules

The focus of the present collection of essays is the "meaning, value and interdependent effects that artificial intelligence (AI) has on society wherever these machines may interact with humans or other autonomous agents."[a] Whether human beings or artificially intelligent systems of the future, autonomous agents are typically afforded a degree of trust commensurate to the set of rules they are expected to follow and their ability to faithfully interpret and act in accordance with those rules. For example, a soldier is expected not only to follow ethical codes but also to have a reasonable understanding of how those codes are to be interpreted. Ideally, the same would be expected of a robot allowed to act autonomously in a similar setting, including robots that are part of a human-machine team.

The rules governing acceptable actions are unavoidably context-dependent. As we have argued in this chapter, these rules, even when they are seemingly simple, contain elements that are informal, open textured, and shared. This situation results in two obstacles:

[☆]This material is based on the work supported by the Air Force Office of Scientific Research under award number FA9550-16-1-0308. Any opinions, finding, and conclusions or recommendations expressed in this material are those of the authors and do not necessarily reflect the views of the US Air Force.

[a]See https://sites.google.com/site/aaai19sharedcontext/.

asymmetry and indeterminacy. Both sustain a margin of error in following open-textured rules (IORs) that cannot be solved by defining more variables in a rule, sharper ones, or using a more nuanced and expansive syntax. We argue that a solution to these problems—a solution often used in law—is to give automated reasoners the ability to properly assess candidate interpretations of given rules by reasoning over their *interpretive arguments* (MacCormick & Summers, 1991; Sartor, Walton, Macagno, & Rotolo, 2014; Summers, 2006; Walton, Sartor, & Macagno, 2016).

Let us consider an example: a robot is commanded to pick up a cup. In the best of cases, it recognizes a cup, extends its open hand, presses snugly, and lifts. It is asked to do so again, albeit with changes: the command given (**C**) is pick up the red cup and there are now three cups on the table: a red, a yellow, and a blue one. It is another success. Again the trial is set up with the same command **C**, except that there are three cups of varying types on the table with similar reddish hues (Fig. 11.1). An argument could be made that each is a red cup, but which, if any, is the intended object? And assuming that the command giver is not available to clarify, how might an intelligent agent decide which action is most likely correct?

An IOR is of this sort, the concepts "red" and "cup" in **C**, are vague to an extent. "Red" is on a color spectrum, which can result in ambiguities, and "cup" may refer to a drinking cup, a trophy cup, a cupping glass, or a cup that holds writing utensils. But the vagueness is magnified and insolvable with IORs—or so we will argue. An IOR occurs when there are concepts that over shoot or under shoot (and not exclusively) the actions, objects, or events that are intended to satisfy them (Licato & Marji, 2018). In other words, there are no definite classes for the informal, open-textured concepts in the rule, though a judgment must be made on whether a rule is satisfied. In the case of **C** applied to the cups in Fig. 11.1, the following arguments might be made:

- Cup (A) is correct because the command giver is a heavy coffee drinker who probably wants coffee.
- Cup (B) is correct because it is the same cup that satisfied command **C** in the past.
- Cup (C) is correct because its coloring is closest to RGB value #FF0000 (the technical definition of "red").

FIG. 11.1 Given the command pick up the red cup, how might a robot determine which action is correct? *Images obtained with permission from Vecteezy.com.*

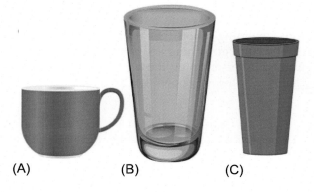

(A)   (B)   (C)

Each of these is interpretive arguments for the "correct" interpretation of the words "cup" and "red" in **C**. It is obvious that each of these draws on some sort of contextual knowledge: the preferences of the command giver (A), the properties and typical uses of the cups (B), a standard definition (C), shared information (A–C), and so on.

There are two definitions that we will assume. An open-textured predicate or category (Hart, 1961) is one in which membership is "highly dependent on context and human intentions [with an] absence of precise conditions for membership" (Branting, 2000, p. 3). Open-textured predicates are pervasive in all contexts in which rules are expressed using natural language, particularly law (Bench-Capon, 2012; da Costa Pereira et al., 2017; Franklin, 2012; Prakken, 2017; Sanders, 1991). For our purposes, a rule can be defined as

> An expression of the connection between a set of conditions, or antecedents, and a conclusion, a consequent, justified by those conditions (Branting, 2000, p. 9).[b]

A rule is an argument in which certain conditions (an item is a cup, the cup is red, etc.), when satisfied, entail a conclusion (that cup, or the intended one, must be picked up). An inference is successfully drawn when the intended act is done. For a rule to be effective, it must be definite enough to clearly apply to certain tasks, yet general enough to operate within varied settings. That is, enactment of a rule depends on certain contextual constants as well as on resilience to variance across settings. For an IOR, one or more of the conjuncts within the antecedent has an informal, open-textured concept, that is, it under- or overshoots the intended events or acts covered by the rule. So the vagueness cannot be overcome by defining more conjuncts. Instead, an autonomous agent must have recourse elsewhere to judge whether an antecedent is satisfied, for example, through interpretive arguments.[c]

Ethical guidelines of behavior, national or international law, and broad moral principles inevitably, if not necessarily, use IORs, and so an agent must learn to cope.[d] Autonomous vehicles, for example, might be required to obey traffic laws such as "drivers should keep to the right as much as possible" (Prakken, 2017). The phrase "as much as possible" is not intended in a physical sense, Prakken remarks, but involves the shared context of traffic at a given time. The phrase assumes situational factors that cannot be defined within a rule's form. For these reasons, there are "divergency gaps" between the form of a rule and its purposive content. These gaps follow from asymmetry and indeterminacy.[e]

11.2 Obstacles of IORs

The example shown in Fig. 11.1 seems harmless enough. By nuancing our lexicon with terms like "paper cup," "glass," and "coffee cup," we avoid the predicate's open texture. If the command was `pick up the red glass`, the problem disappears since we may run a number of

---

[b] Also Walton (2016, p. 79).

[c] IORs incorporate shared constructs.

[d] When we speak of rules or commands, we have these sort of rules in mind.

[e] We are borrowing the phrase "divergency gaps" from Robert Summers, though altering its sense. For him, it describes the gap between law in theory and in practice (Summers, 1997, p. 1185).

successful trials with the added vocabulary. Once we supply a more definite term, which pairs nicely with one of the three cups, the problem is avoided. The generality, scope, or extension of the rule, `pick up the red cup`, has been lost, but with the benefit of removing the open texture that seems to undermine the command. When the rule is an IOR; however, there are no formal strategies for removing an open-textured predicate. Still, our example presents two obstacles for computation that IORs bring about: asymmetry and indeterminacy. We will motivate and explain these obstacles in turn below. With IORs, asymmetry and indeterminacy are heightened to the extent that a command cannot explicitly and precisely define a range of satisfying actions. There is ambiguity in its bounds. If right, and IORs cannot be dealt with through formal changes, like defining more variables or emending them, something akin to a decision or judgment is required (an operation on the basis of an interpretive argument).

11.2.1 Formal languages

For the arguments below to have weight, a few remarks on the formality of AI are in order. According to Dutilh Novaes, a computable process does not have insight or ingenuity (Novaes, 2012, p. 21).[f] Complex operations can be performed with a mechanism, an algorithm or calculator, where all the work required is locating and identifying symbols with respect to an order of input. A formal system can be blindly implemented, and so does not require meaningful symbols.[g] Without assigning meanings to "0" and "1" (or after emptying them of meaning), a binary system can perform various tasks, like driving a car. But there are still people who use the formal apparatus—a mechanism is built and used within a purposive context. As a result, one of the ways a robot can malfunction is behaving "inappropriately" to given a task or setting. Even when the role of an operator is minimized, or nonexistent, the machine succeeds or fails beyond its hardwired connections and programming.

A formal language is often defined as a recursively axiomatized system: There are a finite set of rules joined to a finite vocabulary that can produce an indefinite number of expressions. Dutilh Novaes writes that, in principle, computability can be thought of as a proper subclass of formality since every formal system operates according to explicit rules and, to that extent, is computable (Novaes, 2012, p. 17). When these rules are not recursively axiomatizable—they cannot be mechanically joined to vocabulary in a way that results in an endless stream of well-formed expressions—the system is partially computable. An action can be wholly computed when it is formalized within a recursively axiomatized system, that is, when there is a 1:1 relation between a well-formed expression and an action.

Computability requires a sequential, definite, and finite sequence of steps, besides employing a recursively axiomatized language. Said otherwise, there must be a mechanical application of rules of inference to the vocabulary.[h] There are a few other properties of

---

[f]See also Novaes (2011) for her extensive typology of formality.

[g]Dutilh Novaes distinguishes a computable language from one that is desemantified, or lacking meaning; see Novaes (2012, Chapter 1).

[h]When there is a mechanical application of rules within a language that is not recursively axiomatized, the formality exhibited is mechanical as opposed to computable. Mechanical procedures can be undecidable—the application of rules to formulae may not determine each theorem within a system (Novaes, 2012, p. 19 ft.). Turing machines are an example.

computability worth mentioning: the language is dynamic, or occurs in a given time and space, could be operated by anyone with the same results, and has a predictable output (Novaes, 2012, p. 25). Lastly, "it is important to emphasize the crucial notion of *concrete, external symbolic systems* at the very heart of the notion of computability" (Novaes, 2012, p. 27). Some material inscriptions are required for a vocabulary to be fixed and distinguished from one another. The rules and axioms must be inscribed as well. In sum, content and instruction are explicitly and concretely inscribed for a formal language to be computed.

11.2.2 Asymmetry

A rule has a formal structure. To recall, a rule's antecedents are a conjunction of conditions that represent what must be met for the rule to be actualized. As representations, the antecedents are distinct from the act. For the command, `pick up the red cup`, there are two obvious conjuncts, and these are adequate when a red cup is set before a robot. When there are other cups of similar shades, with the same shade but of different types, or none that are clearly red, those two conjuncts are inadequate for determining which cup is intended. Changes in setting reveal a rule's divergency gaps and one response is to define more conjuncts. But tailoring rules to specific settings, while narrowing its open-endedness, also narrows its generalizability. There are trade-offs between definiteness and generality, which may not be a problem until the shared rules are IORs. Then, asymmetry prevents us from removing the margin of error when enacting the rule. Besides, defining more antecedents with more nuance only goes so far—or too far—resulting in an infinite regress. Such a regress is symptomatic of the problem.

The conclusion that we support further can be briefly stated as: a rule is a type of which its intended acts are tokens.[i] There is an asymmetry between a type and a token because a type is abstract and unique while a token is a concrete particular (e.g., the ink on a page, pixels on a screen, or vibrations in the larynx). This conclusion does not say that the antecedents of a rule are types of which the consequent is a token: the consequent represents the intended act, and so is not identical to it. If right, there cannot be an exhaustive list of antecedents that ensure that an intended act is performed. A margin of error persists even when a program runs correctly: an autonomous agent or human-machine team may not do what was intended, or they may do what was unintended. Since the type/token distinction explains certain failures in programming as well as the possibility of error in spite of successes, the following argument is central to understanding the problem of IORs.

Brun attributes the use of the type/token distinction with respect to principles—specifically, principles grounding logical laws—to Lewis Carroll. While it was recast by Quine, we will follow Brun's (2003, p. 73) interpretation. In a moment we will show how the argument can be adapted to our purposes.

1. Inference *S* has form *V*.
2. According to principle *P*, each inference of form *V* is valid.
3. *S* is valid.

---

[i]See Linda Wetzel's example of a type and a token (Wetzel, 2018).

To justify this argument, another is needed. We will call the above argument inference *T*. Below is inference *U*.

1. Inference *T* has form *W*.
2. According to principle *Q*, each inference of form *W* is valid.
3. *T* is valid.

When we fix variables in the rule, program it accordingly, and the action occurs, we can say that the inference from premise to conclusion has been drawn. Does a successful trial—or an indefinite number of successful trials—ensure that the satisfaction of the premises guarantees the conclusion? We can generalize a principle from those successful trials, which is illustrated in the first argument, inference *T*. Inference *S*, the rule with many successful trials, has a certain form, a certain relation between the variables in the premise and those in the conclusion. Our principle is generalized inductively from the successful trials such that when a rule has a given form, it is valid, that is, we justifiably expect the rule to be successful in the future. So, inference *S* is valid. But, again, why is the argument securing our expectation that the rule will be successful in the future valid? Inference *T* needs to be justified as well as inference *U*, the second argument. So the match between antecedents and consequent in inference *S*, along with the generalized principle, justifies *S* by *T*. Then, the syllogistic form of *T* is placed within inference *U* in order to justify it, and so on.

The argument reveals two worries, one more damning than the other. The first, which Quine discusses, is that an appeal to a principle, or logical law, is circular. A law must evoke an inference it supposedly justifies, and an infinite regress results. This regress is a problem because it means there is no generalizable principle that grounds validity, or the form of our rules (Brun, 2003, pp. 72–73). Quine observes a symptom, though, not asymmetry itself. The second worry, which Brun attributes to Carroll, is that the infinite regress betrays a slight of hand. The successfully drawn inference *S*—the satisfaction(s) of the rule—is not identical to inference *S* when imported into inference *T*. The satisfied variables, which led to the successfully drawn conclusion, are not identical to its formalization as inference *S*. On Brun's and Carroll's reading, not only is there an infinite regress, there is also a categorical difference between the enacted inference and its form, and a principle cannot breach their difference. Criteria of identity are required for matching the satisfaction of the rule and its codified satisfaction, which are not the same.

The command prompting an act is a generalization of select and repeatable features. Though conjuncts can be added to clarify a command and avoid some foreseen hindrances, these parameters cannot ensure that what is intended to be performed via the command is performed. An open-textured predicate lacks definable, constant, and repeatable features. The predicate is open textured in the sense that there are an indefinite number of situations that satisfy it. Because the performance of a command is a token of which the command is a type, whichever explicit criterion we define to match the antecedents with the situations in which the rule should be enacted loosely holds. Further, there is slippage: the antecedents undershoot and/or overshoot the intended act.[j]

---

[j]There is a further implication with respect to criteria of success or adequacy for an operation: there is not only ambiguity when defining the antecedents within a command and the consequent, but also in judging between varying formulations. This second ambiguity is the problem of adequate formalization, which Brun and others handle in depth.

An intended act is computable if it can be formalized within a recursively axiomatized system (Novaes, 2012, p. 17). In other words, an action has an adequately formalized counterpart in a formal language. There is asymmetry between an action or event, on one hand, and the objects within a formal language, on the other. Asymmetry results because the relations between actions or events cannot perfectly align with any single formal system. A rule is enacted in numberless settings, yet a computable language must determine its operation from within, so to speak, or by applying rules to a finite vocabulary, which are taken as substitutes for objects in the world. "Red cup" seems clear enough until there are three cups on the table of similar hues and different types. IORs resist formalization because they rely solely on contextual information and intention, neither of which fit neatly within a recursively axiomatized system.

The other properties of computability are also involved. Computers operate by a sequential, definite, and finite sequence of steps, even in their more complex and simultaneous operations. Our earlier example presents a problem due to the indefiniteness of the concept, "red cup." An open-textured predicate will not accurately or predictably fit within a mechanical procedure. Further, an operation has a predictable end that can be executed by anyone. The three interpretive arguments given earlier show how any of the three cups on the table can be picked up with a supporting reason. One agent may pick up one cup, another agent pick up a different one. So the command, `pick up the red cup`, looks noncomputable after all. As we have argued in the following, asymmetry and indeterminacy do not close off all hope of bringing computers into purposive contexts; these obstacles should lead us to expect a margin of error to persist, and to adapt.

At bottom, computability depends on concrete and external systems; here is where asymmetry has its full force. A symbol is given for an object, operation, or perceptual cue, and the question of token identity arises.[k] Criteria are needed for defining two marks as the same, and they must be the same with respect to their appropriate instances. On one hand, then, a reason must be given for why "A" is the same or different than "*A*," "**A**," or "a." While identity criteria are given within a recursively axiomatized system, the criteria have implications for the deployment of that system within purposive contexts. Is the difference between "A" and "*A*" the same as the difference between "A" and "B" with respect to the representation or function of those marks? If we agree with Dutilh Novaes when she claims that the materiality of notation has certain possibilities, limits, and tendencies, such an explanation will be needed. We must confront the difference between our notation's material and the purposive context in which the notation is used. Is the red cup that satisfied `the red cup` in the past the same red cup when the setting changes? Asymmetry goes beyond our concept and its place in a formal system and compels us to recognize the material difference between the inscription, "red cup," and the cups resting on the table.

Asymmetry effects an infinite regress other than the one Quine observes, which can be shown with another example (Licato & Marji, 2018). Suppose Ann and Bob make a bet, Bob loses and he agrees to buy breakfast for Ann. "Breakfast" is the open-textured predicate in their implicit and largely intuitive agreement. Unfortunately for Ann, Bob is a bad faith antagonist. So on the first day after their bet, Bob shows up with a single cheerio splashed

---

[k] For Dutilh Novaes' discussion, see Novaes (2011, p. 320).

with a drop of milk. Ann is frustrated and tells Bob that the cheerio does not satisfy their agreement: a breakfast must have at least 600 calories worth of food. On the next day, Bob brings uncooked bacon and rotten eggs. Ann rejects the offer, explaining that a breakfast must be of the quality made at a typical restaurant. Because of the asymmetry in the open-textured predicate, Bob could exploit loopholes indefinitely. The conditions Ann sets for what constitutes a breakfast cannot be identical to the meal that would actually satisfy their deal. A gap persists between the formalized variables and the intended action.

The difference between types and tokens does not impede programming generally. The takeaway from Carroll's (Brun, 2003, p. 73) argument is not that formalisms fail to operate in purposive contexts; rather, his point is that a difference holds between an action that satisfies a rule, on one hand, and the antecedents, consequent, and form meant to ensure the rule's satisfaction, on the other. The effects are sometimes trivial. Other times, a setting reveals divergency gaps that threaten to undermine the rule's enactment. With Carroll's distinction in hand, we can explain and anticipate certain challenges when programming in an open context. Our concern is limited to IORs, of course, where the rule and its intended action are misaligned. Any explicit conditions that we fix undershoot or overshoot the satisfying action. This gap occurs because what defines the rule's enactment either relies on a singular context or is given by intention. As a result, another strategy is needed beyond adding more conjuncts or tweaking them. Carroll's argument explains why there is a sizable and persisting margin of error when programming, commanding, or evaluating IORs.

11.2.3 Indeterminacy

Whereas asymmetry concerns the gap between a formula and its intended object, action, or event, our second obstacle, indeterminacy, concerns the words used in IORs. The concept was introduced by Quine (2008), who also uses "inscrutability of reference" or "ontological relativity" in place of indeterminacy.[1] His claim is that a word cannot be fixed to one object or meaning, nor can one object or meaning be fixed to a word. In our example, the word, "cup," has a certain degree of inscrutability.[m] "Cup" can refer to a drinking cup, cupping glass, or trophy cup. Its meaning is relative to a broader linguistic context, or "translation manual," for Quine—a purposive context, more broadly.

1. Radical translation. Quine's argument comes from a thought experiment he calls radical translation. It follows in an abbreviated form. Imagine a linguist confronted with a speaker from an unknown land, speaking a language wholly unlike any she is familiar with. There are no intermediary techniques at her disposal. Instead, she must rely on queries and ostension. As she points to various objects to elicit a response, a rabbit jumps out of the woods. The native turns, points at the rabbit, and says, "Gavagai." The linguist jots down the word "gavagai" and then "rabbit." When another rabbit is seen shortly after, the linguist points and asks, "Gavagai?" and the native assents. Once she does the same with other speakers, our linguist is confident in her translation (Quine, 1960, pp. 28–30). And she should be, though there is indeterminacy in the word pairing. Despite her success, that is, "gavagai"

[1]See Quine (2008) for his breakdown of three indeterminacies, all of which have bearing on our discussion.

[m]The appeal to reference does not commit him to a theory of meaning (Quine, 2008, p. 362).

can mean "rabbit," "undetached rabbit part," "rabbit stage," "the unique appearance of a rabbit's left foot while it is running less than 20 miles per hour," or any number of possible meanings, and no number of queries will settle the matter with complete confidence. Ostension can only make the words' reference so precise.

Quine argues for a persisting indeterminacy in speech dispositions (the proclivities of the native to say "gavagai" and ours for saying "rabbit"). A more complex syntactic apparatus enables the linguist to distinguish rabbits, their parts, and their stages within the native tongue, but that apparatus is relative to a translation manual (an entire catalog of phrase pairings). Once conjunctions, adjectives, prepositions, and so on are introduced, the original indeterminacy seems to disappear. But that is not the case. A totality of speech dispositions can be given multiple translation manuals that account for every phenomena consistently. As Quine writes,

> Rival systems of analytical hypotheses [the basic rules of translation manuals that emerge from many successful pairings, like "gavagai" and "rabbit"] can conform to all speech dispositions within each of the languages concerned and yet dictate, in countless cases, utterly disparate translations [...] each of which would be excluded by the other system of translation (Quine, 1960, p. 73).[n]

Said otherwise, the explanatory power and consistency of one translation manual cannot rule out others. There is no reason other manuals will not have equal power and consistency, and what is more, these manuals may result in translations that conflict. A significant result, for our purposes, is that one language cannot perfectly and uniquely map onto the words, phrases, references, or meanings of another.

Quine's thesis can be seen as a feature of natural language, not a bug, and a feature computable languages do not share. An interpretation of a word is meaningful from a broader translation manual, and there are many that adequately interpret the word. There is indeterminacy, then, between a word and an object pairing. One consequence for programming is obvious and well known, there are many ways to program an operation. Besides trivial changes, like switching natural languages or changing word order, different words can achieve the same results—`pick up the cup` can be replaced by `lift up the cup`. Axioms may be replaced, or a different coding language or formalism adopted.

As said earlier, a computer operates within a formal language without insight or ingenuity. This passivity has specific bearing on our discussion. Though synonymous with respect to our initial example, `pick up the cup` and `lift up the cup` are not the same. When a person is told, first, to pick up a cup, then to pick up a beam, she understands "pick up" in senses appropriate to the task at hand. The different objects change how she interprets the materially identical verb. These changes can be nuanced further since an empty cup is picked up one way, a full cup another, a glass differently than a travel cup. Similarly, we want a robot to pick up a weight, beam, or car differently than how it picks up a cup. One way to achieve these adjustments would be using different verbs: "pick up" for cups and "lift up" for beams. Again, there is a trade-off between definiteness and generality, and, again, ascribing different words ignores a problem rather than solving it. There remains indeterminacy between the words and the intended action. Select words cannot exhaustively capture setting

---

[n]For Quine's definition and more extensive discussion of such hypotheses, see Quine (1960, pp. 68–72).

or intent, which is why two competing languages can adequately express phenomena. Our ordinary use of "pick up" is flexible enough to handle a wide variance across settings; its translation into a computable language, on the other hand, has a more limited extension because it must be within a finite, definite, and sequential procedure that accomplishes a predictable outcome. In this sense, all natural language expressions are open textured, while all computation is closed. When a single command is fine-tuned in isolation from other commands, tailored to a given setting, or supplemented with more variables, not only does the command narrow in scope, it fails to address a persisting problem in IORs: predicates that express an intention or context-given property. To develop Quine's thesis of indeterminacy a bit further, we can turn to the writings of a friend of his, Donald Davidson.

2. Radical interpretation. Indeterminacy occurs within a single language as well as between languages. Expanding and reinterpreting Quine's thesis, Davidson argues that speakers of the same language also deal with indeterminacy. "All understanding of the speech of another involves radical interpretation," or Davidson's amended version of radical translation (Davidson, 2001, p. 125). So the indeterminacy a linguistic faces when translating a wholly foreign language also faces neighbors chatting. The goal of Quine's thought experiment was finding a synonymous expression between languages. A formal structure, embodied by a translation manual, can give a satisfactory output without explaining the meaning of the utterance to be translated. Davidson, on the other hand, emphasizes meaning or semantics. He wants to explain how synonymous expressions are synonymous, including similar expressions by speakers of the same language. Although our focus here are blind languages, Davidson's thesis bears on the limits of programming affected by indeterminacy.

Similar to Quine, Davidson proposes an idealized model of communication to present his argument (Davidson, 2005). A speaker and a hearer have theories for how to interpret expressions, though their theories need not be conscious, devised systems. In successful exchanges, each has two theories. Davidson calls the theories concerning ways of interpreting expressions prior to their exchange, prior theories. They include knowledge of grammar, idioms, definitions, and so on. A hearer anticipates what a speaker's words mean according to his theory while a speaker anticipates how her words will be interpreted. For communication to succeed, Davidson tells us, "what must be shared is the interpreter's and the speaker's understanding of the speaker's words" (Davidson, 2005, p. 96). During an occasion of utterance, certain relevant features will be expressed that could not have been anticipated. These clues are potentially singular, having no bearing on future or prior speech. Thus, a mutual, shared context and occasion-based understanding of a speaker's words make up a passing theory, which is the second theory a speaker and a hearer have in Davidson's model. The whole picture can be summarized as follows: speaker and hearer come together with prior theories and successfully communicate due to converging passing theories. A speaker may have a slip of the tongue, garbled speech, botched grammar, or a malapropism, and a hearer still interpret the speaker as she intends (or prompt the right query for clarification). When that occurs, prior theories and passing theories clearly do not align, yet the hearer successfully interprets the speaker. It is their misaligned prior theories and converging passing theories that reveal indeterminacy.

Whether robots are linguistically competent is beyond the scope of this chapter, though Davidson is interested in such competency. Still, there is a lesson to be gained from his thought experiment. An informal, open-textured predicate must be identified via a passing theory since such a predicate depends on context or intention. Just as a prior theory cannot determine before the moment of exchange what a speaker's words mean, an IOR cannot define a set of actions, objects, or events that satisfy the rule prior to their occurrence. When someone says a malapropism, such as "What a nice derangement of epitaphs" meaning "What a nice arrangement of epithets," the slip of the tongue need not prevent a hearer from rightly interpreting her words. The intended meaning is heard in spite of the verbal mistake.

Recall the proposal for ascribing "pick up" to cups and "lift" to beams. The problem to be solved by the use of two words for two actions was as follows: the act of picking up a cup and the act of picking up a beam are not the same. Where one verb is used for both actions in ordinary speech, changes in setting do not upset the meaning of the verb. The indeterminacy of the word is a feature of its use. A computable language, on the other hand, formalizes an action within a recursively axiomatized system that defines a finite, sequential, and predictable operation. The pull for nuancing our concepts, defining them more precisely or strictly, or changing other properties of our formalism comes from the medium we are working with. Yet it acknowledges indeterminacy without solving it. "A nice derangement of epitaphs" means a nice derangement of epitaphs.

Indeterminacy, then, is an obstacle for programming IORs. Radical translation teaches us that there is, at best, a synonymous relation between "pick up" as we often use the verb and pick up in a computable language. The indeterminacy that furnishes the former with many inflections of meaning cannot translate into the formal language. Yet radical interpretation tells us that pick up within a formal language does not cast off indeterminacy altogether. Changes in setting reveal divergency gaps that persist throughout the use of that concept. This persistence is another reason programming actions within purposive contexts maintain a margin of error. A defeasible interpretation of a formal concept is required given a unique situation. If we accept indeterminacy as a pervasive obstacle in IORs, we may also have a way of addressing the problems noted earlier.

11.3 Interpretive arguments

An IOR is a rule that contains informal, open-textured concepts that must be interpreted. An interpretation is required to determine what satisfies a rule from the symbols codifying those conditions, as well as the indeterminacy of the language used. There is a sharp distinction between a formalism and the purposive context in which it is employed. Formal strategies cannot guarantee the right interpretation. Divergency gaps appear in a command like pick up a cup, yet are often negligible. With IORs, asymmetry and indeterminacy must be addressed. But people at times struggle to decide when an IOR has been satisfied or violated. This uncertainty is most apparent in the courts, a setting in which arguments are regularly given for interpreting an informal, open-textured predicate in a certain way. In fact, resources in law can help us address the problems of IORs. We can adapt the significant work that has already been done on AI's place in law to address the obstacles mentioned earlier.

11.3.1 Statutory interpretation: A working model

A schema for statutory interpretation is one promising avenue for locating and formalizing interpretative arguments, and so addressing IORs. We will use this schema to draw out implications of asymmetry and indeterminacy. The schema is as follows:

> If expression E occurs in document D, E has a setting of S, and E would fit this setting by having interpretation i, then E ought to be interpreted as i (Sartor et al., 2014, pp. 21–28).°

In a court case, a judge must decide whether a law applies to a given context, or setting, of the disputed case. Lawyers give reasons one way or another, and the judge forms an interpretive argument for a certain interpretation of the law to the case at hand. The arguments are defeasible, that is, any conclusions as to whether or not the informal, open-textured predicate was satisfied are always subject to future revisions based on competing arguments or additional information (Walton et al., 2016, p. 56). An interpretation is adopted on the basis of a reason (or the weight of currently known reasons) in its favor.

Looking at the schema, then, the expression, or rule, is defined within a document or domain. The document includes other rules that are similar in various ways: due to relevant actors, actions, events, theme, structure, history, and so on. As will be noted, these similarities can be appealed to when deciding if a rule applies to a case. In addition, a rule has a setting, which is composed of variables that must match a rule's antecedents for the rule to apply. To recall our earlier definition, the antecedents of the rule are the conditions that, when met, entail the rule's consequent. An interpretation either matches the variables of the setting to those of a rule's antecedents so that the rule's consequent is inferred, or it does not. In short, an interpretation is a reason the rule should be understood as satisfied. The last conditional in the schema adds normative force: not only does the expression and setting match, the expression also ought to be interpreted in a given way.

The statutory schema also aligns with a central claim of the present collection: generation, processing, and evaluation of interpretive arguments require a deep representation and understanding of the *context*. An interpretive argument gives reasons that a rule applies to a certain setting on the basis of contextual features. But an informal, open-textured predicate means contextual features cannot be precisely codified in the rule itself. The stand-in variable undershoots and/or overshoots the intended object, action, or event. The schema clarifies our problem: aligning the variables in the expression with those of the setting. The problem can be explained according to asymmetry and indeterminacy.

Our first obstacle, asymmetry: the variables in the expression are concretely and externally inscribed, yet the setting is an event. Or, adding to the difficulty, the setting is a description of an event. The challenge is compounded since the relation of one expression to others (one rule to others) relies on similarities in the settings where those expressions apply. An advantage, however, is that expression, setting, and interpretation can be computed once they are inscribed. Their inscription enables us to further specify the problem of formalizing IORs: the variable standing for the open-textured predicate cannot have an explicit counterpart

---

°Their formulation has been slightly altered.

in the setting's description.[P] An interpretation must fill the gap, so to speak, and ascribing an interpretation requires the appeal to relevant situational factors.

But the meaning of the words themselves cannot be taken for granted either. The words in the expression, the description of the setting, and even the interpretation have an unavoidable degree of indeterminacy. The informal, open-textured predicate within the expression is liable to multiple interpretations, as expected. An event can also be described in various ways without undermining the integrity of the description. If an interpretation is given in words, the interpretation, too, harbors indeterminacy. This is why an explanation, which is also inconclusive, accompanies a judgment. An explanation is given since an interpretive argument has a certain degree of persuasive weight that its words express indeterminately. Of course, an identical argument may not have equal weight in two similar contexts.

11.3.2 Formality of law

An advantage of programming in a legal context is how far the context is already formalized and the kinds of formality exhibited (more work is needed to determine whether a military robot or a smart car share this advantage and, if not, whether such an advantage can be constructed). Not every sense of formality entails computability, and so it does not follow that the law is amenable to computation because it is highly formal. Dutilh Novaes sets computability apart as its own sort of formality and she notes how some formalities lend themselves well to others, though some do not. Still, from the research and programming done, there is reason to believe that large areas within law and decision making are computable. Summers has done extensive analysis on the kinds of formality within the legal system; he argues that a rule brings together a few different kinds of formality (Summers, 1997, 2006). We will lay out these different senses of formality here as a way of situating IORs. Summers' work describes how people have coped with the problem of IORs, and so illumines how its obstacles can be handled.

According to Summers (1997, 2006), a rule has an essential form, or a minimum threshold of formality: prescriptive content, generality, definiteness, and completeness. A rule's content obliges or prohibits an action. As we have already seen, a rule must be general enough to apply to repeatable features or constants of an act, object, subject, event, or setting, yet definite enough to identify those features or constants. A law is complete when it contains everything required to satisfy it. But that property may be misleading. Completeness does not exclude informal, open-textured predicates but rather shows the need for a variable to represent even informal, open-textured predicates. The need for such a variable is significant: when the informal, open-textured predicate is located, an argument can be given for whether or not the predicate is satisfied. A rule is devastatingly incomplete if its informal, open-textured predicates are left out—it cannot be followed or programmed. Again, this narrows the scope of the problem. Completeness ensures that there are other constants that are not open textured. If the closed predicates are unsatisfied, an interpretive argument will not be needed. Another point worth mentioning is that generality, definiteness, and completeness come in degrees,

---

[P]Understandably, and with acknowledgements, Walton et al. (2016) formalize over this problem.

there are trade-offs between them, and they can be joined together in better or worse ways. We will return to this point shortly.

Besides essential form, a rule may also have a structural form, which binds the formal elements together. It is the frame in which the rule is presented, an example being how a rule fits in the schema for statutory interpretation earlier. A rule also has a mode of expression: its explicitness, medium (written, spoken, typed), colloquial or technical vocabulary, and rigor. The more explicit a rule is, the easier it will be to program. Similarly, a written law is easier to program than a spoken one, and a technical vocabulary is easier than colloquial or idiomatic expressions. A law is also within a classificatory mechanism, or rule-set, which Summers calls its encapsalatory form. Examples are constitutional law, statutory law, judge-made law, and customary law. Disputes over whether a law applies assumes a categorization. So disputes within constitutional law, for example, do not carry over into statutory law. These categories have subcategories, relating one law to others in certain ways. Many, if not all, of these senses of formality come into play when the courts pass a judgment.

While these senses define the high level of formality in law, Summers noted that divergency gaps persist between a law's codification and its underlying purpose. These gaps result from and are explained by asymmetry and indeterminacy. The formal elements narrow the asymmetry and indeterminacy that threaten the possibility of judgment and thereby enable interpretive arguments to be given. They achieve this by coming together in a consistent and systematic way. Summers believes that there are two general conditions for a legal system to function. He writes

> It is not possible for any single basic functional element of a legal system to operate entirely on its own to achieve the ends and values of a legal order. Each such element must be combined with others. At the same time, no basic functional element can be combined with other elements in ad hoc, haphazard, and patternless ways and yet be consistently effective. Each element must be systematically combined, integrated, organized, and coordinated within general operational techniques for creating and implementing law (Summers, 1997, p. 1197).

These conditions—the integration of functional elements and the consistency of these elements—are promising for our goal of formalizing IORs. Divergency gaps are defined within a formal system: asymmetry and indeterminacy can be demarcated. While an informal, open-textured predicate cannot be formalized away, its variable defines a space requiring reasons for/or against its satisfaction.[q] A formal system, formally coalescing, is essential to the success of law. Thus, the right formal system coming together in the right way enables judgment.

Summers also argues that the formality of a law shapes its form and content. Decisions about a law's form—how general, definite, and complete it is—changes its content, and vice versa. He gives the following example. Imagine two laws that have the same end, safe driving. The first law is a speed limit of 65 mph. The second is a "drive reasonably" law. Both regulate speed, yet the first is more definite, the second less so. The first is also more complete since greater detail is given for satisfying the law. Both are similarly general since they apply to the

---

[q]This explanation is an oversimplification: there remains the question of whether the formally demarcated space will adequately match the relevant purposive context. A well-formalized system produces interpretive arguments that bear on the relevant contexts. If its judgments are relevant, then it provides evidence of the system's adequacy. Yet asymmetry and indeterminacy suggest that a formal system will not always and unerringly produce relevant reasons.

same streets, cars, and drivers; and, of course, both are prescriptive. There are a number of reasons to prefer the first, like supporting values of predictability, the learnability of a law, and the dignity and efficiency of citizen self-direction. Just as the form of the laws differ, so does their content. Yet Summers observed that indeterminacy persists in both (Summers, 1997, p. 1214). A speed limit of 64 or 66 mph would be as effective, presumably. Besides, there are exceptions to the law, such as emergency vehicles or other situations of distress. Though asymmetry and indeterminacy remain, a certain formality of a law (and more formality is not always best) promotes or obstructs just procedures.

A law is either appropriately formed, malformed, or pathological, as Summers tells us, depending on the senses of formality, their coherence, and the rule's content and purpose. Malformation involves inconsistencies in the formal roles or processes in law, such as when a complainant-oriented adjudicative process is coupled to an impartial and neutral tribunal. In such a case, one is in a biased role and neutral role simultaneously. A pathological form can be under- or over-formal given the purpose behind the rule, procedure, or role. Because malfunction and pathology have many dependencies, there are no general principles for deciding when a law is appropriately formed. Yet legislatures must do their best since "it is only through appropriate form," Summers (1997, p. 1213) adds, "that many necessary law-making choices can be made at all". Summers (1997, p. 1204) emphasize that determining appropriate form "has primacy [in significance] because it is indispensable to legitimate, civic authority." A judgment cannot be made without a dynamic and encompassing formal system in place, exhibited in the structure of any particular law. Only then can a law be applied and an interpretation given.

Still, court decisions cannot proceed by form alone. As Summers (1997, p. 1182) glosses, "Rules are not the whole of the law and much of the remainder is not formal." If law could proceed by form alone, interpretive arguments would not be needed, and the weight and responsibility of court *decisions*, or judgments, would be lost. Divergency gaps limit the extent formalisms can solve the problems of IORs, but they enable interpretations, defeasible and uncertain as they are. From what we have argued, no principle or variable can guarantee that a law applies or does not apply to a case. The different senses of formality and how they come together reveal how the effects of asymmetry and indeterminacy can be circumscribed, yet not overcome. For example, a law's encapsulatory form fixes a domain, determining relevant cases. When the encapsulatory form is appropriate to a given rule, and if that rule is such that its encapsulatory form is highly computable, the cases in which an interpretation must be given can be decided (forming a precedent; Lamond, 2006, 2007) or, a weaker claim, the cases in which an interpretation need not be given can be excluded. Similar tactics can be brought to bear on the others senses of formality.

As a heuristic, the schema for statutory interpretation assists law makers in representing and comparing interpretive arguments. It does not approximate judgment, which is required for addressing IORs. Still, it clarifies our problem and provides a working model for programming interpretive arguments. Summers' research presents the dynamism and holism of formal rules as well as describes how formality can be exploited for narrowing the margin of error in computation. As an alternative to defining better conjuncts or as a guide to defining them, we can change various elements of a rule's formality. Changes here effect how amenable a rule is to computation. Our goal is to compute rules without making them malformed or pathological, so an advantage of the schema of statutory interpretation is its flexibility to varying formalities. A disadvantage is how little it incorporates these senses. A lingering question, then, and one its authors seem to share, is how generally applicable such a schema will be within and beyond law.

11.3.3 Types of interpretive arguments

Jurisprudence arbitrates IORs within a formal system and it does so with a variety of arguments. If we are right about asymmetry and indeterminacy, an artificial agent can handle them or assist us in making judgments through the use or evaluation of interpretive arguments. Since the enactment of an IOR must be based on an interpretation of its informal, open-textured predicate, interpretive arguments are a way for agents to carry out a rule despite asymmetry and indeterminacy, that is, the problem of IORs can be addressed if robots are programmed to offer arguments, compare their force, and act with human partners on their basis.

An interpretation of a legal statute applies a rule: it draws an inference from the antecedents of a rule to the consequent. Since there are informal, open-textured concepts in statutes, and always asymmetry and indeterminacy, too, an interpretive argument is needed to justify the inference. A total of 11 arguments have been identified that are commonly used across legal systems (MacCormick & Summers, 1991; Summers, 1997). Judges and lawyers use these arguments to overcome IORs; such arguments may be adapted for the job of programming moral norms.

1. *Arguments from ordinary meaning*: Standard meaning of the words of a statute within its section or general context.
2. *Arguments from technical meaning*: Legal or nonlegal meaning of word(s) used in a context-sensitive way determined from the context of use, the relevant history of the word(s), or from other evidence.
3. *Arguments from contextual harmonization*: Appeal to contextual features beyond the general context used to interpret the words' ordinary or technical meanings involving the relevant section of the statute or a closely related statute.
4. *Arguments from precedent*: Appeal to past formal interpretations of the statute.
5. *Arguments from analogy*: Appeal to interpretations of relevantly similar statutes.
6. *Arguments from logical implicature*: Appeal to the implications of a recognized legal concept.
7. *Arguments from legal principle*: Appeal to legal principles at work in the relevant field.
8. *Arguments from statutory history*: Appeal to the history of the reception or evolution of the statute.
9. *Arguments from statutory purpose*: Appeal to the purpose a given interpretation of the statute serves.
10. *Arguments from substantive reason*: Use of reasons whose weight does not essentially depend on their authoritativeness.
11. *Arguments from intended meaning*: Appeal to the legislative intention governing the meaning of certain words.[r]

[r] A remaining task, and one that Walton et al. (2016) also noted, is comparing MacCormick's and Summers' list to Tarello's Tarello (1980). While there is overlap, the authors approach interpretive arguments differently, which may offer further insight for this project.

Returning to the schema for statutory interpretation, an interpretive arguments satisfies i, the interpretation that applies an expression to a setting. Here is an example from Walton et al. (2016):

> If *Loss* is in the *Employment Relations Act*, and *Loss* has a setting of *Pecuniary Loss*, and *Loss* fits this setting when interpreted according to its *Ordinary Meaning*, *Loss* should be interpreted as *Pecuniary Loss* (Walton et al., 2016, p. 59).[s]

Another interpretive argument may conclude that *Loss* should not be understood as *Pecuniary Loss* because *Loss* has a technical meaning, or that interpreting it as such violates the context of the rule or breaks from precedent. A judge must decide which interpretive argument carries more weight. By using these kinds of arguments, an interpretation can be given for an informal, open-textured predicate that has persuasive force.

A few comments are in order. The first two arguments—the linguistic arguments from ordinary and technical meaning—have priority. The remaining ones usually support an interpretation of the ordinary or technical meaning of a statute. Sometimes vagueness, or multiple meanings, weakens linguistic arguments so others are needed, but the priority of linguistic arguments is not arbitrary. When an ordinary or technical meaning is readily seen, the onus falls on interpretations that depart from this meaning. As Summers and Taruffo observed, a linguistic argument's force resides in the proximity between linguistic conventions and the lawmaker's choice to use those conventions in expressing their purpose (Summers, 1997, p. 466). It is assumed that how the law should be enforced is indicated in the language used. So recognizing linguistic conventions is the first and obvious guide for deciding whether the antecedents of a law hold. But understanding the words themselves is not the same as deciding whether their meaning bears on a specific case. This determination is why an argument is needed. As we have belabored, it is with respect to applying rules to specific cases that evokes the problems of IORs.

The last argument, an argument from intended meaning, is "transcategorical." This argument sums up the preceding comments: every argument can be framed in terms of legislative intent. Appeal to the purpose of law makers is transcategorical because linguistic, systematic, and teleological arguments concern what law makers intend by the words they use, their desire for consistency, and their motivations. Each type of argument can be framed by intention since each one aligns an interpretation of a law to a specific case according to the intention behind the law. More broadly, a purposive context motivates and regulates the formality of law and any formalism. Judgments are made through an appeal to a purposive context and its context is accessed via interpretive arguments. The "presumption" of legislative intent, or an assumed purposive context, limits possible interpretations. Summers and Taruffo mentioned six presumptions: fluency in the national language and technical legal vocabulary; constitutional validity of law; absurd or manifestly unjust outcomes are not intended; a retroactive effect is not intended; every penal statute requires *mens rea*; and treatises should not be violated (Summers, 1997, p. 471). These presuppositions reaffirm that besides a required formalism, an encompassing purposive context is needed to regulate and apply law. If

---

[s] Again, their formulation has been slightly altered.

interpretive arguments allow us to decide in the face of IORs, we may expect such arguments to enable AI to do the same.

Each type of argument exhibits underlying values of the legal system. The priority of linguistic arguments, for example, results from democratic values like equality before the law and a statute's general intelligibility. Courts weigh values differently, and so there are various appraisals of argument types. But the constant appearance of these types throughout legislative systems suggests that general criteria for evaluating judicial reasons is possible—Summers' and Taruffo's "universal thesis"—which is promising for research in AI. If the use of such criteria were computational, autonomous agents could handle IORs as humans do, by weighing reasons for and against. Researchers are increasingly exploring approaches for such automated evaluations of groups of arguments, but such work is still nascent (Atkinson et al., 2017; Branting, 2000; Dung, 1995; Rahwan & Reed, 2009; Reed & Rowe, 2004; Wachsmuth, Naderi, Habernal, et al., 2017; Wachsmuth, Naderi, Hou, et al., 2017; Walton et al., 2016).

11.4 Conclusion: Ameliorating the problems of IORs

A robot may err in deciding which of the three cups in Fig. 11.1 was meant by the command giver. Even so, it may have reasons for its choice. Such is the potential of adapting interpretive arguments to AI. Whether these reasons are sufficiently human, or intelligible to a human partner, is another matter. It suffices that the reasons have persuasive force for us. Our goal is not to overcome the margin of error and defeasibility of programming moral norms. Asymmetry and indeterminacy should warn us that such a task is futile. But offering interpretive arguments is only one way AI can aid in human decision-making; another is assessing and comparing interpretive arguments; yet another is finding loopholes in the preexisting rules. We have argued that asymmetry and indeterminacy limit our capacity to formalize rules—limits that are magnified in IORs. People, too, are liable to err because of these obstacles, yet we overcome them through interpretive arguments within a formalism and shared purposive context. A similar means for handling informal, open-textured predicates may be available for artificial agents and autonomous human-machine teams.

Either way, for artificial agents to be autonomous, IORs must be dealt with. There are at least three categories of possible solutions, each of which suggest directions for future work.[†] First, in order to advance the study of interpretive arguments, datasets of actual interpretive arguments are sorely needed—to our knowledge, none currently exist. Such datasets may allow researchers to discover whether certain types of interpretive arguments are more acceptable by certain populations in certain contexts. Second, work is needed to automatically evaluate, generate, or improve interpretive arguments. The current state of AI may not yet be at this stage, but the problems described in this chapter suggest that it should be a focus.

Third, and final, it would be useful to have tools that prevent the problems described by creating better IORs in the first place. Such a tool might, given a set of IORs, generate plausible

[†]In our Advancing Machine and Human Reasoning (AMHR) Lab at USF, we are pursuing multiple approaches to tackling the problems described in this chapter.

scenarios and interpretive arguments which exploit the informal, open-textured predicates the IORs rely on. For instance, we have previously described the "loophole task" (Licato & Marji, 2018) in which an antagonistic agent (ideally an artificially intelligent reasoner) tries to find scenarios that fall under literal interpretations of a set of IORs, but go against their intent. As machines increasingly interact with humans, IORs must be dealt with.

References

Atkinson, K., Baroni, P., Giacomin, M., Hunter, A., Prakken, H., Reed, C., … Villata, S. (2017). *AI Magazine, 38*(3), 25–36.

Bench-Capon, T. (2012). Open texture and argumentation: What makes an argument persuasive? In A. Artikis, R. Craven, N. K. Çiçekli, B. Sadighi, & K. Stathis (Eds.), *Logic programs, norms and action: Essays in honor of Marek J. Sergot on the occasion of his 60th birthday.* Berlin and Heidelberg: Springer.

Branting, L. (2000). *Reasoning with rules and precedents: A computational model of legal analysis.* Netherlands: Springer.

Brun, G. (2003). *Die richtige formel: Philosophische probleme der logischen formalisierung.* Frankfurt A. M., München, London, Miami, and New York: Dr. Hansel-Hohenhausen.

da Costa Pereira, C., Tettamanzi, A. G. B., Liao, B., Malerba, A., Rotolo, A., & van der Torre, L. (2017). Combining fuzzy logic and formal argumentation for legal interpretation. *Proceedings of the 16th edition of the international conference on artificial intelligence and law (ICAIL)* (pp. 49–58).

Davidson, D. (2001). *Inquiries into truth and interpretation.* Oxford: Clarendon Press.

Davidson, D. (2005). *Truth, language, and history.* Oxford: Clarendon Press.

Dung, P. M. (1995). On the acceptability of arguments and its fundamental role in nonmonotonic reasoning, logic programming and n-person games. *Artificial Intelligence, 7*(2), 321–358.

Franklin, J. (2012). Discussion paper: How much of commonsense and legal reasoning is formalizable? A review of conceptual obstacles. *Law, Probability and Risk, 11*(2–3), 225–245.

Hart, H. L. A. (1961). *The concept of law.* Oxford and New York: Clarendon Press.

Lamond, G. (2006). Do precedents create rules? *Legal Theory, 11*(1), 1–26.

Lamond, G. (2007). Precedent. *Philosophy Compass, 2*(5), 699–711.

Licato, J., & Marji, Z. (2018). Probing formal/informal misalignment with the loophole task. *Proceedings of the 2018 international conference on robot ethics and standards (ICRES 2018).*

MacCormick, D. N., & Summers, R. S. (1991). *Interpreting statutes: A comparative study.* Abingdon and New York: Routledge.

Novaes, C. D. (2011). The different ways in which logic is (said to be) formal. *History and Philosophy of Logic, 32,* 303–332.

Novaes, C. D. (2012). *Formal languages in logic.* Cambridge: Cambridge University Press.

Prakken, H. (2017). On the problem of making autonomous vehicles conform to traffic law. *Artificial Intelligence and Law, 25*(3), 341–363. https://doi.org/10.1007/s10506-017-9210-0.

Quine, W. V. O. (1960). *Word and object.* Cambridge: MIT Press.

Quine, W. V. O. (2008). Three indeterminacies. In D. Føllesdal & D. B. Quine (Eds.), *Confessions of a confirmed extentionalist: And other essays* (pp. 368–386): Cambridge and London: Harvard University Press.

Rahwan, I., & Reed, C. (2009). The argument interchange format. In G. Simari & I. Rahwan (Eds.), *Argumentation in artificial intelligence.* Dordrecht, Heidelberg, London, and New York: Springer.

Reed, C., & Rowe, G. (2004). Araucaria: Software for argument analysis, diagramming and representation. *International Journal of AI Tools, 14*(3–4), 961–980.

Sanders, K. E. (1991). Representing and reasoning about open-textured predicates. *Proceedings of the 3rd international conference on AI and law (ICAIL '91)* (pp. 137–144).

Sartor, G., Walton, D., Macagno, F., & Rotolo, A. (2014). Argumentation schemes for statutory interpretation: A logical analysis. *Legal knowledge and information systems (Proceedings of JURIX 14)* (pp. 21–28).

Summers, R. S. (1997). How law is formal and why it matters. *Cornell Law Review, 82*(5), 1166–1216.

Summers, R. S. (2006). *Form and function in a legal system: A general study.* Cambridge: Cambridge University Press.

Tarello, G. (1980). *L'interpretaxione della legge.* Milano: Giuffrè.

Wachsmuth, H., Naderi, N., Habernal, I., Hou, Y., Hirst, G., Gurevych, I., & Stein, B. (2017). Argumentation quality assessment: Theory vs. practice. *Proceedings of the 55th annual meeting of the association for computational linguistics (short papers)* (pp. 250–255).

Wachsmuth, H., Naderi, N., Hou, Y., Bilu, Y., Prabhakaran, V., Thijm, T. A., & Stein, B. (2017). Computational argumentation quality assessment in natural language. *Proceedings of the 15th conference of the European chapter of the association for computational linguistics: Volume 1, long papers* (pp. 176–187). Valencia, Spain: Association for Computational Linguistics.

Walton, D. (2016). Some artificial intelligence tools for argument evaluation: An introduction. *Argumentation, 30*(3), 317–340. https://doi.org/10.1007/s10503-015-9387-x.

Walton, D., Sartor, G., & Macagno, F. (2016). An argumentation framework for contested cases of statutory interpretation. *Artificial Intelligence and Law, 24,* 51–91.

Wetzel, L. (2018). Types and tokens. *The Stanford encyclopedia of philosophy.* Stanford University.

12

Engineering for emergence in information fusion systems: A review of some challenges ☆

Ali K. Raz[a], *James Llinas*[b], *Ranjeev Mittu*[c], *William F. Lawless*[d]

[a]**Purdue University, West Lafayette, IN, United States** [b]**University at Buffalo, Buffalo, NY, United States** [c]**Information Management & Decision Architectures Branch, Information Technology Division, US Naval Research Laboratory, Washington, DC, United States** [d]**Department of Mathematics, Sciences and Technology, and Department of Social Sciences, School of Arts and Sciences, Paine College, Augusta, GA, United States**

12.1 Introduction

The design, operational context, and operational concept of future information fusion (IF) system continue to evolve and change dramatically. IF system application is prevalent in a variety of domains that are expected to define our future society. System operational concepts, ranging from smart cities, urban air mobility, industry 4.0, and self-driving cars to multidomain command and control and human space exploration, all require a fundamental functional component of gathering, processing, and fusing information from distributed sources for sense-making—a feat best suited for an IF system. Moreover, with advancing technology, there are many factors that are changing within an IF system, for example, movement to cloud-based environments involving possibly many semiautonomous functional agents [e.g., the Internet of Things (IoT)], the employment of a wide range of processing technologies and methods spread across the agents, an exceptional breadth of types and modalities of available data, human-machine tasking, and diverse and asynchronous communication patterns among independent and interdependent teams and teammates and distributed agents to name a few. These factors and widespread application areas couch such contexts as

---

☆ Adapted from an IEEE Conference proceeding paper with the same title.

"ultra-large-scale systems (ULSS)" as described in Northrop et al. (2006) or system of systems (SoS) (Raz, Kenley, & DeLaurentis, 2017) among other fairly recent papers on ULSS and SoS engineering issues. With evolving operational context and integration of multidisciplinary technology, IF systems are entering a new era that is better characterized as ULSS, SoS, and more appropriately Complex Adaptive Systems (CAS) that are specified as "systems in which a perfect understanding of the individual parts does not automatically convey a perfect understanding of the whole system's behavior" (Complex Adaptive System, 2019)—a phenomenon easily observed in modern IF systems. In ULSS, SoS, and CAS, the end system capabilities emerge due to the interaction of multiple interdependent processes that demand holistic design and engineering. For example, a perfect understanding of only data generation and registration issues does not convey a perfect understanding of how an IF system accomplishes its mission and interacts with its environment and its users.

Traditionally at least, engineers faced with these challenging contexts employ decomposition in an approach for addressing the complexity challenge. This approach incorrectly assumes that a complex system can be designed or replicated by the sum of its individual parts. In such cases, there is an underlying assumption that reductionism is an appropriate mechanism to deal with emergence and complexity that is incorrect because behavior of single ant cannot be extrapolated for developing an understanding of ant colony. As a result, these methods are not able to accurately model all of the interactions between subsystems and components. Unless these interactions are properly understood and their effects on design dealt with, it is almost certain that uncertain behavior will emerge as a characteristic of system-level outputs. Emergent behavior and how to understand and control it are still poorly understood today. Such behavior has various and somewhat contentious definitions that we avoid here (see, e.g., Chalmers, 2006; Fromm, 2005), but one description has it as "Emergent behaviors are unexpected, nontrivial results of relatively simple interactions of relatively simple components" (Chalmers, 2006). The key terms here are "unexpected," "nontrivial," and "interactions," meaning they are results that could portend negative and possibly serious or catastrophic outputs—where the underlying cause is attributed to interactions. Dealing with emergence is very likely an impending challenge for the IF community, especially with the increasing demands of future IF system operational contexts and the growing complexity of engineering component fusion solutions with new technologies such as machine learning (ML).

The impetus for this chapter is to review the emergence challenge from different viewpoints to develop an understanding of the challenges it presents for IF systems and what approaches and principles are needed for future IF system design and development. In particular, we examine emergence from three different viewpoints:

i. a systems engineering (SE) viewpoint that primarily deals with the design and development of ULSS, SoS, and CAS;
ii. a contextual information fusion viewpoint that highlights the role of context in emergence;
iii. an ML viewpoint that elucidates the emergence challenge associated with utilizing ML techniques for engineering solutions.

Even though these emergence viewpoints are discussed individually, our objective here is to synthesize their underlying implications for future IF systems. The choice of these three perspectives is not arbitrary, as the significance of both ML and SE is being actively advocated in the IF community (Blasch, Cruise, Natarajan, Raz, & Kelly, 2018; Ravanbakhsh et al., 2018; Solano & Carbone, 2013), while contextual information fusion is among the few areas of research within the IF community engaged in understanding emergent behavior (Snidaro, Garcia, Llinas, & Blasch, 2016).

12.2 Technical foundations

12.2.1 Data fusion and IF systems

Here, we offer a historical perspective remark with reference to development of IF discipline. The JDL data fusion process model shown in Fig. 12.1 (Hall et al., 2012; Kessler, Askin, & Beck, 1991; White, 1988)—the long-standing paradigm used to frame discussions about the nature of data fusion—has from the beginning been broken into "levels," as is well known. These levels can be broken down into functions, such as data registration and tracking that are then accomplished by dedicated algorithms. Table 12.1, which is adapted from Raz et al. (2017), summarizes the scope of levels and provides example functions pertaining to each level.

Over the past few decades, research and developments of JDL levels and their corresponding functions have received dedicated attention in the IF community. Numerous technological advances have resulted in scientific breakthroughs and novel algorithms that are now capable of achieving the functionality of JDL levels. However, this siloed development of fusion algorithms that focuses on an individual function within a JDL level is analogous to understanding separately the individual parts of a complex system. Notwithstanding, very little has been done in terms of understanding how to proactively design synergistic processing and behavior across and within these interdependent levels; Llinas et al. in Llinas et al. (2004) and again in Llinas (2010) discussed long ago the issue of interlevel synergy and the need to proactively design such feedback-type operations (e.g., to include a stopping criteria). In the status quo today, there is an apparent lack of formal design principles that lay the foundation for realizing such synergy that will eventually lead to detection, exploitation, and/or mitigation of emergent behavior in IF systems. A dedicated field of research focused on developing formal design principles for complex systems, such as IF systems, is SE, which is described next.

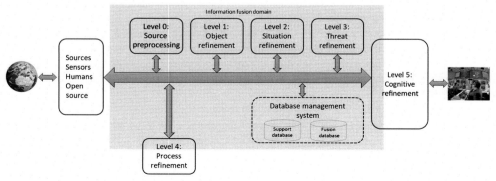

FIG. 12.1   Joint Directorate of Laboratories data fusion model (Hall, Chong, Llinas, & Liggins, 2012).

TABLE 12.1   JDL DFM level scope and example functions (Raz et al., 2017).

JDL data fusion levels	Scope	Functions
Level 0: Source preprocessing	Pixel and signal level data characterization. Signals and features that are determined by measurements and observations	Source detection (signal processing and detection theory). Bias corrections, coordinate transformations, etc.
Level 1: Object assessment	Object location and parametric and kinematic information. Establishment of tracks, IDs, and classification. Combination of multisensor data	Data alignment, data/object correlation, kinematic and attribute estimation, and kinematic and attribute fusion
Level 2: Situation assessment	Contextual interpretation of objects, events, situations, and their relationships	Object aggregation, automated/rule-based reasoning, and complex pattern recognition
Level 3: Threat assessment	Future projections of current situations and consequence determination	Situation aggregation, automated/rule-based reasoning, and complex pattern recognition
Level 4: Process refinement	Resource management and adaptive fusion control in support of mission objectives	Process control, sensor and network modeling, and multiobjective optimization
Level 5: User refinement	Fusion system and human interaction	Knowledge representation and information display

12.2.2 Systems engineering

Most formal definition of a system define it as a "whole" composed of multiple interacting parts that together provide a capability unattainable by the parts alone (Blanchard & Fabrycky, 2011). Hence a system is an entity in which the whole is greater than the sum of its parts. As the parts (sometimes called components or elements) of a system increase in their own complexity, designing their interactions and engineering a system to achieve specific capability become a more complex challenge. Therefore a need for a new discipline emerged for designing and engineering the whole system and not just the parts, for example, engineering an airplane with electronically controlled thrust generating and stabilizing components (i.e., engines, wings, and electronics) or providing space situational awareness by engineering interaction of tracking, fusion, sense-making, and decision-making elements. This technical discipline is called systems engineering (SE).

SE formally guides the realization of a system all the way from its inception to create a capability, through concept development, operations, and retirement. A prime area of concern for SE is to characterize how the different parts and elements of a system will interact with one another to create the desired capability and what interactions may lead to an undesired system effect. SE determines what requirements need to be imposed on the parts, the interfaces, and the interactions, such that the resultant system will meet the defined need and objectives. In other words, SE is the first step toward elucidating, understanding, and controlling emergent behavior.

Recognizing the value SE provides in complex system design and engineering, a number of researchers advocate for the holistic design, engineering, and evaluation of IF systems as offered by the SE principles (Solano & Carbone, 2013; Steinberg, 2000). Steinberg and Snidaro particularly challenge the notion of dividing IF into levels and call for a structured holistic approached based on SE methods for engineering future IF systems (Steinberg & Snidaro, 2015). Nevertheless, the IF community has still to unlock the full potential of SE application for engineering real-world fusion solutions. The earnest need for adoption of SE practices in IF systems is further signified from the fact that future fusion methods (i.e., the parts and the elements of an IF system) are expected to rely on ML methods, which have an emergence challenge of their own.

12.2.3 Machine learning

ML domain is about developing an algorithm to produce an outcome based on previous experience and data (Suciu, Marginean, Kaya, Daume, & Dumitras, 2018). In recent years, ML, primarily housed in computer science, has seen an explosion of research and development and subsequent applicability in multiple application areas, ranging from space application, autonomous machines, to cognitive science and genetic sequencing. The disruptive economic impact of ML has been estimated in trillions of dollars (Brynjolfsson & Mitchell, 2017). The basic idea behind ML methods is that a computer algorithm is trained to "learn" the behavior presented as part of previous experience and/or dataset to the extent that an outcome can be produced by the computer algorithm when it is presented with a never-before-seen dataset or situation.

ML portends a valuable potential for IF systems for learning the underlying data structures and extracting the salient features encountered in fusion, sense-making, and decision-making processes. The recent trends in IF community also point toward an embracing adoption of ML techniques for solving IF problems as evident by the number of ML-related special sessions in the past International Society of Information Fusion (ISIF) conferences. Nonetheless the training and execution of the ML methods—in particular neural networks and deep neural networks—remain a black box to the developers, engineers, and operators. This black box behavior is more often than not dependent on the context of the experience and dataset provided to the ML for training, masks the inner details and working of the algorithm, and subsequently leads to unpredictable emergent behavior.

The susceptibility of ML algorithms to unperceived context and emergent behavior is well documented in both civilian and military domains. A classic example is described in Kherlopian (2019) where a neural network was trained to classify tanks based on training data of pictures with and without tanks. The system worked well in the laboratory environment but failed in operational setting as all the pictures with the tanks were taken on a rainy day and without tanks on a sunny day. This example of emergent behavior (an undesirable outcome in this case) is not an isolated occurrence in the ML developments. Many other researchers, including Google and Microsoft, have experienced similar results in the ML training and developments that have led to initiation of Explainable AI program by DARPA (DARPA, 2019). The overarching question for the IF community, then, is how to utilize SE to incorporate context into the development of future IF systems and mitigate the unintended consequences while exploiting the benefits of emergence and ML.

12.3 Widespread impacts of emergence

This section will first develop key concepts of emergence, what is it and how it is defined in the literature. Second, it will discuss emergence in ML and how the training of ML methods is impacted by it. Finally a characterization of emergence from the SE perspective is introduced, along with a discussion of recent work that addresses emergence in IF and non-IF systems.

12.3.1 Emergence and IF systems

Emergence is defined as an unexpected behavior or outcome due to interacting parts and elements of a systems. In essence, emergence is baked into the very definition of a system where multiple parts come together to create a capability (see Section 12.2.2). The emergent behavior in a system can both be desirable and/or undesirable and can be attributed to the complexity of interactions between system elements. Complex system results in emergent behavior that is challenging to characterize during initial system conceptual formulation. A system can be considered as a complex system when its elements show a great degree of temporal, horizontal, and diagonal interdependence (Taleb, 2007):

- A temporal interdependence implies that a variable (here a system attribute or a particular element's individual behavior) is dependent on its own history.
- A horizontal interdependence implies that a variable is dependent on other variables (i.e., a system outcome results from more than one element).
- A diagonal interdependence refers to a variable's dependence on the history of other variables (Taleb, 2007).

When examined in the light of the aforementioned definition, an IF system—that is, a system based on JDL levels of fusion—unequivocally exhibits all the properties of a complex system and hence is subject to emergent behavior. However, the salient properties of emergent behavior make it rarely attributable to an individual element of a system (Fromm, 2005). Fig. 12.2 illustrates the various sources of emergence in the IF system with the ML algorithms (to include classical fusion algorithms that are susceptible to temporal interdependence) that

FIG. 12.2   Sources of emergence in IF systems.

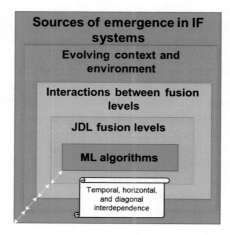

provide the individual capabilities of JDL levels and resulting interactions of JDL levels between different levels and the nature of evolving context and operational environment. The three defining traits of interdependence for a complex system become evident when these sources of emergence are viewed collectively. Levels 0 and 1 algorithms are dependent upon the data and their past history (e.g., a Kalman filter)—that is, a temporal interdependence. Levels 2 and 3 situation refinement and threat refinement are inherently dependent on collecting and fusing data and information from multiple source—that is, a horizontal interdependence. Levels 4 and 5 resource management and user refinement are dependent on what has been observed and on cognitive abilities of users—that is, a diagonal interdependence. For an IF system, this implies that the overall functionality and particularly its emergent behavior cannot be understood or characterized by examining a single fusion level in isolation.

12.3.2 Machine learning and emergence

If the vision of the current wave of evolving capability of artificial intelligence (AI) and ML actually materializes, then future IF systems are expected to be well populated with such technologies, meaning possibly extensive employment of neural network-based agents. As neural networks (NN) can be considered the prototypes of systems exhibiting emergent behaviors (Pessa, 2009), their presence in future systems further substantiates the expectation that IF system design will need to address the issue of emergent behavior.

As emergence or emergent outcomes are the results of unknown dependencies between some agent node and a subordinate, contributing agent node, it can be expected that the accuracy of an ML/NN estimator may be dependent on how well such interagent dependencies are understood. Sheikh-Bahaei argues for the notion of "E-layers" that characterize the degree of dependency knowledge across agent layers as a way to notionally assess the likely performance of ML/NN systems in Sheikh-Bahaei (2017). In this notion, if many so-called E-layers need to be crossed in the multiagent operations, the predictive accuracy of the ML/NN-fused system will degrade. Feature noise is also a factor and the degree of interlevel/interagent dependency knowledge in a given E-layer. Sheikh-Bahaei surveys some literature and presents the results in Table 12.1 as a suggestion that this notion may have merit toward assessing emergence effects on ML/NN predictive accuracy. It can be seen that, as the E-layer or emergence barrier ranges from none to strong, the NN performance degrades; note that, if the emergence barrier is high (weak knowledge regarding interagent dependencies), even low feature noise does not help in regard to output accuracy Table 12.2.

Further along the lines of this theme of emergent behavior along with unpredictable and undesirable behavior in ML systems, Suresh examines the effects of a variety of biases[a] that can creep into ML/NN design and their effects on unintended consequences (Suresh & Guttag, 2019). They identify five classes of such biases (some human) in the processes of design for training data development and for construction of the prototype NN process; these are shown in Fig. 12.3. The issues of emergence and biases (as discussed earlier) along with many other operational and design considerations (Raz & DeLaurentis, 2016) demand the holistic approach of SE for research and development of future IF systems.

---

[a]In this context the term "bias" refers to an unintended or potentially harmful property of the data used in system design and development. It can also be inherent in the algorithms used by the system.

TABLE 12.2 ML prediction success with emergence.

ML problem	Feature noise	Emergence barrier	Prediction success
Character recognition	High	None	High
Speech recognition	High	None	High
Weather prediction	High	Weak	High
Recommendation system	Low	Weak	Moderate
Ad-click prediction	Low	Weak	Moderate
Device failure prediction	High	Weak	Moderate
Healthcare predictions outcome	High	Strong	Low
Melting/boiling point prediction	Low	Strong	Low
Stock prediction	Low	Strong	Low

Adapted from Sheikh-Bahaei, S. (2017). *The E-dimension: Why machine learning doesn't work well for some problems?*

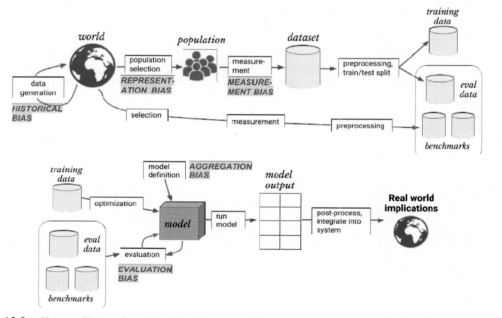

FIG. 12.3 Classes of biases that affect NN design and development (Sheikh-Bahaei, 2017).

12.3.3 Systems engineering and emergence

Detecting, understanding, and leveraging emergence are well-recognized activities in the SE community and especially in the SoS community where the presence of emergent behavior is in the very definition of SoS (Jamshidi, 2008). One of the fundamental endeavors of "system science" is research and development of methods, tools, and processes (MTPs) that addresses the emergent behavior in complex systems. The International Council on Systems Engineering (INCOSE) notes that "research in systems science attempts to compensate for the inherent limitations of classical science, most notably the lack of ways to deal with emergence" (INCOSE, 2015). Although, classical science plays a fundamental role in developing the MTPs for engineering the various parts and elements of a system, system science addresses system-level behavior (including emergence) that arises from the interaction of parts and elements with one another and the operational environment.

A system has system-level properties ("emergent properties") that are properties of the whole system not attributable to individual parts. These emergent properties depend on the system structure that governs the functional flows and information flows in the system, determining the relationship between a system's parts and elements and it's interaction with the environment.

There are a number of papers that address the issue of detecting and recognizing emergent behavior in complex systems (e.g., Birdsey & Szabo, 2014; Haghnevis & Askin, 2012; Santos & Zhao, 2017). Liu, He, Xu, Ding, and Wang (2018) address both detection and suppression of emergent behavior for the case of swarming unmanned aerial vehicles (UAV), using the f-divergence statistic to assess the onset of emergence in the UAV case by assessing swarm spatial diversity and invoking a suppression strategy by selective interplatform communication jamming. Whether such strategies generalize to other complex systems is unknown, IF systems likely will need methods for detecting that their behavior has moved to the emergent class (as a means of self-monitoring). Glinton et al., in a 2009 ISIF conference paper (Glinton, Scerri, & Sycara, 2009), address the modeling of complex systems using mean-field theory to qualitatively describe the state space of the system over a wide range of parameters. That work assessed the evolution of fused belief and trust across the system of agents to yield qualitative assessments of output trends for given system design parameters. Raz et al. (2017) have demonstrated the use of SE techniques for assessing the impact of system structure on the IF system performance and establish that the interactions between the system structure and the fusion algorithms play a key role in IF system performance outcome. Building upon SE techniques, Raz, Wood, Mockus, DeLaurentis, and Llinas (2018) proposes design and evaluation of IF systems using experimental design methods to identify interactions between system components and quantify their impact on performance that can lead to better characterization of emergent behavior. Finally, it should be noted that, as distributed fusion systems are enabled in software, emergent behavior can also be a consequence of various software design and functionality issues, separate from the interagent complexity issue. Mogul reviews these issues in Mogul (2006), arguing for new directions in computer system research to understand how, due specifically to software-specific factors, disruptive emergent behavior can be prevented.

12.4 Emergence challenges for future IF systems

Future IF systems—deployed in both military and civilian domains—will be operating in a highly dynamic and uncertain world and will be faced with competing demands. Asymmetric warfare and the military focus on small, agile forces have altered the framework by which time critical information is digested and acted upon by the decision-makers. Civilian missions involving wide-ranging applications, such as humanitarian assistance and disaster relief, are faced with the extraction of relevant data from ever increasing sources. The phrase "too much data – not enough information" is a common complaint in most operational domains. Finding and integrating decision-relevant information are increasingly difficult in these data-dense environments. Mission and task contexts are often absent (at least in computable and accessible forms) and sparsely/poorly represented in most information systems, thus requiring decision-makers to mentally reconstruct, infer, and extract relevant information through laborious and error-prone internal processes. This problem is compounded as decision-makers must multitask among many competing and often conflicting mission objectives, further complicating the management of information.

Clearly, there is a need for automated mechanisms for the timely extraction of information that has relevance to decisions. Context plays a key role in how information is fused and what the upstream algorithms learn from the fused data. Therefore understanding a complex system from an SE perspective can allow us to ask very challenging questions about the role of context for enabling beneficial properties (decision-relevant information) to emerge. The following brief description provides some samples of challenging problems across the spectrum of IF and ML that will prevail in future IF systems and could benefit from an SE perspective.

12.4.1 Decision models for goal-directed behavior

Future IF system will require instantiation of prescriptive models of decision-making that integrate context-aware information recommendation engines. Furthermore, techniques that can broker across, generalize, or aggregate individual decision models would enable applications in broader contexts such as group behavior. Supporting areas of research may include similarity metrics that enable the selection of the appropriate decision model for a given situation and intuitive decision model visualizations. Other pertinent challenges include the following:

- adequately capturing users' information interaction (seeking) patterns (and subsequently user information biases),
- reasoning about information seeking behaviors to infer a decision-making context,
- instantiating formal models of decision-making based on information seeking behaviors,
- leveraging research from the AI community in plan recognition to infer which decision context (model) is active and which decision model should be active,
- recognizing a decision shift based on work that has been done in the ML community with "concept drift" and assessing how well this approach adapts to noisy data that learns over time.

12.4.2 Information extraction and valuation

Locating, assessing, and enabling through utility-based exploitation, integration, and fusion of high-value information within decision models, particularly in the big data realm, are a research challenge due to the heterogeneous data environment. In addition, techniques that can effectively stage relevant information along a decision trajectory (while representing, reducing, and/or conveying information uncertainty) would enable the wealth of unstructured data to be maximally harnessed.

12.4.3 Decision assessment

Modeling decision "normalcy" to identify decision trajectories that might be considered outliers detrimental to achieving successful outcomes in a given mission context would be areas for additional research. Furthermore, techniques that proactively induce the correct decision trajectory to achieve mission success are also necessary. Lastly, metrics for quantifying decision normalcy in a given context can be used to propose alternate sequences of decisions or induce the exact sequence of decisions. This would require the prestaging of the appropriate information needed to support the evaluation of those decisions and would potentially improve the speed and accuracy of decision-making.

12.4.4 Operator/human issues

Understanding, modeling, and integrating the human decision-making component as an integral part of the aforementioned challenges are needed areas of research. The challenges are to represent human decision-making behavior computationally; to mathematically capture the human assessment of information value, risk, uncertainty, prioritization, projection, and insight; and to computationally represent human foresight and intent. These challenges will require integration of both system science and social science for the development of future IF systems.

12.4.5 Integration of emergence from social sciences

The advent of human-machine teams has elevated the need to determine context computationally, yet social science has had little to offer for their design or operation (Lawless, Mittu, Sofge, & Hiatt, 2019). Recognizing this plight, social scientists argue, and we agree that their science is a repository of an extraordinary amount of qualitative and statistical experience in determining and evaluating contexts for humans and human teams (National Academies of Sciences, 2019). But this situation leaves engineers to seek a quantitative path on their own. Instead, we pursue an integrated path as the better course.

Social psychologists (Gilbert, Fiske, & Lindzey, 1998) recommended the removal of interdependence to make data independent and identically distributed (iid), recommended also by engineers (Fromm, 2005) and information theorists (Conant, 1976). Yet, while the eminent social psychologist, Jones (1998), agreed that interactions were highly interdependent, he concluded that the complexity it caused in the lab is "bewildering." Making it a respected subject of study again, the National Academy of Sciences (National Research Council, 2015) concluded that interdependence, the means of how social effects are transmitted and team behavior emerges, is critical to team performance, the best teams being the most interdependent (Cummings, 2015).

As an example of a system involved in an accident, NTSB News Release (2019) investigated the death of a pedestrian in 2018, finding that the Uber self-driving car saw the pedestrian 6 s early, applied the brakes 1.3 s early, but emergency braking was disabled by Uber engineers to maximize car handling. The human operator saw the pedestrian 1 s early and hit the brakes 1 s after impact. In this case the Uber car did not update the context for the operator when it could have; its lack of interdependence with its operator made it a poor team player.

12.4.6 Interdependence

Three effects characterize interdependence (Lawless, 2017): bistability (two sides to every story, the source of inspiration and innovation, checks and balances, and social reactivity), measurement (produces one-sided stories, consensus-seeking or minority control, and increased uncertainty and errors), and nonfactorability (court cases; proprietary or patent claims; and he said, she said). Measurement, for example, produces an uncertainty relationship that promotes the emergence of trade-offs; for example, from signal detection theory (Cohen, 1995), a narrow waveform yields a wide spectrum, and a wide waveform yields a narrow spectrum, and that both the time waveform and frequency spectrum cannot be made arbitrarily small simultaneously (Fig. 12.4).

12.4.7 Emergence

Emergence, like surprise, can become the weapon that (Von Clausewitz, 1940) claimed caused "confusion and broken courage in the enemy's ranks ..." In competition against an adversary, the goal of a team should be to avoid internal surprise by being sufficiently well trained to manage it, by navigating as a team around obstacles, and by exploiting it when seeking (e.g., emotional) vulnerabilities in an adversary's defenses to cause surprise in the adversary. Teams can emerge as a unit; unlike the Uber car, human-machine teammates can anticipate each other's vulnerabilities to construct contexts in real time to help their team to operate effectively and efficiently in a context shared by a team that they come to trust when their team navigates safely around obstacles (Lawless et al., 2019).

However, to engineer such an emergent behavior in the human-machine teams, an SE perspective that takes into account full spectrum interactions including operational context is deemed necessary.

12.4.8 Machine learning in adversarial environments

For much of the IF community, we are dealing with adversarial environments. This raises the issue of protecting IF systems containing AI and ML components from cyberattacks.[b] In Suciu et al. (2018), a framework for an attacker model is developed, which describes the

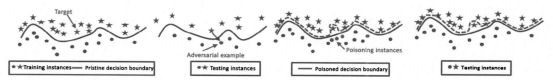

FIG. 12.4 Targeted attacks against machine learning classifiers. *Adapted from Steinberg, A. N., & Snidaro, L. (2015). Levels? In 2015 18th international conference on information fusion (FUSION) (pp. 1985–1992).*

---

[b]Note that AI and ML methods can and have been used as a means to protect software-based systems and in attack systems as well; these are truly "dual-use" technologies. Informal searching suggests that there is more literature on these topics than protecting AI/ML-based systems and components.

adversary's knowledge and control along four dimensions as related to specifically attacking AI/ML capabilities when used largely for classification. Fig. 12.4 shows some of the strategies that adversaries can exploit against an ML/NN classifier that are dependent on adversarial knowledge. On the left is a correctly functioning classifier that correctly labels the target data point. Next is the case of an "evasion" attack where the adversary modifies the target data to cross the friendly classifier decision boundary (adversary learns the boundary); then the next attack is a "poisoning" attack where the adversary perturbs the training data to shift the decision boundary (adversary learns the boundary). These four dimensions are features, algorithms, instances, and leverage. They argue that this approach avoids any implicit assumptions about adversarial capabilities so that the model forms a common basis for modeling adversaries. The four dimensions of their model are as follows: (1) feature knowledge, the subset of features known to the adversary; (2) algorithm knowledge, the learning algorithm that the adversary uses to craft poison data samples; (3) instance knowledge, the labeled training instances available to the adversary; and (4) leverage, the subset of features that the adversary can modify.

Lastly, in considering the broad range of types of unintended consequences, there are also the impacts on the user community (here the IF R&D community and/or IF system users), as described by Cabitza, Rasoini, and Gensini (2017) based on experience in the medical domain. These undesirable factors are as follows:

- reducing the skills of practitioners (both designers and users of the IF system),
- excessive focusing on data and loss of contextual influences,
- dealing with intrinsic uncertainty of the domain need to "open the ML black box" (explain ability, among other needed insights to complex IF and/or AI/ML operations).

12.5 Conclusions and future work

Modern IF systems are faced with evolving operational environments where human and intelligent systems will function as a team to achieve the mission objectives. These evolving operational contexts demand a dynamic response from the IF systems whose behaviors must opportunistically emerge from various complex interactions that take place between different JDL fusion levels (including human interaction) and the environment. Traditionally the IF community has sought a siloed approach for the design and development of these "fusion levels" that does not lend itself to the recognition and characterization of emergent behavior arising at the system-level integration of these levels. Moreover, with the recent technological advancement and profusion of AI/ML, there is an evident push in the IF community to employ these techniques for the respective (yet siloed) design and development of individual fusion levels. However, as discussed in chapter the ML techniques are susceptible to their own emergent behavior, further strengthening the case for a holistic and integrated design of future IF systems. We have argued here that emergence is an impending challenge for the IF community that makes adoption of SE MTPs a necessary step for full spectrum characterization and understanding of IF system emergent behavior.

In this chapter, we have highlighted the various research directions for addressing the emergence challenge of the IF system, such as development of decision models for goal-directed behavior, information valuation, integration of social sciences, and system science for human and intelligent machine teams. The future work will demonstrate how the SE MTPs can be leveraged to advance the state of the art of these research challenges and to incorporate these advancements into future IF systems.

References

Birdsey, L., & Szabo, C. (2014). An architecture for identifying emergent behavior in multi-agent systems. In *Proceedings of the 2014 international conference on autonomous agents and multi-agent systems, Richland, SC* (pp. 1455–1456).

Blanchard, B., & Fabrycky, W. (2011). *Systems engineering and analysis* (5th ed.). New Jersey: Prentice-Hall.

Blasch, E., Cruise, R., Natarajan, S., Raz, A. K., & Kelly, T. (2018). Control diffusion of information collection for situation understanding using boosting MLNs. In *2018 21st international conference on information fusion (FUSION)* (pp. 1–8).

Brynjolfsson, E., & Mitchell, T. (2017). What can machine learning do? Workplace implications. Profound changes are coming, but roles for humans remain. *Science, 358*, 1530–1534.

Cabitza, F., Rasoini, R., & Gensini, G. F. (2017). Unintended consequences of machine learning in medicine. *JAMA, 318*(6), 517–518.

Chalmers, D. J. (2006). Strong and weak emergence. In P. Davies & P. Clayton (Eds.), *The re-emergence of emergence: The emergentist hypothesis from science to religion*: Oxford University Press.

Cohen, L. (1995). *Time-frequency analysis. Vol. 778*. Prentice-Hall.

Complex Adaptive System. (February 08, 2019). *Wikipedia*.

Conant, R. C. (1976). Laws of information which govern systems. *IEEE Transactions on Systems, Man, and Cybernetics, 4*, 240–255.

Cummings, J. (2015). Team science successes and challenges. In *National Science Foundation sponsored workshop on fundamentals of team science and the science of team science, Bethesda, MD*.

DARPA. (2019). *Explainable artificial intelligence*. [Online]. Available from https://www.darpa.mil/program/explainable-artificial-intelligence. (Accessed 18 March 2019).

Fromm, J. (2005). *Types and forms of emergence*. arXiv preprint nlin/0506028.

Gilbert, D. T., Fiske, S. T., & Lindzey, G. (1998). *The handbook of social psychology*. McGraw-Hill.

Glinton, R. T., Scerri, P., & Sycara, K. (2009). Towards the understanding of information dynamics in large scale networked systems. In *2009 12th International conference on information fusion* (pp. 794–801).

Haghnevis, M., & Askin, R. G. (2012). A modeling framework for engineered complex adaptive systems. *IEEE Systems Journal, 6*(3), 520–530.

Hall, D., Chong, C. -Y., Llinas, J., & Liggins, M., II. (2012). *Distributed data fusion for network-centric operations*. CRC Press.

INCOSE. (2015). *INCOSE systems engineering handbook: A guide for system life cycle processes and activities* (4th ed.). Hoboken, NJ: Wiley.

Jamshidi, M. (2008). Introduction to system of systems. In M. J. Chair (Ed.), *System of systems engineering* (pp. 1–20): John Wiley & Sons, Inc.

Jones, E. E. (1998). *Major developments in five decades of social psychology*. New York, NY: McGraw-Hill.

Kessler, O., Askin, K., & Beck, N. (1991). *Functional description of the data fusion process, technical report for the office of naval technology data fusion development strategy*. Naval Air Development Center.

Kherlopian, A. (2019). *Analytic rigor is the key to operationalizing machine learning*. [Online]. Available from https://www.genpact.com/insight/blog/analytic-rigor-is-the-key-to-operationalizing-machine-learning. (Accessed 17 March 2019).

Lawless, W. F. (2017). The physics of teams: Interdependence measurable entropy and computational emotion. *Frontiers of Physics, 5*, 30.

Lawless, W. F., Mittu, R., Sofge, D. A., & Hiatt, L. (2019). Artificial intelligence (AI), autonomy and human-machine teams: Interdependence, context and explainable AI. In *Presented at the AI magazine*.

Liu, Q., He, M., Xu, D., Ding, N., & Wang, Y. (2018). A mechanism for recognizing and suppressing the emergent behavior of UAV swarm. *Mathematical Problems in Engineering, 2018*, 6734923.

Llinas, J. (2010). A survey and analysis of frameworks and framework issues for information fusion applications. In *International conference on hybrid artificial intelligence systems* (pp. 14–23).

Llinas, J., Bowman, C., Rogova, G., Steinberg, A., Waltz, E., & White, F. (2004). *Revisiting the JDL data fusion model II*. DTIC Document.

Mogul, J. C. (2006). Emergent (mis) behavior vs. complex software systems. In *Vol. 40. ACM SIGOPS operating systems review* (pp. 293–304).

National Academies of Sciences. (2019). *A decadal survey of the social and behavioral sciences: A research agenda for advancing intelligence analysis*. Washington, DC: The National Academies Press.

National Research Council. (2015). *Enhancing the effectiveness of team science*. National Academies Press.

Northrop, L., et al. (2006). *Ultra-large-scale systems: The software challenge of the future*. Pittsburgh, PA: Software Engineering Institute Carnegie Mellon University.

NTSB News Release. (2019). *Preliminary report released for crash involving pedestrian, Uber Technologies, Inc., test vehicle*. [Online]. Available from https://www.ntsb.gov/news/press-releases/Pages/NR20180524.aspx. (Accessed 13 March 2019).

Pessa, E. (2009). Self-organization and emergence in neural networks. *Electronic Journal of Theoretical Physics, 6*, 20.

Ravanbakhsh, M., et al. (2018). Learning multi-modal self-awareness models for autonomous vehicles from human driving. In *2018 21st international conference on information fusion (FUSION)* (pp. 1866–1873).

Raz, A. K., & DeLaurentis, D. A. (2016). Design space characterization of information fusion systems by design of experiments. In *2016 19th International conference on information fusion (FUSION), 2016*, IEEE.

Raz, A. K., Kenley, C. R., & DeLaurentis, D. A. (2017). A system-of-systems perspective for information fusion system design and evaluation. *Information Fusion, 35*, 148–165.

Raz, A. K., Wood, P., Mockus, L., DeLaurentis, D. A., & Llinas, J. (2018). Identifying interactions for information fusion system design using machine learning techniques. In *2018 21st International conference on information fusion (FUSION)* (pp. 226–233).

Santos, E., & Zhao, Y. (2017). Automatic emergence detection in complex systems. *Complexity, 2017*, 3460919.

Sheikh-Bahaei, S. (2017). *The E-dimension: Why machine learning doesn't work well for some problems*.

Snidaro, L., Garcia, J., Llinas, J., & Blasch, E. (2016). *Context-enhanced information fusion: Boosting real-world performance with domain knowledge*. Springer International Publishing.

Solano, M. A., & Carbone, J. (2013). Systems engineering for information fusion: Towards enterprise multi-level fusion integration. In *2013 16th international conference on information fusion (FUSION)* (pp. 121–128).

Steinberg, A. N. (2000). Data fusion system engineering. In *Vol. 1. Proceedings of the third international conference on information fusion*. p. MOD5/3-MOD510.

Steinberg, A. N., & Snidaro, L. (2015). Levels? In *2015 18th international conference on information fusion (FUSION)* (pp. 1985–1992).

Suciu, O., Marginean, R., Kaya, Y., Daume, H., III, & Dumitras, T. (2018). When does machine learning FAIL? Generalized transferability for evasion and poisoning attacks. In *27th USENIX security symposium (USENIX Security 18)* (pp. 1299–1316).

Suresh, H., & Guttag, J. V. (2019). *A framework for understanding unintended consequences of machine learning*. arXiv preprint arXiv:1901.10002.

Taleb, N. N. (2007). *The black swan: The impact of the highly improbable*. Random House.

Von Clausewitz, C. (1940). *On war*. Jazzybee Verlag.

White, F. E. (1988). A model for data fusion. In *Vol. 2. Proceedings of the 1st national symposium on sensor fusion* (pp. 149–158).

Integrating expert human decision-making in artificial intelligence applications

Hesham Fouad[a], Ira S. Moskowitz[a], Derek Brock[b], Michael Scott[a]

[a]Information Management and Decision Architectures Branch, US Naval Research Laboratory, Washington, DC, United States [b]Navy Center for Applied Research in Artificial Intelligence, Naval Research Laboratory, Washington, DC, United States

13.1 Introduction

In Fouad, Mittu, and Brock (2019),[a] it was discussed how the advent of low-cost, high-performance computing platforms has made the application of artificial intelligence (AI) technologies practical for many applications. AI technologies are being used in consumer goods, enterprise cloud services, medical applications, and military information domains, among others. One problem that arises in some of the more serious applications of AI is the need to integrate a functional representation of an expert decision maker in the model. In the future, we hope to extend our model to human-machine teams and shared context.

In this chapter, we present an ongoing effort that deals with the problem of human performance degradation in highly multitasked environments. There is ample evidence that humans performing in such environments suffer from increases in cognitive load, fatigue, concerning error rates (Chériff, Wood, Marois, Labonté, & Vachon, 2018; Marois & Ivanoff, 2005), and a weakening of situational awareness (SA; Salmon et al., 2008 for a recent review of SA research). The motivation for this work is to introduce a capability that monitors multiple, incoming streams of information for a user with key representation of expert decision-making that assesses the value of that information to direct the users as attention

---

[a]Please note that, for the sake of readability that we freely borrow from Fouad et al. (2019), with permission of the authors, and without quotations, since some material has been paraphrased. This holds through Section 13.5 only.

to higher priority content. We utilize an automated form of the analytical hierarchy process (AHP) (Saaty, 1980) that builds a model of expert decision-making from observational data and applies the result to prioritize incoming information.

13.2 Background

The value of encapsulating human expertise in an AI system was recognized very early in the advance of AI technologies. One of the early successes in the field was the development of expert systems that captured human knowledge in the form of if-then rules using a structured knowledge engineering process. Inferencing techniques then evaluated these rules against a known world state in a deductive or inductive reasoning process. An early example of a successful application of expert systems was the MYCIN system (Buchanan & Shortliffe, 1984). MYCIN was developed by a team of researchers at the Stanford University to identify a particular strain of bacteria causing severe infections in patients and to then recommend appropriate antibiotics to treat that infection. The system reached a high degree of competence comparable to those of faculty members at Mount Sinai hospital. The performance of the MYCIN system as well as some other early successes generated a flurry of interest in this technology (Leonard-Bareton & Sviokla, 1988). This bubble was, unfortunately, short lived as inherent limitations in the solicitation of knowledge from human experts were soon discovered. The problem faced by knowledge engineers was that human experts were often *not aware of the cognitive processes they used* to make decisions. Experiential knowledge was especially difficult for subject matter experts (SMEs) to identify and convey to knowledge engineers (Feigenbaum, 1984) (see Zang, Cao, Cao, Wu, & Cao, 2013 for a recent survey of the field). More recently, researchers have been investigating modeling human cognitive processes to develop generalized models of human cognition (see Ye, Wang, & Wand, 2018 for a recent survey). These efforts are inherently bound by our limited understanding of how the human brain works. While models of expert human decision-making may come into play in the future, practical approaches are needed in the near term.

13.3 Decision-making background

Decision-making is, in essence, the process of choosing amongst a set of fully articulated competing alternatives with choices based on a set of criteria. Multiple-criteria decision analysis (MCDA) is a subfield of operations research that focuses on devising structured techniques for the analysis of competing alternatives in decision-making. One of the most successful approaches in MCDA is the AHP introduced by Saaty (1980, 2012). AHP is not a computational model, but a business process that guides SMEs in choosing the best alternative among competing choices. The general steps in applying AHP are as follows:

1. Determine a set of domain-specific criteria that will be used to rate alternatives. For example, if one were choosing among candidates for entry into a university, the criteria used might be past scholastic performance, extracurricular activities, standardized test

scores, and the quality of submitted essays. Each of these criteria would likely be weighted differently by the decision makers. These differences lead us to the next step.

2. Determine global weights for each of the criteria using pairwise comparisons for each of the criteria.
3. Perform a comparison between each pair of choices against one of the criteria. For example, applicant A would be compared to applicant B using the scholastic performance criteria. The outcome of this step, once all choices are made, is a scoring matrix E where m is the number of alternative choices and n is the number of criteria. The columns in E are then normalized such that the entries in each column sum to 1. Finally, the values contained in each row are averaged resulting in matrix E'.
4. The final AHP step is to multiply E' by the global criteria weights and use the sum of the resulting products to arrive at the final prioritization of the choices.

In Fouad et al. (2019) the authors concentrated on previous steps 3–4. In this chapter, we concentrate on step 2, and develop a new method using AHP to solve this step.

A detailed description of AHP is beyond the scope of this chapter; the reader is, however, encouraged to read the reference material for further details (i.e., Saaty, 2008). Our motivation in adopting AHP for this work is based on its following stated advantages:

- Wide adoption across commercial, government, and nongovernment entities with a long history of successful application across a broad range of domains.
- Extensively researched and validated.
- Simple, elegant, and low cost.
- Generates an internal consistency check that can flag inconsistent input data.

13.4 Problem domain

One of many tasks navy surface watchstanders must handle is tactical communications, which frequently involves monitoring competing voice and chat messages. Research at the Naval Research Laboratory (NRL) and elsewhere, motivated by the occurrence of information overload in navy combat information centers, has shown that attending to concurrent voices and multiple chat rooms is taxing, promotes weak encoding of content, and can easily result in missed information (e.g., Brock, McClimens, McCurry, & Perzanoswki, 2008; Wallace, Schlichting, & Goff, 2004). Moreover, these issues persist past the acquisition of skill and experience in this and other multitask environments. Related areas of research have shown that even in multimodal contexts (e.g., video with sound), individuals are chiefly only able to focus on one conceptual stream of information at a time whenever there are meaningful differences in thematic content between modes (e.g., Fischer & Plessow, 2016). While some do better than others, switching attention between competing streams with the intent to observe and understand as much as possible requires deliberate effort that is ultimately limited by reasoning abilities, stamina, and other cognitive constraints, all of which are vulnerable to enervation under stress.

To address these operational concerns, a mediated attentional strategy developed at NRL, known as *serial multitasking*, is being studied as an alternative presentation technique for high volumes of incoming tactical communications (Brock, Peres, & McClimens, 2012; Brock, Wasylyshyn, McClimens, & Perzanoswki, 2011; Fouad et al., 2019). Machine mediation of the communications task relieves the effort of deliberating between competing sources by sequencing concurrent messages to be attended to one at a time. As messages arrive, they are stored, assessed, and enqueued for serial presentation and, as needed, for modulated display (e.g., accelerated speech or tagged text for more rapid uptake), allowing the operator to be directed from one message to the next until either high rates of messaging subside, or the operator chooses to suspend the communications task to pursue other matters. In addition, the information storing function facilitates the review of missed messages when the task is resumed and allows spoken communications to be replayed if needed. A specific prospect of the assessment and enqueuing stages of this technique is the potential to sequence communications on the basis of their operational priority. As a first pass, prioritization can be thought of in terms of a message's relevance to the watchstander as a tactical information concern, its explicit or implied degree of urgency, and its time and order of arrival (latency and precedence). As noted earlier, using a given set of criteria to prioritize one message over another can be approached as an MCDA problem. Consequently, our expectation is that once they are enqueued, messages waiting to be seen can be iteratively assessed in terms of these measures, and the AHP methodology can be used to adjust their order for display or, more specifically, to mediate what the operator should attend to next.

Message assessment is one of the key challenges for our proposal. The notions of relevance and urgency may seem to be two of the most important things an operator is likely to want an attention management system to weigh, but in general, these measures will consistently push less relevant messages back in the queue. By taking the increasing latencies of unviewed messages into account, these languishing communications will eventually be pushed forward. Similarly, the role of the static precedence measure (order of arrival) is to preserve the natural sequence of related voice or chat messages whenever this is possible.

It should be noted that a wide range of techniques for, respectively, measuring relevance and urgency on the basis of a user-specified set of terms (i.e., watchstander tactical concerns) is available (e.g., Aggarwal & Zhai, 2012). Voice messages, for instance, can be converted to text to extract their relevance and they can also be aurally processed for affect (e.g., Devillers, Vidrascu, & Layachi, 2010; Kim, Jin, Fuchs, & Fouad, 2010). Serial multitasking envisions a user-centered, interactive, feedback-driven design that will allow operators to suspend and resume the mediated communications task to accommodate the contingencies of their larger workflow and, just as importantly, specify and routinely revise their immediate informational concerns much like a set of search terms. In the approach outlined below, the techniques we employ for these measures are glossed over to focus on a discussion of the issues AHP poses for prioritizing attention to competing information tasks.

13.5 Approach

Our intent is to iteratively apply the AHP methodology to a changing set of enqueued chat and voice messages to obtain a successively prioritized ordering based on the current assessment of each message using the four criteria described earlier (relevance, urgency, latency, and precedence). The problem with applying AHP in our scenario, however, is that we do not know the relative global weights of the four criteria (see AHP step 2 in Section 13.3). These global weights are needed to scale the relative contribution of the assessed criterial measures for each of the n enqueued messages. More to the point, the practical requirement that messages with high latency values are eventually attended to, makes it difficult for SMEs to specifically assess the relative weights of our somewhat nonintuitive mix of criteria using the pairwise comparison methodology prescribed by AHP (again, step 2). We expect that this problem may occur in other domains as well.

We have recently designed an empirical study that should allow us to directly measure AHP global criteria weights based on the manual prioritization of a set of choices by SMEs. The approach works as follows:

A software application successively presents four 8-min segments of a fictional tactical scenario that includes chat and voice messages associated with the scenario's simulated sequence of events. All voice messages in the scenario are transcribed to text. Rather than running the scenario in real time; however, each of the segments is quasirandomly broken into blocks that are posited as resumption points corresponding to the time away from the communications task. During this time away, chat and voice messages arrive and are enqueued for subsequent viewing by participant SMEs. At each resumption point, the currently enqueued chat and text messages are displayed along with a simplified tactical situation display (TACSIT) that depicts a top-down, graphical view of the operational area showing the current position and type of friendly, neutral, and hostile entities. Each participant's task is to score each chat or voice message using a three-level scoring scheme:

1. [] *Read now* indicates that the information is critical to the current state of the scenario and needs to be acted on immediately.
2. [] *Read soon* indicates that the information is important and should be acted on in the near term.
3. [] *Read later* indicates that the information is not immediately relevant to the current state of the scenario.

We map each of these three ratings to corresponding priorities using the same method outlined for assigning weights to criteria and choices in AHP. The resulting priorities are 0.65 for read now, 0.30 for read soon, and 0.05 for read later.

Once a subject rates all of the messages presented for a segment of the scenario and submits the results, the scenario steps to the next logical group of chat and voice messages and the TACSIT display is updated to the current state. Any messages not rated as read now are carried over to the next segment while retaining the same score.

After each SME has completed the study, the result is an $m \times n$ matrix where the columns contain each of the four criteria as well as the priority assigned by the subject. The rows contain the criteria values and the assigned priority for a presentation of a voice or chat message. It is important to note the same message may appear in multiple rows, but will have different calculated criteria values due to latency.

The final step is to use each of the $m \times n$ matrices to derive the criteria weights as follows: Let us say we present a subject with a set of alternatives,

$$\mathbb{A} = \{A_1, A_2, A_3, ..., A_n\}$$

We can express the weight (priority) of the selected alternative as

$$w_s = W_{rel} \cdot w_{srel} + W_{urg} \cdot w_{surg} + W_{lat} \cdot w_{slat} + W_{prec} \cdot w_{sprec}$$

where W_{rel}, W_{urg}, W_{lat}, and W_{prec} are the criteria weights we are trying to find and w_{srel}, w_{surg}, w_{slat}, and w_{sprec} are the selected alternative criteria.

After all selections are made by a subject, we have

$$\begin{bmatrix} w_{0_{srel}} & w_{0_{surg}} & w_{0_{slat}} & w_{0_{sprec}} \\ w_{1_{srel}} & w_{1_{surg}} & w_{1_{slat}} & w_{1_{sprec}} \\ w_{2_{srel}} & w_{2_{surg}} & w_{2_{slat}} & w_{2_{sprec}} \\ \vdots & \vdots & \vdots & \vdots \\ w_{n_{srel}} & w_{n_{surg}} & w_{n_{slat}} & w_{n_{sprec}} \end{bmatrix} \times \begin{bmatrix} W_{rel} \\ W_{urg} \\ W_{lat} \\ W_{prec} \end{bmatrix} = \begin{bmatrix} w_0 \\ w_1 \\ w_2 \\ \vdots \\ w_n \end{bmatrix}$$

The only unknowns in the earlier system of equations are the global weights W_{rel}, W_{urg}, W_{lat}, and W_{prec}. Given that this is an overdetermined system of equations, we can use the method of ordinary least squares to approximate a solution to this system. The problem with this approach is that we are faced with the criteria evaluations of multiple SMEs and must combine their evaluations in a way that insures consistency. The internal consistency-checking method utilized in the AHP process will not work here because the criteria weights are measured from data and are not guaranteed to form a reciprocal matrix. In the following sections, we outline a novel approach to weight the SME responses based on their level of consistency.

13.6 Technical discussion of AHP

We assume that each SME S has a choice of n alternatives. In keeping with AHP doctrine we do not ask the SME for the absolute ranking of one alternative, in terms of "priority" over another. Rather, we ask for a comparison ratio of the alternatives priorities.

13.6.1 SME matrix (comparison ratios)

There are m SMEs, $S_1, \dots, S_m$. Each SME, S_s, ranks each of the n alternatives' A_i priorities p_i, relative to another alternative's priority p_j. This is given by α_{ij}. In practice, one often follows Saaty in his priority rankings, which we reproduce somewhat (Saaty, 1977, 2008; Table 13.1). Note for simplicity, only integers 1–9 and their inverses are used in the table. Our assumptions are that SMEs are good at relative priority ratios, but not with absolute rankings of alternative priorities. That is, if p_i is the priority of A_i, we assume that an SME cannot determine that priority; however, the SME does have knowledge of the priority ratio between the two alternatives. That is, an SME hopes to provide the ratio p_i/p_j as accurately as possible, which is α_{ij} in our notation. What is important to keep in mind is that an SME does not determine the p_i, rather the ratios α_{ij}. From this, we wish

TABLE 13.1 Relative priority ratios p_i/p_j: The benefit of A_i vs. A_j.

Intensity of benefit	Definition	Explanation
1	Equal importance	Two alternatives contributing equally to the mission
2	Weak or slight benefit	—
3	Moderate benefit	Experience and judgment slightly favor one over the other
4	Moderate plus	—
5	Strong benefit	Experience and judgment strongly favor one device over the other
6	Strong plus	—
7	Very strong or demonstrated importance	...; dominance has been demonstrated in practice
8	Very, very strong	—
9	Extreme benefit	The highest possible benefit
Reciprocals	j vs. i instead of i vs. j	We assume SMEs do this correctly!

to determine the absolute priorities. Of course, the ratio p_i/p_j is assumed to be $(p_j/p_i)^{-1}$. This thinking is well documented in the AHP literature (e.g., Saaty, 1977, 2008).

A possible error in this assumption is that the SMEs are often not perfect. We present their priority ratios as α_{ij}, and we wish to determine how close to the actual priority ratio they are. The closer they are, the more they are weighted in our ranking arguments.

Thus, for each SME S_s, we have an $n \times n$ matrix M_{S_s} of alternative priority ratios, where

$$M_{S_s} = \begin{array}{c} \text{alternative} \\ A_1 \\ A_2 \\ \vdots \\ A_n \end{array} \begin{array}{cccc} A_1 & A_2 & \cdots & A_n \end{array} \begin{bmatrix} \alpha_{11} & \alpha_{12} & \cdots & \alpha_{1n} \\ \alpha_{21} & \alpha_{22} & \cdots & \alpha_{2n} \\ \vdots & \vdots & \ddots & \vdots \\ \alpha_{n1} & \alpha_{n2} & \cdots & \alpha_{nn} \end{bmatrix}$$

Assumption 13.1. We assume that the SME presents logical choices for the α_{ij} in that $\alpha_{ij} > 0$ and $\alpha_{ij} = (\alpha_{ji})^{-1}$.

This assumption trivially shows that for an SME $\alpha_{ii} = 1$.

As noted earlier, SMEs need not be perfect. They can make errors in the relative priority ratios of alternatives. A necessary, but not sufficient condition, for an SME to be correct would be for "consistency" (discussed fully below), that is $\alpha_{ik} = \alpha_{ij}\alpha_{jk}, \forall\{i,j,k\}$. This requirement occurs because we view α_{ij} as p_i/p_j, where p_k is the absolute priority of A_k. This condition is the basis for our definition of "consistent" later in the chapter. If this condition is met, all weights can be given relative to any specific device weight, not just to the ratios. Of course, there may still be errors, which is why different SMEs are used, and they are used even if they behave in an inconsistent manner.

13.7 Some matrix definitions

We only consider real matrices in this chapter.

Definition 13.1. We say that a positive square matrix R is a *reciprocal matrix* if

$$a_{ji} = (a_{ij})^{-1} \tag{13.1}$$

Note that a reciprocal matrix has 1s down the main diagonal.

$$R = \begin{pmatrix} 1 & a_{12} & \ldots & a_{1n} \\ 1/a_{12} & 1 & \ldots & a_{2n} \\ \vdots & \vdots & \ddots & \vdots \\ 1/a_{1n} & 1/a_{2n} & \ldots & 1 \end{pmatrix}$$

Theorem 13.1. *An SME always produces a reciprocal matrix, that is, M_{S_s} is always a reciprocal matrix.*

Proof. Trivial.   □

Corollary 13.1. *An SME faced with n alternatives has $1 + 2 + n - 1 = \frac{(n-1)n}{2}$ degrees of freedom.*

Proof. For an SME, once the choices for the entries a_{ij}, $1 \leq i < j \leq n$ of M_{S_s} are chosen, the entire matrix is known.   □

Definition 13.2. We say that a reciprocal matrix is *consistent* if $a_{ik} = a_{ij} \cdot a_{jk}$, $\forall \{i, j, k\}$.

As discussed earlier, if we set $w_i/w_j := a_{ij}$ then it is well defined when the matrix is consistent. Furthermore, being consistent is equivalent to

$$a_{ik} = (a_{ji})^{-1} \cdot a_{jk}, \quad \forall j$$

Let $\vec{r_i}$ be the ith row of a matrix and $\vec{c_j}$ be the jth column of a matrix. We trivially have the following two theorems.

Theorem 13.2. *A reciprocal matrix is consistent if and only if every row is a multiple of another row:*

$$\vec{r_k} = (a_{ik})^{-1} \cdot \vec{r_i} \tag{13.2}$$

Theorem 13.3. *A reciprocal matrix is consistent if and only if every column is a multiple of another column:*

$$\vec{c_k} = a_{ik} \cdot \vec{c_i}, \quad \forall k, i \tag{13.3}$$

Corollary 13.2. *A corollary to either of the previous theorems: A positive square matrix is consistent if and only if it has rank 1.*

This corollary gives us a quick test of whether or not a matrix is consistent. What is interesting from it is that an SME may give an inconsistent M_{S_s} without knowing it. That is, an SME may unknowingly violate the consistency conditions.

Note that a consistent matrix only has $n - 1$ degrees of freedom because the first row, which leads with the number 1, determines the entire matrix.

By definition, a consistent matrix is a reciprocal matrix; what about the converse? The answer is "No." If we consider the following matrix, we see that being reciprocal does not imply being consistent.

$$A = \begin{pmatrix} 1 & 5 & 2 & 3 \\ 1/5 & 1 & 4 & 6 \\ 1/2 & 1/4 & 1 & 3 \\ 1/3 & 1/6 & 1/3 & 1 \end{pmatrix}$$

One can easily see that this matrix is not consistent since it does not obey the row condition given by Eq. (13.2).

The concept of consistency is well discussed in Saaty (1977). It is a necessary condition for the weighting ranks of an SME to be correct. For example, if $a_{12} = 3$ and $a_{23} = 4$, then if the weights are correct, we must have $a_{13} = 12$. However, our SMEs are not always consistent (but again, they always obey the reciprocal condition set by Eq. 13.1).

We will measure the degree of *inconsistency* using AHP techniques and then combine it in a novel manner of weighting (known as EAW) using the maximal eigenvalue of M_{S_s} to get a measure of the benefits/importance of one device over another with respect to a given mission. We refer the reader to the references for the proof of the following theorem.

Theorem 13.4 (Proposition 1 in Osnaga, 2005, and Perron's Theorem in Horn & Johnson, 1985). *A square positive matrix of rank 1 has one nonzero eigenvalue, $\lambda_{\max}$; it is positive and it has a multiplicity of one (a 1-dimensional [1D] eigenspace). Furthermore, we can take the eigenvector corresponding to it to have positive entries.*

If the square positive matrix has a rank greater than 1, there is still one nonzero positive eigenvalue $\lambda_{\max}$ of multiplicity one such that for other nonzero eigenvalues, $\lambda_j, |\lambda_j| < \lambda_{\max}$.

Definition 13.3. We call the unique eigenvector of positive entries that sum to 1 the *Perron vector* (Horn & Johnson, 1985, p. 497).

That is, the Perron vector has an l_1 norm of 1. The following theorem is well documented. We follow the proof as outlined in Saaty (1990).

Theorem 13.5 (From Theorem 1 in Saaty, 1977). *For an $n \times n$ reciprocal matrix R, $\lambda_{\max} \geq n$.*

Proof. Let $\vec{P} = \langle p_1, \ldots, p_n \rangle$ be the Perron vector. $R = (r_{ij})$ and $R\vec{P} = \lambda_{\max}\vec{P}$. Since the $p_i > 0$, we can always find an $\epsilon_{ij} > 0$ such that $r_{ij} = \epsilon_{ij}(p_i/p_j)$. From this condition, R is a reciprocal matrix, $\epsilon_{ii} = 1$, and $\epsilon_{ij} = (\epsilon_{ji})^{-1}$.

Consider the multiplication $R\vec{P}$ with one row of R at a time; we have for the ith row that $\sum_j r_{ij}p_j = \sum_j \epsilon_{ij}p_j$. However, since $\vec{P}$ is an eigenvector for $\lambda_{\max}$, we see that $\sum_j \epsilon_{ij} = \lambda_{\max}$. Because this result holds for every row, we have $\sum_{i,j} \epsilon_{ij} = n\lambda_{\max}$. Now we can write the sum as

$$n\lambda_{\max} = \sum_{i,j} \epsilon_{ij} = \sum_k \epsilon_{kk} + \sum_{1\leq i<j\leq n} \epsilon_{ij} + \sum_{1\leq j<i\leq n} \epsilon_{ij}$$
$$= n + \sum_{1\leq i<j\leq n} \left(\epsilon_{ij} + (\epsilon_{ij})^{-1}\right)$$

Next, we use the trick that Saaty demonstrated. Let $\delta_{ij} := \epsilon_{ij} - 1$; therefore, $\delta_{ij} > -1$ is well defined. Rewriting the above, we have

$$n\lambda_{\max} = \sum_{i,j} \epsilon_{ij} = n + \sum_{1 \le i < j \le n} \left(1 + \delta_{ij} + \frac{1}{1 + \delta_{ij}}\right)$$

$$= n + \sum_{1 \le i < j \le n} \left(\frac{(1 + \delta_{ij})^2 + 1}{1 + \delta_{ij}}\right)$$

$$= n + \sum_{1 \le i < j \le n} \left(\frac{2(1 + \delta_{ij}) + (\delta_{ij})^2}{1 + \delta_{ij}}\right)$$

$$= n + \sum_{1 \le i < j \le n} \left(2 + \frac{(\delta_{ij})^2}{1 + \delta_{ij}}\right)$$

$$= n + n(n-1) + \sum_{1 \le i < j \le n} \left(\frac{(\delta_{ij})^2}{1 + \delta_{ij}}\right); \text{ simplifying and dividing both sides by } n \text{ gives}$$

$$\lambda_{\max} = n + \sum_{1 \le i < j \le n} \left(\frac{(\delta_{ij})^2}{1 + \delta_{ij}}\right) \ge n \qquad\qquad \square$$

Corollary 13.3. *For an $n \times n$ reciprocal matrix R, $\lambda_{\max} = n$ if and only if R is consistent. Furthermore, the Perron vector for a consistent matrix is a normalized column of R.*

Proof. ($\Leftarrow$) If C is consistent, consider the following (keep in mind that it is also a reciprocal matrix):

$$C\left(\vec{c_1}\right) = \begin{pmatrix} 1\,\vec{r_1} \cdot \vec{c_1} \\ a_{21}\,\vec{r_2} \cdot \vec{c_1} \\ \vdots \\ a_{n1}\,\vec{r_n} \cdot \vec{c_1} \end{pmatrix} = \begin{pmatrix} 1 \cdot n \\ a \cdot n \\ \vdots \\ a_{n1} \cdot n \end{pmatrix} = n\,\vec{c_1}$$

Normalize c_1 (or any other column) to get the Perron vector.

($\Rightarrow$) Since $\lambda_{\max} = n$, we know by the proof of the previous theorem that $\delta_{ij} = 0$, $\forall i, j$. Therefore, $r_{ij} = p_i/p_j$, $\forall i, j$ and so $r_{ik} = (p_i/p_j) \cdot (p_j/p_k) = r_{ij} \cdot r_{jk}$, meaning the matrix is consistent. Furthermore, $\vec{c_k}$ is $1/p_k$ times the Perron vector. $\qquad \square$

Saaty (1977) defines $\dfrac{\lambda_{\max} - n}{n-1}$ as the *consistency index* of a reciprocal matrix; it is the proper "statistic" we employ to measure consistency. This step is compared to a similar term derived from random matrices to form the consistency ratio. The values obtained from these random matrices are not concretely tied to theory (Donegan & Dodd, 1991). However, this in no way ignores the huge success of AHP (e.g., Forman & Gass, 2001). These conversations about theoretical justification are beyond the scope of this chapter. Furthermore, we do not need anything from random matrix theory for our approach.

At the same time, is not clear to us that the above is the best definition of the consistency index. It is what Saaty and others in the AHP community use. It has been questioned by some though (Donegan & Dodd, 1991). Various simple experiments with a single matrix perturbation show that in some cases the above formula does not normalize equally as n grows. In fact, they may normalize by multiplying by $n - 1$, rather than by dividing.

However, as n grows the chance of error in the matrix grows. The previous formula is ingrained in the literature and we do not wish to contradict it. We do warn the reader and users that an adjustment may be necessary if we are dealing with an n that involves order of magnitude changes.

What is important to remember is that the consistency index is zero if an SME's reciprocal matrix is in fact consistent, and if its inconsistency grows, the consistency index approaches infinity (albeit slowly). With this in mind, we propose the following definition.

Definition 13.4. The weight of SME S is given by

$$\mathbb{W}_s(\lambda_{\max}) = e^{\frac{n - \lambda_{max_S}}{n - 1}}$$

We use the previous definition of an SME weight because as the consistency index monotonically goes from 0 (most consistent) to ∞ (least consistent), the weight goes from 1 to 0, respectively. That is, the closer an SME is to 1, the more it is weighted. We see this illustrated in Fig. 13.1.

13.7.1 SMEs give actual values

Up to this point we have been assuming that SMEs give the relative rankings of different values as the ratio p_i/p_j. Now we pose the question, what if things are easier for the SME to determine than we assumed and the SMEs give the actual values $p_1,...,p_n$.

From the p_i, we can always form the ratio $a_{ij} = p_i/p_j$. Trivially, we have that the matrix a_{ij} is a reciprocal matrix. Since $p_i/p_k = a_{ij}$, and $a_{ij} \cdot a_{jk} = p_i/p_j \cdot p_j/p_k$, we trivially find that the matrix is consistent, that is, $a_{ik} = a_{ij} \cdot a_{jk}, \forall\{i, j, k\}$.

Therefore, we are always in the state of being consistent. Note this consistency does not mean that the SME is correct. Given the present theory, there is no means to gauge the difference between two consistent SMEs. This difficulty is a topic of future statistical research.

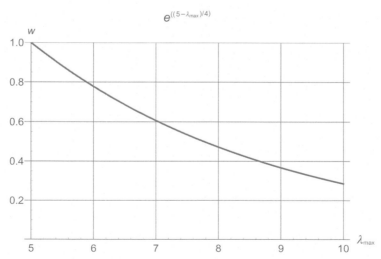

FIG. 13.1   An example of the weight of w_s as a function of $\lambda_{\max}$ for $n = 5$.

One interesting approach would be to test the SMEs afterwards by asking them for the actual weights, and asking them for the relative weights. If the SME does not bother to perform the calculations, we could then see if the reciprocal matrix from that SME is consistent or not, and if inconsistent, we could use the technique described next to combine them. Note the technique below is prefaced by the observation that we are only asking the SMEs about the relative weights they used.

13.8 Exponential additive weighting

Saaty has discussed how the Perron vector can be used as a relative measure of each alternative. We now wish to combine the results for each SME S. Each SME S_s generates a Perron vector from M_{S_s}; we denote this vector as $\vec{P_s}$. We use exponential additive weighting (EAW) to define the weighted sum of the Perron vectors.

Definition 13.5. For n devices and S SMEs, we define the normalized value vector $\vec{N}$ as the positive vector with an l_1 norm of 1:

$$\vec{N} := \left(\frac{1}{\sum_s \mathrm{w}_s} \right) \cdot \sum_{s=1}^{S} \mathrm{w}_s \vec{P_s}$$

The vector $\vec{N}$ then gives us the preferential order of alternatives by ranking them from highest to lowest. It also gives us a measure of how close is each preference. Note the scalar multiple is not necessary to obtain a ranking order; however, we wish to keep everything as a vector of l_1 norm 1.

Definition 13.6. We define the *decision ranking* to be the ranking given to us by $\vec{N}$.

Note that the previous definitions weights each SME by how consistent it is. That is we put more weight in the more consistent SMEs, which makes good modeling sense.

Example 13.1. We attempted to follow the visual brightness example in Saaty (1977), but we had to deviate from it because there is an error in its formulation.

SME 1 produces a relative ranking reciprocal matrix

$$M_{S_1} = \begin{pmatrix} 1 & 4 & 6 & 7 \\ \frac{1}{4} & 1 & 3 & 4 \\ \frac{1}{6} & \frac{1}{3} & 1 & 2 \\ \frac{1}{7} & \frac{1}{4} & \frac{1}{2} & 1 \end{pmatrix}$$

such that $\lambda_{max_1} = 4.10$ with $\vec{P_1} = \begin{pmatrix} 0.61 \\ 0.22 \\ 0.10 \\ 0.06 \end{pmatrix}$ and $\mathrm{w}_1 = 0.97$.

SME 2 produces

$$M_{S_2} = \begin{pmatrix} 1 & 5 & 6 & 7 \\ \frac{1}{5} & 1 & 30 & \frac{1}{2} \\ \frac{1}{6} & \frac{1}{30} & 1 & 2 \\ \frac{1}{7} & 2 & \frac{1}{2} & 1 \end{pmatrix}$$

such that $\lambda_{max_2} = 6.90$ with $\vec{P}_2 = \begin{pmatrix} 0.49 \\ 0.33 \\ 0.06 \\ 0.13 \end{pmatrix}$ and $w_1 = 0.38$.

From the above result, SME S_1 ranks the devices (A_1, A_2, A_3, A_4) to agree with the ranking from S_C. However, SME S_2 ranks them (A_1, A_2, A_4, A_3).

We see that the normalized value vector is

$$\vec{N} := 0.74 \left(0.97 \begin{pmatrix} 0.61 \\ 0.22 \\ 0.10 \\ 0.06 \end{pmatrix} + 0.38 \begin{pmatrix} 0.49 \\ 0.33 \\ 0.06 \\ 0.13 \end{pmatrix} \right) = \begin{pmatrix} 0.59 \\ 0.25 \\ 0.09 \\ 0.08 \end{pmatrix}$$

Therefore, the decision ranking is (A_1, A_2, A_3, A_4); however, the difference between A_3 and A_4 is trivial and we could just as easily (with minor perturbations to the SME's relative rankings) had the ranking be (A_1, A_2, A_4, A_3).

It is possible for both SMEs to be consistent, but have different rankings. Without further information such as a baseline, it is impossible to tell which ranking is correct. However, the Perron vectors do give us the strength of the rankings. By way of an example, consider the following:

Example 13.2. Both of the SMEs below are consistent, an idea that Saaty discussed many times (e.g., Saaty, 1977). However, we include our definition as motivation for our next example.

$$M_{S_1} = \begin{pmatrix} 1 & 1.1 \\ \frac{1}{1.1} & 1 \end{pmatrix}$$

$$M_{S_2} = \begin{pmatrix} 1 & 10 \\ \frac{1}{10} & 1 \end{pmatrix}$$

Both SMEs, S_1 and S_2, rank the devices (A_1, A_2), however, $\vec{P}_1 = \begin{pmatrix} 0.52 \\ 0.48 \end{pmatrix}$ and $\vec{P}_2 = \begin{pmatrix} 0.91 \\ 0.09 \end{pmatrix}$ From this result, we see that the Perron vector describes what the SME matrix is telling us. For S_1, A_1 is valued at 110% of A_2, whereas for S_2, A_1 is greater than 1000% of A_2.

This result leads us to the following definition.

Definition 13.7. We define the *decision matrix* to be the ranking given to us by $\vec{N}$ along with the values of $\vec{N}$.

Of course we can still define the decision matrix if there is only one SME by simply using the Perron vector and its associated matrix. We use the notation D when there is one SME, and $\hat{D}$ if there are multiple SMEs.

Returning to Example 13.1, the decision matrix is

$$\hat{D}_{Ex1} = \begin{pmatrix} A_1 & 0.59 \\ A_2 & 0.25 \\ A_3 & 0.09 \\ A_4 & 0.08 \end{pmatrix}$$

If we compared this matrix to another scenario where

$$\hat{D} = \begin{pmatrix} A_1 & 0.59 \\ A_2 & 0.20 \\ A_3 & 0.14 \\ A_4 & 0.08 \end{pmatrix}$$

we would have the same ranking, but we would have a more confident ranking with A_3 above A_4 in this second scenario.

Revisiting Example 13.2, we have

$$A_{S_1} = \begin{pmatrix} A_1 & 0.52 \\ A_2 & 0.48 \end{pmatrix}$$
$$A_{S_2} = \begin{pmatrix} A_1 & 0.91 \\ A_2 & 0.09 \end{pmatrix}$$

combining both via $\vec{N}$ gives

$$\hat{D} = \begin{pmatrix} A_1 & 0.72 \\ A_2 & 0.29 \end{pmatrix}$$

13.9 Procedure

1. We assume that there are n devices, A_i, and S SMEs, S_s.
2. Given k from 1 to s, each S_k is given to fill in the upper off diagonal part of the $n \times n$ matrix representing the values of A_i with respect to A_j; from this we can obtain the rest of the matrix since it is reciprocal. The diagonals of this matrix are all 1, and the lower off diagonal part of the matrix are the inverses of the upper part.

$$\begin{pmatrix} a_{12} & a_{13} & \cdots & a_{1n} \\ & a_{23} & \cdots & a_{2n} \\ & & \cdots & \vdots \\ & & & a_{n-1\,n} \end{pmatrix} \leadsto M_{S_k} = \begin{pmatrix} a_{11} & a_{12} & \cdots & a_{1n} \\ a_{21} & a_{22} & \cdots & a_{2n} \\ \vdots & \vdots & \ddots & \vdots \\ \vdots & \vdots & \ddots & \vdots \\ a_{n1} & a_{n2} & \cdots & a_{nn} \end{pmatrix}$$

3. Calculate λ_{max_k}.
4. Calculate $\mathbf{w}_k$.

5. Calculate $\vec{P}_k$.
6. Calculate $\vec{N}$.
7. Obtain the ranking from $\vec{N}$.
8. Form the decision matrix D.

13.10 An example with R code

Below is our code:

```
RANK_auto_weight_play1_perturb.R
library(Matrix)
rm(list=ls())
r1<-c(1,5,9)
r2<-c(1/5,1,91/50)
r3<-c(1/9,50/91,1)
M1<-rbind(r1,r2,r3)
eigen(M1)
ev1<-eigen(M1)
vectors1<-ev1$vectors
veigvals1<-Re(ev1$values)
lambda_max1 <-max(veigvals1)
w11<-exp( (3-lambda_max1)/2)
norm11 <-vectors1[1:3]/sum(vectors1[1:3])
norm11
r1<-c(1,19,2)
r2<-c(1/19,1,20/193)
r3<-c(1/2,193/20,1)
M2<-rbind(r1,r2,r3)
eigen(M2)
ev2<-eigen(M2)
vectors2<-ev2$vectors
veigvals2<-Re(ev2$values)
lambda_max2 <-max(veigvals2)
w22<-exp( (3-lambda_max2)/2)
norm12 <-vectors2[1:3]/sum(vectors2[1:3])
norm12
new <-( w11*norm11 + w22*norm12 )/(w11+w22)
print("--------------------------------------")
print("first Perron vector is")
Re(norm11)
print("second Perron vector is")
```

```
Re(norm12)
w11
w22
Re(new)
device<-rbind(1,2,3)
ens<-matrix(Re(new))
pop=data.frame(device=device,ens=ens)
pop[order(pop$ens,decreasing=TRUE) ,]
```

Given M_{S_1} and M_{S_2} below, the output from our code gives

$$M_{S_1} = \begin{pmatrix} 1 & 5 & 9 \\ 1/5 & 1 & 91/50 \\ 1/9 & 50/91 & 1 \end{pmatrix}, \text{ and } M_{S_2} = \begin{pmatrix} 1 & 19 & 2 \\ 1/19 & 1 & 20/193 \\ 1/2 & 193/20 & 1 \end{pmatrix}$$

```
>
> source('~/.../RANK_auto_weight_play1_perturb.R', echo=TRUE)
> library(Matrix)
> rm(list=ls())
> r1<-c(1,5,9)
> r2<-c(1/5,1,91/50)
> r3<-c(1/9,50/91,1)
> M1<-rbind(r1,r2,r3)
> eigen(M1)
eigen() decomposition
$values
[1] 3.000013567+0.00000000i -0.000006783+0.00637964i -0.000006783-
0.00637964i
$vectors
                [,1]                [,2]                [,3]
[1,] -0.9747168+0i  0.97471683+0.00000000i  0.97471683+0.00000000i
[2,] -0.1956627+0i -0.09783136+0.16944889i -0.09783136-0.16944889i
[3,] -0.1079037+0i -0.05395185-0.09344734i -0.05395185+0.09344734i
> ev1<-eigen(M1)
> vectors1<-ev1$vectors
> veigvals1<-Re(ev1$values)
> lambda_max1 <-max(veigvals1)
> w11<-exp( (3-lambda_max1)/2)
> norm11 <-vectors1[1:3]/sum(vectors1[1:3])
> norm11
[1] 0.76252022+0i 0.15306680+0i 0.08441298+0i
> r1<-c(1,19,2)
> r2<-c(1/19,1,20/193)
> r3<-c(1/2,193/20,1)
```

```
> M2<-rbind(r1,r2,r3)
> eigen(M2)
eigen() decomposition
$values
[1] 3.000027270+0.000000000i -0.000013635+0.009044878i -0.000013635-
0.009044878i
$vectors
                        [,1]                    [,2]                    [,3]
[1,] -0.89251355+0i  -0.89251355+0.00000000i  -0.89251355+0.00000000i
[2,] -0.04672973+0i   0.02336487+0.04046914i   0.02336487-0.04046914i
[3,] -0.44859324+0i   0.22429662-0.38849314i   0.22429662+0.38849314i
> ev2<-eigen(M2)
> vectors2<-ev2$vectors
> veigvals2<-Re(ev2$values)
> lambda_max2 <-max(veigvals2)
> w22<-exp( (3-lambda_max2)/2)
> norm12 <-vectors2[1:3]/sum(vectors2[1:3])
> norm12
[1] 0.64309703+0i 0.03367092+0i 0.32323205+0i
> new <-( w11*norm11 + w22*norm12 )/(w11+w22)
> print("-------------------------------------")
[1] "-------------------------------------"
> print("first Perron vector is")
[1] "first Perron vector is"
> Re(norm11)
[1] 0.76252022 0.15306680 0.08441298
> print("second Perron vector is")
[1] "second Perron vector is"
> Re(norm12)
[1] 0.64309703 0.03367092 0.32323205
> w11
[1] 0.9999932
> w22
[1] 0.9999864
> Re(new)
[1] 0.70280883 0.09336906 0.20382210
> device<-rbind(1,2,3)
> ens<-matrix(Re(new))
> pop=data.frame(device=device,ens=ens)
> pop[order(pop$ens,decreasing=TRUE) ,]
 device       ens
1      1 0.70280883
3      3 0.20382210
2      2 0.09336906
>
```

We see then that the decision matrix becomes

$$DM = \begin{pmatrix} 1 & 0.703 \\ 3 & 0.204 \\ 2 & 0.093 \end{pmatrix}$$

Note that both of the $\lambda_{\max}$ are very close to 3, and we end up ranking the devices (A_1, A_3, A_2); we see that there is a good separation (user defined) between the ratings.

13.11 Conclusion

The process we have outlined is one we feel may ultimately play a part in helping machines to express themselves to humans in a way that both humans and machines will understand, formulating the basis for a shared "computational" context.

Acknowledgments

The authors thank William Lawless and Robert Page for their assistance.

References

Aggarwal, C. C., & Zhai, C. (2012). *Mining text data*. New York, NY: Springer.

Brock, D., McClimens, B., McCurry, J. G., & Perzanoswki, D. (2008). Evaluating listeners' attention to and comprehension of spatialized concurrent and serial talkers at normal and a synthetically faster rate of speech. In *Proceedings of the 14th international conference on auditory display (ICAD), Paris, France, June*.

Brock, D., Peres, S. C., & McClimens, B. (2012). Evaluating listeners' attention to, and comprehension of, serially interleaved, rate-accelerated speech. In *Proceedings of the 18th international conference on auditory display (ICAD), Atlanta, GA, June*.

Brock, D., Wasylyshyn, C., McClimens, B., & Perzanoswki, D. (2011). Facilitating the watchstander's voice communications task in future navy operations. In *Proceedings of the IEEE military communications conference (MILCOM), Baltimore, MD, IEEE*.

Buchanan, B. G., & Shortliffe, E. H. (1984). *Rule based expert systems: The MYCIN experiments of the Stanford heuristic programming project*. Boston: Addison-Wesley.

Chériff, L., Wood, V., Marois, A., Labonté, K., & Vachon, F. (2018). Multitasking in the military: Cognitive consequences and potential solutions. *Applied Cognitive Psychology*, 32(4), 429–439.

Devillers, L., Vidrascu, L., & Layachi, O. (2010). Automatic detection of emotion from vocal expression. In K. Scherer, T. Bänziger, & E. Roach (Eds.), *A blueprint for affective computing: A sourcebook* (pp. 232–244). Oxford: Oxford University Press.

Donegan, H. A., & Dodd, F. J. (1991). A note on Saaty's random indexes. *Mathematical and Computer Modelling*, 15(10), 135–137.

Feigenbaum, E. A. (1984). Knowledge engineering: The applied side of artificial intelligence. *Annals of the New York Academy of Sciences*, 426(1), 91–107.

Fischer, R., & Plessow, F. (2016). Efficient multitasking: Parallel versus serial processing of multiple tasks. *Frontiers in Psychology*, 6, 1366.

Forman, E. H., & Gass, S. I. (2001). The analytic hierarchy process—An exposition. *Operations Research*, 49, 469–486.

Fouad, H., Mittu, R., & Brock, D. (2019). Contingent attention management in multitasked environments. In *Proceedings of artificial intelligence and machine learning for multi-domain operations, SPIE defense + commercial sensing, Baltimore, MD*.SPIE.

Horn, R. A., & Johnson, C. R. (1985). *Matrix analysis*. New York, NY: Cambridge University Press.

Kim, J. W., Jin, G., Fuchs, S., & Fouad, H. (2010). Radis: Real time affective state detection and induction system. In *Proceedings of the IADIS international conference on interfaces and human computer interaction (IHCI), Freiburg, Germany*.

Leonard-Bareton, D., & Sviokla, J. (1988). Putting expert systems to WO. *Harvard Business Review, 66*(2), 91–98.

Marois, R., & Ivanoff, J. (2005). Capacity limits of information processing in the brain. *Trends in Cognitive Sciences, 9*(6), 296–305.

Osnaga, S. M. (2005). On rank one matrices and invariant subspaces. *Balkan Journal of Geometry and Its Applications, 10*(1), 145–148.

Saaty, T. L. (1977). A scaling method for priorities in hierarchical structures. *Journal of Mathematical Psychology, 15*, 234–281.

Saaty, T. L. (1980). *The analytic hierarchy process*. New York, NY: McGraw-Hill.

Saaty, T. L. (1990). How to make a decision: The analytic hierarchy process. *European Journal of Operational Research, 48*, 9–26.

Saaty, T. L. (2008). Decision making with the analytic hierarchy process. *International Journal of Services Sciences, 1*(1), 83–98.

Saaty, T. L. (2012). *Decision making for leaders: The analytic hierarchy process for decisions in a complex world* (3rd revised ed.). Pittsburgh, PA: RWS Publications.

Salmon, P. M., Stanton, N. A., Walker, G. H., Baber, C., Jenkins, D. P., McMaster, R., & Young, M. S. (2008). What really is going on? Review of situation awareness models for individuals and teams. *Theoretical Issues in Ergonomics Science, 9*(4), 297–323.

Wallace, D., Schlichting, C., & Goff, U. (2004). *Report on the communications research initiatives in support of integrated command environment (ICE) systems. TR 02/30*. Naval Surface Warfare Center Dahlgren Division.

Ye, P. M., Wang, T., & Wand, F. Y. (2018). A survey of cognitive architectures in the past 20 years. *IEEE Transactions on Cybernetics, 48*(12), 3280–3290.

Zang, L., Cao, C., Cao, Y. N., Wu, Y. M., & Cao, C. G. (2013). A survey of commonsense knowledge acquisition. *Journal of Computer Sciences and Technology, 28*(4), 689–719.

14

A communication paradigm for human-robot interaction during robot failure scenarios

Daniel J. Brooks[a], Dalton J. Curtin[b], James T. Kuczynski[b], Joshua J. Rodriguez[b], Aaron Steinfeld[c], Holly A. Yanco[b]

[a]Toyota Research Institute, Cambridge, MA, United States [b]University of Massachusetts Lowell, Lowell, MA, United States [c]Carnegie Mellon University, Pittsburgh, PA, United States

14.1 Introduction

In public settings, robot systems, including self-driving cars, delivery drones, and cleaning robots, are becoming more common. Soon, people will interact with and live alongside these and other types of autonomous robotic systems on a regular basis. Due to the scale and complexity of these robot systems, we cannot expect every interaction to be flawless even after systems have matured. For example, a robot performing a necessary behavior that is perceived as inexplicable or unpredictable can have a detrimental effect on people's situation awareness and lead to negative user experiences.

Such context issues will affect not only the robots' users but also bystanders, who may have marginal awareness of or interest in the robots' capability or mission. Humans will increasingly be in situations requiring them to make decisions about unsupervised and unfamiliar systems, some of which may be critical to their own safety. To make matters worse, there are currently no standards—de facto or otherwise—to serve as a guide for allowing people to communicate with or to influence the behaviors of these machines. Therefore, we believe that robots need efficient and understandable methods for bidirectional communication, even at a basic level, which could be used for robot operators or for people who are bystanders to the robot. As a first step toward a solution to this need, this chapter describes our findings in an experiment using push and pull notifications on a smartphone to communicate robot information to minimally trained participants.

14.2 Related work

Likely, there will never be perfectly reliable robots, so strategies are needed for mitigating the consequences of failure. Taxonomies have been developed in support of this challenge that categorize faults and provide insight into the many complex ways a system could fail (Carlson & Murphy, 2005; Steinbauer, 2013). Likewise, attributes of "dependable" systems are available (Lussier, Chatila, Ingrand, Killijian, & Powell, 2004) and there is increasing interest in translating internal representations of robot performance into human-understandable forms. Effective methods from prior work include providing advanced warning or confidence feedback, apologizing after failure, asking for help from bystanders, and failure-specific natural language requests (Desai, Kaniarasu, Medvedev, Steinfeld, & Yanco, 2013; Knepper, Tellex, Li, Roy, & Rus, 2015; Lee, Kiesler, Forlizzi, Srinivasa, & Rybski, 2010; Rosenthal, Veloso, & Dey, 2012).

Unfortunately, there are also examples where recovery strategies produce negative effects. For example, inexplicable robot behavior can lead to misalignment of blame and humans often fail to recognize their own correctable mistakes (Kim & Hinds, 2006). Likewise, robot assignment of blame can lead to very negative reactions and lower trust (Groom, Chen, Johnson, Kara, & Nass, 2010; Kaniarasu & Steinfeld, 2014).

There has also been work on how to convey failure to humans. Failures can be expressed implicitly if the robot is able to clearly communicate its intentions in a way that can be contrasted with physical behavior when an error occurs. For example, if a drone were equipped with a light ring direction indicator (e.g., Szafir, Mutlu, & Fong, 2015) that was indicating a straight flight path while the drone was translating to the side, users familiar with the drone's normal operation would be able to immediately discern that something was not right. Likewise, a robot with an arm could point the limb where it believed a person wanted it to go, thereby providing an opportunity to intervene (Hiroi & Ito, 2013). However, the intent which the robot seeks to convey with these methods might not be clear, especially if the recipient is a bystander not familiar with the system.

Explicitly requesting human assistance during failure can also be a valuable failure mitigation strategy in certain situations. For example, Cha, Mataric, and Fong (2016) summarized the process of asking for help as having three phases: (1) getting someone's attention, (2) indicating to the person that help is needed, and (3) conveying the request for help. Likewise, participants in a human-robot teaming study by Barber et al. (2015) expressed an interest in robot failure notifications and communication of robot performance. It is worth noting that self-assessment of performance is still an open challenge for autonomous robots, although this topic is attracting increased attention and new methods are likely to be available in the near future.

For example, there has been work on introspective systems capable of explaining why a robot behaved in a particular manner by tracing and logging the flow of information through a system, and keeping track of which pieces of data were used in making progressively higher level decisions (Brooks, Shultz, Desai, Kovac, & Yanco, 2010). However, providing users with information about the cause of a failure could also make the situation worse. For example, Kim and Hinds (2006) found that robots that attempt to explain their ambiguous actions and errors can actually decrease people's perceived understanding of the system.

There also appear to be nuances in how and when explicit requests of human assistance will be honored. For example, in one study, participants in a public kitchen area were asked for assistance with coffee preparation by an approaching robot (Hüttenrauch & Eklundh, 2006). Only half of the participants complied with the robot's request. The vast majority of the people who helped were not busy concentrating on another task (one of the experimental conditions), while most who were busy ignored the robot, tricked it into thinking they had given it the coffee so it would go away, or shut the door to keep the robot out.

Deciding who to ask for help is also important. Asking the same person for help frequently could quickly become annoying and robots which adapt to training are rated as not annoying (Karami, Sehaba, & Encelle, 2016). Rosenthal et al. (2012) addressed this issue by distributing the burden across an office hallway and anticipating who might be available based on prior behavior. After a few days, many people closed their office doors to avoid being asked by the robot for assistance in moving chairs, writing notes, and informing it of the room number. Similarly, Srinivasan and Takayama (2016) revealed a number of important factors, like politeness, that impact human willingness to help or train robots, including resistance by participants to allocate significant effort to train robots that are developed and maintained by others. This suggests the general public may have differences of opinion between assisting and teaching robots.

There are successful interaction models where humans are willing to assist openly imperfect robots. For example, Yasuda and Matsumoto (2013) hypothesized that people may relate well to imperfect robots, viewing them as similar to children or infants who try but fail in their efforts. They experimented with a robot trashcan that would sometimes spill garbage, but lacking manipulators to clean up after itself. Thus, whenever this would occur, the robot would politely ask a person to pick up the trash for it. The majority of people found the experience to be positive, even when the robot spilled trash. While robot failures could be catastrophic in safety critical applications (e.g., self-driving cars, search and rescue robots) (Kaber & Endsley, 1997), it is likely that many of the robot systems developed in the near term, and into the future as well, will experience failures and will need to ask for assistance from people or other robots.

14.3 Interaction design

Smartphones have rapidly become a ubiquitous technology based on their value in a wide variety of tasks. Due to their market saturation, we believe these devices to be an ideal proxy through which humans and autonomous systems could communicate with each other.

To explore methods for human-robot communication, we used smartphones, with two types of interaction methods. The first type uses *pull-style interactions* to enable participants to query information or communicate with the robot. Pull-style interactions wait in the background for the user to initiate interaction, rather than interrupt the user. The user can view these by tapping on a background notification which will appear as seen in Figs. 14.1 and 14.2. The second type used *push-style interactions* (Fig. 14.3), where the robot initiated communication with nearby participants. Push-style interactions interrupted the participant and were thought to be useful when alerting about hazards or requesting help. These interaction methods were used in conjunction with a balloon popping game that we created for use in the experiment.

We note that robot vacuum manufacturers have been shipping their products with accompanying apps for a few years. For example, Neato Robotics' robot vacuums (Neato Robotics, 2017) have an app that provides four push notifications: "Done Cleaning," "Low Battery," "Base Connected to Power," and "Move Base to New Location" (Neato Robotics, 2015). As another example, iRobot's robot vacuums (iRobot, 2017b) have an app that provides two types of push notifications: "Done Cleaning" and error messages (iRobot, 2017a). iRobot's robot vacuum users can also use the "Care" section of the app to see the status of the robot, its bin, and its extractors (iRobot, 2017c); these notifications are pull notifications. While these manufacturers have developed apps to be used with their robots, we are not aware of any published studies that investigate how these types of interactions influence human-robot interaction for the context when a robot needs assistance.

For both interaction types in the smartphone app that we designed for our experiment, robots were identified with a unique name and an icon that looked like the robot, in order to help identification of the robot(s); see Fig. 14.4 for the set of robots used in the experiment.

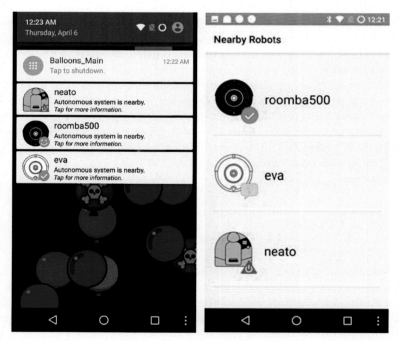

FIG. 14.1 Pull-style notifications: The *left image* shows the pull notifications accessed from within the balloon game. The *right image* shows the pull notifications accessed by opening the smartphone app directly.

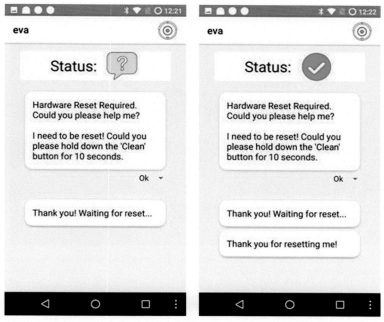

FIG. 14.2 Acting on pull-style notifications: The *left image* shows one robot's help screen reached from the pull notifications within the app and the *right image* shows the robot's help screen after the reset.

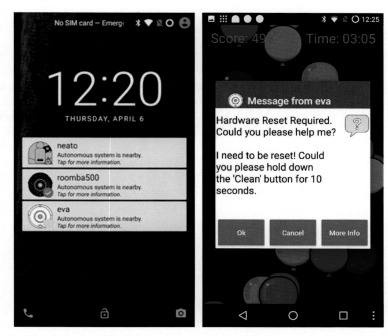

FIG. 14.3 Push-style notifications: The *left image* shows push notifications on the smartphone's lock screen. The *right image* shows a push notification from a robot over the balloon game.

FIG. 14.4   The set of robots used in the experiment, with four Roomba models and one Neato robot. Neato (*far left*) and the Discovery model Roomba (*far right*) were disabled to include "broken" robots in the experiment design.

In the pull-style interactions, the robot's icon also had a small status icon overlaid on its lower right corner, to provide immediate feedback about the robot's state, without needing to open the message.

14.4 Experiment methodology

The experiment described in this section represents our initial investigation into the use of smartphones as a platform for establishing a ubiquitous communication paradigm designed to allow participants to gain basic information from and interact with a variety of autonomous robots. In this experiment, we used several types of robot vacuum cleaners, shown in Fig. 14.4, as our platforms to provide a clearly describable task and to allow interaction with multiple robots in a fairly small space. Four of the five robots were iRobot Roomba robots, each with a different version to provide visual distinction between the robots; the fifth was a Neato robot, rounded on the rear side and flat on the front. The Roombas have a width of 34 cm while the Neato is 33 cm wide; the Roombas are 9.2 cm tall and the Neato is 10.16 cm tall. The enclosure in which the robots were confined was 2.40 m by 2.40 m, as shown in Fig. 14.5.

This study was approved by the University of Massachusetts Lowell's Institutional Review Board. This research has complied with all relevant national regulations and institutional policies.

14.4.1 Communication protocol

The communication between the robots and the user's phone is performed using an underlying communication protocol built on Bluetooth low energy (BLE) and an Android app that makes use of this protocol to allow users to interact with the robots. One of the initial

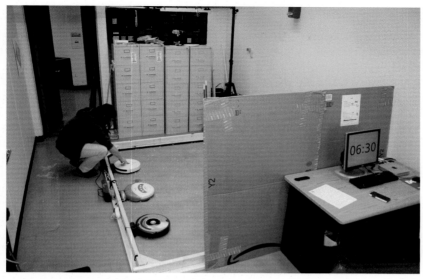

FIG. 14.5   One of the authors demonstrating what a participant might do in the cleaning zone to assist a robot.

challenges addressed was the process through which smartphones and robots could discover each other. The Bluetooth V4.0 specification, also known as Bluetooth Low Energy, was well suited for this task as a relatively short-range communication protocol (about 60 m, unobstructed) that utilizes broadcast messages to allow nearby devices to advertise their presence and the type of service(s) they provide. The software used to facilitate these communications is publicly available.[a]

In order to communicate over Bluetooth, each robot received hardware upgrades, implemented such that there were no visible modifications to the robots' external appearances. The additional electronics that were added shared the same power source as the rest of the robot, thus eliminating the need for additional or modified charging systems. The primary addition was a Raspberry Pi Zero with a Bluegiga BLED112 USB Bluetooth Low Energy dongle, allowing the developers to bypass the Linux kernel's Bluetooth stack and gain greater control of the behavior of the Bluetooth radio.

Status messages consisted of formatted text, optionally attached media resources (an image or icon), a list of commands or responses a user could choose to send back, and whether or not the message should be treated as a *push-style* interaction and displayed as a pop-up. This data was organized according to a JSON definition and serialized. For the commands, the robots offered users the same controls through the Bluetooth interface as the physical button controls found on the robots. The status information sent to the users was derived from the real-time hardware state, or from simulated problems which were generated by the experiment interface.

---

[a]GitHub code repository (https://github.com/uml-robotics/vacuum_trust) contains the software used in this experiment with the exception of data loggers and peripheral programs.

14.4.2 Design

In the experiment, we asked participants to perform two simultaneous tasks: (a) manage a fleet of robot vacuum cleaners while (b) playing a simple video game on a smartphone as a secondary task.

The video game task was a simple, skill-less game of balloon popping. Animated balloons drifted up from the bottom of the screen to the top and "popped" when touched, earning the participant points. Participants needed to pay attention, as balloons marked with skull and crossbones symbols would take away earned points if popped. This game was selected because it does not require prior experience. It provided a secondary task that required monitoring so that participants would not be able to watch the robots constantly.

In parallel, participants were asked to use three apparently standard robot vacuums, which were actually modified and programmed to exhibit the desired behaviors, to collect 6mm × 9mm plastic beads scattered around the floor inside an area fenced off with a 2.4 m^2 low wood frame. Participants were required to remain outside of this area and were not permitted to collect the beads themselves, forcing them to use the robots to accomplish the task. Participants could interact with the robots at the edge of the cleaning zone, as shown in Fig. 14.5.

In order to track time spent physically interacting with or observing the robots, participants were only allowed to play the game when inside a marked game-playing zone that did not have a view of the robots in the cleaning zone (see Fig. 14.6). The game interface was disabled when exiting the game-playing zone. If present in the current experimental condition, the participant could use the app to assess the robots' status or be notified by push

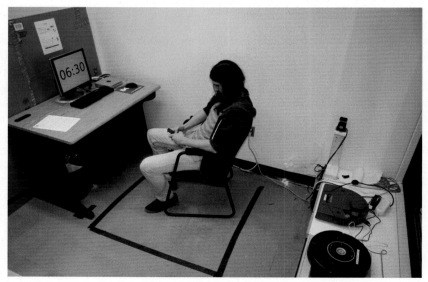

FIG. 14.6   One of the authors demonstrating what a participant would be doing if in the game-playing zone. The participant is not able to see the cleaning zone from this area, due to the cardboard wall obstruction, as can also be seen in the prior figure.

notification when the robots' needed assistance. Alternatively, the user would need to leave the game-playing zone to get the similar information or to interact with the robots.

The robots were secretly modified in a way that allowed them to appear as if they were still standard robot vacuum cleaners. They were programmed to intentionally exhibit various problems with their functionality which the participants would need to address, while the video game acted as a distracting secondary activity for diverting user attention from the robots.

The flaws exhibited by the robots were refusing to start, requiring a reset, returning to the charging dock prematurely, and requesting a dustbin cleaning early. These behaviors were selected for their plausibility to occur in a real scenario, as well as the amount of effort required to correct them. For example, the "dead" robot would never recover, while the one returning prematurely would immediately return to its duty once prompted via the app. Our objective was to gain insight into how participants would manage the two tasks and the robots when provided with access to the different communication styles (i.e., push and pull). Since we wanted to understand the impact on novices, participants were not provided with any training on the use of the app; we also limited training on the robots themselves, as described below.

We used a within-subjects design where each participant experienced two runs—one with only the manufacturer's on-robot interfaces (i.e., smartphone communication *disabled*) and one with the manufacturer's robot interfaces supplemented with our communication app (i.e., smartphone communication *enabled*). In both cases, the participants had access to the on-robot manufacturer's button interfaces.

Our participants were divided into four equally sized groups that were counterbalanced. Groups 1 and 3 shared the same group of robots between runs 1 and 2 with the run the App was enabled alternated between these groups. Groups 2 and 4 were similar in that they also shared the same group of robots but the group was different from 1 and 3. Groups 1 and 2 shared the same order in which the App was enabled, as did 3 and 4 (Table 14.1).

TABLE 14.1 Experiment conditions, as described in Section 14.4.4.

Cond	App support	Run	Robot starting conditions				
			R_A	R_B	R_C	R_D	R_E
1	Enabled	1	Easy	Dead	Help		
1	Disabled	2	Help			Easy	Dead
2	Enabled	1	Easy			Help	Dead
2	Disabled	2	Help	Dead	Easy		
3	Disabled	1	Easy	Dead	Help		
3	Enabled	2	Help			Easy	Dead
4	Disabled	1	Easy			Help	Dead
4	Enabled	2	Help	Dead	Easy		

Participants were not briefed or trained on how symbols on the robot's hardware or beeps the robots communicated to the user would correspond to what was causing the robots to be unable to operate, nor were participants showed how to start the robots. They were shown all the robots that would be used during the experiment including the robots that were to be swapped in on the second run and how to empty the dust bins on each robot. Similarly, participants were not briefed or trained on the use of the smartphone app for robot notifications.

Participants were given 6.5 min to play both the balloons game and use the robots to collect beads. A digital clock in the game-playing zone and a timer in the balloons game provided awareness of this period. Participants were responsible for keeping track of the time remaining by using either a digital clock showing the game time that was positioned inside the game-playing zone, or by using the game timer inside the balloons game (which also showed the experiment time).

While participants earned money based on points scored in the game, the total was adjusted by the fraction corresponding to the percentage of beads collected by the robots (i.e., if they collected 70% of the beads they would get to keep 70% of the points scored in the game). This percentage was determined by measuring the weight of the collected beads, as compared to the known amount scattered on the floor at the start of the run (roughly 100 g). At the end of each run, the beads collected by the robots were measured by weight to calculate the percentage collected, while the remaining beads were removed from the cleaning area by the experimenter. Participants would lose an additional 100 points (approximately 45 s worth of balloons game playtime) for each robot that was not on a charging station when time ran out. Participants received compensation based on the higher of their two final scores. Each person received $5 for simply completing the study, and could earn up to an additional $10 based on their performance, using a score based on the time that the two working robots spent running and the score of the balloons game.

In addition to an informed consent form before the experiment, participants were asked to fill out a pre-experiment questionnaire, two post-run questionnaires, and post-experiment questionnaires to get their opinions and perceptions of the experiment.

14.4.3 Hypotheses

Our hypotheses in this study were as follows:

Hypothesis 1 (H1): Participants would be able to determine which robot they were communicating with using our system, despite similarities between robots.

Hypothesis 2 (H2): Participants would be able to retrieve information about the robots they were working with, identify solutions to problems faster, and allocate their time more appropriately when using the smartphone-based interface compared to only having the default manufacturer interfaces on the robots.

Hypothesis 3 (H3): Participants would prefer having access to the additional information provided by our smartphone-based interface over using the default manufacturer interface on the robot alone.

14.4.4 Independent variables

This experiment used a within-subjects (repeated measures) design in which each participant performed two runs. While both runs included the manufacturers' default interfaces on the robots themselves, our smartphone-based communication was only enabled in one. Between runs, the experimenter replaced two of the three robots used in the previous run in full view of the participant as part of "resetting the task," while the participant filled out the post-run questionnaire. (The two robots not being used in a particular run were on charging stations behind the participant in the game-playing zone, as shown in Fig. 14.6.)

Conditions were counterbalanced by assigning participants into one of four experimental conditions corresponding to the two independent variables in the experiment: the order in which the smartphone app support was used in the runs and the order in which two different starting configurations were used.

The experiment used five robot vacuum cleaners: four iRobot Roombas and one Neato XV11. The four Roombas were two working Roomba 500 models (R_A and R_D), a working Roomba 600 model (R_C), and a nonworking Roomba Discovery model (R_B). The Neato XV11 (R_E) was intentionally programmed to not work. Three of these vacuums were used during the first run, after which two of the three were replaced before starting the next run. There were two combinations of robots that were switched between, each of which consists of two "working" robots and one "nonworking" robot: *Group 1* consisted of R_A, R_B, and R_C while *Group 2* consisted of R_A, R_D, and R_E.

Each of the three robots exhibited a different level of functionality: one robot was "easy" to start, simply requiring the push of a button; one required "help" from the participant before it would start running (it needed to be reset); and the last one played "dead" and would never start working (Table 14.1). The two "working" robots performed their default cleaning behaviors except that the length of time they ran for was shortened and some "problems" were introduced. Two minutes after a robot started cleaning, it would automatically start returning to its dock. After the "easy" robot returned, it would require the participant to come to empty its dustbin before it would be able to start cleaning again. In contrast, the "help" robot could immediately be told to resume cleaning (even before it finished returning to its dock) when its 2 min were up, and never required the dustbin to be emptied.

The robot that needed to be reset flashed a red LED ring around the power button, illuminated a red error symbol in the shape of a circle with an exclamation mark in the center of it, and would periodically play a distinct error tone until the participant pressed and held down on the power button. When the smartphone app was enabled, this robot sent a push-style interaction, causing a message to appear on the smartphone. The reset event occurred at the beginning of each run.

The robot that needed its dustbin emptied illuminated a yellow LED ring around the power button, flashed a blue LED labeled "dirt detect" and would occasionally play a different error tone until the dustbin was removed. When the smartphone app was enabled, participants could view information about the full dustbin on the robot's status page (a pull-style interaction).

Time spent trying to make the third robot work was wasted. One of the dead robots had no lights on and showed no indication it even had power; the other dead robot had a single lit LED light, but showed no other signs of being functional. The dead robot could be viewed using pull-style interactions in the smartphone app, which would reveal the robot's broken status.

14.4.5 Dependent variables

Aside from the three questionnaires, data was logged on the robots and smartphone, in manual notes, and video recordings. After each run, we documented the resting positions of the robots, the percentage of beads collected, and the game score. The post-run questionnaire included the NASA's Task Load Index (TLX) Questionnaire (Hart & Staveland, 1988), as well as questions about participant confidence in the app and where participants thought app information originated.

Logged data included the time in game, the number of times the game was started and stopped, when and how often they left the game zone, and the game score over time. App specific data was also captured, including the number of times each robot's app page was accessed via a pull-style interaction, the time spent viewing each robot's app page, the number of times background notifications were observed, and whether the participant explicitly agreed or declined (via the app dialog buttons) to help the robot.

14.4.6 Participants

Twenty people (14 men and 6 women) between the ages of 18 and 33 participated, all of whom had previous experience with smartphones. Two participants had prior experience using Roombas and one person had used a Philips robot vacuum, while the remaining 17 participants had no prior experience with robot vacuum cleaners.

14.4.7 Analysis methods

The majority of the analyses were 2 × 4 mixed-groups factorial ANOVAs on app status (enabled, disabled) and one of the given conditions (1 through 4) counter balancing the starting conditions of the experiment (Table 14.1). These statistics were computed in R, using the "psych" and "ez" statistics packages. An alpha of 0.05 was used on analyses.

14.5 Results

14.5.1 Robot usage

The app availability had a significant main effect for the combined time the robots spent cleaning [$F(1, 16) = 17.052, P < .001$] (Fig. 14.7). There was a significant interaction between the experiment condition and the presence of the app [$F(3, 16) = 3.49, P = .04$]; however, there was no main effect for condition by itself [$F(3, 16) = 1.064, P = .39$] (Fig. 14.8). A post hoc two-tailed t-test showed that the time the robots spent cleaning was significantly higher during the run in which participants had access to the app ($M_1 = 406, SD_1 = 131$) compared to the run in which it was not provided ($M_2 = 307, SD_2 = 98$); $t(19) = 3.49, P = .002$. SD pooled is $SD_p = 91.7$ and Effect Size was ($M_1 - M_2)/SD_p = 1.08$. In other words, participants were able to keep the robots cleaning for more of the session when using the app. While this was especially true for participants who used the app during the second run, it was also generally true for participants who used the app in the first run.

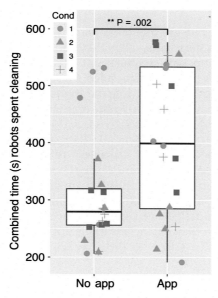

FIG. 14.7 Time robots spent cleaning without (*left*) and with (*right*) the app. Robots spent significantly more time ($P = .002$) cleaning when participants had access to the app.

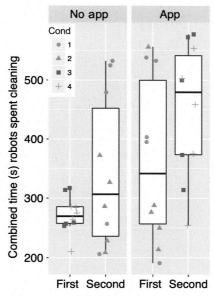

FIG. 14.8 Time robots spent cleaning by the app condition and then the run number in which participants experienced that condition (first or second), demonstrating that there is some learning effect between the first and second runs, regardless of whether the participant started with the app or without it.

14.5.2 Game-playing zone

Participants spent less time outside the game-playing zone, and thus less time watching and physically interacting with the robots, when they used the app. The app was a significant main effect on the amount of time participants spent outside the game-playing zone [$F(1, 16)$ = 4.589, P = .048] (Fig. 14.9). A post hoc two-tailed t-test showed that the time participants spent outside the game-playing zone observing and interacting with robots was significantly less during the run in which they had access to the app (M_1 = 151, SD = 53) compared to the run in which it was not provided (M_2 = 176, SD = 44); $t(19)$ = −2.23, P = .038, SD pooled is SD_p = 37.3 and Effect Size was ($M_1 − M_2$)/SD_p = −0.670.

Participants context switched between tasks less often when provided the app, presumably because it allowed them to determine if the robots needed attention without exiting the game-playing zone. The app was a significant main effect on the number of times participants switched between being inside and outside the game-playing zone [$F(1, 16) = 4.47, P$ = .05] (Fig. 14.10). A post hoc two-tailed t-test showed that the number of switches was significantly less during the run when they had access to the app (M_1 = 4.1, SD = 1.92) compared to the default (M_2 = 5.1, SD = 2.57); $t(19)$ = −2.078, P = .05, SD pooled is SD_p = 1.75 and Effect Size was ($M_1 − M_2$)/SD_p = −0.573.

14.5.3 Balloons game

On average, participants had lower scores on the balloons game when they were also using the app and presence of the app had a significant main effect on the balloons game score [$F(1, 16) = 7.567, P$ = .01]. A post hoc two-tailed t-test showed that participants scored significantly fewer points during the run in which they had access to the app (M_1 = 382, SD = 137)

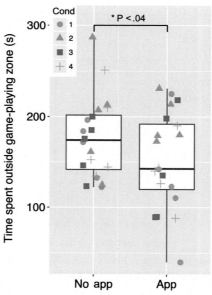

FIG. 14.9 Time spent outside of the game-playing zone without and with the robot status app.

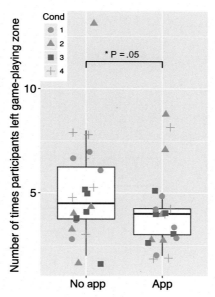

FIG. 14.10 Number of switches in and out of the game-playing zone without and with the robot status app.

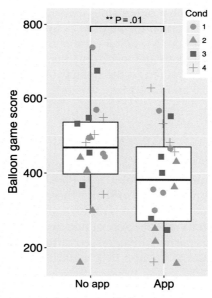

FIG. 14.11 Score in the balloons game, without and with the robot status app.

compared to the default ($M_2 = 463$, $SD = 131$); $t(19) = -2.66$, $P = .01$, SD pooled is $SD_p = 96.0$ and Effect Size was $(M_1 - M_2)/SD_p = 2.62$ (Fig. 14.11).

The lower scores are probably due to a decrease in time spent playing the balloons game, since the rate at which players scored points was similar between conditions, and there was

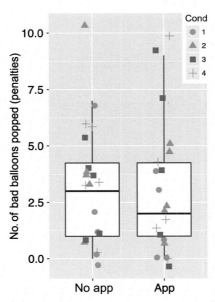

FIG. 14.12   Penalties incurred in the balloons game, without and with the robot status app.

no discernible difference in the number of penalties incurred (Fig. 4.12). This result aligns with the significant main effect for the app on the amount of time spent playing the balloons game [$F(1, 16) = 4.52, P = .05$]. A post hoc two-tailed t-test showed that participants spent significantly less time playing the balloons game during the run in which they had access to the app ($M_1 = 180, SD = 33$), compared to the default ($M_2 = 206, SD = 56$); $t(19) = -2.21$, $P = .04$, SD pooled is $SD_p = 23.6$ and Effect Size was ($M_1 - M_2)/SD_p = -1.10$ (Fig. 14.13).

14.5.4 Robot interactions

There was a weak main effect of having access to the app on the number of times participants pressed buttons on the robots [$F(1, 16) = 3.70, P = .07$]. There was no main effect of the experiment condition [$F(3, 16) = 1.79, P = .18$] and there was no significant interaction between the app and the experiment condition [$F(3, 16) = 1.04, P = .4$] on the number of times participants pressed buttons on the robots. A post hoc two-tailed t-test showed (weak significance) that the number of times participants pressed buttons on the robots was fewer during the run in which they had access to the app ($M_1 = 10.85, SD = 9.6$) compared to the run in which it was disabled ($M_2 = 15.7, SD = 6.56$); $t(19) = -1.92, P = .07$, SD pooled is $SD_p = 6.94$ and Effect Size was ($M_1 - M_2)/SD_p = -0.699$ (see Fig. 14.14). Simply put, participants spent less time using the robots' physical interfaces when they also had access to the app. Two potential explanations for this are that participants were using the app controls instead of the physical controls, and that they potentially had a better understanding of why a robot might not be responding to their actions.

As implied earlier, app availability led to significant differences in participants' physical interactions with robots (Fig. 14.15). Time with robots was calculated by coding each

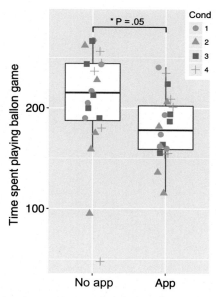

FIG. 14.13   Balloons game-playing time, without and with the robot status app.

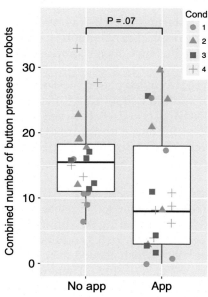

FIG. 14.14   Number of button presses on the robots, without and with the robot status app.

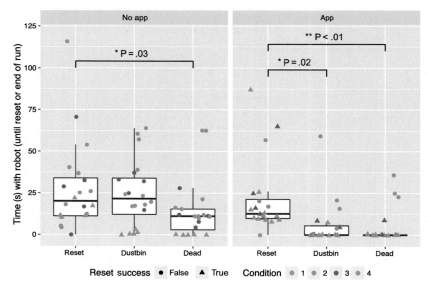

FIG. 14.15   Time physically spent with robots until robot reset, without and with the robot status app.

interaction's start and stop times for every robot up until the time the robot that needed help was reset. Timing started whenever the participant knelt or leaned over a robot while reaching toward, touching, or looking at the robot or the phone. Timing was stopped whenever the user stood up, moved their hand away from the robot, or looked away from the robot or the phone. Time spent working with the dustbins was excluded, with time stopping when the dustbin was removed and restarting once it was replaced. Interrater reliability of two coders (one experimenter and one researcher not involved with data collection, both included on the IRB protocol) was computed using Cohen's kappa and showed significant agreement ($\kappa = 0.87$, $\alpha = 0.05$).

A pairwise comparison using a two-tailed paired t-test on the time spent with robots during the default run without the app showed a significant difference ($P = .03$), SD pooled is $SD_p = 19.1$ and Effect Size was $(M_1 - M_2)/SD_p = 0.691$ between the time spent with the robot that needed to be reset ($M_1 = 28$, $SD = 27$) and with the robot that was playing dead ($M_2 = 14.8$, $SD = 19$). The difference between the robot which needed its dustbin emptied ($M_3 = 24.3$, $SD = 20$) and the robot that needed to be reset was not significant ($P = .6$), SD pooled is $SD_p = 14.4$ and Effect Size was $(M_3 - M_1)/SD_p = -0.257$, nor was there a significant difference between the dustbin robot and the robot playing dead ($P = .1$), SD pooled is $SD_p = 14.3$ and Effect Size was $(M_3 - M_2)/SD_p = 0.665$. In comparison, a pairwise comparison using a two-tailed paired t-test of the time spent with robots during the run with the app showed a larger significant difference ($P = .008$), SD pooled is $SD_p = 15.5$ and Effect Size was $(M_4 - M_5)/SD_p = 1.09$ between the time spent with the robot which needed to be reset ($M_4 = 21.5$, $SD = 22$) and the robot that was playing dead ($M_5 = 4.6$, $SD = 10.5$). There was also a significant difference between the robot which needed to be reset and the robot that needed its dustbin emptied ($M_6 = 6$, $SD = 13.5$, $P = .02$), SD pooled is $SD_p = 15.6$ and Effect Size was $(M_4 - M_6)/SD_p = 0.996$, but not between the robot which needed its dustbin emptied and the robot that needed to be reset ($P = .5$), SD pooled is $SD_p = 10.0$ and Effect Size was $(M_6 - M_4)/SD_p = -1.55$. This suggests the app helped participants more efficiently understand which robot they needed to reset.

Participants are required to hold down the clean button for 7 s in order to reset a robot. This would enable a robot that needed to be reset to continue cleaning; 7 s was chosen to reduce the chance of a user from accidentally resetting the robot. No participant who started without the app held down the clean button to reset the robot that needed help in the first run for longer than 5 s (Fig. 14.16). Participants with the app in their first run appeared to apply their experiences to their second run without the app, as shown by the steadily increasing number of times participants held down the button for over 5 s in the second run. This same group may have also either been uncertain about which robot they needed to reset, or guessed the same technique would work on multiple robots since they also appear to have tried to reset the "dustbin" robot more than in any other situation. Everyone who had the app in their second run successfully reset the robot that needed help, and very few attempts were made at trying to reset a robot that had not requested help.

Half of the participants (10/20) viewed all three robots' status pages using the app. The robot that needed to be reset used a push-style interaction which caused a popup message to appear on the smartphone screen, interrupting what the user was doing. As a result, each of the participants ended up viewing this robot's page at least once. The robot that needed its

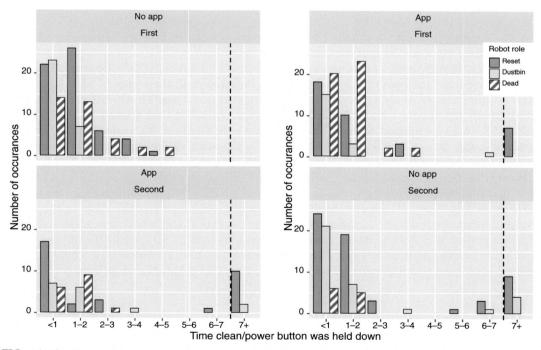

FIG. 14.16 Clean button click/hold times (in seconds). The *two left bar graphs* show one set of participants, who experienced the no app condition first, followed by the app condition second. The *two right bar graphs* show the other set of participants, who experienced the app condition first, followed by the no app condition second.

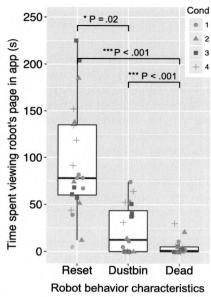

FIG. 14.17   Time spent in the robot status app.

dustbin to be emptied was viewed by 12 of the 20 participants, and the robot that played dead was viewed by 10 of the 20 participants.

Half of the participants were able to use the app to view information about two or more robots. Using the data from the 10 participants who viewed all three robots' status pages, a pairwise comparison using a two-tailed paired t-test showed significant differences on the time participants spent on those app pages between the robot that needed to be reset (M_1 = 88.7, SD = 43.7), needed to have its dustbin emptied (M_2 = 45.3, SD = 17.1), or was nonfunctioning (M_3 = 9, SD = 9) (Fig. 14.17). Participants spent significantly more time looking at the page of the robot that needed to be reset than the robot that needed its dustbin emptied (P = .02), SD pooled is SD_p = 30.2 and Effect Size was ($M_1 - M_2$)/SD_p = 1.43 or the robot that had been disabled (P < .001), SD pooled is SD_p = 30.1 and Effect Size was ($M_1 - M_3$)/SD_p = 2.64. They also spent significantly more time looking at the page of the robot whose dustbin needed to be emptied than that of the robot which had been disabled (P < .001), SD pooled is SD_p = 11.9 and Effect Size was ($M_2 - M_3$)/SD_p = 3.04. In other words, the amount of time participants spent viewing information about the different robots was associated with the appropriate amount of attention needed to get and keep each robot working.

14.5.5 Post-run questionnaires

After each run, participants were asked to fill out a questionnaire asking about their experience with the robots, their perception of what help (if any) they needed to provide to robots, and their workload.

In each of the two runs, each of the three robots engaged in one of three distinct behaviors. One robot immediately required being "reset" before it could begin cleaning, but once this had been completed could continue running without needing any other help. A second robot was immediately available to begin cleaning upon request but thereafter needed to periodically have its dustbin emptied before it could continue cleaning. The last robot played dead, and simply refused to work for the entire duration of the run. During both runs, the two robots that needed help would emit visual (flashing lights) and auditory indicators (beeping sounds) to signal there was a problem until the issue was resolved. Following each run, participants were asked "What kind of help did the robot(s) require or request? Select all that apply." With a single exception, participants' responses were limited to the two actions which they actually needed to take. More participants correctly identified the two solicited actions during the second run (24) than during the first run (19).

The number of participants who understood a robot needed to be reset was significantly higher ($P = .04$ using McNemar's test) during runs when the app was present (12/20) compared to the default (5/20). The run number did not significantly affect participants' understanding of whether or not a robot needed to be reset ($P = .5$). However, the order in which the phone was used did seem to have an effect; 5/10 participants who had access to the app during the first run understood they needed to reset one of the robots, compared to 7/10 who had the app during the second run. In comparison, without the app, only 2/10 participants during the first run and 3/10 from the second run understood that one of the robots needed to be reset.

Participants generally felt that the robots were predictable (Fig. 14.18A) regardless of whether they had access to the app ($M_1 = 3.45$, $SD = 1.19$) or not ($M_2 = 3.35$, $SD = 1.46$) (no significant difference was found using a two-tailed paired t-test; $t(19) = -0.31$, $P = .7$), SD pooled is $SD_p = 1.32$ and Effect Size was $(M_1 - M_2)/SD_p = 0.076$.

Participants were more confident that they understood what robots were doing while using the app. A two-tailed paired t-test showed that participants reported significantly more confidence in their understanding of the robots' behaviors during runs in which they had the app ($M_1 = 4.65$, $SD = 1.57$) compared to runs in which they did not ($M_2 = 3.7$, $SD = 1.42$); $t(19) = 3.13$, $P = .005$, SD pooled is $SD_p = 1.38$ and Effect Size was $(M_1 - M_2)/SD_p = 0.691$ (Fig. 14.18B).

Participants' satisfaction with the robots was higher (weak significance) during the runs when the app was enabled ($M_1 = 4.6$, $SD = 1.19$) than during runs in which it was not ($M_2 = 4.05$, $SD = 1.23$) according to a two-tailed paired t-test; $t(19) = 1.93$, $P = 0.07$, SD pooled is $SD_p = 1.14$ and Effect Size was $(M_1 - M_2)/SD_p = 0.484$ (Fig. 14.18C).

A two-tailed paired t-test also showed that participants found it significantly easier to determine what was needed to keep each robot working during when they had the app ($M_1 = 5$, $SD = 1.26$), compared to the default ($M_2 = 3.7$, $SD = 1.75$); $t(19) = 3.21$, $P = .004$, SD pooled is $SD_p = 1.28$ and Effect Size was $(M_1 - M_2)/SD_p = 1.02$ (Fig. 14.18D).

As part of each post-run questionnaire, participants completed the NASA TLX questionnaire. Six 2×4 mixed-groups factorial ANOVA were performed to examine the effects of using the app and the experiment conditions on mental demand, physical demand, perceived performance, success, how rushed and how discouraged they felt. This analysis was done using the raw TLX data.

There was a weak significant main effect of having access to the app on mental demand [$F(1, 16) = 4.26$, $P = .055$]. Also, there was a significant main effect of the experiment condition

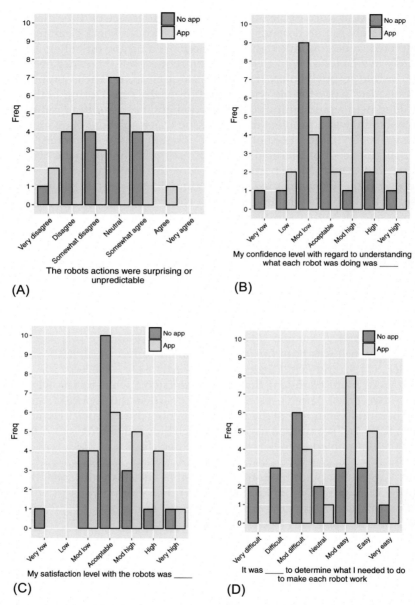

FIG. 14.18   Participant robot reviews, by app usage. (A) Robot predictability; (B) confidence; (C) satisfaction; and (D) obtaining information.

on mental demand [$F(3, 16) = 3.3$, $P = .04$], and a weakly significant interaction between the app and the experiment condition on mental demand [$F(3, 16) = 3.02$, $P = .06$]. A post hoc two-tailed paired t-test showed (with weak significance) that participants tended to have a lower mental demand during the run in which they had the app ($M_1 = 3.7$, $SD = 1.13$) than the run without it ($M_2 = 4.1$, $SD = 1.33$); $t(19) = -1.8$, $P = .088$, SD pooled is $SD_p = 1.13$ and Effect Size was $(M_1 - M_2)/SD_p = -0.355$. A pairwise two-tailed t-test with Holm correction that was used to compare differences in mental demand between experiment conditions found significant differences between Condition 1 ($M_1 = 4.8$, $SD = 1.14$) and Condition 3 ($M_2 = 3.4$, $SD = 0.97$, $P = .048$), SD pooled is $SD_p = 1.05$ and Effect Size was $(M_1 - M_2)/SD_p = 1.33$ and Condition 4 ($M = 3.1$, $SD = 0.074$, $P = .045$), SD pooled is $SD_p = 0.818$ and Effect Size was $(M_1 - M_3)/SD_p = 2.078$, but not between any of the other experiment conditions.

These findings suggest that using the app lowered mental demand, but that perception of workload was influenced by prior experience. We found that participants who were placed in Conditions 3 and 4 had lower mental demands than participants in Condition 1. This result is interesting because participants used the app during their second run for both Conditions 3 and 4, while participants in Condition 1 used the app in the first run (the same was true of Condition 2, but the difference was not as pronounced as in Condition 1).

There was a significant main effect of having access to the app on the physical demand [$F(1, 16) = 4.65$, $P = .046$]; however, there was no main effect for experiment condition [$F(3, 16) = 1.80$, $P = .18$] on physical demand, nor was there a significant interaction between the variables [$F(3, 16) = 1.06$, $P = .39$]. A post hoc two-tailed paired t-test showed that participants tended to have a lower physical demand during with the app ($M_1 = 2.15$, $SD = 0.81$) compared to the default ($M_2 = 2.7$, $SD = 1.34$); $t(19) = -2.15$, $P = .04$, SD pooled is $SD_p = 0.986$ and Effect Size was $(M_1 - M_2)/SD_p = -0.558$. The app allowed participants to substitute walking between different locations in the room to accessing robots with an interaction in the app.

There was a significant main effect of having access to the app on how discouraged participants reported feeling [$F(1, 16) = 5.04$, $P = .04$]; however, there was no main effect of the experiment condition [$F(3, 16) = 1.54$, $P = .24$], nor was there a significant interaction between the variables [$F(3, 16) = 0.34$, $P = .79$]. A post hoc two-tailed paired t-test showed that participants reported feeling less discouraged during when they had the app ($M_1 = 3.4$, $SD = 1.67$) than without it ($M_2 = 4.05$, $SD = 1.62$); $t(19) = -2.37$, $P = .03$, SD pooled is $SD_p = 1.47$ and Effect Size was $(M_1 - M_2)/SD_p = -0.444$. This result is consistent with our findings that participants were more confident about understanding the robots' actions and found it easier to determine what to do to make robots work while using the app.

14.5.6 Post-experiment questionnaires

After the second run, participants were asked to complete a final questionnaire. Nearly all of the participants (18/20) reported that learning how to use the app was easy (Fig. 14.19A). Most also reported that it was easier to figure out what they needed to do with the robots (14/20) and to control them (15/20) by using the app rather than by physically looking at the robots themselves (Fig. 14.19B and C). The majority of participants (14/20) felt that they understood which robot the information in the app was referring to more than half the time, while only 3/20 felt that they "rarely" or "sometimes" understood. A two-tailed t-test did not report significant difference ($t(14.6) = -0.5$, $P = .6$) between ordering conditions.

All 20 participants said they preferred having access to the app (Fig. 14.20A); 19 out of the 20 participants thought the information they received from the app was helpful and

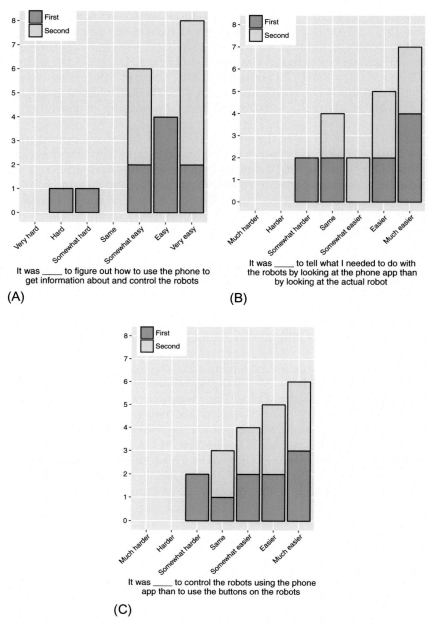

FIG. 14.19   Robot smartphone app characteristics: (A) learnability; (B) information; and (C) control.

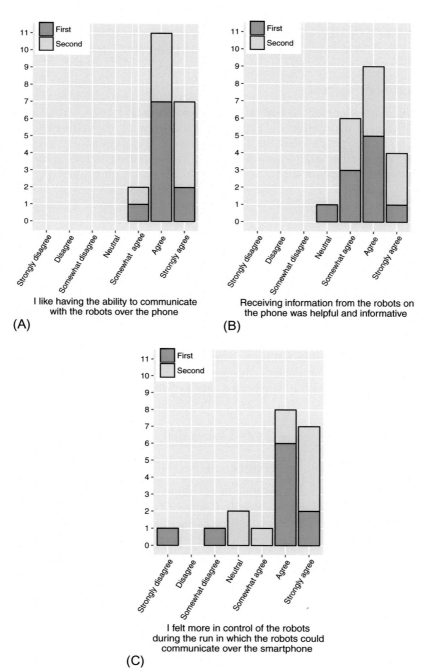

FIG. 14.20 Robot smartphone app preferences: (A) preferred app; (B) app helpful; and (C) feeling of control.

informative, and 16 out of the 20 felt more in control of the robots when they had access to the app (Fig. 14.20B and C). There were no significant differences between run ordering conditions ($P = .3$, $P = .3$, and $P = .4$, respectively, using two-tailed t-tests).

14.5.7 Experiment scores

There was no main effect for the app on experiment score [$F(1, 16) = 1.16, P = .3$]. However, there was a significant main effect for experiment condition on experiment score [$F(3, 16) = 3.18, P = .05$], and there was a weak interaction between the app and experiment [$F(3, 16) = 3.06, P = .06$]. A post hoc pairwise comparison using paired t-tests showed significant differences between Condition 2 ($M_1 = 196$, $SD = 75$) and Condition 1 ($M_2 = 184$, $SD = 92$, $P = .03$), SD pooled is $SD_p = 52.8$ and Effect Size was $(M_1 - M_2)/SD_p = 0.227$ and Condition 3 ($M_3 = 183$, $SD = 78$, $P = .04$), SD pooled is $SD_p = 52.7$ and Effect Size was $(M_1 - M_2)/SD_p = 0.247$.

We have been unable to produce a suitable explanation for why participants in Condition 2 did not perform as well as those in the other three conditions. The low experiment scores were a combination of both low balloon game scores (although the differences were not significant) and low combined time robots spent cleaning. The later was the result of just a single person (out of five) in Condition 2 successfully using more than one robot, compared to four out of five in Condition 1, five out of five in Condition 3, and four out of five in Condition 4. There were no significant differences between Condition 2 and the other conditions with respect to time spent outside the game-playing zone, app usage, time spent playing the balloons game, penalties incurred in the balloons game, or time spent physically interacting with the robots. That said, despite the lack of difference in experiment scores based on the presence of the app, our results still largely supported our hypotheses.

14.6 Discussion

14.6.1 H1 is supported by the results

A majority of participants indicated they could tell which robot was the source of information in the app (70%) and that it was easier to figure out what they needed to do to make the robots work (70%) with the app than by looking at the robots; 6 of the 10 participants who had the app during their first run were able to "reset" the robot that needed help, and 5 out of 10 were able to transfer that knowledge by successfully identifying and resetting a different robot that needed help in their second run without using the app.

In contrast, no one who did not have the app in the first run was able to reset the robot that needed help. However, *all of those same participants* (10/10) were able to successfully reset another robot which needed help when provided the app in their second run.

14.6.2 H2 is partially supported by the results

Participants were able to use the app to retrieve information about the robots and to identify solutions to problems. All of the participants used the app to view the robot that employed a push-style interaction (popup message), and half of the participants viewed all three robots using the app. There are a few possible reasons why more of participants did not view all three robots.

First, while basic use of the Android phone was demonstrated, participants were not provided with any training on how to use the robot smartphone app or its capabilities. The popup message appeared shortly after the run began, as one of the first experiences with the app. Therefore, participants may have believed that any future information would also come in the form of popup messages.

Another related possibility is that some participants may have simply not been interested in viewing the information of some robots, as with two participants who only viewed two of the three robots (both did not view the "dead" robot).

The third possibility is that some participants may not have been able to figure out how to access the information about the other robots. Of the eight participants who only viewed one robot, five of them reported having no prior experience using Android devices.

Participants were able to use the app to identify solutions to problems and allocate their time more appropriately. Participants were much more likely to get two robots working when equipped with the app, with a combined time for robot cleaning that was over a minute and a half longer (on average) than without the app. During app runs, participants tended to focus most of their time and attention on the robot which needed to be reset first.

Participants using the app were also able to get the robots to clean for longer while also spending less time watching and physically interacting with them. We had predicted that this kind of behavior would lead to better performance since participants would have more time to score points in the balloons game and retain a higher percentage of their score. However, despite gaining an average of 30 additional seconds to play the balloons game when the app was enabled, participants using the app actually spent significantly less time playing the balloons game, causing their overall performance to be about the same. Much of the lost time was spent using the app. One potential explanation for this behavior is that the app's ability to communicate with and control the robots had a strong novelty effect on participants, leading them to spend more time with it than with the balloons game. This explanation is supported by the fact that only three participants had previously used a robot vacuum cleaner.

14.6.3 H3 is supported by the results

Participants liked having access to the app, the additional information it provided, and its controls over the robots' built-in interfaces. All of the participants reported that they liked being able to communicate with the robots through the app, and all but one (who was neutral) thought the app was helpful. The majority of participants said they felt more in control using the app. The majority also felt much more confident about understanding what the robots were doing and what needed to be done to make the robots work. According to the NASA TLX questionnaires, participants felt less discouraged while using the app. Unsurprisingly, participants also reported higher levels of satisfaction with using the robots during the run with the app. According to workload data from the NASA TLX questionnaires, the app reduced participants' mental and physical demands.

14.6.4 Effects of run ordering

Some of our results show evidence of an ordering effect. For example, participants who used the app in the first run were able to apply knowledge from their first experience during their second run (e.g., resetting the robot which needed help). Additionally, the 100% increase in participants who could reset the robot in the second run with the app who had previously been unable to without the app suggests that they had a better understanding of the information the app was providing due to their prior experience.

NASA TLX responses from after each run also show ordering effects. Some participants found the app to be distracting (4/20) or its messages confusing (7/20), with most of the complaints coming from participants who used the app during the first run. Participants who used the app during their second run had the additional context on the task. The results from a similar question asked at the end of the experiment support this theory; in that question, all but one participant said they thought the information from the app was helpful.

14.7 Future work

Perhaps the most important limitation of this study is that the participants were not representative of bystanders, who we consider to be an important target audience for this work, ultimately. Instead, participants were acting as operators or supervisors, with the robots' goals being aligned with their own goals. That said, given the lack of training provided, participants did have several characteristics of typical bystanders: a lack of familiarity or prior experience with the robot platform and a lack of training with its user interfaces. In order to measure how the feedback could assist people who are true bystanders to robots, we would test situations in which people must interact with a robot without previously having been informed that a robot would even be involved, but such experiments are difficult to construct. An alternative, less deception oriented experiment might ask people to find and help an autonomous robot carry out a task it has been assigned without prior knowledge of exactly where the robot is, what it looks like, what it is doing, or how to communicate with the robot. We believe that the results of our study are promising for these future bystander experiments, as we have shown that the app is able to convey status information about the context and methods for assisting the robots, an example of shared context.

Another limitation of this work is the lack of explicit comparisons of the effectiveness of *push* versus *pull* interactions. Both interaction styles were used during the experiment; however, they were directly paired with a single type of problem, and always occurred in the same order with participants receiving a *push* interaction popup message shortly after the beginning of the run. Testing the difference in effectiveness of these interaction styles is warranted. Finally, one of the most powerful applications of this work is its potential to be relevant for communicating with a wide variety of different kinds of robotic platforms. Further testing with different kinds of robots, including drones and self-driving cars, is necessary to determine if this technology would be suitable as a ubiquitous method for communicating with publicly deployed autonomous robots.

14.8 Conclusions

The results of this work support the use of smartphones as a ubiquitous interaction method to allow untrained users to communicate with autonomous robot systems. Participants were able to use the app without training and reported that it was easy to learn and use. All of the participants preferred having access to the app and all but one said the app was helpful. Participants were able to retrieve information about nearby robots and could distinguish the source of the information despite similarities in the robots' appearances. With the app, participants felt more confident, they understood what the robots were doing and were more satisfied with the robots' performance. Although participants' experiment scores did not improve with the use of the app, their behavior (specifically, spending less time watching and physically interacting with the robots, and getting more robots working for longer periods of time) created the potential for improved performance. While additional experimentation is needed to better understand the differences between the *push* and *pull* interaction methods and how bystanders might use the system, these results are a promising first step toward building communication between people and the increasing number of autonomous robots in our society.

Acknowledgments

The research in this chapter was supported in part by the National Science Foundation under awards IIS-1552228 and IIS-1552256. Thanks to Chuta Sano and Christopher Munroe for their assistance with aspects of the experiment. Daniel Brooks was a doctoral candidate at the University of Massachusetts Lowell when this work was conducted.

References

Barber, D. J., Abich, J., IV, Phillips, E., Talone, A. B., Jentsch, F., & Hill, S. G. (2015). Field assessment of multimodal communication for dismounted human-robot teams. *Proceedings of the Human Factors and Ergonomics Society Annual Meeting, 59*(1), 921–925. https://doi.org/10.1177/1541931215591280.

Brooks, D. J., Shultz, A., Desai, M., Kovac, P., & Yanco, H. A. (2010). Towards state summarization for autonomous robots. In *AAAI fall symposium series*.

Carlson, J., & Murphy, R. R. (2005). How UGVs physically fail in the field. *IEEE Transactions on Robotics, 21*(3), 423–437.

Cha, E., Mataric, M., & Fong, T. (2016). Nonverbal signaling for non-humanoid robots during human-robot collaboration. In *Proceedings of the 11th ACM/IEEE international conference on human-robot interaction* (pp. 601–602).

Desai, M., Kaniarasu, P., Medvedev, M., Steinfeld, A., & Yanco, H. (2013). Impact of robot failures and feedback on real-time trust. In *Proceedings of the 8th ACM/IEEE international conference on human-robot interaction*. Tokyo, Japan.

Groom, V., Chen, J., Johnson, T., Kara, F. A., & Nass, C. (2010). Critic, compatriot, or chump? Responses to robot blame attribution. In *Proceedings of the 5th ACM/IEEE international conference on human-robot interaction*.

Hart, S. G., & Staveland, L. E. (1988). Development of NASA-TLX (task load index): Results of empirical and theoretical research. *Advances in Psychology, 52*, 139–183.

Hiroi, Y., & Ito, A. (2013). ASAHI: OK for failure: A robot for supporting daily life, equipped with a robot avatar. In *Proceedings of the 8th ACM/IEEE international conference on human-robot interaction* (pp. 141–142).

Hüttenrauch, H., & Eklundh, K. S. (2006). To help or not to help a service robot: Bystander intervention as a resource in human–robot collaboration. *Interaction Studies, 7*(3), 455–477.

iRobot. (2017a). (2017a). *Features of the iRobot HOME app.* https://homesupport.irobot.com/app/answers/detail/a_id/9129/ /features-of-the-irobot-home-app.(Accessed 27 December 2017).

iRobot. (2017b). *iRobot robot vacuums.* http://www.irobot.com/For-the-Home/Vacuuming/Roomba.aspx. (Accessed 27 December 2017).

iRobot. (2017c). *Resetting the iRobot HOME app "Care" status.* https://homesupport.irobot.com/app/answers/detail/a_id/9489. (Accessed 27 December 2017).

Kaber, D. B., & Endsley, M. R. (1997). Out-of-the-loop performance problems and the use of intermediate levels of automation for improved control system functioning and safety. *Process Safety Progress, 16*(3), 126–131.

Kaniarasu, P., & Steinfeld, A. (2014). Effects of blame on trust in human robot interaction. In *The 23rd IEEE international symposium on robot and human interactive communication.*

Karami, A. B., Sehaba, K., & Encelle, B. (2016). Adaptive artificial companions learning from users' feedback. *Adaptive Behavior, 24*(2), 69–86. https://doi.org/10.1177/1059712316634062.

Kim, T., & Hinds, P. (2006). Who should I blame? Effects of autonomy and transparency on attributions in human-robot interaction. In *Proceedings of the 15th IEEE international symposium on robot and human interactive communication.*

Knepper, R. A., Tellex, S., Li, A., Roy, N., & Rus, D. (2015). Recovering from failure by asking for help. *Autonomous Robots, 39*(3), 347–362.

Lee, M. K., Kiesler, S., Forlizzi, J., Srinivasa, S., & Rybski, P. (2010). Gracefully mitigating breakdowns in robotic services. In *Proceedings of the 5th ACM/IEEE international conference on human-robot interaction.*

Lussier, B., Chatila, R., Ingrand, F., Killijian, M. -O., & Powell, D. (2004). On fault tolerance and robustness in autonomous systems. In *3rd IARP-IEEE and RAS-EURON joint workshop on technical challenges for dependable robots in human environments* (pp. 351–358).

Neato Robotics. (2015). *Neato Botvac connected.* https://www.neatorobotics.com/wp-content/uploads/2015/09/botvac-connected-qsg-3-lang.pdf. (Accessed 27 December 2017).

Neato Robotics. (2017). *Neato robot vacuums.* https://www.neatorobotics.com/robot-vacuum/botvac-connected-series/. (Accessed 27 December 2017).

Rosenthal, S., Veloso, M., & Dey, A. K. (2012). Is someone in this office available to help me? *Journal of Intelligent & Robotic Systems, 66*(1), 205–221.

Srinivasan, V., & Takayama, L. (2016). Help me please: Robot politeness strategies for soliciting help from humans. In *Proceedings of the 2016 CHI conference on human factors in computing systems* (pp. 4945–4955). ACM.

Steinbauer, G. (2013). A survey about faults of robots used in RoboCup. In X. Chen, P. Stone, L. E. Sucar, & T. van der Zant (Eds.), *RoboCup 2012: Robot soccer world cup XVI* (pp. 344–355). Berlin, Heidelberg: Springer.

Szafir, D., Mutlu, B., & Fong, T. (2015). Communicating directionality in flying robots. In *Proceedings of the tenth annual ACM/IEEE international conference on human-robot interaction* (pp. 19–26).

Yasuda, H., & Matsumoto, M. (2013). Psychological impact on human when a robot makes mistakes. In *IEEE/SICE international symposium on system integration (SII)* (pp. 335–339).

15

On neural-network training algorithms

Jonathan Barzilai

Dalhousie University, Halifax, NS, Canada

15.1 Introduction

Artificial neural network "training" is the problem of minimizing a large-scale nonconvex cost function. While optimization is a powerful tool, we note in this paper its theoretical and computational limitations: Establishing that an algorithm's convergence point satisfies optimality conditions is itself a difficult problem in the general case. There are no universal necessary and sufficient optimality conditions, and the minimum of a smooth function may be attained at the boundary of a feasible region where no optimality conditions may be satisfied. There are no efficient solutions for the general optimization problem of order 2, since some NP-complete problems are of this order. Constructing a superlinearly convergent algorithm for general quadratic function minimization (including the singular and ill-conditioned cases), or proving that such an algorithm does not exist, is a difficult challenge. For additional details see Chapter 1 in Bertsekas (1999).

We review the relevant issues in the one-dimensional case in Section 15.2 and the multidimensional case in Section 15.3. The implications of these issues for neural-network training are noted in Section 15.4. Throughout this discussion, we assume that the function $f(x)$ has continuous second-order derivatives where the real variable x is a scalar or a column vector and we denote by x^t the transpose of the vector x.

15.2 The one-dimensional case

Denoting by $\Re$ the set of real numbers, assume first that $f(x)$ is defined for all x in $\Re$. Then x is a local minimum of $f(x)$ if $f(x) \leq f(y)$ for all y in a neighborhood of x, and x is a global minimum of $f(x)$ if $f(x) \leq f(y)$ for all $y \in \Re$. For example, the function $f(x) = x^3 - x$ has a local minimum at $x = \sqrt{3}/3$ and a local maximum at $x = -\sqrt{3}/3$. This function has no global minimum or maximum since it is unbounded from above and below. Determining an x value at which

$f(x)$ has a (local) minimum is the problem of (one-dimensional, numerical) unconstrained minimization.

A necessary, but not sufficient, condition for x^* to be a minimum point of $f(x)$ is

$$\left.\frac{df}{dx}\right|_{x^*} = 0, \tag{15.1}$$

that is, the first derivative of $f(x)$ must be zero at x^*. If, in addition, the second derivative of $f(x)$ is positive at x^*:

$$\left.\frac{df}{dx}\right|_{x^*} = 0 \text{ and } \left.\frac{d^2}{dx^2}f(x)\right|_{x^*} > 0 \tag{15.2}$$

then x^* is a (local) minimum point of $f(x)$. If the second derivative is negative, x^* is a (local) maximum point of $f(x)$. If the second derivative is zero, x^* may be neither a minimum nor a maximum point which is the case for $f(x) = x^3$ at its inflection point $x = 0$.

A prototype of iterative algorithms for solving equations is Newton's method. Solving for $g(x^*) = 0$ and denoting the derivative of $g(x)$ at x_k by $g'(x_k) = \left.\dfrac{dg}{dx}\right|_{x_k}$, *under appropriate conditions,* starting with an initial estimate x_0, the formula

$$x_{k+1} = x_k - g'(x_k)^{-1} \cdot g(x_k), \text{ for } k = 0, 1, \ldots \tag{15.3}$$

generates a sequence x_k of estimates for the solution x^*. However, in general, this sequence may converge, diverge, or oscillate. Newton's method is also a prototype of unconstrained minimization algorithms, where we use $g'(x_k) = \frac{d}{dx}f(x)$ in Eq. (15.3) to minimize $f(x)$. Note that a zero of the first derivative of $f(x)$ may be a minimum point, a maximum point, or neither of these. While the minimization problem is closely related to the problem of solving equations, we will see below that these problems are not equivalent.

15.2.1 Convergence and rate of convergence

An effective iterative algorithm generates a sequence of estimates that converges to a solution and achieves this convergence in a small number of iterations. Using Newton's method as a prototype, we note the following: theorems that prove $x_k \to x^*$ for this algorithm assume that the iteration is well-defined (i.e., $g'(x_k) \neq 0$ so that $g'(x_k)^{-1}$ exists for all k), and that the initial estimate x_0 is sufficiently close to x^* (see Luenberger, 1973, Section 7.7). However, an algorithm's step may fail to be defined and, since x^* is unknown, it cannot be known in advance if x_0 is sufficiently close to x^*.

Newton's method converges quickly in the sense that if it does not fail and if x_0 is sufficiently close to x^*, the error sequence $e_k = |x_k - x^*|$ converges to zero, and, roughly speaking, when the error is close to zero and $e_k < 1$, the next error e_{k+1} is of the order of magnitude of the square of e_k. The *asymptotic* rate of convergence of Newton's method is then 2 and we say that this algorithm converges quadratically. It should be emphasized that away from the (unknown) solution, the error may behave differently. For formal definitions and a detailed analysis of convergence rates, see Barzilai and Dempster (1993).

15.2.2 Constrained minimization

Consider next the problem of one-dimensional constrained minimization where x^* is a minimum point of $f(x)$ in an interval $[a, b]$. While a minimum point in the interior of the interval must be a zero point of the derivative of $f(x)$, the minimum may be attained at the interval's boundary, that is, at the interval's end points, where the derivative of $f(x)$ may not be zero.

15.3 The n-dimensional case

In the n-dimensional case, $f(x)$ is a function of a vector x of n real variables. The first and second derivative are replaced with the gradient and the (symmetric) Hessian matrix:

$$g(x) = \nabla f(x) = \left[\frac{\partial}{\partial x_1} f(x), \frac{\partial}{\partial x_2} f(x), \ldots, \frac{\partial}{\partial x_n} f(x) \right]^t$$

and

$$H(x) = \nabla^2 f(x) = \left[\frac{\partial^2}{\partial x_i \partial x_j} f(x) \right].$$

The first-order necessary condition is $g(x^*) = 0$. A point that satisfies the first-order condition may be a minimum point of $f(x)$, a maximum point, or a saddle point—a point where $f(x)$ increases in some directions and decreases in other ones. The positivity of the second derivative is replaced with the requirement that all the eigenvalues of the matrix $H(x^*)$ are positive (the Hessian is positive definite).

We are interested in the class of algorithms of the form

$$x_{k+1} = x_k + \alpha_k d_k \tag{15.4}$$

where starting with an initial estimate vector x_0, at step k a search direction vector d_k, and then a scalar step size α_k are computed (see e.g., Wright & Nocedal, 1999, p. 35). The unmodified n-dimensional Newton's method is then

$$x_{k+1} = x_k - H^{-1}(x_k) \cdot g(x_k) \tag{15.5}$$

where $\{x_k\}$ is a sequence of vectors, the search direction is $d_k = -H^{-1}(x_k) \cdot g(x_k)$ and the step size is $\alpha_k = 1$ for all k. We note the following: (i) for large-scale problems computing the second-order derivatives and the Hessian's eigenvalues (its spectrum) are expensive operations, (ii) each iteration of Newton's method (15.5) requires the solution of the system of equations $d_k = -H^{-1}(x_k) \cdot g(x_k)$.

15.3.1 Convergence and rate of convergence

As in the one-dimensional case, the sequence generated by Newton's method may diverge or converge to minimum, maximum, or saddle points. Its asymptotic rate of convergence is again 2 with the error defined as $e_k = ||x_k - x^*||$ using the Euclidean vector norm $||a|| = \sqrt{\sum_{i=1}^n a_i^2}$.

The actual speed of convergence of the algorithm (15.5) depends on the rate of convergence of the intermediate algorithm for solving the linear equations $H(x_k)d_k = -g(x_k)$ for d_k when they are solved iteratively, which is necessarily the case for large-scale problems. However, all known iterative algorithms for solving systems of linear equations converge linearly, where linear rate of convergence means that the error e_{k+1} is of the order of magnitude of e_k. For example, the sequence defined by $e_{k+1} = 0.9e_k$ converges linearly. It follows that algorithm (15.5) converges linearly when the computational cost of solving its intermediate subproblem is not ignored. The speed of convergence of this subproblem depends on the system's condition number (the ratio of its largest to smallest eigenvalue) and may be very slow. For the same reason, all algorithms that require the solution of a system of linear equations at each iteration converge linearly. For example, the rate of convergence of *Rayleigh Quotient Iteration* for computing an eigenvalue/eigenvector pair is 3, but its actual rate of convergence is 1 (linear convergence) when its intermediate step of solving a linear system of equations is not ignored. For details see Barzilai (2018) and Golub and Loan (1983, pp. 308–309).

15.3.2 Solution of equations versus minimization

In the n-dimensional nonquadratic case, the necessary condition $\nabla f(x) = 0$ constitutes a system of nonlinear equations for the unknowns $x_1,...,x_n$. Reducing the minimization problem to this problem suggests that solving nonlinear equations is easier than solving minimization problems. However, according to the literature of solving nonlinear equations (see e.g., Ortega & Rheinboldt, 1970; Ostrowski, 1966), the only way to solve a system of m nonlinear equations for n unknowns when $m \neq n$ is to reduce it to minimizing the sum $\sum_{i=1}^{m} f_i^2(x)$ which, circularly, requires solving the nonlinear system of equations $\nabla \sum_{i=1}^{m} f_i^2(x) = 0$. Note that if x^* is a *global* minimizer of the sum $\sum_{i=1}^{m} f_i^2(x) = 0$, then $f_i(x^*) = 0$ for all i; but if x^* is not a global minimizer, $\sum_{i=1}^{m} f_i^2(x) > 0$ implies that $f_i(x^*) \neq 0$ for some equations and x^* is not a solution of the equations $f_i(x) = 0$ for all i.

Finally, since the information in the system of equations $\nabla f(x) = 0$ is limited to derivative values and does not include information on the values of the function $f(x)$, the minimization problem is not equivalent to the problem of solving these equations. In Barzilai and Ben-Tal (1982), we show that this is true even in the one-dimensional case.

15.3.3 Steepest descent and conjugate gradients

With the availability of computers, Forsythe and Motzkin (1951) proved that *asymptotically* for $n = 3$ the error $x_k - x^*$ in Cauchy's Steepest Descent algorithm (Cauchy, 1847) converges to a linear combination of the eigenvectors belonging to the largest and smallest eigenvalues of A^tA. A general analysis and proofs of the behavior of this algorithm in the quadratic minimization case are done by Akaike (1959) (for a simpler derivation, see Luenberger (1973, Section 7.6). In the case of minimizing the quadratic function $\frac{1}{2}x^tAx - x^tb + c$ (the simplest minimization problem), the rate is 1, that is, convergence is linear, and asymptotically

$$e_{k+1} \cong \left(\frac{\kappa-1}{\kappa+1}\right)^2 e_k$$

where κ is the condition number of the matrix A (the ratio of its largest to smallest eigenvalues). For example, the condition number of the matrix

$$\begin{bmatrix} 1 & 1 & 1 & 1 & 1 & 1 \\ 1 & 2 & 3 & 4 & 5 & 6 \\ 1 & 3 & 6 & 10 & 15 & 21 \\ 1 & 4 & 10 & 20 & 35 & 56 \\ 1 & 5 & 15 & 35 & 70 & 126 \\ 1 & 6 & 21 & 56 & 126 & 252 \end{bmatrix}$$

(see Golub & Loan, 1983, p.309) is 110,786, which yields $e_{k+1} \cong 0.9999639 e_k$. At this rate, it takes more than 60,000 steepest descent steps to increase the solution's precision by a single digit.

For the Steepest Descent algorithm, the search direction in Eq. (15.4) is the negative gradient $d_k = -\nabla f(x_k) = -g(x_k)$. In the quadratic case, the step size is given explicitly by the formula $\alpha_k = \frac{g(x_k)^t g(x_k)}{g(x_k)^t A g(x_k)}$ but in the nonquadratic case, the step size must be computed by a line search, that is, by a one-dimensional minimization with respect to α of $f(x_k - \alpha \nabla f(x_k))$. Our observations concerning one-dimensional minimization apply to this substep of the algorithm.

Note that although the step size for Newton's method (Eq. 15.5) is constant ($\alpha_k \equiv 1$), in practice this method also requires a line search. Luenberger's framework of global convergence of descent algorithms (Luenberger, 1973, Section 6.5) does not directly take the speed of convergence into account, and it tends to separate the analysis of step size and search direction properties. In Barzilai and Borwein (1988), we show that two methods with the same search direction $d_k = -\nabla f(x_k)$ but different step size behave differently. It follows that in general, and in particular in the case of the Steepest Descent algorithm, the behavior of minimization algorithms cannot be attributed to the choice of search direction only.

Hestenes and Stiefel's method of conjugate gradients (Hestenes & Stiefel, 1952) for quadratic minimization does not require the computation (and storage) of second-order derivatives and it terminates in n steps where n is the problem's size. However, the property of finite termination is irrelevant for large-scale problems. For such systems, this algorithm converges linearly with $e_{k+1} \cong 2 \left(\frac{\sqrt{\kappa} - 1}{\sqrt{\kappa} + 1} \right)^n e_0$. This algorithm may fail (through division by zero) even in the case of quadratic minimization, if the problem is rank deficient—which is typical of big-data problems. In the nonquadratic case, the search directions are in general not conjugate and the algorithm does not terminate in n steps.

15.3.4 Constrained minimization

Boundary and ill-conditioning issues make constrained minimization fundamentally different in the n-dimensional case. Ill-conditioning means that the problem's Hessian condition number is unfavorable at the solution. As in the Linear Programming case, the minimum may be attained at an exponential number of points on the problem's feasible region's boundary.

15.4 Implications for neural-network training

The accuracy of a neural network, that is, the percentage of cases where its output is correct, depends on the quality of its training set, its mathematical structure, and the choice of its minimization algorithm and its starting point. Since computing second-order derivatives of the cost function is expensive and their number is prohibitively large, algorithms that use second-order derivatives cannot be used for large training problems. As a result, the only possible training algorithms *in the literature* are the Steepest Descent or the Conjugate Gradients algorithms and, for the reasons noted above, the only remaining applicable training algorithm is the Steepest Descent method. This method requires a line search to determine a step size (how far to go in the [negative] gradient direction) and its generally poor performance is compounded by the use of fixed step sizes (which is dictated by the high cost of line searches for the training problem).

A new algorithm, Algorithm B67 by this author (see Barzilai, 2018), is stable, fast, and applicable on singular systems. As an example, minimizing the cost function

$$f(x) = (e^x - 1)^2 + (e^y - 2)^2 + (x - y)^2 \tag{15.6}$$

from the initial values $x_0 = 3$ and $y_0 = 4$, B67 converges in 17 steps to a minimum at $x^* = 0.242248978827288$ and $y^* = 0.591497407604927$. In comparison, the Steepest Descent algorithm with a fixed step size of 0.001 requires more than 100,000 steps to converge to this solution.

Note that the total computational effort depends on the effort *per step* and the *number of steps* needed. The effort *per step* for both algorithms does depend on the problem's size, but this effort is the same since both algorithms require the computation of the gradient of the cost function in each step. The *number of steps* depends on the algorithm's rate of convergence which is independent of the problem's size (the rate for Newton's method is 2 regardless of size; other algorithms depend on the problem's condition number which, again, is independent of size). For this reason, Algorithm B67's fast convergence results in orders of magnitude of savings in computational effort for the training problem *regardless of its size*. This also means that it is easy to construct very small neural networks of the simplest structure for which standard training algorithms take an exceedingly large number of steps to converge.

15.5 Summary

Regardless of which neural network model is employed, network training is a minimization problem. For this problem, there is no alternative *in the optimization literature* to the use of the Steepest Descent method with a fixed step-size, but a new, effective, algorithm is now available.

References

Akaike, H. (1959). On a successive transformation of probability distribution and its application to the analysis of the optimum gradient method. *Annals of the Institute of Statistical Mathematics, 11*(1), 1–16.

Barzilai, J. (2018). A spectrum algorithm and optimization notes. *Pure and Applied Functional Analysis, 3*(4), 533–536. A preview is posted at http://scientificmetrics.com/publications.html.

Barzilai, J., & Ben-Tal, A. (1982). Nonpolynomial and inverse interpolation for line search: Synthesis and convergence rates. *SIAM Journal on Numerical Analysis, 19*(6), 1263–1277.

Barzilai, J., & Borwein, J. M. (1988). Two-point step size gradient methods. *IMA Journal of Numerical Analysis, 8*(1), 141–148.

Barzilai, J., & Dempster, M. A. H. (1993). Measuring rates of convergence of numerical algorithms. *Journal of Optimization Theory and Applications, 78*(1), 109–125.

Bertsekas, D. P. (1999). *Nonlinear programming*. Athena Scientific.

Cauchy, A. (1847). Méthode générale pour la résolution des systèmes d'équations simultanées. *Comptes Rendus de l'Acadmie des Sciences, 25*(1847), 536–538.

Forsythe, G. E., & Motzkin, T. S. (1951). Asymptotic properties of the optimum gradient method. *Bulletin of the American Mathematical Society, 57*(3), 183.

Golub, G. H. & Loan, C. F. V. (1983). *Matrix computations*. Johns Hopkins.

Hestenes, M. R., & Stiefel, E. (1952). Methods of conjugate gradients for solving linear systems. *Journal of Research of the National Bureau of Standards, Section B, 49*(6), 409–436.

Luenberger, D. G. (1973). *Introduction to linear and nonlinear programming*. Addison-Wesley.

Ortega, J. M., & Rheinboldt, W. C. (1970). *Iterative solution of nonlinear equations in several variables*. Academic Press.

Ostrowski, A. M. (1966). *Solution of equations and systems of equations* (2nd ed.). Academic Press.

Wright, S., & Nocedal, J. (1999). *Numerical optimization*. Springer.

Identifying distributed incompetence in an organization

Boris Galitsky

Oracle Corporation, Redwood City, CA, United States

16.1 Introduction

In the corpus of research on multiagent systems, distributed knowledge is all the knowledge that a team of agents possesses and leverages in solving a problem. Distributed knowledge (Fagin, Halpern, Moses, & Vardi, 1995) is concerned with what a rational human reasoner knows about what each member of a team knows. Distributed knowledge includes all the knowledge that a community might bring to bear to solve a problem. Distributed knowledge and the wisdom of the crowd demonstrated its superiority over problem-solving of individual agents in a number of domains. In this study, we are interested in the opposite phenomenon that can be observed in some organizations.

In a domain such as customer support, when a customer interacts with multiple human agents, he can be negatively impressed that a team of agents solves his problem in an inferior manner in comparison with how an individual agent would. In a case like this, when a given agent *A* refers to another agent *B* for help with a given problem, *B* further refers to *C* and so forth, and yet the problem is still not solved, distributed intuition becomes a noisy, inconsistent, intractable alteration of the sum of the individual knowledge of *A*, *B*, and *C*. We refer to such deteriorated knowledge as *distributed incompetence* (DI).

In a DI environment, agents have limited authorities over solving problems and limited knowledge about the same of other agents. Passing a customer problem from one agent (who is a rational reasoner within the business domain) to another, a joint multiagent system sometimes stops being a rational reasoner. In some cases, organizations such as insurance companies leverage DI as a means to retain income, trying to make customers give up on their existing claims. Some businesses rely on DI to avoid compensating customers for faulty products and services, in effect reversing transactions. In other cases the upper management of an organization is not in a position to deny compensation, but the DI is a result of a lack of proper

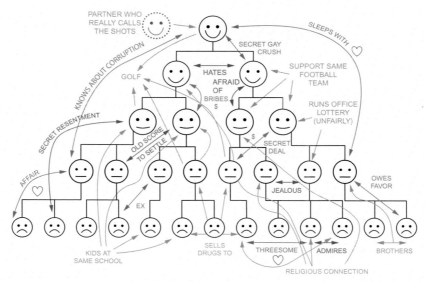

FIG. 16.1 Employees in a customer support organization have all kinds of relations that distract them from acting in the best interests of their company and customers.

management. In many cases, customer support agents (CSAs) are not directly motivated to solve customer problems, but instead, their performance is measured by an abstract user satisfaction score. Frequently, CSAs are either not uniformly motivated to perform their functions or not motivated at all (Fig. 16.1; Integration Training, 2018).

Here is an example of how an external observer describes DI behavior with the terms of how a CSA describes his mission: "The only thing I am authorized to do is to tell you that I am not authorized to do anything."

It has been discovered that a lot of forms of human intellectual and communication activity such as management styles are associated with certain discourse structures of how these activities are described in text. Rhetorical structure theory (RST; in Mann & Thompson, 1987) is a good means to express the correlation between such form of activity and its representation in how associated thoughts are organized in a text. Rhetoric structure theory presents a hierarchical, connected structure of a text as a discourse tree (DT), with rhetorical relations between the parts of it. The smallest text spans are called elementary discourse units (EDUs).

In communicative discourse trees (CDTs), the labels for communicative actions (VerbNet expressions for verbs) are added to the discourse tree edges to show which speech acts are attached to which rhetoric relations. In DI, activity such as *persuasion* is very important in convincing a customer that banks are forced to demand insufficient fund fees to maintain profitability. RST, in particular, helps to understand this form of persuasion as argumentation (Galitsky, Ilvovsky, & Pisarevskaya, 2018).

Logical argumentation needs a certain combination of rhetorical relations of *elaboration*, *contrast*, *cause*, and *attribution* to be sound. Persuasiveness relies on certain structures linking *elaboration*, *attribution*, and *condition* (Berzlánovich, Egg, & Redeker, 2008). Explanation needs to rely on certain chains of *elaboration* relations plus *explanation* and *cause*, and a rhetorical agreement between a question and an answer is based on specific mappings between the rhetorical relations of *contrast, cause, attribution,* and *condition* between the former and the latter (Galitsky, 2019; Galitsky & Parnis, 2019). DTs turned out to be helpful to form a dialogue and to build dialogue from text, to better understand the structure of texts.

In this chapter, we study rhetoric structures correlated with certain forms of verbal activity such as DI as expressed in customer complaints. We intend to discover the distinct features of discourse trees associated with DI. Some of such features can be observed as a result of manual analysis, but most of these features are concealed and need to be tackled by a data-driven approach, so we adjust our customer complaints dataset tagged to detect DI.

16.2 Defining DI

Logically, DI can be inferred when a CSA demonstrates his intention to be other than the well-being of a customer and his company at the same time. Since there is frequently a conflict of interest between a company and a customer, we cannot expect a CSA to always act in the best interests of the customer. However, if a company's interests are not satisfied either, one can conclude that DI is taking place.

When a customer describes her encounter with an individual CSA, she is frequently dissatisfied even when her perception of her opponent is reasonable. However, what makes complainants appalled is an inconsistency between what different CSAs tell them about the same thing. For example, what frequently happens is that one CSA explains the client that his insufficient fund fee (NSF) is due to a too-early withdrawal transaction, whereas another CSA is saying that the deposit transaction has not gone through. This situation puts both client and company at disadvantage that is clearly indicative of a DI. Moreover, when a customer describes this kind of misinformation, it can be trusted in most cases since a customer would need to be too "inventive" to compose a description with this form of inconsistency (it is much easier for a dissatisfied customer to misrepresent an encounter with a single agent [Galitsky, González, & Chesñevar, 2009; Pisarevskaya, Galitsky, Taylor, & Ozerov, 2019]).

Hence a DI can also be defined as a conflict between parties so that these parties behave irrationally by not acting in their best interest as perceived by an impartial judge reading a description of this conflict. In part a case here is a claimed conflict of interest when there is contradiction between the intents of the agents involved. Another case is where a conflict of interest is present but is not attempted to be resolved reasonably.

The problem of a DI is associated with the observed invalid argumentation patterns used by the parties of a conflict. In some cases, if arguments of only one party are faulty, it does not necessarily mean a DI; however, if such an argumentation is systematic, it is natural to conclude that a DI is occurring. The systematic improper use of explainability indicates a DI as well.

Some problems of a DI are associated with a limit on time set by one agent involved in its communication. For example, in the health care industry, doctors commonly interrupt patients explaining their problems in 11 s on average (Singh et al., 2018). Having these reduced descriptions of a problem, it is hard to make a competent decision; therefore certain irrational reasoning patterns can be included, in particular, when referring to other specialist doctors.

A DI is defined in an annotation framework as a decision by a human expert that a CSA has acted irrationally, contradicted another agent, demonstrated a lack of commonsense knowledge, or exhibited a substantial lack of knowledge about company rules or industry regulations. An organization with DI is irrational to an external observer but may well be rational from the expected utility standpoint of an organization's CSA agents who minimize the compensation a user might achieve communicating with such organization.

DI is a key reason customer complaints arise. People usually do not submit formal complaints because of their dissatisfaction with a product or service. To get to the point of a complaint's submission, users usually have to be either handled badly by multiple CSAs or to encounter a DI.

16.3 Observing organizations with DI

16.3.1 DI and management

In his recent research note Grudin (2016) formulates the incompetence problem directly: "How could incompetence be on the rise when knowledge and tools proliferate?" The author cites the Peter Principle (Peter & Hull, 1968) that explains why organizations keep incompetent managers and how they avoid serious harm (Fig. 16.2). Grudin (2016) explores whether managerial incompetence is escalating, despite the greater capability of those who are competent—those, in words of (Peter & Hull, 1968), who have not yet reached their levels of incompetence. The conclusion is that managerial incompetence is accelerating, aided by technology and the weak social changes that strive to level the playing field of competition between employees in an organization. The counterforces rely on weakened hierarchy, but hierarchy remains strong enough to trigger self-preservation maneuvers at the expense of competence.

FIG. 16.2 Illustration for the Peter' principle (Biswa, 2015).

In a DI organization the higher the level of management, the less skillful and capable the respective manager has to be. To be a manager in a DI team, to operate it smoothly, a manager needs to possess a genuine incompetence and a lack of skills. To adequately control and guide lower-rank managers with limited skills and capabilities to produce results, an upper-level manager needs to possess even less skills. If an energetic, highly skilled and result-oriented manager finds herself leading a team of personnel operating in a DI mode, she would not fit in such a team. In a DI team, those members who are doers would be left alone, and those who are not good at doing but who are well in playing politics would be promoted to a managerial position to retain smooth DI operations. Hence, in a DI organization, people with lower delivering capabilities but better communication skills tend to occupy management positions, increasing the stability of DI. Notice that in our model, individual managers are not necessarily incompetent: instead, they lead the whole organization to the distributed incompetence state, possibly achieving their individual managerial goals.

When a company such as Barclays bank (who employed the author of this study) is being sued for a fraud (FCA, 2015), usually due to upper management activities, substantial efforts are often put into training all company employees related to honest business conduct. Most employees are becoming scapegoats blamed for the activities of the upper management, although they would not be authorized to commit a fraud in the first place. Once the same company is charged with another fraud, the training materials for all employees are repeated respectfully, as if the regular employees were also responsible for this new fraud. This form of employee training to prevent a crime these employees would not be authorized to commit anyway is another symptom of a DI and its associated blame games.

16.3.2 DI and whistleblowing

DI is associated with a lack of a number of whistleblowers in an organization. A whistleblower is an agent who exposes any kind of information or activity that is deemed inappropriate, illegal, unethical, or not correct within an organization. The information on alleged wrongdoing can be classified in many ways: violation of company policy/rules, law, and regulation; threat to public interest/national security; fraud; and corruption. Those who become whistleblowers can choose to expose information or allegations to the public either internally or externally. Internally a whistleblower can bring his/her accusations to the attention of other people within the accused organization such as an immediate supervisor. Externally a whistleblower contacts a third party such as a government agency or law enforcement. Whistleblowers, however, take the risk of facing strong reprisal and retaliation from the company being exposed. Once the number of whistleblowers is sufficient or their allegations are supported, the organization can reduce its DI by internal means. Frequently an employee must make a choice to either become a whistleblower, be a quiet opponent of the harmful operations of an organization, or evolve into DI with an organization.

A number of laws exist to protect whistleblowers. Some third-party groups even offer protection to whistleblowers, but that protection can only go so far. Whistleblowers face legal action or even criminal charges, social stigma, and termination from their position or role.

Two other classifications of whistleblowing are private and public. The classifications relate to the type of organizations someone chooses to whistleblow on private sector or public sector. Depending on many factors, both can have varying results. However, whistleblowing in the public sector organization is more likely to result in criminal charges and possible custodial sentences. A whistleblower who chooses to accuse a private sector organization or agency is more likely to face termination, legal and civil charges. In 2010 the Dodd-Frank Wall Street Reform and Consumer Protection Act was enacted in the United States following the crisis to promote the financial stability of the United States and protect whistleblowers (Obama, 2010).

16.3.3 Financial crisis of 2007 and DI

In 2014 the US Justice Department (DOJ) and the banks such as the Bank of America settled several of the DOJ civil investigations related to the packaging, marketing, sale, arrangement, structuring and issuance of residential mortgage-backed securities (RMBS), collateralized debt obligations (CDOs), and the banks' practices concerning the underwriting and origination of mortgage loans. The settlement included a statement of facts, in which the bank acknowledged that it had sold billions of dollars of RMBS without disclosing to investors key facts about the quality and nature of the securitized loans. When the RMBS collapsed, investors, including federally insured financial institutions, had billions of dollars in losses. The bank has also confirmed that it originated risky mortgage loans and made misrepresentations about the quality of those loans to Fannie Mae, Freddie Mac, and the Federal Housing Administration (FHA).

Obviously, each individual financial advisor understood the necessity to disclose the quality of securitized loans to clients. However, such disclosure would jeopardize his career and make selling such shadow financial products more difficult. The most natural way for a bank agent to communicate his attitude is to pretend that she does not understand the problems with financial products she is selling and also pretend that she does not understand that her peers understand the problem with financial products and also pretend that she does not understand this pretense of others. Hence, this form of DI is associated with fairly complex mental states of agents:

```
pretend(agent, not know (agent, problem(fin_product)))
pretend(agent, not understand(agent, know (peer-agent,
problem(fin_product))))
pretend(agent, not understand(agent, pretend(peer-agent, not
know (peer-agent, problem(fin_product)))))
```
We give a definition of pretend
```
pretend (Agent, Pretense): - inform (Agent, Peer-agent, Pretense) &
believe(Agent, not Pretense)) & know (Peer-agent, not believe
(Agent, Pretense)).
```

We go further defining *Coming to believe* using FrameNet (Ruppenhofer et al., 2016). The whole spectrum of finance professionals was hiding behind the curtains of DI, from bank

A person (the Cognizer) comes to believe something (the Content), sometimes after a process of reasoning. This change in belief is usually initiated by a person or piece of Evidence. Occasionally words in this domain are accompanied by phrases expressing Topic, i.e. that which the mental Content is about.
Based on the most recent census I have CONCLUDED that most Americans sleep too much.

Cognizer **Semantic Type:** Sentient	[Cog]	Cognizer is the person who comes to believe something. Sue REALIZED that Bob was lost.
Content **Semantic Type:** Content	[Cont]	With a target verb, the Content is usually expressed as a finite clausal Complement or an Object NP, and may sometimes be expressed by a PP: The President LEARNED that the reporters were hungry. The children DETERMINED the answer.
Evidence [Evid]		Words in this frame may occur with a PP headed by from which expresses the Evidence on which knowledge or belief is based: I have LEARNED from experience that poison oak can be painful.
Means **Semantic Type:** State_of_affairs	[Mns]	An act performed by the Cognizer which enables them to figure something out. A post-mortem examination was unable to ASCERTAIN the cause of death.
Medium [med]		Medium is the text created by the Cognizer to communicate that they came to believe a specified Content.
Topic [Top]		Some verbs in this frame may occur with postverbal Topic expressions: They FOUND OUT about us! More generally verbs in this frame may occur with quantificational nouns followed by Topic expressions: The jury LEARNED something terrible about the suspect.

clerks to university finance professors, to avoid being perceived as nonprofessional. Financial crisis demonstrated how an organization can evolve from being a regular one where recommendations of their financial advisors were reasonable and made sense, to a DI where those advisors pretended they did not understand how risky and meaningless their recommendations were. Not necessarily all advisors understood the problems with their investment recommendations; some might have genuinely believed that they were in the best interest of their clients. For a given bank employee, most of their managers and peers were confirming that their recommendations were valid, complying with bank policies (and maintaining the DI). A DI for an organization is stabilized if no employee wants to stand and blow whistle on higher management.

Bank of America provided $7 billion in the form of relief to aid hundreds of thousands of consumers harmed by the financial crisis precipitated by the unlawful conduct not only of Bank of America, Merrill Lynch, and Countrywide. That relief took various forms, including principal loan reduction modifications that helped many borrowers no longer being underwater on their mortgages and finally having substantial equity in their homes. It also included new loans to creditworthy borrowers experiencing difficulties to get a loan, donations to assist communities in recovering from the financial crisis, and financing for affordable rental housing. Finally, Bank of America has agreed to place over $490 million in a tax relief fund to be used to help defray some of the tax liability incurred by consumers receiving certain types of relief.

Merrill Lynch made misrepresentations to investors in 72 residential mortgage-backed securities throughout 2006 and 2007. Merrill Lynch's employees regularly told investors that the loans it was securitizing were made to borrowers who were likely and able to repay their debts. Merrill Lynch made these representations even though most of its advisors knew, based on the due diligence they had performed on samples of the loans, that a significant number of those loans had material underwriting and compliance defects—including as many as 55% in a single pool. In addition, Merrill Lynch rarely reviewed the loans with limited performance data to ensure that the defects observed in the samples were not present throughout the remainder of the pools. Merrill Lynch also disregarded its own due diligence and securitized loans that the due diligence vendors had identified as defective. This DI practice led one Merrill Lynch consultant to question the purpose of performing due diligence if Merrill Lynch was going to securitize the loans anyway, regardless of the issues that might be identified.

Before the financial crisis, John C. Bogle, founder and chief executive of The Vanguard Group, wrote that a series of challenges facing capitalism that have contributed to past financial crises and have not been sufficiently addressed. He associates the problems of Corporate America with the power of managers who went virtually unchecked by their peers and regulators for a long time. In terms of the current study, as DI penetrated into the management structure of major corporations, the following issues arose, as outlined by Bogle:

- "Manager's capitalism" has replaced "owner's capitalism," meaning a management runs the firm for its benefit rather than for the shareholders, a variation on the principal-agent problem.
- Burgeoning executive compensation.
- The management of earnings focused mainly on share price rather than the creation of genuine value.
- The failure of gatekeepers, including auditors, boards of directors, Wall Street analysts, and career politicians.

The terms to describe the activity of agents responsible for the financial crisis are expressive for articulating DI:

- widespread failure in regulation and supervision;
- dramatic failures of corporate governance and risk management at many systemically important institutions;
- a lack of transparency by service providers, ill preparation, and inconsistent action by higher-level management and decision-making (such as government) that contribute to the uncertainty and panic; and
- a systemic breakdown in accountability and ethics of the agents involved.

Hence an organization with DI sooner or later leads to one or another form of crisis.

A conglomerate of financial organizations, rating agencies, and the government each with its own form of a DI at scale resulted in a crisis so strong that it affected most world economies. A DI in smaller individual organizations such as a company, hospital, or small country usually results in smaller-scale crises that affect a limited number of people. A crisis can also be caused by an organization that is not necessarily in the state of a DI but instead is run by management with a criminal intent but where only a minority of the agents involved are corrupt [such as ENRON Corporation (2001) and the Theranos Corporation (2018)].

Financial crises are not over; a number of authors believe that central banks may be unable to fight future financial bubbles fully given human nature, but at least, they should refrain from boosting these bubbles, in the name of supporting the real economy (Nageswaran, 2014). The author considers the exaggerated oil prices and the cost of shale oil production, profitable when oil prices are about $40 per barrel. He reasons that if the majority of shale oil production in the United States remained viable at around $40 per barrel, then there is still a long way to go before shale oil would cease to be a source of competitive price or existential threat to OPEC oil producers. From this situation the author cites *systemic irrationality* and concludes that what is going on in the oil industry is not a business competition between OPEC and US shale oil producers, but instead is a political, proxy battle where some of the producers in OPEC are acting on behalf of the United States against Russia, under certain conditions of interest to some of these OPEC players.

A DI should be differentiated from the individual incompetence of managers and from criminal intent of managers, which have different mechanisms driving irrational decisions. A DI should also be differentiated from totalitarian regimes, which may or may not be incompetent.

16.3.4 DI and competitive rating

One of the key causes of the financial crisis of 2007 was the lack of competence in credit rating agencies, as has been suggested by multiple authors (Federal Reserve, 2010). The Financial Crisis Inquiry Commission concluded that the financial crisis was avoidable and was caused by "the failures of credit rating agencies" to correctly rate risk.

In academics, there is a long history on the assessment of the quality of an academic study and its contribution based on formal, numerical parameters. A good, objective rating of an academic work is its applicability in practice and deployment in real-world applications. Since this rating is not always applicable to a research work, numerical measures such as citation index is applied. Once the authors target this measure directly, the quality of a work decreases dramatically and can lead to a DI. As publication venues become more competitive, even a higher percentage of authors attempt to directly acquire such rating and the quality and applicability to practice of such research products abruptly drops. In venues where extremely high competitiveness exists, the quality of peer reviews is fairly low as reviewers run out of arguments to perform a fair assessment of a contribution. This failure is another demonstration of how a higher competitiveness leads to a DI. According to the author of the current study, this can be observed in such academic fields as Computational Linguistics and AI.

Galitsky and Levene (2005) simulated the process of possible interactions between a set of competitive services and a set of portals that provide an online rating for these services. The authors claimed that to have a profitable business, these portals are forced to have subscribed services that are rated by the portals. To satisfy the subscribing services, the study relied on an assumption that the portals improve the rating of a given service by one unit per transaction that involves payment. The authors followed the "what-if" methodology, analyzing the strategies that a service may choose to select the best portal for it to subscribe to and strategies for a portal to accept the subscription such that its reputation loss, in terms of the integrity of its ratings, is minimized. The behavior of the simulated agents in accordance with this model turned out to be quite natural from a real-world perspective (Akhremenkov & Galitsky, 2007). One conclusion from these simulations is that under reasonable assumptions, if most of the services and rating portals in a given industry do not accept a subscription policy similar to the one indicated in the preceding text, they will lose, respectively, their ratings and reputations, and, moreover, the rating portals would have problems in making a profit. The prediction made in this study turned out to be plausible for the financial crisis of 2007: the modern portal rating–based economy sector evolved into a subscription process similar to the one suggested in this study, as an alternative to a business model based purely on advertising. Financial rating services contributed substantially to weakening economy for the financial crisis, knowingly providing positive ratings for derivatives that should have been rated poorly.

16.3.5 DI and other forms of irrationality

A DI is a specific form of irrational behavior. The behavioral challenge for how agents make rational or irrational choices is associated with an individual's decision-making. Behavioral irrationality does not necessarily mean or leads to chaos: DI is a good example of it. Most irrational behavior occurs in the course of a reasoning session, where decision-makers do not behave with full knowledge and/or optimal computational power in pursuit of maximizing expected utility. In a DI the behavior of agents is possibly rational for their personal expected utility but definitely irrational for the expected utility of an external user or observer. Yang and Lester (2008) critique the rationality paradigm for judgments and preferences and for exploring the impact of culture on people's economic behavior. Moreover the authors draw attention of researchers to the phenomenon of *systemic irrationality*. Irrationality may exist at the aggregate or societal level, a conclusion based on the observation that large segments of the population are incapable of making decisions in accord with traditional rationality—groups such as those who have a psychiatric disorder, those who are taking medications, those with limited intelligence, those from the lower social classes, children and adolescents, and the elderly. Even those who are not included in these groups, but who take medications for medical conditions, may have their decision-making impaired to some extent. Therefore it is argued that rationality in economic decision-making is more frequently an exception rather than the norm.

Unlike other forms of irrationality, behavior of DI agents is explainable and rational. Conversely, cognitive scientists have known for decades that most humans are inherently irrational. Ariely (2008) introduces a notion *Predictable Irrationality*. The author says that most humans want explanations for why they behave in a certain way and attempt to connect it with how the external world reacts to what they do. Sometimes such "explanations" are not logically valid and are detached from reality. Human irrationality is associated with how humans tell themselves story after story until they come up with a satisfactory explanation that sounds reasonable enough to believe. People also like when such a story that includes favorable explanations portrays them in a positive light. This story mechanism is

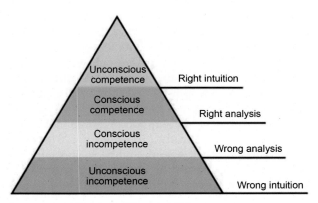

FIG. 16.3   Hierarchy of competence (Curtiss & Warren, 1973).

applicable to DI agents as well: they may believe that they are playing a positive role, having invented a reasonable explanation.

A rational person's behavior is usually guided more by conscious reasoning than by experience and not adversely affected by emotion. An average human is filled with systematic mistakes known to psychologists as *cognitive biases*. These mistakes affect most human decision-making. Cognitive bias makes people spend impulsively, be overly influenced by what other people think, and affects people's beliefs and opinions.

Irrational incompetence can also be considered from the standpoint of an unconscious. An *unconsciously incompetent* person is someone who does not recognize they are doing something wrong and hence go on doing it. For them to unleash their full potential, they must first admit to this incompetence and begin seeing the advantages of acquiring new skills. An employer can play an important role in adding this skill or competency (Fig. 16.3).

A DI is an irrationality of a totally different nature. When agents deviate from normal, rational behavior under the orders of their managers, they are fully aware of what they are doing. They know what they need to know and what they need to believe to perform their duties collectively to satisfy their DI goals. Customer support agents in DI *pretend* they behave in an irrational way, so that an observer of a DI team believes so, but they do not possess the features of irrationality described in the preceding text.

Shuldiner (2019) writes that as we use AI programs more and more, in our attempts to better understand and to manage our private and public affairs, we are injecting more and more opacity into our lives. An average user of a digital camera may not care to know the peculiarities of its operation. In general, for users, AI is proving too difficult to fully understand. So human and machine agents can focus their energy either on operating AI systems or on understanding the underlying technology, but not both at the same time. By embedding AI into the Internet of Things, particularly the intelligent infrastructure that will make up Internet of Things, humans and their technologists are creating a global operating system that is in a large sense opaque. In this chapter, we go further and explain how such a system can evolve into an incompetent one. Various kinds of errors humans make once they form teams are explored in Lawless and Sofge (2016), Mittu, Taylor, Sofge, and Lawless (2016), Moskowitz and Lawless (2016), and Galitsky and Parnis (2017).

Although maintaining privacy is important for consumers, a lot of companies and government organizations use privacy as their excuse for a DI. In healthcare, privacy—related legislation shifts the focus from a customer with medical problems to privacy-related concerns brought upon this customer. It increases the amount of paperwork a customer needs to compete and distracts his attention from the quality of health services being provided.

As customers are distracted from a health-related focus, a healthcare provider can significantly increase profitability and efficiency of its business at the expense of customer well-being. Specialist doctors only spend 11s on average listening to patients before interrupting them, according to a new study (Singh et al., 2018). In primary care visits, 49% of patients were able to explain their agenda, while in specialty visits, only 20% of patients were allowed to explain their reason for visiting. For specialty care visits, however, 8 out of 10 patients were interrupted even if they were allowed to share their agenda.

16.3.6 Aggressive DI

A DI in its extreme form is associated with lies and deceits. When a team wants badly to achieve a goal, it can significantly deviate from rationality by pretending and lying they are not who they actually are to exaggerate their achievement and impress a potential investor. In most cases, what they do lacks domain competence, but they aggressively try to convince the external world in the opposite. We refer to this phenomenon as an *aggressive DI*.

There have always been spectacular stories of lies and deceit in areas in the world where capitalism flourishes, such as Silicon Valley in the United States. There are tales that go on for decades of founders telling partial truths about how their companies were founded and which products were developed; in these cases, CEOs are exaggerating the features of their products to fool the press or to obtain new funding. Some CEOs make false statements about the number of users on their platforms (such as Twitter); some lie to Congress concerning the privacy of their clients, confirming they have complete control over their personal data (Facebook). However, these misrepresentations are nothing compared with the audacious lies of Elizabeth Holmes, the founder and CEO of Theranos (Bilton, 2018).

Starting in the autumn of 2015, the author became interested in the controversy about Theranos, the healthcare company that hoped to make a revolution in blood tests. Some sources, including the *Wall Street Journal*, started claiming that the company's conduct was fraudulent. The claims were made based on the whistleblowing of employees who left Theranos. At some point, FDA got involved, and while the case developed, we were improving our argumentation mining and reasoning techniques (Galitsky et al., 2018; Galitsky, Ilvovsky, & Kuznetsov, 2016) while keeping an eye on Theranos' story. As we scraped discussions about Theranos back in 2016 from the website, the audience believed that the case was initiated by Theranos' competitors who felt jealous about the proposed efficiency of the blood test technique promised by Theranos. However, our argumentation analysis technique showed that Theranos' argumentation patterns were faulty and our findings supported the criminal case against Theranos, which led to its massive fraud verdict. SEC (2018) says that Theranos CEO Elizabeth Holmes raised more than $700 million from investors "through an elaborate, year-long fraud" in which she exaggerated or made false statements about the company's technology and finances.

We build a discourse representation of the arguments and observe if a discourse tree is capable of indicating whether a paragraph communicates both a claim and an argumentation that backs it up. We will then explore what needs to be added to a discourse tree (DT) so that it is possible to judge if it expresses an argumentation pattern or not. Discourse tree is a means to express how author's thoughts are organized in text. Its nonterminal nodes are binary rhetorical relations such as elaboration connecting terminal nodes associated with text fragments (called discourse units).

This is what happened according to (Carreyrou, 2018):

> Since October [2015], the Wall Street Journal has published a series of anonymously sourced accusations that inaccurately portray Theranos. Now, in its latest story ("U.S. Probes Theranos Complaints," Dec. 20), the Journal once again is relying on anonymous sources, this time reporting two undisclosed and unconfirmed complaints that allegedly were filed with the Centers for Medicare and Medicaid Services (CMS) and U.S. Food and Drug Administration (FDA).

Fig. 16.4 shows the communicative discourse tree (CDT) for the following paragraph:

> But Theranos has struggled behind the scenes to turn the excitement over its technology into reality. At the end of 2014, the lab instrument developed as the linchpin of its strategy handled just a small fraction of the tests then sold to consumers, according to four former employees.

Please notice the labels for communicative actions are attached to the edges of discourse trees (on the left and in the middle bottom).

In the following paragraph, Theranos attempts to rebuke the claim of WSJ, but without communicative actions, it remains unclear from its DT (see Fig. 16.5):

> Theranos remains actively engaged with its regulators, including CMS and the FDA, and no one, including the Wall Street Journal, has provided Theranos a copy of the alleged complaints to those agencies. Because Theranos has not seen these alleged complaints, it has no basis on which to evaluate the purported complaints.

We proceed to a CDT that is an attempt by Theranos to get itself off the hook (Fig. 16.6):

> It is not unusual for disgruntled and terminated employees in the heavily regulated health care industry to file complaints in an effort to retaliate against employers for termination of employment. Regulatory agencies have a process for evaluating complaints, many of which are not substantiated. Theranos trusts its regulators to properly investigate any complaints.

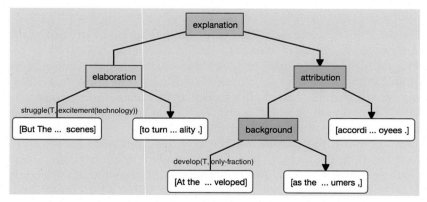

FIG. 16.4   When arbitrary communicative actions are attached to a DT as labels of its terminal arcs, it becomes clear that the author is trying to persuade by bring her point across and not merely sharing a fact.

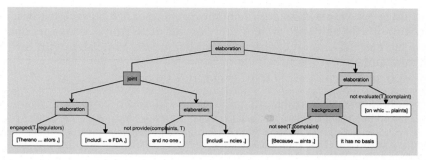

FIG. 16.5 Just from a DT and multiple rhetoric relations of elaboration and a single instance of background, it is unclear whether an author argues with his opponents or enumerates on a list of observations. Relying on communicative actions such as "engage" or "not see," the CDT can express the fact that the author is actually arguing with his opponents. This argumentation CDT is an attempt to make an even stronger rebuff.

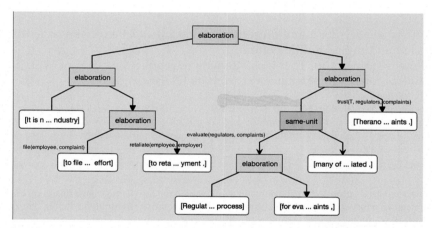

FIG. 16.6 Speech acts as labels for rhetoric relations help to identify a text apart from a heated discussion.

To show the structure of arguments, discourse relations are necessary but insufficient, and speech acts are necessary but insufficient as well (Galitsky et al., 2018).

For this paragraph, we need to know the discourse structure of interactions between agents and what kinds of interactions they are. We need to differentiate between a *neutral default relation of elaboration* (which does not include a speech act) and elaboration relation that includes a speech act with a sentiment such as *not provide(…)* that is correlated with an argument.

We do not need to know the domain of interaction (here, health), the subjects of these interactions (the company, the journal, and the agencies), and what are the entities, but we need to take into account the mental, domain-independent relations among them.

Theranos uses speech acts to show that its opponents' argumentations are faulty. Now, we use the labels for speech acts to show which one are attached to which rhetoric relations (Fig. 16.7; Galitsky, 2019):

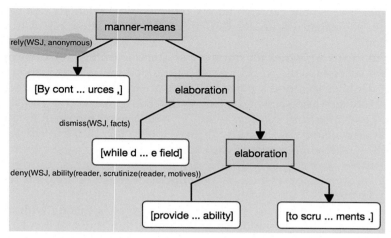

FIG. 16.7 Theranos is arguing that opponent's arguments are faulty.

By continually relying on mostly anonymous sources, while dismissing concrete facts, documents, and expert scientists and engineers in the field provided by Theranos, the Journal denies its readers the ability to scrutinize and weigh the sources' identities, motives, and the veracity of their statements.

From the commonsense reasoning standpoint, Theranos, the company, has two choices to confirm the argument that *his tests are valid*:

(1) Conduct an independent investigation, comparing its results with its peers, opening the data to the public, or confirming that their analysis results are correct.
(2) Defeat the argument by its opponent that their testing results are invalid and providing support for the claim that their opponent is wrong.

Obviously the former argument is much stronger, and we now know that usually the latter argument is chosen when the agent believes that the former argument is too difficult to implement. On one hand the reader might agree with Theranos that *Wall Street Journal* should have provided more evidence for its accusations against the company. On the other hand the reader perhaps disliked the fact that Theranos selects the latter type of argument (2) in the preceding text and therefore the company position is weak.

The authors believe that Theranos' argument is not sound because the company tries to refute the opponent's allegation concerning the complaints about Theranos' services from clients. We believe that Theranos' demand for evidence by inviting the journal to disclose its sources and the nature of its complaints is weak. We claim that a third party (independent investigative agent) would be more reasonable and conclusive. However, some readers might believe that the company's argument (a burden of proof evasion) is logical and valid.

It is hard to verify the validity of argumentation relying on a CDT only (Galitsky et al., 2018). Argumentation analysis should account not only for the information conveyed by the clausal components of the DT (i.e., RST's subject matter) but also for what is inferred, namely, the WSJ writer's intention to motivate the reader to cast doubt at the opponent's accusation of Theranos by inviting him to scrutinize the "proofs" provided.

An argumentation assessment cannot identify the rhetorical relations in a text by relying on the text only; she must essentially rely on context of a situation to fully grasp the arguer's intention.

We proceed to the background for the story of Theranos' CEO, the dedicated Stanford dropout who was set to save the world by making a blood test relying just on a pinprick of blood at a time. Holmes founded a blood testing start-up that was once valued at $6 billion. For years, Holmes was on top of the tech world, being featured at *The New York Times Style Magazine, Forbes, Fortune, Glamour,* and *The New Yorker* and *Inc.,* always wearing a black turtleneck and being associated with Steve Jobs. But as *The Wall Street Journal's* Carreyrou (2018) wrote, almost every word spoken by Holmes as she built and ran her company was either grossly embellished or, in most instances, outright deceptive. Theranos was a DI organization where its incompetence relied on total misrepresentation on all company levels.

As Carreyrou writes the company she built was a web of lies along with threats to employees who discovered these lies and wanted to figure things out. When Holmes tried to impress Walgreens, she created completely false test results from their blood tests. When it was discovered by the Theranos chief financial officer, he was fired right away.

No whistleblowing protections helped any of Theranos employees. The full extent of the whistleblowing is unknown as a number of those involved have remained anonymous; two of youngest among them tried to raise their concerns internally, but they faced bullying in response. They worked in the same lab at Theranos and when they started comparing notes, they realized they were dealing with a conspiracy of lies perpetrated at the highest levels within the organization wrapped in a toxic culture of secrecy and fear. Subsequently, both left the company, but Holmes would not leave them alone, and these employees were put under intense pressure to abstain from sharing information on Theranos. We conclude from this example that the culture of secrecy and fear is the clearest attribute of an aggressive DI.

Holmes told other investors that Theranos was going to make $100 million in revenue in 2014, but in reality the company was only on track to make $100,000 that year. She told the press that her blood testing machine was capable of making over 1000 tests, when in practice it could only do one single type of test. She lied about a contract that Theranos had with the Department of Defense when she said her technology was being used in the battlefield, even though it was not. She repeatedly made up complete stories to the press about everything from her university schooling to company profits to the number of people whose lives would be saved from her bogus technology. And she did all these misrepresentations while ensuring that no one inside or outside her company could publicly challenge the truthfulness of her claims. That is an example of extremely self-consistent and rational behavior in support of the DI in the sense of Section 16.3.5.

16.3.7 DI and unexplainable machine learning

There are various implications related to a DI when organizations use machine learning (ML) systems. If an ML system malfunctions and the company personnel cite it as a reason for an incompetent decision, an organization easily slips into a DI. This slip is especially problematic if an ML system does not possess an explainability feature; its decision is perceived as random and thus is made in an incompetent way.

Although ML is actively deployed and used in industry, user satisfaction is still not very high in most domains. We will present a use case where explainability and interpretability of machine learning decisions is lacking and users experience dissatisfaction in these cases.

Customers of financial services are appalled when they travel and their credit cards are canceled without an obvious reason (Fig. 16.8). The customer explains what happened in detail, and his Facebook friends strongly support his case against the bank. On the top the customer explains his problem; on the bottom, his peers provide recommendations. The banks not only made an error in its decision, according to what the friends write, but also are unable to rectify it and communicate it properly. This situation is a clear indicator of a DI. If this bank used a decision-making system with explainability, there would be a given cause of its decision. Once it is established that this cause does not hold, the bank is expected to be capable of reverting its decision efficiently and retaining the customer.

Computer machines trying to be trusted are a potential reason for a DI. Incompetent workers can first start trusting machines and then blame them for failures of mixed human-machine teams, if these machines lack explainability. Lyons, Wynne, Mahoney, and Roebke (2019) present data from their qualitative study regarding the factors that precede trust for the elements of human-machine teaming. The authors reviewed the construct of human-machine trust and the dimensions of teammate-likeness from a human-robot interaction perspective. They derived the cues of trust from the corpus of human-computer interaction literature on trust to reveal the reasons why individuals might have reported trust of a new technology, such as a machine. The authors found that most subjects reported the technology as a tool rather than as a teammate for human-machine teaming.

Levchuk, Pattipati, Serfaty, Fouse, and McCormack (2019) construct the framework of an energy perspective for a team from which they postulated that optimal multiagent systems can best achieve adaptive behaviors by minimizing a team's free energy, where energy minimization consists of incremental observation, perception, and control phases. In a DI team, first two phases are regular, but the last one is corrupted. This third phase should be minimized in terms of unexplainable control decisions. The authors propose a mechanism with their model for the distribution of decisions jointly made by a team, providing the associated mathematical abstractions and computational mechanisms. Afterward, they test their ideas experimentally to conclude that energy-based agent teams outperform utility-based teams. Models of energy- and utility-based DI teams look like an intriguing subject for a future study.

Both object-level agents and metaagents can display DI. In one possible architecture (Fouad & Moskowitz, 2019), such metaagents are agents existing inside of a software paradigm where they are able to reason and utilize their reasoning to construct and deploy other agents. The authors give an example with a service-oriented architecture, test it with an automated evaluation process, and introduce holonic agents (intelligent agents able to work independently and as part of a hierarchy). Holonic agents are simultaneously complete in and of themselves and are able to interact independently with the environment, while being a part of a hierarchy at the same time. A holon is something that is simultaneously a whole and a part.

September 22 · 👥

Wow. Chase just cancelled my credit cards despite an 18 year relationship.
Apparently my account got flagged for money laundering. Good thing I was brought
an extra credit card on my business trip and that thing called 'cash'. You decide the
best part:
(a) they did not call to talk to me before cancelling
(b) they are informing me with a letter that will arrive in seven days (my cards got cut
off two days ago but I'll find out next Wed!)
(c) they are refusing to refund my annual fees
(d) it took my six calls and two hours on the phone with Chase to decipher this. along
the way, they dropped three calls

Chase sucks and so does JPMorgan Chase & Co.
John China - I need a SVB credit card. Pleassssseeeeeeee?

👍 Like   💬 Comment

👍 1

John   Take the cards (less headache) but make sure you emphasize
to them that they still suck.
Like · Reply · 👍 1 · September 27 at 8:42am

Ben   I'd get new cards .. unforgivable
Like · Reply · 👍 1 · September 27 at 8:43am

Lau   Can you get a detailed report of what exactly led them
to flag your account for laundering, then a formal apology, a higher credit line,
and reduced interest rate?
Like · Reply · 👍 5 · September 27 at 8:55am

Will   you need or want the cards take them back. At least they
changed their mind. Who gets hurt if you don't take them back? Chase won't
notice.
Like · Reply · 👍 1 · September 27 at 8:56am

Ma   Are they reinstating your points? Demand more points or waiving of
annual fees!
Like · Reply · 👍 4 · September 27 at 9:14am

Crai   Make them earn your business back. No simple "water under
the bridge - let's move forward...".
Like · Reply · 👍 2 · September 27 at 9:18am

Tom   Sure, if they throw in some Giants box seats as well
Like · Reply · 👍 3 · September 27 at 9:50am

Pat   New cards. Leave 'em.
Like · Reply · September 27 at 9:55am

Pat   Something with good miles....
Like · Reply · 👍 1 · September 27 at 9:56am

FIG. 16.8   A customer is confused, and his peers are upset when his credit card is canceled but no explanation is
provided.

16.4 Detecting DI in text

The purpose of applying natural language processing to DI phenomena is to find out the DI rate for different organizations. DI ratings obtained from customer feedback texts can be an objective, unbiased assessment of the quality of management in a given organization, in most cases, irrespective of its particular policies and regulations. Once organizations are DI rated, the public would be able to make an informed choice of the products and services provided by them.

16.4.1 An example of discourse-level DI analysis

One of the examples of a DI follows as a response of a customer service representative to a user attempting to resolve a matter and clarifying why a particular operation cannot be performed: *You are asking me to reverse this insufficient fund fee? I cannot do it. The only thing I <CSA> am allowed to do is to tell you that I am not allowed to help you <the customer> with anything. I recommend you trying to ask a branch agent to reverse this fee for you.* This text can be viewed as a credo of a CSA.

Communicative discourse tree for this text is shown in Fig. 16.9A, and parse tree for the second sentence is shown in Fig. 16.9B. Each line shows the text fragment for elementary discourse unit (EDU); expressions in italic are verb frames with substituted semantic roles. The hierarchy is shown from left to right: the level in the discourse tree is shown by the indentation value. The terminal nodes are assigned with EDUs: the fragments of text that are connected by rhetorical relations. Edges of this discourse tree are labeled with speech acts, which are highlighted in EDUs, such as *asking (you, me, …)*. Frames for speech acts are

```
elaboration (LeftToRight)
  elaboration (LeftToRight)
    joint
      EDU: asking(you, me, to reverse this insufficient fund fee) ?
      EDU:I cannot do it .
    elaboration (LeftToRight)
      EDU:The only thing
      attribution (RightToLeft)
        EDU: allowed(me, to do is to tell(me, you, →))
        EDU:that not allowed(I, help(I, you, →))
  elaboration (LeftToRight)
    EDU: recommend(me, you, →)
    enablement (LeftToRight)
      EDU:trying to ask(you, branch agent, →)
      EDU:to reverse this fee for you
```

(A)

FIG. 16.9A   Communicative discourse tree for this text.

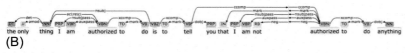

(B)

FIG. 16.9B   Parse tree in the sentence for a "CSA credo."

available at VerbNet (such as http://verbs.colorado.edu/verb-index/vn/allow-64.php—allow-64 for the communicative action *allow*).

The features of this discourse tree can be associated with a DI. The abundance of speech acts and certain interrelations between them indicate a peculiar mental state that should not arise unless a multiagent system evolves into a DI. For example, an inconsistency between *allow (...)* and *not allow (...)* connected by the rhetorical relation of *attribution* is a very special way of a contradiction that should not occur in the normal flow of a business operation, as expressed in this text.

Also, when the statement by a CSA "I cannot do" is strengthened with the *elaboration-attribution* chain, the reader believes that this customer is stuck with her problem and it is impossible for a CSA to provide any help. This perception is the goal of an organization with a DI so that a user can easily give up on his attempts to resolve the matter.

As we collect such texts and form a training set, our ML system detects commonalities between communicative discourse trees for DI texts and automatically builds rules for its detection. Not all such rules can be easily verbalized but a special discourse tree structure is associated with these rules.

16.4.2 A DI detection dataset

We first created a manually tagged set of customer complaints from the financial sector. Annotators were given a definition of a DI and how to classify each complaint as indicative of a DI or not. Then, we built a recognizer program that used this manually tagged set for training and testing. Once our recognizer demonstrated satisfactory performance, we applied it to textual complaints for various banks to estimate their DI rate. Recognition accuracies in the manually tagged dataset allowed us to estimate the value of deviation in the DI rate.

This dataset contains texts where authors do their best to bring their points across by employing all means to show that they (as customers) are right and their opponents (companies) are wrong (Galitsky et al., 2009). Customers always try to blame the company for everything, so the task of the recognizer is to verify if customers' arguments are valid and their stories do not indicate misrepresentations. Complainants are emotionally charged writers who describe problems they have encountered with a financial service, the lack of clarity and transparency as their problem was communicated with CSA, and how they attempted to solve it. Raw complaints were collected from PlanetFeedback.com for a number of banks submitted during the years of the financial crisis of 2007. Four hundred complaints were manually tagged with respect to perceived complaint validity, proper argumentation, detectable misrepresentation, and whether a request for explanation concerning the company's decision occurred.

Judging by these complaints, most complainants were in genuine distress due to a strong deviation between

- what they expected from a product or a service,
- the actual product or service that they received,
- how this deviation was explained, and
- how the problem was communicated by a customer support.

The last two items are directly correlated with a DI. Most complaint authors reported incompetence, flawed policies, ignorance, lack of common sense, inability to understand the reason behind the company's decision, indifference to customers' needs, and misrepresentation from the customer service personnel. The authors are frequently confused, looking for a company's explanation, seeking a recommendation from other users and advice others on avoiding a particular financial service. The focus of a complaint is the proof that the proponent is right and her opponent is wrong, the explanation for why the company decided to act in a certain way, a resolution proposal and a desired outcome. Although a DI is described in an indirect, implicit way, it can be easily identified by a human reader.

The DI tag in the dataset used in the current study is related to the whole text of a complaint, not a paragraph. Three annotators worked with this dataset, and the interannotator agreement exceeded 80%. The set of tagged customer complaints about financial services is available at https://github.com/bgalitsky/relevance-based-on-parse-trees/blob/master/examples/opinionsFinanceTags.xls.

16.4.3 Discourse-level features of DI

In texts where a DI description might occur, one can expect specific discourse-level features. These texts can be an enumeration of the specific mental states of CSA agents, an indication of the conflict with a lack of rationality, or heated arguments among conflicting agents. It is important to differentiate between the emotions of a text's author and the ones describing the mental states and communicative actions of opponents. The complexity of a DI detection is increased by the necessity of grasping the mental state of a team of agents, not an individual one.

Detection accuracy for DI for different types of evidence is shown in Table 16.1. We consider simpler cases, where the detection occurs based on phrases, in the top row. Typical expressions in the row one have an imperative form such as "please explain/clarify/motivate/comment." Also, there are templates here such as "you did this but I expected that" ... "you told me this but I received that."

The middle row contains the data on a level higher evidence for the implicit explanation request case, where multiple fragments of DTs indicate the class. Finally, in the bottom row, we present the case of lower confidence for a single occurrence of a DT associated with an explanation request. The second column shows the counts of complaints per case. The third column gives examples of expressions (which include keywords and phrase types) and rhetoric relations that serve as criteria for an implicit DI. Fourth and fifth columns present the detection rates where the complaints for a given case are mixed with a hundred complaints without a DI.

16.4.4 Implementation of the discourse-level classifier

There are two approaches for discourse-level classification of texts into classes {*DI, no DI*}:

(1) Nearest neighbor learning. For a given text, if it is similar from the discourse standpoint with an element of the positive training dataset and dissimilar with all elements of the negative dataset, then it is classified as belonging to the positive class. The rule for the

TABLE 16.1   Cases of explanation requests and detection accuracies.

Evidence	#	Criteria	P	R
Expressions with the rhetorical relation of *Contrast*	83	Phrases: *A said this … but B said that …*	83	85
		I learned from A one thing … but B informed me about something else		
Double, triple, or more implicit mention of an inconsistency	97	Multiple rhetoric relation of *contrast, explanation, cause,* and *sequence*	74	79
A single implicit mention of an inconsistency	103	A pair of rhetoric relation chains for *contrast* and *cause*	69	75

The left column present the linguistic cue for evidence of DI. The second column from the left gives the counts for each case. The third column presents criteria and examples for the given evidence type. The fourth and fifth columns give the precision and recall recognizing the given evidence type.

negative class is formulated analogously. The similarity of two texts is defined as a cardinality of maximal common discourse structure for the respective discourse structures of these texts, such as discourse trees.

(2) The features of the discourse trees can be represented in a numerical space. The kernel learning approach applies the support vector machine (SVM) learning to the feature space of all subdiscourse trees of the discourse tree for a given text where a DI is being detected. Tree kernel counts the number of common subtrees as the discourse similarity measure between two DTs.

Both approaches are applied for DI detection; we refer the reader to (Galitsky, 2019) for details of both approaches and briefly outline the latter approach below.

We extend the tree kernel definition for the DT, augmenting the DT kernel by the information on speech acts. Tree kernel-based approaches are not very sensitive to errors in parsing (syntactic and rhetoric) because erroneous subtrees are mostly random and will unlikely be common among different elements of a training set.

A DT can be represented by a vector V of integer counts of each subtree type (without taking into account its ancestors):

$V(T) = (\text{\# of subtrees of type } 1, …, \text{\# of subtrees of type } I, …, \text{\# of subtrees of type } n)$. Given two tree segments DT_1 and DT_2, the tree kernel function is defined:

$$K(DT_1, DT_2) \leq V(DT_1), V(CDT_2) >= \Sigma i \, V(CDT_1)[i], V(DT_2)[i] = \Sigma n_1 \Sigma n_2 \, \Sigma_i \, I_i(n_1) * I_i(n_2),$$

where $n_1 \in N_1$, $n_2 \in N_2$, and N_1 and N_2 are the sets of all nodes in CDT_1 and CDT_2, respectively; $I_i(n)$ is the indicator function:

$I_i(n) = \{1 \text{ } iff$ a subtree of type i occurs with a root at a node; 0 otherwise}. Further details for using TK for paragraph level and discourse analysis are available in (Galitsky, 2019).

Only the arcs of the same type of rhetoric relations (presentation relation, such as antithesis; subject matter relation, such as condition; and multinuclear relation, such as list) can be matched when computing common subtrees. We use N for a nucleus or situations presented by this nucleus, and S for a satellite or situations presented by this satellite. Situations are propositions, completed actions or actions in progress, and communicative actions and states (including beliefs, desires, approve, explain, and reconcile). Hence, we have the following expression for an RST-based generalization " ^ " for two texts *text1* and *text2*:

$$text1 \wedge text2 = \cup i, j \, (rstRelation1i, (\ldots, \ldots) \wedge rstRelation2j \, (\ldots, \ldots)),$$

where I ∈ (RST relations in *text1*) and j ∈ (RST relations in *text2*). Further, for a pair of RST relations, their generalization looks as follows:

$$rstRelation1(N1, S1) \wedge rstRelation2\,(N2, S2) = (rstRelation1 \wedge rstRelation2)(N1 \wedge N2, S1 \wedge S2).$$

We define speech acts as a function of the form verb (agent, subject, and cause), where verb characterizes some type of interaction between involved agents (e.g., explain, confirm, remind, disagree, and deny), subject refers to the information transmitted or object described, and cause refers to the motivation or explanation for the subject. To handle the meaning of words expressing the subjects of speech acts, we apply word2vec models.

We combined Stanford NLP parsing, coreferences, entity extraction, DT construction (discourse parser, Joty, Carenini, Ng, & Mehdad, 2013; Surdeanu, Hicks, & Valenzuela-Escarcega, 2015), VerbNet and Tree Kernel builder into one system available at https://github.com/bgalitsky/relevance-based-on-parse-trees.

For EDUs as labels for terminal nodes only the phrase structure is retained; we propose to label the terminal nodes with the sequence of phrase types instead of parse tree fragments. For the evaluation, tree kernel builder tool was used (Galitsky, 2019).

16.4.5 Detection results

Once we confirmed the plausibility of a DI detector on the annotated complaints, we proceeded to assessing the DI rate per organization (Table 16.2). The average DI rate per a customer complaint was 11%.

Recognition accuracies and the resultant DI rates are shown in Table 16.2. We used 300 complaints for each bank to assess the recognition accuracies for explanation request. $79.1 \pm 3.1\%$ looks like a reasonable estimate for recognition accuracy for DI. The last column on the right shows that taking into account the error rate that is less than 20% in DI recognition, $10.9 \pm 3.1\%$ is an adequate estimate of complaints indicating DI, given the set of 1200 complaints. Hence the overall average DI rate for these organizations is about one-tenth.

TABLE 16.2 Discovering DI rates for four banks.

Source	#	Precision	Recall	DI rate
Bank of America	300	79	76	**8.4**
Chase Bank	300	76	80	**11.6**
Citibank	300	77	85	**12.7**
American Express	300	76	84	**11.2**

Bold values are important data of the overall DI rate.

16.5 Conclusions: Handling and repairing DI

DIs naturally appear in organizations due to the human factor. Hence the means to cure a DI can be based on the removal of human factors: making customer support fully formalized by following an established protocol. This approach follows along the lines of, for example, increased safety by means of autonomous systems such as autopilots and navigators. Instead of dealing with a human CSA who has manifold motivations, customers should be handled with an autonomous agent capable of understanding their problems in a limited, vertical domain.

As long as people rely on various products and services to satisfy their needs, they will encounter DIs associated with the frustration of customers and with businesses losing customers. A transition to an autonomous CSA, as long as it is relevant in terms of topic and dialogue appropriateness, would make a DI avoidable. It is hard to overestimate a potential contribution of such a CSA when a broad category of people call financial institutions, travel portals, healthcare and internet providers, or government services such as immigration and revenue agencies.

Task-oriented chatbots for a customer service can provide adequate solutions for a DI. Currently available dialogue systems (Galitsky & Ilvovsky, 2019) with dialogue management and context tracking can be trained from textual descriptions of customer problems and their correct resolution. The resultant functionality of these trained chatbots needs to be formally assessed to avoid hybrid human-machine DI.

The least typical cases of user dissatisfaction, such as the ones associated with the nonsufficient fund fee, can be fully formalized and encoded into the CS chatbot so that human intervention would not be required. A DI-free development team of chatbots should be able to cover the most important cases of product issues and users' misunderstandings to reduce the DI rate significantly from 11%.

In this study, we introduced a new model for a well-known form of behavior for an organization: distributed incompetence (DI). A comparison is drawn between DI and distributed knowledge: in both cases agents reason rationally, but in the former case, the agents pretend to be irrational to achieve certain organizational objective so that external agents would believe that he deals with genuinely incompetent agents. In the latter case of distributed knowledge in a competent organization, knowledge and skills of individual agents help each other to impress an external observer with a superior capability and result-oriented mindset of this organization.

It is not easy to detect distributed incompetence in an organization. Many banks during financial crisis of 2007, ENRON as a public company and also Theranos as a private company succeeded by leading investors by the nose for a long time. Some company managers turn out to be so good liars that neither employees nor customers nor members of the public become suspicious about the company business conduct. The proposed natural language analysis tool is intended to take a corpus of documents (such as internal emails) from an organization and attempt to detect a DI. Our assessment showed that this tool could be plausible in identifying a DI in an arbitrary organization.

References

Akhremenkov, A. A., & Galitsky, B. (2007). Building web infrastructure for providing rating services and subscription to them. *Mathematical Modeling, 19*(2), 23–32.
Ariely, D. (2008). *Predictably irrational.* Harper Collings Publishers.

Berzlánovich, I., Egg, M., & Redeker, G. (2008). Coherence structure and lexical cohesion in expository and persuasive texts. In *Proceedings of the workshop on constraints in discourse III*.

Bilton, N. (2018). *She absolutely has sociopathic Tendencies*. VanityFair. https://www.vanityfair.com/news/2018/06/elizabeth-holmes-is-trying-to-start-a-new-company.

Biswa, P. (2015). *Putt's law, peter principle, dilbert principle of incompetence & parkinson's law*. http://asmilingassasin.blogspot.com/2015/06/putts-law-peter-principle-dilbert.html.

Carreyrou, J. (2018). *Bad blood: Secrets and lies in a silicon valley startup*. Penguin Random House.

Curtiss, P. R., & Warren, P. W. (1973). *The dynamics of life skills coaching. Life skills series* (p. 89). Prince Albert, Saskatchewan: Training Research and Development Station, Dept. of Manpower and Immigration.

Fagin, R., Halpern, J. Y., Moses, Y., & Vardi, M. Y. (1995). *Reasoning about knowledge*. The MIT Press.

FCA. (2015). *FCA fines Barclays £72 million for poor handling of financial crime risks*. https://www.fca.org.uk/news/press-releases/fca-fines-barclays-%C2%A372-million-poor-handling-financial-crime-risks.

Federal Reserve. (2010). *Bernanke-Four Questions*. Federalreserve.gov. April 14, 2009.

Fouad, H., & Moskowitz, I. S. (2019). Meta-agents: Using multiagent networks to manage dynamic changes in the internet of things. In W. F. Lawless, R. Mittu, D. A. Sofge, I. S. Moskowitz, & S. Russell (Eds.), *Artificial intelligence for the internet of everything*: Academic Press/Elsevier.

Galitsky, B. (2019). *Developing enterprise chatbots*. Cham: Springer.

Galitsky, B., González, M. P., & Chesñevar, C. I. (2009). A novel approach for classifying customer complaints through graphs similarities in argumentative dialogues. *Decision Support Systems*, 46(3), 717–729.

Galitsky, B., & Ilvovsky, D. (2019). A demo of a chatbot for a virtual persuasive dialogue. In *Persuasive technologies 14th international conference, Limassol, Cyprus, April 9–11*.

Galitsky, B., Ilvovsky, D., & Kuznetsov, S. O. (2016). Text classification into abstract classes based on discourse structure. In *Proceedings of the international conference recent advances in natural language processing* (pp. 200–207).

Galitsky, B., Ilvovsky, D., & Pisarevskaya, D. (2018). Argumentation in text: Discourse structure matters. In *CICLing 2018*.

Galitsky, B., & Levene, M. (2005). Simulating the conflict between reputation and profitability for online rating portals. *Journal of Artificial Societies and Social Simulation*, 8(2), 1–6.

Galitsky, B., & Parnis, A. (2017). Team formation by children with autism. In W. F. Lawless, R. Mittu, D. Sofge, & S. Russell (Eds.), *Autonomy and artificial intelligence: A threat or savior?* Cham: Springer.

Galitsky, B., & Parnis, A. (2019). Accessing validity of argumentation of agents of the internet of everything. In W. F. Lawless, R. Mittu, D. A. Sofge, I. S. Moskowitz, & S. Russell (Eds.), *Artificial intelligence for the internet of everything*: Academic Press/Elsevier.

Grudin, J. (2016). *The rise of incompetence*: (p. 6). ACM Interactions. 8-1. https://interactions.acm.org/archive/view/january-february-2016/the-rise-of-incompetence.

Integration Training. (2018). IntegrationTraining.co.uk.

Joty, S., Carenini, G., Ng, R. T., & Mehdad, Y. (2013). Combining intra-and multi- sentential rhetorical parsing for document-level discourse analysis. *ACL*, 1, 486–496.

Lawless, W. F., & Sofge, D. A. (2016). AI and the mitigation of error: A thermodynamics of teams. In *AAAI Spring Symposia 2016*.

Levchuk, G., Pattipati, K., Serfaty, D., Fouse, A., & McCormack, R. (2019). Active inference in multiagent systems: Context-driven collaboration and decentralized purpose-driven team adaptation. In W. F. Lawless, R. Mittu, D. A. Sofge, I. S. Moskowitz, & S. Russell (Eds.), *Artificial intelligence for the internet of everything*: Academic Press/Elsevier.

Lyons, J. B., Wynne, K. T., Mahoney, S., & Roebke, M. A. (2019). Trust and human-machine teaming: A qualitative study. In W. F. Lawless, R. Mittu, D. A. Sofge, I. S. Moskowitz, & S. Russell (Eds.), *Artificial intelligence for the internet of everything*: Academic Press/Elsevier.

Mann, W. C., & Thompson, S. A. (1987). *Rhetorical structure theory: Description and construction of text structures*. Dordrecht, The Netherlands: Springer.

Mittu, R., Taylor, G., Sofge, D. A., & Lawless, W. F. (2016). Introduction to the symposium on AI and the mitigation of human error. In *AAAI Spring Symposia 2016*.

Moskowitz, I. S., & Lawless, W. F. (2016). Human caused bifurcations in a hybrid team—A position paper. In *AAAI spring symposia 2016*.

Nageswaran, V. A. (2014). *Systematic irrationality*. https://www.livemint.com/Opinion/reJomN4AkpvUAPHVgRxhDO/Systematic-irrationality.html.

Obama, B. (2010). *Remarks by the president on wall street reform archived 2010-07-23 at the wayback machine.* White House.

Peter, L., & Hull, R. (1968). *The Peter principle: Why things always go wrong.* William Morrow and Company.

Pisarevskaya, D., Galitsky, B., Taylor, J., & Ozerov, A. (2019). An anatomy of a lie. In L. Liu & R. White (Eds.), *Companion proceedings of the 2019 world wide web conference (WWW'19)* (pp. 373–380). New York, NY, USA: ACM.

Ruppenhofer, J., Ellsworth, M., Petruck, M. R. L., Johnson, C. R., Baker, C. F., & Scheffczyk, J. (2016). *FrameNet II: Extended theory and practice.* https://framenet.icsi.berkeley.edu/fndrupal/the_book.

Shuldiner, A. (2019). Raising them right: AI and the internet of big things. In W. F. Lawless, R. Mittu, D. A. Sofge, I. S. Moskowitz, & S. Russell (Eds.), *Artificial intelligence for the internet of everything*: Academic Press/Elsevier.

Singh, O. N., Phillips, K. A., Rodriguez-Gutierrez, R., Castaneda-Guarderas, A., Gionfriddo, M. R., Branda, M. E., et al. (2018). Eliciting the patient's agenda secondary analysis of recorded clinical encounters. *Journal of General Internal Medicine, 34,* 36–40.

Surdeanu, M., Hicks, T., & Valenzuela-Escarcega, M. A. (2015). *Two practical rhetorical structure theory parsers.* NAACL HLT.

Yang, B., & Lester, D. (2008). Reflections on rational choice—The existence of systematic irrationality. *The Journal of Socio-Economics, 37*(3), 1218–1233.

Further reading

Galitsky, B. (2018). Customers' retention requires an explainability feature in machine learning systems they use. In *AAAI spring symposium on "beyond machine intelligence: Understanding cognitive bias and humanity for well-being AI".* Stanford, CA.

Galitsky, B., Ilvovsky, D., & Wohlgenannt, G. (2019). Constructing imaginary discourse trees improves answering convergent questions. In *CICLING, April 7–13, La Rochelle, France.*

Oppong, T. (2018). *What was I thinking? (The science of systematic irrationality).* https://medium.com/kaizen-habits/what-was-i-thinking-the-science-of-systematic-irrationality-e053e5476fcf.

Sharanya, M. (2017). *Overcoming the unconscious incompetence hurdle at work.* https://www.peoplematters.in/article/culture/overcoming-the-unconscious-incompetence-hurdle-at-work-16750?utm_source=peoplematters&utm_medium=interstitial&utm_campaign=learnings-of-the-day.

Begin with the human: Designing for safety and trustworthiness in cyber-physical systems

Elizabeth T. Williams, Ehsan Nabavi, Genevieve Bell, Caitlin M. Bentley, Katherine A. Daniell, Noel Derwort, Zac Hatfield-Dodds, Kobi Leins, Amy K. McLennan

3A Institute, Australian National University, Canberra, ACT, Australia

17.1 Introduction

The constellation of technologies classed as artificial intelligence (AI) are diverse, involving networks of sensors, data, computational models capable of learning[a] and decision-making, and actuators capable of enacting change in the physical world. They may be highly localized or distributed across time[b] and space and have become increasingly ubiquitous in our daily lives. They help us to sort our email, select our news, drive to work, educate our children, monitor our health, and protect our nations.

But as the responsibilities we grant to AI technologies have grown, so too has evidence that the way we design such systems requires critical examination. How do we think about autonomy when designing systems involving AI, and what are the consequences of this for system safety and trust? When we give them agency—the capacity of a person or thing

---

[a] Learning is used loosely here. Rule-based models describing clear responses to particular input data are excluded from this definition; approaches that can be used in scenarios where all possible inputs are difficult to quantify (e.g., search, constraint propagation, and all types of machine learning) are included.

[b] Data taken in the past may be used to train or shape models used to make decisions and prompt action in the present. In this way a system can incorporate elements of both the past and present with the aim of deciding on an action in the future.

---

to act in a given environment or social structure, whether they act individually or collectively—to act on our behalf, how do we ensure that they carry out the task in a way that matches our true (and sometimes unrealized) intentions?

In this chapter, we consider these questions in the broader context of cyber-physical systems (CPSs), defined here as entities composed of interacting arrangements of digital information-processing systems, objects, humans, and environments.[c] CPSs meeting this definition have existed for some time; however, the increasingly common incorporation of computational models capable of learning combined with the rapid ability to extend the reach of such systems far beyond their original testing grounds together presents a new challenge. Take, for example, the differences between one flying drone piloted by a human versus swarms of drones capable of flying on their own. There is a qualitative difference in the challenges needed to design and manage hundreds of drones in our airspace, making decisions about where to go and how. These challenges are compounded when drones may need to transport people or interact with places where people are living.

These challenges indicate a need to think carefully about how we design, manage, and regulate existing and future CPSs. As Wolf and Serpanos (2018) note, the coupling of physical and cyber systems presents risks that are not well accounted for in traditional approaches to thinking about safety and security of new CPSs. The use of AI may present additional design risks. For example, Amodei et al. (2016) argue that the safety problem in AI systems originates from the design process, where systems are created with either an objective function that does not achieve its intended purpose,[d] an objective function that is too expensive to evaluate frequently, or an undesirable behavior during the learning process.[e] However, in addition to thinking about CPSs in terms of their technological capabilities, it is also important to conceptualize CPS subsystem interactions. This gap is something our approach intends to bridge.

The recent appearance of organizations like AI Now, the Cambridge Centre for the Study of Existential Risk, OpenAI, and others with similar missions may reflect a growing concern that, by increasing autonomy in CPSs,[f] the chance that such systems will fail us—possibly with catastrophic results—increases. The prevalent fear is that problems related to CPS safety are more likely to manifest in scenarios where these systems exert direct control over their physical and/or computational components without human knowledge, understanding, or intervention. However, as Elish (2019) discusses, the interactions between human and other system components within a CPS are also problematic: they have been shown to contribute to catastrophic accidents and frequently lead to scenarios where humans acting within the system at a moment of failure are held primarily or solely accountable for the actions of that system. This attribution frequently occurs even when evidence shows the system as a

[c]This is a broad definition of CPS. The term may be more restrictive (in different ways) depending on who is using it; we note very different definitions noted in publications from the United States (Lee, 2015) and Germany (Acatech, 2011), for example.

[d]See Clark and Amodei (2016) for a visual example of a faulty reward function in a game setting.

[e]There's a nice video demonstrating this in Irpan (2018).

[f]We imply here that this is done by models capable of "learning," following the loose definition of the term presented in footnote (a).

whole (via design, contradictory information, or other means) influenced the actions of the humans in question.

The purpose of this work is to chart a systematic path toward thinking about and working through the complexity of such systems, so that we can maximize their potential benefit and minimize their potential for harm. We do so by proposing an analytical framework to be used when designing, creating, managing, and governing such systems. Here, we will illustrate the framework using a well-documented example from history: the 1979 Three Mile Island nuclear reactor accident. We will review incidents involving this safety-critical CPS for two reasons: First, technologies employing fission such as weapon systems and nuclear reactors are typically complex[g] cyber-physical systems with dual-use potential, much like many technologies employing AI; second, if risks are realized, the result of failure in this system is potentially catastrophic, inherently leading to significant regulation, highly complex interactions between human or societal and technical components of the systems, and well-documented incident accounts. The case study of this accident is therefore an excellent opportunity to both present our analytical framework and help us refine it for application to all CPSs.

We begin with a retelling of the story of the Three Mile Island accident, pieced together from Kemeny et al. (1979). We will then follow the story with the demonstration of our framework.

17.2 The Three Mile Island accident

It was March 28, 1979, on Three Mile Island—a slip of flat land perched between the banks of the Susquehanna River near Goldsboro, Pennsylvania, United States. In the predawn darkness the worst commercial nuclear reactor accident in US history was just beginning.

The site featured two reactors—TMI-1, which still operates today,[h] and TMI-2. A schematic of the inside of TMI-2 is shown at the end of this section, in Fig. 17.1. This figure is based on a set of system diagrams from Kemeny et al. (1979, pp. 86–87).

Like all nuclear reactors the goal of TMI-2 is to use the heat generated in the nuclear fission process to generate energy. This goal is achieved by generating steam, which turns a turbine. This type of reactor has a primary water system, which is a closed loop system that is in contact with the fuel cells containing the fissile, radioactive, heat-generating material and control rods in the reactor core. The water in the primary loop is maintained at a high pressure, so it stays liquid at normal operating temperatures. This enhances the system's ability to keep the fuel rods within a safe temperature range. A tank called a pressurizer is central in this. The tank is linked to the primary water system and holds both liquid water and steam (water in its

---

[g]In this case, "complex" means they incorporate two or more subsystems analyzed using different approaches, though both reactors and nuclear weapons are typically also connected to already complicated social, political, environmental, and governance systems, making them potentially very complex indeed. In the chapter, we will consider when and how to bring these elements in as appropriate for a specific line of inquiry.

[h]This statement is correct as of May 2019. Exelon, the company that owns TMI-1, recently announced TMI-1 is scheduled to shut down by September 30, 2019 (Exelon, 2019).

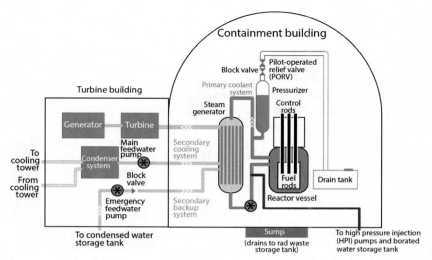

FIG. 17.1   Schematic of relevant components of the Three Mile Island-2 nuclear reactor system. *Based on Kemeny et al. (1979, pp. 86–87).*

gaseous state). The steam in this tank can be heated or cooled to adjust the primary water system pressure; the rest of the water in the primary system is intended to be in a liquid state.

A secondary water system generates steam both for energy production and to carry away some of the heat produced via fission and its daughter products. This secondary system is crucial for keeping the reactor core within an appropriate temperature range: one that ensures that the fuel rods stay intact and any radioactivity from the primary system remains within the containment building. There are automatic backup systems and protections in place to help ensure a safe temperature range is restored if anything fails.

Shortly after 4 a.m. on the day of the accident, the main feedwater pumps responsible for moving water in the secondary system stopped working—an unintended and at the time unrecognized result of some maintenance work on the pipes in the system. Alarms began to sound in the control room, alerting the two operators[i] on duty to the problem.

The first safety system kicked in: the steam turbine and electricity generator shut down automatically. Next the temperature in the reactor core started to rise—no new cool water was coming in, so the heat from the fission reactions within the core was not being dissipated. The pressure in the reactor core increased, automatically triggering the opening of the pilot-operated relief valve (PORV) connected to the pressurizer—and a light in the control room, which told the operators that the valve's electrical system had been activated. The valve, which was supposed to shut 13 s after the main feedwater pumps tripped, remained

---

[i]Two additional personnel—a shift supervisor and shift foreman—would join the operators during the TMI-2 accident not long after the initial alarms started sounding. We refer to them all as operators throughout the story for simplicity.

stuck open, and the light in the control room meant to indicate the status of the PORV turned off—not because the PORV was closed, but because a component involved in triggering the closure had powered off. The operators turned on a pump to begin adding water to the primary system at this point, possibly noting the falling liquid water level in the pressurizer that the decrease in pressure would have induced.

Emergency pumps started trying to feed cooling water into the secondary system, but the valves between the emergency pumps and the secondary system were shut. In the midst of the chaos, operators did not notice two control room lights—one covered by a yellow maintenance tag—that indicated that these were shut. According to Kemeny et al., "No one knows why the second light was missed" (1979, p. 91).

The pressure within the core continued to rise. The reactor control rods dropped in, halting the fission reactions within the core. An emergency system on the primary side kicked in—two high-pressure injection (HPI) pumps began pushing 1000 gal of water per minute into the primary system.

Two minutes later, operators interpreted a high level of water in the pressurizer to mean that the system was full of water and turned off one HPI pump while drastically reducing the flow of water from the second. But, in fact, the liquid water in the core would soon turn to steam, and the primary system, through that open pilot-operated relief valve, would begin boiling dry—much like a forgotten pot of water on a hot stovetop. By the time operators realized this, it was far too late. The fuel rods, consisting of pellets of uranium oxide encased in a zirconium alloy cladding, had already ruptured.

Those two pieces of missed information—the open pilot-operated relief valve and the closed emergency cooling pump valves—would normally have been fairly minor problems. But their presence—and the operators' lack of knowledge about the state of the system—ushered in a series of decisions that led to the loss-of-coolant event and its aftermath. In the next section, we will focus on the early moments of the accident to highlight how our framework can be applied.

17.3 The analytical framework

The framework we present is structured around five question themes—autonomy, agency, assurance, metrics, and interfaces. The themes, introduced in detail in the succeeding text, are designed to help identify the system, its boundaries, and key transition points between different (physical, human, social, environmental, and cyber) components within the system. Each theme aims to bring out key questions and attributes of relevance to the system under investigation; all themes together may be used to help create system maps and feed the creation of system models that can be useful for qualitatively or quantitatively analyzing whether and how the system (imagined or fully realized) determines context to achieve a specified goal. The framework has been developed, tested, and iterated by the 3A Institute Staff and Director D/Prof. Genevieve Bell, Australian National University, over the past 18 months, including with industry and government partners.

In this section, we provide a broad introduction to each question theme and then demonstrate how we apply them to the TMI accident.

17.3.1 Autonomy

Our first question theme centers on autonomy. When we speak of an "autonomous system," we might envision a CPS capable of acting with independence—making decisions on its own with the intention of achieving one or more system goals without direct human influence. In reality, though, just as the word autonomy has many meanings (see, for instance, Huang, Messina, & Albus, 2003; Swaine, 2016), CPSs classed as "autonomous systems" may have vastly different designs resulting from some combination of regulatory requirements, individual or team design visions, and practical decisions resulting from choices regarding the components of the system in question. Here, we loosely define a system as autonomous if it has one or more system goals and can take independent actions toward achieving those goals. When considering a system meeting this definition, then, we might ask the following question: What shapes the decisions driving system action, and when and how are humans involved? In other words, what does autonomy mean for this specific system, and how have system designers translated that meaning into the design of the system?

In the case of TMI-2, one may find this question somewhat puzzling. A 1970s era nuclear reactor is not typically thought of as an autonomous system. The safety systems triggered in the story earlier are controlled deterministically, meaning they operate as they do because one or more human designers have decided to trigger certain actions in a very specific way based on data taken from physical sensor inputs—pressures, temperatures, and so on. There are human operators, maintenance workers, and managers constantly monitoring and intervening. However, the combination of failures encountered in TMI-2 on that day had not been planned for. For the scenario the operators found themselves tasked with handling that day, there were no rules to follow, and no set procedure to draw on. Therefore the human and engineered components of the system together shaped how the system responded to the incident. In other words the TMI-2 system (including its human components) acted autonomously in its attempt to avoid disaster.

As this line of reasoning begins to demonstrate, the question theme of autonomy helps us begin to define system goals and boundaries. In asking about autonomy, we are asking two questions: What are the goals of the system, and how does the system work toward achieving those goals?

For the nuclear reactor at Three Mile Island, the goal of the system was to *safely* produce energy as needed for the US Eastern electrical grid. For the designers, this translated into the following design specifications:

- The system should maintain a well-controlled fission (and therefore energy generation) rate when energy is needed and effectively no fission rate when it is not needed.
- The system must maintain its structural integrity, meaning the radioactivity within the fuel cells should remain within the fuel cells, the primary water system should remain isolated from the outside environment to the extent possible, and the water in both primary and secondary systems should remain in the state(s) each component of the system is designed to accommodate. Note that having the ability to completely suppress the fission rate as quickly as possible is important for meeting this specification.

For all nuclear power plants, the second specification takes precedent over the first because if the structural integrity of the system is threatened, both the safety and energy generation aspects (immediate and enduring) of the system goal will be threatened.

In TMI-2 the structural integrity of the system came under threat when the main feedwater pumps stopped working. The second specification earlier was threatened, triggering a momentary revision[j] of the system's goal, which we can state as follows:

Revised system goal: Maintain the structural integrity of the system, or, failing that, minimize damage to the system.

This revised goal means that energy generation is a secondary concern, and we can exclude the US Eastern energy grid from our system for the purposes of this analysis—excluding it by drawing a boundary before TMI-2's connection to the grid helps us to simplify the system in question. However, we can include all engineered components of the TMI-2 plant involved in the accident within the boundaries of the system and the humans involved in making decisions relating to and acting in concert with these components during the accident. All of these are included within the system because they may have played a role in the accident in question and may therefore be important to consider in our analysis.

It is worth pausing here to reflect on a couple of points the earlier analysis has drawn out. The first relates to the capacity of the system to achieve its goals: what resources or capabilities does the system need to pursue its goal autonomously? Also, how does the notion of autonomy evolve in a given system as a function of time? In other words, how do (or should) the system goals change or be reprioritized as context changes, and how is that reflected (or not) in subsequent system action? And for autonomous human-machine teams, how is shared context constructed?

The questions posed within this aspect of the framework directly translate to systems under development. What are the system goals? How is it expected to achieve them? What does it need to achieve them, and how does that relate to the context in which the system operates?

In the case of TMI-2, the answer to the last two questions regarding goals relates to the actors—human or otherwise—in the system that shape the behavior of the system and the context as a whole. To explore this aspect of the system, we move to our second question theme: agency.

17.3.2 Agency

Agency is another concept with many meanings and interpretations (see, e.g., Giddens, 1979; Luck & D'Inverno, 1995; Sen, 1992). Here, we use the term to refer to the capacity of a person or thing to act. This action can be individual or collective (involving one or more agents) and may be taken within a social structure, an environment, or a computational or engineered system. This question theme might be summed up as follows: Who or what is capable of influencing the state of the system, when, how, and by how much? Who or what decides on the limits or boundaries on each actor's agency within the system?

Consider the first 5 min of the TMI-2 accident, starting from the main feedwater pump failure, which we treat as our time origin. Table 17.1 provides a brief analysis of the agency of various actors (both human and nonhuman) within the system and identifies whether their

---

[j]Note: This might be viewed as a reprioritization rather than a revision of system goals; energy generation is not a primary goal when the system's integrity is threatened. Readers might find it easier to understand our discussion of agent actions during the accident with a specifically redefined goal.

TABLE 17.1   Agency chart for the Three Mile Island accident (first 5 min following the primary feedwater pump failure; the feedwater pump failure is set at $t=0$).

Time	Incident	Actor	Consistent with revised system goal?	Consequence
0 s	Main feedwater pumps fail[a]	Automated system[b]	No	Flow in secondary system halts
2 s	Turbine and generators shut down	Automated system	Yes	Energy generation halts
2–8 s	Pilot-operated relief valve opens	Automated system	Yes	Pressurizer pressure decreases
8 s	Control rods dropped in	Automated system	Yes	Fission halts; heat release 6% of previous rate
~9 s	Three emergency feedwater pumps started	Automated system	Yes	Operators think emergency pumps are working
13 s	Pilot-operated relief valve fails to close	Automated system	No	Primary system remains open
13 s	Operator starts pump to add water to primary system	Human	Yes	Pressurizer water level increases
13+ s	Failure to close block valve in pressurizer system	Human	No	Primary system remains open until 2 h 22 min after start
14 s	Operators miss lights indicating emergency feedwater pump system valves were shut	Human	No	Emergency backup pumps on secondary system fail to introduce water into the system
2 min	High-pressure injection (HPI) pumps start	Automated system	Yes	Primary system coolant replenished
4 min	HPI pump function altered	Human	No	One pump stopped; one pump with reduced flow
~5 min	Pressure, temperature, and water level in the pressurizer are read	Automated system	Yes	Gauges in the control room note pressurizer water level is higher than normal, pressure is falling, and temperature is constant
~5 min	Humans take pressurizer water level to mean system is filling with water, confirming decision to alter HPI pump flow and leading them to drain off primary system cooling water through the let-down system	Human	No	Steam bubbles begin to form in the primary system; loss of coolant event begins

[a] *This was triggered unintentionally by maintenance work. For this incident, there is in fact a considerable chain of events preceding the incident that one could consider, but we will focus our attention to a narrow time slice for the sake of brevity.*
[b] *In this chart, "automated system" refers to an engineered system designed to carry out a specified action when system sensors register a well-defined set of conditions.*
Shaded lines reflect actions that are inconsistent with the revised system goal stated earlier.

actions are consistent with the revised system goal we identified earlier. Here the accident only serves to illustrate our framework, so we choose a small but significant slice of time.

The purpose of Table 17.1 is to allow us to systematically examine how the distributed agency of this system functioned in those crucial first minutes of the accident and to identify the consequences of the actions taken by system actors with agency. "Action" can also mean inaction in scenarios where an actor has (or should have) agency: for example, the first and third incidents at 13 s are both incidents in which action would have been consistent with the revised system goal but was not carried out. In one case the pilot-operated relief valve failed to close; in the second case, operators failed to close the block valve—a valve designed to serve as manual backup to the pilot-operated relief valve.

It is important to note the "actor" column in Table 17.1 is not intended to assign blame in cases where actions inconsistent with the overarching system goals were taken. It is only a reflection of who or what acted within the system; it does not explore why a given action was taken. It is also important to note that the time period of this chart could be expanded in both directions—and indeed may need to be for a full understanding of the incident. Overall, this approach identifies when different components of the system acted against its goals or acted in opposing ways; we can then start asking why those opposing or inconsistent actions were taken.

For TMI-2, there were multiple inconsistent actions in this time range. Unpacking why each failure occurred is in some instances messy, requires investigation beyond the time frame we have picked, and is done fairly thoroughly elsewhere (Kemeny et al., 1979). However, we would like to reflect here on the actions of human actors in TMI-2 who carried out several actions inconsistent with the system goals because they will be particularly instructive when we later address the relevance of the framework here for CPSs involving AI.

As Kemeny et al. (1979) noted, the actions of the humans within the system were based on how they interpreted the context for the limited data from sensors installed within the engineered system. They could not see within the reactor core itself, and they could not directly observe all of the components in the system they had the capacity to influence. Instead, they relied on data from the sensors installed within the system and interpreted these data (as conveyed to them by the system designers), to decide how to proceed.

The humans' interpretation of the system that day was based on the experience they built of the system in normal operation. Why? Their training did not address "minor" events, and tellingly the TMI accident was a chain of minor events, all of which led to a confusing combination of data the human actors had difficulty interpreting in the moment. Arguably the system needed operators with a more complete understanding of the system that day to achieve its goal, and this need could have been fulfilled via appropriate training.

Before we move on to our next theme, it may be helpful to consider how one might apply the framework presented here beyond this investigation. For TMI-2, we are working with evidence of how the incident unfolded, which conveniently narrows our focus for the purpose of this illustration. For a system under development, we might begin with a set of somewhat different questions: What aspects of the system involve a context for decision-making that results in action? What actors exist within the system? What agency do they have? Are there bounds or limits to that agency, either in the form of rule-based code, physical barriers, limitations or failure modes inherent to the components of the system involved in any resulting action? What assumptions, legal frameworks, or design decisions underpin those bounds or limits, and who has decided to impose them? In many cases, all of these factors shaping agency within a system relate closely to the third question theme: assurance.

17.3.3 Assurance

Assurance is a concept that evokes notions of comfort, safety, and security. It has many potential uses, describing everything from a state of mind ["confidence of mind or manner: easy freedom from self-doubt or uncertainty" (Merriam-Webster, 2019)] to anything that "inspires or tends to inspire confidence" (Merriam-Webster, 2019). It also relates to the concepts of trust—another term with many meanings (see, e.g., Hoff & Bashir, 2015; Lee & See, 2004 and references therein)—and risk. This question theme is included to help identify what assurance means in the context of the system under investigation. Who or what is being assured, why, and how? Do the properties of the system requiring assurance shape the system in question, and if so how? Are the assurances being made consistent with system design and function? How do the mechanisms of assurance change with time and context? Are the assurances being made accurate?

In the nuclear industry, both then and now, providing an assurance of safety is a primary concern (see, e.g., He, Mol, Zhang, & Lu, 2014; Squassoni, 2011 and references therein). Because the public is aware of the potential dangers of radiation, building a plant like TMI-2 requires those involved in making its construction possible to assure the surrounding community that those living near the facility will be safe, that radiation will not be released into the environment in normal operations, and that adequate risk mitigation strategies exist to ensure safety even in the event of an unanticipated occurrence. This strategy relates back to the initial system goal we specified, which expressed a desire to produce energy safely.

In exploring the TMI-2 accident and its aftermath, Kemeny et al. (1979) found that TMI-2—and indeed most nuclear reactors in operation at the time were not truly safe.[k] They attributed this to actions of human actors (e.g., operators, managers, regulatory bodies, and local media) in the system. As Kemeny et al. put it,

> We are convinced that if the only problems were equipment problems, this Presidential Commission would never have been created. The equipment was sufficiently good that, except for human failures, the major accident and Three Mile Island would have been a minor incident. Wherever we looked, we found problems with the human beings who operate the plant, with the management that runs the key organization, and with the agency that is charged with assuring the safety of nuclear power plants. *(Kemeny, 1979, p. 8)*

They then elaborate on why they focus on the human components of the system (which, as one can imagine, based on the appearance of so many new actors, has grown considerably):

> The most serious 'mindset' is the preoccupation of everyone with the safety of the equipment, resulting in the down-playing of the importance of the human element in nuclear power generation. We are tempted to say that while an enormous effort was expended to assure that safety-related equipment functioned as well as possible, and that there was backup equipment in depth, what the NRC [Nuclear Regulatory Commission] and the industry have failed to recognize sufficiently is that the human beings who manage and operate the plants constitute an important safety system. *(Kemeny, 1979, p. 10)*

[k]This does not make them unsafe—indeed the primary harm resulting from the TMI-2 accident was mental stress. It simply means the high safety standard expected of a nuclear power plant was not met in the systems being licensed to operate at the time.

This situation implies a level of trust (ignoring for now the complexity this word alone brings in) in the engineered components of the system, which then translated to trust in the system itself. This was despite the fact that humans and engineered components shared agency in nearly every action the system took in the accident in question.

In this contradiction, we find key questions we can learn from TMI-2: Are there contradictions between the stated and manifested mechanisms of assurance in such systems? Have interactions and overlapping agency for all types of actors in the system been identified and properly considered? And do assurances truly apply to the system as a whole, or only a subset of the system?

In TMI-2 the next questioning theme—metrics—played a significant role in shaping how the various actors in the system attempted to restore the system to a safe state.

17.3.4 Metrics

As with most question themes we have introduced thus far, the definition of "metrics" is varied. The Oxford Dictionary defines the term as "a set of figures or statistics that measure results" or "a system or standard of measurement" (2019a). In the case of a system like TMI-2, the appropriate metrics may seem fairly straightforward, typically referring to the measurement of physical quantities best expressed numerically that provide information on the physical state of the system—for example, pressure, temperature, radiation levels, and so on. But in other CPSs and even within certain aspects of the system under investigation here, this question theme becomes much more complex.[1] This complexity is particularly notable when metrics are used as an indirect means to measure or optimize some aspect of a system that is difficult to quantify (O'Neil, 2017). All of this leaves us with a series of new questions to explore: Who decides what metrics to use to create, evaluate, or achieve a task relevant to a system? Why? How are they used? What are the consequences?

For the sake of brevity, we'll focus here on the three key metrics that played a role in the loss of coolant event:

- the water level of the pressurizer,
- the temperature of the primary coolant water,
- the pressure of the primary coolant system.

The first metric was used to indirectly assess the truly crucial question: how much water was in the reactor core? In normal operations, this was a valid indirect metric. At normal operating pressures and temperatures, the water in the primary coolant system was in its liquid state. In the accident that played out in TMI-2, however, this was no longer the case—a mixture of water and steam existed within this system in a condition that, if prolonged, can lead to two things: (1) oxidation of the zirconium alloy fuel rod cladding leading to a loss of integrity and the production of hydrogen gas and (2) temperatures high enough to melt the uranium oxide pellets within the fuel rods. If the primary system is open (as was the case in this incident), this condition can also lead to a situation in which all the water is expelled from the

---

[1]For the sake of brevity, this paper will not address metrics used in the human factor analysis and standards that influenced TMI-2's design. Some discussion of this can be found in Malone et al. (1980). Some of the major issues relating to the human factor component will also be identified later when discussing interfaces.

system. The pressurizer water level was high because steam was pushing up out of the pilot-operated release valve, bringing water with it, not because the primary cooling system was completely filled with water. The operators, assuming the latter, focused on reducing the flow of water into the system to avoid "going solid" (as they called filling the core with water). Therefore this metric led operators to a conclusion about the context they faced—based on their existing understanding of the system, which was true during normal operations—that was incorrect.

The second two metrics were appropriate for assessing the state of the water in the primary coolant system, but only when viewed together and as a function of time. Addressing this requires a short divergence into how pressure and temperature relate to the state of water.

Consider the case in which water is in its liquid state and it is being heated at a constant rate (as was approximately the case within the reactor core after fission was halted, in the first minutes of the accident). The temperature of the water will continue to increase until there is enough energy in the system to trigger a change in phase—from liquid to gas in this scenario. This point is commonly known as the boiling point of water. During the phase change, temperature remains constant. Now the point at which the phase change occurs depends on pressure, and in TMI-2, pressure in the system was decreasing due to the open pilot-operated relief valve. For water in this system, a decrease in pressure at a fixed temperature would lead to a decrease in the boiling-point temperature.

Pressure and temperature were appropriate metrics in the sense that they related to the state of the water in the system. However, the operators had to consider both metrics and think about their significance in light of changes to the system. They had to understand the basic physics earlier and understand why that might in turn lead to a high water level in the pressurizer, which was ultimately (in this case) an indirect measure of the state of the water in the primary coolant system—the part of the system they needed to regain control over. During the accident at TMI-2, the operators focused on one (indirect) indicator of the three to interpret the context and determine how to proceed.

What questions might we draw from this? Let us focus our consideration here on metrics that are essential for enabling the system to achieve its goals. What are they, how are they measured, how are they meant to be used, what actors within the system need to access them, and in what circumstances do they use them? Do the actors have the tools they need to use the metrics adequately? Do they know when to distrust a metric or combination of metrics? Do they know when metrics are direct or indirect measures of the system state of interest? Are the use cases of the metrics clear, and are any assumptions relating to their interpretation known to system actors and/or adequately taken into account in the design of the system (e.g., via system boundaries and limitations to system or actor agency)? When and how are the metrics communicated to system actors, and how does this influence their actions?

As the last question earlier suggests, the ways metrics—and, indeed, data of any kind—are conveyed to actors within the system play an essential role in how that system functions. To investigate this for the TMI-2 accident, we will first introduce our next and final[m] question theme: interfaces.

---

[m] Final for the purposes of this work. This analytical framework is currently a work in progress, so new question themes may emerge with time (context and intent are currently likely additions, for example, as they seem to consistently emerge from this and other work, but we will save their consideration for future publications).

17.3.5 Interfaces

The word interface conjures up the idea of a meeting place or connection point—"a point where two systems, subjects, organizations, etc. meet and interact" (Oxford Dictionaries, 2019b). In this framework, interfaces can occur between subsystems or actors of any kind and can take on many (visible or invisible) forms. In all cases, though, there is an exchange (one-way, two-way, apparent, or hidden) of information that can influence the actions of the system as a whole.

For TMI-2 the control room is the most visible interface of relevance to the accident and is the one we will focus our attention on here. In this case, it is a point of communication between the engineered components monitoring the state of the reactor system and the human operators and managers charged with ensuring the reactor system continues to achieve its goals (whatever they may be at the time). The control room is a complex system in its own right. Kemeny et al. (1979, p. 91) provides a description of the place:

> To a casual visitor, the control room at TMI-2 can be an intimidating place, with messages coming from the loudspeaker of the plant's paging system; panel upon panel of red, green, amber and white lights; and alarms that sound or flash warnings many times each hour.

During the accident the humans interacting with this interface relied too much on one indicator (PORV status). Following this, they chose one metric (the pressurizer water level) to help them interpret the state of the reactor core and ignored two others, which—when combined with the first—told another story entirely. Given the description of the control room, this confusion seems unsurprising—but is it? We will explore this question by reflecting both on the interface design and on the capabilities of the humans required to interface with it.

We will begin with a focus on the design of the interface, paying specific attention to the elements of the interface that appeared to play a role in the TMI-2 accident: the PORV indicator light and the lights indicating the state of the valves connecting the backup pumps to the secondary system.

As noted in the accident story, the PORV indicator shaped the operators' interpretation of the state of the reactor core. In this case the indicator was linked to a switch linked to a solenoid used to open and close the valve. When the solenoid was energized, the light came on; when the solenoid deenergized, the light came off (Malone et al., 1980, p. 30). In normal operations the valve should open and then close in this sequence of events. In the case of TMI-2, the physical closure did not occur when the solenoid deenergized, meaning that the light—which was meant to indicate closure once it switched off—provided operators with information that did not align with the actual state of the system. This contributed to their confusion regarding the state of the system, which in turn influenced their actions on the day of the accident.

When recounting the sequence of events during the accident, we also noted that two lights—indicating that valves between backup pumps to the secondary system were manually shut—were overlooked by the operators on duty that day. In one case the light was covered by a yellow maintenance tag; in the other the reason it was missed was unknown. We will set aside the second missed light, as analysis of this would lean toward conjecture. The light covered by the maintenance tag, however, provides a lesson that is useful: interfaces are not necessarily static objects. Those interacting with the interface may be capable of altering it. When might they do this, and what are the potential consequences?

Some consequences of interface alteration can be positive. Anyone who has worked in complex environments like the one described earlier is likely to have appreciated a colleague's attempt to clarify confusing indicators or share useful tips they learned while trying to get a gauge working again. Others—like the maintenance tag in this example[n]—can be problematic.

The maintenance tag also reminds us of something else: the possibility that some portion of the interface or components sending data to the interface can malfunction. These incidents can lead to confusion even in the case where indicators are designed to accurately reflect the state of the system. If the malfunction is not immediately noticeable, inaccurate or misleading information may be transferred between different subsystems, opening up another potential path toward inappropriate action.

In this account, there is evidence we have learned from TMI-2. Most safety-critical systems take this into account in some way (see, e.g., Morris & Koopman, 2005)—generally by using some type of redundancy within the design of the system. However, it is still important to ask broader questions about when and how this possibility is considered and how these mechanisms for dealing with component or communication failure relate to decisions the system makes.

Another consideration still is the level of understanding subsystems in an autonomous system have about the system as a whole, because this relates to how each subsystem decides on appropriate actions in the face of unanticipated situations unfolding in the form of confusing or previously unencountered information conveyed by an interface within its domain. For TMI-2 the most relevant subsystem to consider is human, and the level of understanding the humans in that system had related directly to two things: (1) their day-to-day experience with the reactor system and (2) their training.[o]

Addressing the first point requires a closer look at the pressure and temperature metrics ignored by the operators on that day. They could have been used to indicate that the water in the coolant system was undergoing a phase change from liquid to gas. Instead, they were ignored. Why? As Kemeny et al. note, "there was no direct indication that the combination of pressure and temperature meant that the cooling water was turning into steam" (1979, p. 11). As knowledge of the state of the cooling water within the system was central to ensuring safe operations, one could suggest that the two metrics of relevance should ideally have been used to indicate the state of the water within the system.

The second point requires a more in-depth investigation than we can carry out in this chapter; however, it is an essential one to consider for any future system. Training refers to that undergone by human operators before they become part of the reactor system. Kemeny et al. note that "[r]eactor operators are trained how to respond and to respond quickly in emergencies. Initial actions are ingrained, almost automatic and unthinking" (1979, p. 91). In the event of any accident at a nuclear plant like TMI-2, rapid responses are necessary to restore system integrity and safe operation; there is little time to think

---

[n]This problem occurs despite the possibly good intentions behind its placement.

[o]There are other factors that we will not go into here for the sake of brevity, as they require a much wider scope. These include the operating procedures used by the operators that day and communication regarding minor safety incidents at reactors at other sites with similar designs. Both are discussed in Kemeny et al. (1979).

through problems before they become difficult to control. This fast tempo is one of the reasons for shared agency in such a system: engineered responses can take much less time than human responses and are therefore sensible to use (with an appropriate level of redundancy) for events requiring quick action.

Not all events can be anticipated, however, and in the case of TMI-2, not all known possible events were planned for. Operators had specific training on how to respond for major incidents, but they did not have the opportunity to develop the skills necessary to respond events that were considered minor. In the case of the TMI-2 accident—a series of minor events that eventually spiraled into one major one—operators found themselves in an unknown situation that they were not equipped to handle appropriately. Kemeny et al. note that the training program was "conceptually weak; emphasis was not given to fundamental understanding of the reactor" (1979, p. 50). That missing understanding—particularly with regard to the state of water within the primary coolant system—may have changed the outcome for TMI-2 that day.

17.4 Discussion and conclusions

In this work, we have used a case study approach to describe an analytical framework we are currently developing at the 3A Institute in consultation with industry partners. We have chosen a historical example not only because it allows us to illustrate the framework while analysis on current systems are ongoing but also because it makes an important point: past CPSs can be used as lessons to help us shape the future of technology.

Using our framework to analyze accidents like TMI-2 allows us to improve it, develop it, and most importantly ensure we are asking the right questions. We can then apply the developed framework to systems in the design, management, or governance[P] stages of a CPS life cycle to help us mitigate or avoid future accidents. Much was learned from TMI-2, but recent events [e.g., Correctional Offender Management Profiling for Alternative Sanctions (COMPAS); see Angwin, Larson, Mattu, & Kirchner, 2016, the Cambridge Analytica scandal; see Cadwalladr & Graham-Harrison, 2018, Stuxnet; see Zetter, 2014, and Air France 447; see Elish, 2019] have made it clear that we still have much more to learn. Our tendency to focus on the individual subsystems of CPSs, rather than on the connections between those subsystems, and indeed on the system as a composite whole has already been shown in time and again to lead to undesirable and unintended outcomes.

There are broader lessons we can take from TMI-2 that apply directly to AI and the idea of a human-machine shared context. For example, the question theme of autonomy brings out the systems aspect of AI: its need to be connected to a larger system—of data, sensors, actuators, humans, and environments—to become useful. This linkage firmly places technology involving AI in a particular context and allows us to ask questions about system goals, possible

[P]Governance is often thought of as something done after the fact, when the new technology has already been invented. It does not always have to be; indeed, some preliminary work we are doing on the German government suggests policy can anticipate technology and, indeed, even help shape it.

autonomous actions, requirements or capabilities enabling those actions, and what happens when that context is changed.

The agency theme brings out questions about actors and boundaries within an AI system: what agency does each of the system components have? What agency should they have? Where is that agency shared, and what are the possible consequences? But the theme can also be interpreted as an opportunity to explore how agents within a system interact to define the agency of the system as a whole.

The assurance theme helps us to ask whether the agency that an AI system has been granted is consistent with what we want. Is it a safe system? Is it trustworthy? Are the assurances being provided for a given system truly meaningful? What assurances are necessary for a system to be released "into the wild"?

The metrics theme plays a significant role in AI systems, where AI models may be designed to optimize metrics without any sense of what those metrics mean or how they relate to our true intentions. Questioning why we use certain metrics and how their specific application might fail within the system (due to design assumptions, changed context, component failure, etc.) is essential for building robust systems of any kind but is particularly important for those involving AI and autonomy.

Finally the interfaces theme brings out the relationship between control and communication in these systems, both of which play central roles in how a system emerges from a diverse collection of subsystems. What does a given actor know when and how does this influence the actions that actor takes? When your AI system must coexist in a dynamic and ever-changing world with humans, how are the intentions of the system communicated to humans or other systems that interact with it? This shared context is particularly important when systems may appear to be physically identical but (due to differences in computational aspects of the system, including AI models) behave very differently.

If anything, TMI-2 teaches us that a safe future with AI—a future where we have a healthy sense of trust in AI technologies—requires us to take a step back and consider any complex technological system as a collection of tightly coupled subsystems that evolve together as a function of time and context (including the humans comprising a component of a system—either directly or indirectly, via physical presence, design intentions, human data, boundaries placed in law, etc.). In our chapter title, we suggest beginning with the human because we are everywhere in these systems—something we tend to forget—and connections with these human components or conceptions about how aspects of a system should work tend to be points of failure. It is our hope that the approach we have presented here is a useful first step toward improving humanity's relationship with a technological future we may not have yet imagined.

Acknowledgments

All of the staff and students at the 3A Institute have contributed indirectly and directly to this work in some way or another; we are profoundly grateful for all of your questions, your sound advice, and your patience in all of our discussions and endless deliberations over this framework, which all of us hope will lead to a new (as of yet unnamed) applied science. E. Williams would especially like to thank Katrina Ashton for her astute questions and careful edits in the final draft stages of this work.

We are also grateful to our funders, the Australian National University and CSIRO's Data-61, and our educational partners, Microsoft Australia, Macquarie Bank, and KPMG, for making it possible for us to deliver some of the content presented here to our first cohort of students.

References

Acatech. (2011). Cyber-physical systems: Driving force for innovation in mobility, health, energy and production. *Acatech Position Paper*, (December). Retrieved from https://www.acatech.de/wp-content/uploads/2018/03/acatech_POSITION_CPS_Englisch_WEB.pdf.

Amodei, D., Olah, C., Steinhardt, J., Christiano, P., Schulman, J., & Mané, D. (2016). *Concrete problems in AI safety*: (pp. 1–29). Retrieved from http://arxiv.org/abs/1606.06565.

Angwin, J., Larson, J., Mattu, S., & Kirchner, L. (2016). *Machine bias*. Retrieved May 20, 2019, from ProPublica website. https://www.propublica.org/article/machine-bias-risk-assessments-in-criminal-sentencing.

Cadwalladr, C., & Graham-Harrison, E. (2018). *Revealed: 50 million Facebook profiles harvested for Cambridge Analytica in major data breach*. Retrieved May 20, 2019, from The Guardian website. https://www.theguardian.com/news/2018/mar/17/cambridge-analytica-facebook-influence-us-election.

Clark, J., & Amodei, D. (2016). *Faulty reward functions in the wild*. Retrieved May 23, 2019, from Open AI Blog website. https://openai.com/blog/faulty-reward-functions/.

Elish, M. C. (2019). Moral crumple zones: Cautionary tales in human-robot interaction (we robot 2016). *Engaging Science, Technology, and Society*, 5, 40–60. https://doi.org/10.2139/ssrn.2757236.

Exelon. (2019). *Three Mile Island unit 1 to shut down by September 30, 2019*. Retrieved May 20, 2019, from https://www.exeloncorp.com/newsroom/Pages/Three-Mile-Island-Unit-1-To-Shut-Down-By-September-30,-2019.aspx.

Giddens, A. (1979). *Central problems in social theory*. https://doi.org/10.1007/978-1-349-16161-4.

He, G., Mol, A. P. J., Zhang, L., & Lu, Y. (2014). Nuclear power in China after Fukushima: Understanding public knowledge, attitudes, and trust. *Journal of Risk Research*, 17(4), 435–451. https://doi.org/10.1080/13669877.2012.726251.

Hoff, K. A., & Bashir, M. (2015). Trust in automation: Integrating empirical evidence on factors that influence trust. *Human Factors*, 57(3), 407–434. https://doi.org/10.1177/0018720814547570.

Huang, H., Messina, E., & Albus, J. (2003). Toward a generic model for autonomy levels for unmanned systems (ALFUS). In *Performance metrics for intelligent systems (PerMIS) workshop*. Retrieved from http://oai.dtic.mil/oai/oai?verb=getRecord&metadataPrefix=html&identifier=ADA515323.

Irpan, A. (2018). *Deep reinforcement learning doesn't work yet*. Retrieved May 23, 2019, from Sorta Insightful (Blog) website. https://www.alexirpan.com/2018/02/14/rl-hard.html.

Kemeny, J. G., Babbitt, B., Haggerty, P. E., Lewis, C., Marks, P. A., Marrett, C. B., et al. (1979). *Report of the President's commission on the accident Three Mile Island: The need for change: The legacy of TMI*.

Lee, E. A. (2015). The past, present and future of cyber-physical systems: A focus on models. *Sensors*, 15(3), 4837–4869. https://doi.org/10.3390/s150304837.

Lee, J. D., & See, K. A. (2004). Trust in automation: Designing for appropriate reliance. *Human Factors*, 46(1), 50–80. https://doi.org/10.1518/hfes.46.1.50_30392.

Luck, M., & D'Inverno, M. (1995). A formal framework for agency and autonomy. In *Proceedings of the first international conference on multiagent systems (ICMAS-95)* (pp. 254–260): AAAI.

Malone, T. B., Kirkpatrick, M., Mallory, K., Eike, D., Johnson, J. H., & Walker, R. W. (1980). *Human factors evaluation of control room design and operator performance at Three Mile Island-2*. (Final Report NUREG/CR-1270-V-1).

Merriam-Webster. (2019). *Assurance*. Retrieved May 17, 2019, from Merriam-Webster Dictionary website. https://www.merriam-webster.com/dictionary/assurance.

Morris, J., & Koopman, P. (2005). Representing design tradeoffs in safety-critical systems. *ACM SIGSOFT Software Engineering Notes*, 30(4), 1. https://doi.org/10.1145/1082983.1083228.

O'Neil, C. (2017). *Weapons of math destruction: How big data increases inequality and threatens democracy* [Reprint]. Broadway Books.

Oxford Dictionaries. (2019a). *Metric*. Retrieved May 19, 2019, from Oxford Dictionaries website. https://en.oxforddictionaries.com/definition/metric.

Oxford Dictionaries. (2019b). Interface. Retrieved May 19, 2019, from Oxford Dictionaries website. https://en.oxforddictionaries.com/definition/interface.

Sen, A. (1992). *Inequality reexamined*. Oxford: Oxford University Press.

Squassoni, S. (2011). *Nuclear power: Between faith and fear*. Retrieved May 19, 2019, from Bulletin of the Atomic Scientists website. https://thebulletin.org/roundtable_entry/nuclear-power-between-faith-and-fear/.

Swaine, L. (2016). The origins of autonomy. In *Vol. XXXVII(2)*. *History of political thought*.

Wolf, M., & Serpanos, D. (2018). Safety and security in cyber-physical systems and internet-of-things systems. *Proceedings of the IEEE*, 106(1), 9–20. https://doi.org/10.1109/JPROC.2017.2781198.

Zetter, K. (2014). *An unprecedented look at Stuxnet, the world's first digital weapon*. Retrieved from Wired website. https://www.wired.com/2014/11/countdown-to-zero-day-stuxnet/.

Digital humanities and the digital economy

Shu-Heng Chen

AI-ECON Research Center, Department of Economics, National Chengchi University, Taipei, Taiwan

18.1 Motivation

In this chapter, we address the relation between the humanities and economics or social sciences in the digital era. Specifically, we address this relation from the perspective of scientific *consilience,* which has been a subject arising in the history of science and perhaps now has already entered its second-wave version. The opening chapter of Slingerland and Collard (2011) extensively motivates the idea of the *second wave of consilience*, which has the following characteristics. First, in the second wave of consilience, "humanists and scientists work together as *equal partners* in constructing a shared framework for inquiry." (Ibid, p. 4; Italics added). Second, with a sort of *nonreductive vertical integration*, the second wave of consilience respects the relative autonomy and heuristic indispensability of human-level concepts and truths and demands so that the flow of explanation and interaction goes both ways in the chain (Ibid, p. 36). Third, it *"contains space for all the disciplines that explore the complexities of human reality,* acknowledging that each possesses its own conceptual tools and methods." (Ibid, p. 36; Italics added).

The question to be posed in this article concerns the role of ICT (stands for information and communication technology) and the digital revolution in this second wave of consilience. We consider this question to be worthy of an examination because the increasing formation of a fully fledged cyberspace has presented humanistic scholars with a new territory that their forerunners could never have had the fortune to experience. With this fresh encounter, we shall make three assertions in this article. First the cyberspace, to be discussed further, can be regarded as a *mapping, projection*, or, by borrowing the ideal from Jean Baudrillard

(1929–2007), a *simulacrum*, of our physical space (the flesh world).[a] Second the gulf between the humanities and economics/social sciences that originally exists in the physical space may become much narrower and hence easier to bridge in this projected cyberspace. Our second argument is based on the fact that the humanities have already earned a new status in this cyberspace, referred to as the *digital humanities*, in which a gateway to the digital economy is emerging. With the emerging gateway, our third argument is that the digital humanities are the foundation of the digital economy, and the digital economy can be perceived as an extension of the digital humanities. The third argument is based on a reflection on the *ontology* of the humanities and the *reinvention of individuality* in the cyberspace.

The rest of this article is organized as follows. Section 18.2 begins with a discussion of what the digital humanities are. After discussing books in the cyberspace and human readers who are empowered with artificial readers, we propose an ontological augmentation of the existing definitions of the digital humanities suitable for the presence of the twin space, that is, the physical space coexisting with the cyberspace. Section 18.3 extends the cyberspace of books and beings with a formal introduction to the twin space to justify our first argument. The twin space is then used as the key analytic framework of this paper, and at this junction, we borrow the idea of *narrative economics* proposed by Robert Shiller, 2012 Nobel Laureate in Economics, to justify the second argument. Justifying the third argument requires a lengthy process in the three subsequent sections. Section 18.4 takes a closer look at the nature of the digital economy, while Section 18.5 shows that the twin space reinvents *individuality* and *identity*, which engenders a new form of the *biography*, a familiar entity in the humanities. This form of biography can only be fully developed with the technology currently running the digital economy, such as cryptocurrencies and blockchains. Section 18.6 shows that the fully developed biography or chorography can be used to solve the matching problem in the cyberspace, and through the *smartness principle* (see Section 18.6.2), many matching problems in the physical space can be solved as well. Using the smartness principle to operate the digital economy is then demonstrated with Sakoda's agent-based model of social interactions (Sakoda, 1971). Hence, from digital biographies to matchmaking, the individuality reinvented is manifested through the thread connecting the humanities with the economy, and this accomplishes our third argument. Section 18.7 provides the concluding remarks.

18.2 What is digital humanities?

The title of this section has long been pursued in the literature. It has become a rich source for incessant intellectual debates, but the subject matter is too voluminous to be reviewed in a single chapter. Fortunately, by briefly mentioning Terras, Nyhan, and Vanhoutte (2013), we can go directly to our departure. In the opening chapter of the book they edited, Terras et al. made a number of crucial points about the definition issue. First, there is no urgency to settle the definition issue; second, it is desirable to have an open, dynamic, inclusive, and pluralistic

---

[a] We may consider using the term *simulacra* due to the postmodernism philosopher Jean Baudrillard. Baudrillard (1981) partly inspired the authoring of this article. It is anticipated that the reader may find the connections while reading this article.

approach to address the issue. "Indeed, at the current time, not only does a comprehensive definition appear to be impossible to formulate, when the breadth of work …is considered… it might ultimately prove unproductive, by fossilising an emerging field and constraining new, boundary-pushing work." (Ibid, p. 6).

In the same vein as their review, we consider that the purview of digital humanities is constantly *evolving*. Its current formation in part originates from its precedent stages, including digital libraries, digital museums, and digital archives. Basically, what these stages did was to transform what people had written, crafted, and performed into digital objects. After these objects were digitalized, the physical places (libraries and museums), which used to accommodate these objects for exhibition purposes, found their incarnations in the cyberspace (digital libraries and digital museums).

18.2.1 Artificial readers

After texts have been digitalized, they can be read not only by humans but also by *artificial readers* (software agents or algorithms).[b] For some kinds of readings and many other things, machines can do it much faster than humans (Davenport & Kirby, 2016). Therefore, by "recruiting" these artificial readers as "assistants," the reading capacity of human readers is substantially expanded. Not only can they now "read" more, but also they can answer many questions that require voluminous reading. Here, we actually come to a point related to what Franco Moretti has proposed the distant reading or the extended reading (Moretti, 2013).

A typical job for the artificial reader is *automated or computational content analysis.*[c] It starts from sentence parsing, keyword identification, word frequency calculation, co-word analysis, topic identification, similarity analysis, network analysis, sentiment analysis, and so on, all the way from the syntactic level of the content to the semantic level using natural language processing, computational linguistics, machine learning, and artificial intelligence.[d] The ultimate goal of the text analysis is to regard reading, an important part of human cognition, as a part of machine dreams, that is, to make machines capable of assisting humans in reading.

[b]The economics of Herbert Simon (1916–2001) has long-positioned agents in economics as *information processing agents*. "Simon's behavioural economics is almost comprehensively demonstrated by his encapsulation of Human Problem Solving and of agents and institutions as Information Processing Systems (Velupillai, 2018, p. 28)." In the cyberspace, nearly all artificial agents are literary information processing agents.

[c]Content analysis is a well-established field. The reader who is less familiar with this field is referred to Neuendorf (2002) and Krippendorff (2013). While both books provide quite a comprehensive review of the development of this field, Cioffi-Revilla (2014) gives an exclusive review of an automated and computational versions within the context of computational social science.

[d]While most of the content that we target in this article are text data, content analysis is increasingly applied to other forms of data, such as graphs, images, audio, and video signal data. See Chen (2018).

18.2.2 Cyberspace of books

Once books (texts) can reside in cyberspace (the digital library), their physical distances from each other, conventionally defined based on their location in the exhibition hall, lose their meaning. Instead, new metrics based on readers' preferences will reshape *the metric space of books*. Since each reader has a different preference, this metric space is *idiosyncratic*, varying among individuals; in addition, since the reader's preference is not time invariant, this metric space could be constantly adapted to it, too. Despite this geometric complexity, this new kind of metric is more consistent with our intuitive understanding of a neighborhood, namely, two books or two texts are *close* if and only if they are *similar* in the eye of the beholder.

The imaginary metric inspires an *agent-based model* for a reader, which simulates the dynamic interactions that can occur in the cyberspace of books. The agent here is not necessarily limited to humans but could encompass books, texts, and other objects. Since the agent-based model is endowed with a metric, it can be endowed with a spatial or network meaning (Namatame & Chen, 2016). Fig. 18.1 gives an example of this network. It is mainly an *ego network* of a human reader (the ego and the focal agent) and the books to which the ego is directly or indirectly connected. This simplification is an excerpt of the full network spanning from humans to humans, humans to books, and books to books. The full network has been used for a discussion of the discovery of a new technology (Johnson, 2010) and the spread of ideas (McCloskey, 2016a).[e]

In Fig. 18.1, when the reader is "interacting" with (reading) one specific book or text (the *red object* in Fig. 18.1), the reader can also interact with its neighboring books (texts; the *purple and*

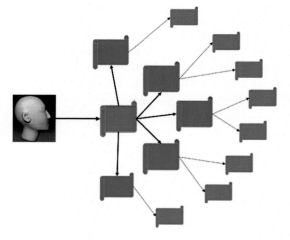

FIG. 18.1   Agent-based modeling of reading in the cyberspace.

[e]The full network is a subject for its own pursuit. For example, the full network can be reorganized into a *bipartite network* of readers and books or even generally to *a multiplex or multilayer network* with many different kind of *things*, each occupying its own layer. In this article, for convenience, only the single-layer network is used, but we should not be subsumed by it when more power of expressiveness is needed.

the blue objects in Fig. 18.1); of course the network would be too complex in that it cannot be automatically visualizable without the involvement of artificial readers, basically the searching algorithms.[f] As our usual concept of social networking, the interactions can progress to the *k degrees of separation* where the parameter *k* is determined by the "sociable" preference of the reader.[g] For example, in Fig. 18.1, the demonstrated specific reader (the *red object*) has the energy to reach the objects with two degrees of separation, but this is just one of the infinitely possible paths that a reader can have in this potentially highly interactive environment.[h]

Up to this point, one may wonder how inanimate books can have interactions with human readers. Indeed, *books are inanimate in physical space*; nevertheless, when it comes to cyberspace, books are basically a sequence of codes that can be triggered with other codes.[i] This is why we claim that books can also be deemed as agents and the agent-based model can be justified as a proper representation for us to understand the complex interactions between human readers and books in this "brave new world."[j]

A typical interaction of artificial readers with the human reader is to gather, from the neighboring objects (books or database), the spatiotemporal information related to the text upon examination by the human reader. For example, the application of the geographic information system to the text enables us to place the text in a frame of space, place, and time, which can be narrated by integrating with other related frames of space, place, and time.[k] This kind of artificial agent is of particular benefit to the humanities since, for those major destinies in the text, "5W1H"[l] can be addressed with the provision of more comprehensive (informative) surroundings.[m]

---

[f]Search engines contribute substantially to the modern economy that has been coined as the *search economy* or, simply, *Google economy*, by John Battelle (Battelle, 2011). When addressing the connection between the digital humanities and the digital economy, one should be reminded of these engines.

[g]This is to follow the well-known *six degrees of separation* initiated by the Hungarian writer Frigyes Karinthy (1887–1938) in his 1929 short story, *Chains*, which was later popularized by the famous small-world experiment led by Stanley Milgram (1933–1984) and Jeffrey Travers (Milgram, 1967; Travers & Milgram, 1969).

[h]The complexity of this kind of dynamics has been eloquently described by Stuart Kauffman's notion of *enablement* and *adjacent possibles* in which agents may constantly experience unanticipated changes (Kauffman, 2000). If humans cannot know what may happen as a result of one of their clicks, then can machines simulate or enumerate all of these possibly infinitely large numbers of paths emanating from that node and make a decision for humans? Hence, if not, machines may not be able to replace human agents in reading, specifically in the decisions emanating from these complex interactions.

[i]To fully appreciate this sentence, a prerequisite for information theory is needed. The humanistic reader with limited exposure to information theory is referred to Campbell (1982).

[j]How possible is it for books to literally interact? Equally interesting to this imagination is the "battle of books" coined by Jonathan Swift (1667–1745), as a title of part of the prolegomena of his book *A Tale of a Tub* in 1704 (Swift, 1968). The battle refers to the controversy between ancient learning and modern learning. In cyberspace the battle is not just a metaphor only; by redrawing Fig. 18.1 the reader can define a battle of books in which he/she is interested.

[k]This is what is known as *spatial humanities* (Bodenhamer, Corrigan, & Harris, 2015).

[l]5W1H refers to "who," "what," "where," "when," "why," and "how."

[m]One example of reading in this more interactive environment can be illustrated with *Text 2.0*, developed by a German research team (Biedert et al., 2010).

One additional remark concerning Fig. 18.1 is made in light of *cyborgs* (Clynes & Kline, 1960). One may consider the network as an extension of the brain and the mind of each reader. The network originally begins with the one internally defined by the brain (Sporns, 2011) and its limited exposure to the outer environment in terms of a book or text but which is now further connected to an external web of knowledge objects. The dynamics (interactions) of the combined networks will be much more intensive and complex than what can occur in the original network.

18.2.3 An ontological augmentation

If reading in the era before *the second machine age*, a term coined by Brynjolfsson and McAfee (2014), is pictured as a primitive *dyadic* relation with limited interactions, what happens now about reading is a complex network with rather extendable interactions. The conventional definitions of the digital humanities (DH) are very much driven from the perspective of machines; by and large, they define DH as the *applications of digital technology* to the study of the humanities. These definitions essentially are from the methodological viewpoints rather than from the ontological viewpoints. We agree with the most conventional definitions in the methodological vein, but we also know that methodological innovation can sometimes have nontrivial ontological implications. Take *mathematical economics* as an example. The *mathematical turn* in (neoclassical) economics is not just the application of mathematics to economics; instead, it goes beyond that and has fundamentally changed its ontology since (Lawson, 2003).[n]

In this article, we propose an *ontological augmentation* of the conventional definition of digital humanities. This ontological turn is motivated by the emergence of the "twin" space as the result of the recent ICT and digital revolution. In this section, we have already had a taste of a small part of the twin space by envisaging books (texts) in the cyberspace and its possible impacts. In the next section, we will formally introduce the twin space and reinvent individuality, which in turn motivates our proposed definition as follows: *Digital humanities is the study of the humanities in the era of the twin space (i.e., the physical space and its twin in cyber space) and there are two directions: in one direction, it is about the development of the humanities in the cyber space, and in the other direction it is about the impact of this development on the conventional humanities.* We provide this definition only to augment existing ones. As stated at the very beginning of this section, we believe that the definition itself will evolve based on what humanistic scholars really need, rather than being fossilized. In the following sections, we will elaborate on these two directions. As we shall see, our proposed definition enables us to see the connection between the digital humanities and the digital economy; specifically, we will observe why the former is the foundation of the latter and the latter is the extension of the former.

---

[n]The reader who is curious about the *mathematical turn* in economics is referred to Mirowski (1989), Stigum (1990), and Weintraub (2002). The consequences of economics becoming increasingly formal have reshaped the ontology of economics in a direction that may make many economists feel disconcerted.

18.3 The twin space

18.3.1 "Cloudy" digital humanities

Following the digital revolution the representations of what people said, thought, and did are not just in the form of paper and books; instead, they are directly prepared in digital form, the so-called *organic data* (Groves, 2011), and archived in the cyberspace or clouds. This activity is contributed to by the current ICT and digital technology, such as wearable devices, ubiquitous computing, and the Internet of Everything. These technologies enable us to map what happens in this physical space back into the cyberspace, which is fashionably referred to as *big data*.[°] Fig. 18.2 summarizes this development.

In Fig. 18.2 the three blocks in the middle portion depict our usual perception of the humanities. Basically, we place humans as the center, archiving their interactions with themselves and with their surroundings, including their natural environment. Every single moment when their minds are moving, such interactions are happening. In addition, these interactions are subject to the tools or technology available at that time, as are the archives of these interactions. Obviously, our technology constraints can only allow a very limited part of these interactions to be archivable, and that also restricts the domain of the humanities. The advent of digital technology, however, has changed the way in which we can archive. For a long time, books have been the means that we have used to archive the aforementioned interactions, but these conventional forms (the upper-left portion of Fig. 18.2) can now be further archived in a digital way (lower left), as Section 18.2 describes, as books in the cyberspace and also those nontextual archives (the artworks).

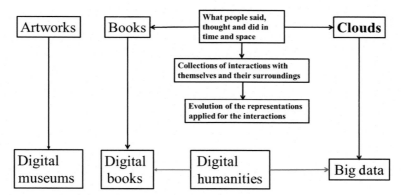

FIG. 18.2   Digital humanities after clouds and becoming cloudy.

<hr/>

[°]We do not wish to evoke another unsettled definition here apart from just mentioning that we follow the definition given by Chen and Venkatachalam (2017); in addition, Chen, Chie, and Tai (2016) have proposed two prototypes, namely, an Internet of cyborgs and an Internet of Things, to categorize the kind of big data collected by modern ICT technology.

In addition, the advent of digital technology has also changed the way in which humans can interact with themselves and their surroundings; interactions with digital technology directly contribute to the formation of archives in the form of clouds, which are digitally organic and are collectively called big data, as shown in the right portion of Fig. 18.2. The working domain of the digital humanities is, therefore, extended from its conventional digital archives to modern big data (the bottom of Fig. 18.2).

Take the literary study of happiness as an example. The usual approach of the digital humanities could begin with a collection of literary texts written in different times, and content analysis can be applied to extract the sentiments from these texts and compare the meaning and degree of happiness in these different times. However, the same approach can be applied to the tweets or big data that document the communications of hundreds of millions of minds, as demonstrated by the *Dow Jones of Happiness* proposed by Peter Dodds and Christopher Danforth (Dodds & Danforth, 2010).

18.3.2 The twin space and consilience

Based on what we have discussed, we can fairly well say that the digital revolution characterized by the current ICT and digital technologies enables us to map what happens in this physical space into its cyber counterpart as if we have two simultaneously co-existing spaces, as shown in Fig. 18.3. One is a society of human agents (the *blue dots* in Fig. 18.3) and "things" in the physical space (the *blue circle*), and the other is the "incarnation" of the former (the *red dots*) in the cyberspace (the *red circle*), further added, assisted, and empowered by a myriad of software agents (the *green dots*) that do not exist in the physical space.

While in the physical space only the present can exist and no one can stop the clock, the past as cumulated in our memory can vividly exist in cyberspace. This legacy is shown in Fig. 18.3 by the *red circles* stacking up over time, which comprise a significant part of big data. In fact, when people spend a substantial part of their daily activities directly in cyberspace, such as chatting over social media, shopping and purchasing in the Internet markets, and conducting various kinds of activities on the corresponding platforms, the act of copying

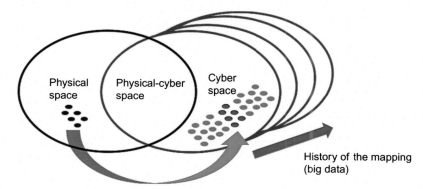

Physical Space Mapped to Cyber Space

FIG. 18.3   Mapping from the physical space to the cyberspace.

is not even required since their digital footprints are the original (organic) documents. Naturally, these identical mappings are automatically performed instantaneously. This synchronizing event could make the distinction between the cyber and the physical space increasingly murky, but that does not affect the mapping from the physical space to the cyberspace. To make the identical mapping explicit, in Fig. 18.3, *the physical cyberspace* is clearly mentioned in the overlap between the physical and cyberspace.

What are the implications of this mapping or the twin space for humanistic scholars? When the cyberspace provides not only the digital archives of the past but also storage "clouds" of the present, how would this impact the humanities? The aforementioned example of the Dow Jones of Happiness shows that, if the digital humanities offer humanistic scholars a key to entering the cyberspace of books and artworks, then we see no particular impediment that could prevent them from getting access to other corners of the (cyber) space. Alternatively put the original disciplinary boundaries in our physical space are less imposed when we come to cyberspace; that is to say, mobility between different disciplines is greatly enhanced.[p] Hence, from the viewpoint of *the unity of knowledge* or the consilience pursuit (Gould, 2003; Morson & Schapiro, 2017; Slingerland & Collard, 2011; Snow, 1959; Wilson, 1998), the cyberspace may provide an alternative consilience route. Indeed, as we mentioned earlier, if the humanities can be understood as the collections of the interactions of humans with themselves and their surroundings, then the tendency to have a broader scope of the humanities in the cyberspace is ineluctable.[q]

Now the opportunity is coming. The presence of the cyberspace can facilitate the linkage attempt between the humanities and economics or other social sciences when all of the data can be integrated in the clouds. In his proposed *narrative economics*, Shiller (2017) points out that social scientists are paying increasing attention to the role of *narratives*, acknowledging their roles in shaping not only individuals' behaviors, judgments, and decisions but also the social dynamics regarding cultures, memes, zeitgeists, ethos, and economic fluctuations. Shiller further points out that "we see little use of enormous databases of written word that might be used to study narratives." (Ibid, p. 969). This lack indicates that social scientists, including economists, can profit by working with humanistic scholars to study the narratives related to economic events, from the past to the present. Therefore, from a methodological viewpoint, the digital humanities constitute the foundation of the digital economy.[r]

---

[p]The cyberspace, thanks to the service performed by a tremendous number of software agents, could once again unexpectedly enlighten us that the world is small, smaller than what we thought, including both the animate and the inanimate. In that sense, we have a new version of the *"small world."*

[q]Recently, we have seen a recurring interest in the dialogue between humanistic scholars and economists, such as McCloskey (1998), Watts (2003), Ruccio and Amariglio (2003), Woodmansee and Osteen (2005), Roy and Zeckhauser (2016), Henderson (2017), Morson and Schapiro (2017), Rossi-Landi (2017), and Shiller (2017). It is interesting to notice that economists have started to believe that the humanities can enable them to delve deeply into the true, radical, and great uncertainty, which is beyond what the probabilistic analytics can generally offer. The dialogue may suggest the following division of labor: construct a mathematical stochastic model when the phenomenon is simple and clear, write a narrative when it gets complex while still manageable, and write a novel when it becomes unmanageably complex.

[r]The digital economy will be defined and discussed in the next section. For the time being, let us just take it as the economy in the cyberspace as we define the digital humanities.

While this discipline is still in its infancy, there are already a number of studies indicating the promising future of this stage (Chen, 2018). Finally, as Shiller also alerts us, narratives from their formation to spreads and the subsequent evolution are very complex: "[t]his is why narratives are difficult to study, and why there are limitations in textual analysis involving word counts or n-gram counts to quantify and study them." (Ibid, p. 971). To grapple with these difficulties, advanced or novel tools are needed, which may help to push the frontier of the digital humanities. Hence, in this regard, the digital economy can be considered to be an extension of the digital humanities.

In addition to the methodological innovation, there is another reason to support our third argument, which is the ontological drive (Sections 18.5 and 18.6). However, before we proceed further, let us make our perception of the digital economy clear.

18.4 The digital economy

Up to now, we have not defined the term "digital economy," it being so popularly used that it seems to be self-evident. Nevertheless, our proposed framework (Fig. 18.3) suggests a definition that may not be shared thoroughly by the existing understanding of the digital economy. In parallel with our earlier definition of the digital humanities, we define the digital economy as the economy operating in cyberspace and its interaction and co-evolution with the economy in the physical space. This definition, albeit broad, has two essential ingredients. First is *autonomy*. While the cyberspace is mapped from the physical space, the agents there are not all puppets; they can have varying degrees of autonomy, specifically for those artificial agents (the *green dots* in Fig. 18.3). Second is *intertwining*. The economy in the physical space and the one in the cyber space are generally highly intertwined and may have both cooperative and competitive relationships. The digital economy refers to both the autonomous and intertwining functions of the economy in cyberspace.

The definition earlier is commensurate with our general understanding of the digital economy (Allen, 2017; Brousseau & Curien, 2007; Goldfarb, Greenstein, & Tucker, 2015), and it is related, while not identical, to the usual conceptions of electronic commerce, namely, the online economy, Internet economy, network economy, search economy, knowledge economy, open-source economy, design economy, platform economy, sharing economy, matching economy, or blockchain economy. They are related because all these economies are underpinned by ICT, but our definition is further underpinned by the Internet of Things (IOT) and the interwoven cyberspace (Fig. 18.3), which may not be fully absorbed by others. In fact, ICT keeps on progressing, and the economy built upon different generations of ICT may have a different structure and operation. For example, the digital economy before and after the era of Web 2.0 or Web 3.0 will be different (Dolgin, 2012); similarly the digital economy before or after the invention of Google search will also be different (Battelle, 2011). The twin space can be considered as the new milestone for these waves of progress; hence the economy, regardless of its emblem as used before, is expected to converge to the digital economy characterized by the twin space.

Fig. 18.4 gives a sketch of the major components of the digital economy defined earlier. The left panel of the figure refers to the technologies that are currently involved in operating

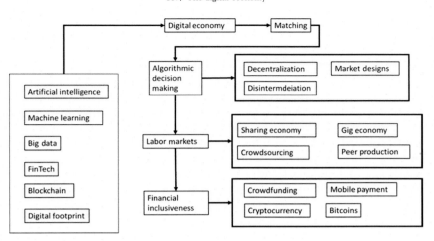

FIG. 18.4 A sketch of a digital economy.

the digital economy. Notice that the list is not exhaustive and that the listed components are not distinct from each other; in fact, they somewhat overlap, depending on our historical perspective. They are put there simply to serve the purpose of the general dialogue needed for this article. Among the six, we have already touched on the first three, artificial intelligence, machine learning, and big data, and the last two will be encountered in the next two sections. The only one that will not be specifically mentioned in this chapter is the fourth item, financial technology (FinTech).[s]

On the head of the figure, we place "matching" right next to the digital economy. In a nutshell the digital economy is about matching. This is so because the digital economy reinvents the idea of *individuality* (Section 18.5), upon which the evolving business models will be further oriented toward *customization* (individual based), and economic activities can be interpreted as the implementation of various matching processes (Section 18.6). This is why we treat matching in essentially the same way as the digital economy. By breaking down its concrete operations, we can see its significance from both the individual and market perspectives (the three blocks in the right panel of Fig. 18.4).

First, in the digital economy, matching is conducted both effectively and massively parallel, through the simultaneous recruitment of a myriad of artificial agents, which in turn help to make automated or semiautomated decisions. Therefore individual decision-making becomes increasingly algorithmic (programmed). The idea of matching also means that the economy is run in a more or fully decentralized fashion, where automated matching no longer requires manned intermediaries, which in turn facilitates the present *disintermediation* trend and *unmanned services*. Matching, as a nontrivial mathematical and computational problem involving a large set of behaviors and cultural considerations, requires a good market or platform design.

Market design is a well-established subject in economics (Bergemann & Morris, 2012; McMillan, 2003; Roth, 2015). In the twin space of modernity, many of the lessons acquired

---

[s]The interested reader is referred to Chishti and Barberis (2016).

in the "old times" still serve as the backbone of platform design; for example, in the *Internet auction*, the design of eBay and Amazon auctions can be considered as a proper extension of pre-Internet auctions (McMillan, 2003). Nonetheless the cyberspace does differ from the physical space in many subtle ways. For instance, it has a huge storage of information (big data)[t] and enjoys an ultraspeed of reaction time[u]; furthermore, man may behave differently when the mask is on (in the cyberspace) as opposed to when it is off (in the physical space)[v]; hence, platform design in many ways is not just a linear extension of the conventional market design on the ground. Because of this similarity and difference, we expect that more job opportunities for real humans will be directed to the design business, as an alternative understanding of the digital economy is the design economy.

Second the idea of matching is rapidly transforming the conventional operation of labor markets. Matching decentralizes the way in which firms or production teams are formed. Production can be accomplished by rather decentralized and fluid teams as exemplified by the various forms of peer production (the wiki economy). Various platforms for *crowdsourcing*, such as Amazon Turks, provide another example. Matching also enhances the place and the schedule of work. Now, there is a new status for the worker, called the *independent contractor*; the economy with this characterization has been given different names, such as the *gig economy*, the *sharing economy*, or the Uber economy (Prassl, 2018). Needless to say, how the labor market in the physical space is operated will be increasingly dependent on how its cyber equivalent is operated and how the matching technology is progressing.

Third the idea of matching also changes everything about money. The traditional role of money in the physical space is twofold: a medium of exchange and a store of wealth. These two functions in cyberspace are just numbers, which, however, need to be verified, for example, through blockchain technology. As long as these numbers are verified and trustful, then payment and wealth bookkeeping can be done in the cyberspace through mobile payments or through cryptocurrencies without even involving a centralized third party. Cashless transactions will become popular with an unmanned service. Matching technology also helps to facilitate direct finance by matching lenders and borrowers. *Crowdfunding* has become the dominant form of microfinance in many countries. The conventional role of financial institutions as financial intermediaries will be affected by the evolution of cyber finance, and this restructuring of the capital market may further support the idea of financial inclusiveness, that is, finance for ordinary people and entrepreneurs (Realini & Mehta, 2015).

---

[t]Because of big data, in its determination of its web-link ranking, the Google search engine developed a sophisticated formula incorporating 250 or so variables, including the use of many social medium network statistics. See Allen (2017).

[u]Perhaps the most illuminating example about the significance of speed to high-frequency finance is what is known as *Flash Boys*. See Lewis (2014).

[v]In the era of the twin space, more often than not, decision-makers have their feet on the ground, but their visions and minds are in deep clouds. Hence, when time is pressing, making a quick decision based on the eye contacts with the screen could be different from what they would be otherwise. See the excellent review of this subject by Benartzi (2015).

18.5 Reinventing individuality

18.5.1 Individuality and the bottom-up history

> England, Goettingen, Wisconsin, are for me no mere locations on a map—they are bodies of ideas in human minds: they would retain their identity if they were to migrate to distant galaxies. *Young (1981, p. 204)*

In Sections 18.2 and 18.3, we have argued that the emergence of the projected cyberspace, accompanied by a large array of artificial agents in cyberspace, has already placed each humanistic scholar in a new network of books and things that can facilitate his/her interdisciplinary mobility and hence may allow us to reexamine the relationship between the digital humanities and the digital economy. This argument is more *methodologically* oriented as if we often experience that what a method commonly shared by two different disciplines may help to enhance the interaction of the two disciplines. However, it is not just methodologically; for in this section, we shall show that the appearance of the cyberspace, *ontologically*, also reinvents *individuality*[w] and that further ties up the relationship between the digital humanities and the digital economy.

Let us first describe the kind of individuality that has been reinvented in the digital era. We define *individuality* simply according to whether an individual can have his or her "*biography*," regardless of his/her social status, achievement, life span, etc. Obviously, in the long past of human history, people who could be given such a privilege are very few. Even though the revolution in printing technology, thanks to Johannes Gutenberg (1400–1468), helped produce publications on a massive scale, this defined individuality remains negligibly low, particularly when compared with the incessant increase in population. Most people came into the world and leave silently, leaving no footprints for latecomers, very much in the way that Marcel Proust (1871–1922) described in his *In Search of Lost Time* (also translated as *Remembrance of Things Past*),

> [w]hen from a long distant past nothing subsists, after the
> people are dead, after the things are broken and scattered,
> taste and smell alone …remain poised a long time
> remembering, waiting, hoping, amid the ruins of all the rest.

For ordinary people, even the "*taste and smell*" are gone. Even though there is *madeleine* (the cake), we can still not find anything since we do not even know what has been lost (Proust, 1982, pp. 50–51).

The history and our memory of the past are publicly shared, but what has been kept in the "menu" are the results of complex social and political processes, beyond the hands of historians and humanistic scholars. Although not distant from the present, we can only limitedly visit the pasts available in the menu, but most ordinary people are not in the menu. Even

---

[w] Here the word *individuality*, instead of individual or individualism, is used because what is intended to be mentioned here is the unique characteristic of each individual, as clearly indicated in the main text. For the *individual* as a moral philosophical subject, we refer to Siedentop (2014), and for *individualism* as a cultural identity, we refer to Hofstede (2001).

though we may become interested in knowing them or being spiritually connected to them, the menu does not leave us a place to click. Partially because of this limited availability, historical scholarship has been long drawn to what is known as *top-down history*, focusing on the grand structure of the society and its centralities but not its peripherals. In the second half of the last century, with a number of influential publications, such as Thompson (1963) and Zinn (1980), *a history of the people* has been crystalized as an alternative genre of historical inquiries, and in contrast to convention, it is called the *bottom-up history* (Lynd, 2014). Bottom-up history seeks to satisfy our desire to know about ordinary, typical, and everyday life; people's fears; and the hope experienced from dawn to sunset; however, if the menu has the same style, then there is really not much "bottom" to conjure up.

The ICT and digital revolution has brought with it a dramatic change to facilitate the pursuit of bottom-up history. With the advent of the twin space, everyone, in principle, can have their "taste and smell" residing in cyberspace; for that, Proust's prose can be adapted as follows:

> [L]*ess* fragile *and* more enduring, more unsubstantial, more
> persistent, more faithful, remain poised a long time, like souls,
> remembering, waiting, hoping, amid the ruins of all the rest; and
> bear unflinchingly, in the tiny and almost impalpable *space* of their *existence, the big data.*
> **(Italics are the adaptations')**

Nowadays, to be a "recluse," one needs to hide oneself in an extremely meticulous way, not using smart phones, avoiding all social media, and reducing one's exposure to the surrounding networked sensors so as to avoid any possible chance of being automatically recognized and archived. These desiderata are difficult to meet; on the contrary, with the increasing precipitation rate of the Internet, eventually all people in the world will have their own biography, the elementary piece of data, for the bottom-up history.

18.5.2 Identity and blockchain

> ...[U]ltimately the whole of a society's history might include not just a public records and document repository, and an Internet archive of all digital activity, but also the *mindfiles of individuals*. Mindfiles could include the recording of every "transaction" in the sense of capturing every thought and emotion of every entity, human and machine, encoding and archiving this activity into *life-logging blockchains*. **Swan (2015, pp. 43–44; Italics added)**

Individuality and identity can be considered as the two sides of the same coin. Presumably, cyberspace can exist for sufficiently long or indefinitely, as will our individuality and identity. The identity that can be shaped in cyberspace is much broader than the conventional one in the physical space. Basically, each individual is identified with the persons or the things that he/she has interacted with in different places over the entire course of his/her life. This information is gigantic and widely spread in time and space, so that only cyberspace can effectively store and handle it; with this *memory-keeping technology*, our individuality can, therefore, be copiously manifested in cyberspace. This demonstration also affects our conception of our identity and behavior cued by that conception (Akerlof & Kranton, 2010).[x]

---

[x] "In every social context, people have *a notion of who they are*, which is associated with beliefs about *how they and others are supposed to behave.*" (Akerlof & Kranton, 2010, p. 4; Italics added).

In the past in physical space, due to the limited exploration of individuality, identity was oversimplified, usually into a list of category variables, such as gender, race, nationality, language, religion, political party, ideological orientation, social status, education, and career. Its items could form a longer list, but these variables are all itemized as they are given. When individuality is reinvented in cyberspace, its richness implies that identities are not categorized in any given way but are constantly shaped or discovered.[y]

Since each individual in cyberspace is uniquely represented by its digital incarnation (projection) in a potentially infinitely dimensional space of big data, as mentioned earlier, one can perceive individuality as the existence of digital biographies or digital autobiographies of an individual; regardless of them being short or long, fragmental or organized, insipid or colorful, or ignored or well circulated, they are all there. If someone wants to read and work on it, they may find ways to get access to it. By the digital convention, each of these biographies is essentially a *sequence of binary digits*. Given its uniqueness, that is, no two individuals can share the same sequence (Harris, 2010); this sequence of bits can serve as the *identification number* of the individual. Thanks to the blockchain technology, or more precisely, *Blockchain 3.0* (Swan, 2015), this form of shaping identity is becoming increasingly familiar and is known with many different terms, such as the *digital identity*, *digital footprint*, and *cyber shadow*. This blockchain technology involves the cryptographic technology used to encrypt this sequence of bits such that the privacy of the individual can be well protected.

The essential spirit of the *blockchain economy*, characterized by the blockchain technology operating in cyberspace, is its pursuit of a decentralization design (Swan, 2015). For the humanities, its implication is the proliferation of the decentralized authorship in the cyber place as the quintessence of the open-source economy.[z] First, each biography is most likely co-authored in the form of peer production, as we have now experienced from Wikipedia, which allows for constant updating. Moreover the person (the protagonist) with which the biography is associated can participate in the authorship by working on his/her biography. The authoring work of the biography may continue even posthumously. In this way the identity of the protagonist will constantly evolve and ceaselessly be reshaped even beyond his/her finite horizon of life.[aa]

Second, and the same as with the other parts of the blockchain economy, artificial agents (artificial readers and artificial editors) could play a major role in this decentralized scheme. Hence, even though a human may not have sufficient time for reading through what has been

---

[y] Akerlof and Kranton did not elaborate on the formation of the *notion* of *who we are* and its dimensionality. In his celebrated model of cultural transmission, Robert Axelrod (Axelrod, 1997) showed that endowing this *notion* with different dimensionality can have substantial effects on the integration (disintegration) of society. In his model, Axelrod assumes that *homophily* is the key driving force for integration. However, whether two individuals share similar traits depends on the list of category variables that are known to them, be they ascribed or acquired. There may be variables that are either *known unknowns* or *unknown unknowns*. The discovery of them in the subsequent social interactions may alter the process of social integration.

[z] As to a review of the evolution of the economy of authorship since the Enlightenment, the interested reader is referred to Woodmansee and Osteen (2005).

[aa] Maybe this is the place where we can see how modern ICT and digital technology accompanied by AI can provide a modern route to read and appreciate Marcel Proust's *Search*.

archived and written about a person, these smart agents may do the verification, compilation, and organization on their behalf.

To sum up, open-sourced information and intelligence, commons-based peer production, and blockchain technology together support a new form of an individual's biography as the digital identity of that individual. This fusion brings a new challenge to the humanities, revolutionizing it not only the way in which we write a biography but also the way in which we conceive of it and use it.

18.6 Matching

The reinvented individuality and identity as delineated in Section 18.5 has far-reaching implications for the economy and business. First, it redirects our attention to matchmaking as underlying all economic activities; second, as a result, in addition to the mass production of homogeneous goods, the customization-oriented production and services become increasingly important. The latter implies that the product and service will become more *malleable* or technically *modularizable*, which in turn also makes matchmaking between *things* critical.[ab] Third, this development further buttresses the transformation from the quantity-oriented economy toward the quality-oriented economy. It would thus be detrimental to those businesses that are not able to distinguish individuals and "respect" them with the needed customization. Finally, by not just being quality based, the economy will also become more *humanistic*, as Deidre McCloskey has long coined the term *humanomics* (McCloskey, 2016b). As we have argued elsewhere (Chen et al., 2016) among others (Benkler, 2011), the advances in matching efficiency from the cyberspace will help to promote prosocial behaviors, altruism-based peer productions, and sharing. The profit-driven, greedy, and selfish portrait of an economic man simply does not describe the whole of humanity. In many cases, if we find meaning or if we are meaningfully matched, it is not necessary to drain ourselves in money games.

18.6.1 Personal web of everything

If networking is the result of social interaction, then the networks to be formed by the "social" interactions of artificial agents, compared with what are normally handled by humans, can be massive.[ac] They are so overwhelming that they can help matching in the physical space, with this not only being limited to *person-to-person* matches but also encompassing *person-to-thing* matches and *thing-to-thing* matches and not only *pair matches*

[ab]In the literature, this development has also been known as the *modular economy* (Chie & Chen, 2013).

[ac]Technically the question posted here concerns the number of connections (the size) for each individual in the physical space and how many more can be added when the corresponding social network is projected into the cyberspace and armed with the help of artificial secretaries. While we do not have an exact figure here, the difference must be tantalizing. This difference is so because, according to the *social brain theory*, the network size that an individual can handle is estimated to be 150, the so-called *Dunbar number*, invented by Robin Dunbar (Dunbar, 2010). Of course, this number can be further examined, but at least it points to the existence of an upper limit for social complexity that a human can afford to handle.

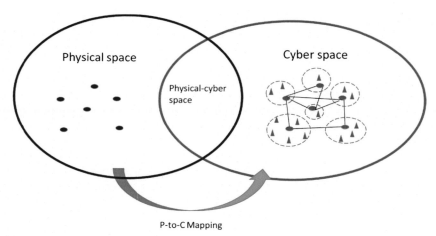

P-to-C Mapping

FIG. 18.5 Customization, matching, and nets.

but also *crowd (team) matches*. This new matching technology is sketched as follows. The physical space is first projected into the cyberspace as shown in Fig. 18.3, but the digital incarnations of humans and things are processed by the voluminous artificial agents (the *green triangle* in Fig. 18.5) residing in cyberspace, who can help reorganize this original network and develop it into what we now call the *Internet of Everything* (Lawless, Mittu, Sofge, Moskowitz, & Russell, 2019). The familiar Uber economy, gig economy, and sharing economy are concrete applications of this technology (Fig. 18.4).

The figure earlier is a zoomed-in version of Fig. 18.3. As in Fig. 18.3, we replicate the twin space. The *blue dots* and the *red dots* represent the individuals in the physical space and their incarnations in the cyberspace, respectively. Furthermore the *green triangles* represent the artificial agents (assistants and secretaries) in the cyberspace only. Each individual in the cyberspace can be served by different numbers of artificial agents, as indicated by the dotted rings with different radii; for example, some install many apps, and some recruit only a few. These artificial agents may not be independent; usually, they are connected by the platform on which they are generated and can work together with other artificial agents under the same or different platforms. Through their teamwork, we can see that the originally isolated individuals in the physical space are now forming a network in the cyberspace.

One essential idea of this reorganization is to treat each individual uniquely and to recognize that the design (configuration) most suitable for each individual is distinctive. The myriad of artificial agents in the cyberspace attempts to learn and know about each individual, called the host (the *red dot* in the respective *red ring* in Fig. 18.5), so that they can possibly do the secretary's or assistant's work for the host, passively or proactively figuring out the list of alternatives and recommending the best choices accordingly.[ad] To some extent, they are replacing the host in making some of his/her decisions, as we have mentioned in Fig. 18.4, the coming of algorithmic decision-making. Of course, how far the replacement can be pursued is not only a technical issue but also an ethical and philosophical issue.

[ad] The familiar examples are Google Assistant, Apple Siri, and Amazon Alexa.

Nevertheless, if the driverless car can be perceived as a list of decisions originally carried out by the host and now taken over by machines, then it is well anticipated that a large proportion of routinized work and decisions can be replaced by these intelligent assistants, too, after they have been given the proper training. With this replacement, humans can be "freed" from the time spent on inconsequential and routinized decisions and can have more social time with others. In addition to driverless cars and unmanned aerial vehicles, the gradual expansion of the *unmanned economy*, such as unmanned check-in counters and unmanned convenience stores, involves the extensive use of algorithmic decision-making technology.

It should be understood that the unmanned economy does not intend to deprive people of their normal social life. In fact, on the contrary, it is the reduction in the amount of time occupied by routines that can provide us with additional time for a more colorful social life. This opportunity is the essential characteristic of the quality-oriented economy. The extensive use of algorithmic decision-making can also be understood from the viewpoint of *algorithmic information theory* (Li & Vitányi, 2008). Routines may imply the *compressibility* of the sequence of bits characterizing the personal biography since routines mean repetitions and hence redundancies. Take an extreme case of a person whose life is so regular or monotonous that it is composed of a small number of routines. In this case, his/her code of life (digital biography) can then be just "all 0s" or "all 1s" or the interchange between 0 and 1 in a predictable manner. Then after the removal of redundancies, his/her life might be *algorithmically* much shorter than that of the genius or talented person who unfortunately died young.[ae] Hence the involvement of algorithmic decision-making is an attempt to preempt the excessive redundancies in life.

Once there is sufficient understanding of the host, the intelligent agents (the *green triangles* inside the *red ring*) may go further to work out the decisions that the host does not make routinely and hence may not be well experienced in finding a house in a new city, finding a partner to work with on a project, finding a job after being laid off, finding a restaurant in a new vicinity, choosing a new IT product, managing investment portfolios in a financial turmoil, and so on. By and large, each problem that these intelligent agents try to help solve can also be characterized as a matching problem, which is to place the host as the focus and ask, within a given context, who and what should become connected to the host so that his/her subjective well-being will be enhanced. Alternatively the intelligent assistants are working toward customizing the *personal web of everything* for the host.

Obviously, not all matching problems triggered by the personal web of everything can be easily solved. Despite this being the case, artificial intelligence has been applied to find out the relation between the host and the possible connections, by studying their similarities or complementarities. This work technically involves applying the chosen metrics and algorithms to a pair of sequences of bits (digital biographies of individuals), with the decision being made based on this derived distance (similarity). For example, for a given host, the *k-nearest neighbor*

[ae] Among the many of these, Frank Ramsey (1903–1930), who died at the age of 26, is the one that I would particularly like to mention here. In his short life, his contribution has been long enough to take a whole paragraph. "In that brief life, he managed to figure out how to measure partial belief and hence lay the groundwork for decision theory and Bayesian statistics; found one branch of mathematics and two branches of economics; and make huge contributions to logic, the foundations of mathematics, semantics, epistemology, the philosophy of science, and truth theory (Misak, 2016, p. 5)."

(KNN) method (Cover & Hart, 1967) or the *case-based reasoning* (Gilboa & Schmeidler, 2001) can propose a collection of individuals whose digital biographies are highly favorable to that of the host. This list may help the host to discover companies that he or she might otherwise only meet based on a black-swan chance.

18.6.2 Great transformation and smartness

In the past, agent-based modeling has already been applied to make it easier for us to imagine what the would-be world built upon the expansion of cyberspace would look. The *Sakoda model of social interactions*, one of the earliest agent-based models in the social sciences (Hegselmann, 2017; Sakoda, 1971) initiated by James Sakoda (1916–2005), provides an illustration. In the Sakoda model, each agent (the host) needs to find a location, a grid in a two-dimensional regular lattice, such that his/her subjective well-being can be maximized. The subjective well-being of each agent is influenced by his/her distance from other agents: Those who are closer have a stronger influence on him/her, and those who are further away have a weaker influence on him/her. More precisely the variables entering into the decision function are the attributes of all agents and their distance from the host's chosen location. James Sakoda proposed this model as a general platform for sociologists to study social interactions and demonstrated the model with many variants, one of which leads to the famous segregation model, also pioneered by Thomas Schelling (1921–2016) (Schelling, 1971).

Back in the 1970s when Sakoda worked on his model, the cyberspace or the digital universe had not been much heard of. To construct an ideal model, Sakoda implicitly assumed that the host could somehow know the attributes of all of the agents in town, regardless of the size of the town and its population. In general, this essentially meant assuming that each agent in the physical space could get access to the biographies of all other agents and could read all of them. Obviously, this assumption is very demanding given the mobility constraints in physical space.[af] Nowadays the Sakoda model has become more likely to happen as long as we assume that everything needed in the Sakoda model has a copy in the projected cyberspace or, simply, that we are working with a cyberspace version of the Sakoda model. As shown in Fig. 18.5, all the artificial agents (*greens*) can use the metric defined by Sakoda (1971) and gain access to the biographies of all other agents (*reds*) and then try to find the best location for their host (the *red* in their ring).

In 1944 Karl Polanyi (1886–1964) published one of the most systematic critiques of the free market idea or the self-regulating market regime, namely, *The Great Transformation: The Political and Economic Origin of Our Time* (Polanyi, 1944). In his analytic framework, the *transformation* refers to some substantial dynamics on the triadic relation of market, society, and government, specifically, the role of government in a society that is constantly threatened by the expansion of a self-regulating economy, as illustrated by our experience with the global financial crisis in 2008.

[af]The Schelling model (Schelling, 1971), therefore, is more realistic in that it assumes that agents can only know the attributes of their adjacent neighbors.

We are now faced with another kind of great transformation. The emergence of the cyber-space as an image of the physical space enables us to have a new solution principle, called the *smartness principle*, for tackling problems that are otherwise difficult to solve in the physical world. The principle is to first *transform* the original problem defined in the physical space into the cyberspace, use tools or software agents available in the cyberspace to solve the problem, and then to *transform* the solution back to the physical space. In this way, we use the cyberspace as an additional tool to solve the problem on the "ground." With this inspiration in mind, the relation between the cyberspace and the physical space can be reconfigured from this projection perspective. There are already many applications in the past, usually embla-zoned with a logo of *smartness*, such as smart cities, smart transportation, smart governance, and smart health management (Chen et al., 2016).[ag]

18.6.3 Feedback loops

Let us use the Sakoda model as an illustration of the use of the transformation (smartness) principle. Once the optimal configuration in the cyberspace is configured by a swarm of artificial agents (the *greens* in Fig. 18.5), we can project the solution back to the physical space, and then the community in the physical space is found accordingly. Therefore this illustration shows that not only can we project the physical space to the cyberspace but also the cyber-space can be projected back (inversely mapped) to the physical space; that is to say, the cyberspace can impact the operation of the physical space. The two then constitute a feedback loop, constantly interacting with each other.

There are two fundamentally different kinds of feedback loops worthy of our attention. In a nutshell, if the increase in the activities (connections) in the cyberspace also causes an increase in the activities (connections) in the physical space, then we say that it has a *positive* feedback; on the other hand, if the expansion in the former causes a contraction in the latter, we can say that it has a *negative* feedback. As an illustration, if the community formation in the cyberspace also helps the community formation in the physical space, as we now show in the left panel of Fig. 18.6 (adapted from Fig. 18.5), the feedback is positive. On the other hand, if the original

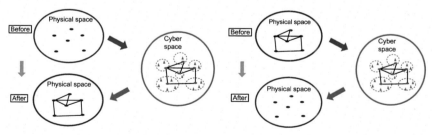

FIG. 18.6 Positive and negative feedback.

[ag]In mathematics, this is a popular way of solving problems. Familiar examples are the Laplace transform and the Fourier transform.

network in the physical space is reduced by the expanding network in the cyberspace, as shown in the right panel of Fig. 18.6, a negative feedback is observed. We may consider that the twin space has a complementary or cooperative relation if the feedback loop is positive and has a substitutionary or competitive relation if the feedback loop is negative.

The aforementioned figure shows that the network formed in the cyberspace may either help activate or prohibit the network in the physical space. The left panel shows the case of the former (the positive feedback), and the right panel shows the case of the latter (the negative feedback).

In addition to the earlier two, the feedback may be *neutral*. In this case the connections for the physical space remain unchanged before and after the cyberspace is included. Let us also ponder this possibility, again in light of agent-based models. Both the Sakoda and Schelling models were introduced in the days when the concept of social networks had not been popularized.[ah] Hence, while we know that physical distance may be independent of social distance, the idea of the neighborhood or neighbor in most earlier agent-based work still relied on the physical network using physical distance. In fact, there is an additional convenience in doing so, that is, visualization. It was easier to visualize the physical models, especially when the graphing tools for social networks, such as UCINET and Pajek, have not been available. Let us illustrate this point using the Sakoda model. In Fig. 18.5, we have a group of individuals *(blues)* who basically have zero interactions with each other in the physical space. Nevertheless, when working on the best configuration for their hosts, the artificial agents *(greens)* solve the Sakoda metric problem and suggest that (recommend that, persuade, and coerce) their hosts have a few specific relations with other agents, as shown in the network in the cyberspace edged by the black lines. Now a community is formed, but this time this community remains in the cyberspace only, and it has no further impact on the physical space. In other words the six *blue-colored dots* continue to be isolated from each other in the physical space, and the projected cyberspace has its own law of motion, which may have little inference with the physical space. One can say that a large proportion of social medium networks still function in this way.

A concrete case of positive feedback can be exemplified by the idea of *glocalization*, a termed derived from *global localization*.[ai] In this case, individuality is expanded into a collective form, that is, a *community*, which typically could be a town or a heritage, but it could also be any attraction in the physical space, such as a school or a coffee shop. If artificial agents can help to match individuals in the cyberspace (Fig. 18.5), then, based on the same smartness principle, we can find the incarnation of the community in the cyberspace, of which identity is its *digital chorography*. This chorography might be initiated by community members but is then further added to and edited by outsiders. This chorography will then be used by a mass of "busy beavers" as a basis for matching communities and people. For example, two

[ah]Freeman (2004) provides an interesting review of social network research from the perspective of the sociology of science.

[ai]Yes, but that still does not answer what global localization means. There are already a number of definitions proposed, and many of them are business oriented. Given its depth and width, we are unable to devote more space to the definition issue. The interested reader is referred to Roudometof (2016) and Hebert and Rykowski (2018). However, as we shall see later, the twin space framework established in this article may provide us with a nascent understanding of whatever definitions have been proposed before.

Austronesian tribes, one in the Philippines and one in Taiwan, may find each other, or the American Indians in Iowa may get interested in the Atayal in Northern Taiwan. Whatever decision we may make for glocalization, the appearance of the twin space will facilitate this trend, since constantly matching with people, things, and places is very natural in the cyberspace, as we have already seen in the cyberspace of books (Section 18.2). In the cyberspace, each chorography keeps on evolving and co-evolving with the rest of the world, functioning similarly to biographies. This co-evolution is probably the gist of glocalization. Of course a positive feedback in this case could further imply a flourish for local tourism businesses.

"Who gets what, and why?" is the title of a book authored by Alvin Roth, the Nobel Laureate in Economics, in 2012. Part of the subtitle is the *New Economics of Matchmaking*. In this article, we argue that the new economics of matchmaking should be built upon digital biographies, digital choreographies, etc. For humanistic scholars, these may constitute the new wine in new bottles, but it is still wine. This space is the place where the humanistic scholars can extend what they have been adept at doing in the humanities or digital humanities. While the current technology can enhance the availability of content, the analysis of the narratives, discourses, rhetoric, sentiments, symbols, and meanings of them demands the participation of humanistic scholars, which cannot just be left to scientists or social scientists, not to mention to artificial agents. The quality of matches depends on the quality of these documents and the artificial agents designed to handle these documents; without the addition of the humanistic refinements, big data in the cyberspace can become another instance of "garbage in, garbage out," a formidable dictum in machine learning.

18.7 Concluding remarks

Ignoring the burden of art and literature and philosophy in

> thinking about the economy is bizarrely unscientific: it throws away, under orders from an unargued and philosophically naive if fiercely held Law of Method, a good deal of the evidence of our human lives.... [E]conomics without meaning is incapable of understanding economic growth, business cycles, or many other of our profane mysteries. *McCloskey (2016b, p. 508)*

It has constantly been a great dream, from politicians to adventurers and from philosophers to scientists, to see the world as a unity, not only physically but also epistemologically. In different times in history, we see that it has happened to different extents, in the Age of Exploration, the Renaissance, the Age of Enlightenment, the Industrial Revolution, and Scientific Consilience, step by step, little by little. In this chapter, we see another dawn, that is, the emergence of the twin space, the cyberspace rising within our real physical world. What can we do with this "new continent?" How will the "Old World" be remembered or forgotten? Five millennia have passed, but we seem to remain just as amazed as Christopher Columbus (1451–1506) and Ferdinand Magellan (1480–1521) were during their times.

Yet, not all memories of these past navigations are pleasant; in fact, they were fraught with the dark side of human nature, which grew together with our expansion in space and in knowledge. Will this time be different? Just look at how people have been publicly shamed in these days in cyberspace (Ronson, 2015). However, this ongoing darkness should not blind us away from the uniqueness of this moment and all the possible adventures that our ancestors were unable to have, that is, *individuality*. While the lands of the world have been physically united, the minds of people have not. In 1492 on his first voyage, Columbus was accompanied by three ships of sailors and further accompanied by many captive natives on his return to Europe in 1493. Almost all of these companies have disappeared completely from our memory as if they never existed. Therefore, although we can come across all of the theaters in the world, we are still unable to see the movies that have been played in them.

In that sense, this time is different. The emergence of the twin space is a historical landmark since people can now be connected or related spatiotemporally by working in the frames of the digital humanities. By considering each of us as a character in a narrative, our characteristics are similar to those of certain others in different times and spaces with specific milieux. Such characteristic analysis may help us to gain more information in matching, not only narrowly for an exchange but also in terms of a relationship from commons-based peer production to other prosocial behaviors. In this way a dream can be weaved together, and another navigation can be organized to cross the Atlantic Ocean. This possibility is why we argue that the digital humanities are the foundation of the digital economy and that the digital economy is an extension of the digital humanities. Even though we are still at the very beginning of a long journey, if someone asks, from a grand viewpoint, where in the end this wave of the industrial revolution will bring us, we believe that this chapter is able to provide the reader with a panoramic view, despite its speculative nature.

Acknowledgments

The paper was presented at the AAAI, 2019 Spring Symposium at Stanford University, March 25–27, 2019. The author is grateful to the organizer of the symposium, Professor William Lawless, for the invitation generously arranged. The author is also grateful for the support this research received from the Ministry of Science and Technology (MOST) (Grant Number MOST 108-2410-H-004-016-MY2).

References

Akerlof, G. A., & Kranton, R. E. (2010). *Identity economics: How our identities shape our work, wages, and well-being.* Princeton University Press.

Allen, J. P. (2017). *Technology and inequality: Concentrated wealth in a digital world.* Springer.

Axelrod, R. (1997). The dissemination of culture: A model with local convergence and global polarization. *Journal of Conflict Resolution, 41*(2), 203–226.

Battelle, J. (2011). *The search: How Google and its rivals rewrote the rules of business and transformed our culture.* Hachette UK.

Baudrillard, J. (1981). *Simulacra and simulation.* University of Michigan Press.

Benartzi, S. (2015). *The smarter screen: Surprising ways to influence and improve online behavior.* Penguin.

Benkler, Y. (2011). *The penguin and the leviathan: How cooperation triumphs over self-interest.* Crown Business.

Bergemann, D., & Morris, S. (2012). *Robust mechanism design: The role of private information and higher order beliefs.* World Scientific.

Biedert, R., Buscher, G., Schwarz, S., Möller, M., Dengel, A., & Lottermann, T. (2010). The text 2.0 framework: Writing web-based gaze-controlled realtime applications quickly and easily. In *Proceedings of the 2010 workshop on Eye gaze in intelligent human machine interaction* (pp. 114–117): ACM.

Bodenhamer, D. J., Corrigan, J., & Harris, T. M. (Eds.), (2015). *Deep maps and spatial narratives*: Indiana University Press.

Brousseau, E., & Curien, N. (Eds.), (2007). *Internet and digital economics: Principles, methods and applications*. Cambridge University Press.

Brynjolfsson, E., & McAfee, A. (2014). *The second machine age: Work, progress, and prosperity in a time of brilliant technologies*. WW Norton & Company.

Campbell, J. (1982). *Grammatical man: Information, entropy, language, and life*. New York: Simon and Schuster.

Chen, S. H. (Ed.), (2018). *Big data in computational social science and humanities*. Cham: Springer.

Chen, S. H., Chie, B. T., & Tai, C. C. (2016). Smart societies. In R. Frantz, S. H. Chen, K. Dopfer, F. Heukelom, & S. Mousavi (Eds.), *Routledge handbook of behavioral economics* (pp. 262–277). Routledge.

Chen, S. H., & Venkatachalam, R. (2017). Agent-based modelling as a foundation for big data. *Journal of Economic Methodology, 24*(4), 362–383.

Chie, B. T., & Chen, S. H. (2013). Non-price competition in a modular economy. An agent-based computational model. *Economia Politica, 30*(3), 273–300.

Chishti, S., & Barberis, J. (2016). *The FinTech book: The financial technology handbook for investors, entrepreneurs and visionaries*. John Wiley & Sons.

Cioffi-Revilla, C. (2014). *Introduction to computational social science*. London and Heidelberg: Springer.

Clynes, M., & Kline, N. (1960). Cyborgs and space. *Astronautics, 5*(9), 26–27, 74–76.

Cover, T. M., & Hart, P. (1967). Nearest neighbor pattern classification. *IEEE Transactions on Information Theory, 13*(1), 21–27.

Davenport, T. H., & Kirby, J. (2016). *Only humans need apply: Winners and losers in the age of smart machines*. New York, NY: Harper Business.

Dodds, P. S., & Danforth, C. M. (2010). Measuring the happiness of large-scale written expression: Songs, blogs, and presidents. *Journal of Happiness Studies, 11*(4), 441–456.

Dolgin, A. (2012). *Manifesto of the new economy: Institutions and business models of the digital society*. Springer.

Dunbar, R. (2010). *How many friends does one person need?: Dunbar's number and other evolutionary quirks*. Faber & Faber.

Freeman, L. C. (2004). *The development of social network analysis: A study in the sociology of science*. Empirical Press.

Gilboa, I., & Schmeidler, D. (2001). *A theory of case-based decisions*. Cambridge University Press.

Goldfarb, A., Greenstein, S. M., & Tucker, C. E. (Eds.), (2015). *Economic analysis of the digital economy*: University of Chicago Press.

Gould, S. J. (2003). *The hedgehog, the fox, and the magister's pox: Mending the gap between science and the humanities*. CA: Three Rivers Press.

Groves, R. M. (2011). Three eras of survey research. *Public Opinion Quarterly, 75*(5), 861–871.

Harris, J. R. (2010). *No two alike: Human nature and human individuality*. WW Norton & Company.

Hebert, D., & Rykowski, M. (Eds.), (2018). *Music Glocalization: Heritage and innovation in a digital age*: Cambridge Scholars Publishing.

Hegselmann, R. (2017). Thomas C. Schelling and James M. Sakoda: The intellectual, technical, and social history of a model. *Journal of Artificial Societies and Social Simulation, 20*(3), 15. http://jasss.soc.surrey.ac.uk/20/3/15.html.

Henderson, W. (2017). *Economics and language*. Routledge.

Hofstede, G. (2001). *Culture's consequences: Comparing values, behaviors, institutions and organizations across nations*. Sage Publications.

Johnson, S. (2010). *Where good ideas come from: The natural history of innovation*. Penguin.

Karinthy, F. (1929). *Chain links*. Reproduced in Newman, M., Barabási, L., & Wtts, D. (Eds.). (2006). *The structure and dynamics of networks* (pp. 21–26). Princeton: Princeton University Press.

Kauffman, S. A. (2000). *Investigations*. Oxford University Press.

Krippendorff, K. (2013). *Content analysis: An introduction to its methodology* (3rd ed.). Sage Publications.

Lawless, W. F., Mittu, R., Sofge, D., Moskowitz, I., & Russell, S. (Eds.), (2019). *Artificial intelligence for the internet of everything*. Academic Press.

Lawson, T. (2003). *Reorienting economics*. Psychology Press.

Lewis, M. (2014). *Flash boys*. New York: WW Norton.

Li, M., & Vitányi, P. (2008). *An introduction to Kolmogorov complexity and its applications*. New York: Springer.

Lynd, S. (2014). *Doing history from the bottom up: On E.P. Thompson, Howard Zinn, and rebuilding the labor movement from below*. Haymarket Books.

McCloskey, D. N. (1998). *The rhetoric of economics*. University of Wisconsin Press.

McCloskey, D. N. (2016a). *Bourgeois equality: How ideas, not capital or institutions, enriched the world*. University of Chicago Press.

McCloskey, D. N. (2016b). Adam Smith did humanomics: So should we. *Eastern Economic Journal, 42*(4), 503–513.

McMillan, J. (2003). *Reinventing the bazaar: A natural history of markets.* WW Norton & Company.

Milgram, S. (1967). The small world problem. *Psychology Today, 2*(1), 60–67.

Mirowski, P. (1989). *More heat than light: Economics as social physics, physics as nature's economics.* Cambridge University Press.

Misak, C. (2016). *Cambridge pragmatism: From Peirce and James to Ramsey and Wittgenstein.* Oxford University Press.

Moretti, F. (2013). *Distant reading.* Verso Books.

Morson, G. S., & Schapiro, M. (2017). *Cents and sensibility: What economics can learn from the humanities.* Princeton University Press.

Namatame, A., & Chen, S. H. (2016). *Agent-based modeling and network dynamics.* Oxford University Press.

Neuendorf, K. A. (2002). *The content analysis guidebook.* Sage.

Polanyi, K. (1944). *The great transformation: The political and economic origins of our time.* New York: Rinehart.

Prassl, J. (2018). *Humans as a service: The promise and perils of work in the gig economy.* Oxford University Press.

Proust, M. (1982). *Remembrance of things past* (C.K. Scott Moncrieff, T. Kilmartin, Trans.). *Vol. 1.* Vintage.

Realini, C., & Mehta, K. (2015). *Financial inclusion at the bottom of the pyramid.* FriesenPress.

Ronson, J. (2015). *So you've been publicly shamed.* Riverhead Books.

Rossi-Landi, F. (2017). *Linguistics and economics.* Walter de Gruyter GmbH & Co KG.

Roth, A. E. (2015). *Who gets what—And why: The new economics of matchmaking and market design.* Houghton Mifflin Harcourt.

Roudometof, V. (2016). *Glocalization: A critical introduction.* Routledge.

Roy, D., & Zeckhauser, R. (2016). Literary light on decision's dark corner. In R. Frantz, S. H. Chen, K. Dopfer, F. Heukelom, & S. Mousavi (Eds.), *Routledge handbook of behavioral economics* (pp. 230–249): Routledge.

Ruccio, D. F., & Amariglio, J. (2003). *Postmodern moments in modern economics.* Princeton University Press.

Sakoda, J. M. (1971). The checkerboard model of social interaction. *Journal of Mathematical Sociology, 1*(1), 119–132.

Schelling, T. C. (1971). Dynamic models of segregation. *Journal of Mathematical Sociology, 1*(2), 143–186.

Shiller, R. J. (2017). Narrative economics. *American Economic Review, 107*(4), 967–1004.

Siedentop, L. (2014). *Inventing the individual: The origins of Western liberalism.* Harvard University Press.

Slingerland, E., & Collard, M. (Eds.), (2011). *Creating consilience: Integrating the sciences and the humanities*: Oxford University Press.

Snow, C. P. (1959). *The two cultures and the scientific revolution.* Cambridge University Press.

Sporns, O. (2011). *Networks of the brain.* MIT Press.

Stigum, B. P. (1990). *Toward a formal science of economics: The axiomatic method in economics and econometrics.* MIT Press.

Swan, M. (2015). *Blockchain: Blueprint for a new economy.* O'Reilly Media, Inc.

Swift, J. (1968). *A tale of a tub: And other satires. Introd. by Lewis Melville.* Dent.

Terras, M., Nyhan, J., & Vanhoutte, E. (Eds.), (2013). *Defining digital humanities: A reader*: Ashgate Publishing, Ltd.

Thompson, E. P. (1963). *The making of the English working class.* New York: Vintage (Revised version, 1968, Penguin Books).

Travers, J., & Milgram, S. (1969). An experimental study of the 'small world' problem. *Sociometry, 32,* 425–443.

Velupillai, K. V. (2018). *Models of Simon.* Routledge.

Watts, M. (Ed.), (2003). *The literary book of economics: Including readings from literature and drama on economic concepts, issues, and themes*: Intercollegiate Studies Institute.

Weintraub, E. R. (2002). *How economics became a mathematical science.* Duke University Press.

Wilson, E. (1998). *Consilience: The unity of knowledge.* New York: Vintage.

Woodmansee, M., & Osteen, M. (2005). *The new economic criticism: Studies at the interface of literature and economics.* Routledge.

Young, L. (1981). *Mathematicians and their times: History of mathematics and mathematics of history.* North-Holland.

Zinn, H. (1980). *A people's history of the United States.* Harper & Row.

Human-machine sense making in context-based computational decision

Olivier Bartheye[a], Laurent Chaudron[b]

[a]CREA, Air Force Academy, Salon-de-Provence, France [b]Theorik Lab, Vernegues, France

19.1 Introduction

The topic of this chapter is focused on knowledge processing (rather than information processing as machine learning for instance), a particular and important field of artificial intelligence. We take into account Judea Pearl's warning for AI scientists "you must build machines that make sense of what goes on in their environment." Making sense for a machine is therefore a crucial issue that was necessarily ignored by machine learning, mainly because algorithms of that kind are based on numbers and cannot handle that way any kind of negation nor any implementation of sense.

Making sense according to a given context is a natural activity for humans. The idea is to define a context as a common knowledge support allowing an indexed family of mixed intelligent agents to collaborate. In particular, what is to be defined is the role of a context as interactions between those families of intelligent agents such that they can help to detect a causal break and to manage it according to the decision process. In other words, decision is crucial to use that context in a collaborative fashion when that context becomes irrelevant.

Roughly speaking, we decide to model sense-making using two separate processes for any intelligent agent: decision and causal knowledge implementation as cognition, and to show that they are the two orthogonal sides of an internal knowledge encoding system. The decision component proposed here is a very special inference called continuous inference. Decision and causal break are merged together in a consistent way in an algebraic structure called a Hopf algebra. We are confident, but we are unable yet to propose a decision algorithm from that structure. The methodological approach of this chapter is mainly conceptual and provides paths to a formal modeling thanks to appropriate theories. Thus, at a metalevel, this article refers to the layers 3 and 4 of the "epistemological quadriptych" EQ (Bartheye & Chaudron, 2018); Fig. 19.1 (by the way, such a bootstrap proves the efficiency of the EQ).

---

1. According to a problem to solve,
2. *Experimental data* from protocols, processes are collected,
3. Then a descriptive *conceptual model* is proposed,
4. A *formal model* is built in order to define formally objects and properties from concepts and to prove the validity of the model,
5. Finally a computer program is *implemented* validating the solution and whose specification agrees with formal properties,
6. Iterate at step 1.

FIG. 19.1   The problem-solving loop sequence for an intelligent agent.

19.2 Basic features of decision based mechanisms

These basic features of a decision mechanism detailed in that chapter are taken mainly from our previous articles on that subject (Bartheye & Chaudron, 2016, 2017, 2018, 2019). The list of keywords identifying these features is the following: *computational context, problem-solving loop, causal break, Hopf algebras*, and *double S-curves*. The aim is to take into account these features and to propose a decision model, or ultimately, let's dream a little bit, a decision algorithm to implement in a standalone machine or in a team of machines.

19.2.1 Computational contexts

Definition 19.1 (Context). A context is an associated set of rules and definitions with certain reproducibility properties.

From the definition in the preceding text, it is clear that nothing is more general and more imprecise than the notion of context. A context seems that way somewhat conceptual; therefore, in Bartheye and Chaudron (2018), we use an epistemological classification in four knowledge basis (Bartheye & Chaudron, 2016): the empirical, the conceptual, the formal, and the methodological basis. If some formal language is used to express rules and definitions, a computational context corresponds clearly to the implementation of an inference process associated with such rules if they have to be used finally by a machine. In effect the real problem for a machine is actually the following: what kind of competence should have an intelligent agent to understand what a context stands for and how to interact with others agents that way? Quite obviously, when one wants to compare the utility of contexts for humans and for machines, one gets a clear answer: a context provides some kind of common knowledge humans can use for collaborative processes. At the opposite, contexts are very complicated to be used for any automaton requiring necessarily some computational capabilities. Various ways to cope with that problem can be proposed: in Reich (2011), to keep things simple, the author selects only first communicative acts and a single action to perform; in other words, sequences of actions are not allowed, and this is a drastic limitation. Restoring sequentiality is undoubtedly richer but definitely more risky. To prepare the inference mechanism whose result will be a combination of actions instances, one should define by the same language both action preconditions and action effects; very often, action effects are the pair (added formulae and deleted formulae). Therefore the classical way to interconnect perception and actions is to use the following orthogonal tools:

(i) predicates as representative tools for situations and (ii) operators or actions as transition tools, which can be fired once a certain situation holds. This is the case in the planning domain definition language (PDDL) (Bartheye & Chaudron, 2016), which is the standard encoding language for "classical" planning tasks. Components of a PDDL planning task are the following:

- Objects: things in the world that interest us.
- Predicates: properties of objects; these can be true or false.
- Initial state: the state of the world that we start in.
- Goal specification: things that we want to be true.
- Operators or actions: ways of changing the state of the world.

That is, both the initial state and the final state are defined according to predicates as representative tools for situations; (quantified) actions are in that case simply transition bundles between elements of a computable set of states. Unfortunately a computational context of that kind with such an inference mechanism computes most of time natural infinite loops.

One can also define a computation context introducing context alteration and context change. The difficulty in that conceptual basis is to detect eventually when a context change may occur since it corresponds to the methodological knowledge basis and not the conceptual one. Conversely, without the knowledge basis, the methodological basis is only "process oriented." We can illustrate these differences and this duality between machine learning and symbolic AI using the problem-solving loop sequence.

19.2.2 The problem solving loop sequence

We postulate that a complex interactivity between an intelligent agent and the environment cannot hold without its internal knowledge representation, which is necessary supported by its own underlying signal carrier. At first sight the physical notion of signal has nothing to do with the concept definition, but the idea is that the signal analysis activity tries to propose a suitable harmonic representation of the environment and provides at the same time the stability of the signal function on which abstraction is gradually and incrementally built. Thanks to that stability, one can build concepts (and therefore contexts) as a signal upper layer. In particular in Bartheye and Chaudron (2018, 2019), it has been shown the dependency of contexts with respect to signal analysis.

It is important to propose an implementation of causality, which is that way based on the signal representation. On one hand the role of the collectivity is to perpetrate a consistent representation of the environment compatible with causal laws, locally implemented according to learning processes and supported by the underlying signal carrier; on the other hand the main contribution of any human individual agent is based on its inference power built on the collective causal knowledge. As in Bartheye and Chaudron (2018), we can illustrate that process according to the problem-solving loop sequence in Fig. 19.1.

It is easy to verify once again that contexts are defined in step 3 corresponding to a conceptual knowledge basis. Step 4 seems more mysterious; in particular a formal model

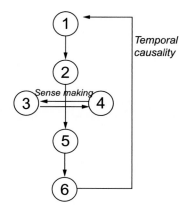

FIG. 19.2   Cross representation between temporal causality and sense making.

is a way to set relevant associations, correspondences, morphisms, equivalences, and to extract consistent properties of that model; this is a way to launch afterward a consistent action that consists to build the proof of such a model. The mental process is similar; once the model extracted from the context is valid enough, a decision is possible. That way, a decision is taken to be a theoretically consistent action. This is not a proof since a decision needs not to be explicit or justified and can eventually be irrelevant. The major drawback is that the effects of the decision could be disastrous without this objective reference.

Without the conceptual step 3 and the formal step 4, a context change cannot be computed. If one aligns, in Fig. 19.2, steps 1, 2, 5, and 6 along a vertical line (or a vertical plane if due to the signal representation, one considers $\mathbb{C}$-numbers), one obtains machine learning as time-oriented information encoding process. The idea is to prepare a decision-making sense as "back and forth" arrows between steps 3 and step 4, which is a "counter time-oriented" process as the horizontal line (or a horizontal plane if due to the signal representation, one considers $\mathbb{C}$-numbers). One can separate the learning process and the decision one according to a cross representation between two orthogonal planes in Fig. 19.2 to propose some $\mathbb{C} \times \mathbb{C}$ structure as a $\mathbb{H}^{a}$-structure:

We will show that full orthogonality between the signal carrier supporting the causality representation and a decision process is the best information system one can define since it provides stability by learning and change by decision once a causal break occurs. The drawback is that changes are quantum transitions generating a disruption one cannot manage from the time-oriented vertical plane. Since artificial intelligence is concerned by collections of intelligent agents and since they often communicate using a common context, the question becomes what are more precisely the relationships between a context and a decision since a context in step 3 comes necessary from step 2 according to the problem-solving loop sequence?

---

[a] In mathematics the quaternions are a number system that extends the complex numbers in the form: $a + b\,\mathbf{i} + c\,\mathbf{j} + d\,\mathbf{k}$ where a, b, c, and d are real numbers and $\mathbf{i}$, $\mathbf{j}$, and $\mathbf{k}$ are the fundamental quaternion units.

19.2.3 The causal break and Hopf algebras

The causal break is really important since we claim that it is the starting point of our investigations. In particular, it has been shown in Bartheye and Chaudron (2018) that any decision process fills a causal break. The notion of causality[b] seems to be somewhat very natural particularly when viewed from our occidental societies. However, it is definitely very complex to capture the exact nature and the exact scope of causality except that it is a time-oriented phenomenon. What is also complicated as well is to propose a representation of the causal function (if any) and in particular, if a causal break holds, to find whether we able to qualify this loss of continuity or even the loss of differentiability. In that case the causal break would be a way to detect either a causal deviation (wrong mode) or even a loss of the causal signal (missing mode). In the case of the wrong mode, the role of the decision process is to restore the causal signal; in the case of the missing mode, its role is to recover the causal signal.

This is an important step toward the formal modeling of causality and decision. We distinguish in that frame the temporal causality and a shift from that temporal causality, which states that sense is actually outside the time scale. It was therefore important to search in Bartheye and Chaudron (2018) for a formal candidate structure able to encode both causality and decision. Since causality is time oriented, we can assume that causality is fully related with some learning process, whereas decision is not since, in the case of the loss of the causal signal (missing mode), it clearly indicates the causal incompleteness of the learning process.

To encode this duality, we proposed to use a very special bi-algebra: a Hopf algebra[c] H although we couldn't provide at the time a well-defined semantic for algebraic operators (μ, η) and co-algebraic operators (Δ, ε) (in a co-algebra, arrows are reversed $x \times y \to z$ becomes $z \to x \times y$). The reader must be patient and content with intuitive arguments. In particular, in a Hopf algebra H, the algebra is a causal information folding process (for instance, machine learning), whereas the co-algebra is a decisional unfolding process. What is important in that bialgebra structure is to define an inverse operator as the antipode S expressing a consistent dependency between causality and decision. In other words, causality and decision can coexist simultaneously in a consistent way in H, and the antipode S expresses a "safe" decision by applying a negation operator on the causal algebraic part (μ, η) of H to deal with the causal break.

---

[b]Causality, also referred to as causation, or cause and effect, is efficacy, by which one process or state, a cause, contributes to the production of another process or state, an effect, where the cause is partly responsible for the effect and the effect is partly dependent on the cause.

[c]A vector space H is a Hopf algebra if it is equipped with morphisms of the following form:

$$
\text{bialgebra} \begin{cases} \text{coalgebra} \begin{cases} \Delta : H \to H \otimes H \\ \varepsilon : H \to k \end{cases} & \\ & \text{antipode } S : H \to H \\ \text{algebra} \begin{cases} \mu : H \otimes H \to H \\ \eta : k \to H \end{cases} & \end{cases}
$$

19.2.4 Double S-curves and disruption

Computational contexts do have a geometrical representation. This geometrical representation is very useful to indicate where a context change must occur. A context is a S-curve, and a context change is a double S-curve. In a paper from a NATO symposium (Hannay, Brathen, & Hyndy, 2015), disruption using S-curves was studied according to double S-curves (Fig. 19.3), where the term adaptive thinking means to change behavior due to a context modification.

The idea is to "disrupt" the planning process by on-the-fly vignettes (see Fig. 19.3) and to cue triggering. The principle of adaptive thinking is to prepare in the face of uncertainty by boosting individual skills. According to Dwight D. Eisenhower's quotation (Hannay et al., 2015): "In preparing for battle, I have always found that plans are useless, but planning is indispensable." The richness of a contextual structure is the ability to host plans first and ultimately decisions. Assume that a S-curve is a generic context; we choose to work on the double S-curves to associate the decision process with a context change.

The adhesion to a context thanks to temporal causality becomes hazardous when the plateau is reached (see Fig. 19.4). A context is valid before the inflection point of the S-curve,

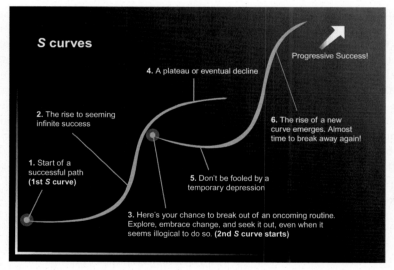

FIG. 19.3 Decision using double S-curves.

FIG. 19.4 Context validity, singular domains, and quantum decision.

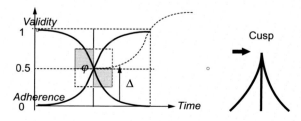

not after. A context is used with a maximal shared adherence (a maximal credit) in the neighborhood of the inflection point. However, a context change must be taken into account when the current context becomes invalid. One can focus around the inflection point:

$$\varphi = \begin{bmatrix} x \\ 0.5 \end{bmatrix}$$

By completion according to the y-axis reflector in Fig. 19.4, one can set that the causal validity decreases from that point φ, the phase inversion point (φ as a cusp[d] is a singularity). The transition from the validity curve to the next context adherence is a quantum step Δ called a decision.

The context curve is a cusp whose left hand side is context adherence and the right side is context validity. This is paradoxical: the context validity query is necessarily performed when the context is invalid; therefore it is deterministic since the answer is necessary no. A context change is required, which is identified by the decision process. The context validity query means that we are already in the singular domain φ. Decision is that way identified by the quantum transition Δ.

We can propose now a very strong criterion: the exact of role of decision is to annihilate locally the temporal signal carrier, which is understood to be the core layer of any local knowledge system. According to this, the signal carrier, as the algebra of the Hopf algebra (μ and η), is a counter model (a model on which negation applies or equivalently an annihilated model), whereas the quantum decision becomes a model as an computable operator and not as an expected result.

19.3 Human-machine agents and characteristics

19.3.1 Human-machine interactions

Take for instance a class of intelligent machines and a class of humans trying to collaborate and interact both in an intraclass mode and in an interclass mode. One can represent the first mode as a hyperconnected graph (i.e., inside the network), whereas the second interaction mode is more regulated by more consistent arrows that must support a sense interpretation. The first class is able to perform a lot of elementary repeatable statements; tests implementing arithmetic operations on numbers; order relations on numbers; and equality between more complex structures such finite trees, lists, finite and acyclic graphs (if operations are parallels, there is some form of conjunction), whereas the second class deals with negation, consistency disjunction, and implication or entailment and sense.

19.3.2 Sense making and computational contexts

The notions of sense and meaning are known to have three subspaces:

— Axiologic: value, quality, etc.;
— Semantic: reasoning, explaining, etc.;
— Teleologic: objectives, aims, etc.

---

[d] A point of transition between two different states.

Thus, by definition, for any a piece of knowledge k (resp. any piece of information) of any agent, its "sense making" is b, a three-dimensional vector (values, reasons, and aims). As far as "decision in context" is considered, it is possible to make fusion of (1) and (3) into (2) so as to make the following approximation: the value and quality of any piece of information or knowledge rely mostly on its capability to provide explanations about itself and from where it comes and conversely its purpose can be expressed by semantic features: aims, intentions, desires, and objectives. Consequently the "sense making" on any piece of information/knowledge can be approximately captured by a set of well-formed formulae. The level of validity and relevance rely on the level of the complexity of the logical model concerned.

Therefore the best representation of computational contexts we are looking for decision should combine both sense (as rationality) and action. In other words, this concerns the ability to classify among suitable actions and unsuitable ones; therefore such a representation should ensure some implementation of consistency. This kind of consistency depends obviously on computational contexts; in other words, sense cannot exist without contexts otherwise its implementation is purely based on deduction. Deduction can be summarized by the slogan: what to say about a thing when precisely nothing is known about it? If something is known by an intelligent agent, one can assume that it is a context and as such is necessary transmittable. But the relationship between sense and context is complicated; the underlying idea allowing sense to be computable is to propose a decision procedure using a special negation that is continuous, otherwise it would not be causal. In other words a context needs separable intelligent agents to communicate, making interactions as a two-sided exchange process between a human and a machine. This has nothing to do with deduction; deduction is a one-sided process. By analogy, one can set the relevance of the Kelvin-Planck statement in physics: the Kelvin-Planck statement (or the heat engine statement) of the second law of thermodynamics states that it is impossible to devise a cyclically operating thermal engine, the sole effect of which is to absorb energy in the form of heat from a single thermal reservoir and to deliver an equivalent amount of work. This implies that it is impossible to build a heat engine that has 100% thermal efficiency. The equivalent statement for consistent information is that is it impossible to implement a one-sided decision process with 100% efficiency. Cognitive exchanges about a consistent knowledge are required, and this is precisely the motivation of the continuous model.

19.3.3 Decision and failures of deductive systems

To encode decision, we have to focus on step 4 in the problem-solving loop sequence. Information managed in step 4 belongs to the formal knowledge basis, where our main preoccupation is to find correspondences and antagonisms between a proof and a decision. This section is mainly concerned with antagonisms and impossibility, whereas the next one is more optimistic.

One can define a deductive system as an unfolding process; using the Hopf algebra notation, it is therefore a co-algebra (Δ, ε) whose graphical representation is a proof tree oriented from the root toward the leaves; this deductive system is a one-co-dimensional projective representation of sense along the proof line. The paradox of that projective representation was mentioned in Girard's quotation (Girard, 1999): "The cut-rule compressing the proof tree has an unbelievable duplicity: (i) it expresses the transitivity of implication. Therefore it corresponds to 90 % of a real proof, which consists in putting together a lemma after or above another lemma. Remember that lemmas concentrate the use of intelligence, and that it may take years to find the right sequence of lemmas that will make their way to the theorem. The other rules are practically never used. (ii) the Hauptsatz paradoxically states that the cut-rule can be eliminated, i.e., that we can prove the same theorem without intelligence. One would then conclude that a machine can do it, and as a matter of fact, the subformula property induces a drastic limitation of the search space."

The above quotation from a logician's point of view expresses incompleteness which is illustrated in this paper using many facets of the notion of "break": causality break of a decision, orthogonality of machines and humans, disruption during choices, differences between contexts, calculus, and formal processes. Various theoretical models are presented to solve or reduce these breaks: Hopf algebras, S-curves, etc.

In the next section a dual and simplified formalism is proposed: the continuous inference model. The idea is precisely not to fill any of the breaks but conversely to capture each of the gaps themselves, for example, current situation/final choice, input/output, and information/intentions. From the sense-making point of view, let us consider the postulate: any explanation of "why" and "how" needed by human beings can be simplified (in the Popper's way) and captured by a set of couples of formulae. Each couple then has the same template: a finite set of literals as hypotheses and a finite set of literals as conclusions. This is the purpose of the continuous inference model.

19.3.4 A plausible integrating model: The continuous inference

The continuous inference, as presented in Chaudron and Maille (1998), is a flexible and general model for the reasoning of cooperating inferential agents, humans $h_1, h_2, \ldots$ or machines $m_1, m_2, \ldots$. Moreover, the continuous inference has a mathematical model providing a "symbolic network" of the knowledge to be captured, more precisely a formal (logical and algebraic) description called the cube lattice structure and its implementation (Chaudron, Maille, & Boyer, 2009). Thanks to a complete problem structure, one can propose a topology of problem-solving spaces. Note that it is essential to keep symbolic information within symbolic spaces and therefore to rely entirely on symbolic data (both for experimental results and for the theoretical model).

The continuous inference is actually a model dedicated to mathematical reasoning tracking, that is, a model capable of capturing a step (the current subproblem) within a mathematical proof, providing comparison capabilities in terms of "size" of deviations between problems. The continuous inference is the wishful name of our model denoting the will of giving a partial answer to the following challenges: when data are symbolic, in so far as it becomes impossible to consider a statement like "formula ζ is an approximation of formula ξ to the nearest 0.25%" nor to define a differential symbolic operator: "formula $\phi + \delta\phi$."

In other words the aim of this subsection is to start from called continuous inference, dedicated to problem representation to propose a structure for decision. According to the problem-solving loop, it is clear that this formal attempt corresponds also to step 4, the formal knowledge basis, where our main preoccupation is to find correspondences and antagonisms between a proof and a decision. Moreover, this formal frame is able to capture links between problems and problem decomposition into subproblems and to build a generic formalized reasoning space for inferential problem-solving. In effect the decomposition of problems into subproblems is considered as a basic action in problem-solving and as a basic principle for intelligent and learning agents.

Another interest of that model is that it is impossible to define the refutation of a proof in a purely syntactic way and without considering any agent: one for the initial proof and one for the refutation. In other words, there is no self-defined refutation. Referring to Lakatos' philosophical works, mathematical problem-solving is a cooperative proof-and-refutation process between (at least) two inferential agents. The demonstration is thus a kind of common language between cooperative and inferential agents. This generic model will be able to capture both the inferential knowledge of each agent and the trace of their cooperative proving activity. Continuous inference is a powerful tool for describing and analyzing cooperative proving situations.

In a dynamic point of view, a mathematical demonstration can be formally represented by a sequence of problems as couples of the form (hypotheses and conclusions), and the most important question is: what kind or algebraic or topological properties is it possible to design? More formally, any mathematical exercise statement can be captured by a couple $(H, C) =$ $(Hypotheses, Conclusion)$: in a problem, in which after the identifiers were presented, the given hypotheses (H) and the conclusion (C) are described. For instance, let us consider the statement of a very simple exercise:

Exercise: "Prove that, if line A is parallel to line B, and lines C and D are parallel, and A is orthogonal to C, then B is orthogonal to D."
This exercise can be reformulated as follows:

H	$(A \parallel B), (C \parallel D), (A \perp C)$
C	$(B \perp D)$

Indeed, the pragmatic of mathematical problem-solving allows classifying cooperative indications in two categories: metaindications and neutral indication. In the metaindication class, one agent gives the other the idea of using a certain kind of method or indicates clearly the theorem that have to be used. In the second category the agent gives to his or her counterpart another smaller problem to solve, the demonstration of which is supposed to reveal the proof of the initial problems what is search for is the "pars pro toto" phenomenon.

Definition 19.2 Let us say that the permanent knowledge of a given reasoning agent α is defined by K_α; a problem $P' = \{H', C'\}$ of K_α is greater than $P = \{H, C\}$ iff$_{\text{def}}$ $K_\alpha \vDash (H' \to C')$ implies $K_\alpha \vDash (H \to C)$. This is denoted by $P \prec P'$.

It is easy to see that the set of problems $(\mathbf{P}, \prec)$ is a preordered set.

Definition 19.3 A problem $P = \{H, C\}$ of K_α is *connected* to $P' =$iff$_\text{def}$; there exists a rule $r = ((f_1, ..., f_n), f)$ element of K_α such that $f \in C$ and $\{f_1, ..., f_n\} \cap H = \{f_1, ..., f_q\}$, then P' is defined as follows:

- $C' = C - \{f\} \cup \{f_{q+1}, ..., f_n\}$
- $H' = H \cup \{f\}$.

Example: If P_1 is

H	a, b
C	c

and if the rule is $r = (d, c)$ (which simply stands for "d implies c") hence the connected problem is P_2:

H	a, b, c
C	d

Note that if P_2 is connected to P_1, then $P_2 \prec P_1$.

A last definition is required so as to generalize the connections between problems:

Definition 19.4 A problem P of K_α is *connectable* to P' iff$_\text{def}$: there exists a sequence of problems $d = (P_1, ..., P_n)$ such that $P_1 = P$, $P_n = P'$, and each P_i is connected to P_{i+1} This is denoted by $P \ll P'$, and $\ll$ is a preorder relation on the set of problems **P**.

From the theoretical point of view, a general topology may appear too ambitious for the modeling of the knowledge space of a cooperative intelligent agent. Thus there is a need for a simplified structure in which the operators may be more efficiently computable. The natural candidate for any algebraic representation of the partial order relation on the set of problems is naturally a lattice structure.[e] Lattice structures give a reasonable improvement of the partially ordered set capabilities as far as noncomparable elements are concerned, while avoiding the strong requirements of totally ordered sets. Here the lattice structure, which is used as a basic tool, offers constructive functionalities for a flexible knowledge model, which is required in any cooperative demonstration process.

Indeed, since "A is parallel to B" (or $A \parallel B$) has to be translated as something like $p(A, B)$, one should ask for a precise definition of the first-order modeling of the hypotheses and conclusions thanks to the "cube model," which will capture both zero-order and first-order questions. The hypotheses and conclusions of problems will be captured by the cube model, which is based on a classical first-order logical language. Elementary hypotheses and conclusions will be represented by literals, and the elements of their power set **C** are called logical cubes as they are interpreted as the conjunction of the literals. Cubes obviously play a dual role besides the classical clauses; hence by default, their variables are existentially quantified.

---

[e] A set E equipped with two internal operators $\sqcap$ (infimum) and $\sqcap$ (supremum) a lattice if $\sqcap$ and $\sqcap$ define the greatest lower bound and the least upper bound of any couple of elements.

We can find now the exact role of the continuous inference: it is a model with which breaks can be ignored whether they can be causal and explanatory, between humans and machines. This shows that the space populated by problems of the form (H, C) is equipped with a negation and has a dedicated topology; (H, C) is at the same time a break and a connection from H toward C.

19.3.5 *Perspectives*

Continuity is necessary related to the context and expresses temporal causality. However, the idea is what kind of continuous structure or what kind of dimensional space can represent context-free structures to deal with causal elasticity. One can assume that in the neighborhood of the causal break, high entropy occurs. That means that the causal break and consequently the decision process are, in best cases, located at the boundaries of the delimited domain and in worst cases "totally out of bounds." Intuitively, that means that the definition domain is unsafe or irregular or equivalently it contains "holes" or "breaks." Consequently, usable contexts require dealing with "out of bounds" algebras as exterior algebras[f] in abstract differential geometry. Take the vertical and the horizontal $\mathbb{C}$-planes in the problem-solving loop sequence: the idea is to build a constructive interaction, the exterior product (Fig. 19.5) manipulating and unfolding these subspaces (here planes) as points of the exterior algebra and curves are plane interactions. That means that the dimensional feature is mixed with the co-dimensional feature, while the continuous feature is mixed with the co-continuous feature using once again the Hopf algebra definition.

Recall that any inference system is a co-algebra and not an algebra. The intuitive meaning of co-continuous is that it is always possible to find a topological correspondence between two connected inference arrows as two-ordered sequences of overlapped open subsets. It is equivalent to set that it always exist a ford of finite length with which one can cross a river from one bank to the other using the topological correspondences between subparts of that ford. Recall that we shall use polarities: the departure bank corresponds to the algebraic component (μ and η) and is called S since it is no longer valid, whereas the middle of the ford F corresponds to the co-algebraic component (Δ, ε) to validate the arrival bank A that we will never be able to represent. The formula $S \vee F$ is the nonclassical version of the implication

FIG. 19.5   Exterior product.

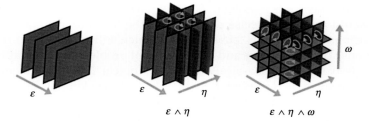

$$\varepsilon \wedge \eta \qquad \varepsilon \wedge \eta \wedge \omega$$

[f] Let F be a field and F^n the n-dimensional vector space; the set $G(k, n)(F)$ of k-planes in F^n is the set of all k-dimensional vector subspaces of F^n with the exterior product $\wedge \cdot$ §.

arrow $S \Longrightarrow F$ that corresponds to the passage at the metalevel. The torsion means that one can only compute the middle of the ford as a sense-making operator, but we can never represent A since it is both connected and disconnected from S, a contradiction.

19.4 Conclusion

One can represent graphically in Fig. 19.6 the correspondences between various algebraic geometrical notions to precise what making sense means for a machine. The center of the picture is the Hopf algebra, mixing the sense making process as a co-algebra (with arrows reversed) and the temporal causality linked by the antipode S that characterizes the disruption between contexts. The co-algebra is crucial since it is a quantum step that is not a time-oriented process, but it is nevertheless highly dependent on it. As a co-algebraic process for sense making, one can propose the continuous inference, which seems actually to exploit the co-continuity, that is the relationship between subplanes, the temporal subplane, and the sense making subplane that is expressed by the exterior product.

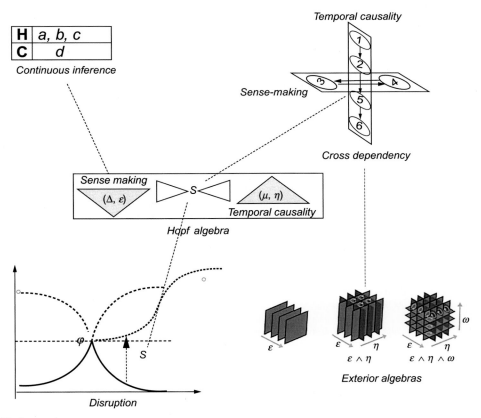

FIG. 19.6   The big picture.

Any decision fills a causal break; any interaction fills a human/machine gap; any explanation aims to fill a sense break; any multiagent model tries to fill the gap between the agents' knowledge and the context. In Fig. 19.6 a big picture shows the formal approaches proposed in this paper so as to capture and fix the various facets of these breaks. Each of them, Hopf algebras, co-algebras, and continuous inference, are components of a general model currently under study: a computable generic decision process thanks to the initial separation between the conceptual knowledge basis and the methodological knowledge basis.

References

Bartheye, O., & Chaudron, L. (2016). Epistemological qualification of valid action plans: Application to UGVs or UAVs in urban areas. In *AAAI Spring Symposia 16, Stanford, USA*.

Bartheye, O., & Chaudron, L. (2017). Context classification using torsion and weak negation: Some criteria for good computational properties. In *AAAI Spring Symposia 17, Stanford, USA*.

Bartheye, O., & Chaudron, L. (2018). Algebraic modeling of the causal break and representation of the decision process in contextual structures. In W. F. Lawless, R. Mittu, & D. Sofge (Eds.), *Computational context: The value, theory and application of context with AI* (1st ed.). CRC Press. ISBN 9781138320642.

Bartheye, O., & Chaudron, L. (2019). Computational contexts, sense and action: How a machine can decide? In *AAAI Spring Symposia 19, Stanford, USA*.

Chaudron, L., & Maille, N. (1998). From students to approximately reasoning agents: the continuous inference model. In *ECAI 98-workshop on synthesis of intelligent agent systems from experimental data, 23/08/1998*.

Chaudron, L., Maille, N., & Boyer, M. (2009). The CUBE lattice model and its applications. *Applied Artificial Intelligence, 17*(3), 207–242.

Girard, J. Y. (1999). On the meaning of logical rules: Syntax vs. semantics. In U. Berger & H. Schwichtenberg (Eds.), *Computational logic* (pp. 215–272). *NATO ASI series* (vol. 165). Berlin, Heidelberg: Springer.

Hannay, J., Brathen, K., & Hyndy, J. I. (2015). On how simulations can support adaptive thinking in operations planning. In *2015 NMSG NATO annual symposium, Munich, October 15th–16th*.

Reich, W. (2011). Toward a computational model of context. In *AAAI Spring Symposia 11, Standford, USA*.

Further reading

Chaudron, L. (1990). Approximate reasoning in mathematics: The "continuous inference". In *ARC'90 Association pour la Recherche Cognitive* (pp. 197–212). Paris: INRIA.

Chaudron, L. (2005). *Simple structures and complex knowledge* (Habilitation thesis). Toulouse, FR: ONERA.

Chaudron, L., & Bartheye, O. (2019). *Symbolic AI strikes back*. In *Bulletin #35 of the 3AF*, (pp. 12–14). https://www.3af.fr/article/edito/editorial-lettre-3af-ndeg35 (in French).

Chaudron, L., Cossart, M. N., & Tessier, C. (1997). A purely symbolic model for dynamic scene interpretation. *International Journal on Artificial Intelligence Tools, 6*(4), 635–664.

Chaudron, L., Erceau, J., Duchon-Doris, C., & Fighiera, V. (2015). Formal approaches for autonomous systems: A generic peace engineering program. In *SMCE 2015, Hong-Kong*.

Chaudron, L., & Lamouroux, G. (1994). Raisonnette, a reasoning support companion. In *International conference on artificial intelligence (ex. Avignon), workshop on cooperative knowledge based sytems, Paris La Defense, (May 1994)* (in French).

Lakatos, I. (1984). *Proofs and refutations*. Cambridge Univ. Press.

Lakatos, I. (1986). In T. Tymoczko (Ed.), *What does a mathematical proof prove?* (pp. 153–162). Birkauser (chapter 2).

Lion, S. (1995). *Une structure de treillis pour l'inférence Continue* (Master's thesis). ENSTA (in French) (1985).

Constructing mutual context in human-robot collaborative problem solving with multimodal input

Michael Wollowski, Tyler Bath, Sophie Brusniak,
Michael Crowell, Sheng Dong, Joseph Knierman, Walt Panfil,
Sooyoung Park, Mitchell Schmidt, Adit Suvarna

Computer Science Department, Rose-Hulman Institute of Technology, Terre Haute, IN,
United States

20.1 Introduction

We are developing a system that is designed for human-robot collaborative problem solving in a shared space. Our system takes advantage of the human's creativity and problem-solving abilities and the robot's strengths of precise repeatability and indefatigability. We consider our system to be representative of the kinds of systems that will eventually revolutionize manufacturing, in particular, for small- to medium-sized companies.

Our system is characterized by two input modalities: speech and gesture. These two modalities afford a more natural way of interacting with a robot, a way that does not require complex descriptions of the locations of objects relative to others, nor an initial phase for naming objects. Our approach simplifies the processing of speech input at the expense of introducing the task of processing gesture and the task of combining the evidence obtained from those two modalities.

FIG. 20.1   Our system.

Our system is designed for a person and a Sawyer robot[a] to solve various wooden block-world assembly problems. The physical system is depicted in Fig. 20.1. We use a Kinect V2 sensor for Xbox One,[b] which contains a depth sensor and a camera. We use a separate microphone. The Kinect and the camera are located in a fixed space, overlooking a table-sized interaction space. The robotic arm has its own camera attached to it near the gripper. The system components are depicted in Fig. 20.2.

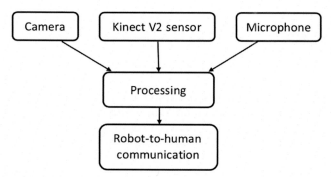

FIG. 20.2   System components.

To manage the information processing tasks, we use the Unstructured Information Processing Architecture (*UIMA*; see UIMA, 2019) that was developed by the IBM Watson team to manage the information processing of their highly successful *Jeopardy!* player. UIMA supports highly modular design and uses what might be considered an additive blackboard representation scheme. The objective of UIMA is to process unstructured information to

[a] https://www.rethinkrobotics.com/sawyer.

[b] https://developer.microsoft.com/en-us/windows/kinect.

discover relevant information (see IBM, 2019). The use of UIMA enables us to represent information about a problem being solved at a fairly high level, information that is easily shared with others. As such the use of UIMA lines up well with the recommendation that "practitioners must ensure that AI-enabled systems are governable; that they are open, transparent, and understandable; that they can work effectively with people; and that their operation will remain consistent with human values and aspirations," from the report on *Preparing for the Future of Artificial Intelligence* by Holdren and Smith (2016).

Since our system is designed for a human and a machine to collaboratively solve problems, there has to be some representation of shared context. In this chapter, we describe the current and near future capabilities of our system to evaluate how shared context can be used to solve problems.

20.2 UIMA

UIMA, the Unstructured Information Processing Architecture (see UIMA, 2019), is a pipeline that enables the processing of information in a highly modular fashion. A key component of UIMA is the "Common Analysis System" (CAS). Similar to a blackboard architecture, it serves to capture information in various stages of refinement. Fig. 20.3 shows a simple example of how one might parse a piece of text in UIMA, capturing information as it is added to the CAS object.

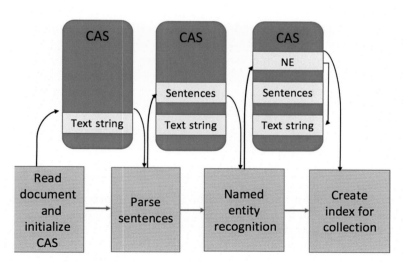

FIG. 20.3   Sample UIMA processing pipeline.

Information is added to a CAS object through software components called *annotators*. Annotators serve as information "gatherers," capturing the outcomes of various information processors. Each annotator interprets the existing data, then adds new data or some combination of both before passing an object to the next annotator in sequence.

In addition to CAS objects, there are also *subjects of analysis (Sofas)*, which are pieces of data referred to within the CAS and stored alongside it. The primary advantage of using Sofas is that a very detailed representation of the state of the world can be made available to each annotator. Still images, depth sensor point clouds, audio recordings, or even video clips can be stored as Sofas and passed between annotators. The advantage of using only a CAS object is that the representation is lightweight. This advantage is important because many of the annotators of our system use communication over HTTP so that they can be independent from the UIMA pipeline, allowing the use of different languages and design strategies. Using only the CAS objects allows us to send HTTP requests with a text body instead of multipart form data. This smaller amount of data being transferred allows the pipeline to run faster.

The parallel version of UIMA, called "UIMA Asynchronous Scaleout" (UIMA-AS) (see UMIA-AS, 2019), enables a highly asynchronous way of processing information. In that version a CAS object can be duplicated for processing by multiple instances of an annotator. Specific to the IBM Watson's *Jeopardy!* player was that it cast a wide net so as to ensure that a potential answer was not missed. This design decision meant that IBM's Watson created thousands of CAS objects as part of answering a given question (for more information, see Epstein et al., 2012). The capacity for parallel processing, however, is something that does not add value to our current system.

IBM took an approach toward processing a given *Jeopardy!* clue that favored the use of many different information-processing components. While the exact number of components was never publicly documented, based on the data we received as part of participating in the "2013 IBM The Great Mind Challenge—Watson Edition," it appeared that IBM Watson used around 200 such components. The exact number is irrelevant; what is relevant is how IBM Watson combined information and associated evidence from all of those components. Using logistic regression, IBM trained a model that is used to perform the final merging and ranking of potential answers. The model is trained to associate regression weights with each of the components of IBM Watson (see Gondek et al., 2012) representing what might be called each component's trustworthiness. While all of this machinery is not necessary for our current system, as the number of annotators in our system increases, we eventually will train some machine learning model.

20.3 Information processing architecture

In this section, we present an overview of the information processing architecture of our system. Fig. 20.4[c] shows the UIMA pipeline with the current annotators and, in *dashed lines*, those that are presently under development.

Memory import and memory storage. These two units are currently under development. The "memory import" unit will read information that is saved as part of the "memory storage" unit. The immediate purpose of these two units is to enable the human collaborator to name entities in the collaboration space so as to refer to them by name, rather than by, say, relative location. These two units will eventually be expanded to store and recall records of problem-solving tasks.

---

[c]Natural language processing.

Object detection. This unit determines the objects of interest in the collaboration space. For our constrained problem, this task is about recognizing the blocks on the table.

Spatial relation generator. This unit parses the data from the "object detection" phase to determine the existing spatial relationships. This step enables the human collaborator to refer to objects by their relative location. Currently, our system is able to process "left," "right," "front," "behind," and "next" relative locations.

Speech-to-text. This unit converts speech to text.

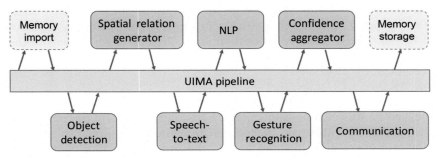

FIG. 20.4   UIMA information processing.

NLP unit. This unit takes the output of the speech-to-text unit; parses the text; and, based on the parse tree, extracts several pieces of information related to the use of color words, spatial relationships, naming of blocks, gesture, and any commands that have been issued.

Gesture recognition. This unit processes a gesture and combines the gesture information with the information added by the NLP unit to add confidence ratings to the objects in our domain.

Confidence aggregator. This unit evaluates various pieces of information compiled in a CAS object. Among others, it determines confidence values for all of the blocks, to indicate which block has been chosen by the human collaborator.

Communication unit. This unit is used to communicate with the human collaborator, whether to acknowledge that the system has sufficient confidence about the instructions received or whether to ask for clarification. Eventually, this unit will grow into a unit that may improve solutions developed by a human collaborator. This collaboration is where context is used to communicate with the human collaborator.

The communication between the UIMA pipeline and the annotators is facilitated through various web services. Fig. 20.5 shows some of the details of this communication. A UIMA request is first sent to our system's routing service that will forward the body of the request to the web service that corresponds to the desired annotator.

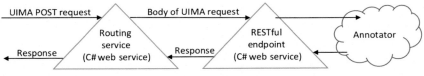

FIG. 20.5   Communication between UIMA pipeline and annotators.

20.4 Object detection

The annotator for object detection is designed to recognize the blocks in our domain. We use the Kinect's built-in RGB camera to perform image transformations that isolate the blocks from the background.

Object identification in a scene is a nontrivial image recognition problem; it is difficult to arbitrarily draw a distinction between what is background and what is foreground within an image. Since object identification is not the primary focus of our work, we simplify some of the details surrounding image recognition in our domain by taking advantage of the background knowledge available in our domain. Namely, we know we are detecting blocks in a fairly static collaboration space. By static, we mean that the physical space does not move; rather, change comes in the form of new objects added to the space or the movement of objects in the static space, as opposed to changing the actual collaboration space itself.

The static collaboration space consists of a white table and blocks of various colors. The camera is focused on this collaboration space. Looking at this from the perspective of context, we assume that all entities are placed on the white table. Given this assumption the system performs a grayscale threshold to find the near-white components in the image. The system assumes that the white collaboration space is the largest contiguous chunk in the image. Once the collaboration space is isolated from the rest of the image, the system performs another grayscale threshold to isolate the colored blocks from the collaboration space. This difference thresholding will produce a block mask where each contiguous chunk is a detected block.

In practice a few additional operations are needed to process noise in the image. In particular, after imaging the collaboration space, we found that the edges of the table were quite rough and extended past the collaboration space. To address this problem the system performs a close-up of the image to remove this noise. Similar morphological operations were performed to isolate the detected blocks and to ensure that the mask capturing these objects was accurate.

For the image processing, our system uses the EmguCV[d] application of the OpenCV[e] image processing module. It provides easy access to the aforementioned image operations. We leave open the opportunity to swap our rudimentary form of image processing for a more sophisticated (albeit time-consuming) form of image processing that works on a larger variety of objects. One such image processing service is provided by Google's object processing[f] service. Consider Fig. 20.6, in which the *green circled objects* were recognized by our system. The centers of the circles represent the identified centers of the blocks.

[d]http://www.emgu.com/wiki/index.php/Main_Page.

[e]https://opencv.org/about/.

[f]https://cloud.google.com/vision/.

FIG. 20.6   Preprocessing of workspace.

Fig. 20.7 shows an excerpt of the CAS object produced by this unit. It corresponds to the example setup shown in Fig. 20.9. In Fig. 20.7 the block with "id" 1.0 corresponds to the block marked "origin" in Fig. 20.9. The setup of Fig. 20.9 assumes that the Kinect is half a meter away from the center of the edge of the table.

```
"DetectedBlock":
[{"id":1.0,
  "center_X":960.0,
  "center_Y":540.0,
  "camera_space_center_X": 0.0,
  "camera_space_center_Y": 0.0,
  "camera_space_depth": 1.5,
  "r_hue":216.0,
  "g_hue":174.0,
  "b_hue":0.0},
 {"id":2.0, ...},
 ...]
```

FIG. 20.7   Excerpt of CAS object after image preprocessing.

20.5 Spatial relation processor

The spatial relation unit processes the data obtained from the "object detection" unit to locate the relative locations of the blocks to each other. This unit enables a human collaborator to refer to objects by their relative locations. Currently, our system is able to process "left," "right," "front," "behind," and "next" relative locations, all from the human collaborator's perspective. Notice this use of relational context; the software automatically calculates relative locations from the human collaborator's perspective.

Fig. 20.8 shows details of how the relative locations are defined and calculated. The inner *dashed circle* in Fig. 20.8 represents blocks that are considered next to the block of interest. Blocks that are next to a given block do not necessarily have to touch that block; they merely have to be physically close. In the current system a block is considered "next" to another block if the distance between them is less or equal to the width of a block, that is, 1.5 in. This measurement was arbitrarily chosen, and a human collaborator may have a different definition of "next." In a future iteration of our system, we plan that the definition of "next" will adapt to a particular human collaborator based on the feedback obtained from them. For example, if a human collaborator repeatedly corrects the robot when the robot picks up a block it considers "next" to a referenced block, the system will adjust its metric for "next."

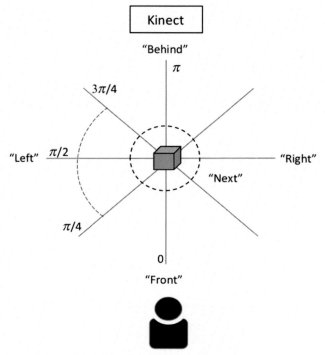

FIG. 20.8   2D spatial relations from the human collaborator's perspective.

The spatial relationships "left," "right," "front," and "behind" are calculated as follows: for each block the system calculates the spatial relationships with all of the other blocks in the collaboration space. Consider Fig. 20.9 for an example. A given block is located at what we call the "origin." For this block the algorithm will loop over all of the other blocks in the collaboration space to classify the block as belonging to one of the four categories and associates a confidence value with that classification. The positions of such a block pair, consisting of the block at the origin and the block to be classified, will be converted into a vector from the "origin" block located at the origin. This vector is then converted into polar coordinates, giving the algorithm location coordinates for the paired block in relation to the "origin" block. The space around the origin is partitioned into four equal-sized sectors.

The confidence value of this classification depends on the distance from the block to the origin. The further away a block is from the reference block, the lower the confidence. Currently, we calculate the confidence as follows:

$$1/\left(1+e^{(x-5)}\right)$$

where x is the normalized distance from the origin, calculated as follows:

$$distance\_from\_origin/(width\_of\_working\_space/2)$$

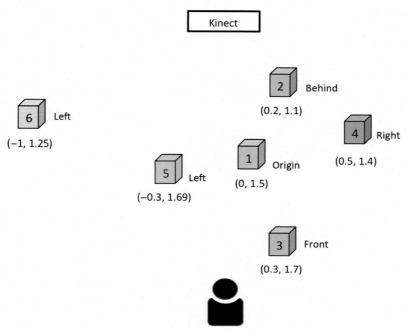

FIG. 20.9   Example of relative locations.

This calculation amounts to a 50% confidence value for about a quarter of the distance across the working space. The tuning factor of 5 gives us a good initial decrease of the confidence as shown in Fig. 20.10.

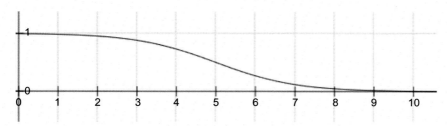

FIG. 20.10   Confidence of spatial relationships based on distance from the origin.

While the system will be initialized with the definitions of the spatial relationships as described, we plan to augment our system so as that it adapts to the human collaborator's common use of the relationship terms. A future version of our system, based on interactions with a human collaborator, will adapt the distance and the size and location of the sectors to the human collaborator's actual use of the relationship terms.

Fig. 20.11 contains an excerpt from a CAS object representing the relationship after processing the setup shown in Fig. 20.9. The data assume that the Kinect is half a meter away from the edge of the center of the table. The data assume that the working space is 2 m wide and 2 m long. The block named "origin" is at the center of table, and block 6 is 1 m to the left of the block named "origin." The block coordinates in Fig. 20.9 have been determined from the perspective of the Kinect and after the spatial relationship labels in Fig. 20.9 have been transposed to the perspective of the human collaborator.

```
"SpatialRelationBlock":
[{"id":1.0,"name":"origin",
  "x":0.00,"y":0.00,"z":1.50,
  "left":"[(5,0.982),(6,0.879)]",
  "right":"[(4,0.978)]",
  "front":"[(3,0.977)]",
  "behind":"[(2,0.990)]"},

 {"id":2.0,"name":"behind",
  "x":0.20,"y":0.00,"z":1.10,
  "left":"[(5,0.979),(6,0.923)]",
  "right":"[(4,0.971)]",
  "front":"[(1,0.990),(3,0.962)]",
  "behind":"[]"},

 {"id":3.0,"name":"front",
  "x":0.30,"y":0.00,"z":1.70,
  "left":"[(5,0.978),(6,0.874)]",
  "right":"[(4,0.966)]",
  "front":"[]",
  "behind":"[(1,0.977),(2,0.962)]"},
 ...]
```

FIG. 20.11   Excerpt from CAS indicating the processing of relationships.

Spatial relationships are stored as lists of tuples for each of the four directions "left," "right," "front," and "behind." The first item of each tuple is a block ID and the second the confidence factor in the classification.

20.6 Speech processing

One of our system's modes of input is spoken language, captured through an external microphone. The speech annotator uses the Google Cloud library's Speech-to-Text service (Google, 2019a). Their service enables us to send an audio snippet and receive back a string representing the spoken text. The string will be translated into a JSON[g] object and passed into the UIMA pipeline. Fig. 20.12 shows the text that was produced when the human collaborator uttered: "pick up the block in front of that block."

[g]https://www.json.org/.

```
"SpokenText":
[{"text":"Pick up the block in front of that block"}]
```
FIG. 20.12   Excerpt of CAS object showing the result of speech processing.

One of the benefits of Google's Cloud Speech-to-Text service is the recognition of names. This quality will eventually aid the natural language processing unit to recognize that a human collaborator is referencing a block by its name.

20.7 Natural language processing

The system's natural language processing (NLP) unit is responsible for parsing a given sentence and for extracting certain pieces of information from it. The NLP unit utilizes Google's Cloud NLP service (see Google, 2019b). It offers a wide range of text analysis, annotation methods, and features that are imperative to understanding language, including sentiment analysis, entity analysis, entity sentiment analysis, syntactic analysis, and content classification.

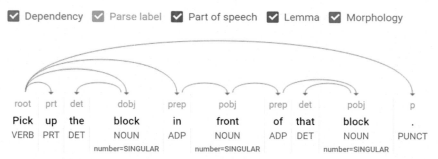

FIG. 20.13   Visual representation of a parsed sentence.

The unit sends a request to the Google Cloud Language library. After the response is received, it is processed to extract the information of interest such as color words, commands, and the suggestive use of pointing to the reference block in our domain. This unit will add the extracted information to the given CAS object.

The current version of the NLP annotator unit relies on Google's syntactic sentence analysis method. This method implements a dependency parser. Fig. 20.13 shows a visual representation of the output from Google's Cloud NLP service for the string: "Pick up the block in front of that block." Table 20.1 explains the abbreviations used.

The NLP annotator creates a *WordProperties* object that is used to hold specific information about every word in a given sentence. It stores fields that keep track of the lemma (text word); part of speech; dependency edge; and its parent word, whether or not it is proper and whether or not it is singular. Parsing the sentence and storing each word in its object format make it much easier to process the sentence and ensure that only necessary information returned from Google's Cloud NLP service is added to the CAS object.

TABLE 20.1   Abbreviations from Fig. 20.13.

Abbreviation	Part of speech
ADP	Adposition (preposition and postposition)
DET	Determiner
NOUN	Noun (common and proper)
PRT	Particle or other function word
PUNCT	Punctuation
VERB	Verb (all tenses and modes)

Next the NLP annotator processes the *WordProperties* object to determine whether the human collaborator (i) uses gesture, (ii) assigns a name to a block, (iii) uses spatial relationships, (iv) issues a command, or (v) uses a color word, as described in the following paragraphs.

20.7.1 Gesture

When the human collaborator uses words like "this" or "that," such as in the sentence "pick up *that* block," the system assigns the Boolean field usesGesture to be true. Gesture words like these are identified by the NLP annotator by searching for words whose dependency edge and part of speech are both "determiner" (DET). Later in the UIMA processing pipeline, the usesGesture field will be used to determine whether or not data from the "gesture recognition" annotator will be used. Our current system assumes that there will be one gesture per sentence.

20.7.2 Naming a block

The string assignedName stores the name to be used by the "memory storage" annotator. To identify a reference name for a specified object, the NLP annotator iterates through the given sentence backward, starting with the last word in the sentence. The code iterates backward because, when a human collaborator issues a naming command, they state the name after describing the entity it refers to. Hence the name appears later in the sentence. Once the NLP annotator identifies a word that is proper, singular, and whose part of speech is "noun," that word is assigned to assignedName. If no such word is found, an empty string is assigned.

20.7.3 Modifiers

The string mods is used to store modifiers, in particular spatial relations. The format of the data in this string is as follows: "[subject]>[modifier 1]|[modifier 2]|...." The ability to store more than one modifier is geared toward future expansion of our system.

The method processing modifiers visits each word in order, beginning with the first word in a sentence. When a word is encountered whose part of speech is a noun, the method creates a new "subject>mods" string. It then iterates backward, from the word before the noun, adding to the string as follows:

- If the word's part of speech is an adjective and its parent is the same noun originally identified, then it adds the adjective to the noun's modifier list with a "|" to separate it from the noun's other identified modifiers.
- Iterate through the list of preestablished directions and check to see if the encountered word is in that list. If it is in that list, then it is added to the current noun's list of modifiers. Directions are stored as a string and contain words such as "front," "behind," "left," "right," and "next." The use of preestablished directions aids in identifying the directional words in a sentence to better correlate them with the "confidence aggregation" unit.

Once these checks have been made for the current noun, the algorithm marks the end of the noun's modifiers list with a comma ",".

20.7.4 Commands

If a human collaborator issues a command, such as "name" or "pick-up," it is stored in the `command` string. After experimenting with several example command sentences for a variety of commands, we determined that the NLP unit may simply search the string representing the spoken text for a number of predefined command strings and then verify that the command, if found in the sentence, is classified as a verb. For commands with multiple words, like pick-up, the system goes a step further by checking the following word or words to ensure that the sequence of words is one of the commands supported by the system. Currently, our system supports the commands "name," "pick-up," and "put-down."

20.7.5 Colors

We use a large dictionary of color words and query the text for their occurrence. Given a color mentioned by the human collaborator, we determine how well it matches the color of the blocks as perceived by the camera. We assign this as the "distance" of a color name to a color perceived by the camera. We use a distance metric to compute a confidence rating of each block, representing the likelihood that a given block is the one identified by the human collaborator.

To calculate the color distance, we first calibrate our object detector to determine correctly the RGB (red, green, and blue) hue values. Each identified color requires an RGB array associated with it, which we previously identified through a collection of HTML defined color values. We translated both sets of values to the CIELAB color space,[h] in which the "L" hue represents the lightness in a pixel, "a" represents the red-green component, and "b" represents the blue-yellow component. In this space, differences in lightness do

[h] https://en.wikipedia.org/wiki/CIELAB_color_space.

not necessarily lead to new colors, a concern that is not handled by RGB values. Within this color space, we compute our confidence as the "delta *E*" value between the two colors; the delta *E* value is the result of a computation that compares the CIELAB values and computes a value that represents the difference as a perceived difference in color from the human eye. Values less than 1 mean two colors are indistinguishable to the human eye, a value from 1 to 2 represents a very slight difference, 2–10 represents a marginal difference, 10–49 represents little similarity, and any larger values up to 100 represent increasingly large differences.

We use this scale because the delta *E* value represents useful information. For instance, when the human collaborator points to a block that is very different in color from what they state, it provides a basis for a useful response to the human collaborator, one that gleans clarification rather than simply requests a new description. This idea of feedback is not explored further in our current implementation but presents the most promising opportunity for the development of shared context if the human and machine can clarify each other's judgments. Hence, this analytical approach to color association produces values that map to human perception, machine perception, and with their mutual feedback construct a shared context.

Fig. 20.14 shows the result of parsing and processing the sentence "Pick up the block in front of that block."

```
"NLPProcessor":
[{"usesGesture":true,
  "assignedName":"",
  "mods":"block>front|,",
  "command":"pick up"}]
```

FIG. 20.14   Excerpt of CAS object showing NLP processing.

20.8 Gesture recognition

Our system uses gesture (see Fig. 20.15) in addition to speech to identify objects. The use of gesture greatly simplifies communication, avoiding the task of having to describe objects and locations in relation to each other or to add a preprocessing phase for naming objects, that is, a phase in which symbols are grounded. We since have become aware of the work by the Japanese company, "Preferred Networks," which too uses gesture in addition to speech to solve tasks for when a robot is asked to tidy up spaces around the home (see Preferred Networks, 2018).

In gesture recognition, there are two primary factors of camera quality: efficacy and cost. These two factors are obvious qualifiers for camera performance, but it is efficacy that needs further discussion. An informal survey of research efforts showed that a wide variety of devices are used; however, the vast majority of projects prefer depth sensors in this domain. To consider why depth sensors are so prominent, it is worth considering the other options that exist in this domain.

At a surface level, depth sensors combine the ease of a single camera with the depth information provided by a stereo camera. Unlike standard cameras a depth sensor forgoes color information in favor of a 3D depth map, whose accuracy tends to outperform the computed values provided by multiple stereo cameras. Many depth sensors use some form of infrared emission followed by infrared detection, which is then combined through various approaches to obtain depth information. One existing methodology projects a grid of dots with the emitter and uses the differences in the spacing of the dots to calculate depth information. More recently, emergent technology uses time-of-flight technology, which uses the time delay between emission and detection to calculate depth information. These variations in depth sensors have various trade-offs that are tied to the individual devices using these technologies, as opposed to the techniques themselves.

FIG. 20.15 Use of gesture.

Across depth sensors the reliance on the "emission-detection loop" means that most depth sensors have short effective ranges, falling prey to noise beyond several meters of operation. This trade-off may limit them for many practical uses, but that is not too concerning for our shared collaboration space. A defined, static working space would likely be no larger than a table's worth of space, easily in the range of detection for a depth sensor. In addition, while cost was not much of a factor with the other cameras, many depth sensors for cameras are relatively cheap (in the range of hundreds compared with thousands of dollars for an industrial stereo camera), making them practical for research.

When looking at individual models of depth sensors, a surprisingly large number of research papers utilized the Xbox Kinect. This device is not particularly robust; however, it is cheap and sufficient for effective, albeit not optimal, gesture recognition. Indeed, one review paper reports that the Kinect "is used by 22 of the 37 papers reviewed" (see Suarez & Murphy, 2012). The Kinect is designed for full-body recognition in gaming applications and is paired with a software development kit (SDK) that affords the flexibility of analyzing depth information to isolate gestures.

The Xbox Kinect V2 library provides utilities that allow easy access to the structural information of a hand skeleton, including its joint information. Using joints in a hand as the basis of estimating a vector in 3D space, we employ a simple heuristic that takes a point from the middle of the palm to the point in a finger furthest from it to be the pointing vector. Our pointing vector is then compared with the center of each block in the collaboration space, to provide a heuristic value that estimates that block's certainty of being identified by gesture. Fig. 20.16 shows an excerpt of the CAS object that represents the confidence that a given block is the one to which the human collaborators point.

```
"Pointing":
[{"id":1.0,"confidence":1},
 {"id":2.0,"confidence":0.35},
 {"id":3.0,"confidence":0.25},
 {"id":4.0,"confidence":0.25},
 {"id":5.0,"confidence":0.35},
 {"id":6.0,"confidence":0}],
```

FIG. 20.16   CAS object after gesture recognition.

20.9 Confidence aggregation

In our current system, each of the units add information to the CAS object paired with a confidence value. To combine all of that information into a single confidence value for each block, we use the product of normalized confidence ratings. We normalize the confidence ratings to ensure that the value of one confidence rating does not distort the value of the aggregate confidence rating. We note that a weighted sum serves a similar purpose, albeit with the added burden of determining weights for each confidence rating to reflect the relative importance of each form of input. The final confidence ratings produced by this unit take into consideration color (see Section 20.7), gesture (see Section 20.7), and spatial relationships (see Section 20.9.1 in the succeeding text).

In the future development of our system for when a more powerful approach becomes necessary, we plan to train a machine learning model to determine the weights for the values produced by the various annotators.

20.9.1 Spatial relationships

To resolve the use of spatial relationships uttered by human collaborators, the spatial relationships extracted by the NLP unit, called "mods," are evaluated based on the data compiled by the "spatial relations generator" unit. The output is a confidence value for each block in the working space, indicating whether it is believed to be the object intended for manipulation.

The algorithm recursively traverses the graph of spatial information compiled by the "spatial relations generator" unit. It begins with a block that was identified through gesture or color identification. It then iterates though the modifiers produced by the NLP unit to retrieve the lists of blocks in that direction/relation. The algorithm recursively calls itself with the shortened list of spatial modifiers. Recursion continues until all modifiers have been used. As explained in Section 20.5, blocks closer to the origin have a higher confidence value for selection. During each iteration the block with the highest confidence value for a given modifier (left, front, etc.) is selected. This value originates from the formula described in Section 20.5. All of the confidence values from each step will be multiplied together to obtain a total confidence value in the overall path taken.

```
"AggregateConfidence":
[{"id":1.0,
  "confidence":0.00,
  "normPointingConf":1,
  "normColorConf":0.00,
  "spatialRelationshipConf":0.00},
 {"id":2.0,
  "confidence":0.00,
  "normPointingConf":0.35,
  "normColorConf":0.00,
  "spatialRelationshipConf":0.00},
 {"id":3.0,
  "confidence":0.997,
  "normPointingConf":0.25,
  "normColorConf":0.00,
  "spatialRelationshipConf":0.977},
  ...],
```

FIG. 20.17 CAS object after confidence aggregation.

If while following the spatial modifiers there are no blocks in a particular direction/relation, then the algorithm will attempt to select the next object in a particular direction based on its confidence level and will continue the calculation with it. If no block is found, a confidence value of 0.0 is assigned.

Given the utterance "pick up the block in front of that block" and assuming the human collaborator points to the block identified as the "origin" in Fig. 20.9, Fig. 20.17 shows an excerpt of the CAS object and the confidence values of three of the six blocks in that domain.

20.10 Communication unit

This unit communicates between the machine and a human collaborator. Here the machine gives its feedback about its level of understanding. It enables a human collaborator and the robot to engage in a dialog while building context for solving a problem. The machine acknowledges when it has a high confidence in an object. Fig. 20.18 shows such a response. If the system has low confidence, it will request more information and restart the UIMA pipeline. A block has high confidence, if no other object has a confidence value within 5% points of the highest value.

```
"Feedback":
[{"feedbackMsg":"I have found the block! I will try to pick
   it up!"}]
```

FIG. 20.18 CAS object with system response.

20.11 Memory

The "memory storage" annotator will work in tandem with the "memory import" annotator to enable a human collaborator to name entities in the domain and to refer to them by name. Eventually, these two units will be expanded to store prior instructions and records of problem-solving tasks. Both of these units are currently under construction, but we expect them to be working soon.

As explained in Section 20.7 on natural language processing, a human collaborator may name entities in the domain. For naming to be useful, names must persist. Since UIMA is a linear processing pipeline, our system needs to write those names to a persistent block of memory to which it has access. Hence, one of the first steps when restarting the pipeline for a new interaction is to initialize the CAS object with any names that were defined.

Our system will store a named block together with its current location. We are currently working on the problem of how to ensure that the system realizes when a block has been moved by the human collaborator. Chiefly the current system does not run in real time, rather it evaluates snapshots of the interaction space whenever the pipeline is run. Tracking the movements of blocks requires real-time processing. While we have the hardware to track movements, we need to evaluate various software solutions.

20.12 Constructing shared context

In this section, we illustrate several occurrences in which the system constructs mutual context. But first, we give an operational definition of mutual or shared context. We do not claim that this definition is definitive; we present it here so that the reader understands what we mean by shared context. The definition in the succeeding text was developed by studying Lawless (2019), Mittu, Sofge, and Lawles (2019), Lawless, Mittu, and Sofge (2017), Mittu, Taylor, Sofge, and Lawless (2015), Burke, Wagner, Sofge, and Lawless (2014), Sofge, Kruijff, and Lawless (2013), and Lawless, Sofge, Klein, and Chaudron (2012).

Definition 20.1 *Shared context* occurs when people or people and machines collaboratively and interactively solve problems. Shared context contains knowledge about the problem at hand and background and common-sense knowledge. In the context of computers, shared context is an artifact that is used to create, record, and maintain the various pieces of knowledge and serves to cooperatively solve problems with human collaborators. A desirable feature of a shared context is that machines can use it to explain their decisions, situations, or perspectives to their human collaborators. Shared context implies that the human and the machine are considered equal; in particular the machine is not subservient to the human. The machine is expected to develop subjective states that allow it to monitor and report on its interpretation of reality or to understand its human collaborator's perspective of reality. Of particular importance to a machine is that the monitoring of its own state may be used to determine whether it has malfunctioned or been compromised.

Since our system is designed for a human and a machine to collaboratively solve problems, there has to be a shared context. We are willing to admit that the shared context in our system is limited at this time. But we are engineering a system from the ground up and are adding functionality to it whenever we add another annotator. We anticipate that shared context grows in functionality as our system grows.

We feel strongly that our approach mirrors that taken by the IBM Watson team when they developed the IBM Watson *Jeopardy!* player (see Ferrucci, 2012). The IBM Watson team took a stepwise engineering approach toward building their *Jeopardy!* player, adding functionality until they were satisfied with their system's performance.

In our system, shared context is implemented through the CAS objects and the way the information in them is processed by the annotators.

20.12.1 Shared context in annotators

The following annotators process information that might be considered common-sense knowledge:

- The "object detection" annotator determines those blocks that appear on the workspace (see Fig. 20.6) by processing the camera image. Using the closed-world assumption, the system is designed to consider only the objects it can process.
- The "spatial relation generator" annotator automatically transposes spatial relationships to a human collaborator's perspective.
- The software that will eventually send instructions to the Sawyer robot performs stereo calibration to reconcile the viewing perspectives of the Kinect and the camera attached to the robot arm.

20.12.2 Context accumulated in the CAS object

The following annotators explicitly represent context by adding information to the CAS object:

- The NLP annotator determines whether a command is given and, if so, which one.
- The NLP annotator determines whether spatial relationships are used by a human collaborator.
- The NLP annotator determines whether a user utters color words or block names.
- The "communication" annotator acknowledges whether or not it has sufficiently high confidence in a human collaborator's directives. The feedback, in particular the positive feedback, is intended to help the human collaborator establish trust in the machine or at least in its level of comprehension.

We will extend the system to ask for more concrete feedback when confidence in a collaborator's directives is not sufficiently strong. We plan to use the robot's arm to point to the most likely block, asking a collaborator whether it is that block that they intend to be manipulated. We will also use corrective feedback from a human collaborator to adapt to their definition of spatial relationships and colors.

After finishing the integration of our system with the robot, we will implement and refine the memory units. The ability to name objects not only aids in identifying objects in our domain but also helps in building trust in the context. After adding memory components, we will add a planning unit. With it the robot can be given higher level instructions. In addition, a planning unit may add to the authority of the machine in a different way. The machine will be able to study instructions given by the human collaborator, to determine whether there is a more efficient way to solve a problem and to relate its findings to its collaborator.

To gain a perspective, key properties of collaboration appear to be the ability to ask questions, take instructions, and give and receive explanations (see Johnson & Vera, 2019). Currently, our system can take instructions and ask questions (or at least indicate that the instructions are ambiguous). Our system serves in a subservient role to the human collaborator. We outlined steps that we will take to bring our system into a state where it assumes a role of a willing apprentice. A key question is whether our system will be able to explain its behavior. We expect that we will be able to implement this behavior. Expert systems of the past inspected their working memory to explain their reasoning (see Buchanan & Shortliffe, 1984). We will be able to inspect the CAS object to do the same. The explanations will be fairly technical, but perhaps, that is desirable.

Johnson and Vera (2019) take a dim view of AI's current ability for successful teaming, stating that "…AI in general has only rudimentary teaming intelligence." They go on to state that "…to ask questions, to take instruction, and to give and receive explanations [are] skills uncommon in the AI world."

Schaefer, Chen, Wright, Aksaray, and Roy (2017) briefly discuss challenges with incorporating context into human-robot teaming. In another paper, Schaefer, Straub, Chen, Putney, and Evans (2017) document their work on communicating intent to develop a shared situation awareness. Chakraborti, Kambhampati, Scheutz, and Zhang (2017) call for an agent-based approach to facilitate human-robot cognitive teaming. Grosz (1996) discusses challenges and potential solutions to facilitate collaborative systems. These proposed methods are currently out of reach of our system but will be introduced as necessary.

20.13 Conclusions

Our system is characterized by two input modalities: speech and gesture. Those two modalities afford a more natural way of interacting with a robot, one that does not require complex descriptions of the locations of objects relative to others nor an initial phase of naming objects. Our approach simplifies the processing of speech input at the expense of introducing the task of gesture processing and the task of combining evidence from processing the information obtained from the two modalities. Due to an information processing architecture intended to be highly modular and designed to use an additive blackboard representation scheme, we are able to represent information about problems, including information considered shared context at a high level. This high level of representation aids in sharing the information with a human collaborator.

We are currently integrating our system with the Sawyer robot to solve physical block-world problems. We use stereo calibration to reconcile the visual views of our system with that of the camera attached to the arm of the Sawyer robot. We are in the process of implementing an annotator that uses the Google Cloud Text-to-Speech[i] service to orally

[i]https://cloud.google.com/text-to-speech/.

communicate with a human collaborator. Google's Text-to-Speech service supports various voices and languages to facilitate a future robotic system that through its voice begins to make it clear that it is an equal partner in problem-solving activities.

FIG. 20.19 Complex block assemblies.

Next, we expect to implement the memory-related features and the ability to address communication failures during collaboration. For example, when the machine has insufficient confidence in a block to be manipulated, rather than asking the human collaborator to clarify their communications, we plan to use the robotic arm to point to the block with the highest confidence and inquire whether the human collaborator meant to identify it, establishing shared context.

Eventually, we expect to add to the system the ability to develop problem-solving plans. This ability would enable the system to receive higher-order commands and to suggest improvements to the human collaborator when the system computed a better plan. Once user testing is under way, we will experiment with problems that we deem to be complex, such as those displayed in Fig. 20.19.

Acknowledgments

We would like to thank James Gibson, Lewis Kelley, Remy Bubulka, and Kieran Groble for developing the initial UIMA setup of our system and for developing a text processing component of our system.

The project described here is part of a larger effort for developing an easy-to-use system for human-robot collaboration. Various components of this project are developed through the collaboration of Carlotta Berry, Yosi Shibberu, Ryder Winck, and Michael Wollowski. We thank our collaborators for making their work available to us.

References

Buchanan, B. G., & Shortliffe, E. H. (1984). *Rule-based expert systems.* Addison-Wesley.

Burke, J., Wagner, A., Sofge, D., & Lawless, W. F. (2014). *Call for participation in the 2014 AAAI Spring Symposium on the intersection of robust intelligence (RI) and trust in autonomous systems.* https://sites.google.com/site/aaairobustintelligence/. (Accessed 6 November 2019).

Chakraborti, T., Kambhampati, S., Scheutz, M., & Zhang, Y. (2017). *AI challenges in human-robot cognitive teaming.* https://arxiv.org/abs/1707.04775. (Accessed 6 November 2019).

Epstein, E. A., Schor, M. I., Iyer, B. S., Lally, A., Brown, E. W., & Cwiklik, J. (2012). Making Watson fast. *IBM Journal of Research and Development, 56*(3/4), 15:1–15:12.

Ferrucci, D. A. (2012). Introduction to "This is Watson". *IBM Journal of Research and Development, 56*(3/4), 1:1–1:15.

Gondek, D. C., Lally, A., Kalyanpur, A., Murdock, J. W., Duboue, P. A., Zhang, L., et al. (2012). A framework for merging and ranking of answers in DeepQA. *IBM Journal of Research and Development, 56*(3/4), 9:1–9:12.

Google. (2019a). *Cloud Speech-to-Text.* https://cloud.google.com/speech-to-text/. (Accessed 6 November 2019).

Google. (2019b). *Natural language.* https://cloud.google.com/natural-language/. (Accessed 6 November 2019).

Grosz, B. (1996). Collaborative systems. *AI Magazine,* (Summer), 67–85.

Holdren, J. P., & Smith, M. (2016). *Preparing for the future of artificial intelligence.* https://obamawhitehouse.archives.gov/sites/default/files/whitehouse_files/microsites/ostp/NSTC/preparing_for_the_future_of_ai.pdf. (Accessed 6 November 2019).

IBM. (2019). *Unstructured information management architecture SDK.* https://www.ibm.com/developerworks/data/downloads/uima/index.html. (Accessed 3 January 2019).

Johnson, M., & Vera, A. H. (2019). No AI is an Island: The case for teaming intelligence. *AI Magazine,* (Spring), 16–28.

Lawless, W. F. (2019). Personal communication (05.08.2019).

Lawless, W. F., Mittu, R., & Sofge, D. (2017). (Computational) context: Why it's important, what it means, can it be computed? In *Technical report of the AAAI 2017 Spring Symposium on computational context: Why it's important, what it means, and can it be computed?*: AAAI Press.

Lawless, W. F., Sofge, D., Klein, M., & Chaudron, L. (2012). *Call for participation in the 2012 AAAI Spring Symposium on AI, the fundamental social aggregation challenge, and the autonomy of hybrid agent groups.* http://www.aaai.org/Symposia/Spring/sss12symposia.php#ss01/. (Accessed 6 November 2019).

Mittu, R., Sofge, D., & Lawles, B. (2019). *Call for participation in the 2019 AAAI Spring Symposium on artificial intelligence (AI), autonomous machines and constructing context: User interventions, social awareness and interdependence.* https://sites.google.com/site/aaai19sharedcontext/. (Accessed 6 November 2019).

Mittu, R., Taylor, G., Sofge, D., & Lawless, W. F. (2015). *Call for participation in the 2015 AAAI Spring Symposium on foundations of autonomy and its (cyber) threats: From individuals to interdependence.* https://sites.google.com/site/foundationsofautonomyaaais2015/. (Accessed 6 November 2019).

Preferred Networks. (2018). *Autonomous tidying-up robot system.* https://projects.preferred.jp/tidying-up-robot/en/\#human_interaction. (Accessed 13 February 2019).

Schaefer, K. E., Chen, J. Y. C., Wright, J., Aksaray, D., & Roy, N. (2017). *Challenges with incorporating context into human-robot teaming* (Technical report SS-17-03). AAAI Press.

Schaefer, K. E., Straub, E. R., Chen, J. Y. C., Putney, J., & Evans, A. W., III. (2017). Communicating intent to develop shared situation awareness and engender trust in human-agent teams. *Cognitive Systems Research, 46*, 26–39.

Sofge, D., Kruijff, G., & Lawless, W. F. (2013). *Call for participation in the 2013 AAAI Spring Symposium on trust and autonomous systems.* https://sites.google.com/site/aaais2013trust/. (Accessed 6 November 2019).

Suarez, J., & Murphy, R. R. (2012). Hand gesture recognition with depth images: A review. In *The 21st IEEE international symposium on robot and human interactive communication.*

UMIA. (2019). *Apache UIMA.* https://uima.apache.org/. (Accessed 6 November 2019).

UMIA-AS. (2019). *Apache UIMA asynchronous scaleout.* https://uima.apache.org/doc-uimaas-what.html. (Accessed 8 January 2019).

Index

Note: Page numbers followed by *f* indicate figures, *t* indicate tables and *np* indicate footnotes.

A

Abbreviated Injury Scale, 151
Activity-based intelligence (ABI), 4
Adversarial approach, 6–8
Adversary forces (AF), 55–56
Agency, 140, 140*f*, 142, 142*f*, 347–350
Agent-based modeling, 362–363
Aggressive distributed incompetence, 326–330
Agile C2 system, 51–52
  aftermath, 60–61
  contingencies, 57–58
  general situation, 55–56
  mission, 56–57
  mission sequence, 59–60
  specific problem, 56
AHP. *See* Analytical hierarchy process (AHP)
AI. *See* Artificial intelligence (AI)
Algorithmic decision-making, 375–376
Algorithmic information theory, 376
AlphaGo Zero, 129–130
Ambassadors, 104
American Recovery and Reinvestment Act of 2009,
    170–171
Analogical mapping, 24–25
Analogical reasoning, robots, 23–24
  analogical mapping, 24–25
  cup-stacking task, 25–26
  interactive object mapping problem, 26
  mapping-by-demonstration (MbD) (*see* Mapping-by-
    demonstration (MbD) approach)
  object mapping (*see* Object mapping, robots)
  "situated mapping" problems, 25–26
  sort-by-color task, 25–26
  transfer learning, 25
Analogy, 9, 24
Analytical framework, CPS, 345–355
Analytical hierarchy process (AHP), 258, 260–261
  advantages, 259
  matrix definitions, 264–268
  SME matrix, 262–263
  SMEs give actual values, 267–268
Analytic hierarchy process, 16

Anchoring and adjustment heuristic, 163
Android minds, 148
Anomaly detection, 4
Anthropomorphization, 148–149
Applied Physics Laboratory (APL), 135–136, 136*f*
Argumentation analysis, 329–330
Artificial agents, 15
Artificial intelligence (AI), 1, 10–11, 13–16, 18, 67–68,
    161–162, 221
  adversarial approach, in courtroom, 8
  agency theme, 356
  apprentice update, 5–6
  assurance theme, 356
  calibration, 7
  context, data, and decision making, 68–69
  discrete wavelet transformation (DWT) (*see* Discrete
    wavelet transformation (DWT))
  general AI, 67–68
  health care, 215
  interdisciplinary approaches, 212
  interfaces theme, 356
  metrics, 6–7, 356
  reasoning systems, goal for, 2–3
  use, in cyber-physical systems (CPSs), 342
  virtual health, role in (*see* Virtual health)
  vs. human learners, in decision making, 216–218
Artificial neural network training, 307
  implications, 311–312
  n-dimensional case, 309–311
  one-dimensional case, 307–309
Asimov's laws of robotics, 11–12
Assembly, 54
Asymmetry, 225–228, 232–233
Attribution processes, 163–164
Augur project, 33
Australian Defense Force, 51
Australian infrastructure systems, 56
Australian Special Forces, 56–57
Autognostic project, 33
Automated/computational content analysis, 361
Autonomous agents, 162, 164–165
Autonomous collaborating systems, 52

Autonomous machines
  deception, use of, 7
  and human users, trust between, 4–6, 8–9
Autonomous robot systems, 16–17
Autonomous systems, 7, 12, 16–17, 135, 346–347, 354
  cognition and implications, for learning systems,
    162–164
  definition, 161–162
  ethical concerns, 165–166
  history, 161–162
  physical, natural and social system interdependencies,
    164–165
Autonomous vehicles, 4–9
Autonomy, 18, 346–347
Availability heuristic, 163

B
Back-end system's design, 131
Balloons game, 290–292, 292–293f
Bayesian network, 48
Bayesian prediction model, 174
Berman Institute of Bioethics, 135–136, 136f
Big data, 365–366
Biomedical information explosion, 206–207
BLE. *See* Bluetooth low energy (BLE)
Blockchain 3.0, 373
Blockchain economy, 373–374
Blockchain technology, 372–374
Bluetooth low energy (BLE), 282–283
Bounded rationality, 162–163
Brain space, 217
Business Process Modeling Notation (BPMN), 130

C
Calibration, 7
Called objects, 104
Canonical C2 system, 51
Captain Simple (CapSim) system, 59
CAS. *See* Complex Adaptive Systems (CAS)
Categoric abstractions, 63
Categoric morphisms, 63
Category theoretic reasoning system, 53–54
Cauchy's Steepest Descent algorithm, 310–311
Causality, 8
Causality theory, 129
CDTs. *See* Communicative discourse trees (CDTs)
Centurions, 148
Channel theory, 61–62
Clinical learning environment, 207, 213–214, 217
Clinical prediction model, 175
Cloud Speech-to-Text service, 409
CME. *See* Continuing medical education (CME)
Cognition, 162–164
Cognitive biases, 325

Cognitive robotics
  reinforcement learning and metareasoning, 24, 32–42
  social learning and analogical reasoning, 24–32
Command and control (C2) systems
  agility (*see* Agile C2 system)
  characteristics, 48–52
  functions, 45–46, 46f
Common Analysis System (CAS), 401, 405, 405f, 408,
    408f
  confidence aggregation, 415, 415f
  context accumulated in CAS object, 417–418
  gesture recognition, 414f
  NLP processing, 412f
  speech processing, 409f
  system response, 415f
Communication protocol, 282–283
Communicative discourse trees (CDTs), 316, 327–328,
    327–328f, 333–334, 333f
Competitive rating and DI, 323–324
Complex Adaptive Systems (CAS), 241–242
Computational contexts, 386–387
Computer vision techniques, 145–146
Conditional interpretation, 96
Confidence aggregation, 414–415, 415f
Confidence-based autonomy (CBA)
    approach, 29
Confirmation bias, 8
Conjugate gradients, 310–312
Consilience, 359, 366–368, 366f
Consistency index, 266–267
Constrained minimization, 309, 311
Content knowledge representation, 217
Contextual variability, 69
Continuing medical education (CME), 206
Continuous inference, 393–396
Convergence, 308–310
Correlation variance, wavelet decomposition, 79–80, 80f
Correspondent inference theory, 163–164
CPSs. *See* Cyber-physical systems (CPSs)
Crowdfunding, 370
Crowdsourcing, 370
Crunchy technology questions, 213–214
Cryptocurrencies, 370
CSAs. *See* Customer support agents
    (CSAs)
Cultural theory, 97
Cup-stacking task, object mapping, 25–26
  assistance phase, 28, 28f
  demonstration phase, 27, 28f
Customer support agents (CSAs), 315–318
Cybercriminals, 56–57
Cybernetics, 161–162
Cyber-physical systems (CPSs), 341–343
  agency, 347–350

analytical framework, 345–355
  assurance, 350–351
  autonomy, 346–347
  interfaces, 353–355
  metrics, 351–352
  Three Mile Island accident, 343–345
Cyberspace, 7, 18–19, 359–360, 365, 369–371, 373
  of books, 362–364, 362f
  physical, 366–367, 366f
Cyber warfare, 7, 56–57, 61
Cyborgs, 364
Cylons, 148

D

DancingFox, 48
Danger-vulnerability matrix, 150
Data fusion process, 243
Data libraries, 3
Data poisoning, 7
Data sharing privacy concerns, 215
Daubechies wavelets, 69–70, 72
Dead robot, 287
Decision assessment, 251
Decision-making models, IF system, 250
Decision matrix, 269, 274
Decision mechanism
  causal break and Hopf algebras, 389
  computational contexts, 386–387
  double S-curves and disruption, 19, 390–391, 390f
  problem solving loop sequence, 386f, 387–388, 388f
Decision ranking, 268–269
Deductive learning, 212–213
Deep Blue, 162
Deep neural network (DNN) model, 175
Deep reinforcement learning (DRL), 153
Dehumanization, 148
Detection accuracy, for DI, 335, 336t
Detection dataset, DI, 334–335
DI. See Distributed incompetence (DI)
Diagonal interdependence, 246
Digital chorography, 379–380
Digital economy, 368–369, 369f
  autonomy, 368
  individuality, reinvention of (see Reinvention of
    individuality)
  intertwining, 368
  matching (see Matching)
Digital engineering ecosystem, 6
Digital health, 14–15, 172f
  consultation, 173
  electronic health services, 170–171
  follow-up, 173
  information, 171–173
  mobile healthcare application, 170–171

technology expansion, 207, 209f
Digital humanities (DH), 18–19, 359–360
  artificial readers, 361
  "cloudy", 365–366, 365f
  cyberspace of books, 362–364, 362f
  definition, 364
  ontological augmentation, 364
Digital system model, 6
Digital technology, 365–366
Diplomacy, information, military, and economic
    (DIME), 50, 58
Discourse-level classifier implementation, 335–337
Discourse-level DI analysis, 333–334
Discourse processes, 129
Discourse tree (DT), 326–327
Discrete wavelet transformations (DWT), 10–11, 69
  decomposition, 70–72
  management decision problem application and
    simulation, 82–89
  orthonormality, 70
  visualizing decomposed wavelet data, 72–77
Distributed common ground station (DCGS), 59
Distributed incompetence (DI), 17–18, 315–317
  aggressive, 326–330
  and competitive rating, 323–324
  defining, 317–318
  detection dataset, 334–335
  detection results, 337
  discourse-level analysis, 333–334
  discourse-level classifier implementation, 335–337
  discourse-level features, 335
  financial crisis of 2007 and, 320–323
  handling and repairing, 338
  and management, 318–319
  and other forms of irrationality, 324–326
  and unexplainable machine learning, 330–332
  and whistleblowing, 319–320
Divergency gaps, 234
Double S-curves, 390–391, 390f
Drone, 278
Drones, 2, 59, 278
Dynamic 4-D medical imaging datasets, 217
Dynamic Second-Wave Services, 55, 55f

E

EDUs. See Elementary discourse units (EDUs)
Ego network, 362
e-health, 13, 171
EHR. See Electronic health record (EHR)
E-layers, 247
Electronic health record (EHR), 218
Electronic health services, 170–171
Electronic medical records (EMR), 207
Electronic warfare, 58

Elementary discourse units (EDUs), 316, 333–334
Emergence and IF systems, 15–16, 246–247, 252
   challenges, 249–253
   integration, from social sciences, 251
EmguCV, 404
Entity labeling, 155, 155f
Entropy, 78
Entropy space, 62
Environment encoding sensors, 34–36
Epistemological quadriptych (EQ), 385
Esthetic design, 127–128
Euclidean statistical manifold, 202
Evasion attack, 252–253
Exponential additive weighting, 268–270
Eye movement desensitization and reprocessing
   (EMDR), 95, 119

F
Facial thermography, 145, 145f, 151
Fast Fourier transformations (FFT), 72
Feedback, in learning theories, 217
FIM. *See* Fisher information matrix (FIM)
Financial crisis of 2007 and DI, 320–323
Fisher distance, 190
Fisher half-plane model, 192
Fisher information matrix (FIM), 188–190
Fisher space-normal distribution, 190–193
Fittedness metric, 54
Fourier transformations, 72
Fractional consumers, 52
FrameNet, 320

G
Game Agent Interactive Adaptation (GAIA)
   projects, 33
Game of Thrones, 113, 116f
Game-playing zone, 290, 290–291f
Gaussian curvature, 191
Gaussian mixture model (GMM), 40
Gazebo experiment, 39–41, 40–41f
Gene activation data, 127
Generalization, 93–94
Generalized knowledge frameworks, 94
Geodesic, 185–187
Gephi, 130
Gesture recognition, 403, 412–414, 413–414f
Gig economy, 370
Glocalization, 379–380
GME. *See* Graduate medical education (GME)
Google Cloud Text-to-Speech service, 418–419
Governance, 104–105, 125–127
Graduate medical education (GME), 206–207
Graph database, 131

Graph isomorphism, 30–31
Group theory, 62
Guardians of the Galaxy, 125

H
Haar wavelet, 70–73, 77, 80–81
Health-care machine learning (ML) applications, 210
HealthTap, 172f, 174
Hessian matrix, 309
Heuristics, 163
Hierarchical Task Networks (HTNs), 33, 36–37
High-pressure injection (HPI) pumps, 345
Holonic agents, 331
Homotopy-type theory, 131
Hopf algebra, 19
Hopf algebras, 385, 389, 391–393, 396–398
Horizontal interdependence, 246
HPI pumps. *See* High-pressure injection (HPI) pumps
Human assistance request, 278
Human-autonomous system interfaces, 215
Human-centric command system, 49
Human cognitive biases, 164
Human decision-making, AI applications, 258–259
   analytical hierarchy process (AHP) methodology,
     260–263
   exponential additive weighting, 268–270
   problem domain, 259–260
   R code, example with, 268–270
Human Genome Project, 166
Human-machine agents
   continuous inference, 393–396
   decision and failures of deductive systems, 392–393
   human-machine interactions, 391
   perspectives, 396–397
   sense making and computational contexts, 391–392
Human-machine teams, 13–14, 16, 252
Humanomics, 374
Human-robot collaboration, 19–20
   annotators, shared context in, 417
   CAS object, context accumulated in, 417–418
   communication unit, 415
   confidence aggregation, 414–415, 415f
   gesture recognition, 412–414, 413–414f
   information processing architecture, 402–403, 403f
   memory, 416
   natural language processing (NLP) (*see* Natural
     language processing (NLP))
   object detection, 404–405, 405f
   spatial relation processor, 405–408, 406–407f
   speech processing, 408–409, 409f
Hyperspectral imaging (HSI), 144–146, 144f
Hypothesis pruning, MbD algorithm
   five-object tasks, 30–31, 30f

seven-object tasks, 30–31, 31*f*
six-object tasks, 30–31, 30*f*

I

Identification number, 373
Imperfect robots, 279
Implicit information, 96–97
Indeterminacy, 228–231
Inductive learning, 213
Inference S, 226
Inference T, 226
Informal, open-textured rules (IORs), 15, 221–223
    ameliorating problems of, 238–239
    asymmetry, 225–228
    formal languages, 224–225
    indeterminacy, 228–231
    interpretive arguments and types, 231–238
    law, formality of, 233–236
    obstacles of, 223–231
    statutory interpretation, 232–233
Information and communication technology (ICT),
        359–360, 364, 368, 372
Information collection systems
    characteristics, 46–48
    functions, 45–46, 46*f*
Information decision systems, 45–46, 46*f*, 48, 52–54
Information fusion (IF) system, 15–16
    adversarial environments, machine learning in,
        252–253
    challenges for, 249–253
    data fusion and, 243
    decision assessment, 251
    emergence, 252
    emergence and, 246–247
    goal-directed behavior, decision models for, 250
    information extraction and valuation, 250
    interdependence, 252
    machine learning, 245, 247
    operator/human issues, 251
    social sciences, integration of emergence from, 251
    sources of, 246*f*
    systems engineering, 244–245, 248–249
Information geometry (IG), 178–180
Information warfare division (IWD), 58
In Search of Lost Time, 371
Integrated autonomous systems, 6–7
Intelligent systems, 149
    fusion system, 58–59
    moral foresight, 138
    pathway to moral action, 138–139, 139*f*
    reasoning system, 127
    values-driven behavior generation for, 152–153
Intentional stance, 147

Interaction design, 279–282
Interdependence, IF systems, 252
Interdependent technologies, 5
Interfaces, 353–355
Internet auction, 369–370
Internet of Everything, 365, 374–375
Internet of things (IOT), 4, 10–11, 368
Interpersonal harm, 141
Interpretive arguments, 221–222, 231–238
Intertask mapping, 26
IORs. *See* Informal, open-textured rules (IORs)
I, Robot, 138
iRobot robot vacuums, 280
iRobot Roombas, 282, 287
Irrational incompetence, 325
Irrationality and DI, 324–326
Isserelis theorem, 194

J

Jeopardy, 211
Johns Hopkins University (JHU), 135–136, 136*f*
Joint Directorate of Laboratories data fusion process
        model, 243, 243*f*, 244*t*, 344*f*
Jointness, 50–51
Joint Operations Command (HQJOC), 58

K

Keynote presentation program, 95, 99–100, 102*f*
    PTSD patient's personal history, influence of, 95,
        119–123
    Red Riding Hood as a Dictator Would Tell It, 108, 109*f*,
        116–119
    vs. Unity gaming platform, 106–107
Kinect V2 sensor, 400
k-nearest neighbor (KNN) method, 376–377
Knowledge, 6
    based prediction model, 174
    processing, 385
    representation, 129
Kolb's learning cycle, 218

L

Legal statute interpretation, 236
Levi-Civita connection, 186–188, 191
Lexpresso, 62–63
Libratus, 129–130
Linguistic arguments, 237
Long-wave infrared (LWIR), 145–146

M

Machine learning (ML), 14–16, 52, 67–68, 214–215
    adversarial approach, in courtroom, 8
    in adversarial environments, 252–253

Machine learning (ML) *(Continued)*
  applications of, 2–3
  calibration, 7
  contextual data, 69
  data and context problems, 2
    building context, 2–5
    generation of new data, 2–4
    mutual determination of context, 2–3, 5, 8–9
  digital twins, 6
  discrete wavelet transformation (DWT) *(see* Discrete
    wavelet transformation (DWT))
  and distributed incompetence, 330–332
  and emergence, 247, 248*t*, 248*f*
  information fusion (IF) system, 245, 247
  metrics, 6–7
  neural networks, 247, 248*f*
  and neural networks (NN) classifier, 252–253
  operational goal, 2–3
  reasoning systems, goal for, 2–3
Machine to machine messages, 13–14
Malmo project, 37–39
Mapping-by-demonstration (MbD) approach, 27
  assistance phase, 27–28, 28*f*
  demonstration phase, 27, 28*f*
  mapping inference phase, 29–31
MapReduce, 62
Market design, 369–370
Matching, 369–370
  cryptocurrencies, 370
  decentralization, 370
  feedback loops, 378–380, 378*f*
  great transformation and smartness, 377–378
  market design, 369–370
  mobile payments, 370
  peer production, 370
  personal web of everything, 374–377, 375*f*
Mathematical economics, 364
Matlab, 72–73, 80–81, 83–84
Matrix definitions, 264–268
Maximum entropy production (MEP), 6
MCDA. *See* Multiple-criteria decision analysis (MCDA)
Mean-field theory, 249
Medical education, 206
  AI hopes, 215
  biomedical information explosion, 206–207
  challenges of, 210
  crunchy technology questions, 213–214
  decisions, 216–218
  digital health technology expansion, 207
  learning challenges, 209–210
  learning contexts, 215–216
  of men and machines, 214
  physician roles, 218

  potential AI application for, 210–212
  shared human—machine contexts in, 212–218
  technology insertion barriers, 208
  use-cases, 211–212
  USMLE step-2 clinical knowledge question, 211–212
Medical learning
  challenges, 209–210
  contexts, 215–216
Medical students, 14–15
Memory-keeping technology, 372–373
Mental demand, experiment condition on, 297–299
Mephisto, 62–63
Merrill Lynch, 322
Message assessment, 260
Metareasoning, 9, 24, 32–42
Meteorological information, 46
Methods, tools, and processes (MTPs), 248–249
Metrics, 6–7, 53*f*, 54, 351–352
mHealth, 13
Microsoft AdventureWorks data, 80
Mind perception, 140–141
Minecraft experiment, 32–33, 32*f*, 37–39, 39*f*
Modeling complex warfighting (MCW) strategic
  investment research program, 54, 62
Mode of interaction, MSA
  human biases, in moral processing, 148–149
  phenomenal stance, 148
  stance adoption, 147
Modern medicine, 214
Moral salience
  affordance/danger qualification of objects, 142–143
  computer vision techniques, 145–146
  integration, 146–147
  interpersonal harm, 141
  materials, 144, 144*f*
  mind perception, 140–141
  minds and their vulnerabilities, 141–142
  moral processing, cognitive and perceptual biases in,
    141
  perceiving, 143, 143*f*
  structural/functional and behavioral, 145, 145*f*
Moral-Scene Assessment (MSA), 11–12, 136–137, 137*f*
  danger-vulnerability matrix, 150
  decision tree, 152*f*
  harm and damage, 149
  harm ontology, 149–150
  insults and injuries, 151
  learning to detect suffering and avoid harming, 151
  mode of interaction, 147–149
  moral salience *(see* Moral salience)
  nonmaleficence, implementation of, 154–156, 154*f*
  pathway to moral action, 138–139, 139*f*
  reasons-responsiveness in physical therapy, 154

synthesis, 151–152
values-driven behavior generation, for intelligent
     systems, 152–153
Moral typecasting, 141
Motion-inducing actuators, 34–36
MTPs. *See* Methods, tools, and processes (MTPs)
Multiple-criteria decision analysis (MCDA), 258
Multivariate normal distribution, 198
MYCIN system, 258

N
Narrative economics, 360, 367–368
Narrative modeling platform, 11, 94
     analogy, 124–125
     conflicting inferences, 113–115
     discrete objects, 103–104
     early version of, 95–96, 95*f*
     general knowledge and interpretation zones, 100–103,
          100*f*
     governance, 125–127
     new system-level representations, 96–100
     operators, 104–106
     PTSD patient's personal history, influence of, 95,
          119–123
     Red Riding Hood example (*see Red Riding Hood as a
          Dictator Would Tell It*)
     research, 129–132
     scale, 127
     2D *vs.* 3D, 106–107
     unexpected information, 127
     unexpected systems, visualization of, 128
NASA's Task Load Index (TLX) questionnaire, 288, 297,
     303
National Academies Keck Futures Initiative, 95–96
Natural language processing (NLP), 169–170, 403, 409,
     414, 417
     colors, 411–412
     commands, 411
     gesture, 410
     modifiers, 410–411
     naming command, 410
     parsed sentence, visual representation of, 409, 409*f*
     technologies, 211, 215
Natural systems, 164–165
Natural visible and infrared facial expression
     (NVIE), 145
n-dimensional case, NN training algorithms, 309–311
     conjugate gradients, 310–311
     constrained minimization, 311
     convergence and rate, 309–310
     equations solution *vs.* minimization, 310
     Newton's method, 309
     nonquadratic case, 310

steepest descent, 310–311
Nearest neighbor learning, 335
Neato Robotics' robot vacuums, 280
Neato XV11 (R_E), 287
Neoj4, 131
Neural networks (NN), 14–15, 17, 247. *See also* n-
     dimensional case, NN training algorithms; One-
     dimensional case, NN training algorithms
Neutrals, 8
Newton's method, 308–309
NLP. *See* Natural language processing (NLP)
Nonurgent primary healthcare, 170
Normalization, 55
Null information, 201–202

O
Object mapping, robots, 25–27
     assistance phase, 27–28, 28*f*
     demonstration phase, 27, 28*f*
     mapping inference phase, 29–31, 30–31*f*
Observe-orient-decide-act (OODA), 48–49, 153
One-dimensional case, NN training algorithms, 307–309
     constrained minimization, 309
     convergence and rate, 308
Ontic realism, 63
OpenCV, 404
Open-source economy, 373
Open-textured predicate, 223, 227–228
Operator/human issues, IF systems, 251
Opportunistic demand model, 55
Organic data, 365

P
Participant robot reviews, 297, 298*f*
Pathway to moral action, 138–139, 139*f*
Patiency, 140, 140*f*, 142, 142*f*
"Patterns-of-life" data, 4
Pearson correlation, 79
Pecuniary loss, 237
Perceptual competence, 138
Perron vector, 265, 268
Persistent structure, 105
Personal health information (PHI), 215, 218
Personal stance, 147
Peter' principle, 318, 318*f*
Phenomenal stance, 147–148
PHI. *See* Personal health information (PHI)
Physical competence, 138
Physical cyberspace, 18–19, 366–367, 366*f*
Physical demand, experiment condition on, 299
Physical harm and insults, 151
Physical interactions, with robots, 292–294, 294*f*
Physical systems, 164–165

Physician roles, 218
PIF. *See* Professional identity formation (PIF)
Pilot-operated relief valve (PORV), 344–345
   indicator, 353
Planning domain definition language (PDDL)
   components of, 386–387
Plausible integrating model, 393–396
Poincaré half-plane model, 192
Poisoning attack, 252–253
Polanyi, Karl, 377
PORV. *See* Pilot-operated relief valve (PORV)
Postexperiment questionnaires, 299–302, 300–301*f*
Post hoc two-tailed paired t-test, 297–299
Post hoc two-tailed t-test, 290–292, 297–299
Postrun questionnaires, 296–299
Posttraumatic stress disorder (PTSD), narrative
      modeling, 95, 119–123
   challenges, 123–124
   complex and nested architecture, 120*f*
   entering and recording text, 121
   representing nested situations, 121–123
Precision education, 205, 213–214
Predetermination, 93–94
Predictable irrationality, 324–325
Professional developmental continuum, 216
Professional identity formation (PIF), 216
Proprietary data, 2–4
Proust, Marcel, 371
Pull-style interactions, 279–280, 280–281*f*
Push-style interactions, 279–280, 281*f*, 283, 295–296
Pythagorean theorem, 184
Python, 36

Q
Q-learner, 34–37, 40, 42
Quasi-Nash equilibrium, 8
Q-values, 39–40, 39*f*, 41*f*

R
Radical interpretation, 230–231
Radical translation, 228–231
Radio-frequency (RF) approaches, 145
Random mapping, MbD algorithm
   five-object tasks, 30–31, 30*f*
   seven-object tasks, 30–31, 31*f*
   six-object tasks, 30–31, 30*f*
Rayleigh Quotient Iteration, 310
R code, example with, 271–274
Reasoning capability, 138
Reasons-responsiveness, 154
Reciprocal matrix, 264
Recurrent neural networks (RNNs), 211
Red-green-blue (RGB) imaging, 144–146
Red LED ring, 287

Red Riding Hood as a Dictator Would Tell It, 95, 107–108
   conflicting inferences, 113–115
   grouping, 111–112
   nested meaning, 111
   new Unity capabilities, 113
   parallel processes, 108–111
   Unity *vs.* Keynote, 116–119
Reflective Evolutionary Mind (REM) project, 33
Reinforcement learning and metareasoning, robots, 24
   algorithm, 36–37, 38*f*
   architecture and concepts, 34
   Augur project, 33
   Autognostic project, 33
   deliberative layer, 35*f*, 36
   Game Agent Interactive Adaptation (GAIA) projects,
      33
   Gazebo experiment, 39–41, 40–41*f*
   knowledge-based frameworks, 33–34
   metareasoning level, 35*f*, 36
   Minecraft experiment, 32–33, 32*f*, 37–39, 39*f*
   object-level layer, 34–36, 35*f*
   Reflective Evolutionary Mind (REM) project, 33
Reinvention of individuality
   identity and blockchain, 372–374
   individuality and history, 371–372
Remote home monitoring, 13
Representation theory, 69
Representative heuristic, 163
Residential mortgage-backed securities (RMBS), 320
"Resonance, integration, and validation" (RI-Val)
      model, 129
Revised system goal, 347
Rhetorical structure theory (RST), 316
Riemannian geometry, 178, 180–190
Riemannian manifold, 184
RMBS. *See* Residential mortgage-backed securities
      (RMBS)
RNNs. *See* Recurrent neural networks (RNNs)
Robot failure scenarios, human-robot interaction during
   analysis methods, 288
   balloons game, 290–292
   based interface, 286
   communication protocol, 282–283
   dependent variables, 288
   design, 284–286
   experiment scores, 302
   game-playing zone, 290, 290–291*f*
   hypothesis 1 (H1), 286, 302
   hypothesis 2 (H2), 286, 302–303
   hypothesis 3 (H3), 286, 303
   independent variables, 285*t*, 287
   interaction design, 279–282
   participants, 288
   postexperiment questionnaires, 299–302, 300–301*f*

postrun questionnaires, 296–299
robot interactions, 292–296, 295–296*f*
robot reset, 295–296, 295*f*
robot usage, 288
run ordering, effects of, 304
time spent, in status app, 296, 296*f*
within-subjects design, 285, 287
Robots, 9, 23–24, 138
    Asimov's law, 137–138, 137*f*
    behavior, 278
    interactions, 292–296, 295–296*f*
    Moral-Scene Assessment (MSA) (*see* Moral-Scene
        Assessment (MSA))
    reinforcement learning and metareasoning, 24,
        32–42
    reset, 295–296, 295*f*
    social learning and analogical reasoning, 24–32
    time spent, in status app, 296, 296*f*
Robot vacuum cleaners, 282, 282*f*, 284
    cleaning zone, 283–284*f*, 284–285
Robust intelligence, 6–7
Runaround, 137
Run ordering, effects of, 304

S

Sakoda model, 377–379
Sawyer robot, 400
Schelling model, 377, 377*np*
Scoring scheme, 261
Self-assembly process, 64
Self-driving cars, 2–4, 8, 135–136
Self-regulated learning (SRL) theory, 217
Semantic segmentation, 146
Semiautonomous system, 136
Sequence of binary digits, 373
Serial multitasking, 259–260
Set theoretic reasoning systems, 53–54, 61–62
Shannon information theory, 6, 13–14
Shared context, 416
    in annotators, 417
    CAS object, 417–418
Sharing economy, 370, 374–375
Simple Hierarchical Ordered Planner
        (SHOP), 36
Simple statistical manifold, 188
Singular value decomposition (SVD), 72
Situated mapping, 25–27
Situatedness metric, 54
Situation theory, 61, 97, 132
Smartness principle, 360, 378–380
Smartphones, 279
    interaction methods, 279–282
    pull-style interactions, 279–280, 280–281*f*
    push-style interactions, 279–280, 281*f*

robot, app characteristics, 299–302, 300–301*f*
    ubiquitous communication paradigm, 282
SME matrix, 262–263
Social learning and analogical reasoning, robots, 23–24
    analogical mapping, 24–25
    cup-stacking task, 25–26
    interactive object mapping problem, 26
    mapping-by-demonstration (MbD) (*see* Mapping-by-
        demonstration (MbD) approach)
    object mapping, 26–27
    "situated mapping" problems, 25–26
    sort-by-color task, 25–26
    transfer learning, 25
Social systems, 164–165
Social warfare, 56
Software development kit (SDK), 413
Sort-by-color task, 25–26
SoS. *See* System of systems (SoS)
Source objects, 104
Sparse data, 3–4
Special Operations Command (SOCOMD), 58
Square positive matrix, 265
SRL. *See* Self-regulated learning (SRL) theory
Static Second-Wave Services, 54, 55*f*
Statistical manifold, 193–200
Statutory interpretation, 232–233
Statutory schema, 232, 235–236
Steepest descent algorithm, 310–312
Subjects of analysis (Sofas), 402
Support vector machine (SVM) learning, 336
Synthesizing operator, 105
Synthetic data, 2–3
Systemic irrationality, 323–324
System-level properties, 249
System of systems (SoS), 241–242
Systems engineering (SE), 15–16, 242, 244–245
    and emergence, 248–249
    information fusion (IF) system, 244–245, 248–249
    methods, tools, and processes (MTPs), 253–254

T

Tactical situation display (TACSIT), 261
Tangent bundle, 181
Tangent space, 181
Task-method-knowledge language (TMKL), 33
Technology insertion barriers, 208
Telemedicine, 13
Telementoring, 13
Temporal causality, 388*f*, 389–391, 396–397
Temporal interdependence, 246
Text manipulation, 121, 122*f*
Textoids, 129
The Human Use of Human Beings, 165–166
Thermography, 145, 145*f*

Third-party advisor, 48
Three-dimensional networks, 94
Three-dimensional spatial location, 105
Three Mile Island (TMI) accident, 18, 343–346
Three Mile Island-2 (TMI-2) nuclear reactor
       system accident, 343–344, 344f, 347
  agency, 347–349, 348t
  assurance, 350
  autonomous system, 346
  engineered components and humans involvement in,
     347
  human actors, actions of, 349
  interfaces, 353–355
  metrics, 351–352
  structural integrity, 347
TMI-1 nuclear reactor, 343, 343np
Trace memory, 36
Transcategorical arguments, 237–238
Transfer learning, 25
Trust
  in autonomous machines, 4–6, 8–9
  metrics, 9–10, 48, 54
t-tests, 86, 87–88t
Two-sorted system, 54
Two-tailed paired t-test, 294–295, 297–299
Type system, 63–64
Type/token distinction, 225

U
UAV. *See* Unmanned aerial vehicles (UAV)
Uber economy, 370, 374–375
Uber self-driving accident, 8
Uber self-driving car, 251
UCR Time-Series Data Mining Archive, 80–81
UIMA Asynchronous Scaleout (UIMA-AS), 402
ULSS. *See* Ultralarge-scale systems (ULSS)
Ultralarge-scale systems (ULSS), 241–242
UME. *See* Undergraduate medical education (UME)
Undergraduate medical education (UME), 206, 206f
Unexpected information, 96–97, 127
Unity gaming platform, 94–95, 97, 99–101, 102f, 103, 105,
     113, 130–131
  vs. Keynote presentation program, 106–107
  PTSD patient's personal history, influence of, 95,
     119–123
  Red Riding Hood as a Dictator Would Tell It, 108–111,
     110f, 115f, 116–119
Unmanned aerial vehicles (UAV), 249
Unmanned economy, 375–376
Unmanned Systems Integrated Roadmap, 3
Unstructured Information Processing Architecture
     (UIMA), 401, 403f, 408, 410, 415
  information processing, 403f
  use of, 400–401

User-induced intervention data, 4
User interface (UI), 98–99, 130
US Justice Department (DOJ, 320
USMLE cases, medical education, 211–212

V
Value of information (VoI)
  and complexity, 200–202
  Fisher information, 188–190
  Fisher space-normal distribution, 190–193
  information geometry (IG), 178–180
  resources allotment, 202–203
  Riemannian geometry, 180–190
Video game task, 284
Virginia Modeling, Analysis and Simulation Center
     (VMASC), 95–96
Virtual health, 13, 169, 173
  advantages of, 169
  consultation, 173
  deep neural network (DNN)
     model, 175
  electronic health services, 170–171
  follow-up, 173
  HealthTap, 172f, 174
  information, 171–173
  limitations, 175
  mobile healthcare application, 170–171
  natural language processing, 169–170
  virtual visits, 169
Virtual patients, 14–15
Virtual reality (VR) approaches, 121

W
Wall Street Journal, 326, 329
Wavelets, 10–11
  decomposition, 70–72
  definition, 69–70
  discrete wavelet transformations (DWT) (*see* Discrete
     wavelet transformations (DWT))
  preferential transformation, for initial resolution-scale,
     77–81
  properties, 70, 89
Whistleblowing and DI, 319–320
Whiteboard representation scheme, 400–401, 418
Wreath product, 62
Wunderkammer, 94, 97–99, 98f

X
Xbox Kinect V2 library, 414
Xbox One, 400

Y
Yellow LED ring, 287

Printed in the United States
By Bookmasters